Conceptions of Knowledge

Berlin Studies
in Knowledge Research

Edited by
Günter Abel
and
James Conant

Volume 4

De Gruyter

Conceptions of Knowledge

Edited by
Stefan Tolksdorf

De Gruyter

Editors

Prof. Dr. Günter Abel
Technische Universität Berlin
Institut für Philosophie
Straße des 17. Juni 135
10623 Berlin
Germany
e-mail: abel@tu-berlin.de

Prof. Dr. James Conant
The University of Chicago
Dept. of Philosophy
1115 E. 58th Street
Chicago IL 60637
USA
e-mail: jconant@uchicago.edu

ISBN 978-3-11-025358-0
e-ISBN 978-3-11-025359-7

Library of Congress Cataloging-in-Publication Data

Conceptions of knowledge / edited by Stefan Tolksdorf.
  p. cm. — (Berlin studies in knowledge research ; v. 4)
English and German.
Includes bibliographical references and index.
ISBN 978-3-11-025358-0 (hardcover : alk. paper)
1. Knowledge, Theory of.   I. Tolksdorf, Stefan.
BD161.C639   2011
121—dc23
                                                                    2011030668

Bibliographic information published by the Deutsche Nationalbibliothek

The Deutsche Nationalbibliothek lists this publication in the Deutsche Nationalbibliografie; detailed bibliographic data are available in the Internet at http://dnb.d-nb.de.

© 2012 Walter de Gruyter GmbH & Co. KG, Berlin/Boston
Printing: Hubert & Co. GmbH & Co. KG, Göttingen
∞ Printed on acid-free paper
Printed in Germany
www.degruyter.com

Preface and Acknowledgements

"Conceptions of Knowledge" is the fourth volume of the series *Berlin Studies in Knowledge Research*. The *Berlin Studies* are a project which is published in co-operation with the Innovationszentrum Wissensforschung (IZW, Center for Knowledge Research) of the Technische Universität Berlin (Technical University Berlin) and the publishing house Walter de Gruyter.

The IZW pursues an inter- and transdisciplinary knowledge research project. Viewed from a philosophical point of view, the focus is on an extensive multifaceted reorientation of analytical epistemology. In this regard, the reader is referred also to the series' first two volumes "Rethinking Epistemology". With reference to the present volume reorientation stands among other things for the discussion of the *pragmatic aspects* of knowledge – *Pragmatic aspects* which try to remove a methodical constriction of classical epistemology. Three of these *pragmatic aspects* which all revolve around the relationship between *knowing and acting* may be suggested at this point:

a) the focus on (the concept of) epistemic abilities as that which precedes knowledge or as that which it consists in;
b) the emphasis on the contextual and discursive aspects of knowledge and justification with reference to their nature and their relevance for the discussion with the skeptic;
c) the account of the variety of forms of knowledge, for instance animal, phenomenal, or practical knowledge.

The reader will not fail to notice that not all of the texts can be made fit into this pragmatic framework. This is intentional. The IZW is, moreover, anxious to generate a discourse on various methodological ways of proceedings and approaches within epistemology. It is to be hoped that the present project may contribute its share to this.

My thanks go to the IZW and to the publishing house Walter de Gruyter for making the realization and publication of this volume possible. My special thanks go to Günter Abel, Claudio Roller and Gertrud Grünkorn.

First and foremost, of course, I also want to thank the authors for their willingness to co-operate and for our very fruitful preliminary discussions. May it continue.

Some texts in this volume have undergone a rather long translation process, either from German into English, or vice versa. The idea behind this is to get closer mutual relations between the German and the English speaking worlds of philosophizing off the ground. The translations were done by Erich Ammereller, Alan Duncan and Ute Feldmann. Many thanks go to them for their good and reliable work. As is well known, translating a philosophical text cannot be separated from philosophy itself.

Can Atli, Hadi Faizi, Timo Hinrichs, Katharina von Laer, Doris Schöps and Martin Wolf helped with the editorial organization and other editorial tasks. Without their help this volume would certainly not have been possible. My special thanks go to them.

Stefan Tolksdorf
Berlin, Summer 2011

Contents

Stefan Tolksdorf
Introduction 1

Chapter One *Knowledge, Ability, and Manifestation*

Part One: Knowledge As Ability

Stephen Hetherington
Knowledge and Knowing: Ability and Manifestation 73

John Hyman
Wie Wissen funktioniert 101

Part Two: Knowledge Through Ability

Ernest Sosa
Knowing Full Well 129

John Greco
Die Natur von Fähigkeiten und der Zweck von Wissen 141

Duncan Pritchard
The Genealogy of the Concept of Knowledge and Anti-Luck
Virtue Epistemology 159

Stefan Tolksdorf
Knowledge, Abilities, and Epistemic Luck: What Is *Anti-Luck Virtue Epistemology* and What Can It Do? 179

Andrea Kern
Knowledge as a Fallible Capacity 215

Part Three: Knowing-How

Günter Abel
Knowing-How: Indispensable but Inscrutable 245

David Löwenstein
Knowledge-How, Linguistic Intellectualism, and Ryle's Return   269

Chapter Two *Knowledge in Situations: Contexts and Contrasts*

Part One: Contextualism

Gerhard Ernst
Two Varieties of Knowledge 307

Nikola Kompa
Nonindexical Contextualism – an Explication and Defense . . . 329

Part Two: Contrastivism

Jonathan Schaffer
What is Contrastivism? 353

Jonathan Schaffer
Contrastive Knowledge 357

Peter Baumann
Contrastivism rather than Something Else? – On the Limits of
Epistemic Contrastivism 395

Jonathan Schaffer
Contrastive Knowledge: Reply to Baumann 411

Peter Baumann
PS: Response to Schaffer's Reply 425

Chapter Three *Challenging Justification – The Nature and Structure of Justification*

Michael Williams
Verantwortlichkeit und Verlässlichkeit 435

Matthias Steup
Justification, Deontology, and Voluntary Control 461

Peter D. Klein
Infinitism and the Epistemic Regress Problem 487

Steven Luper
Das einfache Argument 509

Anthony Brueckner
What Is Transmission Failure? 527

Chapter Four *Varieties and Forms of Knowledge: Animal, Phenomenal, and Practical Knowledge*

Hilary Kornblith
Epistemology and Cognitive Ethology 535

Hans-Johann Glock
Non-Human Knowledge and Non-Human Agency 557

Claudio Roller
Phänomenales Wissen und der Hintergrund 589

Thomas Gil
Rechtliches Wissen 617

Chapter Five *Skepticism: Pragmatic Answers?*

Joachim Schulte
Wittgensteins Zweifel 629

Sebastian Schmoranzer
Skepticism, Contextualism and Entitlement 649

Marie Mcginn
Wittgenstein and Williamson on Knowing and Believing 671

Notes on Contributors 691

Index 697

Introduction

Stefan Tolksdorf

Chapter One:
Knowledge, Ability, and Manifestation

Stephen Hetherington's article "Knowledge and Knowing: Ability and Manifestation" and John Hyman's "Wie Wissen funktioniert" opens the first chapter of this anthology. This volume deals largely, besides other pragmatic topics concerning knowledge and justification, *with the relation between knowledge and acting or being able to act.* One of the key concepts in the articles of Hetherington, Sosa, Greco, Pritchard, Kern, Tolksdorf, Hyman, Abel and Löwenstein is the concept of "epistemic ability" or "epistemic knowing-how", which is brought into play for a variety of purposes. As it were, the first chapter therefore focuses on the question concerning the understanding and status of abilities for knowledge.

First of all it is important to explain which status the concept of ability occupies within this chapter, before I point to a few differences and similarities regarding the use of epistemic abilities. There are three different ways in which abilities and knowledge can both be thought of together. First, we can examine forms of knowledge which consist less in the knowledge of facts than in the fact that the knowing subject is able to do something instead. So called 'knowing-how' is the subject of the articles by Abel and Löwenstein. Secondly, we can ask to what extent the abilities of an agent are responsible for the production of knowledge. Virtue epistemology tries *to ground* knowledge on epistemic abilities. Knowledge is based on virtuous character traits. The issue here is propositional knowledge which itself seems to be in need of knowing-how in order to exist at all. At this point the texts meet. Particulars in this regard can be found in the articles of Sosa, Greco, Pritchard, Tolksdorf and Kern. Thirdly, we can go a step further and claim that propositional knowledge is not just the result of performing an ability but identical with it. Knowledge is an ability. That is the radical thesis of

Hetherington and Hyman. The first chapter proceeds along this tripartite division.

The understanding of epistemic abilities varies from author to author, naturally beginning with the functional role that concept should play in the theory, via the question of how challenging and action-like, that means: how intentionally substantial epistemic abilities should be considered to be, and moving to the question of whether competences of this kind make success reliable or guarantee success, to the relation between epistemic knowing-how and propositional knowledge. But what the authors have in common is the hope that an explanatory potential can be made fertile in epistemic abilities. What for? For traditional questions and problems of epistemology, for instance, like those concerning the nature of knowledge, epistemic normativity, the value of knowledge, our handling of Gettier cases or the question of how epistemic competences are related to human (and animal) activities in general. Hence it is also obvious that the authors are campaigning against a dogma of analytical epistemology with this concept, namely against the distinct separation of theoretical and practical knowledge, which at the same time is associated with the thesis of the intellectual priority of theoretical knowledge. With the concept of competence and of ability the perspective changes, away from the *beliefs* of a *subject* towards a public realm of *performances* of interacting *agents*.

I have started the first part of chapter one (Knowledge As Ability) with Hetherington and Hyman. Both of them defend a radical position. I have begun with Hetherington because due to his recent practicalist conception of knowledge or his practicalism he represents an extreme position measured against the epistemological tradition, a position critics will have to handle if they are to avoid its consequences. The main thesis of practicalism put in a nutshell is: "Knowledge *is* as knowledge *can do*."[1] What Hetherington is striving for is a new orientation of epistemology, the motto of which is: knowledge-that is a kind of knowing-how. He delivers the justification for this assimilation and thesis via an examination of the problem of the criterion.[2] Each theory of knowledge should offer an answer to this problem. It is exactly here that Hetherington sees the strength of his position. But what is the problem exactly? It is the problem of how the connection of general principles of knowledge and specific judgments of knowledge (cases of

---

1   In this volume , 71. On this also cf. his new book: Hetherington (2011).
2   On this cf. Chisholm (1977); Amico (1995).

knowledge) is to be thought of in a non-circular way. This question arises because both sides of this relation seem to be mutually dependent: general epistemic principles must be tested on particular epistemic judgments; and vice versa. So where can we start? I neither want to discuss the problem itself nor Hetherington's solution within this introduction. I think that his theoretical approach to knowledge can be separated from the alleged solution of the problem, and I have my doubts regarding the latter.

Let us take a closer look at how Hetherington considers knowledge and acting/being able to act together. How close is their relation to be seen? This question is of central importance, because the fact *that* both aspects are interrelated is denied only by very few theories of knowledge. Not the *fact* of the interrelation but the *kind* of relation which characterizes his position. Of what kind is this relation? A conceptual relation is involved and not only an evidential one or one concerning rationality. This means: carrying out an act or the manifestation of abilities is not only seen as evidence or reason for the ascription of knowledge. This thesis is often encountered. If an agent can say and justify that p, then we have good reason to also ascribe the knowledge that p to him. But that is not what Hetherington is aiming at. On the other hand, Hetherington also rejects the thesis which claims that knowledge is simply a requirement for or a rational element of acting and practical reasoning. Of course, he does not want to deny that our knowledge has an influence on our actions. He tries to defend the position that knowledge is not something that, itself being conceptually separated from actions, is only *assisting* our practical reasoning and acting. Of course, it is true that when having the knowledge that p it would be rational to do something. But Hetherington goes one step further: Knowledge itself is an ability to act. Compared with Hetherington's practicalist reorientation both the evidential thesis and the normativity approach are to a certain extent only half-hearted. More is at stake for him, he is concerned with a conceptual relation of the following kind: to speak of knowledge means to speak of actions and abilities: "we must conceive of knowledge in such a way as to make effective agency a *part* of it."[3] The state of knowledge a subject is in when she knows that p, is that she is able to act or do something, that she has knowledge of how to act in different ways. According to this conception "*Knowledge* that p" denotes the ability itself, which is to be distinguished from its various man-

---

3   In this volume, 79.

ifestations. For the latter Hetherington reserves the expression "*Knowing that p*". Manifestations of the knowledge that Mount Everest is 8,848 meters high can for instance be that a judgment with this content is accepted, that it is presented as an answer to the respective question, that the subject argues for it, uses this sentence in inferences, etc.

In short: knowing means acting, but knowledge is being able to act. To a certain extent, however, it remains unclear how exactly Hetherington conceives of the relation between knowledge and knowing (being able to act and acting). Which side enjoys conceptual priority? Can we only therefore talk of competences because performances exist? Are not the former mystified independent of the latter? Or is the opposite true: something can only be considered as a manifestation of the type h if type h already exists? Or is the question of the conceptual order itself meaningless, because both concepts require each other and therefore have to be developed and made comprehensible together?[4] I am not sure how Hetherington would answer.

Regarding the present anthology those consequences are of special interest which result from practicalism for contemporary epistemology. If we take this idea seriously it follows that, according to Hetherington, we should say good-bye to a few paradigms of analytical epistemology that we have grown fond of. I would like to point out four consequences:

(a) First of all I would like to start with a question regarding practicalism: If propositional knowledge is generally identified with an ability and if "knowledge that p", as Hetherington says, can also consist of various abilities in different people, then the following question arises: does this imply that with an ascription of the form "S knows that p" to different people different things could be ascribed? Does ascribing different abilities commit us to ascribing a variety of semantic contents as well? Hetherington believes that he can avoid this consequence. How can he do this? Can knowledge, that p be understood as a meta-ability?

(b) The thesis that knowledge does not come in degrees or nuances, similar to being pregnant, is called absolutism about knowledge. In other words: S1 cannot know that p in a better way than S2. Hetherington's ability analysis of knowledge contradicts this thesis. According to *which* abilities an agent has and *how good* they are it makes sense to say that S1 knows better than S2. Abilities come in degrees, someone can

---

4   On similar questions cf. the article by Kern as well as my discussion below.

do something better than someone else, therefore knowledge also comes in degrees.

(c) Absolutism has been abandoned. What about closure? Does the ability analysis of knowledge lead to the abandonment of the closure principle of knowledge too? And if so, is this not a terrible price?

(d) Concerning the relation between knowledge and justification practicalism also comes to an interesting conclusion. The ability to justify a sentence is not a *conceptual* part of the knowledge that p. That is so because the ascribed ability to do something can be multifaceted. Inferential justification is *one* possible ability/manifestation among many. But if justification is not a conceptual part of knowledge then we can rely on the option that weaker forms of knowledge get by without justification.[5]

John Hyman's text "Wie Wissen funktioniert" is, as are the texts of Greco, Williams and Luper, a first German translation of an already published article. We are concerned here with the article "How Knowledge Works" published in 1999.[6] Hyman's text, even though already published in 1999, is of special interest because he presents an understanding of knowledge which anticipates basic insights into virtue epistemology on the one hand, but on the other does not seem to agree completely with this approach either. He is interested rather in how knowledge and action can be identified with each other, similar to how we have seen it done by Hetherington. The text fits perfectly into the concept of the chapter. Hyman, together with Ryle and Wittgenstein, attacks one of the main dogmas of analytical epistemology, namely that knowledge is a kind of *belief*.[7] According to Hyman, however, knowledge is a kind of *ability*. As far as this thesis is concerned it is of a similar radical nature to that of Hetherington. There are a lot of similarities between the two authors.[8]

To put Hyman's point clearly: Knowledge is not (only) the result of the practising of abilities but *identical* with it, even though the former

---

5 On this point also cf. Sosa's animal knowledge in the next section. A further dogma that Hetherington repeatedly takes up is that knowledge precludes epistemic luck. To this Hetherington replies: Knowledge and luck are not always mutually exclusive, there is lucky knowledge. And consequently: a few Gettier situations allow for knowledge. Cf. Hetherington (2011), op.cit.
6 Hyman (1999), 433–451.
7 Cf. McGinn's article in this connection and the question of whether knowledge is a mental state or not.
8 Cf. Hetherington (2011), 34.

may also be true. Wittgenstein writes, for example: "Die Grammatik des Wortes ‚wissen' ist offenbar eng verwandt der Grammatik des Wortes ‚können', ‚imstande sein'."[9] But what can it mean to call knowledge an ability, or, expressed less strongly, to bring the grammar of knowledge and ability into line with each other? A contentual justification of the chapter "Knowledge, Abilities, and Manifestations" consists precisely, with Hetherington and Hyman on the one hand, Sosa and Greco on the other and also including Abel and Löwenstein, in providing the reader with at least three varying conceptions of this thesis. Hyman tackles the question of the relation, by examining the kind of ability this could be. And at this very point he takes a different route from other texts and approaches which are collected in the first chapter. Setting a first course which leads away from the traditional paths of epistemology consists in bringing together theoretical and practical reason, in bringing together knowledge and action. In other words: Hyman suggests that we should not separate the recognition of facts on the one hand from the ability to act for reasons on the other. They rather belong together: facts are possible reasons for actions. As a rule, facts are seen as a genuine object of propositional knowledge. So far, so good. The separation of fact and reason, however, leads to a narrower understanding of factual knowledge, because the dimension of the action guidance of knowledge is not taken into account anymore. Knowledge should be a kind of ability which motivates the knowing subject to do something. Hyman's specific thesis is: "Persönliches propositionales Wissen ist die Fähigkeit, aus Gründen, die Tatsachen sind, zu handeln…"[10] The following is meant here: Let us take the propositional knowledge, for example, that it is raining. You look out of the window and acquire the knowledge that it is raining. Then Hyman goes on to say that the fact that it is raining can be the reason for you to begin different actions. Therefore: S knows that it is raining = S has the ability to do something, the reason being that it is raining: to take an umbrella, to cancel an engagement, to stop watering the flowers, etc. According to this interpretation reasons and knowledge are both interpreted factively: reasons are facts, and knowing that p implies p.

---

9 Wittgenstein (2003), § 150. English translation: "The grammer of the word ‚know' is evidently closely related to the grammar of the words ‚can', ‚is able to'."
10 In this volum, 122. In the original version: "…personal propositional knowledge is the ability to act … for reasons that are facts."

So much for the account of the core idea. What consequences follow from this idea? First I would like to deal with the knowledge of animals and with that illustrate a link between Hyman and Glock (in this anthology). Glock and Kornblith's question concerns the point whether animals can have knowledge or whether they can only have beliefs. It is clear that Hyman does not decide this question directly in favor of one of the two options, but that he is indeed able to make the positions very clear. This is so because in as far as animals can indeed act for reasons (which are facts), they can also have propositional knowledge according to this approach. Glock appeals to Hyman's understanding of knowledge and then answers his question positively: animals can act for reasons, therefore they can also have knowledge.

Secondly, Hyman's thesis implies a criticism of Wittgenstein's statement, that under normal conditions one cannot say "*Ich weiß, dass ich Schmerzen habe (I know that I am in pain).*" (PU § 246) Wittgenstein's point is that with regard to one's own pain the employment of the knowledge operator is without any function in a lot of contexts of saying something. The sentence "I know that I am in pain" actually amounts to saying that one is in pain. But if the fact that I am now in pain can be a reason for my actions, then, according to Hyman, I can also speak of knowledge. And it should be clear that my pain can be a reason for acting.

Finally I would like to draw the reader's attention to a question which I consider to be very interesting, that is the question of the kind of relation which exists between the identification of knowledge with abilities made by Hetherington and that of Hyman. Is practicalism in line with the thesis that knowledge is the ability to act for reasons?[11] At first sight it seems as if Hetherington's ability analysis of knowledge is broader than Hyman's thesis. The abilities which Hetherington is talking of can be of a varying nature, as we have heard. Whoever knows that p *can*, for instance, support a corresponding belief, provide justification, form inferences or *act for reasons* (Hyman). Does Hyman's approach find its way then into Hetherington's practicalism? That one can, of course, understand the phrase "to act for reasons" in a very broad sense would imply that this is not quite right. And that is exactly what Hyman implies when he writes, for instance, that the ability to believe something, to criticize, to doubt, to want, etc. is also of importance. This points rather to similar theories. The reader may want to

---

11 Cf. Hetherington (2011), ch. 2.

try and answer this question, and also decide what relation exists between these two approaches and virtue epistemology. Referring to Hyman, Hetherington himself speaks rather of a slightly different *emphasis* of certain questions and topics.[12]

The third article in the first chapter is by Ernest Sosa and is called "Knowing Full Well". He opens the second part (Knowledge Through Ability) and with this the discussion about virtue epistemology in this volume. Sosa is without doubt one of today's most interesting and most widely discussed epistemologists. Besides his safety-approach (a modal theory of knowledge which responds critically to the condition of sensitivity) this estimation is based especially, and this is of importance for this volume, on the establishment and explication of virtue epistemology. Virtue approaches attribute a key role to the concept of competence.[13] With the help of the concept of intellectual virtues Sosa does not only succeed in indicating a way out of the oscillation between foundationalism and the coherence theory[14], but he also makes clear, with reference to the analogy of the moral virtues, what it means to classify epistemology as a normative discipline and to make concepts like "intuition" fruitful again. Important for the understanding of the concept of epistemic competences (performances) represented by Sosa is the fact that his virtue epistemology is a version of reliabilism. This is important because it first of all allows us to understand the kind of broad basis on which the concept is grounded, that is in what broad sense it is used: every system or every organism has competences when it comes to the reliable fulfillment of aims and functions. Moreover, the follow-up question of how genuinely *human* knowledge should be understood, arises naturally from this broad concept of competence. Sosa addresses this question in his article. He works through animal knowledge to human knowledge step by step. Both forms of knowledge have in common that knowledge is presented as a kind of cognitive achievement. Generally, achievements are success through abilities. Hence, assigned to knowledge it then applies that: knowledge is cognitive achievement, that is: cognitive success through cognitive ability.

---

12 Cf. fn. 11.
13 Cf. for example: BonJour/Sosa (2003); Sosa (2007).
14 Sosa (1980), 3–25.

As Sosa repeatedly claimed, every performance can be normatively judged in a threefold manner:

- *Accurateness*: Was the aim of the performance achieved? Was it successful?
- *Adroitness*: Was an ability manifested?
- *Aptness*: Is success to be explained by ability? Is the result accurate because adroit? In the case of knowledge it means: Does truth (or: true belief) manifest intellectual capacities?

Regarding achievements, the key property is aptness. Whatever generally holds for sporting, musical or practical abilities is also supposed to hold for epistemic competences. Here the aim is the truth of a belief and the way to get there is, for instance, via perception, the ability to draw conclusions, memory, etc. Accordingly Sosa's initial thesis is: animal knowledge is apt belief. Since aptness, as mentioned, is a normative property it follows that: epistemic normativity is a kind of performance normativity.

What has to be added to an apt belief in order for it to become human knowledge? A relatively robust intuition that one encounters again and again is that human knowledge is characterized by being reflective. In order to do justice to this intuition, Sosa introduces the concept of meta-aptness. An apt belief can be a form of knowledge and at the same time be very fragile. That is the case, if the success came about as the result of the manifestation of epistemic abilities but when the conditions of the manifestation are such, however, that the agent could easily have been mistaken. The environment makes the success fragile.[15] In this picture meta-aptness consists in the very varying abilities of an agent to judge his own position. It is necessary to weigh up and assess the conditions of judgment, in order, based on this, to be able to say how high the risk of false beliefs is. "Is my knowledge fragile or built on sand?"– this is the question we ask ourselves. These reflective competences then form the framework for basic aptness. Clearly, a belief can be apt without being meta-apt, and meta-apt without being apt.

According to Sosa the difference between man and animal could therefore be that human knowledge is apt belief because meta-aptness. We speak then of full-aptness. Let us note therefore: human knowledge is a kind of reflective knowledge; and reflective knowledge aims at full aptness, which for its part is to be understood as follows: full aptness =

---

15 Think of the Barney-case. On this cf. Pritchard and Tolksdorf.

df. x is fully apt iff it is apt because meta-apt.[16] We have an apt belief which is aptly believed, if the aptness of the reflective estimation is due to the subject.

So much for the representation of Sosa's thoughts. I now want to suggest some ways in which we could continue, critically and questioningly.

The concept of aptness is at the center of the theory of knowledge in the works of Sosa. But is it sufficient and/or necessary in order to have knowledge? Cases which are supposed to show that knowledge can manage without achievement or that achievement does not always generate knowledge, are presented again and again. We will return to the second question (that is: the condition of necessity) in the discussion of Greco's work (the subject of discussion will be knowledge by testimony), the first question (that is: the condition of sufficiency) is addressed in the articles of Pritchard and Tolksdorf (the subject of discussion will be Barney). The heart of the objection amounts basically to the fact that *robust* virtue epistemologies rely solely on one condition (ability) in order to explain knowledge, but that that perhaps is not enough. Further conditions (perhaps of a modal kind) have to be added.[17]

A further dispute concerns the difference between animal and human knowledge. Not so much in explicating their contents, but rather based on the fact that such a division is performed at all.[18] Should knowledge not be understood as a consistent phenomenon of the same kind?

Sosa has decided to use the concepts "performance" and "capacity" in a very broad way, that is to use them with reference to biological organisms and systems as well. But the question arises whether this conceptual broadening and "intentional anemia" is not obstructing its own explanatory aim, namely to explain epistemic normativity. One might think that there was an important difference between *dispositions* and genuine *abilities*, where it is precisely the intentional increase in the latter which distinguishes the phenomenon of epistemic normativity. In other words: Is it plausible to explain epistemic normativity through reliable dispositions in the broad sense?

In her article Andrea Kern will criticize Sosa's concept of epistemic abilities precisely because firstly it remains unclear what the relation be-

---

16 Cf. Sosa in this volume, 134–137.
17 Cf. Pritchard/Millar/Haddock (2010), ch. 2 and 3.
18 Cf. Hyman, Kornblith und Glock in this volume.

tween abilities, manifestations and normal conditions is, but secondly – and this point is crucial – for Sosa epistemic competences only make *success reliable* but do not *guarantee success*. Kern believes she can show that *such* abilities cannot escape the Gettier problem.

John Greco's text "Die Natur von Fähigkeiten und der Zweck von Wissen" is a translation of his article "The Nature of Ability and the Purpose of Knowledge"[19] which was published in 2007. The article has been published in German for the first time. Beside Sosa and Zagzebski, Greco is one of the leading contemporary virtue epistemologists. As the title of the paper indicates, Greco is concerned with the analysis of the nature of abilities which is, together with the pragmatic question concerning the purpose of knowledge, intended to help us to solve a few tricky problems of analytic epistemology. The mention of the purpose of (the concept of) knowledge refers first to Craig and second to the fact that we employ knowledge in practical reasoning and considerations. Greco links both pragmatic viewpoints together: the purpose of knowledge consists in flagging good informants, namely in the context of practical reasoning. I will go into Craig in more detail when presenting Pritchard.[20]

The central basic virtue epistemological insight, as we have also noted with reference to Sosa, is to say that knowledge is a kind of success from ability, or, and this phrasing is used by Greco more often, S knows that p iff S believes the truth *because* intellectual abilities. The mention of "because" at this point is subject to various interpretations. Greco wants it to be understood in the sense of a causal explanatory story. This means: knowledge is at hand when we are able to *causally explain* the possession of the true belief through the intellectual abilities of the agent. All pragmatic and contextual elements of a causal explanation are then transferred to the nature of knowledge.[21]

Analogously to Sosa, Greco sees epistemic success in analogy to the achievements in other areas of acting. The more general phenomenon in the background is success through abilities, in sports for instance. Vir-

---

19 Cf. Greco (2007), 57–69; also cf. Greco (2010).
20 Also cf. the articles of Ernst and Kompa.
21 To be a little bit more precise: causal explanations depend on the aspect of the cause that seems to be relevant, on the purpose the examination serves and on the pragmatic background as well as on the prior knowledge which backs the explanation.

tue epistemologists, as we have already heard, associate great explanatory hope with this kind of course set and this phenomenon in the background: for example with reference to the value problem of knowledge or to epistemic normativity itself, or associated with the hope of receiving an explanation regarding the incompatibility of knowledge and luck. Greco deals with another question, with the so-called *generality problem*. His answer to this problem is of relevance because it leads us to a more exact analysis of the nature of abilities. I want to say something briefly on this and after that move on to the point concerning how Greco deals with the objection that achievement and success through abilities is a too demanding criterion for knowledge.

The *generality problem* is, simply, that every reliable process of belief formation has to be referred to a certain class of reference, if it is to be accessible to an epistemic evaluation. If the class of reference changes, the epistemic evaluation can also change. Thinking on the relation between epistemic abilities and belief formation we can say that according to which answer we give to the question, which class of reference is relevant, we not only evaluate the reliability of the capacity in question but also say how the individuation of the present epistemic ability is to take place and how it is to be understood. The question now is: how can we know which parameters lead us to the *correct* identification of the ability (via the class of reference)? This is the exact point where Greco refers to the context and to the nature of abilities. The latter always have to be referred already to conditions and environments. This means, for example: Roger Federer is *able* to play tennis, however, not under water or under the influence of drugs. This is why Greco asserts: "S hat eine Fähigkeit F(R/B) relativ zu einer Umgebung U = In einer Menge von einander in relevanter Hinsicht nahe stehenden Welten W, in denen S sich unter B und in U befindet, hat S eine hohe Erfolgsrate darin, R zu erreichen."[22] The conditions which are to be considered normal with regard to the thematized abilities, partially depends on the ability itself (playing tennis) but it partially depends also on the context of making practical judgments and conclusions. The context in which we speak about playing tennis determines how the ability should be understood, that is, under which normal conditions it works. The same holds for knowledge and epistemic abilities. This is so because in the context of

---

22 Cf. the English original citation: "S has an ability A(R/C) relative to environment E = Across the set of relevantly close worlds W where S is in C and in E, S has a high rate of success in achieving R."

practical reasoning we reflect on whether S knows that p and consequently what is actually said when we speak about epistemic abilities.

With Greco, the virtue theoretical approach leads to a further pragmatic shade of the meaning of knowledge beyond the fact that the concept of ability is substantial in that it undergoes a further pragmatization which is achieved by including aspects of the purpose and practical contexts of reasoning. The individuation and establishment of the classes of reference takes place via contextual parameters. To sum up: to solve the generality problem we need two constituent parts: the nature of the ability and the context of thinking about knowledge and abilities.

Let's move on to the second point. There is one standard objection to the thesis that knowledge is an achievement of the agent or more precisely the product of the epistemic abilities of the agent, which was put forward by Jennifer Lackey, using the example of testimonial knowledge.[23] The reference to this form of knowledge is obvious because as a rule knowledge that is gained in this way cannot be explained by the manifestation of the epistemic abilities of the inquirer (the agent), but is based on the competences of the witness. He, not the subject, deserves the actual credit. Greco believes that he can avoid the counter-intuitive assertion that testimonial knowing is not knowledge at all, suggested as being a consequence of virtue epistemology. He draws attention to the fact that the recipient of information is also involved and therefore deserves part of the credit too. The recipient must be able to distinguish good sources of information from bad ones (witnesses), for instance, he has to have the ability to reject certain answers, etc. They both pool their epistemic abilities. In the end Greco defends the idea that: "Die Anerkennung für den Erfolg, der in Kooperation mit anderen erzielt wird, wird nicht von der tüchtigen Leistung anderer zunichte gemacht."[24] For the witness there might be other, more crucial competences at stake than for the recipient, but insofar as both are part of a social collaboration, they both contribute a normative share to the success of the whole. Consequently knowledge by testimony is *also* based on the abilities of the recipient.

Now we may add critically that the question, whether the contribution of the recipient is significant enough, still has to be answered. This

---

23 Cf. Lackey (2004).
24 Cf. Greco in this volume, 151. The English original citation: "…credit for success, gained in cooperation with others, is not swamped by the able performance of others."

has to do with what we are going to find out more about in Pritchard's article, namely whether Greco's answer to the discussed credit problem does not abandon the basic idea of virtue epistemology, explaining knowledge through the abilities of the agent in a *robust* way. Because it is clearly the witness who is *causally salient,* not the inquirer. Is the contribution of the inquirer salient enough for talking about a causal success explanation?

In addition further concerns can be noted. Greco works with a causal interpretation of the word "because". He explains that causal explanations (like all explanations) are pragmatic creatures. If causal explanation is dependent on interests, then so is knowledge. But does a virtue epistemologist have to buy this relativism?

Finally I would like to turn to the articles of Kern and Tolksdorf. Greco, too, merely demands that epistemic abilities are *reliably successful*. Whether this suffices will be discussed later. Tolksdorf will try to show that, in a way, a disjunctive theory of epistemic abilities is not reliant on the 'because'. In my view, cases of knowledge should not be explained by three independent aspects: truth, the manifestation of an ability, and *in addition* a possible *external* causal link between truth and manifestation.

Duncan Pritchard's "The Genealogy of the Concept of Knowledge and Anti-Luck Virtue Epistemology" refers, in part in agreement, in part critically to the virtue epistemological approaches of Sosa and Greco. Both reactions are united in his project of an *Anti-Luck Virtue Epistemology*.[25] Before I go into Pritchard's ability based and modal theory of knowledge, the first part of the title "the genealogy of the concept of knowledge" must be outlined, since it discusses a pragmatic attitude which becomes apparent in many places in this volume. The adoption of a genealogical perspective hinted at, is associated epistemologically with the name of Edward Craig.[26] It inquires about the function, the purpose and the genealogy of the concept of knowledge. The following questions make clear, by way of example, what it can mean to take up such a perspective: What practical value does the concept have? From what pressure to act does it arise? What already backs its formation conceptually?

---

25 On this also cf. Pritchard/Millar/Haddock (2010), ch. 3; cf. Pritchard (2011). And also see the critical examination in Tolksdorf (this volume).
26 Cf. Craig (1990); Gelfert (2011), 67–82; also Tolksdorf (2012).

Craig himself assigns to the concept of knowledge the practical function of identifying good informants.[27] Now it seems natural to associate virtue approaches with genealogical stories of this kind, because epistemic abilities are to a certain extent the basis of good information and informants. Against this background Pritchard would like to show that this appearance is deceptive, that is that Craig's thesis rather safeguards his anti-luck virtue epistemology.

The argumentative route to anti-luck virtue epistemology which, as already mentioned, associates modal elements of knowledge with the concept of ability, is taken essentially by criticizing robust virtue approaches. Pritchard does not deny that the ability intuition is an essential factor of the concept of knowledge. What he doubts, however, is that it alone is capable of explaining knowledge. Linguistically robust ability theories present themselves as follows: "cognitive success should *be because of* the target reliable cognitive ability"; "the cognitive success is *primarily explained by*, and hence *primarily creditable to* the relevant reliable cognitive ability."[28] Formulations of this kind can be found in Sosa and Greco. One can call these virtue approaches *robust* because epistemic abilities are considered to be necessary and sufficient for knowledge. The aim consists in exclusively analyzing knowledge via processes of virtuous belief formation. What can be said against this thesis? On the one hand Pritchard considers the robust approach to be too strong, but on the other too weak. Too strong because it seems to exclude knowledge by testimony. In such cases it seems as if the agent is not primarily creditable for the cognitive success (i.e. true belief). We have already become acquainted with and discussed such cases in connection with Greco's paper in the last section. Greco believed that the inquirer also deserves part of the credit. With regard to this Pritchard would certainly ask: is Greco distancing himself from his original formulation? Is he really still demanding "is *primarily* creditable or explained by"? These questions arise because in order to ward off the objection, it was merely argued that the agent *also* employed epistemic abilities, but not *primarily* so.

Whereas the thesis is too weak because, according to Pritchard, it apparently allows for knowledge where we intuitively do not speak of knowledge, and this matter interests me here. Consider the Barney case: Barney is driving in the countryside with his son. He identifies

---

27 On this cf. also the articles by Greco, Ernst and Kompa.
28 Cf. Pritchard in this volume, 164, 165.

various objects on the landscape as they come into clear view. His eyesight functions very well and the environmental conditions are also good. He sees a barn and forms the belief that there is a barn in the field. This belief is true. Unknown to Barney, the district he has just entered is full of papier-mâché facsimiles of barns. Every other object that looks like a barn is a fake barn.[29] That's the case. Intuitively we would probably say that Barney manifests his epistemic abilities, that his true belief (the success) is to be explained by his perceptual abilities. But then knowledge would exist subsequent to the paradigm of the robust virtue theory of knowledge – which contradicts our intuitive judgment.[30] We do not want to deny the fact that Barney was quite lucky.[31] But knowledge and epistemic luck are mutually exclusive. To be able to handle examples of this kind, Pritchard pleads for a weakening of the robust thesis with a concurrent inclusion of an anti-luck condition: knowledge is the result of exercising epistemic abilities in a modally safe environment. He writes, for example: "S knows that p if and only if S's safe true belief that p is the product of her relevant cognitive abilities."[32] Even though Barney does indeed take his epistemic abilities into account, he does so in a modally inconvenient environment, and so it does not lead to knowledge, as our intuition suggests. Barney's belief is not safe.

The question whether anti-luck virtue epistemology can be associated with a genealogical approach à la Craig leads us back to the beginning of the discussion. Pritchard's reaction consists in tracing the positive answer to this question back to an ambiguity of the concept of the "good informant". On the one hand "to be a good informant" can mean that an agent possesses reliable epistemic abilities and that he comes to have true beliefs on this basis. But it can also mean that we can count (rely on) on the agent. The latter refers to the modal environment. According to Pritchard both interpretations do not coincide because we can rely on an agent, even if he is not a good informant in the first sense, if he does not manifest epistemic abilities – and vice versa.

---

29 Cf. Goldman (1976), 771–791.
30 Cf. Tolksdorf's paper in which this case is addressed in more detail.
31 A belief is considered to be lucky in this context if the agent could easily have been mistaken. This understanding has a modal touch. On this cf. Pritchard (2005).
32 Cf. Pritchard (2011).

Both aspects are rather indicative of two separate conditions of knowledge: a virtue and an anti-luck condition.

Pritchard's theory is inventive and promises high theoretical earnings. The critical discussion of anti-luck virtue epistemology leads us directly to the articles by Kern and Tolksdorf. Both assume, although for different reasons, that the anti-luck condition is useless, strictly speaking, that it does no explanatory work of its own. I do not want to anticipate the arguments at this point but merely adduce questions which point in the direction one could take:

(a) Does Barney really manifest his epistemic abilities in the barn case? I do not think so. Tolksdorf tries to argue in favor of this in his article.

(b) Is modal safety not already an intrinsic part of competence? *In a certain sense*, I think it is. This is my thesis: If we ascribe the ability that we are able to recognize barns, then it is impossible that one could easily have been mistaken. Not generally but with reference to a fake barn. Fake barns undermine the manifestation of the ability via neutralizing its sense. If this is the case, the protective safety clause is too late.

(c) Do the phrases "to rely on" and "good informant through capacities" really denote two separate facets? I do not think they do.

In his "Knowledge, Abilities, and Epistemic Luck: What Is Anti-Luck Virtue Epistemology and What Can It Do?" Stefan Tolksdorf discusses a theory of knowledge which Duncan Pritchard has introduced into his more recent papers. The theory is called *anti-luck virtue epistemology*. It is essential for this approach that two master intuitions are interconnected with regard to knowledge, namely the ability intuition (that is: knowledge arises from ability) on the one hand and on the other the anti-luck intuition (that is: knowledge and epistemic luck are incompatible). Tolksdorf explores the question of whether we really need both conditions. The answer is given in the negative.

With reference to a disjunctive and social-externalistic understanding of epistemic abilities the anti-luck condition is of no concern any more. Put a little more precisely: this condition does not fulfill an independent explanatory function in our understanding of knowledge.

Two theses are in focus here. First of all, the success of epistemic abilities is part of its nature. This contradicts the common definitions of knowledge within virtue epistemology which are reinforced against Gettier-cases as follows: S knows that p iff S believes the truth *because* intellectual ability. The mention of 'because' here is to be understood in such a way that the agent firstly has a true belief, secondly manifests the relevant epistemic ability and thirdly that the success is to be explained by the ability. This definition does not seem to be very problematic. But, I think, appearances are deceptive. This is so because the third condition implies that the first two can even be fulfilled independently of it and also independently of each other. And at this very point Tolksdorf suggests another way: if success belongs essentially to the manifestation of epistemic abilities, then we do not need the external 'because'. Gettier victims may have true beliefs, but in most cases they do not manifest the relevant abilities. If someone is looking at a shaggy dog behind which, luckily, a sheep is hiding, we cannot say that he is looking at a sheep. But in this case *that* would be the knowledge-generating ability.

Another example is of even more importance. Pritchard describes the case of Barney who is driving through a landscape of fake barns and by chance forms the true belief that there is a real barn as an example of so-called environmental luck. Anti-luck virtue epistemology is made for cases like this, for it seems as if pure virtue approaches would have to speak of knowledge here, as Barney has successfully used his epistemic abilities. This, however, is counter-intuitive. Barney does indeed see a real barn, but he does not know. Pritchard's definition of knowledge requires that the abilities be embedded in modally safe environments. Precisely this is not the case with Barney.

Tolksdorf on the other hand comes again to the conclusion that we do not need the additional requirement of modal safety because Barney does not manifest his abilities in fake worlds. This time the explanation does not refer to disjunctivism but to a social-external understanding of abilities. Briefly this means: the self-ascription of abilities and the ascription of abilities from others happens in a realm of actions with certain sense-logical presuppositions. This does not only include our understanding of what it means to distinguish real barns from fake ones in the way presented but also that the ability fulfills a function within the epistemic language game. Both conditions are not fulfilled. In fake-worlds the speech community does not prove the relevant ability to be epistemically significant on the grounds that fakes do look like real barns from the middle distance. What is it supposed to mean that Barney is able to distinguish real from fake barns in this way, when both are indistinguishable from each other? We cannot say that Barney manifests an ability because we do not know, under these conditions, what it is supposed to mean to speak of an ability of this kind. This implies, according to Tolksdorf, that *in a way* epistemic abilities are intrinsically modally safe. So we do not need Pritchard's external anti-luck condition. The latter only conveys the impression of necessity against the background of a false understanding of epistemic abilities.

In her article "Knowledge as a Fallible Capacity" Andrea Kern examines the concept of capacity as it is used in the virtue epistemology of, for example, Sosa, Greco, Pritchard and Zagzebski. The argumentative brunt of the text lies in the fact that she draws attention to a fundamental weakness of the concept. This deficit is supposed to be responsible for the fact that all those attempts can *not* ultimately solve the Gettier problem. On a general level of the description of the problem we can say that Gettier deals with the incompatibility of knowledge and epistemic luck or chance. A philosophical truism is: "knowledge is a cognitive state in which someone grasps the truth of a matter in a non-accidental way."[33] But the fulfillment of this intuition always seems to be more than doubtful when the normative epistemic key quality of a belief, be it justification or the foundation in abilities, does not guarantee its truth. In other words, remembering epistemic disjunctivism: if true and false beliefs can have the same reasons, if they can be the result of the same abilities (or better: if the abilities are also manifested in both cases), then it cannot be understood how the demand that something not be accidental can be obtained. In principle epistemic luck can always squeeze in between reason or competence and truth. Pritchard also draws attention to this weak spot. He writes, for example: "After all, no matter how reliable an epistemic virtue might be, it seems possible that it could generate a belief which is only true as a matter of luck."[34] Interestingly, Pritchard and Kern draw different conclusions from this diagnosis. As mentioned above, Pritchard decides in favor of maintaining the theoretical weak spot of the concept of ability, he provides it, however, with an external anti-luck condition, as a kind of compensation. The latter is intended to solve the problem. Kern, however, focuses on the reference to competence itself.

Taking Sosa as an example, she exemplarily works out two important elements in the concept of epistemic abilities: a success and a condition factor. This should not surprise us, as we have already heard from Greco that every ability is reliable relative to certain environmental con-

---

33   Kern in this volume, 213.
34   Cf. Pritchard/Millar/Haddock (2010), 26.

ditions, that it only has a great *success* rate under these *conditions*. What is vital for Kern now, is the fact that according to this concept the exercise of an ability does not *necessarily* lead to success under normal conditions. But then, according to Kern, in turn the ability cannot explain the success fully, and with that we are back to the Gettier problem. The solution to the problem could consist in only speaking of the manifestation of an epistemic ability when success is guaranteed: such abilities necessarily lead to the truth – virtues are truth guaranteeing. Now such a thesis does not imply, as Kern makes clear, that we must give up our human fallibility. Because making epistemic mistakes can be traced back to the conditions of the agent or the environment according to which an *attempt* was made to manifest certain competences.

With her thesis Kern does not reject the basic reorientation of analytic epistemology as it was initiated by virtue approaches. On the contrary: she subscribes to the shift from the thematization of the properties of *beliefs* to the properties of *agents*. However, she expresses the warning: "Virtue Epistemology ... misunderstands its actual insights and thus falls short of a reinvention of epistemology."[35]

Besides the reliability basis of abilities a cause which correlates with the mentioned misunderstanding exists in the reductionist orientation of contemporary virtues approaches. Attempts are made to understand abilities as being non-epistemic, i.e. via the amalgamation of dispositions and normal conditions. The parts of the analysis are themselves independent of knowledge. However, Kern pleads for a non-reductive procedure: manifestations are manifestations of knowledge-generating abilities.

To better understand how Kern's concept of truth-guaranteeing abilities exactly functions, I would guide the conversation with the following questions:

(a) I have already pointed out the connection between abilities on the one and acts of manifestation on the other hand while discussing Hetherington. Now this point recurs. Kern argues in favor of a conceptual priority of capacities, which more or less means: it is ability which first tells us what it means to speak of a manifestation of the acting type X. Like just said: manifestations are manifestations *of abilities*. So far it is understandable. But can abilities be understood independent of the acts themselves? Does it not rather involve a symmetrical, conceptual relation between abilities and manifestations?

---

35   Kern in this volume, 215.

(b) What relation exists between abilities and their normal conditions? Sometimes the text conveys the impression, that Kern is arguing – against Sosa and Greco – not in favor of an *external* relation, but in favor of an *internal* connection. But first of all I am not sure whether Sosa and Greco do not integrate the normal conditions into the definition of abilities as well. And secondly I would like to know more precisely what role the normal conditions play in Kern's explanation of knowledge. Does she answer: no special role because we have always already (implicitly) digested the normal conditions when we successfully act out our abilities? Everyone knows paradigmatic cases of successfully doing something. Are normal conditions codified in the examples of successful acting?

(c) Of special interest is the Barney case, which Kern does not deal with in detail. Virtue theorists react very differently to it: Sosa sees knowledge being realized in such cases, even if it is fragile, animal knowledge; Pritchard, however, excludes knowledge on account of epistemic luck being present; Greco, being the third in this league, does not see Barney having knowledge because the epistemic abilities are not manifested under such conditions at all.[36] But what is Kern's position on this? In my opinion she is undecided: on the one hand she thinks that nothing can be said against the manifestation of epistemic competence because the case is a successful case. But on the other hand she thinks that it is also valid to say that we cannot completely explain success through abilities. Luck doubtlessly had a hand in this. So how should we judge this?

Günter Abel opens part three of chapter one. After reflecting on the relation between propositional knowledge and ability, and representing the two relata as being identical or as a virtuous grounding process, part three focuses on practical knowledge. Abel and Löwenstein conclude chapter one.

In his paper "Knowing-How: Indispensable but Inscrutable" Günter Abel puts knowing-how at the centre of his investigation. Two aspects of this kind of knowledge are fascinating to Abel. Knowing-how is in some sense indispensable as well as also inscrutable. I would

---

36 See also Tolksdorf. It is not quite clear what Greco's position really is. Sometimes it seems that he is saying: Barney manifests his abilities successfully, but that no causal explanatory link exists between manifestation and success. This is not my position.

like to discuss both aspects in this introduction. The leading question here is: Is knowing-how a mystery?

It applies to this form of knowledge, as Abel makes clear in many places, that it is indispensable for our human self-conception and the conception of others. How can this thesis be justified? With regard to 'indispensability' here are three answers: For example, Abel *first* refers to the fact that we have good reason for believing that knowing-how is a requirement for propositional knowledge. And in as far as we assign a key role to linguistically presented knowledge in modern societies, then thanks to the logical dependency relation this has to apply to *knowing-how* to an even greater degree. However analytic epistemology has not yet discovered particularly illuminating points in this field. In the discussion of the relation between knowing-how and knowing-that Abel deals with a question which is prominent in this anthology, namely the interaction of knowledge and belief on the one hand and our abilities on the other. But there are further reasons for singling out knowing-how as knowledge how to act. *Secondly:* in our practical dealings, for example, a kind of normativity is brought to bear from which other forms of the normative, for example, discursive-inferential relations can be construed. And *thirdly* the knowing-how has a key role not least because, from a moral perspective for example, with regard to the search for truth, the ability to live is always already there. Therefore, one can say: knowing-how is indispensable.

Now to the other aspect: What about 'inscrutability'? What makes knowing-how difficult? How is that kind of knowledge to be understood? Abel understands knowing-how as practical knowledge, as it becomes evident, for example, in abilities and procedural aspects of knowledge.[37] His main thesis, reminiscent of Wittgenstein and Ryle, is: *knowing-how* is not theoretical knowledge, it cannot be reduced to this. This is an attack on the position which became prominent with the writings of Williamson and Stanley.[38] The ability to do something does not coincide with the knowledge of sentences, theories and truths. A person who possesses the best theory of a part of the world of action, may still be a bad agent in that realm of action.

---

37 For a closer analysis of the correlation of *knowing-how*, *knowing-that* and *procedural knowledge* cf. also Löwenstein in this volume.
38 Cf. Stanley/Williamson (2001), 411–444. Löwenstein (in this volume) reconstructs and criticizes the argument of Stanley and Williamson.

A question which is often neglected in the modern debate about knowing-how is: why is practical knowledge actually a form of 'Knowledge'? Abel takes it up and presents the reader with a distinction between knowledge in a *narrow* and knowledge in a *broader* sense. The second meaning is of special interest here. He speaks of knowledge in a broad sense (in contrast to the narrow use in the sense of justified proporsitions) if basic abilities are involved which perform a pre-propositional, although cognitive orientation achievement, by having, for example, the effect of stabilizing actions and making the world accessible. In our abilities cognitive aspects are realized which cannot be reduced to propositional forms of rationality. With this Abel also expands the concepts of "cognition", "reason", "action" and "orientation". From the philosophical point of view the question which arises with regard to the extended employment of these concepts, is the following: what conceptual resources can we draw on to be able to determine broad knowledge (*broad* reason, action and cognition) as cognitively and normatively substantial enough, so that it is more than a causal pattern at the sub-personal level and can fulfill its rational implications as "knowledge"? Abel tries to capture the intrinsic normativity of knowing-how by identifying a practice-internal form of rule-following. A rule-following that refers to regular, normative practice procedures. It is of great importance to realize that Abel differentiates between two kinds of rule-following: one that is characteristic of propositional knowledge and another independent and basal form of rule-following in the realm of knowing-how. Abel tries to understand the latter with reference to practical regularities.

At this point I would like to point to a difficulty which arises from the correlation between *rule-following* and *regularity*. Abel refers to the latter to explicate knowing-how rule-following. He writes: "By regularity I mean practice-internal rule-following in the sense of the regularity of the executions inherent in this practice itself."[39] Two questions occur to me: first, isn't this conceptual determination circular? Is the right kind of regularity defined via rule-following to then distinguish knowing-how rule-following as a kind of regularity? Or is it a question not of a circular definition, but of an intrinsic referential context of both concepts? I'm not sure. And secondly: the attempt to normatively capture the phenomenon of rule-following with reference to regularities can only succeed if regularities themselves are already of a normative na-

---

39 Abel in this volume, 256.

ture. But how can the manner of their normative nature be understood? In what sense are regularities normative? Abel indicates in which direction the reader has to continue thinking with regard to the second question: because he defends the thesis that prelinguistic sensory-perceptual patterns, scenarios, schemes and contents of individuation and discrimination are included and active in perception and action. This is one of Abel's main theses. An answer to the second question is included here if it can be shown that those contents and patterns do not have to be understood biologistically or causalistically, but are already in their own right normative contents which precede propositional structures. The question concerning the logic of non-conceptual reasons and contents in perception and action cannot of course be answered conclusively by this article.[40] But Abel associates the question of knowing-how with those research fields, which deal with pre-linguistic structures. Possible necessary follow-up questions are, for instance: How can these patterns, schemes and contents be understood philosophically? In what way are they present within knowing-how?

David Löwenstein's article "Knowledge-how, Linguistic Intellectualism, and Ryle's Return" deals with the question of how we should understand knowing-how and in which relation it stands to knowing-that. As already indicated, there are many contentual similarities and overlappings between Abel and Löwenstein.

Löwenstein works out exactly how the arguments for the intellectualism of Stanley and Williamson function and how they can be criticized.[41] Like Abel he also rejects this position. 'Intellectualism' is the name given to the position which assumes first that knowing-that is fundamental, and second, in conjunction with that, defends the thesis that knowing-how is a form of knowing-that. In his critical discussion with this position Löwenstein introduces different interpretations of Ryle's *regress argument*. But let's proceed in chronological order.

Stanley and Williamson support their defense of intellectualism essentially on linguistic analyses of the speech form <S knows [how, where, why, etc.] to ride/to look, etc.>. The syntax of this speech form seems to advocate a homogeneous treatment of knowledge which aligns all those knowledge forms (knowledge why, where,

---

40 On this cf. Abel (2004). A few of these questions come up again in the discussion of Roller's article.
41 Cf. Stanley/Williamson (2001), 411–444.

what, etc.) with propositional knowledge. Linguistically there is one propositional analysis of all kinds of knowledge-constructions. Independent of the specific contents of the syntactic argument Löwenstein deals with doubts which arise from the *argument from linguistics* at this point: can a syntactic analysis give answers to philosophical questions? Löwenstein says that it cannot, and I share his intuition.[42]

Löwenstein's interpretation of the knowing-how assigns a key role to the concept of ability, as we have already seen in the case of Abel. This key role cannot be cancelled out by counterexamples of different kinds, as Löwenstein shows. Even Stanley and Williamson's theory does not get by without abilities, when they analyze "S knows how to ride a bicycle", for example, as follows: S entertains the way to do something under a *practical mode of presentation*. But what is a practical mode of presentation in contrast to a theoretical representational mode, if not the ability to do something? All putative counterexamples against the relation between knowing-how and ability can be cancelled out as soon as it becomes clear that the talk of abilities is a dispositional modal manner of speech. S knows how to ski, that of course does not mean that S can go skiing here and now, but that S is able to ski successfully under suitable conditions.[43]

Let's consider Ryle's regress argument now, which is maybe the strongest challenge to intellectualism. A look at the original text, but also at the secondary literature, reveals that there are different arguments that go by the name of "regress argument". Löwenstein distinguishes three of them: a contemplation, an application, and a correctness regress. He decides on the latter. Accordingly, it could be said against intellectualism that, assuming that propositional knowledge is always involved where practical knowledge is concerned, this propositional knowledge can only be relevant and action-guiding if it is *correctly applied*. And as Löwenstein correctly notes: "… to do something correctly requires knowledge how to do so."[44] With that the propositionalist runs the risk of placing knowing-that after knowing-that, he runs into a regress. That is Löwenstein's reconstruction of Ryle's regress argument. In my view, it is a very creative and inventive reading of Ryle.

---

42 The critique concerning the *argument from linguistics* refers to phenomenal knowledge among other things. It is appropriate to include Roller's article on this topic here.
43 Cf. the analysis of the nature of abilities from Greco.
44 Löwenstein in this volume, 290.

Finally I would like to deal with Löwenstein's interpretation of procedural knowledge. His creative approach explicitly refers to Brandom in this regard. If I understand him properly, he interprets the linguistic codification of rules and regulations (procedure) as making an ability explicit (knowing-how).[45] With this kind of speech form we can *say* what is (only) *done* at the level of knowing-how. Therefore quoting Brandom: making it explicit. By transferring mere ability to a public arena of discourse, we make an ability self-aware. That is the theory.

My comment on this is the following: I think it is obvious that this thesis can only be applied in a limited way. And this in two respects. First of all there are a lot of competences for which the procedure of recording and making it explicit seems to make little sense. Procedures cannot always be specified. How, for example, does one construe a good joke? It is nonetheless a cognitive competence. Secondly I would also like to stress that the knowledge of rules is only one possible form of self-realization and self-awareness of human abilities. There might be others. So far Löwenstein might agree.

Now, however, I would like to mention a fundamental objection. Even in those cases for which the picture outlined by Löwenstein is fitting, I have certain doubts about Brandom's idea of making explicit what was already implicitly given. For isn't in these cases an ability "transferred" into knowledge (saying), which is reminiscent rather of a creative *extension* of the ability, of a subsequent action or even of a translation? All these descriptions place a greater value on the status of what is new in procedural knowledge, in opposition to the idea that already existing contents be brought out into the open. The doubts begin exactly at this point: What was already there? What kinds of *contents* are there (because the result seems to be propositional knowledge)? Does the explicit formulation of a rule illustrate an implicit rule? Do such theses not lead to a new intellectualism of knowing-how? These questions primarily concern Brandom, but secondly also Löwenstein, who takes up the idea of 'making it explicit'. I am very curious to know how Löwenstein reacts to these skeptical thoughts.

---

45 For the logic of *making it explicit* and for further examples cf. Brandom (2008), ch. 4.

Chapter Two:
Knowledge in Situations: Contexts and Contrasts

Chapter Two comprises two parts. The first one is concerned with contexts of knowledge and discussions about epistemological contextualism. The second part focuses on contrasts and epistemological contrastivism. Gerhard Ernst opens the first topic in a general way.

A general original insight of contextualism in modern epistemology is the reference to and the explanation of the fact that we tend to evaluate ascriptions of knowledge from different perspectives and contexts in varying ways. Even if not all contextualists would agree with the following definition[46], it can be said, semantically speaking, that the meaning of the word "knowledge" varies according to the context in which it is used. That the concept of knowledge displays semantic varieties, can be understood, for the time being, in a completely general way, that is, not already with reference to the different theories of contextualism.

Let us take a look at Gerhard Ernst's article in this connection which at the same time highlights scopes and limits of contextualism. In "Two Varieties of Knowledge" Ernst shows that epistemologists often miss the point that the word "knowledge" displays at least *two* different ways of use. Based on the works of Oswald Hanfling[47] and on Wittgenstein's insight that the use of our expressions generate a web of resemblances (similarities and differences come and go), Ernst argues that there are two variations of meaning of the concept of knowledge and therefore two kinds of knowledge. In order to follow up both uses he directs the methodical focus of his examination towards the following pragmatic questions: What *function* does the concept perform in the individual situations? What *role* do knowledge sentences play within our form of life? In short: What is the sentence "S knows that p" good for? The question here concerns the practical purpose of the expression.[48] The answers lead us to two different functions of knowledge.

On the one hand Ernst answers this question by saying that a kind of *situational knowledge* is present whenever we express the idea that a subject can be regarded as a good informant (Craig) with sentences of the

---

46 Cf. Kompa's article on this.
47 Cf. Hanfling (2000), 94–110.
48 On this cf. Craig (1990). Craig argues in favor of a change in questions asked in epistemology, a change from analytical 'What-is-questions' to synthetical 'Why-we-use-questions'.

form "S knows that p" (knowledge for the ignoramus). Sometimes knowledge sentences classify agents as good informants with regard to the proposition p. As the fact that S is a good informant concerning p depends on the background information and interests of the ascriber, this use thus amounts to contextualism. Ernst writes: "There is no fact of the matter about whether John knows independently from the point of view we take."[49] The original insight of contextualism is based on this kind of use of "to know". But we should not overlook that there are other uses and functions which could speak for limits of contextualism.

Regarding the contextual nature of the good informant the second kind of knowledge goes a different way. Ernst speaks of the "knowledge for the knower" and thereby refers to situations of use in which the speaker wants to find out whether the subject has got certain information or not, information which the ascriber herself already possesses. Concerning this kind of knowledge there certainly is a need for discussion. In order to facilitate our understanding consider the following case: You know that Paul cannot swim, but being Paul's parent you are interested in knowing whether Claudio, who is taking care of your son for a few hours, knows or knew this. Why do you want to know this? Assume that Paul was allowed to go into the water. In this case it is important to know whether Claudio knew this, in order to be able to evaluate his actions: did it happen on purpose or was it merely due to lack of knowledge (information)? Your question whether Claudio has certain information, whether Claudio *knows*, can also simply have the function of being useful with regard to the exchange of information, that is to find out whether Claudio is a good recipient, as Ernst puts it, for this information. According to Ernst it is interesting that the common question "Does S know that p?" is to be answered positively under the given conditions, if S simply has the true belief p. The only point seems to be whether S is aware of the fact that p. If the story so far is correct, than we have knowledge without justification. Epistemologist's warning bells starts to ring.

It seems that the pure possession of information and beliefs other than the status of the good informant is objective and independent of any additional information the ascriber has. Both uses differ here too. It seems that knowledge for the knower cannot be analyzed in a contextual way.

---

49 Ernst in this volume, 310.

It certainly cannot be denied that this employment of the word corresponds to our use of language. There are situations in which we use the word "knowledge" this way. However, it is still worthy of discussion because epistemologists usually paint a different picture of knowledge, one where knowledge and true belief do not concur precisely.[50] In what way could epistemologists object to this second employment? Here are some possible approaches:

(a) Even *ordinary language* philosophers should not really be interested in how we speak, but in how we *ought to* speak. Philosophy is a normative business, something Wittgenstein repeatedly makes clear despite all his descriptivism and quietism. The motto is: *we rectify a philosophical error*[51]. Concerning our case this means: is the use of "knowledge" in situations which simply involve true beliefs to be accepted or to be criticized? Does it perform a function which is not already involved in the ascription of beliefs? Why, at this point, introduce a higher level epistemic predicate, if the basic concepts are doing all the work?

(b) The first point indicates that the second way in which Ernst uses the concept of knowledge could lead nowhere. This is followed by the assisting consideration that *practical aspects* are less dependent on knowledge than on beliefs, as for example when it comes to explaining and evaluating actions. In other words: does it not suffice that the agent beliefs that p in order to give explanations and evaluations for actions? What does that have to do with knowledge?[52]

(c) Moreover, it is not clear, the critic might argue, whether all those demanding elements which we assume to concern knowledge in the first sense (justified true belief), are not already contained in the manner in which we speak of solid and robust beliefs. That is, rational-normative aspects of justification for instance. Do we really want to know whether Peter solely believed that p, no matter for whatever (irrational) reasons, or does it not also play a role, whether his story concerning his belief is epistemically stable in order for us to be able to evaluate the action and establish whether we are good informants for him? But then the difference between the two kinds of knowledge becomes blurred. Whatever the case may be, it is up to the reader to decide how these critical questions should be dealt with.

---

50 For a critique of the analytical mainstream cf., for example, Sartwell (1991), 157–165; Beckermann (2001), 571–601.
51 Wittgenstein (2000).
52 Cf. Hyman in this regard.

Finally Ernst comes to the convincing conclusion that the meaning of the word "knowledge" is more comprehensive than is thought (philosophically) and that the attempt to define knowledge in terms of justified true belief therefore is doomed: "That is the reason why it isn't possible to find *one* analysis which fits *all* examples."[53] Even if I agree with the conclusion for other reasons, this thesis, however, is central to the present volume.

In "Nonindexical Contextualism – an Explication and Defense" Nikola Kompa refers to Ernst's first kind of knowledge. To be precise, she is concerned with the question of whether we are to understand conversational contextualism in a semantic or pragmatic way.[54] This kind of contextualism is usually semantically underpinned, either by means of an indexical approach or by means of a hidden-structure syntax. In the first case "knowledge" is similar to indexical expressions such as "I" and "here", in the second case, however, the approach is orientated rather towards adjectives such as "flat" and "round". Kompa objects to both alternatives and argues in favor of a pragmatic variety, of nonindexical contextualism.

If conversational contextualism is right, the sentence "S knows that p" can be true in context a, but false in context b, even though the epistemic position of the subject is considered to be stable. What changes are the conversational circumstances of the situation in which the ascriber makes a judgment, that is, the relevance of the information, for instance, or the costs of failure and the value of success, the obviousness of possible mistakes, the course of dialog, etc. All these factors define the standards of knowledge. We can then say that the situation or the context of ascription determines whether the epistemic position of the subject is strong enough to generate knowledge. It can lead to variously demanding epistemic standards depending on what the conversational factors are and how they co-operate. In some the subject S knows that p, in some it does not. Stewart Cohen points to the following example from everyday life:

> Mary and John are at the L.A. airport contemplating taking a certain flight to New York. They want to know whether the flight has a layover in Chi-

---

53 Ernst in this volume, 324.
54 Conversational or semantical contextualism (DeRose, Cohen) is usually distinguished from inferential contextualism (Williams). On this cf.: Cohen (2000), 94–107; DeRose (2009); Williams (1996); Pritchard (2002).

cago. They overhear someone ask a passenger Smith if he knows whether the flight stops in Chicago. Smith looks at the flight itinerary he got from the travel agent and responds, "Yes, I know – it does stop in Chicago". It turns out that Mary and John have a very important business contact they have to make at the Chicago airport. Mary says, "How reliable is that itinerary? It could contain a misprint. They could have changed the schedule at the last minute." Mary and John agree that Smith does not really know that the plane will stop in Chicago. They decide to check with the airline agent.[55]

In this example Mary and John are the ascribers and Smith is the subject/self-ascriber of knowledge. The varying contexts from which judgments are made are responsible for the fact that the self-ascription of Smith and the ascription from others to Smith deviate from each other. Under normal epistemic conditions (that is in everyday contexts of knowledge with low standards) we would agree with Smith and say that he knows that p. The conversational conditions of the more demanding context in which Mary and John find themselves lead to a rise in the standards, so that Smith does not know that p anymore.

The intuitive way of handling diverging ascriptions of knowledge which are expressed in examples such as these is one theoretical advantage of contextualism. Further theoretical advantages are its (apparent) anti-skeptical potential and the compatibility, as Kompa also notes, with pragmatic accounts of knowledge in the sense of Austin, Rorty or Craig. These accounts have in common that the ascription of knowledge often resembles acts of praising, that one indicates that the listener can rely on one or that others can be identified as good informants.

However, as mentioned at the beginning, Kompa focusses on the question of how the context sensitivity of the phrase "to know" is to be explained. If "knowledge" were an indexical expression, we would need to explain how the obvious difference between "knowledge" and "I" came about. Are there hidden indexicals? The question arises because we know no other cases of that linguistic phenomenon. And if so: how is indexical opacity to be explained? Because compared with "I" we seem quite often to miss this property. But this raises the question whether it makes sense to assume something like non-transparent indexicality.

The second approach criticized by Kompa tries to shed light on the context sensitivity via a hidden logical structure. If we say "the table is

---

55 Cf. Cohen (1999), 58.

flat" then the sentence, in a logical sense, has, strictly speaking, another syntactical form, namely: "Relative to standard T the table is flat." "Knowledge" here is not considered to be indexical because "flat" is not one either. So why should we not say that "S knows p" actually stands for "S knows p relative to the epistemic standard T."? One of Kompa's arguments against this approach amounts to the fact that we can say "the table is flatter than the chair" but not "S1 knows that p in a better way than S2."[56] Obviously, there is an important logical difference between "to know" and "flat".

Confronted with the difficulty of indexical varieties Kompa makes the case for nonindexical contextualism. It says essentially that it is probably better not to look for an explanation for context sensitivity on a semantic level, but to capture it through pragmatic aspects. In other words: What can be said against ascribing the same meaning to "knowledge" in all contexts and sentences and explaining the variation in the truth value pragmatically through the eye of the beholder? The ascriber constantly has to evaluate whether the knowledge sentence is true or false which does not necessarily mean that, according to the individual context, she will bring different meanings of the word "knowledge" into play. The evaluation of the truth value is influenced in accordance with the conversational elements, but meaning is stable. This is the suggestion.

My suggestion is that the debate concerning nonindexical contextualism could focus on the following two points. It is certainly right that a position that assigns constant meaning to the word "knowledge" seems to be at an advantage. I think that this is a widespread semantic intuition of competent speakers. But references to semantic intuitions are, of course, a hotly disputed topic within philosophy. That is why Kompa argues that their variety is not troubled by the problems which burden other varieties. Therefore nonindexical contextualism is believed to have *theoretical* advantages. There are, however, *other* questions and possible problems to be considered. For instance:

(a) A key argument for nonindexical and against indexical contextualism is the possibility of the former allowing for epistemic disagree-

---

56 Is that manner of speaking really out of the question? If the context with the higher standards leads to the same positive result as the weaker context, does one then not know that p in a better way? Be that as it may, the thesis of grades of knowledge is defended by Hetherington in his text for this volume (cf. ch. 1). Also cf. Hetherington (2011).

ments. Whoever wants to change the meaning of the knowledge sentence along with the context, is in danger of not allowing real differences of opinion between the contexts. This is so because, strictly speaking, the ascribers are speaking of other things. Verbal differences are not real disagreements because they are not contradictions. Now to the question: Is it a robust piece of data that there are very often such differences in opinion between contexts, and that they are real? I think that they are only apparent in a lot of cases and can be solved in the same way as in the example of "flat", when S1 says: "The table is flat" and S2 (with the microscope in his hand) replies: "Oh no, the table has a lot of surface irregularities." Here we do not have a disagreement. And now, let us take another look at the airport case in this respect. Does it really end in disagreement between Smith and Mary/John concerning the question whether Smith knows that the plane stops in Chicago? I have my doubts. Is it not easy to say that there is no contradiction, since both expressions stem from different contexts? Probably Smith would agree with Mary and John when confronted with the different conversational aspects. Whatever the truth may be, the intuitions concerning this case are anything but clear at this point.

(b) Concerning the theoretical cost/benefit assessment of the two (or three) varieties of conversational contextualism I see, moreover, a great difficulty where Kompa's theory is first of all committed to a *clear separation between semantics and pragmatics*, which, concerning its contents, should be clear enough defined so it can support the key thesis of nonindexical contextualism. This is a little problematic, and it brings us to the second point: Wouldn't we also like to learn what the *constant meaning* of "knowledge" is? That is a way of speaking of meaning which is removed from practical contexts and from specific language games because of a clear division between semantics and pragmatics. Both points are interrelated, because the understanding of Wittgenstein's insight that meaning is use leads in some way to a watering down of the semantic-pragmatic distinction. So what is semantics free from pragmatics? And what is the meaning of "knowledge"? These are my questions.

After situational contexts have been discussed, the second focus of the chapter "Knowledge in Situations: Contexts and Contrasts" is on contrasts as the title already indicates. This addresses a rather new position within analytical epistemology, namely so called contrastivism.[57] In this volume Jonathan Schaffer and Peter Baumann are arguing over the nature and the scope of this position, which quite often is associated with contextualism (or as one variety of it). However, Schaffer's comments show not least that there are not only great differences in content between contextualism and contrastivism, but that differences already become visible on the logical level at which the formulation of positions takes place. But let's proceed in chronological order.

What does contrastivism stand for? It claims that knowledge is a ternary relation between a subject, a knowledge proposition and a contrast proposition. That means: to say that S knows that p is strictly speaking an elliptic formulation, one that hides what is actually said, namely: S knows that p rather than q. It is important that both definitional elements be taken into account. It does not suffice to define contrastivism via the thesis of ternarity of the knowledge relation. This thesis itself is revisionary enough compared with the history and the mainstream of epistemology. For it seems to be a philosophical truism that propositional knowledge is a binary relation between a subject and a proposition. However, as we will see later, it is important to understand exactly how contrastivism got its name: it requires that the third element be defined via contrast classes, that is via contrast propositions.

Let's look at an example of this. Peter sees a robin in his garden. Does Peter know that there is a robin in his garden? According to the conventional view in epistemology this question should be answered with a yes or no. The contrastivist on the other hand refuses to give an answer to this question: "One can't say what is right...", and then asks in return: "It depends on the actual contrast in the situation of the conversation and which contrast is relevant. Please tell me the contrast sentences that compete with 'x is a robin'." Peter might perhaps know that there is a robin rather than a raven, but not that there is a robin rather than a European goldfinch.

Like the contextualist, the contrastivist tries to capture our intuitions which quite frequently fluctuate during the evaluation of epistemic situations. Whereas the contextualist speaks of different contexts from which judgments are passed, the contrastivist refers to varying contrast propositions at this point. The question whether Peter knows or not depends (in some extent) on the contrast.

---

57 For other texts on contrastivism see for example cf. Schaffer (2007), 383–403; Blaauw (2004).

Schaffer defends contrastivism whereas Baumann criticizes it. What can be held against contrastivism? In case that we are following Baumann then, "there are limitations of the theory and certain prizes which have to pay if it wants to retain plausibility."[58] I would like to address two limitations or theoretical costs that Baumann refers to. First he questions the fact that knowledge *always* has to be contrastive. It is not clear what should serve as a contrast proposition for basic mathematical, logical or semantic knowledge. Think of "2+2=4", for instance. Do we know that 2+2 is 4 rather than 5, 0, 8 or -5? All this does not sound very plausible. Schaffer responds to this objection as follows: It might be that the contrast in such cases is practically of no significance, that, because of the missing practical function, it is not seen to be there at all. But if knowledge is contrastive by nature then there have to be contrastive propositions in these cases too. So which ones? Schaffer argues that someone who merely knows the positive integers up to 10 and has learned how to add up using these numbers knows that 2+2=4, and not 20 or -4. I cannot conceal the fact that this answer seems rather artificial and theoretically constrained to me. Baumann brings another objection into play concerning "S knows that 2+2 is 4 rather than 20": if the knowledge subject has merely learned the positive integers up to 10, then she does not *know* the contrastive proposition. Is this objection convincing? I do not think so. It would suffice if the ascriber had the extended system of numbers at her disposal, provided that we acknowledge certain external assumptions regarding knowledge, which is unlikely to be very controversial. It suffices to note that it is not the subject who is the first authority concerning her own knowledge, as knowledge is not an inner state of a person. This, however, is most likely a shared basal belief of contextualism and contrastivism. But I do not want to go into this any further. What Baumann surely rightly refers to, is that there are many cases in which possible confusion, that is the conflict between the knowledge proposition p and the contrast sentences p, r, s, ... simply does not exist in practice. For instance, I do know that there is a bicycle over there. But what, taking contrastive circumstances into consideration, is it supposed to mean if we add: ... and not a car, a scooter or a plane, for instance? For children it can, of course, be important and in the beginning difficult to differentiate between bicycles and scooters. For them the contrast *exists*, but for us it does not. I do not see a way to distinguish those contrasts of a normal

---

58 Baumann in this volume, 366.

conversation which seem to be relevant concerning "x is a bicycle". No one gets things like that mixed up. It is similar with the mathematical example. Anyone who can add up is not likely to say 20 or -4, instead of 4. Such mistakes would rather question whether the person had understood how numbers are added together. That was my point in saying that contrastivism as a general answer seems theoretically constrained. Regarding Schaffer's metaphysical level, some knowledge situations work without contrasts.

Baumann's second objection goes in the following direction: For what reasons should we be committed to merely accept one possibility of the third element being explicated if we assume the ternary nature of knowledge? More precisely: let us recall the basic idea of conversational contextualism and Kompa's article. There we learned that knowledge is a relation between a subject, a proposition and an epistemic standard. Smith knows that the plane has a layover in Chicago measured by everyday standards, but not by the higher standards of Mary and John. Does contrastivism not constitute an unnecessary constriction of the third element? Why only speak of contrastive propositions and not of standards as well? To this Schaffer replies: but aren't epistemic contexts and standards on the one hand and contrastive propositions on the other interrelated? One could say that the standards vary and that they make varying demands on the knowledge subject because through them other contrast classes are brought into play. For Smith it is relevant to preclude, under everyday conditions, that the plane had *no* layover or any other stops *elsewhere* (not in Chicago). However, as a means of contrast, other alternatives come into play for Mary and John: did changes occur at short notice, was the schedule manipulated, etc.? Epistemic standards, thus Schaffer's thesis, have an effect via their implicit and explicit contrasts. If that is correct, a certain theoretical simplification of epistemology would follow as it is easier to theorize contrastive propositions than standards. Or it is the other way around: "The invocation of standards is, in my view, at best an oversimplification for the question of what range of contrasts are generally in play."[59]

Regarding the third element of the knowledge relation I think that Schaffer seems to be right. Contexts generate epistemic standards by exerting an influence on the relevance of contrast classes. If I summarized both points mentioned, I would argue for the following thesis: I do not

---

59 Schaffer in this volume, 376 f.

think that knowledge is always ternary but in case it is, the third element should be defined via contrastive propositions.

It is important to stress that Schaffer and Baumann have argued on two different logical levels so far. Schaffer makes clear that he is concerned with a metaphysical thesis, namely the *nature* of the knowledge relation. Reasoning on this level of course leaves a lot of follow-up questions open and unanswered. For instance: how can we analyze the ternary relation exactly? What relation exists between the nature of knowledge and our linguistic acts of ascribing knowledge? This means: How does metaphysical nature influence the semantics of "to know"? Schaffer does not say anything in particular in this regard, except that contextualism is a semantic thesis regarding the concept of knowledge, whereas contrastivism is to be understood in a metaphysical way.[60] If I understand Baumann correctly, he often argues on the level of *ascriptions* and of the practical uses of knowledge. He thematizes *contrastive knowledge attributions* and finds out that certain situations of ascription obviously get by without contrasts. There is a danger, I think, that both authors might be arguing at cross purposes as they are working on different levels.

Finally, I would like to indicate which intuitive relations I see between contrastivism and contextualism. The origin of contrastivism, I think, lies in the theory of relevant alternatives which is the founding manifesto of contextualism itself. The relevant alternatives are one possible way of defining the contrast of a knowledge sentence. In the epistemic dialog between subjects there is repeated (implicit) reference to those alternatives with regard to which it must be decided whether someone knows that p. What becomes apparent in a dialog, is expressed by the words 'rather than'. That means that contrastivism makes explicit what is often a silent or implicit part of epistemic conversations. In the course of the conversation the class of relevant alternatives can repeatedly change which leads to the contents of the knowledge ascription also being influenced by the varying 'rather than'.

The paradigmatic field of the application of contrastivism is the discourse and the Socratic situation of being able to ask and answer questions. This is so because every questioning only makes sense with reference to a background of possible answers. But as mentioned above, not every situation is of this kind. Sometimes there is no conversation and no real questions because the situation is clear.

---

60 But cf. Schaffer in this volume (*Contrastive Knowledge*).

Chapter Three:
Challenging Justification –
The Nature and Structure of Justification

In "Verantwortlichkeit und Verlässlichkeit"[61] Michael Williams tries to bring together two approaches in contemporary epistemology: responsibilism and reliabilism. Both positions provide answers to questions concerning the nature and structure of justification, at least as long as reliabilism does not completely abandon the concept of justification. Their answers, however, are often given in such a way that the other position disappears from view. If this is the case, then, according to Williams, we run the risk of not being able to understand human knowledge adequately. Epistemic justification has to combine responsibility and reliability.

Responsibilism often comes as a deontological approach, i.e. linked to the idea, that justification is to some extent concerned with responsibility and the performance of duty.[62] Generally speaking: being justified means arriving at cognitive attitudes guided by epistemic norms. This line of thought leads to problems, if the deontological approach is interpreted in a (hyper)-intellectual way, when, with regard to knowledge, it is *always* claimed that the knowledge subject must have used ways of justification to arrive at reasons which, in the sense of internalism, are known to the subject. In short: First, the subject has to have reasons, then, based on this, she can acquire knowledge. Under these very demanding conditions many intuitive knowledge cases are no longer included in the epistemic picture.

If I understand Williams correctly, he argues as follows: he takes up the position of responsibilism, criticizes intellectualistic versions of the same and tries to include the insight of reliabilism via more balanced and weaker forms of (responsibility–style of) epistemic normativity. Here the basic belief in the background is: responsibility is indispensable, if we want to be able to explain the normative dimension of human knowledge.[63] Responsibility without reliability, however, is epistemi-

---

61 Cf. also the original, Williams (2008), 1–26.
62 On this cf. Steup's article. Williams does not go into further detail and give a specific explanation of deontological theories. It is an interesting question, whether Steup's version is hyper-intellectual, that is, whether it is criticized by Williams or not.
63 Cf. Klein's article in this anthology for instance.

cally worthless. Then again, *pure* reliability leads nowhere, normatively speaking, and thus misses the actual phenomenon.

How can both approaches be brought together again? Williams' key move consists in substituting the traditional model of the structure of justification, which is facilitated by the *Prior Grounding* model, with another structure which still identifies normativity by the obeying of epistemic rules, without getting involved in mentalist ideas.[64] It is of course the *default-and-challenge* model of justification which is being referred to here. What is the difference between the two models? To put it briefly: following the default-and-challenge model, the knowledge subject does not, in every case, have to have passed through a previous route of positive authorization of a belief in order for knowledge to be present. As a rule, the ascription of knowledge is a sort of *default position* which is associated with an obligation to argue in favor of the normative position taken *in case of doubt* (that means not always and not under all conditions). A challenge has to be warded off. Whoever is attentive and has not made any epistemic mistakes can acquire knowledge, even if they did not justify explicitly what they believed to know.

Two kinds of epistemic rules emerge in the default-and-challenge structure of justification, *ought-to-do* and *ought-to-be* rules. It is precisely the latter, understood as an indication of normal conditions of justification and therefore of a form of assessment and criticism of a belief, which strengthens the deontological approach because firstly these rules avoid intellectualism due to describing rules concerning the future of a belief, and secondly the classical objection of doxastic involuntarism is removed.[65]

According to Williams one crucial element of default-and-challenge responsibilism is the inclusion of reliability. This happens in a more emphatic way than we can observe, for example, in the works of Brandom. Brandom places the so called reliability inferences with the ascriber. The latter proceeds from a disposition of classification to having knowledge, via the identification of the agent's disposition as being *reliable*.[66] Williams assigns even greater significance to the knowledge of reliability. In his opinion it is, in basal cases, indispensable for the agent himself

---

64 For the presentation of both models cf. also: Williams (2001).
65 For a different strategy of dealing with this objection cf. Steup in the present anthology. It is not clear how far apart Steup and Williams are. Both defend their deontological approaches differently.
66 Cf. Brandom (1994), ch. 4 and (2000), ch. 3.

to come to the conclusion that one's own epistemic abilities are reliable – and this in conceptual and epistemic respects. If this knowledge is not at hand, the agent is not considered to be a competent epistemic speaker, because he can neither judge whether a challenge is relevant and entitled to be made, nor can he himself put forward challenges. We should therefore only in exceptional cases remove reliability inferences from the hands of the agent. Williams writes: "Sellars behauptet, dass jemand, der bezüglich dieser Fähigkeit [z. Bsp. einfache Fähigkeiten der Farbklassifikation, S.T.] nicht in der Lage ist, auf Verlässlichkeit zu schließen, nicht an dem Spiel teilnehmen würde…"[67]

Finally I would like to sum up by suggesting the following characteristics of the default-and-challenge model: first of all, justification is normative; the involved normativity is to be understood in the deontological sense, as a kind of rule-following, regarding what is considered to be epistemically good. Here this position avoids extreme internalism and equally radical externalism. Challenges have to be rejected after they have been made, not beforehand. However, challenges themselves are rational moves within the language game, i.e. they have to be justified. This gets the skeptic into difficulties. Questions and answers are to be located at one level, epistemically speaking, unlike, for example, the *Prior Grounding* model in which doubting and questioning were always appropriate, that is, where we find an asymmetry between questions on the one hand and ascriptions and claims on the other, an asymmetry that is in favor of the skeptical question. 'Challenges for free' are rejected.

For various reasons "Justification, Deontology, and Voluntary Control" by Matthias Steup fits in well with the general alignment of the present volume. On the one hand he discusses an essential dimension of human-discursive knowledge that we became acquainted with in the first chapter and also in Williams' text, namely the dimension of normativity. On the other hand, his deontological view of epistemic justification which contains a certain answer to the question concerning epistemic normativity also connects *knowledge* and *acting*, as has been done in many other articles.

---

67 Williams in this volume, 413. Original citation: "Sellars's claim is that someone incapable of the reliability inference with respect to these capacities would not be situated in the game of giving and asking for reasons in the way required by the possession of genuine conceptual capacities."

Let's take a closer look at this. In terms of the goods or objects of justification – we are concerned with beliefs – Steup explicitly speaks of action-like performances: believing is acting or belief formation is a form of agency. As a rule, this linking of believing to acting is interpreted as a theoretical weakness, but with reference to this volume, to me it rather seems to be a strength.

What does the deontological approach amount to? First of all it points to concepts like duty, rule, and blamelessness. A special form of normativity is clearly being brought into play by all these concepts. If the matter is one of e*pistemic duty* the approach has to refer to an *epistemic ought*. Since an agent is distinguished positively if he or she has fulfilled epistemic duties, the point should be that he or she has acted in ways one epistemically ought to act in such situations. In this context Steup defines justification as follows: "S is justified in believing that p = df. it is not the case that S ought to refrain from believing that p."[68]

As is already known, the main argument against this definition will not be long in coming and is involved in what is called doxastic involuntarism. The position addressed in this case (doxastic involuntarism) proceeds from the intuitively plausible thesis that our beliefs are, contrary to our actions for instance, not controlled, not deliberate, that they cannot be presented as the result of a decision. "Given our evidence, we cannot believe otherwise."[69] According to that, the reproach is that of a category mistake: the deontological approach treats beliefs like actions, and because it deals with the former in the sense of an ought which cannot be applied to cognitive states the position is committed to a category mistake. But is doxastic involuntarism true? Steup answers this question in the negative. The fact that we are able to deliberately control our beliefs can also mean that we form and defend them in the light of rational reasons. With that the focus has shifted, namely to the question, what we mean reasonably, when we say and decide whether an act is being deliberately controlled or not. If we consider the formation of a belief and move the debate about the deontological approach closer to compatibilism concerning free will, the following analogical answer might be suggested: a causal antecedent by itself does not per se preclude deliberate control but the right kind of causation is a sign of that same control. In other words: the fact that we form beliefs in the light of rational reason is a sign of rational control. Therefore

---

68 Steup in this volume, 423.
69 Steup in this volume, 431.

this means that beliefs are under our voluntary control. I agree with Steup.

In my opinion we can yet further strengthen Steup's position in a way that he does not himself deal with. Let's take a look at the defense or adherence of a belief rather than at its formation. Assuming Williams and Brandom are right regarding the basic idea of the default-and-challenge model of justification[70] then the subject of knowledge commits itself in case of doubt to defend the default entitlement against objections and criticism. The discussion of doxastic decision and freedom acquires a new and different meaning in the light of the beliefs, which we have with regard to the default-and-challenge structure because it involves *acts of defending and assessing* – and these are types of acting. The agent has to react to criticism and possibly sacrifice his normative position.

To sum up: *Having a belief,* in the epistemic sense, has a strong normative flavor. The causal and rational prologue plays a role, as does the causal and rational epilogue. That is why I agree with Steup when he says that epistemic normativiy is to be understood by an epistemic ought, as the prologue and epilogue mentioned above are both an indication of epistemic duties. I would even go a step further: *Having a belief* is in part the ability *to defend* the belief. Therefore doxastic involuntarism seems to be wrong.

As so often, the devil is in the detail: a lot depends on how strong the concept of duty is made and on how narrowly the deontological approach is interpreted. In my view Steup opts for a weaker interpretation, one that I find convincing.

In his paper published here "Infinitism and the Epistemic Regress Problem" Peter Klein makes another attempt at explaining and defending infinitism in epistemology.[71] At first sight the reader might get the impression that infinitism does not fit well in the place of this chapter, framed as it is by Williams and Steup. Why not place it near the more formal texts by Luper and Brueckner? Because I think that the logical structure of justification which leads Klein to infinitism also has pragmatic roots. This is how I read Klein.

Let's begin with the question: what is infinitism? The answer is that this position involves a reaction to the old, well known regress problem. The problem of regress concerns the structure of reasons, or more pre-

---

70 Cf. Williams in this volume, and Brandom (1994).
71 For former attempts cf. Klein (2007), 1–17 and (2011), 245–256.

cisely: the processes of justification which we are committed to when knowledge is involved. Assuming I claim that p on the basis of r1. Now I am confronted with the question of how reliable the reasons r1 are. Why do I think that I can rely on these evidences? Now I am obviously forced to adduce other reasons which are capable of supporting r1, for instance r2. The problem is, that it is not obvious why this game or process of justification should end here. In principle reasons can be challenged any number of times. That means that we are confronted with a regress.

The following three options suggest themselves as possible reactions to the regress: first of all, the dogmatic insistence on selected reasons without adducing any further reasons, secondly, epistemic foundationalism, and thirdly, the coherence theory. Let's exclude dogmatism. Klein believes that neither of the other two options can solve the problem, that they themselves in fact end in infinitism. Why? Foundationalism thinks that it can escape regress with the help of so called basic beliefs. Basic beliefs are immediately justified beliefs, that is they are justifiers that do not need any further justification. The coherence theory, on the other hand, wants to support a selected belief epistemically by making it part of a coherent system. Neither answer can have the final say according to Klein because in both cases we *can* ask ourselves for what reasons the theoretician believes that the property E (to be a basic belief or to be a member of a coherent system) classifies beliefs as being epistemically supported. What makes systems of beliefs or basic beliefs into special epistemic properties? One more time thus we can question the reasons. But with this question we are again confronted with a regress, or rather we are on the trail of infinitism. That is so because all that infinitism initially says is that there is no answer to the question concerning reasons which cannot itself in turn be questioned and challenged: "the central claim of infinitism ... [is] that there is no privileged belief that is immune to further interrogation."[72]

Even if we do not always question the adduced reasons in practice, it is not logically impossible to do so. Klein does not consider it problematic that this possibility always remains. Why is he so unconcerned here? We are looking for an answer to the question whether the process of justification is able to strengthen our beliefs. Concerning this question infinitism tells us: human knowledge is guided by the normative imperative which says: "Please look for reasons!" In the course of epistemic

---

72 Klein in this volume, 462.

conversations and dialogs we question our justifications and look for reasons of our reasons, etc. In order that the activity of justification can have epistemic weight, it has to improve our beliefs. And that is exactly what happens, as the justification moves on step by step. The dialog between A and B penetrates deeper and deeper into the rational foundation. With that, according to Klein, we would have arguments against the initial suspicion which expresses itself in the regress problem, namely that justifications could be epistemically worthless moves in the language game of knowledge: "…the act of justifying a belief gives it a positive epistemic status that the reason might not yet enjoy."[73] And we can add: even if those acts always renew and repeat themselves. The giving and demanding of reasons does not stop, it is an essential part of the language game of knowledge.

This is how I understand Klein. For me infinitism is an analysis of the continuous progress of epistemic conversations. Logics and pragmatics meet at this point.

(But one question remains: How do default-and-challenge justification and infinitism interrelate? I do not see a contradiction here. We can always separate default claims from this status and question them with regard to their epistemic strength.)

The articles by Steven Luper and Anthony Brueckner discuss rather more formal aspects of the structure of justification. Here two principles are at the centre of the discussion: the *closure* principle of knowledge on the one hand and the principle of *transmission* of evidential warrant across known entailment on the other. Both principles do not coincide and are the subject of contemporary debates.

Steven Luper's paper "Das einfache Argument" is a translation of the English article "The Easy Argument".[74] Luper discusses the closure principle of knowledge, he reacts, more precisely, to a problem concerning the principle that knowledge is closed under known entailment, which has become predominant during the past few years.

To put it quite simply, closure means the following: if S knows that p and S also knows that p entails q, then S also knows that q. Knowledge is closed under known entailment. With this simple wording the principle is open to many attacks and counterexamples. To reinforce it, Hawthorne suggests a more detailed wording which is intended to

---

73 Klein in this volume, 468.
74 Luper (2008), 321–331.

take the wind out of the sails of some objections. He writes: "If one knows P and competently deduces Q from P, thereby coming to believe Q, while retaining one's knowledge that P, one comes to know that Q."[75] At this point I do not want to go into any other stronger versions of this formulation in greater detail. Let us assume that the principle presented or a similar wording has a certain initial plausibility.

On what grounds can closure be challenged? The principle is the subject of epistemological debates, not least because it is of great importance for the discussion with the skeptic. Since, as is known, the *modus ponens* of the anti-skeptic is the *modus tollens* of the skeptic:

(1) If S knows that p and if S also knows that p entails q, then S also knows that q.
(2) S knows that p.
(K1) Therefore: S also knows that q.

(1) If S knows that p and if S also knows that p entails q, then S also knows that q.
(2 ★) S does not know that q.
(K2) Therefore: S does not know that p either.

In both arguments the principle of closure is presupposed with regard to the first premise, the skeptic, however, proceeds from the negation of knowing that q to the negation of knowing that p.

Luper is not concerned with the discussion with the skeptic. However, this debate makes it clear that critics of closure ask over and over again whether knowledge is really closed with regard to *all* implications. Does it not suggest itself that certain heavyweight implications (negated skeptical hypotheses, for example) should not be included in the knowledge operator?[76] Luper concentrates on precisely this kind of question. In doing so he discusses a putative type of counterexample, in which knowledge is purported to be too easily generated. Stewart Cohen has introduced the following case into the discussion: S looks at his table and arrives at the knowledge that the table is red. S also knows that 'the table is red' entails that 'it is not the case that the table is white but illuminated by a red light'.[77] If closure held, one could (too?) easily rule out such illusions. Critics now point out that closure

---

75 Hawthorne (2005), 29.
76 On this cf. Dretske (2005), 13–26.
77 Cf. Cohen (2002), 309–329.

too easily entails the knowledge that such illusive situations are not the case. To put it briefly, the reproach is: is it not circular to infer normal perceptual conditions, if they themselves are, strictly speaking, preconditions of the perceptual belief "this table is red"?

Luper confronts the reader with a theoretical cost-benefit calculation. Every answer to the problem of easy knowledge is associated with costs. One can abandon closure on the one hand which leads to very implausible consequences. Or alternatively one can reinforce the claim for knowledge that p is the case, in the hope that skepticism will not be an issue, but that at the same time knowledge which is derived too easily will be included as a sort of precondition for the knowledge that p. But the demand for independent reasons for the implication q, if p is to be known, opens up the way for the skeptic. Luper is of the opinion that the concession that easy knowledge is possible provides the best cost-benefit calculation: "Wenn ich Recht habe, können wir die Möglichkeit einfachen Wissens nicht ausschließen, ohne entweder die Geschlossenheit aufzugeben oder eine Analyse mit inakzeptablen skeptischen Konsequenzen anzunehmen. In der Annahme, dass keine dieser Alternativen akzeptabel ist, können wir den Schluss ziehen, dass Wissen manchmal eben tatsächlich einfach *ist*."[78]

Now, is easy knowledge possible? Luper says 'Yes'. Maybe this thesis can also be supported in a different way. Let's take another look at Williams. With the aid of the default-and-challenge model it can be said that so called easy knowledge has a default status with reference to perceptual conditions. If there are no good reasons to doubt that things are the same color as they appear to be in our perception, then we can assume that the circumstances are normal. Hence it is a case of default-knowledge. In a way, the knowledge of the initial premise p, i.e. 'this table is red', is not of this nature, because it has an evidential back-up. But we should not demand of the closure principle that it only gives one kind of answer to the question of *how* knowledge can be generated. All that closure needs to be true is the fact that the one cannot be known without the other. Knowledge that the table is red is associated with the knowledge that the conditions of the situation are normal, that

---

[78] Luper in this volume, 477. Original citation: "If I am correct, we cannot rule out the possibility of easy knowledge without either abandoning closure or adopting an analysis with unacceptable skeptical consequences. Assuming that neither alternative is acceptable, we can conclude that sometimes knowledge just *is* easy."

is, that the table is not white and illuminated by a red light. Both knowledge contents stand and fall together, irrespective of whether one of the two propositions has a default status and the other hasn't. If q does not have such a status, then p cannot be claimed either.[79]

In my opinion it certainly remains correct that the conclusion could seem circular, because the assumption that the perceptual conditions are normal always precedes or encase the perceptual belief. But closure does not demand, something which Brueckner addresses in the next passage, that evidential warrant is transferred from the premises to the conclusion. That is the difference between *closure* and *transmission*. More about that now.

Anthony Brueckner's "What is Transmission Failure?" is concerned with the question of how we should understand the transmission of evidential warrant and what, in this connection, transmission failure can be in the process of justification. The transmission principle of warrant across known entailment does not coincide with the closure principle discussed by Luper. Crispin Wright has repeatedly pointed to the difference.[80] I would like to offer the reader some theoretical prerequisites which should make it easier to follow Brueckner's line of thought. The difference between closure and transmission of warrant consists in the fact that the latter is of a more particular kind: it shows *how* somebody arrives at a warrant for a proposition, namely via the inference from the premises to the conclusion, which transports the warrant via the argument. Closure on the other hand says nothing at this point, and quite rightly so, because the *way* of recognizing that p is the case is in most situations not a way of recognizing what is implied in p (i.e. that q is the case). In other words: our reasons for p are not always reasons for q as well. We see that the table is red but this way of recognizing does not enable us to see that the table has not been manipulated.

By *cogent argument* Crispin Wright understands an inference via which a first-time warrant is transferred from the premises to the conclusion, just as it is required by the transmission of evidential warrant. Now interestingly, we can note that some arguments are of this nature, whereas others are not. The epistemological relevance of the principle of transmission consists in the fact that, among other things, some

---

79 Cf. also Schmoranzer in this volume.
80 Cf. Wright (2003).

anti-skeptical arguments – think of Moore's 'refutation' of the skeptic – are suspected of being examples of transmission failure.

Let us say that warrant is transported, if the following conditions are fulfilled: first time warrant for p is based on evidence E; S deduces the conclusion c from the premise p; and thereby receives a first time warrant for c based on p (and E). Transmission failure means then that warrant for the premise is possible only if the conclusion is already warranted. If one needs independent reasons for c, before p can be considered as warranted, then evidential warrant cannot be transferred from the premises to the conclusion.

For example:

> ...consider [SOCCER], involving as evidence: (e) Jones has just headed the ball into the net, he is being congratulated by team-mates and the crowd has gone wild. That provides a defeasible warrant for: (P) Jones has just scored a goal, which entails ... that: (I) A game of soccer is taking place.[81]

Wright's thought here is that the fact that a soccer game is taking place is already required, if the premise 'Jones has just scored a goal' is to be warranted. Only if the actions by Jones are carried out within a soccer match does it make sense to say that he has scored a goal. If so, then transmission of evidential warrant from p to c fails. The same holds for Moore who wanted to move from "Here is a hand" to "There is a material world". In whatever way Moore believed it was possible to refute the skeptic, it does not seem possible by means of transmission of evidential warrant. His argument is not *cogent*.

In his paper Brueckner deals critically with Silins who argues that there is no coherent formulation of a transmission failure which still makes genuine cases of such errors possible.[82] After dealing with Silins Brueckner follows him in pursuing the distinction between *doxastic* warrant and *propositional* warrant. As warrant is involved in the principle of transmission, it is essential to know what form of warrant it is. At the end of his text he offers the reader the following formulation regarding transmission failure: "If S believes C at t, then S cannot acquire his first warrant for believing C at a later time t' when S reasons from P to C..."[83] With this formulation we are back on stage and can pursue our question where Moore goes wrong.

---

81 Cf. Wright (2004), 25.
82 Cf. Silins (2005), 71–102.
83 Cf. Brueckner in this volume, 495.

Chapter Four:
Varieties and Forms of Knowledge –
Animal, Phenomenal, and Practical Knowledge

On the one hand the chapter "Varieties and Forms of Knowledge" deals with possible extensions of analytical epistemology presented by the thematization of forms of knowledge which have been most widely neglected on the basis of a prevalent *propositional* paradigm. Usually epistemologists understand knowledge as "knowing that something is the case." But there are other kinds, for instance animal or phenomenal knowledge.

On the other hand methodological concerns regarding the analytical-conceptual project of knowledge are also addressed. This critique opens the door for new methods (and also new kinds) of knowledge.

Let us start with the latter. "Epistemology and Cognitive Ethology", the article by Hilary Kornblith, expresses doubt regarding the scope and relevancy of the traditional procedures of analytical epistemology and tries to tie philosophical questions of knowledge to empirical methods of investigation. His central theme is: There are not two or more separate phenomena here, there is not knowledge for philosophers that is to be conceptually examined on the one and knowledge as an empirical phenomenon in the area of nature on the other hand, but there is merely one phenomenon that philosophers and empirical scientists should examine *together*. He himself sums up his thesis as follows: "An examination of work in cognitive ethology thus serves as a useful corrective to the traditional focus of epistemologists on the human case."[84] In other words: The category of human knowledge can be understood more closely and in a better way, if we look at how knowledge works in the case of animals.

The reorientation of the relationship between philosophical epistemology and cognitive science being addressed in the article of Kornblith is to be seen against the background of critical reflexions regarding the traditional analytical-conceptual method of epistemology. Kornblith doubts that the question concerning the *nature* of knowledge can in detail be clarified by answers given to questions concerning the *concept* of knowledge. Other than commonly assumed such a transformation of the

---

84 Cf. Kornblith in this volume, 501.

question (from the nature to the concept) does not involve a better reformulation of the original topic, but simply a new object of examination.[85]

At this point the following dilemma arises for the analytical philosopher, as Kornblith sees it: Either the analysis of concepts is or is not important for epistemology. If it is not, then the analytical method becomes less important (horn two). But even if the analysis of concepts remains substantial for epistemology, we should pursue it *empirically* (horn one). On the one hand it seems to be true that, even *if* the concept of knowledge reveals essential properties of the phenomenon of 'knowledge' the philosopher is well advised to rely less on his own semantic intuitions but instead to gather those data in a *social-scientific*, exact way, for instance in terms of empirical experimental philosophy.[86] In addition, if the possession and acquisition of concepts matters with regard to philosophical questions, empirical input is also believed to be helpful. As modern research in psychology has shown, philosophical concept theories seriously differ from those in psychology. Therefore: if the analysis of concepts is important, then, it seems, that there is no way around the empirical (experimental, psychological) investigation of concepts.

Now to the second horn: Kornblith's fundamental critique focuses on the other side of the dilemma, as epistemology does not concern the *concept* of knowledge at all. According to him philosophers should not examine the concept of knowledge but knowledge itself. They should broadly examine it in the same way that we examine gold, water, or tigers, that is by directly examining examples and not by examining them via the concepts "gold", "water", or "tigers". All these examples concern natural kinds, the essence and nature of which was and is always just partially and imperfectly expressed in the meaning of the individual sign. Applied to epistemological objects the key thesis is then: knowledge is a natural kind and should be examined like all natural kinds: by empirically examining individual examples.

What does all that have to do with cognitive ethology? Kornblith's naturalism brings cognitive ethology into play and the knowledge of animals along with it because he classifies the possession of reliable processes of belief formation as evolutionarily beneficial. Here we have a va-

---

85 On this cf. Kornblith (2002), and (2006), 10–25.
86 On this cf. Weinberg/Nichols/Stich (2001), 429–460; and Weinberg et. al. (2010), 331–355.

riety of reliablism at work. Knowledge as a natural kind is therefore understood via the evolutionary function of that kind, which can be understood much more clearly with reference to animals. The knowledge of animals is principally of the same kind as the knowledge of humans. Humans are merely in possession of reliability structures on a meta level (higher-order belief forming processes). Therefore we can directly utilize the results of cognitive ethology for epistemology.

Radical approaches entail a broad range of possible critique. I would like to draw attention to a few points regarding the argumentative dispute, which are common in the current debate.

(a) Basically two types of intuition are confronting each other. Those who regard knowledge as a natural kind on the one hand and those who, for example, following Wittgenstein, Williams, and Brandom on the other, thematize knowledge as a social phenomenon which is concerned with practices of attributions of knowledge. As a social phenomenon it has a normative character in various ways.[87] However this dispute is settled, the case can be made for the fact that rational aspects are a vital part of *human* knowledge, so that cognitive ethology can indeed say something about the knowledge of *animals*, but is of no direct philosophical relevance because human knowledge is of a different kind. Whoever abstracts from concepts like responsibility, obligation and rule-following appears to be, according to a possible thesis, discussing another phenomenon. Epistemic justification does not only serve the probability of truth. Within social and discursive contexts it is also a manifestation of our human self-conception as acting agents.[88]

Of course, Kornblith need not disagree. In that case, however, he is stuck for a story on how we get to epistemic normativity taking the conceptual requirements of cognitive ethology into considertion. But can such a story be told? (I do no think so.)

Assuming genuine human epistemic normativity, it can also be shown with reference to human knowledge, in objection to Kornblith, that the dualism of the *phenomenon* of knowledge and the *concept* of knowledge is not sustainable. The phenomenon of human knowledge

---

87 Furthermore, Williams argues against the theoretical homogeneity of the concept of knowledge. Should he be right and should knowledge therefore be in the possession of a lot of facets and contextual coloring, then the plausibility of a homogenous constitution of a specific kind, as Kornblith assumes, vanishes. Cf. Williams (1996), ch. 3.

88 On this cf. also the articles of Hetherington, Steup and Klein in this volume.

cannot be separated from its concept, it is a thick socio-normative phenomenon. Under these assumptions it correspondingly applies that the understanding of the concept of knowledge *is* an understanding of the nature of knowledge and we achieve the former by giving an account of the practice of the *ascription* of "to know". A counter project could start like this, for instance.

(b) But even if we defer this critique, a possible question is also implied when taking Kornblith into consideration. Namely, is cognitive ethology actually reliant on *knowledge?* Is it theoretically necessary to ascribe knowledge to animals and not just beliefs? This is so because the suspicion is raised that the talk of beliefs and pro/contra-attitudes is sufficient to explain behavior. At this point we encounter our next contribution, because this topic is taken up again by Hans-Johann Glock, whose article we now want to turn to.

The question is thus: Animal Knowledge or Animal Belief? In "Non-Human Knowledge and Non-Human Agency" Hans-Johann Glock argues for the former. Even if the impression is created that Kornblith and Glock agree concerning the knowledge of animals, their approaches are very different from each other. Glock does not use non-human knowledge as an argument against analytical epistemology in every respect and his approach is motivated essentially in a language philosophical way. At those points where he distances himself from the paradigm of analytical epistemology he appeals rather to Hyman and Wittgenstein than to cognitive ethology.

Glock proceeds from the general idea that the concepts of "knowledge" and "action" have to be thought of together.[89] To be more precise: according to this tradition of thought, epistemic concepts are conceptually tied to practical concepts. The original question of whether or not animals have knowledge shifts to whether animals are acting subjects or whether they act for reasons. As is known, such questions allow for two extreme positions, assimilationist and differentialist ones. Glock decides in favor of a weak form of assimilationism: "The[se] basics of knowledge and action are shared by humans and animals."[90] With regard to the realm of acting, everyday language appears to support this point: we ascribe intentional states of various kinds to animals in order to be able to explain their behavior. In order to be able to establish

---

89 On this explicitly cf. Hyman's article.
90 Glock in this volume, 549.

a relation to knowledge on this level, Glock appeals to a thesis of Hyman (see ch. 1), according to which propositional knowledge is presented as an ability to act for reasons. This means: knowledge that p is the ability to act for the reason that p. Thus Glock's conclusion is: animals can act for reasons, they are therefore in possession of propositional knowledge.

Following this thesis a few questions arise. First of all: Are reasons not very demanding, inner entities the ascription of which is full of mental and intentional requirements and which therefore can at best be understood in a metaphorical way where animals are concerned? Secondly: the discussion of reasons and knowledge brings with it the concept of *proposition*. Do we really want to say that there can be a relation between animals and such abstract objects? Glock addresses both questions. He reacts with a factive understanding of reasons with regard to the first objection. Concerning reasons, his thesis is that it is not a question of inner states but of objective circumstances, of facts. If that is the case the actions of animals can, of course, also be motivated by facts. I find this interpretation of the basal concept of reason very plausible and promising. His reply to the second objection, however, is still not quite clear to me. Glock writes "…the idea that an intentional state is a relation between a subject and a proposition is problematic."[91] Glock essentially offers semantic arguments for his thesis. The reader may decide whether this attack on language philosophical orthodoxy is successful because Glock attacks nothing less than the standard interpretation of our way of speaking of intentional states.

Finally I would like to record that Glock does indeed draw attention to the difference between animal knowledge and human knowledge. Therefore his assimilationism, as noted above, is moderate. In the above quote there is talk of the "basics" being the only thing shared in both cases. In the basic or less strict sense of the word, animals have knowledge – and on this level the ascription is not to be understood in a metaphorical way. Human knowledge, however, goes beyond the basics. How is this "more" to be understood? To this Glock says, it involves a different scope: "It lies rather in the fact that we can believe, know and do *more*."[92] In my opinion Glock does not only aim for a difference in quantity at this point, but also for qualitative differences which are coupled with a *more* in believing and acting.

---

91 Glock in this volume, 545.
92 Glock in this volume, 549.

But does he go as far as to speak of a *kind* of difference? This question remains open. As repeatedly mentioned above there is indeed conceptual scope for the thesis that, thanks to normative-rational commitments, human knowledge is of a different kind. The question concerning the nature of animal and human knowledge, that is of which kind animal and human knowledge is, is indeed relevant to Glock's assimilationism. This is so because in the attempt to deal with the question concerning qualitative similarities and differences a further question arises, namely one concerning the concept and understanding of *concepts*. If we ascribe reasons, actions, and knowledge to animals we cannot help ascribing concepts to them as well, at least I would adhere to this thesis. And Glock, too, hesitates approaching the field of non-conceptual contents. But this line of thought forces us to reconsider the logical presuppositions of assimilationism. Because: when we ascribe concepts to animals, we obviously ascribe to them *something other* than to competent speakers. Here I am thinking of two paradigms of concept possession which dominate philosophical literature: the cognitive scientific one on the one hand and the inferential one on the other.[93] If animals come within the first one and humans, on the other hand, within the second, the question arises whether we really ascribe (human) knowledge to animals? Therefore my closing question is: what is the point of assimilationism?

In "Phänomenales Wissen und Hintergrund" Claudio Roller examines, as the title indicates, a form of knowledge that entered the realm of analytical epistemology quite late and which has (compared with propositional knowledge) hardly been dealt with. Here it is a question of phenomenal knowledge or of experiential knowledge, that is of knowing what-it-is-like or how-it-feels to have an experience, to see something red or to taste raspberries, for instance. This form of knowledge is known by the name "qualia" from the philosophy of mind. The focus of the article is on the question concerning the nature of this knowledge, more precisely, on the relation it bears to propositional and to practical knowledge. The two positions which Roller moves between throughout, are represented by Hugh Mellor (phenomenal knowledge is knowing-how) and Tim Crane (phenomenal knowledge is a form of propositional factual knowledge). He deals critically with both of them, although his sympathies lie more with the relation be-

---

93 On this cf. Brandom (2000).

tween experiential knowledge and knowing-how. Roller tries to make clear that *knowing-how* and to an even greater extent *knowing-that* both "entered the scene" at a fairly late stage, compared to phenomenal or experiential knowledge. Experiential knowledge and knowledge by acquaintance are classified as fundamental, as being the basis on which both abilities and theoretical forms of knowledge can be built. According to Roller a philosophical genealogical reconstruction of human knowledge has to begin with phenomenal knowledge and proceed then to theoretical knowledge via practical knowing-how. That is Roller's major topic.

Mellor, for example, addresses the basal human growth of experiential knowledge as a growth of corresponding competences, for instance the ability to identify or to imagine colors. Roller's objection to this thesis is, in a nutshell, that abilities and competences of this kind require an acquaintanceship with colors and a corresponding experiential knowledge. These abilities cannot be understood unless one has actually had these experiences, therefore how to know does not merge in how it is or feels. What Roller regards and defends as an essential insight of Mellor is the assumption that phenomenal knowledge is of a non-propositional kind.

In order to hint at a possible dispute with Roller's text, I would like, at this point, to let the *propositionalist* have a say and play the *advocates diaboli*. Here is a first thought. Whoever deals with Roller's critique of propositionalism will note that he makes use of a specific dualism with language on the one and experiences on the other side. His point is: The propositionalist does indeed have concepts such as "this shade of color" or "red" but he does not yet have the corresponding experience with them. One could object to this point, however, that this dualism is anything but an essential component of the propositional theoretical structure. On the contrary. One key insight of propositionalism is that it makes both sides of this dualism more than incomprehensible, as McDowell has repeatedly pointed out.[94] Concepts and experiences belong together. This means: during the process of acquisition but also often while using color concepts patterns and color experiences are not separable from the concepts. *That* is the way we learn and use "red". Unlike the way philosophical thought experiments suggest, the pattern and experience is not added to the concept afterwards. Language (meaning, content) is, this could be stressed in accordance with McDo-

---

94   Cf. McDowell (1996).

well, a *thick* phenomenon, an interwoven network of linguistic and non-linguistic elements. The competent use of color concepts goes hand in hand with color experiences. Or in other words: to have our concept of 'red' is to have *color experiences,* and vice versa. What is a concept of 'red' supposed to be without *experiences?*

And: If the dualism of language and experience were plausible, this would mean that not only concepts would be in danger of seeming incomprehensible but experiences as well. This is so because on the other hand non-conceptual experience is in danger of becoming a great mystery, because in that case we would have the argumentative duty to specify what a non-conceptual content is in more detail. Such "contents" are certainly very popular. But do we know what we are being offered here? Or do we succumb to the myth of the given? Can we understand the demand that is being made here? Contents are essentially of a normative and inferential kind, otherwise it could not be shown how the content that p is to be distinguished from the content that q. But how can these aspects be captured on the non-conceptual level?

To sum up: In a certain respect propositionalism is the attempt to escape this kind of dualism by claiming that conceptuality and experientiality are bound to each other. But it seems to me that Roller is committed to that kind of dualism.

Why do I follow the strategy of arguing in favor of propositionalism? Because it seems to me that the answers to these questions are of central importance for Roller's project. Let's take a look at the following: Roller criticizes propositionalism in that it cannot adequately describe how we acquire language.[95] The problem is that the conceptual resources which are needed to make language acquisition comprehensible as an accomplishment or *achievement* of an *agent* become useless due to the propositional interpretation of meaning and content. Following propositionalism, content, normativity, reason, and action are understood in such extensive ways that they are not available on the level of children who do not yet speak. If these concepts are missing, the question arises of how non-normative and non-acting beings can actually *become* users of language. Or rather: if we cannot describe language acquisition with concepts like 'acting', 'reason' and 'sense', then a non-normative process remains. But how then can the transmission to normative spaces of acting be possible?

---

95 On this reproach cf. also Tolksdorf (2011).

My supposition is that Roller is going to face a very similar problem. As I have shown elsewhere[96], I am trying in the context of his problem to speak of a continuum of sense which will allow us to keep the realm of acting and the realm of propositional content separate. This continuum is intended to enable an approach to genealogical transitions between forms of sense (Sinnformen). Roller uses this picture on various occasions, but he wants – and this is the crucial point for me – to go further back, that is he wants to begin at a lower point to tell the genealogical story. Here I see a start-up problem which, at its core, is connected with the question concerning non-conceptual content and with Roller's charge against propositionalism. Anyone who considers color experiences as being more basic than the most simple, normative forms of action and sense and who, on the pre-lingual level, assigns to them a constitutive role for a later conceptual meaning and normativity, must be able to say with what non-causal vocabulary these initial stages are to be described. At this stage the reference to non-conceptual content or to Searle's background does not seem to explain anything to me. In a nutshell, the problem is: what makes these basic abilities of discrimination (on the sub-personal level) and the equally basic experiences of red become *abilities* and *experiences* in a non-cognitive scientific sense? Since, in my view, only an understanding which goes beyond causal-cognitive concepts enables a transition from one *form of sense* to another and thereby the possibility of an *adequate* description of language acquisition. If Roller withdraws to the sub-personal level, however, it holds that the discrimination of colors on a sub-personal level runs the risk of pursuing the naturalistic dream of painting a normative picture with non-normative elements. So what is the possible way out of this dilemma?

With his article "Rechtliches Wissen" Thomas Gil, like Roller, also works against a background where forms of knowledge are distinguished as propositional knowledge, practical knowing-how, and phenomenal experiential knowledge. Unlike Roller, however, Gil's focus is not on experiential knowledge. The object of research being legal knowledge means that the focus is on the practical forms of knowledge in this case. The question is: is legal knowledge a knowing-how?

Gil assumes that all three forms of knowledge are to be *genuinely* understood, that is, that it is not possible, to, for instance, reinterpret prac-

---

96 Ibid.

tical knowledge in a propositional way. In the case of practical knowledge theoretical independence lies in the fact that someone is in the possession of knowing-how if he or she is competent in *doing* certain things, e.g. is able to do something.[97]

Relating this thesis to the juridical practice of working and judging, Gil comes to the following conclusion: the *abilities* of a jurist are essentially those of applying general norms to individual situations, of identifying individual cases *as individual cases of this and that kind*, and of making creative decisions. The competences listed of *applying* theoretical knowledge in this connection, as well as decision-making cannot themselves again be of a theoretical kind or be reduced to a knowledge of rules. Even though jurists have to be in possession of the knowledge of rules and sentences, their core competence is the above-mentioned knowing-how. In this sense jurisdiction is an (meta-)ability. In Thomas Gil's words: "Rechtliches Wissen wäre nach all dem Gesagten ein praktisches Können, das in rechtlich vermittelten Kommunikationsverhältnissen Vieles und Verschiedenes zu tun ermöglicht…"[98]

Chapter Five:
Skepticism: Pragmatic Answers?

The discussion with the skeptic has always been part of philosophy, especially of epistemology. Answers to skeptical arguments can be sorted according to different aspects.[99] Let's be guided by the following classification:

(a) *direct answers* to skepticism try to show, in an epistemic way, that we can have that knowledge which has been called into question, namely even under the preconditions of the skeptical argument. That means: what the skeptic is saying is intelligible but he has overlooked the fact that everyday knowledge (but maybe also the knowledge of oneself not being a brain in a vat) is possible for us humans. There is a *solution* to the skeptical paradox.

(b) *indirect (diagnostic) answers*, however, take a step back and a somewhat closer look at the skeptical argument itself. They do not adopt the

---

97 Cf. also Abel and Löwenstein in this volume.
98 Gil in this volume, 592.
99 Cf. Conant (2004) for a detailed account and differentiation of skeptical variants.

argument as it is, they refuse to continue under the semantic and epistemic requirements of skepticism. That is to say: there is a *dissolution* to the skeptical paradox. In this domain Michael Williams distinguishes between *therapeutic* and *theoretical* indirect strategies.[100] The therapist believes that he can prove that the skeptic did not give any meaning to his concepts and sentences, or, if he speaks meaningfully, that the ascribed meaning does not generate a philosophical problem or puzzle. In some sense, the meaningfulness of the skeptical figure of doubt is called into question. Do we still know what the skeptic means when he talks of radical and all encompassing doubt? Here we find also transcendental approaches to skepticism.

Williams himself is arguing in a theoretical way, however, when he points to the fact that there is a certain epistemological theory (epistemic realism) which, being in the background, gets the skeptical argument going in the first place. This theory is intelligible (directed against the therapist) but it is optional for one thing and false for another.

The articles presented in this chapter deal, more or less, with indirect answers to the skeptical problem.[101] The Wittgenstein of Schulte pursues a moderate therapeutic strategy, whereas the Williams of Schmoranzer reveals a theoretical option which helps, *so far successfully*, to avoid skeptical consequences. Let's look at it step by step.

Joachim Schulte's "Wittgensteins Zweifel" examines to what extent Wittgenstein's therapeutic procedure is able to classify the philosophical doubt first as a *pathological* doubt, but then also to explain whether the pathological doubt is *nonsense*. In this context Schulte accounts for a figure of argumentation in Wittgenstein, which can subsequently often be found, for example, in neo-pragmatic refutations of empiricist theses (see, for example, Brandom's Kant-Sellars-thesis, or Sellars' discussion of looks-talk). It is claimed in that kind of argumentation that vocabularies and types of actions are put in a pragmatic-logical order in a way that displays pragmatic and semantic dependencies between different vocabularies and types of actions.[102] More precisely this means that:

---

100 Cf. Dancy/Sosa/Steup (2010), '*Michael Williams*'; cf. Williams (1996).
101 Skepticism is not the actual object of examination for Mcginn. She is concerned rather with the question of whether knowledge is a mental state or not. However, she, too, gets onto the subject of pragmatic answers to skepticism.
102 For a thematization of pragmatic-genealogical orders between concepts or actions cf. Tolksdorf (2011).

the figure of doubt arrives fairly late in our "cognitive household", as it requires basal forms of language and thought with which we directly and naturally react to the world. Only when the child has learned what it means to tell the truth or to report something, can it proceed to doubt a claim of truth. Analogous to this, the lie comes after the sincere report. Schulte says that doubt is the exception to the rule. So what we find here is the thesis that doubt requires a certain logical environment in order to be meaningful: there has to be the possibility of assurance, of justification and rejection, of the resolution of a doubt, etc.

At that point when these insights are transferred to radical skeptical doubt it becomes interesting. For such a doubt it is characteristic that it passes from a local to a global error, from the possibility that some of our judgments here and now could be false to the stronger assumption that *all* judgments (asserted under whatever conditions) could be false. However, this means that the logical environment, that is the background which breathed life into the doubt in the first place, is removed.

What are the consequences of this removal? Schulte argues very warily and cautiously, he shows that Wittgenstein himself was undecided. Why this restraint? Clearly the problem is that it is anything but easy to decide whether a doubt without the prospect of removal is conceivable but *exaggerated,* or on the other hand *meaningless.* The skeptic certainly changes our intuitive concept of doubt. But is the thesis of meaninglessness the consequence of the remoteness from common use? We must examine it exactly, as Schulte and Wittgenstein advise, and find out whether the analogy was overstretched – and this can only happen by looking at individual cases. At this point *my* intuition is quite clear: I don't see what the concept of doubt is supposed to mean when still used by the radical skeptic. The reversal of the general case (rule) and the exception (or even stronger: the suspension of such a contrast, since there are no cases of success anymore) makes it impossible for me to see what *function* the figure of doubt and the act of doubting could have any more. And in a certain sense the danger of nonsense, originating in the pseudo-concept of doubt left over, spreads to the contents of those sentences which are doubted. Because if somebody claims that it is in principle always possible to be wrong about the color of the cat or whether there is a table standing here, for instance, that person takes away the ground from beneath us, the ground on which we have learnt to talk about tables, cats and colors. In other words: What does the skeptic actually claim at this point? But that is only my intuition. Schulte argues more carefully and relegates us to the specific cases in question.

Let me sum up: in the comments of Schulte and Wittgenstein I see a certain form of semantic-pragmatic reaction to the skeptical figure of doubt, which is revealed in the pragmatic-logical order of some concepts and actions which we cannot do without. Certain competences of a linguistic and non-linguistic kind make it possible to doubt in a concept-logical way. Without these competences, 'to doubt' would be "on holiday" (to use a Wittgensteinian phrase).

Sebastian Schmoranzer pursues another strategy in his article "Skepticism, Contextualism and Entitlement". He examines a facet of Williams' theoretical epistemic approach. This consists essentially of drawing attention to ways of reaching a positive status of the justification of a sentence, even and especially when there is no evidence or are no reasons in a narrower sense. Since the non-evidential support refers to relations between actions and propositions in epistemic contexts, I see a pragmatic handling of the skeptic at work in this project as well.

But let us take a closer look at this matter. As Schmoranzer shows, Williams links his inferential contextualism to a theory of epistemic entitlement.[103] In this connection the concept of entitlement is intended to show that a positive epistemic characterization of a belief or an agent is also possible if the agent does not possess evidence, that is, if the belief is not supported by reasons. Directed against the skeptic the thesis means that in everyday contexts we are, for example, *entitled* to think that we are not brains in a vat and that this form of entitlement generates the corresponding knowledge under these circumstances. Of course, reacting to the skeptic this way is tempting because we have problems offering reasons for negated global skeptical hypothesis.

But how does Williams arrive at this thesis? An important link is certainly the commitment to the so called default-and-challenge model of epistemic justification which, as mentioned, broadly maintains that "…a belief is prima facie personally justified as long as there is no reason to think that it is false."[104] So let us assume that negations of skeptical hypotheses possess a default status in everyday life, that they are therefore considered to be justified until we have good reason to

---

103 On inferential contextualism cf. Williams (1996), (2001), 165–187 and (2003).
104 Schmoranzer in this volume, 599. On the default-and-challenge model also cf. Williams in this volume, furthermore cf. Brandom (1994).

doubt that we are not brains in a vat. Therefore we are *entitled* to believe that we are not brains in a vat. Of course this is not yet sufficient to refute the skeptic. What we need is a more exact definition of what epistemic entitlement is and how it works. Schmoranzer works out different approaches, among them for example a methodological variety of epistemic entitlement as we can find them in Williams' writings, for instance in connection with the concept of methodological necessities. The idea behind this is the following: every context has its own typical, methodological logic which arises out of the inferential connections between the allowed and natural asking and answering of questions on the one hand and sentences which are more like presuppositions on the other. Some questions and answers are movable elements in the river of investigation, whereas others belong to the riverbed, to the methodological assumptions and requirements of the investigation. This reminds one of Wittgenstein's metaphor of the riverbed in "On Certainty". Remember:

> Man könnte sich vorstellen, dass gewisse Sätze von der Form der Erfahrungssätze erstarrt wären und als Leitung für die nicht erstarrten, flüssigen Erfahrungssätze funktionierten; und dass sich dies Verhältnis mit der Zeit änderte, indem flüssige Sätze erstarrten und feste flüssig würden.
>
> Wenn ich experimentiere, so zweifle ich nicht an der Existenz des Apparates, den ich vor den Augen habe. Ich habe eine Menge Zweifel, aber nicht *den*. Wenn ich eine Rechnung mache, so glaube ich, ohne Zweifel, dass sich die Ziffern auf dem Papier nicht von selbst vertauschen.[105]

That means therefore, if we move within a certain context, some sentences, according to Williams, are methodologically necessarily true. We cannot carry out any historical investigations if doubts about the past are features of the language game. Regarding the concept of epistemic entitlement we can then note: taking into account the methodological conditions of asking and answering historical questions which straddle a certain inferential space, we are *entitled* to think that the earth has existed for more than 5 minutes. If epistemic entitlement

---

[105] Wittgenstein (1999), § 96 und 337. In English: "It might be imagined that some propositions, of the form of empirical propositions, were hardened and functioned as channels for such empirical propositions as were not hardened but fluid; and that this relation altered with time, in that fluid propositions hardened, and hard ones became fluid." (OC 96). "If I make an experiment I do not doubt the existence of the apparatus before my eyes. I have plenty of doubts, but not *that*. If I do a calculation I believe, without any doubts, that the figures on the paper aren't switching of their own accord." (OC 337).

can generate knowledge, we can know the negation of the corresponding skeptical hypothesis. And even more generally: as it is methodologically necessary for most (all?) types of action that we are not brains in a vat, we (ordinary people, historian) seem to be in possession of global epistemic entitlement, unlike the skeptic who thinks that we are not. We are thus able to know that we are not brains in a vat.

It seems to me that this reply to the skeptic is a pragmatic answer in that it relies on the concept of methodological necessities, which itself must be explained by the inferential structures of the areas of investigations and practices. It is at this very point, however, that Schmoranzer now expresses concern. How does Williams, this is how I understand Schmoranzer, get from a thesis of *pragmatic-methodological* relations to a thesis of positive *epistemic* status? And he answers: he doesn't – "Methodological entitlement does not imply epistemic entitlement."[106] The problem seems to be that the positive epistemic status depends in addition on whether the contextual method of investigation and inquiry is an *epistemically* valuable one. Methodological necessities refer to the internal logic of the context, but who can tell us that the context itself is epistemically good? That we are inclined to ask this question shows that the question concerning the epistemic status of entitlement is now directed at the context itself. But how can it be answered? Schmoranzer makes it clear that it cannot already be considered as answered solely on the grounds that we are concerned with a practice or context that has developed historically, is stable and holistically connected. All these criteria can be examined anew with regard to their epistemic value.

But now the following question arises: on what grounds *at all* can we tell which epistemic status a sentence or a context has? I would like to raise the following doubt here: it seems as if Schmoranzer wants to detach epistemic standards of assessment from any kind of context and any methodical embedding. But how plausible is this account? How plausible is the separation of pragmatics and epistemology on this fundamental level? Is it not true that every epistemic question has in play some methodological constraints? I agree with Schmoranzer that we can always ask whether certain contexts and methods of investigation are instrumental to truth. But this question is always part of a context itself, either in the same or in a different one. A belief can be a methodological necessity in a certain context and thus put the agent into the status of entitlement measured against the standards of her

---

106 Schmoranzer in this volume, 605.

own context. Regarding epistemic goodness from which context does Schmoranzer's assessment of the contexts and the pragmatic entitlements take place? From a philosophical context? If so, did Williams not suggest questioning the plausibility of such a theory or meta-point of view? However it is, is not Williams' point that, *in general*, epistemic questions do not exist in a vacuum, but have pragmatic foundations?

In "Wittgenstein and Williamson on Knowing and Believing" Marie Mcginn deals with the question of whether knowledge is a mental state or not.[107] In "Knowledge and its Limits"[108] Williamson answers this question positively, whereas Wittgenstein believes he has good reasons for assuming that knowledge is not a mental state of a person. The latter writes among other things: "‚Ich weiß es', sage ich dem Andern; und hier gibt es eine Rechtfertigung. Aber für meinen Glauben gibt es keine." (ÜG 175); "Es wäre richtig zu sagen: ‚Ich glaube …' hat eine subjektive Wahrheit; aber ‚Ich weiß …' nicht." (ÜG 179); "Oder auch: ‚Ich glaube …' ist eine Äußerung, nicht aber ‚Ich weiß …'" (ÜG 180).[109]

Is there a real difference of opinion here between both philosophers, or is it merely a terminological difference? The question of whether knowledge is a mental state of a person, comes up over and over again and is very salient in different parts of this volume. Related to the concentration on epistemic abilities and their transformatory role in analytic epistemology it appears, for example, as follows: is the idea of a mental state part of non-performance based epistemology? In other words: if knowledge is bound more or less closely to actions and abilities, does it then still make sense to talk of a mental state? Or: if our perspective changes by moving away from beliefs towards

---

107 Mcginn's text could certainly have been included in different parts of this volume, for instance in ch. 1 or 3. It has been included here because a central idea of the question of what is meant by considering knowledge as a mental state points to the discussion with the skeptic. Mcginn takes up the reference to Wittgenstein, also made by Schulte, and also points to pragmatic strategies in dealing with the skeptic.
108 Cf. Williamson (2000).
109 Cf. Wittgenstein (1999). English translation: "‚I know it' I say to someone else; and here there is a justification. But there is none for my belief." (OC 175); "It would be correct to say: 'I believe …' has a subjective truth; but 'I know …' not." (OC 179); "Or again: 'I believe …' is an 'expression', but not 'I know …'." (OC180).

agents, how illuminating is the supposition then still that knowledge is something *within* a person?

As we have seen in the first chapter, however, the matter is not so easy or unambiguous, which is partly (not only) due to the ambiguity of the concept ‚mental state'. Virtue approaches do not negate the image of mental states in all cases. Hyman seems rather to be skeptical where this idea is concerned, whereas Hetherington explicitly accepts and defends it. However, I cannot deny that both understand something different by it. If knowledge *is* an ability or performance, then this affects the ascription of the state: to be in the state of knowing-how is something different from being in the state of a feeling or thinking. The latter are paradigmatic mental states. On the other hand Sosa and Greco are interested primarily in the ability-based prologue to a *belief*, so that the old way of speaking of knowledge as a mental state is preserved to a certain extent. Here knowledge is not an ability, but rather the *result* of a performance. Thus it is convenient that we can touch on the topic once more at the end of the volume. The circle closes.

Whatever the case may be, with her question about whether there is a real controversy between Wittgenstein and Williamson, it is precisely with these ambiguities that Mcginn is fighting. She introduces different interpretations and comes to the conclusion, roughly speaking, that the two of them do not contradict each other in many respects.

Let me sum up her discussion as follows: Williamson directs his thesis concerning mental states against internalism and defends an externalistic, factive interpretation of knowledge. Wittgenstein does not challenge these points. On the other hand, Wittgenstein wants to note the fact that from the sincere *assurance* of "I know that p" it does not follow that the speaker knows that p. That is, however, precisely what holds for many mental states: he who assures sincerely that he believes that p, is thereby in the state of having a belief. Williamson does not doubt this however. Both also agree on the fact that mental states are not always transparent in this way.

Mcginn then turns to the discussion with the skeptic. Her assumption is: "The question whether there is a real disagreement between Wittgenstein and Williamson might be thought to depend ... not on what each has to say about how the concept of knowing functions, but on the role that Williamson's claim that knowing is a mental state plays in his response to the sceptic."[110] What makes her say that? Witt-

---

110 Mcginn in this volume, 648.

genstein rejects the reference to mental states of knowledge at those points at which Moore tries to refute the skeptic, by *assuring* that he knows that p. Here there is an alignment of 'knowledge' and 'belief'. Wittgenstein writes roughly: "Der falsche Gebrauch, den Moore von dem Satz ‚Ich weiß …' macht, liegt darin, dass er ihn als eine Äußerung betrachtet, die so wenig anzuzweifeln ist wie etwa ‚Ich habe Schmerzen'." (ÜG 178).[111] On this, however, Williamson also agrees with Wittgenstein. Williamson's anti-skeptical strategy relies primarily on disjunctive arguments: the evidence in cases of success and error are not identical, therefore the skeptic cannot show that knowledge of the material world is impossible by pointing to error cases.

At that point where Moore treats knowledge like a mental state, Williamson, more in line with Wittgenstein, reverts to pragmatic answers. But what was Moore's point? Why does a new skeptical challenge possibly emerge at this point? Or putting the question in another way: Why does Moore feel that it is still pressing to answer the skeptic, even after disjunctivist arguments have been put forward? It is so because against disjunctivism one can always bring a sort of meta-skepticism into play, because it has merely been shown that we are *either* in a good *or* in a bad situation now. Disjunctivism delivers a disjunctive conclusion, but not one that tells us that we are presently dealing with a case of success. Referring to this pressure Moore says: but I know that this is a hand. Here it can be seen clearly that Moore attacks a different skeptical question than Williamson. Williamson seems to be attacking this form of skepticism pragmatically when he asks: but should this challenge of the skeptic not also be founded rationally?[112] Is it not more useful not to doubt everything in order to find the truth? Should we not rely on what is obvious if we want to make progress? Here too, a real controversy between Wittgenstein and Williamson is not the result.

At the end, however, Mcginn makes out a possible disagreement. Williamson wants to classify knowledge as a fundamental, non-analyzable mental state. Under these circumstances the distinction between knowledge and evidence becomes blurred. The field of application of the phrase ‚to know' broadens. Wittgenstein on the other hand argues in favor of a narrower way of understanding and using 'to know'.

---

111 English translation: "The wrong use made by Moore of the proposition 'I know…' lies in his regarding it as an utterance as little subject to doubt as 'I am in pain'" (OC 178).
112 On this cf. the articles by Schulte and Williams in this volume.

This means: where we speak of knowledge, we also commit ourselves to giving reasons, for example: because one sees, hears, concludes or remembers something. But in such an epistemic chain these reasons themselves are not knowledge because we (as a rule) do not insist again on reasons for why one sees or remembers something. The question "*Why* do you see ...?" obviously functions differently from "*How* did you come to know ...?" Wittgenstein makes an intuitive distinction between "I know ..." and "I see ...". It is misleading to treat seeing like knowing because this leads to the question concerning the corresponding reasons with regard to seeing and we are then forced, possibly, towards theories of the kind which make us name internal *seemings* as reasons for seeing something.

But also with reference to world-picture sentences and hinge-propositions Wittgenstein rejects the classification under the category ‚knowledge'. Such sentences are there, so to speak, without a reason, they are a precondition in the epistemic language game, they always back our questions and investigations. Strictly speaking there is no justification for them. The difference between Wittgenstein and Williamson seems to consist in the fact that Wittgenstein considers knowledge to be a higher level phenomenon which only evolves after many concepts and abilities have – in a sense-logical way – already been in play. For Williamson on the other hand knowledge is fundamental. It is up to the reader to decide, how important and of what theoretical consequence this discrepancy is for epistemology.[113]

References

Abel (2004): Günter Abel, *Zeichen der Wirklichkeit*, Frankfurt/Main.
Amico (1995): Robert P. Amico, *The Problem of the Criterion*, Rowman/Littlefield.
Beckermann (2001): Ansgar Beckermann, "Zur Inkohärenz und Irrelevanz des Wissensbegriffs. Plädoyer für eine neue ‚Agenda in der Erkenntnistheorie'", in: *Zeitschrift für philosophische Forschung* 55, 571–601.
Blaauw (2004): Martijn Blaauw, *Contrastivism: Reconciling Skeptical Doubt with Ordinary Knowledge*, (Diss.), Amsterdam.
BonJour/Sosa (2007): Laurence BonJour/Ernest Sosa, *Epistemic Justification*, Blackwell.
Brandom (1994): Robert Brandom, *Making It Explicit*, Harvard.
Brandom (2000): Robert Brandom, *Articulating Reasons*, Harvard.

---

113 Translation from German by Ute Feldmann.

Brandom (2008): Robert Brandom, *Between Saying and Doing*, Oxford.
Chisholm (1977): Roderick Chisholm, *Theory of Knowledge*, Prentice-Hall.
Cohen (1999): Stewart Cohen, "Contextualism, Skepticism, and the Structure of Reasons", in: *Philosophical Perspectives* 13, 57–90.
Cohen (2000): Stewart Cohen, "Contextualism and Skepticism", in: *Philosophical Issues* 10, 94–107.
Cohen (2002): Stewart Cohen, "Basic knowledge and the problem of easy knowledge", in: *Philosophy and Phenomenological Research* 65, 309–329.
Conant (2004): James Conant, "Varieties of Skepticism", in: D. McManus (ed.), *Wittgenstein and Skepticism*, London/New York, 97–136.
Craig (1990): Edward Craig, *Knowledge and the State of Nature*, Oxford.
Dancy/Sosa/Steup (2010): Jonathan Dancy/Ernest Sosa/Matthias Steup (eds.), *A Companion to Epistemology*, 2nd Edition, Blackwell.
DeRose (2009): Keith DeRose, *The Case for Contextualism*, Oxford.
Dretske (2005): Fred Dretske, "The Case against Closure", in: M. Steup/E. Sosa (eds.), *Contemporary Debates in Epistemology*, Blackwell, 13–26.
Gelfert (2011): Axel Gelfert, "Genealogies of the Concept of Knowledge and their cognitive-ecological Dimension", in: *Episteme* 8 (2011), 67–82.
Goldman (1976): Alvin Goldman, "Discrimination and Perceptual Knowledge", in: *The Journal of Philosophy* 73, 771–791.
Greco (2007): John Greco, "The Nature of Ability and the Purpose of Knowledge", in: *Philosophical Issues* 17, 57–69.
Greco (2010): John Greco, *Achieving Knowledge*, Cambridge.
Hanfling (2000a): Oswald Hanfling, "A Situational Account of Knowledge", in: *The Monist* 68(1995), 40–56.
Hanfling (2000b): Oswald Hanfling, *Philosophy and Ordinary Language*, London/New York, 94–110.
Hawthorne (2005): John Hawthorne, "The Case for Closure", in: M. Steup/E. Sosa (eds.), *Contemporary Debates in Epistemology*, Blackwell, 26–43.
Hetherington (2011): Stephen Hetherington, *How to Know*, Blackwell.
Hyman (1990): John Hyman, "How Knowledge Works", in: *The Philosophical Quarterly* 49, 433–451.
Klein (2007): Peter Klein, "Human Knowledge and the Infinite Progress of Reasoning", in: *Philosophical Studies* 134), 1–17.
Klein (2007): Peter Klein, "Infinitism", in: Sven Bernecker/Duncan Pritchard (eds.), *Routledge Companion to Epistemology*, Routledge, 245–56.
Kornblith (2006a): Hilary Kornblith, *Knowledge and its Place in Nature*, Oxford.
Kornblith (2006b): Hilary Kornblith, "Appeals to Intuition and the Ambitions of Epistemology", in: S. Hetherington (ed.), *Epistemology Futures*, Oxford, 10–25.
Lackey (2004): Jennifer Lackey, "Review of M. DePaul/L. Zagzebski (eds.): Intellectual Virtues", in: *NotreDame Philosophical Review*.
Luper (2008): Steven Luper, "The Easy Argument", in: *Acta Analytica* 22, 321–331.
McDowell (1996): John McDowell, *Mind and World*, Harvard.
Pritchard (2002): Duncan Pritchard, "Two Forms of Epistemological Contextualism", in: *Grazer Philosophische Studien*, 64.

Pritchard (2005): Duncan Pritchard, *Epistemic Luck*, Oxford.
Pritchard/Millar/Haddock (2010): Duncan Pritchard/Alan Millar/Adrian Haddock, *The Nature and Value of Knowledge*, Oxford.
Pritchard (2011): Duncan Pritchard, "Anti-Luck Virtue Epistemology", in: *The Journal of Philosophy*.
Schaffer (2007): Jonathan Schaffer, "Knowing the Answer", in: *Philosophy and Phenomenological Research* 75, 383–403.
Silins (2005): Nicholas Silins, "Transmission Failure Failure", in: *Philosophical Studies* 126, 71–102.
Sosa (1980): Ernest Sosa, "The Raft and the Pyramid: Coherence versus Foundations in the Theory of Knowledge", in: *Midwest Studies in Philosophy* 5, 3–25.
Sosa (2007): Ernest Sosa, *A Virtue Epistemology*, Oxford.
Stanley/Williamson (2001): Jason Stanley/Timothy Williamson, "Knowing How", in: *Journal of Philosophy* 98, 411–444.
Sartwell (1991): Crispin Sartwell, "Knowledge is Merely True Belief", in: *American Philosophical Quarterly* 28, 157–165.
Tolksdorf (2011): Stefan Tolksdorf, "Wittgenstein und das Projekt einer pragmatisch-genealogischen Philosophie der Sprache", in: *Wittgenstein-Studien* 2(2011), 103–135.
Tolksdorf (2012): Stefan Tolksdorf, "Überlegungen zur pragmatischen Genealogie des Wissensbegriffs", in: D. Koppelberg/S. Tolksdorf (eds.), *Erkenntnistheorie – wie und wozu?*, Paderborn.
Weinberg/Nichols/Stich (2001): Jonathan Weinberg/Shaun Nichols/ Stephen Stich, "Normativity and Epistemic Intuitions", in: *Philosophical Topics* 29, 429–460.
Weinberg et. al. (2010): Jonathan Weinberg/Chad Gonnerman/Cameron Buckner/Joshua Alexander, "Are Philosophers Expert Intuiters?", in: *Philosophical Psychology* 23, 331–355.
Williams (1996): Michael Williams, *Unnatural Doubts*, Princeton.
Williams (2001a): Michael Williams, *Problems of Knowledge*, Oxford.
Williams (2001b): Michael Williams, "Kontextualismus, Externalismus und epistemische Maßstäbe", in: T. Grundmann (ed.): *Erkenntnistheorie – Positionen zwischen Tradition und Gegenwart*, Paderborn, 165–187.
Williams (2003): Michael Williams, "Skeptizismus und der Kontext der Philosophie", in: *Deutsche Zeitschrift für Philosophie* 6.
Williams (2008): Michael Williams, "Responsibility and Reliability", in: *Philosophical Papers* 37, 1–26.
Williamson (2000): Timothy Williamson, *Knowledge and its Limits*, Oxford.
Wittgenstein (1999): Ludwig Wittgenstein, *Über Gewißheit*, Frankfurt/Main.
Wittgenstein (2000): Ludwig Wittgenstein, *The Big Typescript*, Vienna edition, Frankfurt/Main.
Wittgenstein (2003): Ludwig Wittgenstein, *Philosophische Untersuchungen*, Frankfurt/Main.
Wright (2003): Crispin Wright, "Some Reflections on the Acquisition of Warrant by Inference", in: S. Nuccetelli (ed.), *New Essays on Semantic Externalism and Self-Knowledge*, Cambridge.

Wright (2004): Crispin Wright, "Wittgensteinian Certainties", in: D. McManus (ed.), *Wittgenstein and Skepticism*, London/New York, 22–55.

Chapter One
Knowledge, Ability, and Manifestation

Part One:
Knowledge As Ability

Knowledge and Knowing: Ability and Manifestation*

Stephen Hetherington

Epistemology has often sought to tell us what knowledge is; so often, indeed, and with so little agreement, as to have generated much frustration at the apparent lack of progress in our attaining a settled conception of knowledge's nature. What *should* epistemologists say about knowledge? Should we decline to seek a conceptual analysis of it – a cessation encouraged by Timothy Williamson?[1] We could, but we need not; for we might instead diagnose that history of epistemological frustration quite differently. If this paper is right, the frustration has arisen, to some crucial extent, from a widely guiding yet equally overlooked misconception of what *kind* of thing knowledge is. How might we come to realise this? My approach will be the indirect one of gesturing at an alternative conception – saying what else knowledge might be, with the departure from epistemologically standard conceptions of knowledge thereby being manifest. My aim will be to effect what I call a *practicalist* reorientation of this segment of epistemology. Knowledge *is* as knowledge *can do*. That will be my verdict.

1. The problem of the criterion

I will reach that verdict by attending initially to a classic epistemological concern – the problem of the criterion – as to how we *could* ever hope to understand the nature of knowledge. Rightly, Roderick Chisholm regarded that problem as conceptually central to epistemology:[2] if we are to understand the nature of knowledge, we need to understand – at least often enough – *when* it is ever present and *why* it is ever present. That is, we must recognise instances and criteria. Paradigmatically, therefore, epistemologists formulate general *principles* about what it

---

* I am grateful to John Bengson for his excellent comments (questioning and critical) on a draft of this paper.
1 Williamson (2000), ch.1.
2 Chisholm (1982), ch. 5 and (1989), 6–7.

takes for knowledge to be present. Also paradigmatically, epistemological discussions may be centred upon many specific *judgements* about when knowledge is present. And which of those principles and judgements are true? Epistemologists offer more or less detailed arguments (at their simplest, these remain appeals to intuition) in support of various principles and judgements.

In order to understand how that problem arises, I will focus upon a simple example, concerning one kind of knowledge and one attribution or judgement of some such knowledge's presence. Let P be this epistemic principle: 'Other things being equal, perception is a way of gaining knowledge of many aspects of the physical world.' And let J be this epistemic judgement: 'I know that I am seeing a kangaroo' – a judgement reflecting your belief (itself reflecting your apparently perceiving in favourable circumstances) that you are seeing just such an animal. All else being equal, we could well be inclined to accept both P and J as true – and thereby as elements within an accurate theory of knowledge (of what it is like and of where it is within the world). Still, what epistemic support do we have for the truth of those assessments? In particular, can we know them to be true? Almost effortlessly, that question leads us to develop the problem of the criterion in the following way.

1. Suppose you accept P. But what would make your acceptance knowledge? P is known only if it is justified epistemically. Your epistemic support for it must include some specific epistemic judgement(s) such as J. (After all, P is about perceptual knowledge; as is J.) What is also needed, however, is that J be true: P's truth is established only insofar as *accurate* epistemic judgements are supporting it.

2. Yet what *makes* an epistemic judgement accurate? A specific judgement as to something's being knowledge is accurate only if it satisfies an accurate epistemic principle: J is accurate only *by* satisfying a principle such as P.

3. Suppose, for simplicity, that J is the only epistemic judgement to which P is answerable and that P is the only epistemic principle to which J is answerable – in each case, if they are to be accurate. Then 1 implies that P is known only if J is true and only if J supports P. And 2 implies that J is knowledge only if P is true and only if P supports J.

4. Now imagine arguing (congruently with 3) in the following two ways, as we seek to establish both P's truth and J's truth:

J is true, and J supports P. So, P is true.
P is true, and P supports J. So, J is true.

Clearly, we cannot sensibly argue in both of those ways together, so as to detach even to one of J and P having been established as true. Hence, at least one of J and P must *independently* be established as true – independently, that is, of these two arguments. In other words, even if at least one of J and P can be established via the other, *only* one could be; that epistemic favour cannot be returned.

5. But there is no independent way of knowing P or of knowing J.[3] A general epistemic principle must be tested on particular epistemic judgements; *and* vice versa.

6. From 4 and 5: we cannot know both P and J. This constitutes (in a simplified form) our failing to know which epistemic principles are true; *or* which epistemic judgements, if any, are true; *or* even one of those two states of affairs.

7. From 3, 5, and 6: indeed, given our not knowing both of P and J, we do not know *either* of them. The knowledge of either one of them depends upon knowing the other one of them. Consequently, if we do not know J, we do not know P. And if we do not know P, we do not know J.

And *that* is hardly an uplifting conclusion. Does it amount to our lacking all epistemological knowledge?[4] It could well do so. It does do so if epistemology's knowing something at all must somehow involve knowledge of the truth of some general epistemic principles and/or of some particular epistemic judgements.[5]

---

3   (i) We may consider enlarging the scope of 'P' and 'J', so as to encompass a pleasing *array* of epistemic principles and epistemic judgements. Nonetheless, the same problem will continue to arise, even if not still so immediately. (ii) A similar conclusion would follow even if we were to allow that the truth of an epistemic principle or judgement (respectively) could be known via *another* such principle or judgement. For the question would arise (in an epistemologically familiar way) of how the *new* epistemic principle or judgement is itself known. Thus, we would not have left behind our initial question, the one which initiates the problem of the criterion.

4   That is a conclusion for which I have argued elsewhere (1992; 2010), on grounds independent of the problem of the criterion.

5   This section's argument may also be formulated, *mutatis mutandis*, in terms of epistemic justification rather than of knowledge. I note this because we might wonder whether one instance of the associated form of reasoning – the instance which speaks of knowledge, as against that which is about justification – is conceptually *primary*. For example, is there a problem with knowl-

2. Wilfrid Sellars

Confronted by section 1's version of the problem of the criterion, how should we respond as epistemologists? Acceptance of its disturbing conclusion is possible — but not, we may hope, obligatory. Can we find a non-sceptical solution to the problem? Might there even be a way of dissolving the problem from its outset?[6]

Maybe so; maybe so; and we might discern a helpful hint, even if only a hint, in a response by Wilfrid Sellars.[7] His own favoured answer to the problem of the criterion talked of *explanatory coherence*. His version of the problem was formulated in terms of epistemic IPM — introspective, perceptual, and memory — principles and judgements. This is a more realistic version of the problem than section 1's, which made do with a single principle, a single judgement, both of these being only perceptual. But no matter: the fundamental form of the problem persists, the same in Sellars' hands as it was in section 1. *Some* way is still being sought of providing epistemic support for, respectively, our epistemic principles and our epistemic judgements — a way which does not already presuppose this having occurred. And how is this to be done? For Sellars, we may embed the principles and judgements within a larger theory:

> It is reasonable to accept [the epistemic IPM principles] because they are elements in a theory T which coheres with our introspections, perceptions and memories. Our ostensible introspections, perceptions and memories are likely to be true because they fall under [the principles].[8]

Why is that at all helpful?

> How, we are inclined to expostulate, could it be reasonable ... to accept T *because* it is supported by our introspective, perceptual and memory judg-

---

edge only because there is one for justification? 'Yes' is probably the usual answer to that question. But section 9 will dispute that answer; in the meantime, I will continue to focus directly upon knowledge.

6 A clarificatory point: the problem of the criterion is not a sceptical argument for our having no knowledge. Hence, it is not to be answered by the observation, possibly an externalist one, that knowing is not generally dependent upon knowing an epistemic principle. The problem of the criterion challenges our having higher-level knowledge, such as might be part of epistemological understanding that some knowledge is present on a particular occasion.

7 Sellars (1979).

8 Ibid. 177 f.

ments (IPM judgments), if it is *because* they fall under [the epistemic IPM principles] that it is reasonable to accept these IPM judgments?[9]

That is indeed the core of the problem of the criterion. Sellars' answer to it incorporates a few aspects:

> If asked why it is reasonable to accept [the epistemic IPM principles], I would have argued that they are elements in a conceptual framework which defines what it is to be a finite knower in a world one never made ... In short I would have appealed to a more encompassing version of what I have been calling theory T.[10]

> [This] expanded account might well be called 'Epistemic Evaluation as Vindication'. Its central theme would be that achieving a certain end or goal can be (deductively) shown to require a certain integrated system of means. ... [That] end can be characterized as that of being in a *general* position, so far as in us lies, to *act*, i.e., to bring about changes in ourselves and our environment in order to realize *specific* purposes or intentions.[11]

> [As regards the 'rationality of accepting' the epistemic IPM principles,] ... since agency, to be effective, involves having reliable cognitive maps of ourselves and our environment, the concept of effective agency involves that of our IPM judgments being likely to be true .... [U]nless they *are* likely to be true, the concept of effective agency has no application.[12]

3. *Ernest Sosa*

There is something helpful in that last remark by Sellars; precisely what, though? Ernest Sosa dismisses Sellars' suggestion thus:

> But how could this explain our *epistemic* justification for accepting the T principles? We want effective agency, true enough, and it might be suggested that this somehow gives us reason to accept the T principles. Even *if* it does, however, it will not be *epistemic* reason.
>
> Thus, if a foundation offers a big prize to those who can get themselves to believe the T principles, this gives a reason of sorts for doing so, but that would not help us with the traditional epistemic problematic. We would not thereby have found the right sort of reason, an epistemic reason, for accepting the T principles. ... Suppose we want X and realize we won't have it unless p. To suppose that this gives any reason to believe that p is to indulge in wishful thinking. ... Can this possibly be what Sellars has in mind?

---

9 Ibid. 178.
10 Ibid. 179.
11 Ibid. 178 f.
12 Ibid. 180.

> Certainly not, but it is not easy to turn up a more plausible alternative. ... Consider the fact that we cannot act effectively unless our IPM judgments are reliable. Why should that fact give us an *epistemic* reason for thinking that our IPM judgments *are* reliable. [sic] This takes us back to pragmatic vindication, with its attendant problems.[13]

Quite so: Sosa has made clear what moral we should *not* take from Sellars' comments. What lesson *should* they teach us, then? Is there one?

4. Knowing and effective agency

There *is* a way in which the concept of effective agency can help us here. But it is not quite what Sellars has advocated. In effect, Sosa interprets Sellars as using the concept of effective agency to tell us that we are not effective agents unless our IPM judgements are generally true, and hence unless congruently supported IPM principles are generally true. Do we know, however, that people *are* effective agents? We could know this only by knowing people's intentions, knowing how their actions express or implement those intentions, and knowing the outcomes of those actions. Yet such knowledge will largely be IPM knowledge itself: we could have it only if there *are* true IPM principles which we satisfy and/or IPM judgements which are known to be true; and until the problem of the criterion is solved, we cannot know which, if any, IPM judgements or IPM principles are true.[14]

Confronted by this worry, Sellars might have replied that his point does not require us to know ourselves to be effective agents; we need only *be* such agents. Such a reply would be mistaken, though. The question *is* one of having that knowledge – just as the problem of the criterion is about our knowing the IPM principles and IPM judgements to be true. Even if Sellars was right to introduce the concept of effective agency when saying why some IPM judgements and IPM principles *are* true, our epistemological challenge remains that of *knowing* these truths.

---

13 Sosa (2009), 105 f.
14 So, the problem here is not one about self-knowledge as opposed to others-knowledge. We might have envisaged having this knowledge of oneself before extrapolating to gain – even if more fallibly – such knowledge of other people. But that knowledge would remain IPM knowledge, even if only of oneself; and the problem of the criterion would remain. That problem concerns the kind of knowledge in question, not the identity of whoever would have it.

That point may also be made in the following way. Sellars is treating effective agency as a *further* aspect of ourselves and the world, something to be mentioned by our epistemological account in *addition* to any articulation we offer of various IPM principles and IPM judgements. As epistemologists, we then aim to know the presence of this new aspect – namely, our being effective agents – so that we will *thereby* come to know, as epistemologists, various epistemic IPM principles and IPM judgements to be true. These principles and judgements are thereby characterised by our epistemological account as describing features of ourselves and the world *beyond* our effective agency – features knowable partly by *means* of our epistemically prior knowledge of our effective agency. Sellars has gestured at there being some sort of interlinking of our effective agency's presence with the truth of at least some non-trivial body of our IPM principles and IPM judgements. (And this is the only such interlinking being described, even gesturally, by Sellars.) Hence, if his discussion is to be understood as alerting us to how we could know such principles or judgements to be true, it is by his implying our needing to know that the effective agency is present in the first place.

Consequently, we return to the earlier worry. If the problem of the criterion afflicts our prospects of having IPM knowledge, we *cannot* know when, if ever, we exercise effective agency. Sellars proffers the concept of effective agency as a way of orienting us helpfully towards the presence of knowledge of IPM judgements and of IPM principles. Equally, though, that help can hinder – and seriously so. The concept of effective agency, once introduced as a genuinely explanatory element in the epistemological story, functions as *just one more aspect of the world which we need to know before* we could have those fundamental kinds of knowledge. Yet to have knowledge of that particular aspect of the world would itself be to have some instance of one or more of those fundamental kinds of knowledge. In short, we would not have escaped the problem of the criterion.

That is our epistemological problem. Is there an alternative way for us to use the concept of effective agency?[15] In spite of having hinted that

---

15 Could we, for example, call on Anscombe's (1963) concept of knowledge-in-intention? It is not clear that we can. First, knowledge-in-intention need not be knowledge of *effective* agency – the intention's *succeeding* in bringing about the intended result (ibid. 82). Second, Sellars' thinking might be general enough to apply to the rest of the Anscombean intention anyway (the intention consid-

there is one, I am yet to describe it. Still, section 5 will do so – by building upon a constraint outlined in this section, regarding how the concept of effective agency could help us to understand knowledge's presence. That constraint is as follows.

We have found just now that we remain trapped by the problem of the criterion if effective agency appears within our epistemological story as an element conceptually *separate* from the desired IPM knowledge. And that separateness has indeed been present in the story so far: on Sellars' behalf, we have posited some sort of *dependence*, in one or both directions, between the effective agency and the IPM knowledge. I say 'some sort' and 'one or both' because none of those details are made clear by Sellars. Sosa (in section 3) parsed the dependence in a way which treats the presence of effective agency as evidence for – and hence as conceptually separate from – the truth of IPM principles or IPM judgements. But possibly the dependence is transcendental instead – such as if Sellars had meant that IPM knowledge's availability is a precondition of our having even a concept of effective agency (a concept which we do seem to have). Even so, conceptual separateness would remain: we would need to know that what we take to be a concept of effective agency *is* a concept of effective agency rather than of only-almost-effective agency, say; and then – if IPM knowledge is necessary for our having a concept of effective agency – part of our knowing that we do have this concept would be our knowing that we have IPM knowledge. The problem of the criterion would thus remain, too.

Consequently, it is not enough, for defusing the problem of the criterion, that we simply *have* a concept of effective agency. As explained above, we would require some related knowledge. We would need to know either (i) that such a concept is *satisfied* (perhaps by ourselves) or (ii) that *it* – and not merely some similar concept – really is present. Either of these would be a *prior* determination, if we are to use Sellars' point for reaching an understanding of ourselves as having IPM knowl-

---

ered apart from its success component); for he is talking of introspection also, not only of memory and perception, in talking of IPM judgements. Third, the main epistemological interest in Anscombe's challenge is the idea of having knowledge (yet not inductively, it seems) of what one is about to do, *before* one does it. And even if she would be right to deny that such knowledge is strictly IPM knowledge, we could respond by extending Sellars' discussion so as to apply it to IPMN knowledge – 'N' for 'intentional'. The problem of the criterion itself can be generalised accordingly.

edge. And, as explained above, each of those prior determinations will be of the presence of IPM knowledge.

Once more, therefore, we encounter the problem of the criterion. In effect, on Sellars' picture effective agency is posited as something for which knowledge is *helpful*; or it is offered to epistemologists as something *towards* which knowledge can lead us; or it is thought of as something for which knowledge can *suit* us; or .... None of these options, however, allows us to transcend the problem of the criterion.

5. *Effective agency within knowledge*

An effective alternative is available. We may think of the relationship between knowledge and effective agency as one of *constitutiveness* rather than of dependence. I will offer an account of knowledge on which the presence of effective agency is part of one's knowing. I will thereby fashion part of a conception of knowledge, rendering talk of effective agency a necessary part of the conception's putative description of the presence of knowledge.

Section 4 shows why even an especially close form of dependence (such as a transcendental one) leaves the concept of effective agency as too *extrinsic* to the concept of knowledge. What we need instead is a far more intimate linking of the two; so much so that we need a sense of how knowledge is to be understood partly as involving effective agency *within* itself. That is, we must conceive of knowledge in such a way as to make effective agency a *part* of it. In this way, effective agency must not (as it is in section 4) be merely an aspect of the world always separate from knowledge – not even an aspect which helps us, once we notice its presence, to take a significant step towards noticing also the presence of knowledge.

How might we gain such a conception of knowledge? We may begin by reflecting upon the *state* of having some piece of knowledge. Routinely, epistemologists call knowledge a state of a person; as indeed it might well be. Yet there are also many actions which we would regard as *manifestations* or *expressions* of that state. And these actions often themselves involve effective agency. What connections exist, then, between such actions – along with the effective agency they incorporate – and any state of knowledge they manifest or express?

For example, let us suppose that you know yourself to be a person. There are various actions you perform – with effective agency – which express at least this knowledge. You call yourself a person; you believe that you are a person; you respond in perceptually predictable ways to others who regard themselves similarly; you engage in inferences which build upon some or all of that; and so on. Many epistemologists would explicate *normatively* the connections between your knowledge and those actions. The rough idea is that, by having the knowledge of being a person, it becomes normatively apt for you to engage in such actions. The knowledge would render the beliefs normatively apt; or it would render the assertions normatively apt; or it would render the related actions normatively apt; or so on.[16]

Even roughly, however, is that quite the best way of describing the connections if our aim is to understand knowledge's presence? Perhaps not, because even those normative connections could seem needlessly extrinsic (in section 4's sense). To see this, consider the following two kinds of case, corresponding in turn to whether we would regard the normative connections as reflecting, or instead as implying, the knowledge's presence. (i) *Reflecting*. Suppose we say that the knowledge's presence is sufficient (other things being equal) for one or more of these kinds of normative aptness. This would not help us to evade the problem of the criterion, because we need to show the knowledge's presence in the first place. (ii) *Implying*. Suppose we argue, conversely, that the knowledge's presence is implied by the normative aptness of one or more of those kinds of action. We then face an adaptation of the problem of the criterion. An action is normatively apt only if it satisfies a true principle of normative aptness. So, we know it has that status or property, only if we already know the truth of some such principle (one which the action satisfies). But we know the truth of some such principle only if we already know, of some instantiations of the principle, that they do have this status or property (with the principle thereby delivering correct verdicts). Consequently, we cannot have either sort of knowledge – either of the principle's truth or of a particular action's being normatively apt. Knowledge of the latter should therefore not yet be treated as our way of knowing that a particular piece of knowledge is present.

Again, therefore, it seems that we need to isolate a closer, a more constitutively immediate, connection than such normative ones between the knowledge and those actions. This is why I am suggesting in-

---

16 Regarding such normative links, see Williamson (2000), ch. 11, on knowledge and assertion, and Hawthorne and Stanley (2008) on knowledge and action.

stead that, when having some knowledge, you are thereby in a state which *inherently* – not extrinsically – admits of being expressed in one or more of those kinds of action.[17] What sort of state is that? We might contemplate different possibilities here; I will develop one of the stronger ones. For I will advocate conceiving of the knowledge as being a state of being *able to* act in those ways. Indeed, it is a state of having *knowledge how* to act in those ways. It is *that* sort of state. *This* is what knowledge is. Knowledge-that would *be* a kind of knowledge-how.

And there it is. *There* is the paper's key idea.[18] Immediately it will incur an objection along these lines:

> We are trying to understand knowledge-that – knowledge of some truth or state of affairs. And epistemologists standardly *distinguish* knowledge-that from knowledge-how. At the very least, they do not treat knowledge-that as itself a *kind* of knowledge-how. (Sometimes, they seek a contrary conceptual reduction, of knowledge-how to knowledge-that. Probably more often, they assume a fundamental and irresolvable conceptual distinction between the two.)

Yes, but epistemologists could be mistaken in that respect. Let us reflect for a while upon whether we *could* sensibly conceive of knowledge-that as being a kind of knowledge-how. What would it look like if it *was* to be like that?[19]

---

17 *Which* kinds of action? As the example above indicates, I offer no precise characterisation of this range. Indeed, I allow the following possibility. The actions relevantly related to the knowledge that *p* might bear more or less directly and narrowly upon *p*. And so, equally, some or all of them might bear – less or more directly and narrowly – upon *q*, *r*, *s*, and so forth (each of these being distinct from *p*). This would amount to there being some constitutive overlap between knowledge that *p* and knowledge that *q*, knowledge that *r*, knowledge that *s*, etc. (This possibility will matter later in the paper.)
18 Note that I am not providing an analysis in the form of necessary and sufficient conditions for all possible circumstances. Rather, my conception possesses this form: To have some knowledge that *p* is to be in a state which could be manifested in any *or* some *or* all of the following ways: $W_1, W_2, ..., W_n$ – where n could differ for different values of '*p*' as well as for the same '*p*' in different settings, yet where effective agency is necessary to each W_i ($1 \leq i \leq n$) anyway. This form of conception leaves open the possibility of different instances of knowledge that *p* being manifested in different ways. I will talk, nonetheless, of knowledge's being *constituted* whenever it is present. On constitution as a more fully determinate relation than this, see Johnston (2005).
19 What follows is a brief sketch. For a more detailed account of knowledge-that as a kind of knowledge-how, see Hetherington (2006; 2008; 2011, ch. 2). My

I have presaged that it would be an ability, a complex ability.[20] What will this involve? Because of the complexity of the ability in question, there can be various possible ways of manifesting or expressing it. Traditionally, knowledge is said to be a kind of belief – an augmented belief, but a belief nonetheless. In contrast, on my account belief is a possible way of *expressing* the knowledge (rather than itself *being* the knowledge). And the present account's departure from traditional epistemology does not end there. Sometimes, similarly, knowledge is said to be a kind of acceptance (rather than a kind of belief);[21] whereas on my account acceptance (like belief) is just a further possible way of *expressing* the knowledge.[22]

Already, therefore, we have those two possibilities for distinguishing between knowledge and expressions of it – one possibility regarding belief, another for acceptance. But there are even more, besides. They are not difficult to find. Think of the many further *uses* to which (as epistemologists may traditionally have said) we typically put our knowledge.

---

focus here is mainly upon knowledge-how only in that respect – in other words, the kind of knowledge-how which is suited to be knowledge-that. (See note 27 below.) I am not offering an account of knowledge-how, considered just in itself and in full generality. On the latter challenge, see Bengson and Moffett (forthcoming *a*; forthcoming *b*) for a wide range of conceptual options.

20 'But,' it will be objected from the outset, 'there are cases where a person knows how to do X, while no longer having the ability to do X.' (For some such cases, see Snowdon 2003.) That objection fails. A chef who still knows how to make a specific complicated meal, yet who is now physically unable to make it, now knows how to do it only in the sense of knowing *how it is that* the deed is to be done. And the latter knowledge is knowledge-*that*. It is not (as this distinction is standardly applied) knowledge-how. (For a dissenting interpretation, see Bengson and Moffett, forthcoming *b*.) Moreover, even if such cases *are* ones where there is genuine knowledge-how without the corresponding physical ability, that disparity is beside the immediate point. For that disparity obtains between some cognitive knowledge-how and an inability within 'the rest of the body' to implement that knowledge-how: cognitively, the chef knows what is to be done, even as her bodily infirmity renders her unable to put that knowledge into action. In contrast, on the idea I am developing, that disparity is absent. Both the knowledge-how and the ability are cognitive, since it is knowledge-that of which each is being used to provide an understanding. If one is present, therefore, so is the other. And if one is absent, so is the other.

21 See, for example, Lehrer (1990).

22 'Is every acceptance an expression of knowledge? Surely that would be too generous.' I will return to this below. But right now we may reply thus: 'Not necessarily. It depends on whether the acceptance is expressing a pertinent knowledge-how.'

For instance, it would be routine for epistemologists to regard the ability to raise knowledgeable questions, the ability to tell a justificatory story, the ability to pursue knowledgeable inferences, abilities to act congruently in various ways, and so on, as being present *because* – causally because – the knowledge already is. These would naturally be deemed present *as* uses of the already-existing knowledge. Yet that is not the only available interpretation of their presence. Instead, on my account all of these are possible ways of *expressing* or *manifesting* the knowledge. And that is not quite the same as their *using* the knowledge (as they would standardly be regarded as doing).

Even when related knowledge is present, we need not reach for the usual interpretation – of these actions as being *uses* of the state which is the knowledge. Even if we say that, in such circumstances, none of those actions would happen if one did not know some specified truth, *why* – we may also ask – do these actions occur, given one's having the knowledge that p, say? Is it because one 'moves from' the knowledge that p to these actions? Is it because one is 'building upon' the knowledge in these active ways, by using it to enrich or animate the rest of one's life? We need not say so; and I have described a conceptual danger in saying so. Again, I offer a simpler picture: One is merely *expressing* or *manifesting* the knowledge that p. One is doing so *in* performing these actions.

This alternative interpretation allows, as it should, that the state which is the knowledge is thereby *constitutively* at the core of all this activity.[23] But my explanation of that location for the knowledge is not the traditional epistemological one. I am arguing that the knowledge is constitutively at the core of all that activity because it is – it really is – the ability *to* be manifested in such ways. In short, the knowledge is the conceptually constitutive – and not (as is usually said) just a causally efficacious – locus for these actions. To say that they happen only because they can, *given* the knowledge that p, is to leave open that vital choice; for '*given*' is ambiguous between the constitutive reading and the causal one. Here is how to make the point more carefully: Those actions happen because they can, as *part* of knowing that p. This is where the account must talk, too, of effective agency: not as being a necessary part of knowledge, but as being a necessary part of knowing; which it-

---

23 'Where, then, is the effective agency? Constitutively speaking, where is *it?*' We are about to see.

self is not a necessary part of knowledge, but which is conceptually understandable only as part of or fashioning a concept of knowledge.

The idea is that we may talk of knowledge that *p* and — quite distinctly — of knowing that *p*.[24] Standardly, epistemology has not treated this as a substantive difference at all. The distinction has been regarded as a variation merely of syntax. 'She knows that *p*' is typically presumed to be interchangeable with 'She has the knowledge that *p*' — obviously not in all syntactic respects, but at least in what is being *portrayed*. The standard epistemological view is that only one state of affairs is being portrayed — by each of those two sentences, interchangeably. Nevertheless, that standard epistemological presumption is metaphysically questionable, as we should appreciate by contemplating an alternative conception like this paper's.

On this conception, we allow that, whenever there is a state of knowledge that *p*, expressions or manifestations of it are possible. We also respect the fact that (i) the state which is the knowledge that *p*, and (ii) the expressions or manifestations of that state, are not identical aspects of the world. Thus, an ability need never be expressed or manifested; and even once it is, it remains something distinct from the manifesting of it. This metaphysical distinction is what I will attempt to reflect by talking of knowledge that *p* and — separately — of knowing that *p*.

Here is my suggestion for how we may do that. Let an *expressing* or *manifesting* of some knowledge that *p* be an instance of knowing that *p*. Let the knowledge itself that *p* be the knowledge-how, the ability which might — but also might not — *be* manifested or expressed. It sounds quite odd, of course, to talk of knowing that *p* — as some action distinct from one's being in a state which includes having the knowledge that *p*. But we may treat such talk of knowing as a shorthand. When knowing that *p*, one does not perform this action directly. One is knowing, by doing something else directly — something of which it does not sound odd to say, for example, that it lasted for ten minutes.

For instance, you could be knowing that *p* purely by asserting accurately that *p*. At any rate, this is a way of knowing that *p* *if* it is an expression of your knowledge that *p*. Correlatively, the knowledge that *p* is your ability — your knowledge-how — *to* do such things as asserting accurately that *p*. The knowledge that *p* is the ability for itself to *be* ex-

---

[24] Perhaps such talk will be somewhat revisionary in philosophical terms. Still, we should at least test it.

pressed or manifested in such ways. I use the terms 'such things' and 'such ways' non-prescriptively, as designating a potentially shifting collection – one which could, *but* need not, include your asserting accurately that p, say. It might also – or even instead – include *other* possible ways of manifesting the knowledge. These could, but need not, include some or all of the following: believing accurately, inferring accurately, perceiving accurately, questioning accurately, remembering accurately, acting accurately, etc. As I have been emphasising, in principle there are many possible ways to be acting, each of which (I suggest) can be parsed as *knowing* a truth p – with all of them thereby being expressions or manifestations of the *knowledge* that p.[25]

Where does Sellars' concept of effective agency (from section 2) fit into this story? Within this setting, effective agency is – in different ways – part of knowledge *and* of knowing. Unmanifested, it is part of knowledge. Manifested, it is part of knowing. To know that p is to have the knowledge that p. This is (in other words) to know how to manifest the knowledge that p: it is the ability to manifest or express itself in various pertinent ways – asserting accurately, perceiving accurately, etc. This amounts to the knowledge how to act in some or all of those various available ways, any one of which would thereby constitute a manifestation or an expression of the knowledge that p.[26] And my suggestion – a *practicalist* one, I call it – is that to know that p *is* literally to have that knowledge-how.[27] To know is, in part, to *have* effective agency; whereas to be knowing is, in part, to be *manifesting* effective agency.[28]

---

25 All of them, *as* manifestations of knowledge-how, will manifest something further. Each will also be manifesting knowledge-*to*. In general, doing A as a manifestation of an ability to do A involves knowing *to* do A in the specific circumstance. We may think of the knowledge-to as an enabling *link* between the knowledge-how to do A and the doing of A. For more on knowledge-to, see Mason and Spence (1999).

26 Of course, not all knowledge-that is just *any* kind of knowledge-how. Generally speaking, knowledge-that can be manifested in ways too many to be enumerated or delineated; not, even so, in just any way.

27 I am not saying that, conversely, all knowledge-how is knowledge-that. See Gilbert Ryle's famous arguments (1949; 1971) against that implication. See Stanley and Williamson (2001) on Ryle on this. See Hetherington (2006, sec. 2; 2011, sec. 2.2) on why Stanley's and Williamson's anti-Rylean argument fails.

28 Does that picture already succumb to a vicious infinite regress, along the following lines? "On the paper's account, (1) to know that p is (2) to know how to manifest the knowledge that p. But (2) is also knowledge-that: it is

6. Defusing the problem of the criterion

Section 5's picture is programmatic but already helpfully suggestive. For a start, it points us towards a form of solution – strictly, a kind of dissolution – of the problem of the criterion. It does this by outlining an alternative conception of how we could know general epistemic principles and particular epistemic judgements.

We may see this by returning, for convenience, to section 2's simplified example involving principle P and judgement J. What section 5 has said about knowledge in general also applies to knowledge that P and to knowledge that J. Any knowledge of either of these is knowledge-how. It is likewise a complex ability. But note that there need not be merely a *single* complex ability which constitutes the knowledge that P or, equally, the knowledge that J. In general, different instances of knowledge that p – even when they are directed at a single p – could be at least somewhat different abilities. My own knowledge that p and yours can differ: mine might be an ability to act in ways which are not quite those available to you; nevertheless, your ability to act in various p-related ways could be as real as mine, even if its manifestations will be different to mine. All of which leads to these two related points:

> First, different *abilities* might constitute different instances of knowledge that P. The same is true of knowledge that J. Second, there could be different ways in which even a single such ability – a single instance of knowledge that P, or of knowledge that J – can be *manifested* or *expressed*.

Here is one possible application of that general point about the dimensions of complexity available in principle. To know that P is to have an ability to do … what? A number of things, most likely; such as accurately explicating and defending P, asserting P accurately, believing P accurately, accepting P accurately, …, and generally and accurately trusting individual perceptions in various ways, such as in subsequent actions. (After all, P *says* that perceptions give us knowledge.) To know that

---

knowledge that $p^\star$ – for some $p^\star \neq p$. So, what was required of (1) is required of (2). Hence, there is knowledge that p only if (3) there is knowledge how to manifest the knowledge that $p^\star$ – the knowledge which is (2). But (3) is knowledge-that: it is knowledge that $p^{\star\star}$ – for some $p^{\star\star} \neq p^\star \neq p$. And so forth, *ad infinitum*; unwelcomely, too". That objection founders because (2) is not knowledge that $p^\star$ – for $p^\star \neq p$. It *is* knowledge that p. The paper's account treats (2) *as* (1), not just as a necessary condition of (1). Consequently, depending upon how simple p is, for example, knowledge that p need not involve any further knowledge-that.

P is thus the ability to do some or all of those things. But they are themselves manifestations of what we may term *sub*-abilities, relative to the knowledge that P. That is, the ability which is the knowledge that P somehow comprises further abilities, such as some or all of those specific ones. However, practicalism allows that whatever is a sub-ability, relative to one piece of knowledge, could also be an ability which is itself a *further* piece of knowledge. For instance, the last-named sub-ability (relative to the ability which is the knowledge that P) — namely, the ability generally to trust individual perceptions aptly in various ways — can in turn be manifested by actions which will themselves be manifestations of the ability which is the knowledge that J. Maybe these actions are manifesting even *more* directly the knowledge that J than the knowledge that P. Nonetheless, these same actions could be manifestations — more *or* less directly, as it happens — of these two pieces of knowledge at once. You could be manifesting the knowledge that P, although less directly, *by* manifesting more directly the knowledge that J.

In a similar vein, one way — albeit a less direct way — of manifesting the knowledge that J could be by knowing that P. You might manifest directly the knowledge that P, such as by asserting accurately that P, by believing accurately that P, reasoning accurately from P, etc. — committing yourself directly in one or more such ways to P. And along such lines you could well be going beyond what is *needed* for manifesting the knowledge that J. The latter knowledge, concerning a particular epistemic judgement, is quite specific in its content. Comparatively direct manifestations of it will be similarly specific, tied narrowly to J in the content they manifest or express. Still, knowledge that P is an ability bearing upon those same manifestations of J. It can also be manifested by them, even if less directly so.

Those points allow direct manifestations of, say, J not to be manifesting the ability which is the knowledge that P. And the same compatibility is true in reverse: you *could* be manifesting immediately the knowledge that P without having the ability which is the knowledge that J.

We thus have a way of bypassing — indeed, of setting aside — the problem of the criterion. For we see how knowledge that P and knowledge that J are *not* reciprocally dependent.[29] There can be knowledge

---

29 I am not saying that *only* in a practicalist way such as mine could we hope to see this. In principle (as John Bengson rightly reminded me), non-practicalists may also endorse this view. What matters in all such cases is whether the view can in

that P without knowledge that J, just as knowledge that J is possible even in the absence of knowledge that P. These possibilities may be actualised in either or both of the following two ways. (i) *Abilities*. Each of those pieces of knowledge is an ability, a complex ability which may – but need not – include the other as a sub-ability. In each case, there can be other abilities instead whose presence, as sub-abilities, would suffice for the knowledge in question. (ii) *Manifestations*. *A fortiori*, each piece of knowledge may be manifested in ways which *can* also be manifesting the other. (And so we explain the *prima facie* power of the problem of the criterion.) Yet neither of those two pieces of knowledge *need* be manifested, even so, in a way which is manifesting the other. Accordingly, the problem of the criterion ceases to be a problem. It does not arise. (And so we explain the *ultima facie* disappearance of the problem of the criterion. *Qua* problem, its existence is only *prima facie*.)

7. Knowledge and absolutism

A doubt could well remain, nonetheless:

> If you are manifesting directly the knowledge that P, this *must* involve your manifesting the knowledge that J, even if not also directly.

But that 'must' is misplaced. Certainly you *could* be manifesting at once the two pieces of knowledge: a single action, such as a single inference, might be expressing both pieces of knowledge. This is not required, however. Suppose that your manifestations of the knowledge that P are reflectively philosophical: you defend P by locating it learnedly among kindred principles. Suppose also that your manifestations of the knowledge that J are more animal than reflective.[30] Then you are manifesting in respectively quite different ways your knowledge that P and your knowledge that J. This could reflect your respective associated abilities being similarly different.

Thus, that potential independence, of each piece of knowledge from the other, is manifest within a practicalist conception of knowledge.

---

turn be grounded within, or explained by, a larger epistemological picture. I am offering one possible such picture, a practicalist one; I leave to others the challenge of seeking an adequate non-practicalist one.

30 As Sosa (2009) might say.

Why is it *not* so clear within traditional (non-practicalist) theories of knowledge?

Note first that epistemologists have usually presumed an *absolutism* about knowledge that p. By this, I mean a view on which it is impossible to know a single truth p more or less fully, more or less well. This is often parsed as the view that there cannot be any disparate *degrees* or *grades* of knowledge that p (for a particular p). Proponents of that view will generally allow the possibility of there being more or less good justificatory support for p (or, more generally, a better or worse epistemic position regarding p). Few, however, regard knowledge similarly. Most epistemologists, it seems, accept that sort of knowledge-absolutism. But how often is their acceptance of it based on much *argument*?[31] Rarely; which is unfortunate, because this is not simply an 'intuitive' matter. Instead, it is quite theoretical, requiring us to evaluate carefully the epistemological costs of one commitment as against another. Accordingly, we should *examine* whether knowledge-absolutism is epistemologically mandatory.

In fact, such absolutism readily becomes less clearly correct once we embrace an *ability* analysis of knowledge-that – conceiving of knowledge-that as knowledge-how – such as section 5's practicalism has advocated. In general, abilities admit of degrees or grades, at least roughly so. They can be more *or* less pronounced or developed, stronger *or* weaker. So too, correlatively, is any instance of knowledge that p, insofar as it *is* an ability. This is especially so, given the complexity – along the following two dimensions – of the ability which will be the knowledge that p. First, sub-abilities which can constitute a particular case of knowledge that p can themselves be more, *or* they can be less, pronounced and developed. Second, there could be more, *or* there could be fewer, of these present anyway within a given case.

Why would we want to deny that possibility, by embracing knowledge-absolutism? Recall epistemology's standardly deeming knowledge to be a state. I have been arguing that the state in question could be one of potentiality, an ability. But many epistemologists, as far as I can tell,

---

31 See Hetherington (2001; 2006; 2011), for arguments *against* epistemology's needing to incorporate knowledge-absolutism. And I am not alone in this stance. I have some welcome company. Fellow non-absolutists about knowledge-that include de Morgan, Malcolm, Carnap, Quine, Hintikka, Peacocke, Alvin Goldman, David Lewis, Sosa, and Reed. For details of these philosophers' non-absolutism about knowledge-that, see Hetherington (2011, sec. 2.8).

implicitly treat that initial concession, of knowledge's being a state, as if the concession implies that any instance of knowledge is *a definite thing* – in the sense of something which, in having properties, is akin to a *determinate substance*. After all, on that traditional picture, even when describing you as *knowing* that *p* we mean that you *have the thing* which is the knowledge that *p* – and that you thereby have something which, once present, can never become *more* present. It is a thing which is present or not; and that is that. There it is; or no, it is not. In that respect, Fred Dretske compares knowledge with pregnancy:[32] there cannot be either more or less of it; there *is* it, or there is *not* it. And that is his argument – all of it – for knowledge-absolutism. In reply to which, Baron Reed remarks aptly that 'a woman carrying twins into the ninth month is clearly more pregnant than a woman with one six-weeks-old embryo.'[33]

I have been discussing this issue because one of the theoretical costs of knowledge-absolutism is a susceptibility, such as we have been discussing, to the problem of the criterion. When that problem arises for an epistemologist, this is partly *because* of her being an absolutist about the knowledge which is being discussed, such as knowledge that P and knowledge that J. One sign of this is the fact that section 6's dissolution of the problem of the criterion was possible partly because of what we can now recognise as having been a *non*-absolutism about these cases of knowledge. I mentioned a few possible sub-abilities which could be constituting a particular instance of the knowledge that P; but no specific one of them, *and* no specific number of them, was deemed essential to the ability which was constituting that instance of knowledge that P. Implicitly, therefore, this picture is non-absolutist: there could be more *or* fewer of those sub-abilities present as part of the ability which is the knowledge that P – with the latter being itself more *or* less fully developed, accordingly. And now we should appreciate how such a picture permits an instance of knowledge that P (or, for that matter, knowledge that J) to be *more or less good* as knowledge of its particular truth. This then allows the epistemological story to welcome the possibility of one's having the knowledge that P in a way which is less good than it might have been – *even* while one is nonetheless having knowledge that P. The same is true, *mutatis mutandis*, of the knowledge that J. So, we may welcome the possibility of an instance of knowledge that P's

---

32 Dretske (1981), 363.
33 Reed (2010), 242, n. 43.

having a lessened quality as knowledge that P – with this being *due* in part to the absence of the knowledge that J.

Both of these non-absolutist possibilities can thus be realised, and indeed explained, within section 6's picture. An instance of knowledge that P could be a more or less extensive and strong ability, as could an instance of knowledge that J. Those abilities could have at least somewhat differing sub-abilities. And although each instance of knowledge (each of those two abilities) could be manifested in some shared ways, not all of their manifestations need be shared. The epistemological story about knowledge's nature should become far more flexible in these ways than a standard knowledge-absolutism would have us believe it must be. Once it does, the problem of the criterion disappears.[34]

8. Knowledge and justification

Often, the problem of the criterion is motivated in terms of the epistemic *justification* which is thought to be required within the respective pieces of knowledge. Yet my account in this paper has proceeded without relying upon that sort of formulation. Why so?

Epistemic justification takes one of two general forms. It could be externalist, such as when reliably accurate perception supports – simply by being so reliable – a given belief that p. Or it could be internalist, such as when good evidence or reasons – in part by being present to the epistemic agent's awareness – are supporting the belief that p. But in either of those kinds of case, we may think of the presence of the justification as itself an ability – specifically, an ability which can be *just one more* of the sub-abilities available to be manifested or expressed, within the ability which is one's knowledge that p. Perceiving reliably, and responding aptly with a belief or acceptance; reasoning well in support of a position; the diligent marshalling, weighing, and retaining of evidence: any of these (and more) could be justificatory aspects – in turn, externalist ones or internalist ones – of how one is knowing that

---

[34] For more details on how a non-absolutism about knowledge is sufficient to unseat the problem of the criterion, see Hetherington (2001, sec. 6.3). But that account is not also grounded – as this paper's account is – upon a larger epistemological picture of knowledge's nature and point. If knowledge-practicalism is true, then so is non-absolutism about knowledge; and practicalism is a fuller picture of the nature and point of knowledge and knowing.

p. The respective abilities which these various actions express or manifest may, in turn, be regarded as justificatory aspects of how the knowledge that p can be present.

Notice the qualifiers – 'could', 'may', and 'can' – in that account. This paper's practicalist, or ability, analysis of knowledge allows us not to *require* any of these justificatory aspects to be present as part of the knowledge that p's presence.[35] Accordingly, although (in section 1) the problem of the criterion could have been presented in terms of justification rather than knowledge, if this paper's practicalist conception is correct then we would have been overlooking what is most pressing about the putative challenge. We would have been focussing on justification, presumably as a way of trying to *derive* a problem about knowledge; whereas the apparent problem should be discussed *directly* in terms of knowledge.

Or could we choose to derive the problem *purely* as one about justification? Of course; but justification is arguably not of independent or prior epistemological interest anyway. That is,[36] maybe the epistemologically more 'intuitive' notion is that of knowledge. In any event, it could be the phenomenon about which people *care* more readily. Current epistemological interest in the possibility of what Timothy Williamson calls *knowledge-first* epistemology is pertinent, too.[37] That approach, supported also by Jonathan Sutton,[38] would have us think about justification in terms of knowledge, not vice versa. And that is, in effect, what I am doing here.

---

35 In saying this, am I allowing knowledge and knowing to be present *without* justification and justifying being present? I am; and this is a further view for which I have argued in detail elsewhere, in different ways: Hetherington (2001, ch. 4; 2007; 2011, ch. 4). Nevertheless, we may also say that (with all else being equal) when justification *is* present the knowledge as such is thereby improved. It would be better in accord with section 7's non-absolutism about knowledge – a view which does admit, after all, the possibility of improving one's knowledge that p. The knowledge would be better *as* knowledge of that truth of which it is knowledge. It could be better in a particular case *by* being an ability which includes justificatory abilities.
36 See also William Alston's (2005) doubts about the unitary theoretical strength of the concept of epistemic justification.
37 Williamson (2000).
38 Sutton (2007); and possibly by Hetherington (2011), ch. 5.

9. Knowledge and truth

Section 8 was prepared to discard justification as a conceptually *necessary* component of knowledge. On this paper's picture, justificatory factors remain welcome, even actively sought, within knowledge – but possibly not therefore conceptually *needed* within it. This is not to deny that perhaps all *actual* instances of knowledge within this world include a justificatory element. In any event, the paper's practicalism – its ability analysis – unequivocally retains *truth* as a conceptually necessary condition of knowing. It has done this by talking, not simply about agency (in terms of ability), but about *effective* agency. Sellars was right to seize (even if he did so only gesturally) upon that phenomenon; for effectiveness amounts to truth, to accuracy.

At any rate, it does so in the setting we are discussing. Recall (from section 5) how knowing that p is a matter of acting in various ways such as asserting, inferring, answering, etc. And note how each of those actions succeeds only in some way directed at p. We recognised this in section 5 by including an *accuracy* condition within each of those sub-abilities potentially involved in any case of the complex ability which (for a particular person) is knowledge that p (for some given p). Knowing that p would be expressed or manifested, not simply in one's asserting that p and believing that p, for instance. One's *accurately* asserting that p and one's *accurately* believing that p would (as section 5 explained) be the apposite expressions or manifestations.

Even that will not seem, to most epistemologists, to *suffice* for knowing. Nevertheless, section 8 has explained why justification might not always be a conceptually necessary component of knowledge. And section 7 has told us why, at least in conceptual principle, some cases of knowledge that p could be lesser knowledge that p – perhaps (in the spirit of section 8) *because* of an absence of justification – while still being knowledge. Even if an instance of such knowledge is not everything we could want within knowledge (even within knowledge of the particular p in question), in principle non-absolutism about knowledge might still allow that lesser instance to *be* knowledge. Again, the result would simply be a *lower* grade of knowledge that p. There might be many ways – not all of which need involve the presence of epistemic justification – in which a piece of knowledge can be manifested with effective agency.

10. Knowledge and tethers

Why, then, are epistemologists so standardly committed to the idea of knowledge's having to include epistemic justification? It is an idea with a powerful and ancient philosophical genesis. Commonly, the idea is motivated among epistemologists by Socrates's remarks in the *Meno*[39] about the difference between knowledge and true belief ('correct opinion'). The difference, he argued, is the presence of a *tether*. Socrates described tethers in this way:[40]

> true opinions, as long as they remain, are a fine thing and all they do is good, but they are not willing to remain long, and they escape from a man's mind, so that they are not worth much until one ties them down by (giving) an account of the reason why. And that, Meno my friend, is recollection, as we previously agreed. After they are tied down, in the first place they become knowledge, and then they remain in place. That is why knowledge is prized higher than correct opinion, and knowledge differs from correct opinion in being tied down.[41]

That picture is appealingly simple; too simple, though. There are three interweaving problems with it. (i) Socrates's argument is *fallacious* unless supplemented with a further constraint. The tether he describes could itself become frayed, worn through, unreliable. How might he avoid that shortcoming? (ii) A strong tether, one not worn through, would suffice. However, this natural suggestion is only metaphorical. And rendering it less so could well make it quite *uninformative*. It would be so if it is requiring the tether (e.g., as recollection) to be knowledge itself – and thereby impervious to that possibility of being too frayed. That idea would be uninformative, for Socrates's purposes, because he is seeking to understand knowledge not in terms at all of knowledge. (iii) A better response is available; yet it is one which moves us more *towards* than away from this paper's practicalism. Suppose we ask what the point is of a tether anyway. Socrates, it seems, would answer thus: '... so that the correct opinion can be *used*, time and again as needed, in this and that circumstance as needed.' But such uses are naturally understandable as being expressions or manifestations of the ability *to* express or manifest them. They are expressions or manifestations of the forms of effective agency available within knowledge. In effect, therefore, we would

---

39 Socrates *Meno*, 97a–98c.
40 Ibid. 98a.
41 The translation is from Grube (1981), 86.

seem to be forming a view of knowledge as knowledge-how – knowledge as the ability to do various things, such as with a correct opinion.

The example envisaged by Socrates concerned one's having a correct opinion as to how to reach the desired destination of Larissa. Socrates seems to have viewed the desired tether as allowing that correct opinion to stay in place, remaining available so as to enable the person with the opinion to continue using it in the single way for which it is useful – specifically, his successfully making the journey to Larissa. Yet Socrates thereby understates that particular opinion's potentially relevant usefulness. It admits of many further embeddings within one's life. We may also use that tethered correct opinion to answer questions about journeys to Larissa (and some questions about other journeys), or to help others to walk there. We may even use that correct opinion later, when thinking about distances to different places. A tether, we see, need not be so narrowly characterised as to be what epistemologists call epistemic justification. Even Socrates's example, simple though it appears initially, need not be interpreted so narrowly. We may conceive of the tether far more wide-rangingly. We may permit *various* possible ways of manifesting a tether; and we may let a tether be the complex potentiality for there to *be* these different possible ways of its being manifested. This makes the tether potentially more powerful, in that it could be better suited for a *range* of possible circumstances. And, as I said, it *allows* the tether, in a given case, not to be justificatory. There are manifestations or expressions which Socrates could well have been trying to encompass with his talk of tethers. So we may infer, at any rate, once we adopt a practicalist interpretation of knowledge, such as this paper has begun to provide.

References

Alston (2005): William Payne Alston, *Beyond 'Justification': Dimensions of Epistemic Evaluation*, Ithaca/NY.

Anscombe (1963 [1957]): Gertrude Elizabeth Margaret Anscombe, *Intention*, 2nd edtion, Oxford.

Bengson/Moffett (forthcoming *a*): John Bengson/Marc Moffett, "Two Conceptions of Mind and Action: Knowing How and the Philosophical Theory of Intelligence", in: J. Bengson/M. Moffett (eds.), *Knowing How: Essays on Knowledge, Mind, and Action*, Oxford.

Bengson/Moffett (forthcoming *b*): John Bengson/Marc Moffett, "Non-Propositional Intellectualism", in: J. Bengson/M. A. Moffett (eds.), *Knowing How: Essays on Knowledge, Mind, and Action*, Oxford.

Chisholm (1982): Roderick Milton Chisholm, *The Foundations of Knowing*, Minneapolis.
Chisholm (1989): Roderick Milton Chisholm, *Theory of Knowledge*, 3rd edition, Englewood Cliffs/NJ.
Dretske, (1981): Fred Dretske, "The Pragmatic Dimension of Knowledge", *Philosophical Studies* 40, 363–78.
Grube (1981): George Maximilian Anthony Grube (trans.), *Plato: Five Dialogues*, Indianapolis.
Hawthorne/Stanley (2008): John Hawthorne/Jason Stanley, "Knowledge and Action" *The Journal of Philosophy* 105, 571–90.
Hetherington (1992): Stephen Hetherington, *Epistemology's Paradox: Is a Theory of Knowledge Possible?*, Savage/Maryland.
Hetherington (2001): Stephen Hetherington, *Good Knowledge, Bad Knowledge: On Two Dogmas of Epistemology*, Oxford.
Hetherington (2006): Stephen Hetherington, "How To Know (That Knowledge-That Is Knowledge-How)", in: S. Hetherington (ed.), *Epistemology Futures*, Oxford, 71–94.
Hetherington (2007): Stephen Hetherington, "Is This a World Where Knowledge Has to Include Justification?" *Philosophy and Phenomenological Research* 75, 41–69.
Hetherington (2008): Stephen Hetherington, "Knowing-That, Knowing-How, and Knowing Philosophically", *Grazer Philosophische Studien* 77, 307–24.
Hetherington (2010): Stephen Hetherington, "Elusive Epistemological Justification", *Synthese* 174, 315–30.
Hetherington (2011): Stephen Hetherington, *How To Know: A Practicalist Conception of Knowledge*, Wiley-Blackwell.
Johnston (2005): Mark Johnston, "Constitution", in: F. Jackson/M. Smith (eds.), *The Oxford Handbook of Contemporary Philosophy*, New York, 636–77.
Lehrer (1990): Keith Lehrer, *Theory of Knowledge*, Boulder/Colo.
Mason/Spence (1999): John Mason/Mary Spence, "Beyond Mere Knowledge of Mathematics: The Importance of Knowing-To Act in the Moment", *Educational Studies in Mathematics* 38, 135–61.
Reed (2010): Baron Reed, "A Defense of Stable Invariantism", *Noûs* 44, 224–44.
Ryle (1949): Gilbert Ryle, *The Concept of Mind*, London.
Ryle (1971 [1946]): Gilbert Ryle, "Knowing How and Knowing That", in: *Collected Papers*, Vol. II., London, 212–25.
Sellars (1979): Wilfrid Stalker Sellars, "More on Givenness and Explanatory Coherence", in G. S. Pappas (ed.), *Justification and Knowledge: New Studies in Epistemology*, Dordrecht, 169–82.
Snowdon (2003): Paul Snowdon, "Knowing How and Knowing That: A Distinction Reconsidered", *Proceedings of the Aristotelian Society* 104, 1–29.
Sosa (2009): Ernest Sosa, *Reflective Knowledge: Apt Belief and Reflective Knowledge*, Vol. II., Oxford.

Stanley/Williamson (2001): Jason Stanley/Timothy Williamson, "Knowing How", *The Journal of Philosophy* 98, 411–44.
Sutton (2007): Jonathan Sutton, *Without Justification*, Cambridge, Mass.
Williamson (2000): Timothy Williamson, *Knowledge and Its Limits*, Oxford.

Wie Wissen funktioniert*
John Hyman

I

Ich werde mich hauptsächlich mit der Frage „Was ist persönliches propositionales Wissen?" beschäftigen. Diese Frage richtet sich offensichtlich auf einen äußerst beschränkten Gegenstand, und das in dreifacher Hinsicht. Erstens gibt es sowohl unpersönliches als auch persönliches Wissen. Zweitens unterscheidet man häufig zwischen propositionalem und praktischem Wissen. Drittens schließlich fragen wir nicht nur, was Wissen ist, sondern wir können auch fragen, ob und wie Wissen verschiedener Art erworben werden kann: kausales Wissen, apriorisches Wissen, moralisches Wissen u.s.w. Ich werde zunächst jeden dieser drei Punkte kurz erläutern.

Als erstes unterscheidet man zwischen persönlichem und unpersönlichem Wissen – mit anderen Worten, zwischen dem psychologischen und dem sozialen Wissensbegriff.[1] Wir verwenden den Begriff des Wissens, um den kognitiven Zustand von einzelnen Personen zu beschreiben, wir verwenden ihn aber auch, um den Fortschritt der naturwissenschaftlichen und historischen Forschung zu beschreiben. So können wir zum Beispiel vom Wissensstand auf einem gewissen Gebiet der Biologie oder Geschichte sprechen oder uns danach erkundigen. In diesem Falle geht es uns offenkundig nicht darum, was irgendjemand zum Beispiel über die Genetik der Fruchtfliege oder das Leben Karls des Großen weiß, sondern was die wissenschaftliche oder akademische Gemeinschaft weiß. Aber natürlich gibt es eine enge Verbindung zwischen persönlichem und unpersönlichem Wissen. „Man weiß, dass p" bedeutet jedoch nicht einfach nur „Irgendjemand weiß, dass p". Dies anzunehmen, hieße zu ignorieren, welch wichtige Rolle in der Ökonomie des Wissens Dokumenten, Archiven und Bibliotheken zukommt. Die Er-

---

* Originally published in *Philosophical Quarterly* 50 (1999), pp. 433–451. Reprinted and translated by permission of the publisher, John Wiley and Sons.
1 Vgl. Williamson (1973), 3.

findung der Schrift bedeutete, dass jeder einzelne von uns vergessen kann, was er weiß, ohne dass wir als Kollektiv unser Wissen verlieren. Deshalb hatte auch Thamus, der mythische König Ägyptens, von dem Sokrates im *Phädrus* spricht, Recht, als er sagte, die Schrift sei ein Mittel für die Erinnerung und nicht für das Gedächtnis, aber er hatte Unrecht, als er daraus den Schluss zog, dass durch sie nicht das Wissen erweitert werden könne, sondern nur der Schein von Wissen.

Zum zweiten wird häufig von einem Unterschied zwischen praktischem und propositionalem Wissen gesprochen – eine Unterscheidung, die Ryle unter der Überschrift „Wissen, wie und Wissen, dass" erörterte.[2] Wie viele Kommentatoren festgestellt haben, sind diese Etiketten jedoch irreführend, denn „A weiß, dass ..." ist nicht die einzige Konstruktion, mit der man jemandem propositionales Wissen zuzuschreiben kann. „A weiß, ob es morgen regnen wird", „A weiß, wann und wo Alexander der Große geboren wurde" und „A weiß, wie sich Schwämme fortpflanzen", zum Beispiel, schreiben alle A propositionales Wissen zu. Fraglich ist erstens, ob wissen, wie man etwas macht, dasselbe ist wie die Fähigkeit zu haben, es zu tun, oder geschickt darin zu sein; zweitens fragt sich, ob wissen, wie man etwas macht, und wissen, dass etwas der Fall ist, ihrem Wesen nach unterschiedliche Arten des Wissens sind. Skeptikern wird es nicht schwer fallen, Beispiele zu finden. Penelope zum Beispiel weiß, wie man einen Teppich knüpft, noch lange nachdem sie die Kraft in ihren Fingern verloren hat, dies zu tun. (Wenn sie dies weiß, aber nicht mehr tun kann, mag das natürlich daran liegen, dass sie zu schwach dazu ist oder blind, aber es kann nicht an ihrem Unwissen liegen.) Und „Viktor weiß, wie man ein Kaninchen häutet" kann durch „Für einige ø gilt: Viktor weiß, dass er ø-en muss, um ein Kaninchen zu häuten". Diese Beispiele liefern jedoch kein zwingendes Argument; und die hier aufgeworfenen Fragen verdienen eine geduldigere Behandlung, als ich sie hier vornehmen kann. Sie ist ihnen glücklicherweise auch zuteil geworden.[3]

Drittens befasst sich die Erkenntnistheorie nicht nur mit der Frage, was Wissen ist, sondern auch mit den Fragen, ob und wie Wissen verschiedener Art erworben werden kann. Diese knappe Formulierung fasst natürlich eine ganze Reihe schwieriger und umstrittener Probleme zusammen. Mir ist es wichtig zu betonen, dass die Fragen, was Wissen ist und wie Wissen erworben werden kann, zwei unterschiedliche, wenn

---

2   Vgl. Ryle (1990), 212–25; Ryle (1986), Kap. 2.
3   Eine detaillierte und skeptische Erörterung, in deren Schuld ich in diesem Absatz stehe, findet sich in Brown (1971), 213–48; White (1982), Kap. 2.

auch miteinander verknüpfte Fragen sind. Es ist eines zu sagen, wie Wissen erworben werden kann und wie nicht, und wie deshalb Wissensansprüche getestet werden können; und es ist etwas ganz anderes zu sagen, was Wissen ist; ebenso wie es eines ist zu sagen, wie ein Recht oder eine Pflicht erworben werden kann und wie man deshalb entscheiden kann, ob jemand ein solches Recht oder eine solche Pflicht hat, und etwas ganz anderes zu sagen, was ein Recht oder eine Pflicht ist.

In der Forschungsliteratur gibt es eine Tendenz, den Unterschied zwischen diesen beiden Fragen zu verwischen, und dies hauptsächlich aus zwei Gründen. Erstens gehört zu den traditionellen Aufgaben der Erkenntnistheorie die Auseinandersetzung mit der skeptischen Frage, ob wir wirklich die verschiedenen Dinge wissen, die wir gewöhnlich und unreflektiert zu wissen glauben. Aber die Behauptung, wir wüssten diese Dinge – über Ursachen, die Vergangenheit, die Gedanken anderer Menschen etc. – kann nur gerechtfertigt werden, indem gezeigt wird, dass es eine zufrieden stellende Antwort auf die Frage gibt, wie wir diese Dinge wissen. Wenn eine Wissensdefinition also den Skeptiker widerlegen soll, wird sie nicht nur erklären müssen, was Wissen ist, sondern auch, wie es erworben werden kann. Zweitens wird weithin angenommen, dass Wissen eine Art von Überzeugung ist. Aber wenn wir diese Annahme machen, dann kann es leicht so scheinen, als liefe die Entscheidung, ob A weiß, dass p, oder nur glaubt, dass p, darauf hinaus, ob As Überzeugung auf eine Weise erworben wurde, die uns berechtigt, sie als Wissen gelten zu lassen. Und wir werden deshalb wahrscheinlich die Frage, wie Wissen erworben werden kann, als Teil der größeren Frage betrachten, was es ist.

Aus diesen und vielleicht noch anderen Gründen gibt es in der Erkenntnistheorie eine gewisse Neigung zu dem, was die Presseleute „mission creep" (eine schleichende Ausweitung des Kampfauftrags, AdÜ) nennen. Zunächst wollen wir nur sagen, was Wissen ist, aber schon bald werden wir in die Frage verwickelt, wie es erworben werden kann; und binnen kurzem müssen wir mit dem Hubschrauber evakuiert werden und hinterlassen ein Chaos. Ich werde mich nur mit der Frage beschäftigen, was Wissen ist. Um die Fragen, wie Wissen von verschiedener Art erworben werden kann und ob und, wenn ja, wie die Skepsis in der einen oder anderen Form widerlegt werden kann, werde ich mich dagegen nicht bemühen.

II

Was ist persönliches propositionales Wissen? (Nach den einleitenden Bemerkungen werde ich im Folgenden die Einschränkung weglassen und einfach nur von Wissen sprechen.) Nach der immer noch vorherrschenden Lehre ist Wissen eine Art von Überzeugung. In den vergangenen Jahren hat indes eine weniger einflussreiche Ansicht Aufmerksamkeit auf sich gezogen und Anhänger gefunden. Der Ansicht der Minderheit zufolge ist Wissen nicht eine Art von Überzeugung: Es ist eine Art von Fähigkeit.[4]

Die Unzufriedenheit mit der vorherrschenden Auffassung ist verständlich. Seit der Veröffentlichung von Gettiers viel zitiertem Artikel sind sich die Philosophen weitgehend einig, dass Wissen nicht als gerechtfertigte wahre Meinung definiert werden kann.[5] Aber auch unter denen, die behaupten, Wissen sei eine Art von Überzeugung, endet hier die Einigkeit. Trotz einer ungeheuren Anzahl von Arbeiten konnte keine Definition von Wissen als Überzeugung allgemeine Zustimmung erlangen. Wie es scheint, hat die Konstruktion von Gegenbeispielen den Einfallsreichtum der Kritiker bisher keineswegs erschöpft;[6] und zwangsläufig wird es mit der zunehmenden Komplexität der Definitionen umso wahrscheinlicher, dass sogar eine Definition, die allen vorstellbaren Gegenbeispielen standhielte, zu offenkundig *ad hoc* wäre, als dass sie großes Gewicht haben könnte. Es wäre, mit anderen Worten, schwer zu verstehen, was der Witz eines so komplizierten Begriffs sein könnte oder warum etwas davon abhängt, ob jemand etwas weiß. Es überrascht deshalb nicht, dass die Aussichten für eine Definition von Wissen als Überzeugung mittlerweile von vielen als sehr skeptisch eingeschätzt werden.[7] Selbst die Auffassung, dass Wissen, im Gegensatz zu gerechtfertigter Überzeugung, nicht wirklich wichtig sei, ist schon laut

---

[4] Die negative Ansicht scheint aus der Schlussfolgerung zu folgen, zu der Sokrates in Platons *Theaitetos* (210a-b) kommt, nicht dagegen die positive Ansicht. Vgl. auch *Politeia* 476–9. Einige Autoren, die behaupten, aus „A weiß, dass p" folge, dass A glaubt, dass p, räumen dennoch ein, dass Wissen keine Art von Überzeugung sei. Vgl. etwa Chisholm (1957), 17 f.

[5] Gettier (1963), 121 ff.

[6] Shope (1983) ist eine Herkulesarbeit, die bestätigt, dass die Bemühungen um Gettiers Problem bis zum Zeitpunkt ihrer Veröffentlichung bestenfalls zu keinem eindeutigen Ergebnis gelangt waren.

[7] Vgl. Craig (1990) und Williamson (1995).

geworden.⁸ Man könnte also meinen, es sei an der Zeit, der Minderheit aufmerksamer zuzuhören.

Falls Wissen eine Art von Überzeugung ist, so bleibt ungewiss, um welche Art es sich dabei handelt. Aber auch die Ausarbeitung der von der Minderheit vorgeschlagenen Auffassung war bisher nicht erfolgreich. Wittgenstein bemerkt: „Die Grammatik des Wortes ‚wissen' ist offenbar eng verwandt der Grammatik des Wortes ‚können', ‚imstande sein'."⁹ Und er unterzieht diese Beziehung einer sorgfältigen Untersuchung in dem besonderen Fall des Verstehens, d. h. des Wissens der Bedeutung. Ryle sagt, „wissen" gehöre zur Familie der „Fertigkeitswörter".¹⁰ Aber die Definition der Art von Fertigkeit, die Wissen sein soll, wurde bisher kaum weiter entwickelt.

Ein Grund hierfür ist eine Neigung seitens der von Wittgenstein und Ryle beeinflussten Philosophen, Wissen zu eng an den Gebrauch der Sprache für die Beantwortung von Fragen und das Geben von Informationen zu knüpfen.¹¹ Alan White etwa behauptet, Wissen sei „die Fähigkeit, die richtige Antwort auf eine mögliche Frage zu liefern".¹² Aber die richtige Antwort auf eine Frage zu liefern, heißt nach der natürlichsten Deutung, diese Antwort vorzutragen; und in diesem Sinne kann man wissen, dass p der Fall ist, ohne die richtige Antwort auf die Frage liefern zu können, ob p der Fall ist. Unter gewissen Umständen möchten wir vielleicht sagen, ein Hund wisse, dass es Zeit sei, Gassi zu gehen, könne es aber nicht sagen. White räumt ausdrücklich ein, dass es „keinen Grund" gebe, „warum wir nicht davon sprechen sollten, dass kleine Kinder und Tiere viele Dinge wüssten ... [z.B.] dass es Zeit sei für einen Spaziergang", und er bestreitet, dass die Fähigkeit, die richtige Antwort auf eine mögliche Frage zu liefern, impliziere, „dass sie diese auf sprachliche Weise äußern" oder – vermutlich – überhaupt äußern könnten. Aber er gibt keine Erklärung dafür, wie die Ausübung dieser Fähigkeit genau zu definieren sei.

Vielleicht dachte White, die richtige Antwort auf eine mögliche Frage zu liefern, bestehe bloß darin, jemanden in die Lage zu versetzen, die Antwort zu geben; denn ein Hund kann seinen Besitzer freilich auf

---

8 Vgl. Kaplan (1985), 354 ff.
9 Wittgenstein PU § 150.
10 Ryle (1986), 178. Die Auffassung der Minorität kann ihren Stammbaum ebenfalls bis zu Platon (*Theaitetos* 196c-199c) zurückverfolgen. Vgl. auch Aristoteles (*De Anima* 417a 21-b 2).
11 Margolis (1972), 74–82; White (1983), Kap. 6; Craig (1990).
12 White (1983), 119; Vgl. Wittgenstein ÜG, § 586.

die Tatsache aufmerksam machen, dass es Zeit ist, Gassi zu gehen, und ihn dadurch in die Lage versetzen, diese Tatsache festzustellen. Aber diese Definition wäre zu großzügig. Denn im selben Sinne könnte auch das Lackmuspapier, das selbst nichts wissen kann, die richtige Antwort auf die Frage liefern, ob eine Lösung säurehaltig ist. Als Alternative könnte man vielleicht sagen, die richtige Antwort zu liefern, bestehe darin, jemanden *absichtlich* in die Lage zu versetzen, die Antwort zu geben (vgl. White S. 120). Dies wäre jedoch zu streng. Denn selbst wenn es möglich ist, dass ein Hund das Gassigehen herbeizuführen beabsichtigt oder jemanden dazu bringen will, dass Gassi gegangen wird, indem er auf die Tür zuspringt, ist es doch gewiss *nicht* möglich, dass er die Absicht hat, jemanden in die Lage zu versetzen, festzustellen, dass es Zeit sei, Gassi zu gehen. Whites Definition befindet sich in einem unglücklichen Schwebezustand zwischen einer Tautologie und einer Unwahrheit: zu wissen, ob p, bedeutet nichts anderes, als die Antwort auf die Frage zu wissen, ob p; aber es bedeutet nicht, die Antwort auf die Frage, ob p, geben zu können.

Was wir über Tiere zu sagen geneigt sind, so mag man einwenden, sollte nicht unser Hauptgrund dafür sein, eine bestimmte Wissenstheorie zu verwerfen. Da sich sprachlose Tiere der Tatsachen allenfalls in einem verminderten Maße bewusst sind, sollten wir uns beim Philosophieren über Wissen an kompetenten Sprechern einer Sprache orientieren und unsere Ansicht über die kognitiven Vermögen von Tieren von unserer Erkenntnistheorie abhängig machen und nicht umgekehrt. Ich gebe zu, dass dieser Einwand von beträchtlicher Überzeugungskraft ist, und zwar trotz der oben erwähnten Tatsache, dass Whites Wissenstheorie damit vereinbar sein sollte, Tieren Wissen zuzuschreiben. Aber in jedem Fall spielt Wissen in unserem Leben eine sehr viel umfassendere Rolle als die Fähigkeit, Antworten auf Fragen geben zu können, und eine zufrieden stellende Definition sollte diesen Sachverhalt widerspiegeln. Die Lehre, Wissen sei gerechtfertigte wahre Überzeugung, war zu eng auf das zugeschnitten, was Bernard Williams die Situation des Prüfers genannt hat – „die Situation, in der sich sachkundige Fragesteller dafür interessieren, wie gut A über bestimmte Wissensinhalte Bescheid weiß"[13] – die, wie Williams feststellt, in der Praxis kaum typisch ist. Whites Wissenstheorie war dagegen auf das zugeschnitten, was man die Situation des Gutachters nennen könnte – die Situation, in der sachunkundige Fragesteller daran interessiert sind, von jemandem, der es wissen sollte, zu erfahren, ob p der Fall ist. Natürlich kommen diese beiden Situationen vor; aber es ist

---

13 Williams (1972), 3.

schwer einzusehen, warum man glauben sollte, dass sie den Schlüssel zur Natur des Wissens liefern könnten.

Einige zur Tradition der Minderheit zählende Autoren haben überzeugende Argumente dafür geliefert, dass Wissen eine Art von Fähigkeit ist[14]. Aber sie haben entweder zu wenig darüber gesagt, welche spezifische Art von Fähigkeit Wissen sein soll, oder das, was sie gesagt haben, war unbefriedigend. Zu genau diesem Problem möchte ich einen Lösungsvorschlag präsentieren. Falls diejenigen, die der Minderheit angehören, Recht haben, so können wir nicht behaupten, dass wir verstehen, was Wissen ist, wenn wir nicht erklären können, wie es sich im Denken und Verhalten äußert. Aber an diesem Punkt sind ihre Bemühungen ins Stocken geraten. Glücklicherweise gibt es hierfür jedoch eine relativ einfache Erklärung. Dafür werde ich jedenfalls argumentieren.

III

Ich werde zunächst eine Definition von Wissen betrachten, die Anthony Kenny vorgeschlagen hat, ein weiterer Philosoph, dessen Auffassung von Wissen durch Wittgenstein und Ryle beeinflusst ist. Wissen, so Kenny, ist „eine Fähigkeit sui generis". Aber er bezweifelt, dass man auch nur einigermaßen genau sagen kann, wozu es eine Fähigkeit ist:

> Es lässt sich nicht leicht bestimmen, wie sich Wissen im Verhalten äußert, und manches Wissen wirkt sich möglicherweise niemals auf das Verhalten aus. Wir können bestenfalls sagen, dass Wissen in der Fähigkeit besteht, das eigene Verhalten auf unbestimmte Weise so abzuwandeln, wie es für die Verfolgung der eigenen Ziele relevant ist.[15]

Zweierlei ist richtig an dieser Definition, und zweierlei ist falsch. Als erstes spricht für sie, dass, falls Wissen eine Fähigkeit ist, eine Definition von Wissen, wie Kenny unterstellt, angeben muss, worin sich Wissen äußert oder manifestiert. Hier wird ein ganz allgemeines Merkmal jeglicher Art von Vermögen oder Potentialen angesprochen. Dispositionen, Fähigkeiten, Fertigkeiten, Neigungen und Anfälligkeiten sind alles Vermögen; und Vermögen werden durch das definiert, was als ihre Realisierung oder Ausübung gilt, d. h. indem man sagt, wozu sie ein Vermögen sind. Kenny hat zweitens Recht, wenn er die eigentümliche Flexibilität von Wissen betont. Wissen kann sich auf eine unbestimmte Vielzahl von Weisen

---

14 Z.B. White (1982), Kap. 6.
15 Kenny (1989), 108 f.

äußern. Zum Beispiel kann sich Toms Kenntnis der Tatsache darin äußern, dass der Kurs des Rubels eingebrochen ist, dass er eine Ferienreise nach Russland bucht, Aktien von Gazprom erwirbt oder seinem Freund in Moskau Dollars schickt.

Auf der anderen Seite scheint Kenny die Frage, wie sich Wissen im Verhalten äußert, mit der Frage gleichzusetzen, wozu Wissen eine Fähigkeit ist. Das ist jedoch ein Fehler. Denn wenn Wissen eine Fähigkeit ist, dann ist es eine Fähigkeit, deren Ausübung ebenso im Denken bestehen kann wie im Sprechen oder im Verhalten. Eine Entscheidung zu treffen, eine Folgerung zu ziehen, Kopfrechnen, etwas zu bezweifeln, zu glauben oder sich etwas zu erhoffen, einen Wunsch zu erwerben oder eine Absicht auszubilden, sind alles Dinge, in denen sich Wissen ebenso äußern oder bekunden kann wie im Verhalten. Toms Kenntnis der Tatsache zum Beispiel, dass der Kurs des Rubels eingebrochen ist, kann sich in seiner Entscheidung äußern, eine Ferienreise nach Russland zu buchen, ganz gleichgültig, ob er dies tun wird oder nicht, und ebenso in seiner Hoffnung, dass der Freund seine Ersparnisse in Dollars angelegt hat, statt darin, ihm das Geld zu schicken.

Die zweite Schwäche von Kennys Wissenstheorie ist, dass sie nicht zu erklären vermag, was die heterogene Vielfalt von Phänomenen verbindet, die das Wissen, dass p, im Gegensatz zum Wissen, dass q, zum Ausdruck bringen können. Wissen, so sagt er, sei die Fähigkeit, das eigene Verhalten auf unbestimmte Weise so abzuwandeln, wie es für das Verfolgen der eigenen Ziele relevant ist. Aber wenn Wissen eine Art von Fähigkeit ist und wir nicht mehr darüber sagen können, wie diese Fähigkeit ausgeübt wird, dann muss der Unterschied zwischen dem Wissen von etwas Bestimmten und dem Wissen von etwas anderem im Dunklen bleiben.

Aber ist das wirklich eine Schwäche? Die Antwort auf diese Frage hängt natürlich davon ab, wie eine Erklärung des Unterschieds zwischen dem Wissen, dass p, und dem Wissen, dass q, aussehen soll. Wenn wir aber eine Formel suchen, die spezifische Handlungen und geistige Akte mit dem Besitz von spezifischen Wissensinhalten verbindet, so könnte man einwenden, dann ist diese Suche, wie sich leicht zeigen lässt, vergeblich. Zwar gibt es einen trivialen Sinn, in dem den verschiedenen Abwandlungen des eigenen Verhaltens, in denen sich ein bestimmtes Wissen äußert, etwas gemeinsam ist, da sie alle durch dieses Wissen *beeinflusst* oder *bestimmt* sind. Wenn also (zum Beispiel) Toms Wissen, dass der Kurs des Rubels eingebrochen ist, eine Fähigkeit ist, dann kann man durchaus sagen, dass die Ausübung dieser Fähigkeit in Handlungen und geistigen Akten bestehen wird, die durch das Wissen beeinflusst und bestimmt sind, dass der Kurs des Rubels eingebrochen ist. Aber sehr erhellend ist dies nicht. Und es führt uns in die Irre, wenn wir deshalb glauben, wir könnten konkret sagen, welche Handlungen und geistigen Akte Tom genau dann zu vollziehen in der Lage ist, wenn er weiß, dass der Kurs des Rubels eingebrochen ist. Denn wenn A weiß, dass p, dann folgt daraus nicht, dass A fähig ist, *all* das zu tun, was durch das Wissen, dass p, beeinflusst und bestimmt sein könnte. Wenn Tom weiß, dass der Kurs des Rubels eingebrochen ist, dann folgt daraus zum Beispiel nicht, dass er in der Lage ist, bei der Weltbank einen Kredit zu bekommen oder den russischen Premierminister zu entlassen. Und wenn A dazu in der Lage ist, *zumindest eines* der Dinge zu tun, die durch das Wissen, dass p, beeinflusst und bestimmt sein könnten, folgt daraus nicht, dass A weiß, dass p. Eine Investition bei Gazprom zum Beispiel mag durch das Wissen beeinflusst und bestimmt sein, dass der Kurs des Rubels eingebrochen ist, aber Tom muss nicht unbedingt wissen, dass der Kurs des Rubels eingebrochen ist, um Aktien von Gazprom zu kaufen.

Auf diesen Einwand ist zu erwidern, dass der Unterschied zwischen dem Wissen von etwas und dem Wissen von etwas anderem nicht erklärt werden kann, indem man sagt, welche spezifischen Handlungen und geistigen Akte das Wissen, dass p, ausdrücken könnten. Aber daraus folgt nicht, dass wir nicht erklären können, wozu das Wissen, dass p, eine Fähigkeit ist. Betrachten wir zum Vergleich die Frage „Was ist Begeisterungsfähigkeit?". Begeisterungsfähigkeit ist offensichtlich eine Charaktereigenschaft, eine Disposition oder eine Neigung; aber es ist nicht eine Neigung, etwas ganz Bestimmtes zu tun. Begeisterte Sportler hüpfen nicht ständig von einem Fuß auf den anderen und springen vor Freude in die Luft; und begeisterte Philosophen zittern nur selten vor Erregung und erzählen einander, wie viel Freude ihnen das Philosophieren bereitet. Begeisterungsfähigkeit ist (zum Teil) eine Neigung oder Disposition, viele Dinge mit Begeisterung zu tun. Es ist, wenn man das so sagen kann, eine *adverbiale* Neigung, eine Neigung, Dinge mit Begeisterung zu tun. Ganz entsprechend ist Unpünktlichkeit eine Neigung, viele Dinge, wie etwa zu einem Treffen erscheinen, die Steuererklärung abgeben und Briefe beantworten, nicht rechtzeitig, sondern mit Verspätung zu tun. Wie es ein anonymer Gutachter hilfreich formuliert hat, kann man Handlungen nur dadurch als unpünktlich charakterisieren, dass man sagt, sie würden mit Verspätung getan, also in Relation zu einer Uhrzeit und nicht im Hinblick darauf, was es für Handlungen sind. Unpünktlichkeit ist also eine adverbiale Neigung, obschon in diesem Fall das Adverb kein modales, sondern ein temporales Adverb ist.

Diese Beispiele lehren, dass uns nichts davon abhält, eine bestimmte Antwort auf die Frage zu geben, wozu Begeisterungsfähigkeit und Unpünktlichkeit Neigungen sind, auch wenn es keine speziellen Handlungen und geistigen Akte gibt, die zu vollziehen – seien es einige von ihnen oder alle – sie Neigungen sind. Aber ist es auch möglich, eine analoge Antwort auf die Frage zu geben, was das Wissen, dass p, für eine Fähigkeit ist? Falls ja, so ist Wissen eine adverbiale Fähigkeit, und zwar in dem Sinne, in dem Begeisterungsfähigkeit und Unpünktlichkeit adverbiale Neigungen oder Dispositionen sind. Wissen ist, mit anderen Worten, nicht die Fähigkeit, dies oder jenes zu tun: Es ist vielmehr die Fähigkeit, etwas auf eine adverbial bestimmte Weise zu tun, ebenso wie Unpünktlichkeit die Neigung ist, etwas mit Verspätung zu tun. Wenn dem nicht so ist, bleibt der Einwand bestehen, und alles was wir darüber sagen können, wie sich Wissen im Denken und Verhalten ausdrückt, vermag nicht den Unterschied zwischen einem bestimmten Wissen und einem anderen zu erklären.

Das ist also der Stand der Dinge: Die verschiedenen Abwandlungen des eigenen Denkens oder Verhaltens, die ein bestimmtes Wissen zum Ausdruck bringen, sind jene, die durch dieses Wissen beeinflusst oder bestimmt sind. Aber wir können nicht erklären, wie Toms Wissen, dass der Kurs des Rubels eingebrochen ist, zum Ausdruck gebracht wird, indem wir sagen, welche Handlungen und geistigen Akte durch sein Wissen beeinflusst und bestimmt werden kann. Die Frage ist also, ob wir dies stattdessen mithilfe einer adverbialen Paraphrase des zweiten Glieds der folgenden Konjunktion erklären können.

1. Tom ø-te, und Toms Ø-en wurde durch das Wissen, dass der Kurs des Rubels eingebrochen ist, beeinflusst oder bestimmt.

Das ist allerdings keine besonders schwierige Aufgabe. Denn wir können genau dieselbe Information vermitteln, indem wir entweder sagen, dass Toms Ø-en durch das Wissen, dass der Kurs des Rubels eingebrochen war, beeinflusst oder bestimmt wurde, oder dass die Tatsache, dass der Kurs des Rubels eingebrochen war, eine der Tatsachen ist, angesichts derer oder in deren Licht Tom ø-te. Aber eine Tatsache, angesichts derer oder in deren Licht Tom ø-te, ist eine der Tatsachen, weshalb Tom ø-te, und zwar in dem Sinne von „weshalb", der einen Grund dafür anführt, etwas Bestimmtes zu tun oder nicht zu tun, oder etwas Bestimmtes zu glauben, zu wollen oder zu bezweifeln. Eine mögliche Paraphrase für (1) wäre also:

2. Tom ø-te aufgrund der Tatsache, dass der Kurs des Rubels eingebrochen war.

Das Adverb in (2) ist natürlich kein modales oder temporales, sondern ein sogenanntes thematisches Adverb; es ist vergleichbar mit „zögerlich" oder „absichtlich". Wenn man sagt, Tom habe etwas zögerlich getan, so muss das nicht heißen, dass er es auf zögerliche Weise getan hat; und wenn man sagt, er habe etwas absichtlich getan, so kann dies nicht bedeuten, dass er es auf absichtliche Weise getan hat, denn eine solche Weise gibt es nicht. „Tom stimmte nur zögerlich zu" heißt normalerweise, dass Tom zustimmte, aber dies nur zögerlich tat; und „Tom hustete absichtlich" bedeutet, dass Tom hustete und dies aus einem Grund tat. (2) impliziert, dass Tom absichtlich ø-te; aber zusätzlich identifiziert es den Grund für sein Ø-en, die Tatsache nämlich, dass der Kurs des Rubels eingebrochen war.

IV

Falls die bisherige Argumentation korrekt ist, leuchtet es ein, dass Wissen eine Fähigkeit ist, etwas aus Gründen, die Tatsachen sind, zu tun oder zu unterlassen, zu glauben, zu wollen oder zu bezweifeln. Das heißt, es leuchtet ein, wenn wir uns bei unserer Konzeption von Wissen daran orientieren, wie sich Wissen in unserem geistigen Leben äußert, statt daran, wie wir Wissen erwerben; und wenn wir folglich nicht vergessen, dass die Liste – Tun, Unterlassen, Glauben, Wollen und Zweifeln – nicht erschöpfend ist. Ein jedes Verb, das in dem Satz „As Grund zu ø-en war, dass p" vorkommen kann, lässt sich dieser Liste hinzufügen.

Wenn dies der richtige Ansatz ist, dann lässt sich eine Definition von Wissen auf den Gedanken gründen, dass die Tatsachen, deren wir uns bewusst sind, diejenigen Tatsachen sind, durch die unsere Gedanken und Handlungen geleitet werden können. Und die sich daraus ergebende Definition bietet die nötige Kombination aus Flexibilität und Präzision. Sie hat das richtige Maß an Flexibilität, da die Vielfalt von Dingen, die A aus dem Grund tun kann, dass p, genauso heterogen ist wie die Vielfalt von Dingen, die A tun kann und deren Tun durch das Wissen, dass p, beeinflusst und bestimmt werden kann. Und sie ist in dem Sinne präzise, in dem sie genau erkennen lässt, welcher Unterschied zwischen dem Wissen, dass p, und dem Wissen, dass q, besteht. A weiß, dass p, genau dann, wenn die Tatsache, dass p, As Grund dafür sein kann, etwas zu tun, zu unterlassen, zu glauben, zu wollen oder zu bezweifeln; und A weiß, dass q, genau dann, wenn die Tatsache, dass q As Grund dafür sein kann, etwas zu tun, zu unterlassen, zu glauben, zu wollen oder zu bezweifeln.

Im restlichen Teil dieses Aufsatzes werde ich etwas zu den Begriffen sagen, mit denen ich Wissen definieren möchte, also zu Tatsachen und Gründen. Ich werde auf einige potentielle Einwände eingehen; und ich werde kurz zu Wittgensteins Behauptung Stellung nehmen, dass man von mir nicht sagen könne, ich wüsste, dass ich Schmerzen habe.

V

Ganz offensichtlich muss etwas zu Tatsachen und Gründen gesagt werden – etwas, aber nicht alles. Ich habe nicht gesagt, was Tatsachen sind, und ich habe auch nicht vor, dies zu tun. Tatsachen sind weder Ereignisse noch Verbindungen von Gegenständen, denn sie haben keinen Ort in Raum und Zeit. (Wer dies bezweifeln möchte, sollte anfangen, sich über negative und konditionale Tatsachen Gedanken zu machen.) Wir reden manchmal so, als hätten Tatsachen einen Ort in Raum und Zeit, etwa wenn wir danach fragen, wo eine bestimmte Tatsache zu finden oder zutage getreten sei. Aber diese Redewendungen zeigen nur, dass eine Tatsache an einem bestimmten Ort festgestellt oder zu einer bestimmten Zeit entdeckt werden kann. Tatsachen sind keine Situationen, denn im Gegensatz zu Situationen kann man Tatsachen behaupten; und im Gegensatz zu Tatsachen haben Situationen einen Beginn und sind von einer bestimmten Dauer. Vielleicht ist eine Tatsache einfach das, was eine wahre Behauptung behauptet, wie Strawson meint.[16] Aber es ist nicht nötig zu entscheiden, ob diese Formel akzeptabel ist, denn, gleichgültig was Tatsachen sind, empirisches Wissen ist die Kenntnis von Tatsachen. Falls Strawsons Formel korrekt ist und falls es moralische und ästhetische Wahrheiten gibt, so gibt es auch moralische und ästhetische Tatsachen, und moralisches und ästhetisches Wissen ist die Kenntnis dieser Tatsachen. Wenn die Formel dagegen falsch ist, muss die hier verteidigte Analyse von Wissen so erweitert werden, dass sie auch moralische und ästhetische Phänomene einbezieht; was aber eine relativ einfache Aufgabe wäre.

Was Tatsachen auch immer sein mögen, sie können auf jeden Fall Gründe sein. Das habe ich bisher vorausgesetzt, aber ich bin bereit, es zu verteidigen. Betrachtet man die handlungstheoretische Literatur, so hat es

---

16 Strawson (1971), 196.

den Anschein, als herrsche einige Verwirrung darüber, was Gründe sind. Davidson zum Beispiel sagt, Gründe bestünden aus geistigen Zuständen und Dispositionen; von Wright sagt, eine Bitte könne ein Grund sein; und sowohl Kenny als auch Audi behaupten, Ziele seien Gründe. (Audi fügt hinzu, ein Ziel sei „der Inhalt eines Wunsches und [werde] ausgedrückt durch die Infinitivphrase, die typischerweise dazu verwendet [werde], das anzugeben, was gewünscht wird, z. B. ‚philosophisches Denken zu fördern'".[17]) Aber alle diese Behauptungen sind falsch.

Um zu verstehen, warum, muss man sich drei fundamentale Tatsachen über Gründe vor Augen führen. Erstens: Wie Raz betont, spielen Gründe eine Rolle in praktischen Schlussfolgerungen;[18] und sie spielen auch in theoretischen Schlussfolgerungen eine Rolle: As Grund dafür, etwas zu tun, kann Bs Grund dafür sein, etwas zu glauben. Beispielsweise kann Arthurs Grund dafür, zu glauben, dass die Erde kalkhaltig ist, nämlich dass die Azalee verwelkt ist, Audreys Grund dafür sein, den Gärtner zu entlassen. Mit einem Wort: Gründe können als Prämissen fungieren. Zweitens: Gründe können dargelegt oder gegeben werden; und die kanonische Form des Satzes, der den Grund einer Person, etwas zu tun oder zu glauben, darlegt oder angibt, lautet: ‚A ø-t, weil p' oder ‚B glaubt, dass q, weil p'. Daraus, dass „weil" ein Junktor ist, folgt, dass die kanonische Form des sprachlichen Ausdrucks für einen Grund ein Satz im Indikativ ist, obwohl auch gerundivische und andere Konstruktionen gebräuchlich sind, z. B. „Angelas Heben der Stimme war der Grund, warum Peter hinausging" oder „Angelas Kommen war Peters Grund dafür wegzugehen". Drittens: Erklärungen sind faktiv, was erst recht für Erklärungen gilt, die den Grund einer Person angeben, etwas Bestimmtes zu tun oder zu glauben: „A ø-te, weil p" impliziert, dass p; und das gleiche gilt für „B glaubt, dass q, weil p".

Diese drei Tatsachen schließen aus, dass geistige Zustände, Forderungen und Ziele Gründe sind. Wenn Sybille für James Austern zubereitet, weil sie glaubt, Austern seien ein Aphrodisiakum, dann kann man ihre Überzeugung etwas ungenau als einen geistigen Zustand beschreiben; aber „Sybilles Überzeugung, dass Austern ein Aphrodisiakum sind" kann keinen Satz ergänzen, der mit „Sybille bereitete für James Austern zu, weil ..." oder „Es ist wahr, dass ..." beginnt. Sybilles Grund war nicht ihre Überzeugung, dass Austern ein Aphrodisiakum sind, sondern viel-

---

17 Davidson (1990), 20; von Wright (1983), 54; aber vgl. von Wright (1998), 10 f.; Audi (1993), 15 f.
18 Raz (1990), 17.

mehr *dass sie glaubte*, dass Austern ein Aphrodisiakum sind. Dieselben Tests werden bestätigen, dass auch Bitten und Ziele keine Gründe sein können. Wenn Paul Jeremy das Salz reichte, weil Jeremy ihn darum bat, war sein Grund, *dass* Jeremy ihn darum gebeten hatte: nicht Jeremys Bitte, Paul möge ihm das Salz reichen, sondern dass er die Bitte geäußert hatte. Und wenn Martin hustete, um Paulines Aufmerksamkeit zu erregen, war sein Grund nicht sein Ziel, nämlich Paulines Aufmerksamkeit zu erregen, sondern *dass* das Husten Paulines Aufmerksamkeit erregen werde oder dass er dies glaubte.

Obwohl wir absichtliche Handlungen oft durch Bezugnahme auf geistige Zustände oder Dispositionen, Bitten oder Ziele erklären können, so lautet das Fazit, sind sie keine Gründe. Gründe sind Tatsachen oder Wahrheiten.

VI

Es ist ein Axiom, dass Überzeugungen Handlungen erklären können. Aber wenn, wie ich behauptet habe, die Tatsache, dass p, nicht As Grund dafür sein kann, etwas zu tun, wenn A nicht weiß, dass p, was war dann Martins Grund zu husten, wenn Martin nicht wusste, dass Husten Paulines Aufmerksamkeit erregen würde, aber wenn er hustete, weil er dies glaubte? Die Antwort, die ich gerade implizit gegeben habe, lautet, dass Martins Grund war, dass er glaubte, sein Husten werde Paulines Aufmerksamkeit erregen. Es ist aber wichtig, darauf hinzuweisen, dass die Tatsache, dass A glaubt, dass p, nur gelegentlich in genau derselben Beziehung zu As Handlung steht, in der die Tatsache, dass der Kurs des Rubels eingebrochen war, zu Toms Investition in Gazpromaktien stand. Das will ich erklären.

Nehmen wir an, Roger glaube, er werde vom Geheimdienst verfolgt. In dieser Situation könnte er Verschiedenes tun. Er könnte beispielsweise nach Brasilien fliegen, seine Briefe verbrennen oder sich bei dem Abgeordneten seines Wahlkreises beschweren. Aber nehmen wir stattdessen an, er suche seinen Arzt auf. Wenn wir erklären, dass er seinen Arzt aufsuchte, weil er glaubte, vom Geheimdienst verfolgt zu werden, so fassen wir wahrscheinlich eine andere Art von Beziehung zwischen der Überzeugung und der Handlung ins Auge, als wenn wir sagten, dass dies sein Grund dafür sei, seine Briefe zu verbrennen. Eine erste Annäherung an eine Erklärung dieses Unterschieds wäre es, zu sagen, dass die Tatsache oder vermeintliche Tatsache, dass er vom Geheimdienst verfolgt wurde, nicht die Tatsache war, derentwegen Roger seinen Arzt aufsuchte. Denn nicht das, *was* Roger glaubte, bestimmte seine Entscheidung, sondern die Tatsache, dass er es glaubte. Nehmen wir ferner an, Ruth räsonniere folgendermaßen:

> Ich glaube, dass Eigentum Diebstahl ist.
> Leute, die glauben, dass Eigentum Diebstahl ist, sollten in die Arbeiterpartei eintreten.
> Also sollte ich eintreten.

Sie tritt also ein. Die Tatsache, dass sie glaubt, Eigentum sei Diebstahl, ist einer ihrer Gründe, die Tatsache oder vermeintliche Tatsache, dass Eigentum Diebstahl ist, dagegen nicht.

In diesen Beispielen stehen die Tatsache, dass Roger glaubt, er werde vom Geheimdienst verfolgt, und die Tatsache, dass Ruth glaubt, Eigentum sei Diebstahl, in genau derselben Beziehung zu ihren Handlungen wie die Tatsache, dass der Kurs des Rubels eingebrochen war, zu Toms Investition. Aber hier haben wir es mit ungewöhnlichen Fällen zu tun. Welche Art von Verbindung zwischen Überzeugung und Handlung fassen wir also unter gewöhnlicheren Umständen ins Auge, wenn wir sagen, der Grund einer Person, etwas Bestimmtes zu tun, sei gewesen, dass er geglaubt habe, dass p? Welche Art von Verbindung stellen wir uns zum Beispiel zwischen Martins Überzeugung, sein Husten werde Paulines Aufmerksamkeit erregen, und seinem tatsächlichem Husten vor, wenn wir sagen, sein Grund, zu husten, wäre gewesen, dass er glaubte, es werde Paulines Aufmerksamkeit erregen?

Wir können zu einer Antwort gelangen, indem wir zwei zentrale Aspekte der Beziehung zwischen Glauben und Wissen zur Kenntnis nehmen. Erstens: „Ich glaube ..." ist die Position, auf die wir uns zurückziehen, wenn „Ich weiß ..." durch die Tatsachen widerlegt ist. Zweitens: In dem Maße, in dem As Überzeugung, dass p, As Verhalten (oder seine anderen Überzeugungen und Einstellungen) beeinflusst oder bestimmt, wird es dies tendenziell auf dieselbe Weise tun wie As Wissen, dass p. Natürlich könnte As Überzeugung, dass p, ihn im geringeren Maße beeinflussen, wenn er sich beispielsweise der Tatsache bewusst wäre, dass er unter dem Einfluss von Vorurteilen steht oder dass seine Belege nicht schlüssig sind. Unter diesen Umständen wird das Maß, in dem er durch die Überzeugung beeinflusst ist, von dem Maß abhängen, in dem er kontrollieren kann, was er glaubt, empfindet oder tut, indem er sich diese Tatsachen in Erinnerung ruft. Trotzdem gilt: Wenn A ø-en (oder glauben, dass p, oder B bewundern) würde, wenn er wüsste, dass p, dann wird A dazu tendieren zu ø-en (oder zu glauben, dass p, oder B zu bewundern), wenn er glaubt, dass p.

Nehmen wir also an, Helen sage, und zwar aufrichtig, ihr Grund, in Eile aufzubrechen, sei gewesen, dass sie spät dran war, oder dass sie in Eile aufbrach, weil sie spät dran war, aber es stelle sich heraus, dass sie überhaupt nicht spät dran war. Falls Helen akzeptiert, dass sie irrtümlicherweise glaubte, spät dran zu sein, steht zu erwarten, dass sie ihre Erklärung ändert. Denn wenn sie sagt „Mein Grund, in Eile aufzubrechen, war, dass ich spät dran war" oder „Ich brach in Eile auf, weil ich spät dran war", setzt sie voraus, dass sie *tatsächlich* spät dran war; ebenso wie wenn sie sagen würde „Ich wusste, dass ich spät dran war". Wenn sie sich nicht widerspricht, wird sich Helen also auf eine Erklärung zurückziehen, die, in Strawsons Formulierung, „all die schwere Last abwirft, die man auf sich nimmt, wenn man sich auf Aussagen über die Welt festlegt", nämlich „Ich brach in Eile auf, weil ich glaubte (dachte, annahm), dass ich spät dran war"[19]. (Die Festlegung, die man aufgibt, betrifft natürlich die Erklärung und nicht die Handlung.) Man nehme zur Kenntnis, dass die revidierte Erklärung den Grund identifiziert, aus dem, *wie es ihr schien*, Helen in Eile aufbrach, nämlich dass sie spät dran war. Aber sie sagt nicht, dass dies ihr Grund *war*. Im Gegenteil.

Wenn wir erklären, warum Helen in Eile aufbrach, indem wir sagen, ihr Grund sei gewesen, dass sie glaubte, spät dran zu sein, dann ist die Kraft der Erklärung meiner Meinung nach mit einem Wort die folgende: Sie führt nicht die Tatsache an, angesichts derer Helen handelte, aber indem sie die Tatsache anführt, dass sie glaubte, spät dran zu sein, identifiziert sie die Antwort, die Helen gegeben hätte, wenn man sie zur Zeit der Handlung nach ihrem Grund gefragt und sie aufrichtig geantwortet hätte. Sowohl

3. As Grund zu ø-en, war, dass sie glaubte, dass p

als auch

4. As Grund zu ø-en, war, dass p

sollen die Erklärung dafür geben, weshalb A ø-te. Aber (4) soll die Tatsache anführen, angesichts derer A ø-te, während (3) – in den allermeisten Fällen – dies nicht tut. Und obschon sowohl (3) als auch (4) vorgeben, den Grund zu identifizieren, den A dafür gegeben hätte, dass er

---

19 Strawson (1988), 94.

ø-te, sagt (4), dass dies sein Grund *war*, während (3) – in den allermeisten Fällen – dies nicht tut. Ryle schreibt in *Der Begriff des Geistes*:

> [W]enn man sagt, dass er am Rande bleibt, weil er weiß, dass das Eis dünn ist, verwendet man einen ganz anderen Sinn von ‚weil' oder gibt eine ganz andere Art von ‚Erklärung', als wenn man sagt, er bleibe am Rande, weil er glaubt, das Eis sei dünn.[20]

Das trifft es genau. Im ersten Fall ist der Grund des Mannes, dass das Eis dünn ist, im zweiten Fall, dass er glaubt, das Eis sei dünn. Aber der Grund des Mannes steht zu seiner Handlung in den beiden Fällen in einer unterschiedlichen Beziehung, und die Art von Erklärung, die gegeben wird, indem man seinen Grund identifiziert, unterscheidet sich dementsprechend.

VII

Wir müssen folgenden Einwand erörtern. Ich habe die Auffassung vertreten, dass die Tatsache, dass p, nicht As Grund dafür sein kann, etwas zu tun, wenn A nicht weiß, dass p; und wenn Martin nicht wusste, dass sein Husten Paulines Aufmerksamkeit erregen würde, sondern deshalb hustete, weil er glaubte, dies werde geschehen, so war sein Grund für das Husten, dass er glaubte, dies werde Paulines Aufmerksamkeit erregen. Aber das von mir im Detail erörterte Beispiel betraf eine falsche Überzeugung, nämlich Helens Überzeugung, dass sie spät dran war. Es ist also in Wahrheit vielleicht so, dass die Tatsache, dass p, nicht As Grund dafür sein kann, etwas zu tun, wenn A entweder nicht weiß oder nicht richtigerweise glaubt, dass p. Wenn beispielsweise die Tatsache, dass Mary Trüffel liebt, Jims Grund dafür war, Trüffel zuzubereiten, folgt dann daraus, dass Jim wusste, dass Mary Trüffel liebt, wie ich behauptet habe, oder folgt daraus nur, dass er *entweder* wusste *oder* richtigerweise glaubte, dass Mary Trüffel liebt?

Wir können uns dieser Frage zuwenden, indem wir zunächst zugestehen, dass die Tatsache, dass p, die Erklärung für die Tatsache, dass A ø-te, sein kann, obwohl A nicht wusste, dass p. Wenn zum Beispiel der Pfeffer in der Suppe Sally zum Niesen brachte, dann erklärt die Tatsache, dass Pfeffer in der Suppe war, die Tatsache, dass Sally niesen musste, gleichgültig, ob Sally wusste, dass Pfeffer in der Suppe war, oder nicht. Aber das ist nicht der Fall, mit dem wir es hier zu tun haben, weil die

---

20 Ryle (1986), 180.

Tatsache, dass Pfeffer in der Suppe war, nicht Sallys Grund zu niesen war; sie war einfach nur der Grund, warum Sally niesen musste. Unsere Frage lautet, ob die Tatsache, dass p, As Grund dafür sein kann, etwas Bestimmtes zu tun, wenn A nicht weiß, dass p. Und die Antwort darauf muss sicherlich nein sein. Denn angenommen, es bestehe Einigkeit, dass Jim nicht wusste, dass Mary Trüffel liebt, aber sie zubereitete, weil er glaubte, sie täte dies. Sein Grund für die Zubereitung von Trüffeln kann nicht variieren, je nachdem, ob seine Überzeugung wahr oder falsch ist, denn wir haben bereits genug gesagt, um zu wissen, was genau sein Grund war, ohne festzustellen, ob Mary Trüffel liebt. Aber wenn seine Überzeugung falsch war, konnte die Tatsache, dass Mary Trüffel liebt, nicht Jims Grund für ihre Zubereitung gewesen sein, weil es keine solche Tatsache gab. Deshalb war die Tatsache, dass Mary sie liebt, auch dann nicht sein Grund, wenn seine Überzeugung wahr war.

Der Einwand schlägt also fehl. Wenn A nicht weiß, dass p, dann mag sein Grund dafür, etwas Bestimmtes zu tun, sein, dass er glaubte, dass p; oder dass p wahrscheinlich war oder sogar dass p möglich war. Aber die Tatsache, dass p, kann nicht As Grund dafür sein, etwas Bestimmtes zu tun, wenn A nicht weiß, dass p; und genauso wenig kann sie As Grund dafür sein, eine bestimmte Handlung zu unterlassen, oder dafür, etwas zu glauben, zu wollen oder zu bezweifeln.

Die Unzulänglichkeit wahrer Überzeugung wird dann besonders deutlich, wenn wir einen Fall betrachten, bei dem sich die Frage nicht stellen kann, ob jemand etwas weiß, weil es nichts ist, was man wissen kann. Beispielsweise kann niemand wissen, wer den Grand National gewinnen wird – dies ist einfach zu sehr vom Zufall abhängig. Aber nehmen wir an, dass in einem bestimmten Jahr Fred glaubt, Pegasus werde gewinnen. Vielleicht hat er eine Vorahnung; vielleicht hat er auch beobachtet, in welcher Form sich die Pferde befinden. Fred ruft jedenfalls seinen Buchmacher an und setzt auf Pegasus, weil er glaubt, Pegasus werde gewinnen. Angenommen nun, Pegasus *wird* gewinnen, obwohl dies natürlich noch niemand weiß. Ist die Tatsache, dass Pegasus gewinnen würde, Freds Grund, auf ihn zu setzen? Offensichtlich nicht. Und können wir, wenn das Ereignis stattgefunden hat, wahrheitsgemäß sagen, dass Fred auf Pegasus setzte, weil Pegasus gewinnen würde. Offensichtlich auch dann nicht.

Betrachten wir schließlich noch ein wohlbekanntes Beispiel für eine gerechtfertigte wahre Überzeugung, die nicht das Zeug zum Wissen hat:

An einem Nachmittag im Juni sitzt Henry vor dem Fernseher. Es ist der Tag des Herrenfinales in Wimbledon, und das Fernsehen zeigt, wie McEnroe Conners schlägt. Es steht zwei zu null in Sätzen und McEnroe steht vor dem Match Point im dritten Satz. McEnroe macht den Punkt. Henry glaubt gerechtfertigtermaßen, dass
1. er gerade gesehen hat, wie McEnroe das diesjährige Wimbledonfinale gewinnt
und schließt daraus vernünftigerweise, dass
2. McEnroe der diesjährige Wimbledon-Champion ist.
Tatsächlich jedoch funktionieren die Kameras in Wimbledon nicht mehr, und das Fernsehen zeigt die Ausstrahlung des Spiels vom Vorjahr. Aber währenddessen ist McEnroe dabei, das Gemetzel vom Vorjahr zu wiederholen. Henrys Überzeugung (2) ist also wahr und er ist sicher gerechtfertigt, (2) zu glauben. Aber wir würden kaum sagen wollen, dass Henry (2) weiß.[21]

Angenommen, Henry, der sich daran erinnert, dass sein Bruder auf McEnroe gesetzt hat und im Falle seines Siegs 100 Pfund gewinnen wird, käme zu dem Schluss, dass sein Bruder 100 Pfund gewonnen hat. Ist die Tatsache, dass McEnroe der diesjährige Champion ist, Henrys Grund zu glauben, dass sein Bruder 100 Pfund gewonnen hat? Offensichtlich nicht. Sein Grund ist vielmehr, dass er *glaubt*, McEnroe sei der diesjährige Champion. Wir können wahrheitsgemäß sagen, dass Henry glaubt, sein Bruder habe 100 Pfund gewonnen, weil er glaubt, dass McEnroe der diesjährige Champion ist, aber nicht, dass er glaubt, sein Bruder habe 100 Pfund gewonnen, weil McEnroe der diesjährige Champion *ist*.

Diese Beispiele stützen meine Widerlegung des Einwands: Ich akzeptiere natürlich, dass die Tatsache, dass p, die Tatsache, dass A ø-te, erklären kann, gleichgültig ob A wusste, dass p, oder nicht; aber wenn die Erklärung behauptet, dass die Tatsache, dass p, As Grund zu ø-en war, und damit impliziert, dass es vernünftig oder unvernünftig von A gewesen sein könnte, zu ø-en, dann impliziert sie auch, dass A wusste, dass p. Dasselbe ist, nebenbei gesagt, wahr, wenn man es mit Wahrnehmungs- statt mit Tatsachenbewusstsein zu tun hat. Wenn sich in As Umgebung irgendein Stoff oder Ding befindet, dann mag das erklären, warum A ø-te, ohne zu implizieren, dass A diesen Stoff oder das Ding wahrnahm. Wenn der Pfeffer in Marks Suppe ihn zum Niesen oder ein Gas ihn zum Lachen oder Gähnen brachte, folgt daraus nicht, dass Mark den Pfeffer oder das Gas sah oder roch. Und wenn irgendeine chemische Substanz in seinem Essen ihn wütend oder ängstlich machte, folgt daraus nicht, dass er diese Substanz schmeckte. Aber wenn die Erklärung impliziert, dass es ver-

---
21 Dancy (1985), 25. Das Beispiel wird Brian Garrett zugeschrieben.

nünftig oder unvernünftig von A sein konnte zu ø-en, dann impliziert das, dass A den Stoff oder Gegenstand wahrnahm, der ihn dazu brachte zu ø-en. Wenn zum Beispiel eine Rede Joe wütend machte, dann hörte oder las er die Rede; und wenn eine Feierlichkeit ihn stolz oder ängstlich machte, dann sah oder hörte er die Zeremonie.

VIII

Aus diesen Gründen, so scheint es, kann die Tatsache, dass p, nicht As Grund dafür sein, etwas Bestimmtes zu tun, wenn A nicht weiß, dass p. Sollte uns dieses Ergebnis überraschen? Ich glaube nicht.[22] Denn wenn A nicht weiß, dass p, dann ist er sich der Tatsache, dass p, nicht bewusst, und wenn er sich einer Tatsache nicht bewusst ist, wie könnte diese Tatsache dann sein Grund sein?

Aber die Behauptung, dass die Tatsache, dass p, As Grund dafür sein kann, etwas Bestimmtes zu tun, wenn A weiß, dass p, könnte ebenfalls auf einen Einwand stoßen. Denn ich habe weiter oben eingeräumt, dass es Umstände geben könnte, unter denen wir sagen möchten, ein Hund wüsste, dass es Zeit sei, Gassi zu gehen. Aber, so mag man einwenden, da Hunde keine Gründe für ihr Handeln geben können, können sie nicht aus Gründen handeln; und deshalb kann die Tatsache, dass es Zeit sei, Gassi zu gehen, nicht ein Grund des Hundes dafür sein, etwas Bestimmtes zu tun.[23]

Offensichtlich können Hunde keine Gründe für ihre Handlungen geben, weil sie über keine Sprache verfügen. Aber der Einwand ist schwach, und zwar aus zwei Gründen. Erstens ist es zweifelhaft, ob ein Wesen nichts aus einem Grund tun kann, wenn es keinen Grund für seine Handlung geben kann; und tatsächlich gibt es wohlbekannte Beispiele von Tieren, die etwas tun und sich dabei auf Überlegungen stützen, wie etwa die Geschichte von Chrysipps Jagdhund. Seiner Beute dicht auf den Fersen kam er zu einer Stelle, an der sich der Weg in drei Pfade ver-

---

22 Manchen erschien das offensichtlich. Prichard z. B. sah keine Notwendigkeit, dafür zu argumentieren: „[Einer bestimmten Ansicht über Pflichten zufolge] können wir, im strengen Sinne, niemals eine Pflicht tun, wenn wir eine haben, weil es eine Pflicht ist, d. h. weil wir wissen, dass es eine Pflicht ist. ... Bestenfalls können wir, wenn wir eine Pflicht haben, diese tun, weil wir fraglos denken oder glauben oder es zumindest für möglich halten, dass es Pflicht ist, so zu handeln. ‚Duty and Ignorance of Fact‘, wiederabgedr. in Prichard (1949), 24.

23 Vgl. etwa Kenny (1989) 37 f.

zweigte; er schnüffelte an einem Pfad, konnte aber die Witterung seiner Beute nicht aufnehmen; er schnüffelte am zweiten und zog wieder eine Niete; und nahm den dritten Pfad *ohne zu schnüffeln*. Annas und Barnes kommentieren die Geschichte wie folgt:

> Wie ist das, was er tat, zu erklären? Chrysipp vertritt die Auffassung, er müsse eine einfache Überlegung angestellt haben: Er sagte zu sich: ‚Entweder A oder B oder C; aber nicht A und nicht B: also C'.... Erklärungsbedürftig ist die Tatsache, dass der Hund den dritten Weg ohne ein weiteres Experiment wählt – und die von Chrysipp angebotene Erklärung ist höchst plausibel.[24]

Wenn das richtig ist, dann gibt der Syllogismus die Gründe des Hundes wieder, den dritten Pfad zu wählen, trotz der Tatsache, dass der Hund weder diesen noch einen anderen Grund hätte geben können.

Was Annas und Barnes sagen, ist für Philosophen untypisch. Denn obwohl weithin angenommen wird, dass die ethologische Literatur reichlich Hinweise auf Überlegungen bzw. Schlussfolgerungen bei Hunden und Primaten liefert, pflegen Philosophen gegenüber intellektuellen Fähigkeiten von Tieren, die über keine Sprache verfügen, skeptischer zu sein als Nichtphilosophen. Aber – und das ist der zweite Grund, weshalb der Einwand schwach ist – angenommen, es gäbe zwingende Argumente, die zeigten, dass die empirischen Hinweise weitgehend falsch bewertet wurden, und dass Chrysipps Hund keine Überlegungen im strengen Sinn angestellt und auch nicht im strengen Sinn aus dem Grund gehandelt hat, den der Syllogismus wiedergibt. Auch dann wäre der Einwand nicht überzeugend, wenn diese oder andere Argumente auch bewiesen, dass sich der Hund nicht im strengen Sinne der Tatsache bewusst war, dass seine Beute den dritten Weg genommen hatte. Gewiss, die Begriffe, mit denen wir die Ausübung rationaler Vermögen beim Menschen beschreiben, treffen auf viele Tiere nur in einem abgeschwächten und analogen Sinne zu. Welche Tiere das sind, ist umstritten, aber die allgemeine Behauptung ist es nicht. Aber dasselbe gilt für kognitive Fähigkeiten. Wenn der Einwand also Biss haben soll, dann muss man zeigen, dass dort, wo man nicht mehr von einem Handeln aus Gründen sprechen kann, Wissen intakt bleibt. Aber jene Argumente, die Philosophen überzeugt haben, dass allein der Mensch aus Gründen handeln kann, zeigen das nicht. Sie treiben keinen Keil zwischen das Erkennen von Tatsachen und die Fähigkeit, aus Gründen zu handeln. Im

---

24 Annas u. Barnes (1985), 47 f.; vgl. Sorabji (1993), Kap. 7. Die Geschichte wird erzählt von Philo: *On Animals* 45–6 und Sextus Empiricus: *Outlines of Pyrrhonism* I § 69.

Gegenteil. Davidson zum Beispiel hat die Auffassung vertreten, dass nur die Angehörigen einer Sprachgemeinschaft aus einem Grund handeln können, weil ein Wesen nicht aus einem Grund handeln kann, wenn es keine Überzeugungen haben kann, und nur ein Angehöriger einer Sprachgemeinschaft Überzeugungen haben kann.[25] Aber ein Wesen, das keine Überzeugungen haben könne, könne auch nichts wissen.

Davidsons Grund für die Behauptung, dass nur ein Angehöriger einer Sprachgemeinschaft Überzeugungen haben kann, lautet, dass ein Wesen keine Überzeugung haben kann, wenn es nicht die Möglichkeit des Irrtums versteht; aber „dazu ist nötig, dass man den Gegensatz zwischen Wahrheit und Irrtum − zwischen wahrem Glauben und falschem Glauben − begreift" − ein Gegensatz, der sich, wie er behauptet, nur in einer Sprachgemeinschaft herausbilden kann[26]. Der unverbesserliche Hundeliebhaber wird unverzagt bleiben, denn es versteht sich nicht von selbst, dass ein Geschöpf keine Überzeugung haben kann, wenn es nicht die Möglichkeit des Irrtums begreift. Ein Hund, so wird er argumentieren, kann hungrig oder lüstern sein, oder er kann einen Knochen vergraben wollen, gleichgültig, ob er die Möglichkeit der Frustration oder Enttäuschung begreifen kann oder nicht, und gleichgültig, ob er den Gegensatz von Erfolg und Misserfolg erfassen kann; und wenn diese Analogie falsch ist, so sagt Davidson nicht, warum sie falsch ist. Aber die Stichhaltigkeit von Davidsons Argument ist nebensächlich. Für unsere Belange zählt, dass Davidsons skeptische Folgerung in Bezug auf Tiere nicht die Aussage in Zweifel zieht, dass die Tatsache, dass p, As Grund dafür sein kann, etwas Bestimmtes zu tun, wenn A weiß, dass p. Ja, weit davon entfernt, dass Davidson die Verbindung zwischen Erkenntnis und Vernunft schwächen würde, wird diese von ihm sogar gestärkt. Denn er argumentiert ausdrücklich dafür[27], dass es nur in dem Maße sinnvoll sei, einem Geschöpf Überzeugungen und Wünsche − und folglich auch Wissen − zuzuschreiben, in dem diese Zuschreibung ein allgemeines Muster der Vernünftigkeit in seinem Verhalten ans Licht bringe.

Die Argumentation in diesem Artikel steht zu der skeptischen Ansicht über Tiere, die Davidson und, aus anderen Gründen, Aristoteles, Thomas von Aquin und Descartes befürworten, weder im Widerspruch, noch bestätigt sie diese. Aber sie bestätigt die Behauptung, in der ihre Argumente konvergieren, dass nämlich das Erkennen von Tatsachen und die

---

25 Davidson (1990), 224−47.
26 Davidson (1990), 246.
27 Davidson (1990), 226.

Fähigkeit aus Gründen zu handeln, die Tatsachen sind, zusammen auftreten oder nicht auftreten. Wenn die von mir verteidigte Auffassung von Wissen stimmt, könnte der Grund dafür nicht simpler sein: Sie sind identisch.

IX

Wittgenstein bemerkte, dass die Grammatik des Wortes ‚wissen' jener des Wortes ‚können', ‚imstande sein' offenbar eng verwandt sei. Die von mir vorgebrachte Argumentation bestätigt dies. Aber sie widerspricht Wittgensteins berühmter Behauptung: „Von mir kann man überhaupt nicht sagen (außer etwa im Spaß), ich wisse, dass ich Schmerzen habe."[28] Denn die Tatsache, dass ich Schmerzen habe, kann sicherlich mein Grund dafür sein, etwas Bestimmtes zu tun, zu wollen oder zu glauben – z. B. ein Aspirin zu nehmen, mich hinlegen zu wollen oder zu glauben, dass ich zu lange in der Sonne war. Wenn also die von mir verteidigte Auffassung von Wissen korrekt ist, so kann man von mir sinnvoll und wahrheitsgemäß sagen, dass ich weiß, dass ich Schmerzen habe.

Ich glaube, dass dies eher ein Grund ist, Wittgensteins Lehre zu bestreiten, als die von mir vorgeschlagene Definition von Wissen zurückzuweisen oder abzuwandeln. Wir möchten sagen, dass unter normalen Umständen ein erwachsener Mensch weiß, ob er Schmerzen hat oder nicht, aber dass ein Hase oder ein neugeborenes Baby dies nicht weiß. Die von mir vertretene Wissensauffassung vermag dies zu erklären. Ein Hase oder ein neugeborenes Baby können sich der Tatsache, dass sie Schmerzen haben, nicht bewusst sein – obwohl sie natürlich Schmerzen haben können – weil die Tatsache, dass ein Hase oder ein Baby Schmerzen hat, nicht sein Grund dafür sein kann, etwas Bestimmtes zu tun. Aber im Falle eines erwachsenen Menschen kann ihm eine Tatsache bezüglich seines momentanen Bewusstseinszustands als Grund dienen, genauso gut wie jede andere Tatsache; und mehr ist nicht nötig, um von Wissen reden zu können. Dennoch stellen Wittgensteins Lehre und die dafür vorgebrachten Argumente eine Herausforderung dar, und sie sind von großer Bedeutung. Ich hoffe, diese Bemerkungen bei einer anderen Gelegenheit weiter ausführen zu können.

---

28 Wittgenstein PU, §246; vgl. Wittgenstein ÜG, §§502, 504.

X

Die von mir verteidigte Auffassung von Wissen ist simpel: Persönliches propositionales Wissen ist die Fähigkeit, aus Gründen, die Tatsachen sind, zu handeln und auf Handeln zu verzichten, zu glauben, zu wünschen oder zu zweifeln. Ich habe nicht behauptet, dass wir nicht erklären können, warum jemand in bestimmter Weise gehandelt hat, etwas Bestimmtes geglaubt oder gewollt hat, wenn wir nicht Tatsachen anführen können, deren er sich bewusst war. Im Gegenteil. Ebenso wenig habe ich behauptet, dass allein Tatsachen Gründe sein können. Ich habe vielmehr behauptet, dass die Tatsachen, deren wir uns bewusst sind, die Tatsachen sind, die wir in Erwägung ziehen können, oder besser gesagt – um Wissen nicht zu sehr zu intellektualisieren – die Tatsachen, die unsere Gründe sein können. Wenn wir uns einer Tatsache bewusst sind, kann sie unser Grund sein; und wenn nicht, dann nicht.[29,30]

References

Annas/Barnes (1985): Julia Annas/Jonathan Barnes, *The Modes of Scepticism*, Cambridge.
Aristoteles, *De Anima,* 417a 21-b 2.
Audi (1993): Robert Audi, *Action, Intention and Reason*, Cornell.
Brown (1971): D.G. Brown, „Knowing How and Knowing That, What", in: O.P. Wood/G. Pitcher (eds.), *Ryle*, London, 213–48.
Chisholm (1957): Roderick M. Chisholm *Perceiving*, Cornell.
Craig (1990): Edward Craig, *Knowledge and the State of Nature*, Oxford.
Dancy (1985): Jonathan Dancy, Introduction to Contemporary Epistemology, Oxford.
Davidson (1990): Donald Davidson, *Handlung und Ereignis,* Frankfurt/Main.
Gettier (1963): Edmund L. Gettier, „Is Justified True Belief Knowledge?", in: *Analysis,* 23.
Kaplan (1985): Mark Kaplan, „It's Not What You Know That Counts", in: *Journal of Philosophy,* 82.
Kenny (1989): Anthony J.P. Kenny, *The Metaphysics of Mind*, Oxford.
Margolis (1972): Joseph Margolis, „Knowledge, Belief and Thought", in: *Ratio,* 14.
Philo: *On Animals.*

---

29 Freunden und Kollegen in München, Oxford und Tel Aviv sowie einem anonymen Gutachter des *Philosophical Quarterly* bin ich für ihre Kommentare zu früheren Entwürfen dieses Artikel dankbar.
30 Aus dem Englischen übersetzt von Erich Ammereller.

Platon: *Theaitetos*.
Prichard (1949): Harold A. Prichard, *Moral Obligation*, Oxford, 18–39.
Raz (1990): Joseph Raz, *Practical Reason and Norms*, Princeton.
Ryle (1990): Gilbert Ryle, „Knowing How and Knowing That", in: *Collected Papers*, Vol. II, Bristol.
Ryle (1986): Gilbert Ryle, *Der Begriff des Geistes*, Ditzingen.
Shope (1983): Robert K. Shope, *The Analysis of Knowing*, Princeton.
Sorabji (1993): Richard Sorybji, *Animal Minds and Human Morals*, London.
Strawson (1971): Peter F. Strawson, „Truth", in: *Logico-Linguistic Papers*, London.
Strawson (1988): Peter F. Strawson, „Perception and its Objects", in: J. Dancy (eds.), *Perceptual Knowledge*, Oxford.
Sextus Empiricus: *Outlines of Pyrrhonism*.
White (1982): Alan R. White, *The Nature of Knowledge*, Rowman.
Williams (1972): Bernard A. O. Williams, „Knowledge and Reasons", in: G.H. von Wright (eds.): *Problems in the Theory of Knowledge,* The Hague.
Williamson (1995): Timothy Williamson, „Is Knowing a State of Mind?", in: *Mind*, 104.
Wittgenstein (1999): Ludwig Wittgenstein, *Philosophische Untersuchungen*, (PU).
Wittgenstein (1999): Ludwig Wittgenstein, *Über Gewißheit*, (ÜG).
von Wright (1983): Georg H. von Wright, *Practical Reason*, Oxford.
von Wright (1998): Georg H. von Wright, „Of Human Freedom", in: *In the Shadow of Descartes*, Dordrecht.

Part Two:
Knowledge Through Ability

Knowing Full Well*

Ernest Sosa

Belief is a kind of performance, which attains one level of success if it is true (or accurate), a second level if it is competent (or adroit), and a third if its truth manifests the believer's competence (i.e., if it is apt). Knowledge on one level (the animal level) is apt belief. The epistemic normativity constitutive of such knowledge is thus a kind of performance normativity. A problem is posed for this account, however, by the fact that suspension of belief falls under the same sort of epistemic normativity as does belief itself, even though to suspend is of course precisely *not* to perform, at least not with the aim of truth. The solution in what follows distinguishes orders of performance normativity, including a first order where execution competence is in play, and a second order where the performer must assess the risks attendant on issuing a first-order performance. This imports a level of reflective knowledge above the animal level.

Two of Plato's best-known dialogues are inquiries about knowledge. The *Theaetetus* inquires into its nature, the *Meno* also into its value. Each dialogue, I will suggest, involves the same more basic question: What sort of normativity is constitutive of our knowledge? A belief that falls short of knowledge is thereby inferior. It is better to know than to get it wrong, of course, and also better than to get it right just by luck. What is involved in such evaluation? An answer to this more basic question enables a solution for both Platonic problems.

We shall assume that knowledge requires at a minimum a belief that is true. Our inquiry into the nature of knowledge thus takes a more specific form. In this paper our question is this: What condition must a belief satisfy, in addition to being true, in order to constitute knowledge? The question of the nature of knowledge has been central to epistemology in recent decades, as it was for Plato.

Edmund Gettier showed us that the further condition a belief must satisfy cannot be just its being competently held, competently acquired

---

* Originally published in *Philosophical Studies* 142 (2009), pp. 5–15.

or sustained. This is so because, for one thing, a belief can be false despite being competent. If the believer then competently deduces something true from his false belief, this true conclusion cannot *thereby* amount to knowledge. Yet, if we competently deduce a conclusion from a premise that we competently believe (even after drawing the conclusion), we thereby competently believe that conclusion as well. So a belief can be both true and competently held without amounting to knowledge.

Post-Gettier, the Platonic problem takes this form: What further condition, added to, or in place of, being competently held, must a true belief satisfy in order to constitute knowledge?

On the contemporary scene, the second Platonic problem, that of the value of knowledge, has more recently moved to center stage. For Plato this was the problem of how knowledge can be quite generally more valuable than its corresponding true belief, if a merely true belief would be no less useful. A true belief as to the location of Larissa, for example, will guide you there no less efficiently than would the corresponding knowledge. In line with this, we ask: How if at all does knowledge as such always improve on the corresponding merely true belief?

In connection with both problems, we will assume that there is some further condition (however simple or complex) that a belief must satisfy in order to constitute knowledge, beyond being a belief and being true. This condition must add normatively positive content, moreover, sufficient to explain how it is that knowledge, which must satisfy this further condition, is as such always better than would be the corresponding merely true belief. When one ponders a question, for example, there is some respect in which it would always be better to answer knowledgeably than to answer correctly but just by luck.

Knowledge as a special case

All sorts of things can "perform" well or ill when put to the test. Rational agents can do so, but so can biological organs, designed instruments, and even structures with a function, such as a bridge. A bridge can perform well its function as part of a traffic artery. When a thermostat activates a furnace, it may perform well in keeping the ambient temperature comfortable. When a heart beats, it may perform well in helping the blood circulate. And so on.

A puppet performs well under the control of a puppeteer if its hinges are smooth, not rusty, and well oiled, so that its limbs are smoothly responsive. A bridge might perform well by withstanding a storm. We credit the puppet, as we do the bridge, if its good performance flows appropriately from its state and constitution.

The puppet "performs" (well or ill), as does the bridge, and thus produces performances. But it would be quite a stretch to consider it an "agent." Human beings are different, in any case, if only because we are rational agents. Not only are there reasons why we perform as we do. There are also reasons that we have for so performing, and for which, motivated by which, we perform as we do. This is not just a matter of having aims in so performing. After all, the thermostat and the heart do have their aims. But they are motivated by no such aim; no such aim gives them reasons motivated by which they perform as they do.[1]

Human motivation is on another level, even when the performance is physical, as in athletic or artistic performance.

The archer's shot is a good example. The shot aims to hit the target, and its success can be judged by whether it does so or not, by its accuracy. However accurate it may be, there is a further dimension of evaluation: namely, how skillful a shot it is, how much skill it manifests, how adroit it is. A shot might hit the bull's-eye, however, and might even manifest great skill, while failing utterly, as a shot, on a further dimension. Consider a shot diverted by a gust of wind initially, so that it would miss the target altogether but for a second gust that puts it back on track to hit the bull's-eye. This shot is both accurate and adroit, yet it is not accurate because adroit, so as to manifest the archer's skill and competence. It thus fails on a third dimension of evaluation, besides those of accuracy and adroitness: it fails to be apt.

Performances generally admit this threefold distinction: accuracy, adroitness, aptness. At least so do performances with an aim (assuming any performance could ever be wholly aimless).

---

1 True, we could perhaps, just barely, make sense of an extended sort of "motivation" even in those cases, as when a nearby torch fools the thermostat into activating the air conditioner even when the room is already cool. It still in some broad sense has a reason for performing as it does, a "motivating reason." Despite the non-trivial resemblance, nonetheless, this is clearly a metaphorical extension, if only because of the vastly greater complexity involved in human motivation. In any case, a thermostat does not literally have a mind, or any motives.

A performance is better than otherwise for not having failed, i. e., for not having fallen short of its objective. In line with that, it is good if it succeeds, if it reaches its objective. A performance is at least good as such for succeeding, even if it is a murderer's shot. The shot itself may still be an excellent shot, despite how deplorable is the broader performance in which it is embedded.

A performance that attains its first-order aim without thereby manifesting any competence of the performer's is a lesser performance. The wind-aided shot scores by luck, without thereby manifesting appropriate competence. It is hence a lesser shot by comparison with one that in hitting the mark manifests the archer's competence.[2] A blazing tennis ace is a lesser shot if it is a wild exception from the racket of a hacker, by comparison with one that manifests superb competence by a champion in control. And so on. Take any performance with a first-order aim, such as the archery shot and the tennis serve. That performance then has the induced aim of attaining its first-order aim. A performance X attains its aim <p>, finally, not just through the fact that p, but through the fact that it brings it about that p.[3]

The case of knowledge is just the special case where the performance is cognitive or doxastic. Such belief aims at truth, and is accurate or correct if true. And it has accordingly the induced aim of attaining that objective. Such belief aims therefore not just at accuracy (truth), but also at aptness (knowledge). A belief that attains both aims, that of truth and that of knowledge, is for that reason better than one that attains merely the first. That then is a way in which knowledge is as such better than merely true belief.[4]

---

[2] A shot might manifest an archer's competence without its accuracy doing so. The shot with the two intervening gusts is a case in point. How does that shot manifest the archer's competence? By having at the moment of release a direction and speed that would take it to the bull's-eye, in relevantly normal conditions.

[3] Just as its being true that p entails its being true that it is true that p, so one's bringing it about that p may entail that one brings it about that one brings it about that p, assuming such iteration always makes sense.

[4] Even if performances do not have the automatically induced aims just suggested, we still retain an account of why knowledge is better than merely true belief, since apt performances, in general, are as such better than those that attain success only by luck. So, beliefs provide just a special case of that general truth. This account still depends of course on our view of knowledge as apt belief, belief that manifests the relevant competence of the believer in reaching its aim of truth.

The account of epistemic normativity as a sort of performance normativity has thus two virtues. It provides an explanation of the nature of knowledge, which amounts to belief that is apt, belief that is an apt epistemic performance, one that manifests the relevant competence of the believer in attaining the truth. And, secondly, it explains also the extra value of knowledge beyond that of merely true belief.

Unfortunately, the account encounters a troubling objection, which we next consider.

The problem of withholding

What's the problem?

The normative judgment that knowledge is as such better than merely true belief is of a piece with the normative judgment that withholding is better than believing when the evidence is insufficient. Since both judgments are epistemically normative, one would expect them to be closely akin. But that is not what one finds on first inspection.

If truth is the first-order aim of our cognitive endeavors, it is not obvious how to assess suspension of judgment with respect to that objective. Accordingly, it is also unobvious how to apply our AAA normative structure of performances to such withholdings. These are after all precisely *non*-performances. How then can they be brought within the sphere of our performance normativity? And if they are not thus assimilable, serious doubt is cast on our claim to have uncovered the most relevant epistemic normativity involved in our intuition that knowledge is as such better than merely true belief.

Let our archer now be a hunter rather than a competitor athlete. Once it is his turn, the competitor must shoot, with no relevant choice. True, he might have avoided the competition altogether, but once in it, no relevant shot selection is allowed. The hunter by contrast needs to pick his shots, with whatever skill and care he can muster. Selecting targets of appropriate value is integral to hunting, and he must also pick his shots so as to secure a reasonable chance of success. The shot of a hunter can therefore be assessed in more respects than that of a competitor/athlete. The hunter's shot can be assessed twice over for what is manifest in it: not only in respect of its execution competence, but also in respect of the competence manifest in the target's selection and in the pick of the shot.

Not taking a shot at a particular target may or may not involve a performance. You might fail to take that shot because at the time you are asleep, for example. Alternatively, you might intentionally and even deliberately forbear. If your deliberate forbearing has an aim, moreover, and if the aim is attained, then your forbearing succeeds, and may even be a performance, indeed one that is apt.

Suppose a domain in which an agent puts in performances with an aim, whether athletic, artistic, academic, etc. This yields a derivative aim: to avoid failure. You can aim to avoid failure, moreover, without aiming to attain success, at least not ground-level success. When a hunter decides not to take a shot at a certain high-value target, for example, his performance, his forbearing, has its own aim of avoiding failure. To forbear is precisely not to aim at first-order success. Nevertheless, forbearing has an aim of its own: namely, avoiding failure.

Take then a hunter's performance of forbearing, which succeeds in avoiding ground-level failure. It does attain that aim. Is it thereby apt? Yes, so it is by our account; that is what we have to say. The forbearing is, after all, a performance with an aim of its own, and it does attain that aim, in doing which it does manifest a sort of competence.

What if it is a shot that the hunter very obviously should have taken? What if he makes a big mistake forbearing?

How do we avoid the unwelcome result that the forbearing is apt despite being one that obviously should not even have occurred? We can grant that it is a narrowly apt performance, while defining a broader aptness that it lacks. Let us explore this option.

Consider Diana's forced choice between taking a shot and forbearing from doing so. If she opts to take the shot, then her archery skills come into play. If they produce a hit, then her performance, her shot, manifests her narrow competence, and is hence narrowly apt. Compatibly with this, nonetheless, her shot selection might have been incompetent.

That is one way for a narrowly apt shot to be broadly objectionable. The huntress who forbears taking a shot that she obviously should take fails in her performance of forbearing. Her forbearing avoids ground-level failure, but is deplorable nonetheless.

Varieties of aptness

A performance is apt if its success manifests a competence seated in the agent (in relevantly appropriate conditions). It does not matter how fragile was the continued presence of the competence, or its appropriate conditions, when the agent issued the performance. A performance can thus easily fail to be "meta-apt," because the agent handles risk poorly, either by taking too much or by taking too little. The agent may fail to perceive the risk, when he should be more perceptive; or he may respond to the perceived risk with either foolhardiness or cowardice. He might perform on the ground level although the risk of failure is too high; or he might forbear although it is pusillanimous of him not to plunge ahead.

The aptness of a performance is thus to be distinguished from its meta-aptness. Either one can be present without the other.

An archer's/hunter's shot selection and risk taking may be excellent, for example, and in taking a certain shot he may manifest his competence at assessing risk, while the shot itself nevertheless fails, being unsuccessful (inaccurate) and hence inapt. The shot is hence meta-apt without being apt.

Conversely, the hunter may take excessive risk in shooting at a certain target, given his perceived level of competence (he has been drinking) and the assessed potential for wind (it is stormy). When he shoots, he may still fall just below the level of competence-denying inebriation, however, and the wind may happen to fall calm, so that his shot is (through that stroke of luck) quite apt. Here the shot is apt without being meta-apt.

Our shift from the competitor archer to the hunter archer, with his much wider latitude for target or shot selection, imports therefore the following distinction.

> A shot is apt iff the success it attains, its hitting the target, manifests the agent's first-order competence, his skillful marksmanship.
> A shot is meta-apt iff it is well-selected: i.e., iff it takes appropriate risk, and its doing so manifests the agent's competence for target and shot selection.

Neither aptness nor meta-aptness is sufficient for the other. They vary independently.

If Diana shoots, her shot might itself be both apt and meta-apt. If she forbears, her forbearing might be meta-apt, though of course it will not be apt on the ground level, since it does not even aim for success on that level. The forbearing might be meta-apt, nevertheless, in being a proper response to the perceived level of risk, a response that manifests her meta-competence.

Sometimes an agent responds properly by performing on the ground level, in which case that positive performance is meta-apt; sometimes the proper response is to forbear, so that the forbearing is meta-apt.

Arguably, a shot could be both apt and meta-apt while still falling short in that it is not in virtue of being meta-apt that it is apt. Thus, a shot might manifest a hunter's risk-assessment competence, and it might issue from his competence as an archer, in conditions appropriate for such shots, while yet its aptness does not so much manifest the archer's meta-competence as display a kind of luck. Diana might assess risk aptly and then just toss a coin to decide whether to shoot.

Full aptness and reflective knowledge

A performance attains thus a special status when it is apt at the ground level while its aptness manifests competent risk assessment. Suppose this risk assessment issues in the performer's knowing that his situation (constitutional and circumstantial) is favorable (where the risk of failure is low enough) for issuing such a performance. If these conditions all obtain, then the performance's aptness might manifest its meta-aptness; thus, its aptness might be relevantly explicable as manifesting the performer's meta-knowledge that his first-order performance is likely enough to succeed and be apt.

This applies to performances such as a shot that hits its prey. That shot is superior, more admirable and creditable, if it is not only apt, but also meta-apt, and, further, fully apt: that is, apt because meta-apt. This happens, for example, when the aptness of Diana's shot stems from her meta-competence in assessing risk properly, so that the shot's aptness manifests her competence for taking apt shots, a competence that essentially includes her ability to assess risk well.

Aptness comes in degrees. One shot is more apt than another, for example, if it manifests a more reliable competence. On one dimension, a shot by a tennis champion may be no better than a similarly paced and placed shot by a hacker. On another dimension, however, the champion's shot manifests his prowess on the court, while the hacker's nearly identical shot is just lucky, and skillful only minimally or not at all. The champion's shot manifests competence, moreover, on two levels. It manifests his sheer athletic ability to hit with good pace and placement, and with impressively good percentage. But it can and normally does manifest also her good shot selection, including her ability to attempt shots with an appropriate percentage of success. The hacker's shot falls short on both dimensions.

The champion's shots are apt, meta-apt, and fully apt: i.e., apt relevantly because meta-apt. For a shot to have the property of being apt is for its success to manifest a competence seated in the agent. This whole arrangement is itself something that the agent might be able to arrange (or not), and not simply by exercising the first-order competence seated in him. The agent might be able to choose when and where to exercise that competence, for one thing, and might manifest more or less competence in such a choice.

The same is true of the archer's/hunter's shot. It can be apt in that its success, its accuracy, manifests the agent's competence in relevantly appropriate conditions (no wind, enough light, distance within proper bounds, and so on). But it, and its aptness, can also manifest the agent's meta-competence for target and shot selection. If so, then it is no accident that the shot is made in specific conditions where the archer's competence is up to the task of producing success with a high enough percentage. In other words, the agent's risk perception is then competent enough, and this competence is manifest in his knowledge that the level of risk is appropriate. On one level, how apt the shot is depends on the degree of competence manifest by its success. But, on another level, the full aptness of the shot depends also on the meta-competence manifest by its aptness and by its success. What is required for this fuller aptness is that the agent's first-order aptness derive sufficiently from his assessment, albeit implicit, of the chances of such success (and, correlatively, of the risk of failure).

Here the agent is on a meta-level. He must take into account the likelihood that his competence is (and will remain) intact and that the relevant conditions are (and will remain) appropriate, and he must assess how likely it is that his action from such a competence in such conditions will succeed. Suppose he takes his chances of such success to be high enough (and the risk of failure low enough), and he is right, knowledgeably so, the chances being as he takes them to be, and his competence and conditions being relevantly as envisaged. Suppose further that he exercises his competence accordingly, so that the (first-order) aptness of his shot is owed sufficiently to his meta-competence, is owed sufficiently to his getting it right about the chances of success, and to his getting this right as a manifestation of that meta-competence. The agent's shot is then more fully apt and more fully creditable in proportion to how fully all of that falls into place.

We have thus found a further level of performance-based normativity. Epistemic normativity is, once again, a special case also in this more complex and subtle way. Animal knowledge is first-order apt belief. Reflective knowledge is animal belief aptly meta-endorsed by the subject. We can now see that knowing something full well requires that one have animal and reflective knowledge of it, but also that one know it with full aptness. It requires, that is to say, that the correctness of one's first order belief manifest not only the animal, first-order competences that reliably enough yield the correctness of the beliefs produced. One's first-order belief falls short if it is not appropriately guided by one's relevant meta-competence. This meta-competence governs whether or not one should form a belief at all on the question at issue, or should rather withhold. It is only if this meta-competence is operative in one's forming a belief at all on that subject matter that one's belief can reach the epistemic heights. One's first-order belief is apt in proportion to how reliable is the first-order competence manifest in its success. What is more, it is more fully apt in proportion to how reliable is the meta-competence that its success also manifests. This meta-competence is manifest at a remove, however, because the meta-knowledge that it is a belief likely enough to be apt on the ground level is constituted by the fact that the correctness of the corresponding meta-belief itself manifests the subject's relevant meta-competence.

Fully apt performances are in general better as performances than those that succeed without being apt at all, and also than those that are apt without being fully apt. Diana's apt shot that kills its prey is a better shot for being apt than it would be if successful only by luck and not through competence. Moreover, it is also a better, more admirable, more creditable shot, if its success flows also from her target-selecting, shot-picking competences. Her shot is more creditable in that case than it is when the right competence is manifest in conditions required for a successful first-order performance, but only by luck external to any such selection meta-competence on her part.

Epistemic normativity is again just a special case of all that. Apt belief, animal knowledge, is better than belief that succeeds in its aim, being true, without being apt. Apt belief aptly noted, reflective knowledge, is better than mere apt belief or animal knowledge, especially when the reflective knowledge helps to guide the first-order belief so that it is apt.[5] In such a case the belief is fully apt, and the subject knows full well.

---

5 In fact proper reflective knowledge will always guide or help to guide its corresponding animal belief. Proper reflective knowledge will after all satisfy requirements of coherence, which means not just logical or probabilistic coherence of the respective belief contents, but also the mutual basing relations that can properly reflect such coherence among the contents. Cross-level coherence, from the object to the meta, and conversely, is a special case of such coherence, and it imports "guidance" of the animal belief by the relevant meta-beliefs (or, in other words, basing of the former on the latter). It bears emphasis that the meta-aptness of a belief, which we have found to be an important factor in its epistemic evaluation, requires ascent to a good enough perspective concerning the first level potential attitudes among which the subject must opt (whether he opts with full conscious deliberation or through a less explicit procedure). Coherence among first-level attitudes is not enough. The subject must ascend to a level wherein he assesses relevant risk, whether in full consciousness or less explicitly, and opts on that basis. Included in that analysis is perforce some assessment of one's relevant competence(s) and situation, and this must itself be performed adequately, if it is to yield a fully creditable first-level performance. Its assessment as thus fully creditable is moreover epistemic. For it is an assessment based on epistemic standards as to whether belief is the proper response to one's situation rather than suspension of belief.

Die Natur von Fähigkeiten und der Zweck von Wissen*

John Greco

Eine Reihe von Autoren, zu denen auch ich zähle, hat die Auffassung verteidigt, dass Wissen wahre Überzeugung ist, die sich auf intellektuelle Tugend gründet.[1] Wenn wir intellektuelle Tugenden als Fähigkeiten (oder Vermögen) des Wissenden begreifen, dann lautet ihre These, dass Wissen wahre Überzeugung ist, die sich auf intellektuelle Fähigkeiten gründet. Diese Vorstellung ist eng mit einer anderen verknüpft: dass Wissen *anerkennenswerte* wahre Überzeugung ist. Diese Vorstellungen sind miteinander verknüpft, da einem aus Fähigkeiten resultierenden Erfolg eine bestimmte Art von Anerkennung zusteht, und nach der hier vertretenen Theorie ist Wissen eine Art von Erfolg, der auf Fähigkeiten beruht.[2]

Eine solche Auffassung von Wissen hat verschiedene Vorteile. Erstens und vor allem gestattet sie uns, ein uraltes Problem bezüglich der Natur des Wissens zu lösen. Wir können davon ausgehen, dass die Erkenntnistheorie eine normative Disziplin ist und Wissen eine normative (oder evaluative) Dimension hat. Was aber ist die Natur dieser normativen oder evaluativen Dimension des Wissens? Die hier vertretene Theorie beantwortet diese Frage, indem sie Wissen als ein Beispiel für eine allgemeinere Art von Phänomenen betrachtet, mit der wir aufs beste vertraut sind. Wie gesagt, nach der hier vertretenen Theorie ist Wissen eine Art von Erfolg, der auf Fähigkeiten beruht, und als solcher erbt es die verschiedenen normativen und evaluativen Eigenschaften, die im Allgemeinen mit Erfolgen verknüpft sind, die auf Fähigkeiten beruhen.

Aus Fähigkeiten resultierender Erfolg ist ganz offensichtlich Erfolg, für den der Handelnde Anerkennung verdient. Indem man Wissen zuschreibt, zollt man Anerkennung: Wenn wir sagen, jemand wisse etwas,

---

* Originally publishd in *Philosophical Issues* 17 (2007), pp. 37–49. Reprinted and translated by permission of the publisher, John Wiley and Sons.
1 Vgl. zum Beispiel: Sosa (1991), Zagzebski (1996) und (1999), Greco (1999) und (2003), Lehrer (2000), Riggs (2002).
2 Diese Idee wird besonders betont in Greco (2003).

so zollen wir ihm dafür Anerkennung, dass er richtig liegt. Wenn wir bestreiten, dass jemand etwas weiß, verweigern wir ihm die Anerkennung dafür, richtig zu liegen. In einem Typ von Fällen verweigern wir die Anerkennung für einen Erfolg, da kein Erfolg erzielt wurde – S hat eine falsche Überzeugung. In anderen Fällen verweigern wir die Anerkennung, da ein Erfolg zwar erzielt wurde, aber nicht auf Fähigkeit beruht – S glaubt die Wahrheit, aber dies ist ein Zufallstreffer oder es verdankt sich einem Denkfehler. Worum es hier – allgemeiner ausgedrückt – geht, ist die Tatsache, dass die Art von Anerkennung oder Wertschätzung, die mit Erfolg, der aus Fähigkeiten (Tüchtigkeit oder Tugend) resultiert, einhergeht, im Leben der Menschen allgegenwärtig ist. Beispiele hierfür finden sich im Bereich der Moral, des Sports, der Kunst und vielen anderen Bereichen. Praktisch überall, wo es menschliche Tüchtigkeit oder Fähigkeit gibt, gibt es eine mit ihnen verbundene normative Praxis. Die hier vertretene Auffassung sieht im Wissen und in der epistemischen Bewertung ein weiteres Beispiel für diese allgemeinere Art von Normativität, die uns wohlvertraut ist.

Neben diesem Vorzug hat diese Auffassung noch einige, eng damit verbundene Vorteile. Zum einen liefert sie uns eine schöne Erläuterung der Vorstellung, dass Wissen mit glücklichem Zufall unvereinbar ist. Das scheint zu stimmen, aber was genau bedeutet es? In welcher *Weise* ist Wissen mit glücklichem Zufall unvereinbar?[3] Nach der hier vertretenen Auffassung können wir sagen, dass Wissen auf die gleiche Weise mit glücklichem Zufall unvereinbar ist wie ein auf Tugend beruhender Erfolg. Das heißt, es gibt eine Bedeutung des Worts „glücklicher Zufall", in der ein glücklicher bzw. zufälliger Erfolg genau der Gegensatz ist zu einem Erfolg, der auf Tugenden oder Fähigkeiten beruht, zum Beispiel wenn Tiger Woods ein ausgezeichneter Schlag gelingt, mit dem er den Golfball auf dem Grün platziert, im Gegensatz zum schwachen Schlag eines schlechteren Spielers, bei dem der Ball auf einen Baum trifft und von dort auf das Grün zurückspringt. Es gibt einen klaren und vertrauten Sinn, in dem der Erfolg des letzteren Spielers glücklich war und der von Tiger Woods nicht. Nach der hier vertretenen Auffassung können wir sagen, dass Wissen in ganz derselben Weise im Gegensatz zum glücklichen Zufall steht: Im Falle von Wissen erzielt man einen intellektuellen Erfolg (d. h. man glaubt etwas Wahres) und dieser Erfolg verdankt sich der eigenen Fähigkeit. Um es noch einmal zu wiederholen, aus Fähigkeiten

---

3 Für eine ausführliche Behandlung dieser Frage vgl. Pritchard (2005).

resultierender Erfolg ist beispielhaft für einen Erfolg, der im Gegensatz steht zu einem bloß glücklichen bzw. zufälligen Erfolg. Schließlich gibt uns die hier vertretene Auffassung eine elegante und systematische Antwort auf das Wertproblem, d. h. das Problem, wie man erklären soll, dass Wissen wertvoller ist als bloße wahre Überzeugung.[4] Wir zollen dem aus Fähigkeiten resultierenden Erfolg größere Anerkennung als dem bloß glücklichen Erfolg. Aber wir *schätzen* auch den aus Fähigkeiten resultierenden Erfolg mehr als den bloß glücklichen Erfolg. Tatsächlich gibt es eine lange Tradition, die den tugendhaften Erfolg, also den Erfolg, der aus Tugend oder Tüchtigkeit resultiert, mit dem höchsten Gut des Menschen identifiziert: Dieser Erfolg ist selbst von intrinsischem Wert und konstitutiv für das Gedeihen des Menschen. So schreibt Aristoteles in der *Nikomachischen Ethik*: „Das Gut des Menschen erweist sich als Tätigkeit der Seele im Sinne der Gutheit."[5] Natürlich müssen wir nicht ganz so weit gehen wie Aristoteles, um zu der hier vertretenen Antwort auf das Wertproblem zu gelangen. Es genügt, dass aus Fähigkeiten resultierender Erfolg wertvoller ist als Erfolg, der auf andere Weise zustande kommt. Und diese schwächere Behauptung scheint offensichtlich richtig zu sein.

Die Behauptung, Wissen sei eine Art von Erfolg, der aus Fähigkeiten resultiert, kann also eine ganze Menge erklären. Nichtsdestotrotz sieht sich diese Ansicht mit einigen Problemen konfrontiert. In diesem Artikel möchte ich auf drei dieser Einwände eingehen, die, wie mir scheint, besonders schwerwiegend sind. Allerdings nicht so schwerwiegend, dass sie nicht entkräftet werden können. Aber letzteres erfordert doch einige Anstrengung. Es erfordert insbesondere, die Ansicht weiter zu entwickeln, indem wir sie mit zusätzlichen Thesen verbinden. Damit, so behaupte ich, versetzen wir sie in die Lage, eine angemessene Erwiderung auf alle diese Einwände zu erlauben. Im ersten Abschnitt werde ich die drei Einwände kurz darstellen und im zweiten Abschnitt werde ich zwei Ideen vorstellen, die uns, wie ich glaube, helfen werden, diese Einwände zu entkräften. In den nachfolgenden Abschnitten werde ich dann auf die einzelnen Einwände detailliert eingehen.

---

4 Vgl. Greco (2009). Für eine ausführliche Behandlung des Wertproblems vgl. Kvanvig (2003).
5 Vgl. Aristoteles: *Nikomachische Ethik* I.7.

1. Drei Einwände

Der erste Einwand ist eine Variante des Allgemeinheitsproblems, wie es sich für den Reliabilismus stellt.[6] Dieses Problem wird gewöhnlich als ein Problem für den Prozessreliabilismus dargestellt, also für die Ansicht, dass eine Überzeugung nur dann epistemisch gerechtfertigt ist, wenn sie durch einen verlässlichen kognitiven Prozess erzeugt wurde. Das Problem besteht darin, dass sich die Frage der Rechtfertigung in Bezug auf einzelne Überzeugungen stellt, während Verlässlichkeit eine Eigenschaft ist, die bestimmten Typen von kognitiven Prozessen zukommt. Aber jede einzelne Überzeugung fällt unter viele Typen von Prozessen. Zum Beispiel ist meine Überzeugung, dass jetzt gerade Kaffee in meiner Tasse ist, durch Wahrnehmung hervorgerufen, durch visuelle Wahrnehmung, visuelle Wahrnehmung unter guten Lichtverhältnissen etc. Und natürlich variieren diese Prozesstypen, was den Grad ihrer Verlässlichkeit angeht. Das Problem für den Reliabilismus besteht darin, zu bestimmen, welcher Grad von Allgemeinheit zum Zwecke der Bewertung der fraglichen Einzelüberzeugung am besten geeignet ist. Dieses Problem wird zu einem Einwand, wenn man zu dem Schluss kommt, dass die Aufgabe nicht erfüllbar ist. Dieser Einwand lautet, dass sich der relevante Grad von Allgemeinheit für Prozesstypen nicht angemessen bestimmen lässt und deshalb das reliabilistische Projekt, auf diese Weise Rechtfertigung zu definieren, scheitert. Für unsere gegenwärtigen Belange müssen wir bloß zur Kenntnis nehmen, dass sich eine Variante des Allgemeinheitsproblems auch für die hier vertretene Wissenstheorie stellt. Die Auffassung, dass Wissen aus Fähigkeiten resultierender Erfolg ist, wirft, mit einem Wort, die Frage auf, wie wir die Identität von Fähigkeiten bestimmen sollen. Genauer gesagt: Wie sollen wir die Identität von Fähigkeiten für die Zwecke epistemischer Bewertung bestimmen? Hier ergibt sich erneut das Allgemeinheitsproblem.

Unser zweiter Einwand wird von Jennifer Lackey vorgetragen und richtet sich auf eine zentrale These der hier vertretenen Auffassung.[7] Kurz gesagt behauptet Lackey, nicht alles Wissen sei anerkennenswerte wahre Überzeugung, und als typisches Beispiel führt sie Wissen an, das auf dem Zeugnis anderer beruht. Insbesondere gibt es Fälle von Wissen, dass auf dem Zeugnis anderer beruht, bei denen die Anerkennung für die wahre Überzeugung von S nicht S selbst, sondern der Person gezollt wird, die

---

6 Für eine klassische Darstellung des Problems vgl. Conee/Feldman (1998).
7 Vgl. Lackey (2004), (2007).

das Zeugnis gegeben hat. Nehmen wir beispielsweise an, dass ein glänzender Mathematiker ein schwieriges Theorem beweist und mich dann über das Ergebnis informiert. Es ist plausibel anzunehmen, dass ich deshalb weiß, dass das Theorem wahr ist. Aber die Anerkennung hierfür erhält der Mathematiker. Anders gesagt, nicht meine, sondern seine Fähigkeiten liefern die Erklärung dafür, wie ich zu der wahren Überzeugung gekommen bin.

Unser dritter Einwand wird von Dennis Whitcomb erhoben und lautet, dass es der hier vertretenen Auffassung nicht gelingt, das Wertproblem zu lösen.[8] Insbesondere behauptet Whitcomb, dass Wissen kein Fall von etwas sei, das seiner Art nach wertvoller ist, und deshalb der Wert von Wissen nicht auf diese Weise erklärt werden könne. Whitcombs Argument ist kompliziert, weshalb ich es hier noch nicht detailliert darstelle, sondern erst später.

2. *Zwei Ideen*

Die These, dass Wissen eine Art von Erfolg ist, der aus Fähigkeiten resultiert, sieht sich mit schwierigen Problemen konfrontiert. Ich möchte nun kurz zwei Ideen vorstellen, die uns meines Erachtens die Mittel an die Hand geben, diese Probleme zu bewältigen. Beide Ideen werden in den nachfolgenden Abschnitten, in denen ich zeige, wie nützlich sie sind, weiterentwickelt.

Die erste Idee betrifft die Natur von Fähigkeiten. Fähigkeiten im Allgemeinen und intellektuelle Fähigkeiten im Besonderen haben einige wesentliche Eigenschaften und weisen eine gewisse Struktur auf. Wir kommen mit den oben aufgezählten Problemen voran, indem wir uns diese Eigenschaften und Struktur zunutze machen. In der Tat benötigen wir eine „Metaphysik der Fähigkeiten".

Die zweite Idee betrifft den Zweck von Wissen. Genauer gesagt, sie betrifft die Zwecke, die Wissen erfüllt, und unseren Begriff von Wissen. Hier berühren sich zwei Themen, die in der neueren Literatur eine prominente Rolle spielen, auf interessante Weise. Das eine Thema wird unter anderem von Edward Craig hervorgehoben: dass der Begriff des Wissens die Funktion hat, gute Information und gute Informationsquellen (Informanten) zu kennzeichnen.[9] Das andere wird unter anderem

---
8 Vgl. Whitcomb (Manuskript).
9 Vgl. Craig (1999).

von John Hawthorne und Jason Stanley hervorgehoben: dass Wissen für praktische Überlegungen verwendet wird.[10] Fügen wir beides zusammen: Der Begriff des Wissens hat die Funktion, gute Information und gute Informationsquellen zum Gebrauch in praktischen Überlegungen zu kennzeichnen. Das ist die zweite Idee, die wir uns in der Auseinandersetzung mit den oben aufgezählten Problemen zunutze machen können.

3. Das Allgemeinheitsproblem

Wie ich sagte, ergibt sich eine Variante des Allgemeinheitsproblems auch für die hier vertretene Auffassung von Wissen als einem auf Fähigkeiten beruhenden Erfolg. Um besser zu verstehen, weshalb das so ist, sollen zunächst einige Eigenschaften von Fähigkeiten im Allgemeinen betrachtet werden.

Erstens: Zu sagen, jemand habe eine Fähigkeit, heißt, dass man sich darauf verlassen kann, dass er auf eine gewisse, für die fragliche Fähigkeit relevante Weise erfolgreich ist. Zweitens: Fähigkeiten sind an eine Reihe relevanter Bedingungen geknüpft. Wenn wir beispielsweise sagen, Jeter habe die Fähigkeit, Baseballs zu schlagen, so unterstellen wir, dass man sich darauf verlassen kann, dass er unter für das Baseballspiel geeigneten Bedingungen beim Schlagen von Baseballs erfolgreich ist. Es tut Jeters Fähigkeit keinen Abbruch, dass er zum Beispiel im Dunklen oder mit Sand in den Augen nicht in der Lage ist, Baseballs zu schlagen.

Drittens: Fähigkeiten sind immer relativ zu einer bestimmten Umgebung. Das folgt daraus, dass Verlässlichkeit immer relativ zu einer bestimmten Umgebung ist und der Besitz einer Fähigkeit Verlässlichkeit impliziert. Beispielsweise hat Jeter die Fähigkeit, Baseballs zu schlagen, relativ zu einer für Baseball charakteristischen Umgebung. Er hat sie nicht, wenn er sich in einem Kriegsgebiet befindet, wo es ihm an der nötigen Konzentration für das Schlagen von Baseballs fehlt. Man beachte, dass sich die Begriffe „Bedingung" und „Umgebung" überschneiden – einige Sachverhalte mögen in der Beschreibung von beiden enthalten sein. Für unsere gegenwärtigen Belange können wir „Umgebungen" als Mengen relativ stabiler Umstände betrachten und „Bedingungen" als Mengen veränderlicher Umstände innerhalb einer Umgebung.

---

10 Vgl. Hawthorne (2004), Stanley (2005). Darüber hinaus Williamson (2000) und Fantl/McGrath (2002).

Schließlich: Wenn man sagt, jemand habe die Fähigkeit, ein bestimmtes Resultat zu erreichen, sagt man gleichzeitig mehr und weniger, als dass er eine gute Erfolgsbilanz darin hat, dieses Resultat zu erreichen. Das liegt daran, dass Fähigkeiten dispositionale Eigenschaften sind: Zu sagen, dass S die Fähigkeit hat, Resultat R zu erreichen, bedeutet, dass S die Disposition oder Tendenz hat, R in – in relevanter Weise – nahen Welten zu erreichen. Die tatsächlichen Erfolgsbilanzen können das Ergebnis eines glücklichen Zufalls sein statt aus einer Fähigkeit zu resultieren. Tatsächliche Erfolgsbilanzen können aber ebenso das Ergebnis eines *unglücklichen* Zufalls sein wie das Ergebnis *mangelnder* Fähigkeit. Mit einem Wort: Wenn man sagt, S habe eine bestimmte Fähigkeit, so heißt das, dass S eine hohe Erfolgsrate in solchen möglichen Welten hat, die einander in relevanter Hinsicht nahe stehen.

Wenn wir diese Beobachtungen zusammenfassen, können wir den Schluss ziehen, dass Fähigkeiten die folgende Struktur aufweisen:

S hat eine Fähigkeit F(R/B) relativ zu einer Umgebung U = In einer Menge von einander in relevanter Hinsicht nahe stehenden Welten W, in denen S sich unter B und in U befindet, hat S eine hohe Erfolgsrate darin, R zu erreichen.

Jetzt zeigt sich, warum die hier vertretene Wissenstheorie mit einer Variante des Allgemeinheitsproblems konfrontiert ist. Zu sagen, S wisse *p*, impliziert nach dieser Theorie, dass S bezüglich *p* aufgrund seiner intellektuellen Fähigkeit die Wahrheit glaubt, wobei eine Fähigkeit eine Disposition ist, das besagte Resultat mit einer hinreichend hohen Erfolgsrate zu erreichen. Aber jede wahre Einzelüberzeugung wird das Resultat mehrerer Typen von Dispositionen mit der oben angegebenen Struktur sein. Darüber hinaus werden wir, was die wahren Überzeugungen von S angeht, unterschiedliche Erfolgsraten erhalten, je nachdem, wie wir die relevanten W, B und U bestimmen. Es ist zum Beispiel möglich, dass die Erfolgsrate von S sehr hoch ist, wenn die Bedingungen enger definiert werden, aber sehr niedrig, wenn diese Bedingungen weiter definiert sind. Wie sollen wir die relevanten Parameter bestimmen, um diejenige Disposition herauszugreifen, die für die Bewertung der Überzeugung von S relevant ist?

An diesem Punkt, so möchte ich nun darlegen, können wir von unserer zweiten Idee Gebrauch machen, dass nämlich der Begriff des Wissens den Zwecken praktischer Überlegung dient. Insbesondere dient der Begriff des Wissens der Kennzeichnung guter Information und guter Informationsquellen zur Verwendung in praktischen Überlegungen.

Wenn das richtig ist, dann verfügen wir über eine Lösung des Allgemeinheitsproblems: Die relevanten Parameter sollten den Interessen und Zwecken der relevanten praktischen Überlegungen entsprechend bestimmt werden.

Diese Idee entspricht genau unserer allgemeinen Auffassung von Fähigkeiten. Wenn wir beispielsweise sagen, dass S die Fähigkeit hat, Baseballs zu schlagen, dann hilft uns der Kontext praktischer Überlegungen, das zu bestimmen, was ich hier behaupte. Wenn ich ein Baseballmanager in einer Diskussion darüber bin, ob Jeter eingetauscht werden soll, werde ich etwas ganz anderes behaupten als der Trainer der Little League, der überlegt, wie er einen neuen Siebenjährigen aufstellen soll. Beispielsweise wird sich hier dramatisch ändern, welche Bedingungen relevant sind und was als relevante Umgebung zählt. Im Allgemeinen werden diese Erwägungen sowohl durch (a) die Natur der fraglichen Fähigkeit bestimmt werden, als auch durch (b) die Natur des Kontexts praktischer Überlegungen, in dem die Frage relevant ist.

Die hier diskutierte Idee ähnelt einem Vorschlag von Mark Heller, wie man das Allgemeinheitsproblem für den Reliabilismus lösen kann.[11] Heller zufolge begehen Reliabilisten einen Fehler, wenn sie die Herausforderung annehmen, mit der sie das Allgemeinheitsproblem konfrontiert: nämlich die, eine systematische Regel zur Bestimmung der relevanten Allgemeinheitsgrade anzugeben. Dies ist deshalb ein Fehler, wie Heller argumentiert, weil die relevanten Allgemeinheitsgrade durch den Kontext bestimmt werden.

> ‚Verlässlich' ist ein ganz gewöhnliches Wort, das in ganz gewöhnlichen Situationen für Vorkommnisse gebraucht wird, die unter mehrere Typen fallen, denen unterschiedliche Grade an Verlässlichkeit zu kommen. Irgendwie gelingt es uns aber dennoch, das Wort im gewöhnlichen Gespräch ohne Schwierigkeit zu verwenden. Ebenso kontextrelativ wie der Gebrauch dieses Ausdrucks im gewöhnlichen Gespräch ist, so kontextabhängig ist ‚verlässlich' im Wissensdiskurs. Wenn wir diese wenig überraschende Tatsache einmal zur Kenntnis genommen haben, sollten wir erkennen, dass das Allgemeinheitsproblem nur aufgrund unvernünftiger Forderungen entsteht, die man an den Reliabilisten stellt. Es ist unvernünftig, ein feststehendes Prinzip für die Wahl des korrekten Allgemeinheitsgrades zu fordern, wenn das, was als korrekt gilt, von Kontext zu Kontext variiert.[12]

Heller präsentiert seine Ansicht als eine Variante des Zuschreiber-Kontextualismus. „‚Verlässlich' ist im besonderen Maße vom Kontext des

---

11 Vgl. Heller (1995).
12 Ebd. 502 f.

Bewertenden abhängig."¹³ Es ist bemerkenswert, dass es sich hierbei um keinen wesentlichen Aspekt von Hellers Lösung des Allgemeinheitsproblems handelt. Um dies einzusehen, müssen wir die vertraute Unterscheidung zwischen dem Kontext des Zuschreibers (oder Bewertenden) und dem Kontext des Subjekts treffen. In Hellers Lösung des Allgemeinheitsproblems kommt die Hauptfunktion der Tatsache zu, dass die Bestimmungen der Allgemeinheit kontextabhängig sind. Wir landen beim Zuschreiber-Kontextualismus, wenn diese Bestimmungen, wie Heller meint, vom Kontext des Zuschreibenden abhängig sind. Aber „subjektsensitive Invariantisten" wie Hawthorne und Stanley können eine ähnliche Strategie anwenden, indem sie nämlich die Bestimmungen der Allgemeinheit von den Interessen und Zwecken des Subjektkontexts abhängig machen. Solange die Interessen und Zwecke relativ zu den verschiedenen Kontexten der Subjekte variieren, lässt sich der relevante Mechanismus von Hellers Lösung erhalten.

Die von mir verteidigte Variante der Hellerschen Lösung ist, technisch gesehen, eine Variante des Zuschreiber-Kontextualismus, obwohl weder der Kontext des Subjekts noch der Kontext des Zuschreibers *als solche* für die Bestimmung der relevanten Allgemeinheitsgrade wichtig sind. Wichtig hierfür ist vielmehr der Kontext praktischer Überlegung, der sowohl der Kontext des Subjekts als auch der des Zuschreibenden oder der einer dritten Partei sein kann. Insbesondere die relevanten Parameter werden durch die Interessen und Zwecke festgelegt, die in dem relevanten Kontext praktischer Überlegung wirksam sind. Wenn wir beispielsweise entscheiden wollen, was *wir* tun sollen, werden die Parameter durch die Anliegen festgelegt, die unsere praktischen Überlegungen leiten. Wenn wir dagegen entscheiden, was *S* tun sollte, werden die Parameter durch die Anliegen festgelegt, die ihre praktischen Überlegungen bestimmen. Die hieraus resultierende Ansicht kommt gut mit den schwierigen Fällen für den Zuschreiber-Kontextualismus und den subjektsensitiven Invariantismus zurecht, was wir allerdings im Rahmen dieses Artikels nicht vertiefen können. Hier geht es vielmehr darum, dass wir jetzt über eine vernünftige Lösung für das Allgemeinheitsproblem verfügen.¹⁴

---

13 Ebd. 503.
14 Diese Variante des Kontextualismus ist ausführlicher entwickelt und verteidigt in Greco (2008).

4. Wissen und Anerkennung

Man betrachte den folgenden, von Jennifer Lackey beschriebenen Fall:

> Kurz nach seiner Ankunft am Bahnhof von Chicago möchte sich Morris erkundigen, wie man zum Sears Tower kommt. Er sieht sich um, geht willkürlich auf einen Passanten zu und fragt ihn, wie man das gewünschte Ziel erreicht. Der Passant, der, wie es der Zufall will, in Chicago wohnt und die Stadt ausgezeichnet kennt, gibt Morris eine Wegbeschreibung, mit der er sein Ziel nicht verfehlen kann.

Lackey schreibt:

> Die Erklärung dafür, dass Morris den richtigen Weg wusste, hat fast nichts, was von epistemischen Interesse wäre, mit ihm zu tun, und fast alles, was von epistemischen Interesse ist, mit dem Passanten. Die Erklärung dafür, dass Morris zu einer wahren statt zu einer falschen Überzeugung gelangte, ist insbesondere, dass der Passant mit der Stadt Chicago vertraut ist und sie gut kennt. (…) Obwohl man plausiblerweise sagen kann, dass Morris von dem Passanten Wissen erwarb, so scheint es, gibt es keinen substantiellen Sinn, in dem Morris Anerkennung dafür verdient, dass er die wahre Überzeugung hat.[15]

Dies ist ein schwer zu entkräftender Einwand. Wir müssen vorsichtig vorgehen und Schritt für Schritt. Zunächst müssen wir uns klarer darüber werden, wie eine tugendtheoretische Position Wissen auffassen soll, das auf dem Zeugnis anderer beruht. Die Theorien solchen Wissens spalten sich häufig in zwei Lager. Der ersten Theorie zufolge kommt es für ein solches Wissen darauf an, dass die Quelle des Zeugnisses tatsächlich zuverlässig ist. Der zweiten Theorie zufolge ist es dafür auch wichtig, dass der Glaubende weiß oder zumindest gerechtfertigterweise glaubt, dass die Quelle zuverlässig ist. Aus tugendtheoretischer Perspektive wird jedoch

---

15 Vgl. Lackey (2004), Übersetzung Ute Feldmann.
Im Original: „Having just arrived at the train station in Chicago, Morris wishes to obtain directions to the Sears Tower. He looks around, randomly approaches the first passerby that he sees, and asks how to get to his desired destination. The passerby, who happens to be a Chicago resident who knows the city extraordinarily well, provides Morris with impeccable directions to the Sears Tower. What explains why Morris got things right has nearly nothing of epistemic interest to do with him and nearly everything of epistemic interest to do with the passerby. In particular, it is the passerby's experience with and knowledge of the city of Chicago that explains why Morris ended up with a true belief rather than a false belief. . . Thus, though it is plausible to say that Morris acquired knowledge from the passerby, there seems to be no substantive sense in which Morris deserves credit for holding the true belief that he does."

eine dritte Art von Theorie plausibel, dass nämlich Wissen, das auf dem Zeugnis anderer beruht, erfordert, dass der *Glaubende* ein zuverlässiger *Empfänger* von Informationen ist. Es kommt also nicht so sehr darauf an, dass derjenige, der das Zeugnis gibt, zuverlässig ist, oder dass der Glaubende dies weiß, sondern vielmehr darauf, dass der Glaubende selber zuverlässig ist, was den Empfang und die Bewertung von Informationen anbelangt. Es leuchtet ein, dass dies von ihm verlangt, zuverlässig zwischen zuverlässigen und unzuverlässigen Zeugnisquellen unterscheiden zu können.

Angenommen, der dritte Ansatz sei der richtige. Dann müssen wir bei Lackeys Beispiel zwei Fälle unterscheiden: den Fall, in dem Morris ein zuverlässiger Empfänger von Informationen ist, und den Fall, in dem er dies nicht ist. Aus der Perspektive einer Tugendtheorie weiß Morris nur in einem Fall der ersten Art, wo sein Ziel zu finden ist. Aber in einem solchen Fall verdient Morris auch Anerkennung dafür, dass er zu der entsprechenden Überzeugung kommt. Das heißt, sein Erfolg gründet sich auf seine Fähigkeit, zwischen einem guten und einem schlechten Zeugnis anderer zu unterscheiden und kann deshalb ihm zugeschrieben werden.

Aber das bisher Gesagte ist unzureichend. Denn so wie Lackey ihren Einwand formuliert, verdient derjenige, der das Zeugnis abgibt, die Anerkennung und *nicht* Morris. Lackey schreibt: „Die Erklärung dafür, dass Morris den richtigen Weg wusste, hat fast nichts, was von epistemischem Interesse wäre, mit ihm zu tun, und fast alles, was von epistemischem Interesse ist, mit dem Passanten."[16] Aus der gegenwärtigen Perspektive ist das, was Lackey sagt, allerdings nicht ganz richtig. Denn in Fällen der ersten Art hat die Erklärung dafür, dass Morris zur richtigen Überzeugung kam, etwas, das von epistemischen Interesse ist, mit ihm zu tun: nämlich seine Fähigkeit, zwischen einem guten und einem schlechten Zeugnis anderer zu unterscheiden. Das ist der wichtige Unterschied zwischen der ersten Art von Fall, bei dem Morris etwas weiß, und der zweiten Art von Fall, bei dem Morris nichts weiß. Aber vielleicht ist Lackeys Überlegung folgende: Morris selbst hat *relativ* wenig Anteil an seinem Erfolg. Er hat so wenig Anteil daran, so die Überlegung, dass die Bedeutung des Beitrags von Morris hinter der Bedeutung des Beitrags des Zeugen verschwindet.

Ein solcher Einwand gewinnt an Überzeugungskraft, wenn man Fälle betrachtet, bei denen wir es mit dem Zeugnis eines Experten zu tun haben. Erinnern wir uns beispielsweise an den Fall des glänzenden Ma-

---

16 Ebd.

thematikers. Er beweist ein schwieriges Theorem und teilt mir sein Ergebnis mit. Die Mitteilung, so kann man plausiblerweise sagen, ist die Quelle meines Wissens, dass das Theorem wahr ist. Dem hier erörterten Einwand zufolge verdiene ich in diesem Fall jedoch überhaupt keine Anerkennung für meine wahre Überzeugung. Oder, um den Einwand etwas vorsichtiger zu formulieren, ich verdiene nicht „genug" Anerkennung, da meine eigenen Fähigkeiten für die Erklärung, warum ich hier die Wahrheit glaube, nicht „wichtig genug" sind.

Eine Reaktion hierauf wäre, einfach auf stur zu schalten. Das heißt, wir könnten darauf beharren, dass mein Beitrag einen hinreichend großen Anteil an der Erklärung *hat*. Man überlege sich: Wenn ich, was die Wahrheit schwieriger mathematischer Theoreme angeht, jeder beliebigen Person Glauben schenkte, hätte ich auch in jenem Fall kein Wissen, in dem ich zufällig von einer zuverlässigen Quelle Zeugnis erhielte. Diese Art von Pattsituation wäre jedoch unbefriedigend, und Lackey bringt diesbezüglich eine berechtigte Sorge zum Ausdruck: dass wir nämlich unsere Intuitionen im Hinblick darauf, ob der Beitrag von S „hinreichend bedeutsam" ist, von unseren Intuitionen bezüglich der Frage, ob S Wissen besitzt, bestimmen lassen. Das heißt, wir entscheiden *zuerst* darüber, ob S Wissen hat, und *dann* erst (auf dieser Grundlage) ob der Beitrag von S im fraglichen Fall „hinreichend bedeutsam" ist. Wenn dem so ist, verliert die Theorie viel von ihrer Erklärungskraft. Insbesondere verliert sie das Potential, in einem breiten Spektrum von Fällen zwischen Wissen und Nichtwissen zu unterscheiden.

Was können wir also tun, um eine Pattsituation zu vermeiden und die Bedenken zu zerstreuen? Wir können zum einen Analogien zu nichtepistemischen Fällen herstellen, in denen unsere Intuitionen sowohl fest als auch unkontrovers sind. Zweitens können wir eine systematische Erklärung der Analogien geben.

Man betrachte als erstes einen unkontroversen Fall von Anerkennung für einen Erfolg. In einem Fußballspiel erhält Ted einen glänzenden, fast unmöglichen Pass und schießt dann ein leicht zu erzielendes Tor. In dem hier vorgestellten Fall sind es die athletischen Fähigkeiten des Spielers, der den Pass gibt, die herausragen. Der Pass war glänzend, die Annahme leicht. Wir können uns auch vorstellen, dass dieser Spieler, bevor er den Pass gab, einem anderen auf glänzende Weise den Ball abgenommen hatte. Nichtsdestotrotz verdient Ted Anerkennung für das Tor. Wie groß dabei die Hilfe anderer auch war, er war derjenige, der den Ball ins Netz schob. Das heißt nun nicht, dass derjenige, der ihm den Pass gab, keine Anerkennung für das Tor verdient, oder dass er nicht mehr Anerkennung verdient als Ted. Es heißt jedoch, dass Ted auf die richtige Art und Weise am Erfolg beteiligt war, um Anerkennung zu finden. Vergleichen wir diesen Fall mit einem anderen: Ted ist an einem Fußballspiel beteiligt, aber unaufmerksam. Obwohl er den Ball nicht sieht, prallt ein glänzender Pass von seinem Kopf ins Tor. Hier verdient Ted keine Anerkennung für das Tor. Er war an ihm beteiligt, aber nicht auf die richtige Art und Weise.

Ich behaupte hier natürlich, dass der erste Fall in relevanter Hinsicht analog zu dem Wissen ist, das auf dem Zeugnis des Experten beruht. Die systematische Erklärung lautet: Die Anerkennung für einen Erfolg, der in Kooperation mit anderen erzielt wird, wird nicht von der tüchtigen Leistung anderer zunichte gemacht. Sie wird nicht einmal von der hervorragenden Leistung anderer zunichte gemacht. So lange die eigenen Anstrengungen und Fähigkeiten daran in angemessener Weise beteiligt sind, verdient man für den fraglichen Erfolg Anerkennung.

Wir können die Erklärung für diese Fälle vertiefen, indem wir zu der zweiten der oben eingeführten Ideen zurückkehren: dass nämlich unser Begriff des Wissens den Zwecken praktischer Überlegung dient. In der Tat können wir uns diese Idee für eine Erklärung zunutze machen, warum in Fällen von Wissen, die auf dem Zeugnis von Experten beruhen, und ganz allgemein von Wissen, das auf dem Zeugnis anderer beruht, im Allgemeinen Anerkennung nicht zunichte gemacht wird. Kurz gesagt: Der zuverlässige Empfang von Zeugnissen im Allgemeinen und Zeugnissen von Experten im Besonderen leistet für die Zwecke praktischer Überlegungen einen guten Dienst. Das heißt, in Fällen von Wissen, das auf dem Zeugnis anderer beruht, hat S die richtige Art von Fähigkeit und verwendet sie auf die richtige Art und Weise, um damit den Zwecken praktischer Überlegungen zu dienen, d.h. jenen von S und jenen der Gruppe, die sich auf S als gute Informationsquelle verlassen muss. Etwas Ähnliches können wir sagen, um zu erklären, warum Ted dafür Anerkennung erhält, dass er ein leicht zu erzielendes Tor schießt: Man leistet dem Zweck des Fußballspiels einen guten Dienst, wenn man ein zuverlässiger Vollstrecker leicht zu erzielender Tore ist. Das heißt, im Fußballbeispiel hat Ted die richtige Art von Fähigkeit, und er macht von ihr auf die richtige Art und Weise Gebrauch, um damit den Zwecken des Fußballspiels zu dienen, d.h. seinen eigenen und denen des Teams, das sich darauf verlassen muss, dass Ted (leicht oder schwer zu erreichende) Pässe annimmt und Tore schießt.

5. Der Wert von Wissen

Am Anfang des Artikels habe ich behauptet, dass eine Tugendtheorie eine elegante Lösung des Wertproblems erlaubt, also des Problems, warum Wissen wertvoller ist als bloß wahre Überzeugung. Sie erklärt den Wert von Wissen dadurch, dass sie ihn auf den Wert von etwas zurückführt, das seiner Art nach allgemeiner ist als Wissen. Kurz gesagt: Wissen ist deshalb wertvoll, weil es eine Art von Erfolg ist, der auf Fähigkeiten beruht, und ein derartiger Erfolg hat im Allgemeinen einen besonderen Wert, der den Wert bloßen Erfolgs übersteigt. Dennis Whitcomb hat die Auffassung vertreten, dass es dieser Theorie an der Erklärungskraft mangelt, die ich für sie in Anspruch nehme.

Zur Begründung dieser Behauptung empfiehlt er uns, das folgende Beispiel näher betrachten:

> An einem Schießstand beschweren Strolche die meisten Pfeilspitzen mit Gewichten. Die Meisterschützen schießen ihre Pfeile ab und verfehlen wegen der Gewichte das Ziel. Auch ich schieße und durch Zufall bekomme ich den einzigen Köcher mit ungewichteten Pfeilen. Aufgrund von Fähigkeiten, mit denen man fast immer erfolgreich ist, treffe ich ins Ziel. Meine Schüsse sind erfolgreich, und sie sind überdies erfolgreich *aufgrund* meiner Tugend.[17]

Betrachten wir nun ein zweites Beispiel.

> Auch bei einer Zeitung arbeiten Strolche, und kurz bevor die Druckmaschinen starten, ersetzen sie eine der Wahrheiten, die in der Zeitung stehen, nämlich *p*, durch die Unwahrheit non-*p*. Als die Zeitung fast fertig gedruckt ist, fällt den Herausgebern der Fehler auf und sie lassen einige korrigierte Exemplare drucken. Durch Zufall lese ich ein korrigiertes Exemplar. Dadurch gelange ich zu der Überzeugung, dass *p*, aber ich gelange nicht zu dem Wissen, dass *p*.[18]

Whitcomb behauptet, die beiden Fälle zeigten, dass die hier vertretene Auffassung den Wert von Wissen nicht auf den Wert von etwas zurückführt, das seiner Art nach allgemeiner ist als Wissen. Er schreibt:

> Die beiden Fälle sind völlig analog. In jedem Sinne, in dem wir es im ersten Fall mit einer Tugend zu tun haben, haben wir es auch im zweiten Fall mit einer Tugend zu tun. Da ich im zweiten Fall kein Wissen habe, kann also wahre Überzeugung nicht durch Tugend zu Wissen werden, zumindest

---

17 Vgl. Whitcomb (Manuskript).
18 Ebd.

nicht in dem Sinne von Wissen, in dem Erfolg auf anderen Gebieten zu Wissen-aufgrund-von-Tugend auf diesen Gebieten wird.[19]

Meine Erwiderung auf diesen Einwand stellt die erste Behauptung der letzteren Passage in Frage, dass nämlich die beiden Fälle völlig analog sind. Insbesondere zeigt eine genauere Betrachtung der Natur von Fähigkeiten, warum der erste Fall ein Beispiel für einen Erfolg ist, der auf Tugend beruht, der zweite Fall dagegen nicht. Das ist der wichtige Unterschied zwischen den beiden Fällen und die Erklärung dafür, dass wir im zweiten Fall kein Wissen zuschreiben.

Erinnern wir uns an die oben verteidigte Behauptung, dass Fähigkeiten im Allgemeinen die folgende Struktur aufweisen:

> S hat eine Fähigkeit $F(R/B)$ relativ zu einer Umgebung U = In einer Menge von einander in relevanter Hinsicht nahen Welten W, in denen S sich unter B und in U befindet, hat S eine hohe Erfolgsrate darin, R zu erreichen.

Wie diese Struktur auszufüllen ist, hängt, wie wir festgestellt haben, von der fraglichen Fähigkeit ab. So werden beispielsweise unterschiedliche Fähigkeiten unterschiedliche R als die relevanten Erfolge festlegen, die diesen Fähigkeiten entsprechen. Ebenso werden unterschiedliche Fähigkeiten unterschiedliche Bedingungen, die für die Ausübung der fraglichen Fähigkeit relevant sind, festlegen. Die Bedingungen, zum Beispiel unter denen man von einem guten Schlagmann erwartet, dass er den Baseball trifft, unterscheiden sich von den Bedingungen, unter denen man von einem guten Sänger erwartet, einen Ton zu treffen. Die Spezifikation der relevanten Werte für R, B und U hängen des weiteren vom Kontext ab: Wenn ich sage, Jeter sei ein guter Schlagmann, so meine ich nicht ganz dasselbe, als wenn ich sage, mein siebenjähriger Sohn sei ein guter Schlagmann (was er übrigens tatsächlich ist).

Wir können diese Überlegungen wie folgt auf Whitcombs zwei Beispiele anwenden: Die Fähigkeit, ein Ziel zu treffen, ist wie jede andere Fähigkeit relativ zu Bedingungen definiert, die sich für diese Art von Fähigkeit eignen. Insbesondere verlangen wir nicht, dass ein Bogenschütze unter Bedingungen (relativ zu einer bestimmten Umgebung) zuverlässig ist, zu denen Strolche gehören, die Pfeile gewichtet. Dementsprechend gelten Welten, in denen manipulierende Strolche die Leistung beeinflussen, nicht als relevant für die Bestimmung, ob S die fragliche Fähigkeit hat, selbst dann nicht, wenn die manipulierenden Strolche in der tatsächlichen Welt von S auftreten oder wenn die Welten,

---

19 Ebd.

in denen sie die Leistung von S beeinflussen, entsprechend einer anderen Ordnung „nahe" sind. Es verhält sich ganz ähnlich wie bei Jeters Fähigkeit, Baseballs im Yankee Stadium zu schlagen – es spielt keine Rolle, ob sich im Stadium ein Trickbetrüger aufhält, der leicht das Licht abschalten könnte.

Bei intellektuellen Fähigkeiten sieht die Situation allerdings anders aus. Hier kommt es darauf an, wie sich das Manipulieren der Information durch Strolche, die sich in der Umgebung aufhalten, auf die Leistung von S auswirken würde. Gegeben die Natur und der Zweck unseres Wissensbegriffs, kommt es hier wesentlich darauf an, ob S solche Aspekte seiner Umgebung zuverlässig bewältigen kann. Das ist auch der Grund, weshalb wir in dem Zeitungsfall sagen können, dass S die Wahrheit nicht aufgrund seiner Fähigkeit glaubt. Relativ zu der Umgebung, in der er sich befindet, hat S nicht einmal die Fähigkeit, zu einer wahren Überzeugung der relevanten Art zu kommen.

Nun könnten wir das Beispiel mit den Bogenschützen so abändern, dass in ihrer Umgebung keine Betrüger auftreten und kein absichtlicher Betrug in „nahen" Welten stattfindet. Das Vorherrschen gewichteter Pfeile in der Umgebung beispielsweise könnte das Ergebnis eines unbeabsichtigten mechanischen Versagens im Herstellungsprozess sein. Aber die Erklärung bleibt dieselbe – die Fähigkeit von S, das Ziel zu treffen, wird nicht durch seine Leistung bei mangelhafter Ausrüstung definiert. Aber die Fähigkeit, wahre Überzeugungen auszubilden *wird* dagegen durch seine Leistung bei irreführenden Quellen in der Umgebung definiert.

Zum Abschluss möchte ich noch einen weiteren Fall betrachten. Stellen wir uns ein Tom-Grabit-Beispiel vor, bei dem S sieht, wie Tom ein Buch aus der Bibliothek entwendet.[20] In dieser Variante des Beispiels hat Tom keinen Zwillingsbruder, aber dafür eine verrückte Mutter, die behauptet, er hätte einen. Die Geschichte der Mutter ist der Polizei wohlbekannt, die ebenfalls weiß, dass die Mutter verrückt ist und dass Tom keinen Zwillingsbruder hat. Dieses Beispiel ist analog zu dem mit der Zeitung, bei dem nur wenige irreführende Zeitungsexemplare im Umlauf sind und jeder davon weiß und weiß, dass in Wirklichkeit *p* der Fall ist. S liest eine nicht manipulierte Zeitung und glaubt auf dieser Grundlage wahrheitsgemäß, dass p. In der Literatur findet sich die Tendenz, in einem derartigen Falle, Wissen zuzugestehen. Wir gestehen

---

[20] Jonathan Kvanvig (2003) führt es als Beispiel gegen eine tugendtheoretische Auffassung an.

mit anderen Worten dann bereitwilliger Wissen zu, wenn die potentiell irreführende Evidenz anderen wohlbekannt ist.

Ich möchte hierfür folgende Erklärung anbieten, die sich abermals die Vorstellung zunutze macht, dass Wissenszuschreibungen dazu gebraucht werden, (a) gute Information und (b) gute Informationsquellen zu kennzeichnen. Insofern, als wir uns auf den Zweck (b) konzentrieren, tendieren wir dazu, streng zu sein und darauf zu achten, welche Leistungen S in der relevanten Umgebung erbringen würde. Insofern wir uns auf (a) konzentrieren, tendieren wir dazu, uns dann zu entspannen, wenn sich *p* bereits „im Fluss" guter Informationen befindet. Wir schreiben mit anderen Worten S dann bereitwilliger Wissen zu, wenn die fragliche Information bereits wohlbekannt ist.

Dieselben Überlegungen erklären, warum wir in manchen Fällen bereitwilliger Leuten Wissen zuschreiben, die auf Fragen antworten, deren Antworten bekannt sind, wie zum Beispiel in einer Prüfungssituation. Wenn ein Kind die Antwort gibt, dass Providence die Hauptstadt von Rhode Island ist, sagen wir häufig ohne zu zögern, dass es dies wisse. Angenommen aber, unser Augenmerk richte sich nicht darauf, ob das Kind die richtige Antwort gibt, sondern vielmehr auf seine Fähigkeiten. Jetzt werden wir wahrscheinlich nicht so leicht sagen, dass es dies wisse – jetzt wollen wir wissen, ob es geraten hat.

Ich komme zum Schluss. Zu Beginn dieses Artikels habe ich drei Einwände gegen die Ansicht erörtert, dass Wissen eine Art von Erfolg ist, der aus Fähigkeiten resultiert. Danach habe ich zwei Ideen vorgestellt, mit deren Hilfe diese Einwände entkräftet werden sollten. Die erste Idee betraf die Natur beziehungsweise Metaphysik von Fähigkeiten. Genauer gesagt: Fähigkeiten im Allgemeinen sind dispositionale Eigenschaften, die eine charakteristische Natur aufweisen. Die zweite Idee betraf den Zweck von Wissen. Genauer gesagt: Wissenszuschreibungen dienen dazu, gute Information und gute Informationsquellen zum Gebrauch in praktischen Überlegungen zu kennzeichnen. Indem wir diese Ideen mit der hier vertretenen Auffassung von Wissen verbinden, so habe ich behauptet, verhelfen wir dieser dazu, die gegen sie vorgebrachten Einwände zu entkräften.[21,22]

---

21 Ich danke Berit Brogaard, Jeremy Fantl, John Hawthorne, Jennifer Lackey, Matt McGrath, Duncan Pritchard, Joe Salerno, Ernest Sosa und Dennis Whitcomb für hilfreiche Hinweise und Bemerkungen zu früheren Fassungen und vergleichbaren Themen.
22 Aus dem Englischen übersetzt von Erich Ammereller.

References

Conee/Feldman (1998): Earl Conee/Richard Feldman, „The Generality Problem for Reliabilism", in: *Philosophical Studies* 89, 1–29.
Craig (1999): Edward Craig, *Knowledge and the State of Nature*, New York.
Fantl/McGrath (2002): Jeremy Fantl/Matthew McGrath, „Evidence, Pragmatics, and Justification", in: *Philosophical Review* 111, 6–94.
Greco (1999): John Greco, „Agent Reliabilism", in: *Philosophical Perspectives* 13.
Greco (2003): John Greco, „Knowledge as Credit for True Belief", in: M. DePaul et al. (eds.), *Intellectual Virtue: Perspectives from Ethics and Epistemology*, Oxford.
Greco (2009): John Greco, „The Value Problem", in: A. Haddock/A. Millar/D. Pritchard, *Epistemic Value*, Oxford.
Greco (2008): John Greco, „What's Wrong with Contextualism?", in: *Philosophical Quarterly* 58, 416–436.
Hawthorne (2004): John Hawthorne, *Knowledge and Lotteries*, Oxford.
Heller (1995): Mark Heller, „The Simple Solution to the Generality Problem", in: *Nous* 29, 501–515.
Kvanvig (2003): Jonathan Kvanvig, *The Value of Knowledge and the Pursuit of Understanding*, Cambridge.
Lackey (2004): Jennifer Lackey, *Review of M. DePaul and L. Zagzebski (eds.) (2003): Intellectual Virtue*, Notre Dame.
Lackey (2007): Jenniger Lackey, „Why We Don't Deserve Credit for Everything We Know", *Synthese* 158, 345–361.
Lehrer (2000): Keith Lehrer, *Theory of Knowledge*, 2nd edition, Westview Press.
Pritchard (2005): Duncan Pritchard, *Epistemic Luck*, Oxford.
Riggs (2002): Wayne Riggs, „Reliability and the Value of Knowledge", in: *Philosophy and Phenomenological Research* 64, 79–96.
Sosa (1991): Ernest Sosa, *Knowledge in Perspective*, Cambridge.
Stanley (2005): Jason Stanley, *Knowledge and Practical Interests*, Oxford.
Whitcomb (manuskript): Dennis Whitcomb, *Knowledge, Virtue, and Truth*, typescript.
Williamson (2002): Timothy Williamson, *Knowledge and Its Limits*, Oxford.
Zagzebski (1996): Linda Zagzebski, *Virtues of the Mind*, Cambridge.

The Genealogy of the Concept of Knowledge and Anti-Luck Virtue Epistemology

Duncan Pritchard

1. Craig on the genealogy of the concept of knowledge

In a highly influential work, Edward Craig has argued for a distinctive way of approaching the theory of knowledge, one that looks to what we might broadly speaking call the *genealogy* of the concept of knowledge.[1] His idea is that instead of conducting the traditional epistemological enterprise whereby we reflect on our ordinary usage of the concept of knowledge and then try to figure out how best to analyse the concept in light of this usage, we should instead begin by reflecting on what practical purpose the concept of knowledge might serve and proceed from that starting-point. To this end, Craig asks us to consider an imaginary society of cognitive agents who are very similar to us except that they lack the concept of knowledge. Like us, these agents need true beliefs in order to successfully navigate their environment, and they can either acquire such true beliefs via their own on-board cognitive resources (e.g., their perceptual faculties) or they can make use of the on-board cognitive resources of others in the community by seeking them out as informants. Here is the question that Craig asks: what would prompt such a society which lacks the concept of knowledge to introduce it?

Craig's suggestion is that it would be very useful in such a community to have the conceptual resources to flag reliable informants. After all, if one is forced to depend only on one's own on-board cognitive resources then one will be severely limited in the true beliefs that one can form about one's environment. But if making use of others in the community as informants is to assist us in this regard then it had better

---

1 Cf. Craig (1990). I say that the proposal is 'broadly speaking' genealogical because while Craig does consider the question of what practical purpose might have conceivably prompted us to acquire such a concept, he is not offering a historical account of how this concept came into being.

be the case that these informants are reliable, since otherwise they could just as well be leading us astray rather than furnishing us with true beliefs. We could thus imagine a concept very like knowledge – a kind of proto-knowledge concept – being employed for just this purpose. Call this proto-knowledge, 'knowledge*', and call anyone who possesses knowledge* a 'knower*'. The idea is then that it would be useful to label good informants as knowers* with regard to the range of propositions which they are good informants about, and accordingly to label the accurate information that they offer on subjects about which they are good informants, knowledge*.

So, for example, imagine that John lives on a hill and so has a particularly good view of what is happening in the valley below (and that he is generally truthful and helpful, etc.,). He would thus be a reliable informant when it comes to a range of propositions concerning what is happening in the valley. It would clearly be practically useful for us to flag the fact that John is a good informant in this regard, and we can do this by calling him a knower* as regards these propositions, in that his true beliefs in these propositions amount to knowledge*.

Note that knowledge* is not yet the same as our concept of knowledge. For one thing, this concept only applies to other people's true beliefs, while we also use the concept of knowledge to classify our own beliefs. In addition, in deciding whether an agent is a knower* we are only assessing how good an informant is relative to the actual circumstances that she finds herself in – i.e., the 'live' error-possibilities that are in play in her environment. In the case of John just described, for example, all that is at issue is whether he has a good view of the valley and the ability (and inclination) to make use of this advantage. The salient error-possibilities when it comes to the question of whether he has knowledge* are thus such things as whether there is something in his environment which is obscuring his view (a heavy fog, say). Note, however, that our concept of knowledge treats a far greater range of error-possibilities as salient. In particular, it is also responsive to potential error-possibilities, even if they are not actual. So, for example, we do not treat someone as having knowledge if they formed their cognitive success is due to luck, even if in the actual circumstances that obtained there was in fact no impediment to the acquisition of true belief (we will consider an example – the 'Barney case – which illustrates this point in §3).

Interestingly, however, we would expect the proto-concept which is designed to pick out reliable informants to evolve over time so that it begins to resemble our concept of knowledge. For example, we could imagine knowledge★ ultimately being used to classify oneself and not just others, and the application of the concept being 'stretched' so that it is responsive to non-actual but potential error-possibilities (a process that Craig calls *objectification*). Over time, then, we would expect knowledge★ to evolve into knowledge.

Call this Craig-style story about the genealogy of the concept of knowledge the *genealogical account*. Many philosophers find the genealogical account very compelling, at least in broad outline.[2] That is, while many will quibble over the details, I think most epistemologists would be inclined to grant the general thesis of the genealogical account that the fundamental point of the concept of knowledge is to flag reliable informants.[3] My goal in this paper is not to defend the genealogical account, but rather to explore what consequences this widely endorsed view has for our thinking about knowledge since, as we will see, I think this proposal may well end up supporting a very different account of knowledge than many suppose.

2. From the genealogical account to virtue epistemology

On the face of it, the genealogical account would seem to favour those theories of knowledge which put reliable cognitive abilities at the centre of their theory. This is because a necessary condition of a reliable informant is surely that the informant forms her beliefs in the target propositions via her own reliable on-board cognitive abilities. Accordingly, if the fundamental purpose of the concept of knowledge is to flag reliable informants, then one would expect any viable theory of knowledge to make essential appeal to cognitive abilities.

In the contemporary epistemological literature those theories of knowledge which make essential appeal to reliable cognitive abilities

---

[2] Although Craig's proposal has been highly influential within contemporary epistemology, until quire recently there have been relatively few published discussions of it. For some useful discussions of this proposal, see Lane (1999), Williams (2002), Neta (2006), Greco (2007); (2008), Fricker (2007); (2010), Kusch (2009); (2011), Kappel (2010), Gelfert (2011), Henderson (2011), Kelp (2011) and Kornblith (2011).

[3] For two sceptical treatments of the genealogical account, see Kelp (2011) and Kornblith (2011).

are known as *virtue epistemologies*.[4] Thus we might conclude from the foregoing that the genealogical account lends support for virtue epistemology. In general terms, I think this is entirely correct, though since there are a wide range of virtue-theoretic proposals in this regard this still leaves an awful lot of room for further discussion. In particular, it will be a further question whether the genealogical account lends support for a particular form of virtue epistemology.

Before we get to this further question, however, let us first explore in a little more detail the motivation (the implications of the genealogical account aside) for having an ability condition play a central role in one's theory of knowledge. It is certainly the case that we have a strong intuition that knowledge demands cognitive ability. This can be brought out quite nicely by considering cases where agents are forming beliefs which are guaranteed to be true but where this cognitive success in no way reflects the cognitive abilities of the agent concerned. In such cases we are strongly disinclined to attribute knowledge.

Consider first the following case, which we will call 'Temp':

Temp
Temp forms his beliefs about the temperature in the room by consulting a thermometer. His beliefs, so formed, are highly reliable, in that any belief he forms on this basis will always be correct. Moreover, he has no reason for thinking that there is anything amiss with this thermometer. But the thermometer is in fact broken, and is fluctuating randomly within a given range. Unbeknownst to Temp, there is an agent hidden in the room who is in control of the thermostat whose job it is to ensure that every time Temp consults the thermometer the 'reading' on the thermometer corresponds to the temperature in the room.[5]

---

4 Note that this is to construe virtue epistemology in rather broad fashion, albeit in a way that I think will be familiar to many readers. For example, this characterisation of virtue epistemology would treat Plantinga's (1993) 'proper function' account of knowledge as a kind of virtue epistemology, even though he has explicitly disavowed this description of his view. Clearly, though, Plantinga is here thinking of virtue epistemology as involving more than just the idea that the employment of reliable cognitive abilities is central to the acquisition of knowledge. For some of the key defences of virtue epistemology, see Sosa (1991); (2007); (2009), Kvanvig (1992), Montmarquet (1993), Zagzebski (1996); (1999) and Greco (1999); (2000); (2009*a*). For two very useful overviews of the literature on virtue epistemology, see Axtell (1997) and Greco/Turri (2009).

5 I put forward, and discuss, the Temp case in a number of places. See, for example, Pritchard (2009*b*), ch. 2; (2010) and Pritchard, Millar/Haddock (2010), ch. 3.

I take it we have a strong intuition that Temp cannot acquire knowledge in this fashion, since one simply cannot gain knowledge of the temperature of the room by consulting what is, unbeknownst to one, a broken thermometer. Interestingly, as this example demonstrates, this remains the case even if even the scenario is explicitly set up so that Temp is *guaranteed* to be correct in the beliefs that he forms by consulting this broken thermometer. The problem is that even despite this guarantee of cognitive success there is simply the wrong direction of fit between Temp's beliefs and the corresponding facts, in that the facts are changing to fit with what Temp believes rather than Temp's beliefs being responsive to the facts. This is because Temp's cognitive success is nothing to do with his cognitive abilities and everything to do with a feature of his environment – *viz.*, the hidden 'helper'. In contrast, in genuine cases of knowledge the cognitive success in question is significantly related to the cognitive abilities of the agent.[6]

Consider also this second case, which we will call 'Alvin':

Alvin
Alvin has a brain lesion. An odd fact about the brain lesion that Alvin has, however, is that it causes the sufferer to form the (true) belief that he has a brain lesion. Accordingly, Alvin truly believes that he has a brain lesion.[7]

Given how Alvin is forming his beliefs he is guaranteed to be right. Clearly, though, Alvin does not have knowledge in this case, and the reason for this is that his beliefs are true *despite* his cognitive abilities and not as a result of them. Indeed, the Alvin case is an example of a *cognitive malfunction*, albeit a cognitive malfunction that just happens to

---

6   There is, admittedly, a certain amount of 'noise' in this example. After all, it is not as if Temp is playing no part at all in the cognitive process that results in his cognitive success – for one thing, his perceptual abilities are presumably functioning as they should be as part of his checking of the reading on the (broken) thermometer. Even so, I think we can easily see that whatever cognitive ability Temp is displaying in this case it is irrelevant to his cognitive success. Nonetheless, if one prefers a 'cleaner' example then the obvious way to do this is to make the epistemic helper a benevolent demon of some sort. For example, we could imagine an agent forming beliefs in an epistemically terrible fashion – by tossing coins, say – but who is guaranteed to be cognitively successful because the benevolent demon will reliably ensure that whatever our hero believes is true. As with Temp, then, there is the wrong direction of fit between belief and fact, in that the facts are responsive to what the agent believes rather than *vice versa*.
7   This case is due to Plantinga (1993), 199.

be reliable. As such, the reliability of this belief-forming process cannot reflect the cognitive abilities of the agent concerned.

Cases like this demonstrate that one of the core intuitions we have about knowledge concerns the fact that knowledge entails a cognitive success that is in some substantive sense due to the agent's reliable cognitive ability. Call this the *ability intuition*. The genealogical account can explain why we have this intuition, since given that account we would expect our concept of knowledge to be responsive to whether an agent is forming her beliefs in a way that reflects her reliable cognitive abilities. This is because a reliable informant about a certain subject matter will be an informant who is forming true beliefs about that subject matter via her reliable cognitive abilities. On this view, then, it is no wonder that we have the ability intuition.

So the genealogical account can explain why we have the ability intuition, and thereby offer support for those virtue-theoretic accounts of knowledge which place reliable cognitive abilities at their heart. On the face of it, however, it also seems to offer support for a specifically robust rendering of virtue epistemology, whereby the appropriate employment of reliable cognitive abilities is not only necessary for knowledge, but also (along with true belief) *sufficient*. After all, if it were to turn out that one's virtue-theoretic account of knowledge invoked other conditions beside an ability condition, then so long as one accepted the genealogical account one would be faced with a puzzle – *viz.*, why did the concept of knowledge evolve out of the concept of knowledge* in such a way that it required a further condition over and above an ability condition?

In order to make this concern vivid, suppose that one offered a theory of knowledge which incorporated both an ability condition and a further condition which is specifically invoked in order to deal with Gettier-style cases.[8] This would be an understandable way to go, since Gettier-style cases often do seem to involve agents appropriately employing their reliable cognitive abilities in order to attain a true belief, and yet such cases are explicitly designed to elicit the intuition that the cognitive success at issue is just too lucky to count as knowledge. Accordingly, it would seem that an ability condition will not by itself suffice, with true belief, for knowledge.

---

8   This is just the sort of view that Greco (1999); (2000) proposes in his early work on virtue epistemology.

Consider, for instance, the following example, which we will call 'Roddy':

Roddy
Using his reliable perceptual faculties, Roddy non-inferentially forms a true belief that there is a sheep in the field before him. His belief is also true. Unbeknownst to Roddy, however, the truth of his belief is completely unconnected to the manner in which he acquired this belief since the object he is looking at in the field is not a sheep at all, but rather a sheep-shaped object which is obscuring from view the real sheep hidden behind.[9]

Intuitively, Roddy is employing his reliable cognitive abilities entirely appropriately and coming, thereby, to form a true belief in the target proposition. And yet equally intuitively he lacks knowledge, in that it is simply a matter of luck that his belief is true, and luck of this sort seems entirely incompatible with knowledge possession. Thus, in order to deal with cases like that of Roddy, one might be inclined to supplement one's virtue-theoretic account of knowledge with some sort of condition which excludes these cases, such as an anti-luck condition of some sort (i.e., that it should not be the case that one's belief is only true as a matter of luck). The problem, however, is that from the point of view of the genealogical account it would seem to be just plain mysterious why we would have ended up with a concept of knowledge which treated knowledge as being mostly about the employment of reliable cognitive ability, but which also demanded that a further codicil be met so as to avoid Gettier-style cases.

Interestingly, a dominant trend in virtue epistemology has been to opt for a more robust rendering of this thesis which does away with the need to appeal to any further epistemic condition over and above the ability condition. Call any such view a *robust virtue epistemology*, in contrast to a *modest virtue epistemology* which also makes appeal to further (non-virtue-theoretic) epistemic conditions. Clearly one advantage of robust virtue epistemology is its theoretical simplicity when compared with its modest counterpart.[10] Moreover, given the foregoing it

---

9 This case is adapted from one offered by Chisholm (1977), 105.
10 Another theoretical advantage is its apparent ability to be able to offer a compelling account of the distinctive value of knowledge. See, for example, Greco (2009*b*) for a clear statement of this putative advantage of the view. For critical discussion of this general claim, see Pritchard (2009*d*); cf. Pritchard (2008); (2009*a*); (2009*c*) and Pritchard, Millar/Haddock (2010). See also Pritchard (2007*b*); (2007*c*).

would also seem that the genealogical account lends additional *prima facie* support to going down the simpler robust virtue-theoretic route.[11]

If robust virtue epistemology were a sound position, then this would be all to the good, but unfortunately, as we'll see in the next section, this proposal faces some pretty stiff problems. We are thus faced with a puzzle, in that the genealogical account seems to favour robust virtue epistemology over modest virtue epistemology, and yet robust virtue epistemology seems unsustainable. Resolving that puzzle will be the task of §4.

3. Contra robust virtue epistemology

As just noted, it is without question that robust virtue epistemology is a proposal with many theoretical virtues. Unfortunately, it is also a proposal that faces some pretty stiff problems too. Before we get to the problems facing the view, however, we first need to explain what a robust virtue epistemology is, and in particular how it evades the problem posed by Getter-style cases that was noted earlier.

In essence, robust virtue epistemologies grant that knowledge is more than just the conjunction of cognitive success (i.e., true belief) and reliable cognitive ability, since a mere conjunction of cognitive success and reliable cognitive ability will not exclude Gettier-style cases (as, indeed, we saw above). Nonetheless, they maintain that we do not need to introduce a further non-virtue-theoretic condition – such as a Gettier-excluding anti-luck condition – into our theory of knowledge. Instead, what is required is simply that we specify the relationship that the cognitive success must bear to the reliable cognitive ability – *viz.*, that the cognitive success should *be because of* the target reliable cognitive ability.[12]

The natural way to read the 'because of' here, I take it, is in causal explanatory terms, such that what is being claimed is that the cognitive success is primarily explained by, and hence primarily creditable to, the

---

11 Greco (2008); (2009a) is one proponent of robust virtue epistemology who has explicitly argued that the genealogical account lends support to this kind of view.
12 For the key virtue-theoretic proposals of this sort, see Sosa (1991); (2007); (2009), Zagzebski (1996); (1999) and Greco (2009a); cf. Greco (2003); (2007a); (2008).

relevant reliable cognitive ability.[13] So construed, this modification to the view seems to comfortably solve the problem posed for modest virtue epistemology by the Gettier-style cases, since these cases do appear to involve a cognitive success which is precisely *not* primarily creditable to the reliable cognitive ability of the subject but rather explained by factors entirely outwith the subject's cognitive agency. In the Roddy case, for example, what explains Roddy's cognitive success is not his reliable perceptual abilities but merely the fact that there happens to be a sheep hidden from view behind the sheep-shaped object that he is looking at.

So far so good for robust virtue epistemology, then. The problem comes once we start to consider other cases of knowledge-undermining epistemic luck beside the cases that fit the standard Gettier-style cases. In particular, consider the following familiar case, which we will call 'Barney':

Barney
Using his reliable perceptual faculties, Barney non-inferentially forms a true belief that the object in front of him is a barn. Barney is indeed looking at a barn. Unbeknownst to Barney, however, he is in an epistemically unfriendly environment when it comes to making observations of this sort, since most objects that look like barns in these parts are in fact barn façades.[14]

Now Barney's cognitive success is clearly lucky, given the environment he is in. After all, most of the things that look to Barney like barns in this locale are in fact barn façades, and hence he is very lucky to have formed a true belief in this scenario. On this score, the case is analogous to a normal Gettier-style case like Roddy. Where it differs, however, is in how the agent concerned really is seeing what he takes himself to see – *viz.*, he really is looking at a genuine barn. The contrast with the Roddy case is instructive here, since it is vital to that case that Roddy is not looking at what he thinks he is looking at, even if the belief he forms as a result of what he sees happens to be true.

---

13 This is the line taken by Greco (2008); (2009a), for example. In contrast, Zagzebski e.g., (1999) treats this relation as an undefined primitive, while Sosa (2007); (2009) understands it in terms of the manifestation of a power. For reasons of space, and because I discuss them at some length elsewhere – see, in particular, Pritchard (2009a); (2010) and Pritchard, Millar/Haddock (2010), chs. 2 – 3 – I will not be exploring these alternative proposals here.

14 The barn-façade case was first put forward in print by Goldman (1976), who credits the example to Carl Ginet.

This point is important since it makes a big difference to our assessment of what explains Barney's cognitive success. For while we saw above that Roddy's cognitive success is clearly not primarily creditable to his reliable cognitive ability, given that Barney really is seeing a genuine barn it does seem that his cognitive success *is* primarily creditable to his reliable cognitive ability. After all, and unlike the Roddy case, it is not as if there is something other than his reliable cognitive ability which is primarily creditable for his cognitive success; instead, it is the fact that he is appropriately using his reliable perceptual faculties in observing the barn which explains why he truly believes that there is a barn before him. But if that's right, then it seems that merely appealing to a 'because of' relation will not suffice to ensure that one's robust virtue epistemology can deal with all cases of knowledge-undermining epistemic luck.[15]

If this were not a serious enough problem for robust virtue epistemology, a second difficulty is waiting in the wings. Consider the following example, which will call 'Jenny':

Jenny
Jenny gets off the train in an unfamiliar city and asks the first person that she meets for directions. The person that she asks is indeed knowledgeable about the area, and helpfully gives her directions. Jenny believes what she is told and goes on her way to her intended destination.[16]

According to standard views in the epistemology of testimony, Jenny gains knowledge in this case. Indeed, it is usually argued that if we are unwilling to ascribe knowledge in such cases where an agent trusts a knowledgeable informant, then we will have to endorse a widespread scepticism about much of our testimonial knowledge, given that so much of it is acquired in a similar fashion. The problem, however, is that it is hard to see how crediting knowledge to Jenny can be squared with robust virtue epistemology. After all, given that she forms her be-

---

15 Elsewhere, I diagnose this inability on the part of robust virtue epistemology to handle the Barney case in terms of a more general failure on the part of robust virtue epistemology to recognise an important distinction between two types of knowledge-undermining epistemic luck, what I call 'intervening' and 'environmental' epistemic luck (where the kind of epistemic luck specifically at issue in the Barney case is of the latter variety). For more on this distinction and its application to robust virtue epistemology, see Pritchard, Millar/Haddock (2010), ch. 2 and Pritchard (2010).
16 This case is adapted from one offered by Lackey (2007), albeit to demonstrate a slightly different point.

lief by, for the most part, trusting the word of another, Jenny's cognitive success does not seem to be explained by *her* reliable cognitive abilities specifically at all, but rather by her informant's. If that's right, then it seems that robust virtue epistemology should deny knowledge in these cases, despite this being a counterintuitive result, and accordingly align themselves with a 'sceptical' view regarding the epistemology of testimony.[17]

Crucially, notice that this problem exacerbates the difficulty posed by the kind of knowledge-undermining epistemic luck in play in the Barney case. This is because while the Barney case shows that robust virtue epistemology is too *weak* a theory of knowledge, in that it wrongly counts cases of cognitive success as knowledge, the Jenny case shows that robust virtue epistemology is also too *strong*, in that it wrongly prevents certain cases of cognitive success counting as knowledge. Collectively, then, these two problems pull the proponent of robust virtue epistemology in opposing directions, since they call for both a weakening and a strengthening of the view. For this reason, it will be very difficult for the defender of robust virtue epistemology to offer a principled defence of the position which simultaneously deals with both difficulties.[18]

There is a good reason why robust virtue epistemology faces these challenges, and it concerns the fact that there is no appropriate rendering of the ability condition on knowledge which can deal with the quandary posed by knowledge-undermining epistemic luck. As the Barney case illustrates, even if you in effect 'beef-up' the ability condition by adding a 'because of' relation between the target cognitive success and the target reliable cognitive ability, it is still possible for the cognitive success in question to be subject to knowledge-undermining epistemic luck. But the problem is that in beefing up the ability condition in order to try to eliminate knowledge-undermining epistemic luck the proponent of robust virtue epistemology ends up with a theory of knowledge which is now unable to accommodate certain cases of *bona fide* knowledge, such as the testimonial knowledge at issue in the Jenny case.

---

17 Despite being counterintuitive, this view of the epistemology of testimony—known as *reductionism*—is not without its adherents. See especially Fricker e.g., (1995).
18 I explore in detail elsewhere how proponents of robust virtue epistemology might respond to these problems, and why such responses are unsatisfactory. See especially, Pritchard, Millar/Haddock (2010), chs. 2–4 and Pritchard (2010).

I suggest that what this demonstrates is the need for an anti-luck condition in one's theory of knowledge in addition to an ability condition. Moreover, I maintain that this way of thinking about knowledge is not an *ad hoc* response to the Gettier problem, but rather reflects the fact that these conditions are responding to two distinct master intuitions that we have about knowledge. The first is the ability intuition that we noted above. The second is the *anti-luck intuition* that knowledge requires cognitive success that isn't due to luck. Now at first blush one might think that these two intuitions are essentially the same, in that for one's cognitive success to be due to one's ability as the ability intuition demands is surely for it to not be due to luck, and for one's cognitive success to not be due to luck as the anti-luck intuition demands is surely for it to be due to one's cognitive ability. Closer inspection, however, reveals that they make distinct demands on one's theory of knowledge.

We have already see that one can satisfy the ability intuition in a robust fashion and yet still fail to satisfy the anti-luck intuition – that was precisely the moral of the Barney case discussed above. We can also illustrate how one can satisfy the anti-luck intuition without thereby satisfying the ability intuition by appealing to the Temp case that we outlined in §2 in support of the ability intuition. For recall that what was significant about that case was that the agent concerned was actually *guaranteed* to be cognitive successful, given how he was forming his beliefs. Accordingly, it cannot possibly be the case that his cognitive success is a matter of luck. Nonetheless, Temp does not acquire knowledge in this case, and the reason for this, as we noted, is that his cognitive success is not due to his reliable cognitive abilities at all, but rather entirely due to the assistance of a hidden helper.[19]

Given that these two intuitions impose distinct demands on one's theory of knowledge, it follows that one will need distinct epistemic conditions in order to accommodate them. We are thus led to a theory of knowledge that has both an anti-luck and an ability condition, a view that I call *anti-luck virtue epistemology*. Since it incorporates an ability condition this view is a form of modest virtue epistemology, albeit one which gives equal weight to both the anti-luck condition and the ability condition (i.e., it does not regard the anti-luck condition as being a

---

19 One moral of cases like Temp is thus that an anti-luck epistemology which did not incorporate an ability condition would be doomed to failure. For discussion of anti-luck epistemology, see Pritchard (2005); (2007*a*).

mere codicil which is tacked-onto one's theory of knowledge in order to deal with certain problem cases involving knowledge-undermining epistemic luck). I defend this proposal at length elsewhere,[20] but it ought to be clear from the foregoing what advantages such a view has.

To begin with, notice that if you have an anti-luck condition in your theory of knowledge then you can thereby deal with those troublesome epistemological cases which trade on knowledge-undermining luck, including both standard Gettier-style cases like Roddy and non-standard Gettier-style cases like Barney. For another, your ability condition will deal with those epistemological cases which trade on the ability intuition, such as Temp and Alvin. And since one has the anti-luck condition to appeal to, one does not need to beef-up one's ability condition in order to try to eliminate knowledge-undermining luck. Accordingly, one does not make the mistake made by robust virtue epistemology of setting the bar for knowledge too high and thereby excluding certain *bona fide* cases of knowledge, such that present in the Jenny case. In short, with both conditions working together in one's theory of knowledge, one is able to satisfactorily deal with a wide range of problem cases in epistemology.

There is, however, one point on which anti-luck virtue epistemology seems to be at a major theoretical disadvantage, and that concerns the motivation for the view. In particular, while I think it is undeniable that we have these two intuitions about knowledge and that they make distinct demands upon us, a worry still remains about why our concept of knowledge should incorporate these two discrete epistemic conditions. The puzzle seems to be exacerbated once one reflects on the plausibility of the genealogical account, for while that offers a cogent rationale for why we might have the ability condition, it does not seem to explain at all how a separate anti-luck condition may have come about. If that's right, then it is a fairly serious strike against anti-luck virtue epistemology.

More generally, we seem to be faced with a dilemma here. On the one hand, insofar as we accept the genealogical account then we seem to be led towards endorsing a form of robust virtue epistemology, a position which we have found to be untenable. On the other hand, insofar as we opt for the alternative anti-luck virtue epistemology which can

---

20 See especially, Pritchard, Millar/Haddock (2010), chs. 2–4 and Pritchard (2010).

avoid the problems facing robust virtue epistemology, then we seem to be forced to reject the highly intuitive genealogical account.

Fortunately, as we will see in the next section, there is a crucial ambiguity in the genealogical account, and once this is brought to light this account *does* offer a good explanation of why our concept of knowledge should have two separate epistemic conditions of this sort. On closer analysis, then, far from favouring robust virtue epistemology, the genealogical account in fact favours anti-luck virtue epistemology. Thus, the dilemma just set out is in fact entirely illusory, in that one does not need to choose between anti-luck virtue epistemology and the genealogical account.

4. Rethinking the genealogical account

The ambiguity that I have in mind in the genealogical account concerns the very notion of a reliable informant. In one sense, it can mean an informant who possesses a reliable cognitive ability with regard to the target subject matter (and who is willing to sincerely communicate what she believes, something that we will take for granted in what follows). In another sense, it means an informant whom one can rely on (i.e., whose information will not lead you astray). Now one might naturally think that this is a distinction without a difference, in that informants who possess reliable cognitive abilities in the sense just specified are thereby informants one can rely on, and *vice versa*. Closer inspection, however, reveals that first appearances are deceptive on this score. In order to see this, we just need to notice that it can be appropriate to rely on an informant who is forming her true belief via an unreliable cognitive ability, and also that it can be inappropriate to rely on an informant who nevertheless is forming a true belief via a reliable cognitive ability.

First, consider a potential informant who possesses a reliable cognitive ability as regards a certain subject matter but who is in an environment in which there exists a misleading defeater, one which you know about, but the prospective informant does not, and one which moreover you are unable to defeat. An example might be an informant who is a reliable barn detector, but where you have been given a misleading ground (e.g., false testimony from a good source) for supposing that the informant is in barn façade county. Given that this is a misleading defeater, the informant is in fact a *reliable* informant about the relevant subject matter. But given also that you know about the misleading defeater, and are aware that you are unable to defeat that defeater, would you be able to *rely on* this informant? Surely not.

The converse point also holds. In particular, we can imagine a case where there are compensating factors in play, known only to us, which mean that we can rely on the information presented to us by an informant even though this information is not the product of the informant's reliable cognitive abilities. Imagine, for example, an informant who thinks that they have clairvoyant powers, but in fact is mistaken on this score (and we know this). Suppose further that we also know that this informant's wife is a very powerful person who wants her husband to continue to believe that he has this power and hence does what she can, where possible, to make sure that events turn out in the way that her husband predicts. Finally, suppose that we know that the informant's wife can fix the result of any horse race. With this knowledge in hand, the testimony of the informant regarding who will win tomorrow's horse race would certainly be information that one could rely on, even though the informant's true belief in this regard is in no way the product of a reliable cognitive ability.

In general, what is key to both of these kinds of cases is the role that luck is playing. In cases in which the informant's relevant cognitive abilities are reliable but where we are nonetheless unable to rely on the information she provides, the problem is that a dose of bad epistemic luck is cancelling out the good epistemic luck that our informant possesses the relevant reliable cognitive abilities (and thus is in this sense a good informant). In the case described above, for example, this bad epistemic luck is the presence of the undefeated misleading defeater regarding the barn façades. In contrast, in cases in which the informant lacks the relevant reliable cognitive abilities but is nonetheless providing us with information that we can rely on, a dose of good epistemic luck on our part is cancelling out the poor epistemic luck that our informant lacks the relevant reliable cognitive abilities (and thus is in this sense a bad informant). In the 'clairvoyant' case described above, for example, this good epistemic luck is our knowledge of the compensating factors in play.

With this point in mind, it ought to be clear why this ambiguity in the idea of a reliable informant explains why the concept of knowledge that evolves from the proto-concept will generate *both* the anti-luck and the ability intuition. For as the range of cases which the concept of knowledge is meant to apply to widens, so the distinction will open up between good informants who are reliable and good informants that we can rely on, and we would expect the concept of knowledge that results to respect both sides of this distinction. In particular, examples where an agent possesses the relevant reliable cognitive abilities but where the presence of epistemic luck means that we would not be able to rely on this agent *qua* informant would not be counted as cases of knowledge. Similarly, those cases in which an agent forms a true belief in an epistemically friendly environment – such that any true belief so formed would not be subject to epistemic luck – would not be counted as cases of knowledge so long as the agent concerned failed to exhibit the relevant reliable cognitive abilities (even though we could rely on this agent *qua* informant). In short, the concept of knowledge that results will both (i) disallow cases of true belief as knowledge where the belief isn't appropriately due to the relevant cognitive abilities on the part of the agent, and (ii) disallow cases of true belief as knowledge where the truth of the belief is substantively due to luck.

A very plausible and popular story about the genealogy of the concept of knowledge thus lends support to anti-luck virtue epistemology after all, despite first appearances. In fact, if I am right that the goal of picking out reliable informants is ambiguous in the way just described, then contrary to the prevailing wisdom on this score, this 'just so' account of the concept of knowledge actually *favours* anti-luck virtue epistemology over rival proposals, such as robust virtue epistemology.

5. Concluding remarks

I was very open right from the off that my purpose here was not to defend the genealogical account, but merely to note its plausibility and consider what implications it had for our thinking about knowledge. I have now argued that, despite first appearances, such a proposal in fact lends support to the account of knowledge that I favour as opposed to a competing account. Nonetheless, the point remains that I have not offered a detailed defence of this claim, and so one might naturally be concerned that this 'result' is hostage to whether the genealogical account stands the test of time.

While this worry is, strictly speaking, entirely sound, I think we should be wary about overstating it. For one thing, let us not forget that there is as yet no competing proposal to the genealogical account available in the literature, and hence no alternative standard against which to evaluate the merits of anti-luck virtue epistemology on this score. Accordingly, it is hard to avoid taking the genealogical account as the default view. But a more important issue here is that the success of anti-luck virtue epistemology in dealing with cases that other popular theories of knowledge struggle with itself offers supporting grounds for the genealogical account, at least once we recognise, as I have argued here, that the notion of a reliable informant which is central to the genealogical account is crucially ambiguous. We thus have a highly plausible account of why we have the concept of knowledge that we do and a highly plausible account of knowledge itself which are mutually supporting. It is not then as if we have simply taken the genealogical account as read and then motivated anti-luck virtue epistemology as a result. Rather, we have independently motivated anti-luck virtue epistemology and then shown how it accords with the genealogical account, properly construed. In this sense, then, the genealogical account now enjoys *additional* theoretical support that it lacked when we began this project.[21]

References

Axtell (1997): Guy S. Axtell, "Recent Work in Virtue Epistemology", in: *American Philosophical Quarterly* 34, 410–30.

Chisholm (1977): Roderick M. Chisholm, *Theory of Knowledge*, 2nd edition, Englewood Cliffs/New Jersey.

Craig, (1990): Edward Craig, *Knowledge and the State of Nature: An Essay in Conceptual Synthesis*, Oxford.

Fricker (1995): Elizabeth Fricker, "Telling and Trusting: Reductionism and Anti-Reductionism in the Epistemology of Testimony", in: *Mind* 104, 393–411.

Fricker (2007): Miranda Fricker, *Epistemic Injustice: Power and the Ethics of Knowing*, Oxford.

Fricker (2010): Miranda Fricker, "Scepticism and the Genealogy of Knowledge: Situating Epistemology in Time", in: A. Haddock/A. Millar/D. H. Pritchard (eds.), *Social Epistemology*, Oxford, 51–68.

Gelfert (2011): Axel Gelfert, "Genealogies of the Concept of Knowledge and Their Cognitive-Ecological Dimension", in: *Episteme* 8, 67–82.

---

21 Thanks to David Bloor, Georgi Gardiner, Axel Gelfert, Mikkel Gerken, Sandy Goldberg, Alvin Goldman, Peter Graham, John Greco, David Henderson, Klemens Kappel, Hilary Kornblith, Martin Kusch, Christoph Kelp, Ram Neta and Shane Ryan for helpful discussion on related topics. Special thanks to Stefan Tolksdorf for detailed comments on an earlier version. This paper was written while I was in receipt of a Phillip Leverhulme Prize.

Goldman (1976): A. Goldman, 'Discrimination and Perceptual Knowledge', in: *Journal of Philosophy* 73, 771–91.
Greco (1999): John Greco, "Agent Reliabilism", in: *Philosophical Perspectives* 13, 273–96.
Greco(2000): John Greco, *Putting Skeptics in Their Place: The Nature of Skeptical Arguments and Their Role in Philosophical Inquiry*, Cambridge.
Greco(2003): John Greco, "Knowledge as Credit for True Belief", in: M. DePaul/L. Zagzebski (eds.), *Intellectual Virtue: Perspectives from Ethics and Epistemology*, Oxford, 111–34.
Greco(2007): John Greco, "The Nature of Ability and the Purpose of Knowledge", in: *Philosophical Issues* 17, 57–69.
Greco(2008): John Greco, "What's Wrong With Contextualism?", in: *The Philosophical Quarterly* 58, 416–36.
Greco(2009a): John Greco, *Achieving Knowledge*, Cambridge.
Greco(2009b): John Greco, "The Value Problem", in: A. Haddock/A. Millar/D. H. Pritchard (eds.), *Epistemic Value*, Oxford, 313–21.
Greco/Turri (2009): John Greco/John Turri, "Virtue Epistemology", in: E. Zalta (ed.), *Stanford Encyclopaedia of Philosophy*, http://plato.stanford.edu/entries/epistemology-virtue/.
Henderson (2011): David Henderson, "Gate-Keeping Contextualism", in: *Episteme* 8, 83–98.
Kappel (2010): Klemens Kappel, "On Saying that Someone Knows: Themes from Craig", in: A. Haddock/A. Millar/D. H. Pritchard (eds.), *Social Epistemology*, Oxford, 69–88.
Kornblith (2011): Hilary Kornblith, "Why Should We Care About the Concept of Knowledge?", in: *Episteme* 8, 38–52.
Kelp (2011): Christoph Kelp, "What's the Point of 'Knowledge' Anyway?", in: *Episteme* 8, 53–66.
Kusch (2009): Martin Kusch, "Testimony and the Value of Knowledge', in: A. Haddock/A. Millar/D. H. Pritchard (eds.), *Epistemic Value*, Oxford, 60–94.
Kusch(2011): Martin Kusch, "Knowledge and Certainties in the Epistemic State of Nature", in: *Episteme* 8, 6–23.
Kvanvig (1992): Jonathan L. Kvanvig, *The Intellectual Virtues and the Life of the Mind*, Savage/MD.
Lackey (2007): Jennifer Lackey, "Why We Don't Deserve Credit for Everything We Know", in: *Synthese* 158, 345–61.
Lane (1999): Melissa Lane, "States of Nature, Epistemic and Political", in: *Proceedings of the Aristotelian Society* 99, 211–24.
Montmarquet (1993): James A. Montmarquet, *Epistemic Virtue and Doxastic Responsibility*, Lanham/ NJ.
Neta (2006): Ram Neta, "Epistemology Factualized: New Contractarian Foundations for Epistemology", in: *Synthese* 150, 247–80.
Plantinga (1993): Alvin C. Plantinga, *Warrant: The Current Debate*, Oxford.
Pritchard (2005): Duncan H. Pritchard, *Epistemic Luck*, Oxford.
Pritchard (2007a): Duncan H. Pritchard, "Anti-Luck Epistemology", in: *Synthese* 158, 277–97.

Pritchard (2007b): Duncan H. Pritchard, "Recent Work on Epistemic Value", in: *American Philosophical Quarterly* 44, 85–110.
Pritchard (2007c): Duncan H. Pritchard, "The Value of Knowledge", in: E. Zalta (ed.), *Stanford Encyclopædia of Philosophy*, http://plato.stanford.edu/entries/knowledge-value/.
Pritchard (2008): Duncan H. Pritchard, "Radical Scepticism, Epistemic Luck and Epistemic Value", in: *Proceedings and Addresses of the Aristotelian Society* (suppl. vol.) 82, 19–41.
Pritchard (2009a): Duncan H. Pritchard, "Apt Performance and Epistemic Value", in: *Philosophical Studies* 143, 407–16.
Pritchard (2009b): Duncan H. Pritchard, *Knowledge*, London.
Pritchard (2009c): Duncan H. Pritchard, "Knowledge, Understanding and Epistemic Value", in: A. O'Hear (ed.), *Epistemology (Royal Institute of Philosophy Lectures)*, Cambridge, 19–43.
Pritchard (2009d): Duncan H. Pritchard, "The Value of Knowledge", in: *Harvard Review of Philosophy* 16, 2–19.
Pritchard (2010): Duncan H. Pritchard, "Anti-Luck Virtue Epistemology", forthcoming in: *The Journal of Philosophy*.
Pritchard/Millar/Haddock (2010): Duncan H. Pritchard, Alan Millar/Adrian Haddock, *The Nature and Value of Knowledge: Three Investigations*, Oxford.
Sosa (1991): Ernest Sosa, *Knowledge in Perspective: Selected Essays in Epistemology*, Cambridge.
Sosa (2007): Ernest Sosa, *A Virtue Epistemology: Apt Belief and Reflective Knowledge*, Oxford.
Sosa (2009): Ernest Sosa, *Reflective Knowledge: Apt Belief and Reflective Knowledge*, Oxford.
Williams (2002): Bernard Williams, *Truth and Truthfulness: An Essay in Genealogy*, Princeton.
Zagzebski (1996): Linda Zagzebski, *Virtues of the Mind: An Inquiry into the Nature of Virtue and the Ethical Foundations of Knowledge*, Cambridge.
Zagzebski (1999): Linda Zagzebski, "What is Knowledge?", in: J. Greco/E. Sosa (eds.), *The Blackwell Guide to Epistemology*, Oxford.

Knowledge, Abilities, and Epistemic Luck: What Is *Anti-Luck Virtue Epistemology* and What Can It Do?

Stefan Tolksdorf

1. Duncan Pritchard repeatedly defended the thesis that, when it comes to knowledge, there are two master intuitions, the connection of knowledge to abilities on the one hand, and in some way the incompatibility of knowledge and luck on the other, which both ought to find their way into our theories of knowledge. He writes:

> "Given that these two intuitions impose distinct demands on one's theory of knowledge, it follows that one will need distinct epistemic conditions in order to accommodate them. We are thus led to a theory of knowledge that has both an anti-luck and an ability condition, a view that I call *anti-luck virtue epistemology*."[1]

In this quote a theory of knowledge is hinted at that in the spirit of analytic philosophy presents a definition of knowledge in which two strains of present epistemology are connected with each other in a special way: anti-luck theories are married to virtue approaches.[2]

I shall pursue the question whether we actually need both conditions for a theory of knowledge. My thesis is: the anti-luck condition accomplishes no independent explanatory task, but already inheres in the ability condition.

2. How can the two master intuitions be more precisely characterised? What can be inferred from the phrases 'knowledge excludes luck' and 'knowledge arises from ability'? Let us begin with the reference to abilities, i. e. one through which it is supposed to be brought to expression that we regard knowledge as a sort of cognitive achievement and accomplishment for which the agent takes responsibility and deserves credit. For this reason, attributions of knowledge are normative

---

1   Cf. Pritchard (2011); also Pritchard (this volume); Pritchard (2010), ch. 2, 3.
2   Whoever rejects the strong demands of a conceptual analysis can regard the two master intuitions as *necessary* conditions of *paradigmatic* cases of knowledge.

moves in the epistemic language games, because, aside from the passive elements, there are also active aspects in the acquisition of knowledge, for example, the manifestation of a technique of knowledge, or an epistemic ability. The fundamental idea of virtue epistemology is, simply put, that knowledge is a special form of a more general phenomenon, namely success through abilities, which in turn means: knowledge is cognitive success (truth) through cognitive abilities (perception, memory, etc.). Or, to cite Greco: "S knows that p if and only if S believes the truth because S's belief that p is produced by intellectual ability".[3] If the success is based upon abilities, we speak of achievements. Knowledge is a type of achievement. Roger Federer's success when he plays a winning forehand can either be lucky or the result of his athletic competence. In the latter case we praise and honour him for it, and he enjoys the status of a special form of normativity. The analogy is intended to suggest that epistemic agents are to be regarded from a certain perspective as athletes, artisans or musicians. All these cases are about abilities.

The root of one strain of present day virtue epistemology lies in reliabilism. What is sought is, so to speak, *a more precisely determinable* class of reliable belief formation processes. It is necessary to determine the class more precisely, because there can be reliable processes at the sub-personal level that are neither part of the agent's character nor of his/her realm of action and that we do not regard as knowledge generating for that reason.[4] Reliable belief formation processes are therefore knowledge generating when the *agent's* epistemic *abilities* are at issue: epistemic capacities and abilities which produce, under normal conditions, a high rate of cognitive success and which are, in a sense, part of the cognitive character.

To illustrate the central idea of virtue epistemology and thereby the role of abilities for knowledge, let us consider a case of would-be "clairvoyance". Under presently normal conditions we attribute no knowledge to the subject, when it comes to predicting the future and making statements about the world through clairvoyance. The reason for this has to do with the fact that we do not regard would-be "clairvoyance" as an epistemically significant capacity. Such techniques are not part of the epistemically social space of reasons and actions. To the extent that clairvoyance is not an epistemic ability, perception, memory, intuition and reasoning are.

---

3   Cf. Greco (2010), 71; also Sosa (2007), 80; Sosa (2011).
4   Reminiscent of Plantinga's brain lesion case, in Plantinga (1993).

Naturally much more must be said if the concept of epistemic abilities is to be provided with sufficient substance. The following shall serve further clarification: In general it can be said that epistemic abilities are in a sense answers to ‚how is it possible' – questions; to questions of the sort: *How* can one know such a thing? The answers that determine the 'how' more precisely name epistemic abilities and constitute the backbone of the epistemic language game. My recommendation is that we should speak of epistemic abilities on at least two different levels of abstraction, the varying talk being a reaction to the different ways in which we can react to such ‚how is it-possible'-questions. On the first level, the concept of epistemic abilities reminds us that we can, for instance, make a distinction between perception on the one hand and conjecture or would be "clairvoyance" on the other. The first strategy in answering the *how* hence leads us to sources of knowledge, to the senses and activities of the mind. The reader may think of seeing, hearing, feeling, remembering and reasoning. Such capacities, in the broadest sense of the word, are means and ways of finding something out about the world. I will distinguish from this a second, more specific level of speaking of epistemic ability. For we answer such questions as "How do you know that the train leaves at such-and-such a time?" or "How do you know what time it is?" not only with reference to sources of knowledge in general, but with the citation of specific types of action: because I *looked at the schedule*, or because I *looked at my watch*. The answer thus refers to concrete grounding actions, to *techniques* and *methods* of recognizing or finding something out, in which epistemic capacities of the former level are involved. *Seeing* is an essential part of *looking at a watch*, yet it is integrated in concrete contexts and actions. What epistemically competent subjects must learn is precisely which techniques of knowledge (epistemic abilities on the second level) can be applied in regard to which questions and in which situations. Seeing, as a general faculty, does not help with this specific point.

This distinction points to different interpretations of the concept of epistemic abilities. The opinions are usually split into virtue reliabilists and virtue responsibilists. The latter fortify the concept of virtue in a rather Aristotelian way, speaking less of faculties than of epistemic character traits, such as open-mindedness, attentiveness, carefulness and impartiality.[5] I decided above to speak of reliable abilities that may be (in-

---

5   Cf. for a detailed distinction within virtue epistemology Baehr (2008); and for a virtue responsibilist approach in particular Zagzebski (1996).

nate) faculties as in the case of perception, or that may be types of action which have been learned in the course of epistemic education. Note the latter: because I have spoken of concrete courses of action and not only of our senses/faculties, I would like to point out a *third* possible way to understand the concept of epistemic abilities, namely, understood as concrete types of action in the epistemic language game. I am thinking of an interpretation along the lines of Wittgenstein. This is not about stable and/or innate faculties, but concrete types of action whose epistemic relevance must be controlled and trained by the agent, if he is to be able to move competently in the epistemic language games. This is what I mean by a "technique of knowledge". So we can distinguish between epistemic abilities as character virtues, as reliable faculties and as ways of acting in a language game. For short: virtues, faculties and techniques. Pritchard essentially discusses epistemic abilities as reliable faculties and I would like to follow him in doing so for our purposes here. But let me say that I am inspired by the Wittgensteinian interpretation of epistemic abilities. All key aspects of the following analysis are, in my opinion, also valid for this interpretation.

This sketch is admittedly still vague. But what has been said suffices to make it clear that there are good reasons to hold on to the basality of the *ability condition* along with Pritchard and others. To speak of knowledge is to speak of abilities. If someone luckily happens upon the truth or remains reliably on its trail through a brain lesion, then we do not attribute knowledge.

How, then, is the *anti-luck condition* to be understood and evaluated? Here, too, it appears as though we are dealing with a philosophical commonplace. A glance at the recent history of analytic epistemology suggests that there were nothing more obvious than the thesis that *knowledge is non-accidentally (non-luckily) true belief*. The different theories are, in a way, nothing but alternative spellings of the demand for ‚non–accidentality'.[6] This means that in all approaches it is shown in different ways that the agent is not accidentally, or luckily, in possession of a true belief, i.e. that the truth does not owe itself to epistemic luck. So what we seek is precisely an anti-luck condition. For this reason we say that the owner of a ticket in a fair lottery, by reading the results in the newspaper, can come to know that his ticket is a loser, but not that such knowledge is possible solely on the grounds of statistical val-

---

[6] In this sense, justification, causality, sensitivity, or safety ought to ensure ther non-accidentality of a true belief.

ues. For even if true, luck still plays an important role in the second case. A very improbable win could be modally near-by: you could easily have won. The truth (holding a blank) remains, in a sense, lucky. Or another example: Assuming you form the belief that the mailman is standing at your door every time your dog barks. Some of your beliefs are true. Your success *now*, though, is in some sense based on luck, because the dog also barks when a bitch or your neighbour is near.

Let us examine the topic luck more closely. If it is demanded that the belief must not be true accidentally, then with this demand the first step is taken to modal analyses of knowledge. For if the factual correspondence of belief and truth can be a matter of luck, then it obviously makes sense, instead of factual correlation, to demand modal stability. To find out whether a subject is lucky in having a true belief we ask whether she would have had this belief, if the conditions had been minimally different. E. g. if it is not actually the postman, but a bitch at your door, then the persistent belief that the postman were at the door would be false. So the belief in the first case was luckily true. In this way we test the modal stability of our beliefs, which apparently has some effect on the attribution of knowledge. So the question is whether the truth value of the belief would change if the world were another in a certain respect. With regard to the definition of luck, this means, for instance, according to the *safety approach*: a belief is accidentally true if it could easily have been false. I shall explain this with an example, but first the consequences for the concept of knowledge shall be inferred, namely: If one knows then it ought not be the case that one's true belief could easily have been false. The lottery- and mailman statements can easily be false, while the belief gained through the newspaper or a look out the window is in no danger of becoming false in near-by possible worlds.

There is therefore a natural connection between anti-luck conditions and full-blooded modal theories of knowledge, for example, as portrayed in safety approaches. The counterfactual phrase ‚S could not easily have been wrong' is, in the sense of a possible-worlds semantic, interpreted as follows: In close possible worlds in which S believes that p, p is also the case.[7] The belief is *safe*.

---

[7] Somewhat more thoroughly and more precisely, as well: "For all S, q, S's belief in a contingent proposition, q, is intermediately safe if (i) in all very close near-by possible worlds in which S forms the belief that q in the same way as in the actual world, S's belief is true; and (ii) in most other near-by possible worlds in

A multiplicity of examples appears to render the striving for modal stability plausible. Exemplarily, we shall point to the following case: In the morning, S looks at his clock under normal lighting circumstances and becomes convinced that it is 8:30. She forms the belief that it is 8:30 now. Unfortunately, the clock stopped yesterday at exactly 8:30. S's belief is therefore true at 8:30. Here we would not speak of knowledge, though, because in many near-by possible worlds – in such in which it is now 8:29 or 8:31, but in which the worlds do not otherwise differ – this would be a false belief. S's belief is not *safe,* a matter of luck, and therefore no knowledge. On the other side, if the clock worked well the belief would be safe because in near-by possible worlds S would believe that it is 8:30 only if this were the case.

3. Now, I do not intend to assert that the anti-luck intuition were false. This is certainly not the case. We are concerned with two plausible intuitions regarding knowledge: knowledge arises from ability and knowledge excludes luck. There is, however, in my opinion, good reason to speak against a *full-blooded* modal theory of knowledge, i.e. against a theory that relies solely on modal safety, and thus believes itself to be able to renounce abilities, or purports to retrieve these through the exclusion of luck. My point is, in a word: The exclusive addressing of possible worlds and so of modal stability does not lead to an appropriate understanding of the concept of knowledge. Safety is not an *independent* explanatory part of our understanding of knowledge. The anti-luck condition is in some way already inherent in the ability condition. This is what I intend to demonstrate.

The critical reasons at issue here against full-blooded modal theories mainly have to do with the radical externalism, and therefore with the extensional and action-free structure of such anti-luck approaches and hence with their inability to capture the intentional facet of our epistemic practices. The exclusive focus on the anti-luck condition that neglects to address epistemic abilities, yields an unacceptable gulf between

---

which S forms the belief that q in the same way as in the actual world, S's belief is true." (cf. Pritchard (2008)). This formulation first refers to the distinction between very close near-by and near-by possible worlds, which is necessary in order to handle inductive knowledge on the one hand and with lottery cases on the other; secondly, the safety of the belief is bound to belief-forming processes, and thirdly, there is an effective restriction that the safety approach is primarily plausible for contingent propositions.

knowledge on the one hand and the space of reasons and actions on the other. I shall illustrate this by making a few points.

Let us turn our attention to some selected objections to the safety approach as a full-blooded modal theory:

(a) First, there are many counterexamples of the sort in which certain beliefs that are not based on abilities do not fall under the category of knowledge, *if safe or not*. Let us consider the example of necessarily true sentences. Such sentences are true by their definition in all possible worlds, regardless of the way in which the subject comes to them. Following the safety condition all such beliefs are safe. Let the possession of an according belief be connected with an absurd method for gaining it, and ask then: is knowledge in this case assured alone by safe truth? Certainly not.[8]

Or let us consider the following known case: Petra's clairvoyant intuitions lead her to beliefs about the whereabouts of the German chancellor. For whatever reasons, her fellow humans are interested in ensuring true beliefs for her in such affairs. This means: they bring the chancellor to each predicted place. Each particular belief formed in this way is thus safe, as in all near-by possible worlds, i.e. in such in which Petra believes the chancellor to be in Berlin, on vacation at Hiddensee, etc. (otherwise, everything is the same as in our world), she believes something true. Here we would certainly not speak of knowledge either.

Finally, let skepticism be considered. Assuming our world is as we believe it to be. If this is so, then brain-in-a-vat worlds are surely quite distant worlds: much would need to change, compared to our actual world. So all subjects have safe anti-sceptical beliefs because in all near-by worlds the thought "I am not a brain-in-a-vat" is true. But do we know this? I will not discuss this case. Suffice it to say that the question whether one can ground anti-sceptical knowledge in this way is a point of conflict. The problem is that it is really unclear *how* such things can be known. But "knowledge that p" without an answer to the question how that kind of knowledge is possible makes the epistemic stance mysterious.

---

8   But now, who would claim that through the addition of the belief-forming method of necessary sentences this problem could be gotten rid of, forgets that the question whether a belief-forming process (in contrast to the belief itself) be safe or not, has already left the full-blooded safety approach behind. With that topic we are on the way to properties of *epistemic abilities*. See also footnote 9.

These examples bring us to the following systematic point:

(b) The *safety* of a belief owes its modal properties solely to the correlation between truth values and possible worlds. But the question is not posed *how* the modal stability arises, *how* it is to be explained. It is precisely this *how* – not the pure fact of safety – , that decides in favour of positive or negative attributions of knowledge. If we ignore the *how*, then, under certain circumstances, "'knowledge' that is epistemically for free" arises: as soon as the arrangement of possible worlds leads to the impossibility or implausibility of a belief's falsity in near-by worlds, there is knowledge, regardless of whether the agent has the according epistemic abilities to track such facts or not. And this consequence is more than counterintuitive. If this thesis were plausible, then we would have to count on cases of knowledge of which we could not say *how* one even *can* know such a thing.

My critique of full-blooded modal theories amounts to this: if modal stability is the only epistemic concern, then the central question is whether a correlation between the two relata exists. But correlations alone express no explanatory dependencies, no asymmetry between the relata. This very dependency, or asymmetry, between the relation links, though, appears to be central to our treatment of knowledge. We demand a certain explanatory direction, a *direction of fit*: if knowledge is supposedly given, then we expect the agent to be *sensitive* to certain facts, and in the process of recognition (seeing, hearing, etc.) these sensitivities are manifested. Instead of correlation, then, we demand that the agents be connected to the world in the *right way*. And the fact that we happen to live in a world that finds itself in a certain range of possible worlds is surely too weak to guarantee the right sort of world-contact.[9]

---

9   Defenders of the safety approach can object that I ignored that the reference to methods of belief forming is part of the safety definition, and that this very well answers the *how-possible* question. I deny this, though. The role of belief-forming processes in this theory does not aim at the epistemic *direction of fit*, but is more a means to the end of the possible-worlds semantic. Pritchard writes, for example: "…the possible world that we need to consider in order to evaluate whether a belief is sensitive is the nearest possible world in which the target proposition is false and the agent forms a belief in that proposition using the same belief-forming method as in the actual world." (Pritchard (2009), 32). Now, here are my comments. First of all, the concept of the belief forming process is completely under-determined. It is still unclear how we should understand the processes, and whether they fulfill the required asymmetry in explanation. Secondly, it is used merely as a means to an end. It is correctly recognised that we must address methods and processes. The function of this ref-

Safety, therefore, does not eliminate all kinds of epistemic luck. If luck is incorporated in the direction of fit, then a safe belief could be luckily true. The asymmetrical fortification of the relation between world and agent thus suggested, which goes beyond correlations, leads us to epistemic abilities – the *basis* or *reason* of modal stability and safety, as I would like to claim. Abilities are ways to answer the world.

(c) One final point directly affects the possible-worlds semantic taken as a basis. To my mind, such an analysis of epistemic counterfactuals shows that the concept of epistemic abilities is inevitable. Or in other words: The anti-luck condition is implicitly reliant on the context of epistemic abilities. What does that mean? Remember that a belief is safe iff in most near-by possible worlds in which S beliefs that p, the belief is true. And now my point is: The talk of *close*, *near-by* and *far away* possible worlds presupposes a concept of the similarity of worlds that is not only to be understood *quantitatively*, but *qualitatively*: the important issue is to push certain aspects of similarity to the fore, and to neglect others. Slight possible changes are not all the same. Only some of them are really *relevant* to epistemic evaluations. Contextual emphases of this sort are not to be grasped extensionally, though. The world does not distribute the range of similarity of possible worlds itself, and we receive other distributions according to varying contextual facets. And if contexts involve epistemic abilities, then it follows that to determine which worlds are close, near-by and far away, we need to know how the abilities should be understood.

To illustrate this with an example, let us take the belief "3 bottles of milk are in the refrigerator". Starting off from this belief *alone*, nothing epistemically meaningful can be said about the range of possible worlds. So let us add the knowledge generating epistemic ability to this: the belief is based upon the perception of the 3 bottles. And let us assume that the belief is true. Is it also safe? To fulfill this demand, as already stated, the subject, presuming it manifested the same ability, would have to come to this very belief in most of the near-by possible worlds, when 3 bottles are in the refrigerator. According to the definition, a possible world is near-by if the changes are minimal in comparison with the actual world.

---

erence, though, consists only in determining the right reference class of possible worlds. The search is one for those near-by worlds in which the same process of forming beliefs is used. What processes these are and how they affect the *how-possible* question, all these questions remain unanswered.

I would like to argue that this way of speaking is worthless, epistemically speaking. Intuitively, the distinction between near-by and far away worlds is convincing: a world in which other natural laws are valid appears to be farther away from the actual world than one in which 4 bottles are in the refrigerator. The latter is more similar to the actual world, because fewer changes are necessary. But, epistemically speaking, what is the use of the talk of *minimal* changes and *similarities*? If no further aspects are added, then the possible-worlds semantic is a dull sword in epistemological wars. For what we need for the epistemic evaluation is a difference between *relevant* and *irrelevant* alternative world courses. In other words: there could be very close worlds in which the agents form a false belief, but because the worlds are epistemically irrelevant they nonetheless know, that p. It could very well be the case that the agent could have been easily in error, but that we would still say he knows that 3 bottles are there. Let us assume there was a great amount of luck in play, as it was alone due to lucky circumstances that the agent did not dim or turn the light off by mistake. In many near-by possible worlds, then, the light is poorer or off, which leads to the agent possibly forming false beliefs: perhaps believing he sees 2 or 4 bottles, not recognising them as milk bottles, etc. We can see now that near-by or very close worlds can be completely irrelevant for the question of knowledge, for we do not demand that perception functions perfectly in the dark or under poor lighting conditions. This considerations place the epistemic ability itself at the focus of our reflections. The nature of the ability in question and the context of manifestation tells us which close worlds are relevant, and which ones are irrelevant. Pure modal similarity between possible worlds is without epistemic abilities too coarse-grained. We are primarily concerned with the ability, its manifestation and its normal conditions. The Cartesian world of deception is quite far away from the actual situation; therefore we should not take it into consideration. The poor conditions for perception, however, can be quite near-by, but we should not take these into consideration either. *Both worlds are not relevant, measured against the epistemic ability*.

It appears to me that the plausibility of the safety approach consists inter alia in the fact that it sometimes accidentally takes the right worlds into view. Let us regard the epistemic ability responsible for the production of knowledge. What we want to know is whether it assures cognitive success reliably under *normal conditions*. We have heard that alterations of the normal conditions (lighting conditions) and the sense-logical presuppositions (deceiver god) allow no statement on the epistemic strength of the ability. In neither case does the success or failure says anything about the epistemic status of the ability. We can afford to ignore such options.[10] But irrelevant worlds are *usually* far away, and relevant worlds near-by. In most of the examples cited, the near-by worlds are those in which normal conditions for the abilities are retained. Yet this need not necessarily be the case. Because the *possible*-worlds spectrum only accidentally accords with *relevant* worlds, my recommendation is: Take the epistemic ability, examine it in its context, and test whether it accomplishes the goal under its normal conditions. Only the applied epistemic ability, its function and the language game in which it comes to manifestation grounds the talk of possible worlds, making the idiom of near-by and far away possible worlds intelligible to us. If we know what function the ability takes on in a concrete situation, we can say what worlds are near-by and relevant, and which, on the other hand, cannot undermine the attribution of the ability, and are consequently irrelevant. Epistemic closeness is not identical to modal closeness.

For the reasons cited against full-blooded modal theories of knowledge I draw the following conclusion: The objections and counterexamples mentioned make it clear that full-blooded modal theories hover strangely in the air. The reason for this is that these anti-luck approaches make themselves guilty of a confusion of *reason* and *consequence*. The modal stability that is an important part of our intuitions about knowledge, and which should not be denied as a part of our epistemic attributions, *follows* from the concept of epistemic abilities. Whoever places his money only on the consequence, neglecting the history and the actual *reason* of the modal stability, falls prey to counterexamples and objections of the sort cited here. This consequence shall be rendered more plausible in what follows.

4. Where do we stand now? I have attempted to make it clear that both master intuitions seem quite plausible, and that we do not succeed in interpreting the demand of luck-exclusion resolutely, i.e. as sole condition of a theory of knowledge, from which the ability condition perhaps might be inferred as secondary. This hope remains unfulfilled. Does not this alone already speak for Pritchard's thesis that we need an *anti-luck virtue epistemology?* Not necessarily, for the option still remains that

---

10 More on this later.

full-blooded ability theories might be able to capture our anti-luck intuitions. This strategy sounds considerably more promising than the other way, in the light of what has been said here, as abilities always bring us in the normative realm of intentionality and acting by their very nature, and they are certainly one way for excluding epistemic luck. As I said above, the would-be "clairvoyant" therefore has a *luckily* true belief, because would-be "clairvoyance" is not an epistemic ability: measured against our present social standards of justification, it is rather akin to a type of guessing that here and now rather coincidentally leads to the truth. Abilities, however, provide us with a systematic sense for the truths. A competent basketball player will consistently sink free throws. And analogously: Who has learned, on the basis of the exercise of corresponding perception-based capacities to determine the contents of his refrigerator, will usually come to no false beliefs under normal circumstances.

Luck exclusion and the disposal of epistemically relevant abilities hence appear to be connected. This impression is strengthened when we come back to the aforementioned safety conception of epistemic luck: who comes *by perception* to the knowledge that a large dog is sitting in front of the door, has a *safe* belief precisely because the belief is the product of epistemic abilities. In all close, and in many near-by possible worlds in which the subject forms the belief that there is a dog in this way, the belief is true. The basis of safety is the epistemic ability of perception.

The question that follows naturally is: What speaks against the attempt to defend *robust* ability approaches in epistemology? And, connected to this: does the *anti-luck condition* play an independent role?

5. Before I take up these questions again, I would like first to clarify to which theses Pritchard actually commits himself with his *anti-luck virtue epistemology*. It will then be easier for us to comprehend which logical status is assigned to the two intuitions and conditions.

In principle we can classify theories of knowledge according to which of the two intuitions is placed at the explanatory centre, and thus which intuition takes over the role of the *primary* master intuition. Against the asymmetry between anti-luck and ability brought to expression in such a classification, Pritchard offers his own theory as a variant in which the same weight and status is attributed to both conditions.

In the last section it was rather suggested that we ought to place all our money on the abilities, and to find in this intuition and the according condition (almost) everything of relevance for a treatment of knowledge. Pritchard holds this very idea to be false:

> Virtue Epistemology ... comes close to gaining a correct understanding of knowledge, but ultimately fails precisely because it misunderstands the fundamental intuitions that a theory of knowledge must answer to.[11]

Positively formulated:

> What we need, in short, is an anti-luck virtue epistemology: an account of knowledge which gives equal weight to both of the master intuitions and so incorporates both an anti-luck and an ability condition.[12]

In these and other passages it becomes clear that Pritchard commits himself to the following three claims:

(1) the two master intuitions are *different in content,*
(2) the two master intuitions are *independent* or function independently,
(3) the two master intuitions are of *equal weight.*

Obviously the three claims do not completely overlap. The first thesis says that the connection of knowledge to epistemic abilities and the incompatibility of knowledge and epistemic luck are two separate conceptual demands. In other words, both conditions focus on different aspects of knowledge with varying vocabularies. But the claim is involved that the one perspective and vocabulary cannot be *reduced* to the other. The second demand for independency goes beyond that, as it is additionally presumed that e.g. the anti-luck condition cannot be *derived* from abilities. And thirdly, according to Pritchard: both conditions have the same explanatory value in the theory.

The picture presented to us in these theses is one in which we deal not with *one* epistemic coin that can now be investigated from one side (robust anti-luck theories) and now from the other (robust ability theories). Instead, there are *two* different coins that must be brought together in the theory.

I am of the opinion that this picture is misleading, that, in other words, Pritchard's claims about the relation of both intuitions to one another are not fully right. We need no **anti-luck** *virtue epistemology*. I intend to demonstrate this in what follows.

The three aforementioned claims simultaneously guide us to possible critical reactions:

---

11 Cf. Pritchard (2010), 51.
12 Ibid. 54.

Non-(1): *Reduction* of one of the two vocabularies to the other, which after the implausibility of the direction 'abilities-speech can be reduced to anti-luck-speech' can only mean: the anti-luck condition can be reduced to the ability condition,

Non-(2): *Deriving* the anti-luck condition from the talk, or from the nature of epistemic abilities,

Non-(3): Demonstrate the different explanatory weight the two master intuitions possess, which now means: abilities do most of the explanatory work to understand knowledge.

For semantic reasons, I take a critical view of the plan of reduction. I do not believe that we can reduce the conditions or intuitions to one another. They each stress a different conceptual aspect of our understanding of knowledge. The chances for Non-(2) and Non-(3), however, are considerably better in my opinion. But here it must be remembered that the two strategies each have another potential for critique as well. Non-(2) threatens the *anti-luck virtue epistemology* across the board, replacing it with a *robust virtue epistemology*. Non-(3), on the other hand, is to be understood in a weaker sense, as long as the thesis of the independency of both intuitions is maintained in this procedure, and only the attribution of equal standing is eliminated. Because, for reasons already mentioned, the asymmetry of the conditions will always favour the ability intuition, the following question poses itself in connection with Non-(3): if the conditions are not equivalent, then where is the difference in content between *modest* ability approaches and Pritchard's *anti-luck virtue epistemology*? Pritchard characterizes the former as follows: "S knows that p if and only if S's true *non-Gettierised* belief that p is the product of the reliable cognitive traits that make up her cognitive character."[13] The anti-luck condition functions in modest ability theories solely as an ad hoc attachment, taken up to exclude Gettier cases. If it could be shown that both conditions find their place in the theory of knowledge with a massive mismatch, will not the *anti-luck virtue epistemology* then become a *modest virtue epistemology*? The problem with this is that Pritchard has good reasons against the last type of theory.[14]

---

13 Cf. Pritchard (2009), 61.
14 Why should this be a problem? Modest ability theories in this sense are firstly ad hoc theories, and hence always to be taken with a grain of salt. Secondly they appear to be theoretically unmotivated: how and why should our knowledge concept be essentially ability-based, but then have the additive that has the sole function of excluding all those cases that we cannot intuitively manage

The following two further options could be added to the three critical strategies (Non-1-Non-3) already mentioned:

(4) the *anti-luck virtue epistemology* does not keep its word, i. e. it does not satisfy its own explanatory promises,
(5) the *anti-luck virtue epistemology* is an unmotivated epistemological position.

(4) is aimed at the possibility that by means of this approach many epistemological problems and questions (the Gettier problem, the lottery paradox, the closure principle of knowledge, skepticism, etc.) might not be solved or answered. That means: the theory is plausible, maybe true, but explanatory weaker than expected. This consequence would be unacceptable for Pritchard, who emphasises the theoretical benefit of the theory again and again. The lack of motivation asserted in (5) can have two foundations. Firstly: if it could be demonstrated that robust ability theories were theoretically possible and had the same problem solving competency (the same explanatory potential), why should we then decide for a more heterogeneous, theoretically more complex approach? A second and related question arises: why should (the concept of) knowledge have *two distinct parts or conditions*? Pritchard believes it possible, with the aid of a genealogical story in Craig's[15] sense, to react to this satisfactorily.

In the next section I shall first pursue the question of what reasons Pritchard offers to suggest that we were concerned with two *independent* master intuitions. What is the argument for defending (2)? In this context two kinds of epistemic luck are distinguished. Then I want to show that, regardless of substantial thoughts on epistemic abilities, the thesis of equal explanatory weight seems to be wrong (Non-3). At the centre of my critique, though, is the subsequent argumentation for Non-(2). Finally, it shall be demonstrated that the *anti-luck virtue epistemology* is not only implausible but also unmotivated. So (5) seems to be true.

6. Let us return to the question of the reasons why Pritchard believes we need an anti-luck condition separated from the abilities. What speaks in favour of the independency of both conditions? If we hold on to both master intuitions as they have hitherto been described, then it would

---

as knowledge under robust virtue conditions? Pritchard himself sees these problems, and therefore attempts to avoid equivalent treatment.
15 Cf. Craig (1990); also Craig (1993).

take the wind right out of the sails of robust ability theories if it could be demonstrated that the fulfilment of the ability condition does not necessarily guarantee the modal safety of the belief. In other words: could epistemic abilities be *unsafe*? This would mean: The manifestation of an epistemic ability leads to a true belief, yet the subject would in many near-by possible worlds, in spite of the exercise of the ability, come to false beliefs.[16] If that is the case, then epistemic abilities would be compatible with luckily true beliefs.

Is it really that way? Can robust ability approaches be criticised in this way? Pritchard attempts to answer this question positively, first by pointing to a distinction between two kinds of epistemic luck that are both supposed to prevent knowledge. What he addresses is called *intervening luck* on the one hand, and *environmental luck* on the other. The thesis is that the former kind poses no problem for robust abilities, while the latter does. In the latter case it should prove demonstrable how *manifestation of abilities* and *modal safety of belief* can come apart.

The paradigmatic example of *intervening luck*, i. e. for epistemically relevant luck, in which the luck occurs between agent and world (or rather: between manifestation of the ability and the truth of the belief), is the shepherd Knut. Knut is out on his meadow, looking at a sheep-like animal under good conditions for perception, and is thus convinced that a sheep is located in the immediate vicinity. The belief is true, although the animal that the shepherd has seen is no sheep, but a big shaggy dog (*bad-luck factor*), behind which a sheep is luckily hidden (*good-luck factor*).[17] Now, we do not want to say that Knut knows that there is a sheep in his immediate vicinity. It seems interesting, though, that he has a true belief that has come about through the exercise of epistemic abilities (perception). Does the *virtue epistemology* fail at this point? No. Representatives of this approach usually react by strengthening the relation between truth and manifestation as follows: out of "knowledge is true belief that is the product of an epistemically virtuous belief-forming process" comes "S knows that p if and only if S believes the truth

---

16 We are going to return to the following questions later: Must epistemic abilities really be safe, should knowledge be given? What speaks against epistemic abilities also generating knowledge under modally unsafe conditions?

17 This maneuver illustrates the standard recipe on the construction of Gettier cases: (a) a belief is justified, but due to *bad luck* not true; (b) *good luck* neutralises the *bad luck* factor, and makes the belief true and justified.

because S's belief that p is produced by intellectual ability".[18] The strengthening consists in the transition from *"is the product of"* to *"is true because of"*.

In what way does the 'because' strengthen the theory? One answer is: What is needed is no longer only that the epistemic subject firstly has a true belief AND secondly that by the belief production epistemic abilities are in play, but also the fact that the subject's true belief has to be *explained* by the manifestation of the relevant epistemic abilities. Does the subject believe something true because he/she has used his/her epistemic ability? Does the reference to abilities provide the best explanation of having the truth? Is competency an *essential* factor of success? In this ways the 'because' goes beyond the demand 'the belief is true and the product of epistemic abilities'.

This formulations provoke questions and explications about what 'causal explanation' is supposed to mean and can mean in these cases, but these questions and explications need not concern us for purposes of the present enquiry. It is certainly intuitively clear that the truth of Knut's sheep-belief is not essentially to be explained through the exercise of his perception, but rather through the fortunate circumstance that a sheep is standing behind the shaggy dog. The explanation of having the truth must *essentially* refer to this *lucky event*, which is knowledge-destructive. Therefore the ability is causally not salient enough.

So much for the treatment of the first kind of epistemic luck under ability-based circumstances. Before I come to the second kind of luck, the portrayed strategy of robust approaches in dealing with Gettier-cases should be critically illuminated. My question is: do we really need the *causal because*? Robust virtues theorists like Greco and Sosa say: yes, we do. This answer presupposes that Knut manifests his epistemic abilities in such scenarios. Taking this almost for granted, Pritchard writes: "Roddy [Knut, S.T.] is employing his reliable cognitive abilities entirely appropriately...".[19] This assumption builds the framework of classic Gettier-situations, in which a justified belief can be false. Justification is no guarantee for truth. In terms of abilities: the exercise of an epistemic ability is compatible with the falsity of the belief. The *because* only comes into play, firstly, if an ability has been executed, and secondly if the success (truth) is given, but not given through the execution of the

---

18 Cf. e.g. Greco (2010),71 f.; also Greco (this volume). Sosa also understands aptness as accurate performance because of adroitness. Cf. Sosa (2007).
19 Cf. Pritchard (2011).

relevant ability. The causal connection thus amounts to an external relation between ability and truth. What does this all mean then for Knut's epistemic abilities in the shepherd example? Let us turn our attention to the following case in comparison: an agent looks at a stopped clock that luckily displays the correct time. According to the strategy portrayed, one would have to say here: truth is given, and an ability has been manifested, yet it is not the manifestation of the ability that explains the having of the true belief. And now, against this picture I ask: *Which epistemic abilities are actually in play here?* This question, I hope, helps us to recognize the right connection between manifestation and success.

Seen from the first person perspective, the procedure is like the standard case of determining the time. We have learned to react to such questions with a technique of knowledge, e.g. with a glance at the clock. We can recognize what time it is by looking at a clock. So far, so good. But now it certainly cannot be denied that the actually executed "act of justification" is defect in a significant way. Looking at a stopped clock is no epistemic technique or ability, when it comes to questions of time. Without further information, nobody can recognize what time it is by looking at a stopped clock. Defective clocks do not make any access to the facts of time available to us.

The reader can already see what my point is: spoken in the spirit of epistemic disjunctivism, manifestation of an ability and success are bound together intrinsically. In other words: epistemic or athletic abilities are represented linguistically by success verbs, which means that success belongs to their essence.[20] We speak of *seeing a sheep, recognising the time* and *hitting the ball*. If the normal conditions of the manifestation are met, then the ability leads necessarily to success. Naturally there is a difference between "attempts to recognise (to see, to hit)" and "recognise" (to see, to hit). What we must ask ourselves is whether the agent, if he looks at a stopped clock, manifests the epistemic ability *in question*, or only believes to do so. To my view, a normal condition, or a sense-logical presupposition of the ability is not fulfilled if the clock is defective, which in turn means that the ability with which we are concerned is not manifested. The person *tries* to recognise the time, and she does in fact manifest some other abilities, for example, looking (at a clock). So she may come to know that there is a clock, but she does not acquire knowledge about the time because the relevant capacity for this kind of knowledge is not manifested.

---

20 Cf. McDowell (1998), (2011); also Kern (in this volume).

This result can now be applied to Knut without any problems. Indubitably he exercises a number of epistemic abilities, and even comes to knowledge in these areas. He sees his meadow, animals and much more. And it is also correct that he believes he sees a sheep. For him it looks as though he were manifesting that ability which leads us to true sheep-beliefs. But the ability of 'seeing-x' certainly cannot be exercised if before the x an x-like object obscures the view. Knut tries to see a sheep, but he does not succeed.

What do I want to say with this? I have doubts about the necessity of an external causal relation in the context of robust ability theories. Disjunctivists do not need the causal appendix. If the conditions for seeing a sheep were normal, then we would need no external strengthening by means of causal connections, because success in this view internally belongs to the manifestation of the ability. If *intervening luck* destroys the connection between agent and world, then it follows that this kind of epistemic luck undermines the manifestation of the ability. The defect does not only affect the causal relation between manifestation and success, but already the very manifestation of the ability. The *causal because* names no (external) strengthening, because success belongs to the meaning of ability. It is rather like a toothless gear in the machinery of epistemic abilities whose existence simultaneously reveals a deep misunderstanding of epistemic abilities.

Here an aspect becomes clear in which my conception of epistemic abilities differs from present, robust theories.[21] Naturally, I do not reject the parlance "cognitive success is to be explained *through* the manifestation of an ability". If the ‚because' amounts to this and nothing else, then I have no problem with it: precisely that is the point of an epistemic ability. What I would like to emphasise, though, is that, in my opinion, not *three* separate aspects are given here: success, the manifestation and additionally the external causal relation. Intervening luck cases are quite simply explainable through the non-manifestation of the ability: no knowledge because no relevant epistemic ability is manifested. To foreshadow a bit, I would like to point out to the reader that I am going to treat the second kind of epistemic luck (next section) similarly. Yet the explanation is different, disjunctivism no longer being

---

21 Principally, my concept of epistemic abilities appears to distinguish itself in the following points: it is action-like, intentionally rich, disjunctivist and extensional. I shall return to speak of the last point later on.

able to help at that point. But instead a *social externalism* of the individuation of abilities does come into play.

7. Let us now turn our attention to the second kind of epistemic luck. In this, the luck frames the exercise of the ability, and does not present itself, as in the first, between the agent and the world. Such cases are built by placing the exercise of an ability into an *unsafe* environment (or arrangement of possible worlds). Naturally we are talking about poor Barney, who drives through a landscape of fake barns that are indistinguishable from real barns. By mere accident he looks at the only real barn there, and so comes to a true barn-belief – and yet does not know that it is a real barn. This is the description of the case, and the standard interpretation. Pritchard's intuition regarding such cases is as follows: Barney sees a real barn owing to the exercise of his epistemic abilities (perception). The conditions for seeing barns are good. Barney's eyes function perfectly as well. So the disjunctivists' 'world'-condition and/or the causal condition of robust approaches is fulfilled, as we explain having a true belief through the perception of the barn. Barney really sees a barn. What should undermine such an explanation if luck does not step in between subject and world? The abilities seem to react to the world. According to the standard interpretation of such cases there is a manifestation of an epistemic ability, but no knowledge, because epistemic luck is still a significant factor – a kind of luck that cannot be eliminated by a concept of epistemic abilities alone: "It is, after all, *because* of his skill that he is successful, even though he could very easily have not been successful in this case."[22] The belief is modally unsafe, i.e.: under slightly modified conditions the agent could have formed a false belief. In the present, actual case the belief is true, because the agent has applied his epistemic abilities, but he very easily could have been formed a false belief.

It is this kind of epistemic luck that has led to fascinating debates in contemporary epistemology. Are knowledge and environmental luck really irreconcilable, and if so, does the concept of ability not already exclude unsafe beliefs? It seems fitting at this point, before discussing the Barney case any further, to close the circle first and to bring the synthesis of anti-luck and abilities in the anti-luck virtue approach to a definition of knowledge. Pritchard writes:

---

22 Cf. Pritchard (2010), 35.

"Knowledge is *safe* belief that *arises out of* the reliable cognitive traits that make up one's cognitive character, such that one's cognitive success is *to a significant degree creditable* to one's cognitive character."[23]

Let us ignore the details for now. The gist of the definition can be summarised thus: knowledge is given when an agent applies his epistemic abilities in a *modally safe environment*. Barney admittedly manifests his epistemic ability in perceiving the barn, but in an unsafe environment, so that he could easily have formed a false belief. In this case he did not gain *knowledge*, because the second condition is not fulfilled.[24]

The following two aspects belong to the details of the defintion. First, Pritchard works without the causal strengthening between manifestation and truth. He thus returns to the original, modest formulation of virtue epistemology. The talk is merely of '…*arising out of*…', no longer of '…*is true because of*…'. Second and associated with this, it is not required that the agent is primarily creditable or to be praised for the cognitive success. Here, too, Pritchard weakens the condition of '*primarily creditable*' to the point of '*is to a significant degree creditable*'. Both aspects together serve the explanatory potential of the theory, or more exactly the problem solving competency with respect to knowledge by testimony and the treatment of Gettier examples.[25]

8. One possibility of attacking *anti-luck virtue epistemology* consists in the rejection of the thesis of explanatory equality between both master intuitions (Non-(3)), as already explained above. I actually do assume that we have finally achieved more than mere Non-(3). I plead for the stronger thesis Non-(2), according to which the anti-luck condition can in some sense be derived from the condition of ability. If this is successful (i. e. if the derivation works), we can clearly say that the two conditions

---

23 Ibid. 54.
24 In epistemically friendly environments (in safe worlds) the relevance of abilities can be reduced; in unfriendly ones, however, we expect an accordingly higher degree of competency on the part of the subject. On this, see ibid. 55: "The degree of cognitive ability that is required in order to know thus varies in line with how epistemically friendly one's environment is.".
25 The following shall suffice as a brief explanation: Knowledge by testimony is to a considerable extent dependent upon the witness' knowledge and capacities. It is not me who *primarily* deserves credit, but the informant. Should this knowledge not be eliminated by ability approaches, then a corresponding weakening of the knowledge conditions is called for. Against this cf. Greco in this volume; also Greco (2010).

cannot have the same epistemological status: the exclusion of epistemic luck inheres in a certain way already in the abilities, which are epistemically primary. From Non-(2) follows Non-(3).

In this section, though, no reference shall be made to later arguments. The question is hence: are there pre-theoretical reasons that ensure Non-(3) that Pritchard can also respect, and which he therefore would also have to refute? My answer is yes.

As we already learned, robust anti-luck theories break down at a much more fundamental level than robust ability approaches (if these also fail). For extensional criteria of luck exclusion run the risk of not even reaching that region of the world of human action in which the talk of (human) knowledge is at home; that region in which we are in a space of reasons, in which responsibility and normativity are addressed and in which a thick concept of abilities really works. The talk of abilities logically precedes every discourse on the exclusion of epistemic luck, because it assures that a *category mistake* is avoided through the intentional nature of abilities. It may be the case that the ability concept does not do all the epistemological work, or that many theories of this classification are *false*. Falsehood presupposes meaningfulness, though, and it is the latter which can cause robust modal theories of knowledge to break down, namely, that they cannot serve as theories of *knowledge* at all. Talk of abilities is basal to philosophy in any case. Only if it is ensured that we are concerned with contexts of *competency* the question whether further epistemic luck factors are to be excluded makes sense. The latter is at most an addition at a second level. We can express this idea as follows: under normal conditions we attribute knowledge to an agent if he has the right competencies, while we never make this attribution if only the *anti-luck condition* is fulfilled. Safety of a belief without manifestation of abilities may seem interesting, but never tells us anything about human knowledge.[26]

---

[26] I am not certain whether Pritchard would agree with all this. Probably not. Sosa, Greco and Pritchard work with a reliablist concept of abilities that often has a slightly naturalistic aftertaste. It seems to me, however, that the ability intuition he also defends amounts to the very same points. The way away from pure reliabilism to agent reliabilism and further to virtue epistemology makes clear that the determination and the role of epistemic abilities shifts even more strongly into the focus. The interesting question is, of course, how strong and thick the concept of epistemic ability must be for human knowledge and epistemic normativity to be explained. Here we appear to differ. Sosa's talk of organisms with goals, for instance, is far too weak for me. Re-

In this case, the question whether the attribution of knowledge is true or not does not arise beacause we are not in the space of knowledge. This conclusion seems to be supported by our pre-theoretical intuitions. Normally we clearly do not speak of knowledge unless abilities are at work, while those cases in which abilities are present, and yet in which epistemic luck might be involved, are often discussed *controversially*. There is an asymmetry here. Obviously we do not treat both conditions equally. The inequality expressed in our intuitions also suggests that the two epistemic kinds of luck are not to be placed on one and the same rung of the ladder. Concerning intervening luck the *bad luck factor* precedes the *good luck factor*. The first factor alone makes it easy to see that the exercise of the ability is interrupted, that the agent does not achieve his goal. The sheep-like, shaggy dog obscures the view of the sheep, for which reason we can say that the agent is not connected to the world in the right way. Even the *good luck factor* does not change this. Knowledge cannot be present in such cases precisely because the epistemic ability does not achieve its intrinsic goal. The subject is only *apparently* on the track of a sheep. This much is perhaps undisputable. Our intuitions are homogenous with regard to the former kind of epistemic luck. It is often undecided, though, whether *environmental luck* destroys knowledge with the same radicality and on the same *pre-theoretical* basis. The fact that there are debates on the question whether Barney manifests his epistemic abilities and so comes to knowledge or not, demonstrates that we are rather undecided here. We cannot recognise the sheep if a dog is in front of it, but why does the pure possibility that the agent could easily have not exercised his ability prevent the benefits and achievements of the actual ability-based performances? It seems to me that, for now, this question is real and open. The cases in question are no clear paradigmatic applications of the term 'knowledge', which, as examples of this sort show, are essentially decided by the existence of epistemic abilities. Perhaps there are theoretical reasons for taking up independent anti-luck criteria into our judgments of knowledge. Even if it turns out to be that way, it is in fact a theoretical supplement to the established practices of knowledge attributions, which intuitively are based firstly on abilities.

---

liable dispositions are not *abilities*. They never lead to the right type of intentionality and normativity. Much seems to depend upon this question, but I will not pursue it here.

My conclusion is therefore: at least at the level of our intuitions – and Pritchard speaks of master *intuitions* – we are not dealing with two equivalent conditions of knowledge.

9. Let us turn to the stronger thesis Non-(2). If it is to be shown that the *anti-luck condition* is in some sense a consequence of the concept of epistemic abilities, then one must succeed in repudiating some of the talk of *unsafe* epistemic abilities.

Let us take a closer second look at Barney. Much depends upon whether he manifests his abilities under these conditions or not. Champions of the ability approach answer this question affirmatively in most cases, although they differ with regard to what *follows* from this affirmative answer. Here are some sketchy answers:

(a) because epistemic abilities are manifested, a type of knowledge (animal knowledge) is also present (Sosa);

(b) abilities are present and manifested, yet the because-condition is not fulfilled, because we do not explain the possession of the *true* belief primarily through epistemic abilities, but through the lucky circumstance of looking at the only real barn – so no knowledge because the performance is not the best causal explanation of the success ("Greco"[27]);

(c) Barney applies epistemic abilities, but knowledge is not present, because his belief is *unsafe*: he applies his capacities in an unsafe environment (Pritchard).

The debate between Sosa and Pritchard, for instance, amounts to that the former sees no essential problem for knowledge in unsafe worlds. Environmental luck does not destroy animal knowledge, which consists in apt belief (i.e. accurate belief through adroitness). Following this route it is correct to say that this kind of epistemic luck renders the abilities *fragile*. But knowledge asks for aptness, not for safety in this sense. Pritchard disagrees.

I, on the other hand, would like to propose a position beyond the variants (a)-(c). Little attention was paid to the thesis that, in a certain

---

27 In Greco (2010) there are different approaches for treating this question. On the one hand, it seems obvious to assert, analogous to the reaction to *intervening luck*, that the truth does not owe itself to ability in the case of *environmental luck* either. On the other hand, Greco starts in a direction similar to mine, first not speaking of a manifestation of epistemic abilities at all. But then the logical role of the 'causal because' is unclear to me.

respect, Barney does not really manifest the relevant epistemic ability and due to this fact does not acquire knowledge. If that sounds convincing, then what we epistemically need in Barney-cases are robust abilities only. More generally stated: epistemic abilities *cannot be realised in modal unsafe environments*. For this I want to argue here, the central foothold of the argument being a sort of *ability externalism*.

One reason why this position is often overlooked certainly has to do with a widespread *internalism* with regard to the individuation and the manifestation of abilities. As a rule, it is a firm illusion that abilities are *internal dispositions* of a subject or organism: *inner items* or *inner objects*, the existence of these dispositions being entirely independent of external factors. This sort of internalism conceptualizes abilities as dispositions to react in a certain way to a sense impression or seemings. Wherever the organism goes, the abilities follow. Thus construed, with regard to the ability, success is an external factor. The dispositions are successful if they are laid into an environment that *coincidentally* fits. The inner *equipment* is constant, but its success rate depends upon the configurations of the world.

To support internalism, thought experiments of the following sort have been developed: Barney is compared to his double, Barney★. Both have the same barn impressions, the same stimuli, sufficiently similar neuronal patterns, etc. And now the internalist asks: do we really want to claim, due to this and other internal similarities between both, that accidental environmental differences (Barney is in another world than Barney★, in his world there are barn facades, etc.) influence the existence and the manifestation of the ability? Do coincidental environmental factors put Barney into a worse position than Barney★? In Pritchard's words: "Given that all that is different about the two cases are incidental features of the environment, it is hard to see why there should be any difference in the cognitive characters."[28]

But this is precisely where my doubts begin. I think internalism is wrong. Externalistic ability approaches can assume different forms. Either it can be interpreted as purely causal-referential dependencies of an ability upon the world, or it can be understood as social and genealogical externalism in an broader sense. This is the interpretation I favor. Here the role of the epistemic *community* and the *acquisition* of an ability plays a key role for individuation. And of course, the world is already contained in these aspects from the very outset. If we attend not to

---

28 Cf. Pritchard (2008).

an organism, but to abilities as capacities for epistemic transactions, whose nature is inseparable from their social-functional role, then the environment of a successful manifestation belongs internally to the understanding and to the nature of the ability itself. This is my thesis. Epistemic abilities are part of epistemic language games which in turn are placed in a social space of reasons. It is the epistemic realm of action that gives epistemic abilities relevance, says which abilities are relevant, which ones are not. The question is: how does such a social externalism alter the evaluation of Barney's situation?

Let us examine the example somewhat more closely. Barney, a competent ‚barn recogniser', gets lost, and winds up in a landscape of fake barns without knowing it. Two questions must be distinguished, in my opinion, whose answers bring external aspects both of the individuation and manifestation of abilities to light, though:

(a) *Does* Barney still *have* the ability in question during his drive through the fake barn landscape?
(b) *Does* Barney *manifest* the epistemic ability by looking at the only real barn?

On (a): The answer to this question is connected to how agents can acquire and lose abilities. It was assumed that normally Barney is competent in such matters, and thus that he has acquired an ability through practice and training that has already been manifested many times. In normal landscapes he is a good 'barn recogniser'. We now assume that the loss of such abilities can be *conditioned* either by the *agent* or by the *environment*. The former could mean e.g. that neuronal disorders lead to the loss of the capacities, or that a lack of exercise over an extended period of time may destroy 'bodily know-how'. Even Roger Federer can lose a great deal of his ability after a twenty year break from tennis.[29] Neither of these forms of agent-conditioned loss is present in Barney: his brain works flawlessly, nor can a break in exercise be spoken of. Let us turn to environmental factors. It is obvious that massive long-term changes in the environment can affect human actions. This variant of externalism should be no topic of debate. If, through some cosmic accident, the colour red happened to disappear, then the ability to distinguish red from green would naturally vanish with it. Or let us

---

29 This type of loss admittedly pertains rather to athletic and musical competencies, and to a much lesser degree to epistemic abilities. The latter, under normal conditions, seldom fall into disuse over a longer period of time.

assume that tennis balls suddenly begin to move chaotically once they make contact with the racket. Under these conditions a learned ability (how to play tennis) loses its *sense*. Every language game and the actions involved therein have certain natural presuppositions. The same is true of barns and fake barns: if the abnormal landscape becomes a global and constant rule, then men lose a certain kind of classification through perception.

What does that mean for Barney? How do the given environmental factors in the case affect the first question? I think we have the intuition that Barney is in possession of the epistemic ability throughout his journey through the fake barn landscape. I agree. To say that Barney (still) has the ability can mean, for example, that back in his home world he can recognise barns at the end of the street with perfect accuracy. The external factors mentioned are not radical enough to destroy an acquired competency. Barney can still distinguish barns from fakes at many times and in different places. The world of error is local, and is surrounded by good functional worlds. The illusions are temporally and spatially limited so that they have no effect on the existence of the ability. But here an external aspect, this time of social nature, is also decisive for this judgment: We say that Barney still *has* the ability, because the *attribution* of the ability remains a social issue. The corresponding competency is still meaningful, and still has a place in the language game. For our epistemic actions the reference to this knowledge capacity is still a relevant move in many contexts, a reference that fulfils its function – even though we have learned of certain limits. The social space of reasons identifies the ability as epistemically significant. The social externalism regarding abilities traced here binds the existence of a capacity to the language- and action- community's recognition of a purpose in it that thus assigns a function to the ability in the realm of actions. And this attribution is still given.

This result accords with our intuitions. Because if it were otherwise, i. e. if Barney no longer had the ability, we would be faced with the absurd consequence that epistemic abilities could come and go temporally and spatially. We will certainly not say that Barney lost and regained his capacity so-and-so often during his journey through normal and fake barn landscapes.

In summary: *Having* an epistemic ability depends, among other things, conceptually upon the fact that the ability is identified as epistemically relevant (– and with this comes a story about acquisition, function, etc. of the ability). For Barney this fact is given. Therefore, it makes sense to say that he still *can* distinguish real barns from fakes.

10. But social-external factors are also of significance, especially wherever one is concerned with the question whether Barney *manifests* his epistemic abilities, whose existence was principally admitted in the previous section. To my mind, the external factors now lead rather to a negative answer. It must be emphasised that this question and its answer ought to interest us especially. For regarding knowledge it is not important whether the agent is in possession of an ability, in whatever sense, but whether the situation is such that the attribution or denial of the manifestation makes sense. And the latter depends largely upon external factors, what I would now like to show.

It is indubitably the case that the manifestation of epistemic abilities, and abilities in general, are understood relative to conditions and environments. This idea is not controversial. The question whether agents manifest their abilities is connected to the question under what conditions such an execution is attempted. We do not expect Barney to recognise barns at night or in a state of blindness, just as we would react with reasonable doubts and scruples if barns could turn into fake barns indiscernible to the beholder. It is controversial, though, what role normal conditions play in the individuation of abilities. Reminiscent of Wittgenstein's difference between the (natural, physiological, causal, etc.) presuppositions of concepts in a language game and the actual use and semantic properties of concepts itself in such a language game, much appears to me to speak for the claim that the conditions just mentioned do not go into the explicit *description* and into the semantic *definition* of the abilities. A competent agent certainly knows under what *paradigmatic* conditions it makes sense to undertake the manifestation of his ability and under which ones it is better to let it be. So we expect as a rule that between useful and non-useful conditions at least a practical distinction can be made. Yet this does not mean that whoever acts has an all-embracing explicit or implicit understanding of the normal conditions at his disposal that transcends the standard descriptions of paradigmatic cases. And a second point that is partially connected to this is also worthy of mention. Even all those circumstances that every competent agent can easily mention, when asked, do not go completely into the individuation of the ability.

All this suggests the thesis that our capacities are not individuated fine-grained, in the sense of the specification of normal conditions.

We speak of the ability of 'riding a bicycle', but not of 'riding a bicycle in a world with gravity – in a healthy state – without a storm …'. In Alan Millar's words: "But the claim that someone can ride a bicycle is not shorthand for a longer statement to the effect that the person can ride a bicycle provided that this, that or the other condition obtains."[30] So the understanding of an ability implies in a *limited way* an understanding of *paradigmatic* conditions of application. Whatever the details may be, the distinction between coarse-grained and fine-grained individuation does not answer my question. Nonetheless, the normal conditions matter. So my question whether Barney manifests his ability under those conditions is not only a verbal attack, that is, not a question about how to name the ability. I would now like to show that changes of the conditions, or of the environment of a competency, can lead to the question of an ability's manifestation becoming pointless.

Let us consider a case of successful exercise of an epistemic ability, e. g. Barney's perception of a barn in his home world. The environmental conditions can now be manipulated in a threefold way, compared to the successful opening case:

(a) changes in which a failure makes us doubt the attribution of the ability to Barney, for example, when he fails to apply it under normal circumstances;

(b) changes in which a failure does *not* make us doubt the attribution of the ability. We do not expect Barney to be a good 'barn recogniser' under the influence of drugs or in the dark. The failure is epistemically insignificant, but success can speak in favour of a special competency level of the agent.

The first two types of changes refer to conditions of good execution of an ability.

But of especial significance are (c) changes in which neither success nor failure is brought into connection with the epistemic ability. Both possible results of the apparent manifestation are epistemically irrelevant because under these circumstances the result allows no statement about the ability. Certain sense-logical presuppositions are unfulfilled. The changes rob the abilities of their established functions at the conceptual level. Here we are not concerned with conditions of good execution, but with basic conditions that are supposed to make it possible to speak of the execution of an ability at all. In a certain respect, of course,

---

30 Cf. Millar (2009), 232.

they are similar to the changes of the (b)-type: in both cases I emphasised that the conditions render the capacity epistemically irrelevant. In both cases we are faced with a sort of slippage. But still there are important differences in the form of the drainage. In the one case an ability does not come to application for good reasons; one ought not rely on it. In the other case, however, it is rather a 'free spinning gear in the epistemic machinery'. *Sense-logical presuppositions*, in my opinion, should not be taken into the narrower category of *normal conditions*. Naturally both changes are of such a sort that the executions are not normal. But it would be better to say that, under conditions of the (c)-type, the sense-logical presuppositions that make the ability and the attempt at manifestation possible in the first place disappear. One consequence of this distinction is that the success in the drug example can still speak for the manifestation of the ability, while under altered sense-logical presuppositions neither success nor failure speaks for or against the epistemic ability, because the type of action itself is undermined. My thesis is then: the fake barns directly affect the nature, or the essence of the ability; they undermine the goal and purpose of the ability, understood as perception-based identification of barns. Darkness and drugs, however, leave the ability intact; they rather pose *external* troubles. The fake barns are thus ability-*internal* disturbances in a sense. They affect our *understanding* of the ability: What, if anything, is the statement, that an agent can recognise barns based on perception from a medium distance supposed to mean under these conditions, (namely) if barns cannot be distinguished from fake barns in this way?

The difference between alterations of the normal conditions that preserve the meaningfulness of the discourse about and the application of the ability and those that do not is somewhat blurry. What I wish to point out, however, is, to put it in Wittgenstein's terms, that under altered external conditions a concept, but also an ability can spin free, having no hold in our epistemic processes anymore. At this point, "language goes on holiday" – and with it the ability in question. If we consider changes of the (b)-type, we can still imagine what it means to try to see a barn even if the lighting is poor or the agent is under the influence of drugs. Yet even this option is missing as soon as the barns cannot be distinguished from facades. What can it mean to try to separate both types of edifice via perception? That means: we do not *understand* what it means to classify between barns and fake-barns *in this way*.

It now seems to me that Barney's journey through the fake barn landscape amounts to a change of the (c)-type. This is to say that under these conditions the language community brackets the epistemic ability in a sense, excludes it from the game of 'reason giving'. The existence of fakes that are not distinguishable from real barns first undermines the *basis* of the ability, and secondly, having to do with this, also the ability's *function* in the language game of knowledge. As I already emphasised: without any function, though, the ability begins to spin freely, and is no longer a gear in the machinery of epistemic actions. In an environment with fakes the perceptual basis is lost. The difference in appearance, to which our perceptual capacity reacts, is missing. As long as fake barns look like real ones, what sense does it make to talk of perception-based discriminations? The consequence of this is that the ability in question loses its grounding power.

This can be further illustrated with Craig: Let us assume that a central function of the concept of knowledge consists in identifying good information via flagging good informants. Epistemic abilities are then the backbone of this language game (i.e. to flag good informants), because they determine what must be fulfilled for an agent to be a good informant. If we return to Barney, then it is obvious that in a landscape of fake barns he certainly cannot be a good informant in these matters. The social-epistemic space of reasons no longer admits this knowledge-generating way, when it comes to the difference between good and less good informants. Naturally there are still other ways to find out facts of this sort. That makes the difference between local and global sceptical hypotheses. Independent of this option, though, it is certain that Barney's epistemic ability, which he has already manifested repeatedly under other circumstances, is *pointless* in the fake world.

The upshot is: Even if there are good reasons to assume that Barney still *has* his epistemic ability, we still have to admit that he cannot manifest it, because the social and external factors do not identify the ability in question as such a one and as epistemically relevant. In the fake world Barney cannot do something that he could still do at home, namely, distinguishing barns from fake barns in a certain way. A certain move in the language game has become worthless, because we do not understand how to distinguish between barns and fake barns under the conditions of the thought experiment and how the epistemic ability in question functions concretely at this juncture.

11. The following two additions belong to the defence of the picture portrayed:

(1) Barney's defect is not of an epistemic global nature. Nothing of what I said in the last section implies that Barney is not able to recognise objects anymore, or that he lost other related abilities. This is clearly not the case: the external factors do not pertain to the ability of distinguishing houses from trees, for example. It is not the 'epistemic language game itself' that has collapsed, but only a small part of it. Therefore I would in parts very well agree with Pritchard when he writes:

> Intuitively the cognitive abilities that Barney employs in this case are just the normal cognitive abilities that he would employ in a wide range of cases which involve identifying medium-sized objects at relatively close range in good cognitive conditions.[31]

I answer: yes and no. Barney still has many abilities. But it does not follow from that that a certain technique applied to barns still works. He can achieve knowledge through perception about houses, cars and trees, but not about barns, because in the landscape described one way to do something does not work.

(2) One further point is important in order to avoid possible misunderstandings. It is naturally right to say that Barney factually manifests *certain* epistemic abilities in the situation described, just not the one at issue. So it is not only the case that we can still principally attribute epistemic abilities to Barney in the fake barn landscape, but also in the more specific sense that in the situation described many of these are manifested. Barney *sees* something, e.g. an edifice, or he is *looking at a meadow*, etc. In many respects, Barney is an epistemic agent.

12. What conclusion should we draw from the considerations expressed here about the key question of the article? On the one hand, it was demonstrated, against Pritchard, that *environmental luck* is not in the position to prove that, aside from an ability condition, we *also* need an anti-luck condition on equal standing with, and independent of the former. The discussion of the Barney case tends to support the claim that the epistemic ability is not manifested and the counterexample is therefore excluded through the *first* condition of knowledge. Our intuitive judgments can be explained very well in terms of robust abilities.

---

31 Cf. Pritchard (2009), 66.

Are there any further, more systematic consequences? At the beginning of the text, I suggested that we need no *anti-luck virtue epistemology*, because the anti-luck condition *in a way* is already inherent in the more basic ability condition. Have we shown that epistemic abilities are *necessarily* modally *safe*? At this very point we must proceed with caution. For this thesis is certainly not defensible in its conceptual generality, even if its *opposite* is extremely implausible. Everthing depends upon how the restriction 'in a way' that I use is to be understood. Now I would like to say something about this.

First of all: Of course, we cannot principally exclude that an agent finds himself in an environment in which he might easily have made mistakes. What is decisive for the epistemic abilities, though, is an exact look at the type of mistakes. The reader will remember the difference between (b)-type worlds and (c)-type worlds in this context. Presumed it could easily have been the case that the normal conditions for the manifestation of a competence were not good. One of 100 drinks in the bar did not contain a drug affecting perception. The agent was lucky and took this one. The modal unsafety of this type undermines neither the manifestation of the ability nor the acquisition of knowledge. So epistemic abilities are not principally *(b)-type safe*. Naturally we admit such unsafety only as an exception, when the normal conditions for the execution of the ability are sufficiently common. Otherwise the competence loses its seat in the world of action. So I would agree with Sosa that epistemic abilities can be fragile in exceptional cases. If fragility is the rule, though, then the ability quite probably dies out.

In another respect, though, epistemic abilities are safe. I am speaking here of a sort of *(c)-typ safety*. The fact that we speak of *possession* and of the *manifestation* of an ability such as that of recognising a barn implies at a conceptual level that deceptive worlds of the sort described, ones that undermine the sense and the function of the ability, are far away worlds. We can only speak of a manifestation if real barns and fake barns can be distinguished from one another in the necessary way.

To conclude: Barney's judgment that there is a barn on the meadow, if made in his home region, is a case of knowledge, because he manifests an epistemic ability. This ability is, on the one hand, more or less *fragile*, but on the other, *modally safe*. An inadvertently ingested drug could have led Barney to perceptive errors easily, but the *talk of the manifestation* of the ability under these circumstances excludes the possibility that under good circumstances Barney could easily have confused barns with fake barns.

13. At the end I would like to speak about one last criticism of *anti-luck virtue epistemology* that we described above as follows: the theory is claimed to be an *unmotivated* epistemological position (5). Such an accusation can principally stand on two legs: *firstly* if the promised explanatory potential can also be expected from other, simpler approaches. This point leads explicitly to robust ability theories which are simpler in their argumentative structure, because they only address *one* master condition, and which are also in the position to provide a satisfactory answer to Gettier cases, lottery propositions, closure, etc. This is in fact my opinion. What I find interesting here, however, is *secondly* the leg that the *anti-luck virtue epistemology* is unmotivated for the reason that it cannot explain why our concept of knowledge should have two independent conditions at its disposal. More precisely: Craig's genealogical story binds the concept of knowledge to the purpose of flagging good informants, from which it can then be inferred that the ability intuition is the central trait of the knowledge concept. But how can the fundamental thesis of the *anti-luck virtue epistemology* be derived from this story? Pritchard's surprising answer is: "On closer analysis, then, far from favouring robust virtue epistemology, the genealogical account in fact favours anti-luck virtue epistemology."[32]

The argument behind this thesis goes as follows: the concept of a good informant is itself ambiguous, implying two aspects, firstly, that the informant has *reliable* epistemic abilities at his disposal, but secondly, that we can also *rely on* him. Only if both conditions are fulfilled do we speak of knowledge: S knows that p if S is an informant who comes to his belief based upon abilities, and is also someone on whom we can rely. In order to keep both meanings of "good informant" separated from each other logically (for it could also appear as though an agent were reliable, precisely because he has epistemic abilities), Pritchard thinks of cases in which they seem to come apart.

Case 1: Someone can use reliable abilities in a situation, yet certain misleading defeaters on the side of the attributers are responsible for the fact that we cannot rely on the agent. Here Pritchard is thinking of Barney and the additional information that he is driving through a landscape of fake barns, although this is not the case (misleading defeater).

Case 2: Clairvoyance-man is married to a powerful wife who will, in each case of clairvoyance, arrange the world in the right way so that her husband has a true belief. We know all this, and so we can rely on

---

32 Pritchard (this volume), 170.

the claims of the clairvoyant. This notwithstanding, his supposed clairvoyance is not an epistemic ability.

I do not see that these cases speak against my robust ability approach, and for Pritchard's *anti-luck virtue epistemology*. He does not succeed in driving a wedge between ‚reliable capacity' on the one hand and ‚rely on' on the other hand. For in the former case there is still the question from what perspective judgments are made. If I am in possession of the misleading defeater, but do not know that it is misleading, then I do not rely on the agent. So far I agree with Pritchard. But why do not we rely on him? Because under the conditions we presuppose he manifests no reliable ability. In fake worlds Barney's ability is without value. Therefore I attribute no ability-manifestation to him, and therefore I do not rely on him. But if I judge from Pritchard's perspective, knowing that the defeater is misleading, then I can rely on Barney, simply because I can also attribute an epistemic ability to him. Hence, in the case of a constant perspective, both aspects Pritchard distinguishes vary together.

Case 2 is to be evaluated differently, but it presents no problem for me either. In this kind of case Pritchard considers situations in which someone does not apply any epistemic ability, but can still be a reliable informant for us, due to additional knowledge. Such cases are easy to undermine, though, as Craig notes, because the agent is treated in such cases less as a *good informant* than as a *good source of information*.[33] And I also agree with Craig that the latter is too weak for knowledge. As a rule, our additional knowledge refers to epistemic abilities of another sort, or another person, from whence we infer 'knowledge' then in connection with the statements of the information source. This description, however, does not speak against robust ability theories, as once again reliability is to be explained through reliable epistemic abilities. First of all the other abilities are responsible for the fact that we can rely on somebody. And then we can rely on the source of information in a derivative sense.

Of course, my answer to Pritchard's attempt to generate a gulf depends on the story I told about epistemic abilities over the preceding pages. As a rule, *reliability* is attached to *reliable epistemic abilities* explana-

---

33 On this distinction cf. Craig (1990), 37 ff.

torily. We rely upon S, *because* he has the corresponding abilities. Both meanings of the expression "good informant" vary together.[34,35]

References

Baehr (2008): Jason Baehr, "Four Varieties of Character-Based Virtue Epistemology", *Southern Journal of Philosophy* 46, 469–502.
BonJour/Sosa (2003): Laurence BonJour/Ernest Sosa (eds.), *Epistemic Justification*, Malden.
Craig (1990): Edward Craig, *Knowledge and the State of Nature*, Oxford.
Craig (1993): Edward Craig, *Was wir wissen können*, Frankfurt/Main.
Greco (2010): John Greco, *Achieving Knowledge*, Cambridge.
Greco (this volume): John Greco, "Die Natur von Fähigkeiten und der Zweck von Wissen", in: S. Tolksdorf (ed.), *Conceptions of Knowledge*, Berlin/New York.
Kern (this volume): Andrea Kern, "Knowledge as a Fallible Capcity", in: S. Tolksdorf (ed.), *Conceptions of Knowledge*, Berlin/New York.
McDowell (1998): John McDowell, "Knowledge and the Internal", in: McDowell, *Meaning, Knowledge, and Reality*, Harvard.
McDowell (2011): John McDowell, *Perception as a Capacity for Knowledge*, Marquette.
Millar (2009): Alan Millar, "What is it that Cognitive Abilities are Abilities to Do?", *Acta Analytica* 24, 223–236.
Plantinga (1993): Alvin Plantinga, *Warrant and Proper Function*, Oxford.
Pritchard (2008): Duncan Pritchard, "Virtue Epistemology and Epistemic Luck, Revisited", *Metaphilosophy* 39, 66–88.
Pritchard (2009): Duncan Pritchard, *Knowledge*, Palgrave/Macmillan.
Pritchard (2010): Duncan Pritchard, "Knowledge and Final Value" (ch.2), and "Anti-Luck Virtue Epistemology (ch.3)", in: D. Pritchard/A. Millar/A. Haddock (eds.), *The Nature and Value of Knowledge*, Oxford.
Pritchard (2011): Duncan Pritchard, "Anti-Luck Virtue Epistemology", *The Journal of Philosophy*.
Pritchard (this volume): Duncan Pritchard, "The Genealogy of the Concept of Knowledge and Anti-Luck Virtue Epistemology", in: S. Tolksdorf (ed.), *Conceptions of Knowledge*, Berlin/New York.
Sosa (2007): Ernest Sosa, *A Virtue Epistemology*, Oxford.
Sosa (2011): Ernest Sosa, *Knowing Full Well*, Princeton.
Zagzebski (1996): Linda Zagzebski, *Virtues of the Mind*, Cambridge.

---

34 Thanks to Peter Baumann, Alan Duncan, Gerhard Ernst, Stephen Hetherington, Dirk Koppelberg, Katharina von Laer, David Löwenstein, Duncan Pritchard, Hans Julius Schneider and Ernest Sosa for helpful comments and discussions.
35 Translated from German by Alan Duncan.

Knowledge as a Fallible Capacity
Andrea Kern

1. In her essay "What is Knowledge?" Linda Zagzebski concludes that the so-called Gettier problem is unavoidable on a certain definition of knowledge. It is the central problem confronting every account of the concept of knowledge that conceives of it as true belief plus a further element, where that further element is closely tied to the truth of the belief, but does not contain it.[1] As a reminder: the so-called Gettier problem consists in the fact that there seem to be cases, like those in Gettier's examples, in which someone has a true and justified belief, without having knowledge, because the truth of his belief is purely accidental. Gettier's examples were meant to show that therefore knowledge cannot be defined as true justified belief.

Now (almost) all authors that worked on the concept of knowledge in the wake of Gettier's examples agree that Gettier pointed out a feature of the concept of knowledge that is fundamental to our understanding of this concept. This feature is the fact that knowledge is a cognitive state in which someone grasps the truth of a matter in a non-accidental way. That truth is non-accidental is central to knowledge, and it is what distinguishes knowledge over other cognitive states. As long as we cannot account for this feature, we indeed cannot understand the concept of knowledge. Zagzebski's analysis of Gettier's examples has the merit that it shows how every such definition of knowledge is inevitably susceptible to counterexamples, in which the following holds:

> All that is necessary is that there be a small gap between truth and the component of knowledge in addition to true belief in the definition. Call this component Q [...] The conclusion is that as long as the concept of knowledge closely connects the component Q and the component of truth but permits some degree of independence between them, no definition of knowledge as true belief plus Q will succeed.[2]

From this, Zagzebski concludes that knowledge cannot be conceived of as a sum of elements, with the element of truth on the one side and

---

1 Zagzebski (1999), 101.
2 Ibid.

other elements, whatever they may be, on the other. According to the traditional definition of knowledge as true justified belief, this other component is understood as a normative component. This means that it is to be understood as a component that describes a norm fulfilled by someone who has knowledge. However, according to some authors, it is clear that the concept of knowledge is a normative concept already by virtue of containing the idea of truth. In the case of propositional knowledge we can understand this as follows: propositional knowledge is grounded in beliefs, for which it is constitutive that they make truth claims. That beliefs constitutively make truth claims means that they refer to the idea of truth as a norm that they claim to fulfill, or at least to be close to fulfilling. Clearly, beliefs do not always fulfill this norm. But the fact that beliefs all too often do not fulfill it obviously does not prove that not all beliefs are *aimed at* this norm. Rather, it only shows that beliefs are not always the way we think they are. On the contrary, the fact that we take a belief back as soon as we realize that it is not true proves precisely that beliefs are, as such, aimed at truth.

However, according to the traditional definition of the concept of truth, the normativity of the concept of knowledge goes beyond the normativity of beliefs and their reference to truth. The fact that the concept of knowledge is a normative concept not only means that it contains the norm of truth. For an accidentally true belief is indeed a belief, but it is not knowledge. In addition, it means that the truth of the belief must first of all be *explained* through something that removes the accidental character of truth, and secondly also has the character of a norm. This means that it represents something one strives to fulfill whenever one makes a claim to knowledge. Now, Zagzebski's thesis is that no normative property of belief, such as e.g. its being justified, is able to account for the feature we have named above: the feature of the non-accidentality of truth. For this, so the argument goes, could only be the case if this further component of the concept of knowledge, which is added to truth, already contained truth itself. This however, according to Zagzebski, is impossible: "[N]o normative property of a belief guarantees its truth".[3]

But if this is the case, i. e. if it is impossible to solve the accidentality problem through a further normative property of beliefs, such as its being justified, then we have to look to a different logical level in our search for that component of knowledge that combines truth with

---

3   Ibid. 105.

non-accidence—so conclude Linda Zagzebski and others like Ernest Sosa and John Greco. Instead of looking for properties (other than truth) that beliefs must have in order to be knowledge, we need to look for properties that people need to have, in order for their beliefs to have the status of knowledge. The key concept, with which these authors explicate the concept of knowledge, is that of intellectual virtues. Intellectual virtues are supposed to be precisely those properties that, according to these authors, provide for the normative component of the concept of knowledge, which is responsible for truth being non-accidental.

In the following I want to show that the so-called virtue epistemology that claims to set epistemology on a new foundation by focusing, not on acts of knowledge, but on the people who produce these acts, misunderstands its actual insight and thus falls short of a reinvention of epistemology. I will show this by discussing two very different virtue theoretical approaches, those of Zagzebski and Sosa. With the concept of virtue as they understand it, both of them give the wrong answer to a correctly conceived problem. The concept of virtue, as it is understood here, falls short of its goal, because it is still in the thrall of precisely the assumption that is responsible for the failure of traditional epistemology.

2. We said above that an explication of knowledge must search for that very component that needs to be added to the truth of a belief so that it has the status of knowledge. We must do that in order to rule out the possibility that the belief is merely accidentally true. Our insight is that this additional component can only do that if it already contains the truth of the belief as such, i.e. if fulfilling this additional component as such already answers the question whether the belief containing the component is true. The norm of truth, as related to the concept of knowledge, must accordingly be redundant. It must already be contained in the norm that the additional component in question describes. Let us call the additional component in question Q. Now, given that any belief explained through Q is true, we would get the following formal explanation:

Someone knows that p, if and only if his belief that p is explained through Q.

First I will consider how the version of virtue epistemology, as Linda Zagzebski has developed it, thinks to satisfy this formal explanation. Her definition is: "Knowledge is belief arising out of acts of intellectual virtue.⁴" To understand this explanation, we must first ask what intellectual virtues are. Virtues, as Zagzebski explicates, are enduring properties of people, which have essentially two components: they have a motivation component and a success component. Someone has a virtue, according to Zagzebski's definition, if he is motivated to achieve a certain goal, and he is reliable in achieving the goal of this motivation.[5] Aristotle famously distinguishes between ethical and intellectual virtues. While we can say with Aristotle that the common goal of all ethical virtues is justice, Zagzebski suggests that we are to understand intellectual virtues as virtues that have as their common goal the achievement of knowledge. To have an intellectual virtue accordingly means being motivated by the goal of achieving knowledge, and being reliable in the acquisition of knowledge. In the following we want to understand how an intellectual virtue can be that component Q which rules out that the belief it explains is merely accidentally true. Therefore, we must ask how exactly we are to think the interrelation between motivation and success on this view. Zagzebski writes:

> Intellectually virtuous motivations lead the agent to guide her belief-forming processes in certain ways. They make her receptive to processes known to her epistemic community to be truth conducive and motivate her to use them, even if it means overcoming contrary inclinations.[6]

If someone has an intellectual virtue, then he is motivated to acquire knowledge, which brings him to use methods of producing beliefs that his epistemic community knows are truth conducive. What does this mean? By a truth conducive method Zagzebski essentially means what is commonly meant in so-called reliability theories. Namely, the truth conduciveness of a method is understood to be a function of the number of true beliefs, and the proportion of true and false beliefs that are produced with this method. According to a common interpretation, this means that a method is truth conducive if *most* beliefs it produces are true. Zagzebski finds this determination too narrow, for she thinks that there are fields in which there is knowledge even though their methods produce only few true beliefs (such as for instance in philosophy). She writes:

---

4   Zagzebski (1999), 109.
5   Cf. Zagzebski (1996), 166.
6   Ibid. 176.

> I suggest that we may legitimately call a trait or procedure truth conducive if it is a necessary condition for advancing knowledge in some area even though it generates very few true beliefs and even if a high percentage of beliefs formed as the result of this trait or procedure are false.[7]

As we will more precisely see below, all virtue epistemologies are characterized by the thought that the property, which is supposed to play the key role in the explanation of knowledge, must be truth conducive. The spectrum of positions relating to truth conduciveness is distributed on a scale of probabilities, in which each determines a different number of true beliefs that must be present, in order to be able to call a given property—named "virtue"—truth conducive. The authors usually call for a high probability, but one need not, as is the case with Zagzebski. However, both ends of the spectrum are ruled out: it is both excluded that the exercise of the virtue *always* leads to a true belief, as also that the exercise of the virtue *never* leads to a true belief. Why? The first case, it is thought, would contradict the idea of essential fallibility of human reason. The second case would contradict the idea of virtue, which essentially contains a success component, i.e. it represents a property that conceptually includes being successful in producing that act or state through which it is motivationally defined. In other words: there is no virtue if there are no acts that realize the motivational goal of the virtue, and which realize it not just in any way, but precisely by doing exactly what someone with this virtue would do under these circumstances. According to virtue epistemologists, this description of the success component of virtues leaves open *how* successful the virtues have to be, in order to be understood as virtues. That is why here we have a spectrum of probabilities, or, more precisely, probabilities of success.

3. To recapitulate: on this view, virtues are properties of people and the exercise of them leads to successful acts with a certain (however specified) degree of probability, i.e. to acts that realize the motivational goal of the virtue. This means two things.

First, it means that the exercise of the virtue as such does not guarantee that the motivational goal of the virtue is actually realized. It can happen that someone exercises an intellectual virtue, for instance the virtue of intellectual openness or intellectual curiosity, without acquiring knowledge through it. Intellectual openness towards other beliefs does not guarantee that the beliefs that are acquired through this open-

---

7   Ibid. 182.

ness are also true. Intellectual virtues are *truth conducive,* but not *truth guaranteeing.*

Second, it means that whenever someone carries out an act that is successful in regard to the virtue, the success of this act is *not completely* to be traced back to the exercise of the virtue in question. This would only then be the case, if it were ruled out that someone could exercise the virtue in question without success. If intellectual openness as such does not guarantee that the beliefs I acquire by being intellectually open are true, then the truth of a belief that I have acquired by being intellectually open cannot be completely explained through this virtue.

Let us consider how Zagzebski determines a virtuous act. She defines it as follows:

> Let us call an act an act of virtue A if and only if it arises from the motivational component of A, it is something a person with virtue A would (probably) do in the circumstances, and it is successful in bringing about the end (if any) of virtue A because of these features of the act.[8]

So, a virtuous act is defined by three elements: (1) motivation, (2) activities proper to the virtue, and (3) success. According to this view there is a crucial difference between virtue as a power and a virtuous act. While a virtue, conceived as a power, contains the success component of the virtue merely as a probability, a virtuous act contains the actual success. There is therefore a gap between virtue as a power and virtue as an act: the gap of success. That someone performs a virtuous act says something about the success of his activity. That someone has a virtue as a power only says something about the probability of success of his activity.

However, if this is so, then it means, as we have just seen, that virtue as a power cannot be what explains the successful realization of the motivational goal of the virtue. Virtue as a power is, on this view, neither explanatorily sufficient for a successful act, nor even necessary. Therefore, a consequence of Zagzebski's conception is that, on her view, someone can carry out a virtuous act, without himself being in possession of a virtue.[9] For her conception of a virtuous act it is merely central, first, that one is motivated through the goal of the virtue, second, that one performs activities that are proper to the virtue, and finally, that one

---

8   Ibid. 248.
9   Zagzebski writes: "It is important to notice that on this definition it is not necessary that the agent possess virtue A in order to perform an act of virtue A." (Zagzebski (1999), 108).

fulfils the goal of the virtue precisely through those activities. However, all three conditions can be fulfilled on Zagzebski's view, *without* one being in possession of the virtue as a power. Therefore, virtue as a power does not play any role in the explanation of a virtuous act. The role of virtue is another one: we have to refer to virtue as a power, she thinks, in order to explain what it means to perform activities proper to the virtue, which are part of the definition of a virtuous act. For activities proper to the virtue are per definitionem those activities which someone who has a certain virtue would carry out under certain circumstances. The virtue as a power therefore does not play any *explanatory* role in reference to the virtuous acts, but merely a *conceptual* role in the definition of such acts.

When asking what it means to have knowledge, Zagzebski concludes from this that the normative component Q we are looking for, which is supposed to explain the truth of the belief, cannot be the *virtue as a power*, but *virtuous acts* in the sense described above. This way Zagzebski comes to the definition of knowledge above, in which knowledge is a belief that arises from virtuous acts: "Knowledge is belief arising out of acts of intellectual virtue."[10]

The question of what explains the truth of a belief—as we showed in the beginning—is of central importance for any virtue epistemology. For this theory claims to supply a solution for the non-accidence demand that Gettier cases remind us of so vividly and problematically. The non-accidence demand consists in it being part of the definition of knowledge that the truth of belief must not be accidental. The only way that this can be ensured in the definition of knowledge—according to Zagzebski's programmatic thesis—is by defining knowledge in such a way that the truth of the belief is not conceived as an additional component over and above the normative component of the concept of knowledge (call it Q)—i.e. as a further condition that needs to be fulfilled for the act to have the status of knowledge. Rather, it must already be contained in the component Q.

Zagzebski believes to have found such a conception. Her view of knowledge is that knowledge is a belief that arises from acts of intellectual virtues. It is *acts* of intellectual virtues that explain knowledge. For acts of intellectual virtues realize per definitionem the goal of these virtues, namely truth. And that is precisely why acts of intellectual virtues represent the normative component Q in question. For, they define

---

10 Zagzebski (1999), 109.

knowledge in a way that already contains the truth of the belief. On Zagzebski's view, that is precisely what rules out those Gettier cases in which someone fulfils the component Q, despite the fact that her belief is only accidentally true.

But let us consider the matter more precisely: how exactly are these cases excluded? An act of intellectual virtue as such contains the truth of a belief, because it is defined as realizing the goal of the virtue (truth) precisely *in virtue of* (1) being motivated by this goal and (2) being based on activities proper to the virtue. Therefore, that which explains knowledge is the presence of (1) and (2), *plus* the fact that the presence of (1) and (2) is the explanation for the belief being true.

According to this conception it is therefore possible that (1) and (2) are present *without* producing a true belief, or that a true belief is indeed produced, but that it is not explained through the presence of (1) and (2). Let us consider the virtue of attention. If someone is highly attentive in the process of forming beliefs, this does not as such entail that the belief formed this way is true. Even someone highly attentive can be wrong. If this is so, i.e. if the presence of the components (1) and (2) do not as such mean that the successful case obtains, then this means that the successful case is dependent on something *beyond* the presence of components (1) and (2). But if that is so, then it means that the successful case is *not completely* explained through components (1) and (2). What explains the successful case cannot in any case be completely ascribed to the presence of (1) and (2). Otherwise it would have to be ruled out that (1) and (2) might be present without the successful case obtaining. It follows that, when explaining the truth of a belief one needs to refer back to accidence even in the best possible case. The demand for non-accidence is not fulfilled. With that the theory fails to meet its own requirement.

Virtue epistemology is motivated by the attempt to solve the accidentality problem that confronts the definition of knowledge. Instead of solving this problem, virtue epistemology gets tangled up in the problem of not allowing any single case to fulfill the non-accidence demand. Even the best possible case is one in which good luck needs to come to our aid. The Gettier case here becomes the normal case.

4. Happily, our diagnosis above has pointed us towards the reason for this failure. The central thought above is that we need a definition of knowledge on which the truth of a belief is explained through the nor-

mative component Q.[11] Now virtue epistemology does not fail because this thought is wrong. On the contrary, this insight is indeed the key for solving the problem. A certain form of explanation of knowledge must be a part of the definition of knowledge. Rather, virtue epistemology fails because it cannot account for its own insight. For the normative component Q cited by virtue epistemology—the presence of an act of an intellectual virtue—is essentially characterized by the fact that it *cannot completely* explain the successful case. It cannot explain it not because the component Q—the concept of a virtuous act—fails to contain the successful case by definition. Here Zagzebski is completely faithful to her insight. If an act of intellectual virtue is present, then a true belief is present. Rather, the problem is that whenever the success component (3) is present (and the belief is accordingly true), its presence is not completely explained through the presence of (1) and (2), i.e. the appropriate motivation and the activities proper to the virtue. Rather, accident is always invoked in the explanation as well. The accidence problem is not solved here, but it is only shifted to a different level. We conclude from this that we need an explication of knowledge according to which the normative component Q completely explains the successful case. Now it is clear that the normative component Q cannot completely explain the successful case as long as we understand Q in terms of *specific acts*, which *precede* the belief in question without themselves already being acts of knowledge. This is precisely what characterizes acts as proper to the virtue. For in order to have a complete explanation for the truth of a belief, on this model, it would have to be possible to derive the truth of the belief from the presence of specific acts proper to the virtue. However, it is impossible to derive the truth of an act from other acts, which are not themselves acts of knowledge. If that is impossible, then it means that, on this model, it is in principle impossible to have a *complete* explanation of the successful case. Therefore, we must look for a candidate for the normative component Q that obeys a different explanatory logic than acts do.

Now, we have seen above that the idea of virtue as a power does not play any *explanatory* role in Zagzebski's virtue epistemology. It is neither an explanatorily necessary nor an explanatorily sufficient condition for the successful case. As we will see in the following, that is precisely the reason for its failure: the idea of virtue as a power is exactly the

---

11 Zagzebski writes: "This means that the concept of reaching A because of B is a key element in the definition". (Zagzebski (1999), 111).

idea that we need in order to get the kind of explanation of knowledge we are looking for. This is the point of Ernest Sosa's conception of virtue epistemology which I want to consider in the following. The basic explication of the successful case, i.e. an act of knowledge, must for Sosa be an explication that contains a specific form of the explanation of the truth of the belief: an explanation of the truth of the belief through a power, through a "competence", through a "virtue".[12] That, according to Sosa, is the solution for the accidentality problem of knowledge. The only real alternative to a belief, whose truth is accidental, is a belief, whose truth is explained through a "competence", i.e. a capacity. A shot at a target can hit the bull's eye, without this success being the manifestation of a competence. We call such a success accidental. But the shot can also hit the bull's eye because the shooter has the necessary competence to achieve this. A competent shooter does not hit the target accidentally; rather, here we have an explanation for his success: a competence that explains why he hits the target. And that is exactly how beliefs can be evaluated. A belief can be true by accident: namely exactly when no capacity is manifested in it. And a belief can be true because of a capacity. Thus, for Sosa, what ensures the non-accidence of a belief's truth in the relevant sense is not certain acts, which precede the belief in question, but rather a certain "competence", which explains the truth of the belief.[13]

Now Sosa calls the normative property that only applies to acts, when their source is an appropriate competence, the "aptness" of acts.[14] That means it is a part of the definition of an "apt" act that this act is explained in a certain way: namely, through an appropriate competence. Only a competent subject can carry out acts which are "apt" in this sense: "What is required for the shot to be apt is that it be (…) successful because competent".[15]

Acts can therefore be judged according to different normative aspects, e.g. whether they are merely successful, or whether they are actually "apt", i.e. successful *because* competent. It is precisely this normative aspect, i.e. the aspect of "aptness" that distinguishes the concept of knowledge. The concept of knowledge describes a belief that is "apt", i.e. that reaches the "goal" of every belief, namely to be true, precisely

---

12 Cf. Sosa (2007).
13 Ibid. 23.
14 Ibid. 23 f.
15 Ibid. 29.

through and because it is the result of an exercise of a certain competence. Sosa's definition of knowledge is thus: "Belief amounts to knowledge when apt: that is to say, when its correctness is attributable to a competence exercised in appropriate conditions."[16]

Therefore, on Sosa's view it is the idea of a certain competence—also called virtue, which is the explanatory part of the concept of knowledge—that plays the key role in solving the problem of non-accidence. What imbues a belief with the status of knowledge are not, or not simply, certain properties which the belief has—as the traditional definition of knowledge as true justified belief assumes. Rather, it is the fact that the belief is connected with a certain form of explanation, i.e. that it has a certain "source".

5. What does Sosa mean by a "competence"? Sosa writes:

> [A] competence is a disposition, one with a basis resident in the competent agent, one that would in appropriately normal conditions ensure (or make highly likely) the success of any relevant performance issued by it.[17]

Therefore, abilities in the relevant sense are characterized through two features: first, they have a "success factor", and secondly a "condition factor". This means that their successful exercise is relative to certain conditions which define the competence. It characterizes competences that they cannot be successfully exercised under all circumstances, but only under certain circumstances. Now, how does Sosa describe the "success factor" of abilities? For this, let us consider his explication of what makes up an epistemic competence: Sosa differentiates two kinds of epistemic competences. The first kind of epistemic competences are "dispositions to host a distinctive range of deliverances in certain coordinated circumstances. These deliverances are intellectual seemings".[18] Examples for this are e.g. our senses, memory, or reflection. Sosa also calls this first kind of epistemic competences "epistemic sources", because they deliver logically basic acts or states. It is on their grounding that we can gain knowledge.[19] The second kind of epistemic competences are "dispositions to accept such deliverances at face value, absent any sign to the contrary".[20] Therefore, this second kind of epis-

---

16 Ibid. 92.
17 Ibid. 29.
18 Ibid. 106.
19 Ibid.
20 Ibid.

temic competences consists in a "disposition implicitly to trust a source".[21]

Human knowledge, according to Sosa, is based on the possession and exercise of both kinds of epistemic competence. Now, it is clear that the mere idea of a disposition to deliver intellectual seemings, bound up with the mere idea of a disposition to trust such seemings, absent any sign that they are illusory, cannot yet have the status of an epistemic competence. For, epistemic competences are essentially characterized through a "success factor". But the idea of intellectual seemings leaves in itself open, whether these seemings are *true* and it is therefore right to trust them and accordingly possible to cognize through them how things are, or whether they are *illusory* and it is therefore wrong to trust them because they are misleading. Sosa describes the necessary "success factor" as follows:

> Such a disposition [i.e. a disposition of the second kind, which consists in trusting a particular epistemic source, A.K.] can be a "competence" only if its contained source is sufficiently reliable, at least in its distinctively appropriate conditions.[22]

In order for a disposition of the second kind—i.e. the disposition to trust acts and states that arise from a disposition of the first kind—to be sufficiently reliable and therefore to be able to have the status of an *epistemic competence* according to Sosa, the disposition of the first kind must be sufficiently reliable. Accordingly, it must itself have the status of an epistemic competence. The status of the disposition of the second kind is therefore dependent on the status of the disposition of the first kind. If the disposition of the first kind has the status of an epistemic competence, then the disposition of the second kind, which is grounded in the first, has it, too. But what is it exactly, on Sosa's view, which qualifies a mere disposition in the sense described above to be an epistemic competence?

It is clear that it must achieve a certain explanatory role. But which? We can best clarify this by stating what it is, on Sosa's view, that *must not* characterize a disposition: what makes a disposition an epistemic competence is not that this disposition represents a sufficient condition for an act of knowledge, so that it would be possible to completely explain an act of knowledge through this disposition. Sosa does not hold this ex-

---

21 Ibid.
22 Ibid.

planatory achievement to be an essential feature of competences. This can be seen in two places in his explication: first, an act of knowledge is, according to him, a compound of two different epistemic competences. In order to explain knowledge, we need two different kinds of epistemic competence, which means that neither competence is itself capable of delivering a complete explanation of knowledge. The first kind of epistemic competence only explains how there can so much as be states and acts that fall under the concept of "intellectual seemings", without themselves having the status of knowledge. The second kind of epistemic competence only explains how beliefs are formed on the grounds of such seemings, but without themselves being able to explain these seemings. For Sosa, if someone has an epistemic competence, this does not already mean that he is in possession of something that delivers a complete explanation for an act of knowledge.

Second, let us imagine that someone is in possession of both kinds of epistemic competence according to Sosa's conception. This means that he has a disposition, which is "sufficiently reliable", as he says, "at least in its distinctively appropriate conditions". Epistemic competences have, as we expressed it above, a "success factor" and a "condition factor". The success factor consists in someone, who possesses the epistemic competence, producing the successful case—as defined by the competence—in sufficient frequency. The criterion that distinguishes a mere disposition from a competence is therefore a statistical one. Now, this criterion should be relative to certain conditions. The relevant statistical frequency, which determines if someone is in possession of a competence, is relative to certain conditions. The question is not whether someone produces the successful case sufficiently frequently *under all conditions*, but rather, whether he produces it sufficiently frequently under certain "distinctively appropriate conditions". "Failed attempts in abnormal circumstances do not show lack of the capacity. (...) What is required is only that your attempts tend to succeed when circumstances are normal".[23]

Let us, for the moment, assume we understand what is meant by these "distinctively appropriate conditions", or, as they are also called, "normal circumstances". We will return to this point, for I doubt we have really understood it on this model. But let us assume, for the argument's sake, that we do understand it. Thus it is obvious that the capacity to see cannot be exercised under all conditions, but only under cer-

---

23 Ibid. 83 f.

tain conditions. Now, on Sosa's view the following case is possible: someone has the competence, the conditions are normal, and yet he still does not produce the successful case, but falls short of it. This case is possible because the possession of the competence does not in fact mean that the exercise of the competence *always* succeeds under normal conditions. Rather, it only means that it *mostly* succeeds. Under so-called normal conditions two cases are therefore logically possible: the exercise of the competence succeeds, or it does not succeed.

But what does this mean? It means that whenever an exercise of a competence succeeds under normal conditions, this must be a matter of luck, *a matter of accident*. This is because, given Sosa's description of the case, *there is nothing* through which we could explain the success in this case. For, there is ex hypothesi nothing in this case that distinguishes it from a case in which the exercise of the competence fails. We can explain the case *neither* through the competence itself, for it is merely so defined that its exercise succeeds in most cases under normal circumstances. Thus the competence cannot be the complete explanation for the successful case. *Nor* can we explain the successful case by appealing to certain circumstances that explain why the exercise of the competence succeeded in this case. For these cannot per definitionem also be present in a case in which the exercise of the competence fails. But if we cannot explain the successful case either through the competence or through the circumstances, then it can only be a matter of accident.

Therefore, Sosa's version of virtue epistemology also fails to solve the very problem which provided the actual motive for virtue epistemology. Sosa's original insight was that the fundamental concept of epistemology must be the concept of a competence. The concept of a competence should explain what it means for a belief to have the status of knowledge by explaining the presence of this belief in a certain way. Therefore, the point of the concept of competence is, for Sosa, that it connects two things, and precisely by doing that and because of that it can solve the accidentality problem: the concept of a competence connects the question "What is X?" with the question "How is X explained?". The concept of a competence connects these two by making the answer to the second question a *constitutive* element of the answer to the first question. If knowledge is a capacity, then the question how knowledge is explained is not subordinate to the question what knowledge is. Rather it is part of *the same question*. If knowledge is a capacity, then this means that the explication of what it means to have knowledge, in the sense of a single act of knowledge, necessarily contains a certain form of the explanation of the act in question—namely an explanation through the capacity in question. Accordingly, someone can be said to have a belief with the status of knowledge, if and only if he has acquired the belief through the exercise of his epistemic competence. A belief—even a true one—that is not explained with recourse to what Sosa calls "epistemic competence", cannot per definitionem be an act of knowledge.

Sosa's version of virtue epistemology fails precisely—as I will show in the following—because he does not consistently hold on to this fundamental insight. Sosa's mistake is that he believes epistemic abilities cannot *in any case* deliver a complete explanation of knowledge. But if that is so, then the concept of an "epistemic competence" cannot do what it is actually supposed to do: namely, solve the accidentality problem. If the concept of an epistemic competence is really to play the key role in the explication of knowledge—what all virtue epistemologists claim—then the concept of an epistemic competence should have a different bearing on the explanation of knowledge than it has had in the conceptions considered so far. Namely, it should be capable of delivering a complete explanation of knowledge.

7. Duncan Pritchard has come up with a similar result via a different route, namely that the versions of the virtue epistemology we have discussed so far cannot solve the accidentality problem of epistemology.[24] But, as I will argue in the following, he drew the wrong conclusion—that there can be no motive for holding a virtue epistemology. Virtue epistemology, Pritchard concludes, is as good and as bad as numerous other candidates, like traditional reliabilism or causal theory etc. Because virtue epistemology fails in its own demands, according to Pritchard, it undermines itself.

But the confession that the accidentality problem of cognition cannot be solved weighs heavy, if it is accurate. For it would mean nothing less than that the concept of knowledge is empty: a chimera describing an act or a state that is not any different from the one when we correctly guess something by luck. No skeptic denies that we can get lucky. But every skeptic denies that the concept of knowledge can meaningfully be applied to acts that human subjects perform. And we would agree with exactly this skeptical thought, if we agreed that the accidentality prob-

---

24 See Pritchard (2003).

lem could not be solved. The concept of knowledge would be empty. The solution of the accidentality problem is inextricably intertwined with the concept of knowledge.

8. I said above that the strength of virtue epistemology lies in its being motivated by the insight into the crucial nature of the accidence problem. Epistemological difficulties hinge fundamentally on the solution of the latter. It fails, because it cannot see *how* it can solve this problem by introducing its central concept, the concept of the epistemic capacity. It fails because it sees itself caught in the following dilemma:

As a first step, it wants to claim that we can explain knowledge by ascribing it to an epistemic competence. The first thesis is thus:

> (1) Having knowledge means having a belief that is not accidentally true, precisely because it is the result of an exercise of an epistemic competence.

As a second step, it sees itself forced to explicate the idea of an epistemic competence in accordance with the second thesis:

> (2) Having an epistemic competence that explains knowledge means that, under the conditions proper to the competence in question, one sufficiently frequently produces a true belief on the basis of a true seeming.

However, theses (1) and (2) are not compatible. According to thesis (1), the fact that a belief is the result of an epistemic competence should be responsible for the belief not being accidentally true. Let us first clarify how one comes up with introducing the concept of an epistemic competence, in order to use it to explain how there can be non-accidentally true beliefs. That a belief is non-accidentally true must generally mean that it is necessarily true. That a belief is necessarily true must generally mean that there is a "law" that explains why a belief that falls under this law is true. This "law" obviously cannot refer to anything other than the manner in which the belief is formed. A belief whose formation falls under this "law", so the thought goes, is necessarily true. Now, the idea of an epistemic competence should be precisely that "law" we are looking for. A belief that is produced by an epistemic competence—and so explained through it—is not accidentally, but necessarily true.

That a belief, arising from an epistemic competence, is necessarily true, implies that a belief, arising from an epistemic competence, is *always* true. The reverse obviously does not hold. That a belief, formed in a certain way, is always true, does not as such imply, that it is necessarily true. Let us for instance imagine someone, who adopts the principle to always believe the opposite of what his brother believes. And accidentally it turns out that his beliefs are always true. That his beliefs are always true, does not mean that they are necessarily true, since the truth of his beliefs is not explained by the manner in which he forms them. Rather, the principle according to which he forms them is purely accidentally linked to the truth. However, if an epistemic competence is to be a "law" which ensures that beliefs which fall under it are necessarily true, then this means that this law needs to link beliefs with the truth in such a way that it follows that beliefs which fall under this law cannot but be true.

Now, according to thesis (2), an epistemic competence cannot consist in the fact that someone who exercises the competence *always* has a true belief. Rather, it consists in the fact that, in *sufficiently many cases*, in which conditions appropriate to the competence in question are present, someone has true beliefs. More precisely, it consists in the fact that, *in sufficiently many cases,* in which conditions appropriate to the competence in question are present, he has true seemings and trusts them, absent signs that they could be false. Therefore, according to thesis (2), the epistemic competence does not always produce true beliefs, but only sufficiently frequently. For, according to thesis (2), it is possible that all conditions appropriate to the competence in question are present and yet someone forms a false belief nevertheless. For, the seeming he confronts may not be true, but he might nonetheless trust it because he does not have any signs that it is false. But that means that we cannot say that when a subject with the competence in question exercises this competence under conditions appropriate to it, he necessarily forms a *true belief*, but merely, that he forms a *belief* that is probably true. Even if the belief is in fact true, it is not necessarily true. For—given these conditions—it was not ruled out that it could have been false. Thus, in each case truth of a belief is a matter of accident. Theses (1) and (2) are therefore incompatible.

9. If we want to hold on to thesis (1), then we have to understand an epistemic competence differently. We have said above that an epistemic competence can only take the place of the law we are looking for—the law that ensures that a belief that falls under it is necessarily true—if the fact that someone has an epistemic competence implies that the beliefs produced by it are *always* true.

Here the following objection arises—and an objection of this sort is presumably the reason why Sosa does not even consider this thought, rather than excluding it from the very beginning: if we say that the fact that someone has an epistemic competence implies that the beliefs brought about by this competence are *always* true, then this means, so the thought goes, that we must demand *more* of someone who is in possession of an epistemic competence than Sosa does. While Sosa only demands that someone *frequently* has a true belief under appropriate conditions, we demand that he *always* have true beliefs. But that cannot be reasonable. For it would mean, so the objection runs, that we demanded *epistemic infallibility* from someone in possession of an epistemic competence. For it would mean that someone only has the capacity to acquire knowledge, if possessing this capacity rules out his being wrong. However, that idea of knowledge cannot reasonably be applied to human beings. The thought that human beings can have knowledge cannot reasonably be interpreted in a way that implies that they would have to be epistemically infallible in order to have it.

However, this objection is based on a misunderstanding. The objection is based on a false identification of two thoughts, that are to be held apart: namely, it confuses the thought

(3) that the idea of an epistemic competence implies that beliefs produced by this competence are always true,

with the thought

(4) that the bearer of an epistemic competence is epistemically infallible.

But how does one come to identify these two thoughts? Obviously, there is an alternative way of doing justice to the idea of the fallibility of human beliefs without having to deny thought (3). Let us first clarify this alternative understanding of human fallibility in terms of a competence familiar to us all: the capacity to speak. That someone has the capacity to speak means, if we follow the thought (3), that whenever the appropriate conditions for the exercise of this capacity are present, it is *impossible* that the exercise of this capacity fails. Of course it could happen that the conditions appropriate for the exercise of a capacity are present, but the bearer of this capacity decides not to exercise it. Anthony Kenny, who, more than anyone else, famously places the concept of capacities at the center of his thought, uses the example of a speaker who stands in front of an audience, but then decides not to say anything after all.[25] What is ruled out are cases in which conditions appropriate to a capacity are present and its exercise fails anyway. Nevertheless, the thought that someone can speak is obviously not identical with the thought that he can never make mistakes when speaking. Someone who can speak can also misspeak, can make a grammatical mistake, can use a word incorrectly, etc. How does that fit together? It's clear how we *cannot* interpret such cases: namely, as cases in which appropriate conditions are present, but the exercise of the capacity fails. But from that we can already see how we must understand these cases: namely, as cases in which the exercise of the capacity fails, *because the appropriate conditions for its exercise are not present*, more precisely: because there are circumstances that prevent or limit the successful exercise of the capacity.

If we interpret cases of success and failure in this way, we can fulfill the demand articulated above: that we need an understanding of epistemic competences, according to which the epistemic competence plays the role of a law which ensures that a belief which falls under it is not accidentally true. For a belief that is the result of an epistemic competence, in the sense above, is not accidentally true since its truth has an explanation: its truth is based in its being a result of an exercise of an epistemic competence. This is exactly what defines an epistemic competence in the understanding described above: having an epistemic competence means that, whenever it is exercised, it produces a true belief. And, on the other hand, we can do justice to the possibility of error. For this interpretation does not rule out, but rather encompasses the fact that there can be conditions under which someone cannot exercise his epistemic competence "correctly" or "really" or "successfully", because he is prevented or limited in its exercise. That someone can exercise his epistemic competence only limitedly or not at all under certain conditions, does not have to mean that the belief he forms, as far as he forms one, is wrong. It may be dark outside, so that the conditions are inappropriate for perception. That need not prevent someone from forming a belief about the color of the car in the far corner of the parking lot. And it can happen that his belief that it is a green car is correct. But if this is so, then the truth of his belief is not *completely* explained by his capacity of epistemic perception. For its exercise was per definitionem limited because of the unfavorable conditions for perception. He was a bit lucky. Having unfavorable epistemic conditions therefore does not necessarily mean forming a false belief, rather it only means,

---

25 Cf. Kenny (1975), 52 ff.

that if the belief is true, its truth cannot be completely explained by the epistemic capacity. By contrast, under favorable epistemic conditions, the capacity completely explains the successful case.

According to this understanding of abilities, we can therefore combine two things: a successful case that is completely explained by the capacity, and the possibility of failure that must be explained by the presence of unfavorable conditions. Herewith we have the concept of a *fallible competence*. That a competence is fallible means that it cannot be successfully exercised under all possible conditions, but rather that its successful exercise is dependent on the presence of favorable conditions. On the other hand, this does not mean—as Sosa thinks—that under favorable conditions its successful exercise is only *very probable*. No: under favorable conditions its exercise *necessarily* leads to success.[26]

10. Why do representatives of virtue epistemology not see this alternative? In conclusion, I will answer this question in a way that makes clear that the alternative we are suggesting is linked to an understanding of abilities which challenges an assumption which dominates (but is not limited to) contemporary epistemology. This assumption has the character of a dogma: above, I said it was Sosa's central insight to see that the accidentality problem of epistemology can only be solved if a certain kind of explanation, namely an explanation by an epistemic competence, plays a key role in the explanation of what it means to have knowledge. His problem is, as I have shown, that he cannot hold onto this insight consistently. He does not succeed in using the idea of an epistemic competence to completely explain knowledge. Accident is not eliminated.

Sosa wants to say that capacities have an explanatory role in relation to the acts that fall under them. This role is *constitutive* for the determination of the identity of these acts. That is his central insight. Let's call it the constitution thesis. But what follows from this thesis? We come closer to the meaning of this insight, if we remind ourselves of a distinction John Rawls makes in a different context: namely, the distinction between constitutive practice rules and regulative rules. This distinction will help us to more precisely understand the constitution thesis above with reference to capacities. For in terms of their constitutive character, capacities relate to the particular cases in which they are actualized ex-

---

26 For the concept of a fallible competence cf. the more extensive Kern (2006), 292 ff.

actly as Rawls's practice rules relate to the cases in which they are actualized. Rawls's example of practice rules are the rules of baseball. He describes their status as follows:

> Striking out, stealing a base, balking, etc., are all actions which can only happen in a game. No matter what a person did, what he did would not be described as stealing a base or striking out or drawing a walk unless he could also be described as playing baseball, and for him to be doing this presupposes the rule-like practice which constitutes the game. The practice is logically prior to particular cases: unless there is the practice the terms referring to actions specified by it lack a sense.[27]

Rawls characterizes practice rules by saying that for such rules the practice "is logically prior to particular cases", in which they are actualized. For Rawls, the claim that the practice is *logically prior* to the particular case involves three thoughts which make up the central content of this claim: first, the claim holds that certain concepts do not make any *sense* independently of a reference to the practice. From that it follows, second, that some actions can only exist *as* instances of a praxis, because it is only by reference to the practice that the concepts under which they fall obtain their content. And it follows, third, that there are certain concepts that can only *exist* if that very practice exists on which their meaning depends.

If we follow Rawls's explication and apply it to the relation between abilities and their acts, then the constitution thesis means, first, that acts which fall under a certain capacity cannot be explicated without reference to the capacity in question, under which they fall. And it means, second, that a specific capacity cannot be explicated through acts prior to this capacity, or rather acts that do not themselves already presuppose this capacity.

Let us, however, consider Sosa's explication of capacities: Sosa says that epistemic capacities are dispositions to produce seemings that would, under favorable conditions, in sufficiently many cases lead to a true belief if the subject trusted them. However, the notion of constitution that is claimed here is, at the same time, not thought through. For, Sosa here explicates what an epistemic capacity is by means of acts, namely seemings, whose identity is completely independent of the epistemic capacity under which they are supposed to fall. That a subject has a seeming in this sense, does *not* necessarily mean that he is in possession of an epistemic capacity. Rather, the opposite is the case. Someone

---

27 Rawls (1999), 37.

counts as possessing not simply such a disposition, but an epistemic capacity, if the totality of his seemings fulfill a certain criterion: namely, if sufficiently many of them lead to true beliefs. The difference between the seemings of someone who has a mere disposition and the seemings of someone who has an epistemic capacity is therefore not *ontological*, but *statistical*. It does not consist in the fact that the particular seemings, which they both have, are each *of a different kind*. It consists only in the fact that—statistically—the majority of seemings of the one are true, while those of the other are not.

Saying that the one has an epistemic capacity while the other does not, therefore does not consist in him having seemings that one can *only* have if one has an epistemic capacity. This means that the source of those seemings that constitute knowledge is by no means the epistemic capacity as such—which we define through them—but rather a disposition that one can also have even if one is incapable of having knowledge. It follows that the meaning of the statement "S has an epistemic capacity" is, according to Sosa, reducible to the following two statements: "S has seemings" and "Most of S's seemings lead to true beliefs".

Let us contrast how one must understand these so-called seemings, if one takes seriously the conceptual priority of capacities which defines their constitutive character: if one takes this thought seriously, then it is ruled out that an epistemic capacity can be explicated by seemings whose identity is determined independently of this capacity. The seemings which explicate what it means to have an epistemic capacity are rather to be understood in such a way that one can only *have* them if one has an epistemic capacity. Having an epistemic capacity then means that *all* acts that explicate what it means to have knowledge cannot have their source in anything other than the capacity. If that is so, then it is impossible to analyze the statement "S has an epistemic capacity" into two component claims about seemings, independent of this capacity and grounding its meaning. For the understanding of seemings which explicate what it means to have an epistemic capacity cannot be more fundamental than the understanding of the epistemic capacity itself.

For someone to have an epistemic capacity entails, therefore, that every single seeming he has is defined by falling under an epistemic capacity. This does not mean, as we have already said above, that *all* seemings that the subject of an epistemic capacity has are such that they lead to true beliefs. This also need not mean, that *most* of these seemings do. It would, after all, be possible, that—for contingent reasons—a subject of epistemic capacities lives under conditions that are very unfavorable for the exercise of this capacity (e.g. the lighting conditions are rarely normal, but it is mostly misty, or dark etc.). Statistically, most of his seemings would not lead to a true belief. But it does mean that *all* seemings which the subject has can only be had *if* and *because* he has this capacity. Explicating knowledge through the idea of an epistemic capacity means to explicate knowledge through acts that have their source in this capacity. And this capacity is defined precisely by producing acts of knowledge.

11. Virtue theorists of epistemology fail, I argued above, because they are not capable of taking their insight into the constitutive character of epistemic capacities to its ultimate consequences. On the one hand, they want to say that epistemic capacities are constitutive for acts of knowledge—as far as something can only then be an act of knowledge, if it is ascribed to such a capacity. On the other hand, this is exactly what one cannot say, if abilities are explicated through acts that can just as well be produced without epistemic abilities. For if abilities are explicated in such a way, explaining an act of knowledge *completely* through an epistemic capacity is ruled out in principle. For then, in each case in which one has a true belief, the truth of the belief is only made *probable* through the capacity. It always remains a matter of accident if the belief—as produced by such a capacity—turns out to be true. We could perhaps say that it is then not *merely* a matter of accident, but it is indeed accidental if it does turn out to be true. Virtue epistemology is blind to the thought that the idea of a capacity is an idea of something that completely explains the act which falls under it. The idea of a complete explanation, in this sense, is incomprehensible to them. Virtue theorists, however, do not substantiate the claim that capacities cannot deliver such an explanation. Rather, they take it for granted to such an extent in their considerations that they do not ever question it.

If the thought that capacities can deliver a complete explanation is ruled out from the very beginning, then the difference between knowledge and a merely accidentally true belief obviously cannot be described by saying that, in the former case the truth is explained by the epistemic capacity and in the latter it is not. I.e. another criterion is needed. John Greco concluded from this that we need something like a theory of "explanatory salience" in order to articulate this difference.[28] If the differ-

---

28 Greco (2003), 364.

ence between knowledge and merely accidentally true belief cannot consist in the fact that in the former case the belief is completely explained through the capacity while in the latter case it is not—rather, even in the *best possible* case, the belief can only *partially* be explained through the capacity, it follows that the difference between the two cases can only be one of degree. When explaining the belief, it is described as a difference in the weight that is ascribed to the capacity in the different cases. Then it is conceivable to imagine the different cases of true belief on a scale, the case in which the capacity plays no role in the explanation being on the lower end and the case in which the capacity plays a crucial role being on the higher end. Knowledge would reside at the top of such a scale. That is, in the case of knowledge, the capacity would represent the *salient* feature of the explanation of belief. According to Greco, given that it is ruled out in principle that a true belief is completely explained through an epistemic capacity, we have to draw the following conclusion for our understanding of the concept of knowledge:

> When we say that in some (...) cases, but not others, S believes the truth *because* she believes out of intellectual virtue, this must reflect different levels of salience in the various cases. In cases of knowledge, S's intellectual abilities have an especially important place in an explanation regarding why S has a true belief.[29]

That obviously raises a question regarding the basis on which we might say that an epistemic capacity is the explanatorily salient feature in one particular case but not in another. Greco's answer is that the basis essentially consists in our "interests and purposes".[30] The question of whether a true belief is explained through an epistemic capacity and therefore constitutes knowledge is essentially a matter of our "interests and purposes". For it depends on these interests and purposes whether we consider the capacity to be the explanatorily salient feature of a situation or not. However, it is clear that our interests and purposes can change or simply be different. This would not only mean that our answer to the question as to whether someone has knowledge or not would change. It would also mean that there is, in principle, no objective criterion for deciding this question, precisely because every answer to this question must refer to the idea of "salience"—which for Greco is precisely not an objective criterion.

---

29 Ibid.
30 Ibid.

12. As we have argued above, we need to be able to understand capacities in such a way that an act of knowledge is completely explained through an epistemic capacity. Only then is the accidentality problem really solved. As we have shown, in order to make this possible, we need to think through the constitutive character of capacities. It follows that there needs to be a different relation between the "success factor" and the "condition factor" in abilities than the one Sosa assumes. For Sosa, as we have seen, favorable circumstances play a central role in the explanation of the successful case. For the successful case is, for Sosa, explained by three components: (1) that the subject has a non-epistemic disposition, (2) that certain circumstances are present, under which this disposition very frequently produces true acts, and (3) a grain of luck. By contrast, if we take the thought seriously that epistemic capacities are constitutive for the acts that fall under it, then the talk of "favorable circumstances" *cannot have any explanatory power* in reference to the successful case of a capacity. For such an explication rules out that we could have an understanding of what it is to exercise the epistemic capacity in question independently of an understanding of the conditions favorable to the exercise of this capacity. And, in fact, our understanding of what it means to exercise an epistemic capacity is *dependent* on our understanding of a successful case of an exercise of this capacity. Such a case is—trivially—contained in the favorable circumstances. Favorable circumstances are then nothing other than those circumstances that are present in such a case. Therefore, they cannot contribute anything to an understanding of such a case, rather they themselves are to be understood in terms of such a case. What explains why someone has knowledge is, therefore, not that he is exercising an epistemic capacity together with the fact that the circumstances are favorable for this capacity. Rather, it is nothing other than the exercise of the epistemic capacity itself, which contains the so-called favorable circumstances, because this capacity cannot even be understood independently of those circumstances.[31]

13. To conclude: it was my intention to show that the introduction of the idea of an epistemic capacity is in fact capable of solving the key problem that so persistently engages epistemology. For the idea of a capacity, whatever else it may be, is the idea of a certain form of explanation of a normatively distinguished act or state—exactly that act or

---

31 Cf. my argumentation in Kern (2006), 281 ff.

state, which defines the capacity. Consequently, two things are intertwined in the idea of a capacity: the concept of a particular act—like an act of knowledge—and a particular form of explanation. It is part of the concept of acts which fall under a capacity that they are explained in a certain way—namely, through the capacity under which they fall. This thought already finds its natural expression when we say that acts *actualize* or *exercise* the capacities under which they fall. The relation we are describing when we say that an act "falls under" a capacity is therefore more precisely described as "actualizing" the capacity. Epistemic abilities—this is the basic idea—are the irreducible sources of knowledge. I.e. an act is only an act of knowledge if it actualizes a capacity that is explicated through precisely these acts, which it explains. If an act actualizes a capacity which it defines, then this means that we *do not need anything* except the reference to the capacity itself in order to explain the success of this act. It is exactly this logical feature of abilities that makes them indispensable for the solution of the accidence problem.

My intention in the discussion of contemporary virtue epistemology was to show that this logical feature of capacities—which makes them so central to epistemology—is incompatible with a reductive understanding of capacities. By a reductive understanding of capacities, I mean, as I have shown above, a concept that takes capacities—whose logical role should lie in explaining a particular normatively distinguished successful case—to be analyzable into (1) a disposition that produces acts neutral towards the successful case, and (2) certain circumstances, under which the acts of the disposition are frequently successful. According to this reductive understanding of abilities, it is logically ruled out that a capacity can completely explain the successful case. In each case, luck must come to our aid. However, this dissolves the logical role of the concept of capacity.

I have still said too little above as to how we are to understand the conceptual priority of capacities over the acts which fall under them. For clearly capacities can only be made out if there are corresponding acts which are explained through these abilities. There cannot be abilities without their proper acts. Thus, the thesis of a conceptual priority cannot oblige one to claim that there is "something", called a "capacity", invisibly lingering behind the scenes like Ryle's ghost in the machine, and living its own life independently of our knowledge of it. Perhaps it is a fear of this kind that is the reason why virtue theorists of epistemology lose sight of the constitutive character of epistemic capacities, which they see with only one eye. However, the fact that abilities have a conceptual priority over the acts which they explain does oblige one to see that there are things in the world called "capacities" that cannot be understood by a reduction to empirically observable single events or acts. Rather, capacities must always already be understood, if one is to understand such particular events or acts such as knowledge in fact is.[32]

References

Greco (2003): John Greco, "Virtue and Luck, Epistemic and Otherwise", *Metaphilosophy* 34, 353–366.
Kenny (1975): Anthony Kenny, *Will, Freedom and Power*, London.
Kern (2006): Andrea Kern, *Quellen des Wissens*, Frankfurt/Main.
Pritchard (2003): Duncan Pritchard, "Virtue Epistemology and Epistemic Luck", *Metaphilosophy* 34, 106–130.
Rawls (1999): John Rawls, "Two Concepts of Rules", in: S. Freeman (ed.), *Collected Papers*, Cambridge, 20–46.
Sosa (2007): Ernest Sosa, *A Virtue Epistemology. Apt Belief and Reflective Knowledge*, vol. 1, Oxford.
Zagzebski (1996): Linda Zagzebski, *Virtues of the Mind. An inquiry into the nature of virtue and the ethical foundations of knowledge*, Cambridge.
Zagzebski (1999): Linda Zagzebski, "What is Knowledge?", in: J. Greco/Ernest Sosa (eds.), *The Blackwell Guide to Epistemology*, Oxford, 92–116.

---

32 Translation from German by Tea Jankovic

Part Three: Knowing-How

Knowing-How: Indispensable but Inscrutable

Günter Abel

I. The Relevance and Status of Knowing-How

1. Knowing-How as a Practical Skill and Procedural Knowledge

Mario knows how to prepare delicious mocha ice cream. He knows how to ride a bicycle and how to play the cello, a volley in tennis, and a hand in poker. He also knows in general how to follow rules in acting, speaking, and thinking. Obviously, knowing-how (in the sense of practical skills and procedural knowledge) is in continuous demand and successfully put to use in Mario's life and the lives of other people. Examples abound in science, technology, philosophy, and the arts. Peter knows how to conduct a scientific experiment, and how to guarantee the functionality of technological systems. Markus knows how to clarify fundamental terminology and pursue logical analysis in philosophy. Yvette, a mathematician, knows how to carry out a proof. Claus the painter knows how to produce color fields and counterpose them, just as the musician Benjamin knows how to create them with timbres. Most people are quite familiar with such abilities, capabilities, competencies, and customs, which all go by the name "knowing-how," each in a different sense. Humans are constantly acting within them.[1]

---

1   I consistently use the expression "knowing-how" instead of "knowledge-how" or "know-how". When speaking of "knowing-how" the dynamic and procedural character of the processes and phenomena I describe are better expressed than do the terms "knowledge-how" and "know-how," which convey something rather static. Within the word family of *knowing-how*, one must differentiate between several members. In this article I do not try to elucidate the following fine-grained distinctions between them in all their detail and interaction, but they are constantly present in the background: *Skills* (e.g., playing cello, reading, or calculating) are trained and improved through *abilities* to learn them. By *practical abilities* I mean the capabilities and capacities by which means people behave or do something. Briefly, one's knowing how

When successful, knowing-how works so naturally that people neither pay special attention to it nor think about what different components work together in it and how they do so. If swimmers, for example, were to contemplate exactly how they were executing their actions, they would fall prey to the well-known millipede syndrome. Once the millipede is asked to demonstrate explicitly how it manages to keep all of its feet moving smoothly, it instantly gets tangled up. The ballerina who, in the midst of her refined motions, begins to reflect on how she manages to make these motions successfully instantly loses her grace. The threat of paralysis through analysis arises.

The difference between practical and theoretical knowledge is, of course, also fundamental in this context. I know *that* Angela Merkel is the federal chancellor. And I know *how* to maintain my balance while riding a bicycle. But the former statement imparts a theoretical knowledge of facts that I can linguistically articulate and communicate in a that-proposition. The how-statement, on the other hand, communicates practical and procedural knowledge, an ability composed of skills, capabilities, and expertise that inscrutably defies propositional articulation and analysis.

It is also revealing to realize how the expression "knowing-how," as familiar as it is, works, and what its peculiarities are. One can identify at least the following three constructions of knowing-how: (a) "knowing how something works," (b) "knowing how it is to be or to have an x," and (c) "knowing how to do something." A construction of the first kind is stated by such sentences as "Do you know *how* the espresso machine works?" This question can be answered (beyond a simple "Yes" or "No") with a propositional construction ("I know *that* it works in such and such a way").

---

to act is determined by practical abilities. *Expertise* refers to ability, skill, and talent. Whoever has talent has largely developed an ability and is able to acquire new skills quickly in order to avoid errors and unnecessary effort.

Competence is usually taken to mean a general ability, that is, the general capacity to speak and take action, the ability of a speaker or hearer to produce and understand intelligible utterances in a language, and the ability of an agent to engage in actions, execute them, and understand other persons' actions. Abilities, skills, talents, and competencies are articulated and executed within a space of habits that are traditional or yet to be established. By habits I mean the general setting of common and conventionalized modes of behavior in practice and theory. The points addressed in this article are to be treated in greater detail in the first two chapters of Abel (forthcoming 2012). For an earlier treatment in German, see Abel (2010a).

My inquiry does not focus on the expression "knowing how it is to be serene" [sad, in love, jealous, and so on] or on the knowledge of how it feels from within to go through these states. To be sure, such knowing-how-it-is constructions and the corresponding phenomena, states, and processes already have to do with sensory and experiential abilities without which a person would be unable to have the experiences mentioned. Instead, I am primarily concerned in this article with the construction "knowing how to do something," that is, with practical skills, capabilities, and competencies. The central issue is whether a person can perform certain actions, operations, practices, and motions. In many cases of such "knowing how to do something," people simply speak of an ability, of adroitness and expertise. In my opinion, though, it is important not to disguise the components of practical knowledge also embodied technically in adroitness or to make them disappear altogether. The practical skills, capabilities, and competencies brought to mind by the expression "knowing-how" are worth being understood and addressed as knowledge in a broad sense, which I elucidated below. But this sense of practical and procedural knowledge does not fall under the theoretical (or linguistically propositional) concept of "knowledge-that." One could speak of an "ability-knowledge," but that term sounds awkward and needs explanation. So let us instead use the apt English expression "knowing-how."

It is important to distinguish a narrow and a broad sense of knowledge.[2] The narrow concept of knowledge means knowledge that is methodically gained, organized, and bound to truth and justification. It is necessary to be able to speak of this knowledge and to be able to express, communicate, intersubjectively verify, and *salva veritate* substitute it in propositions.

The broad concept of knowledge refers to the ability to grasp and appropriately comprehend what a given something is about (e.g., a sentence or a picture). It also has to do with human procedural and practical abilities manifest in successful skills, capabilities, practices, and competencies (e.g., swimming or playing cello). This procedural ability obviously plays a cognitive, action-stabilizing, and orienting function. It is usually exercised so naturally that one explicitly notices it only when (a) it ceases to function smoothly, leading to interruptions in fluent acting, speaking, and thinking and (b) one must learn, practice, and improve skills and competencies (e.g., proper performance of a waltz or

---

2 See Abel (2004, chapter 10; 2007; 2011).

the correct steps for solving an algebra problem). Knowing-how skills and competencies can be understood as knowledge in this broad sense.

Several arguments support this view. The first one centers on the internal connection between practical knowing-how skills and what it means to have experiences. Experience can be regarded as a mélange of various components in which information and skills are not isolated but rather acquired together and found together in their interpenetrations. Limiting the talk of "knowledge" to its narrow sense of gaining and dealing with information, one would quickly be entangled in gaining and executing skills, especially knowing-how skills. Hence, it is no surprise that people use the word "knowledge" to mean not only "experience" in general but also its heuristically differentiated components (information and skills).[3] With these points in mind, I now address the practical abilities of knowing-how not merely as skills in a practical and technical sense.

Knowing-how skills are not simply inherent predispositions. They are skills that must first be acquired through practice and improvement. I therefore address all abilities and skills that concern human experience in the triangle of I–we–world, or rather in the triangular relations of subject, other subjects or agents, and the world—as a knowing in the broad sense of the term sketched above. Knowing how to cope with oneself, with other persons, and with the world in this triangle is neither a biologically inherent quality nor theoretically propositional knowledge. This intermediate position makes it seem reasonable to speak of knowing-how not only as a practical ability but also as a procedural knowledge.[4]

Knowing-how does not consist of a theoretical knowledge of the correspondence between attributive sentences and states of affairs. Knowing-how is not a matter of "truth." It is not concerned with conditions of theoretical truth but rather of practical conditions of satisfaction. Knowing-how encompasses ability and knowledge with respect to successful and appropriate acting, that is, knowledge in the broad sense of successful correctness. To that extent, being acquainted with a practice is expressed in the practical knowing-how skills. And bringing these skills to action can really be seen as analogous to the use of conceptual knowledge schemata in the narrow sense of knowledge.

---

3 Cf. Lewis (1990), 516 f.
4 The triangular relation of I–we–world and the broad sense of knowledge is detailed in Abel (2011).

In this context two aspects are especially revealing. First, lack of training and development of practical knowing-how skills, as with playing tennis, in many cases means that the actual tennis match and the attendant experiences do not occur at all. Even having the best possible theoretical concepts and mental images of playing tennis does not lead to actual tennis-playing, or even to an adroitness in serving and volleying. Second, it is often the acquisition and improvement of practical knowing-how skills that can trigger, create, favor, and further a "knowing-*that*." Examples of such outcomes are easy to find.[5] If I am an expert at the waltz, I can, at the end of a given dance step, predict the next steps (including possible variations) and can thus generate a theoretical knowledge-that. If I am a competent native speaker of German, I can decide and assess whether sentences that may occur are well-formulated in that language. (And this ability does not require me to know all the syntactic and semantic structures of every sentence possible in the German language.)

In fluently functioning practice and performance, and thus in the successful execution of knowing-how (e.g., how to keep balance while riding a bicycle or dancing), the person who possesses the knowing-how instantiates the biological, motoric, and physical regularities involved in bicycling or dancing. These instantiations usually happen unconsciously and without any explicit intention. They happen in a manner somewhat analogous to how I see the outlines of objects according to the functional mode of my visual system while watching the world. I can see these outlines without needing any antecedent linguistically propositional knowledge or algorithmic or otherwise formal theory about the functionality of the visual system.[6]

I could easily cite additional examples to delineate the practical knowing-how from the theoretical knowing-that. "Learning to ride a bicycle" and "factually knowing how to ride a bike" do not require knowledge of the regularities and physical laws of the bicycle. And acquiring or possessing competence in using a natural language (e.g., German) neither consists in nor presupposes the acquaintance with the syntactic form and semantic content of all sentences that can be uttered in the German language. In other words, construing a relation to a realm of

---

5 The following two examples are taken from Nemirow (2007), 38.
6 Within Marr's (1982) algorithmic approach, the first step of the visual system's activities concerning object perception consists in discerning the corners and edges and, hence, the perimeters of the object.

theoretical knowledge and linguistic propositions is not necessary, previously or conditionally, for an agent's acquisition and exercise of the knowing-how practices in order to begin executing the practice (e. g., bicycling or dancing). Talk of such a realm immediately reminds the philosopher of Russellian "propositions", Fregean "thoughts", or a set of "possible worlds". Consequently, the practice of, say, actually riding a bicycle must be clearly distinguished from the syntax and semantics of those sentences of ascription, report, and evaluation by means of which one attributes the ability to ride a bicycle to Peter, for example, or reports to other persons *that* Peter can ride a bicycle.

It is crucial to see that neither instantiation nor the syntax and semantics of linguistic sentences of ascription is at issue in the actual execution of knowing-how as a practical skill.[7] What pertains to instantiation becomes the object of a scientific analysis of the processes correlated with knowing-how (e. g., neurobiological and physical processes). The questions concerning the sentences of ascription are the object of syntactic and semantic analysis in the philosophy of language and in linguistics. Neither of these two perspectives, instantiation or ascription, though, also grasps the performative character of the practice (e. g., of actually riding a bicycle). The peculiar nature of practical skills, capabilities, competences, and executions itself, which I subsume under the term "knowing-how", is not a question of the instantiation of theoretical (e. g., neurobiological or linguistic) rules. In the argument I defended in this article, it is instead a question of the practical, internal knowing-*how* in every case and of the rule-following ability inherent in each. Thus, the ballerina does not have to be acquainted with neurobiology and the mechanics of bodily movements before her elegant and expressive movements in order to execute them. Even if the ballerina is assumed to know the best possible neurobiology and mechanics of bodily movement, that knowledge would still not enhance her performance. Indeed, one would have to be glad if the propositional knowing-that did not hinder the performance.

---

7   Stanley and Williamson (2001) take quite a different position. They base their argumentation on the syntax and semantics of attributive sentences in order to define knowing-how merely as a version of knowing-that. Stanley and Williamson's presentation is formally brilliant in its development, but in my opinion it entirely fails to reflect the genuine character of knowing-how. Though this article is not about a critical examination of Stanley and Williamson's views, much of what I present here can be seen as a criticism of their thesis.

2. Knowing-How and Propositional Knowledge

In the above examples of fluently functioning practice, the issue is neither conscious intentions nor propositional knowledge. Nor is it the inferential relations that are characteristic of propositions. The central concern is with the executions as executions, not with making the practice (e.g., of bicycling) depend on the application of conscious intentions, linguistic propositions, and logical inferences in order to enter into and to perform fluently functioning practice of bicycling or dancing. Having the concept of an activity, such as swimming, does not constitute swimming, nor does it help the ability to swim. Even if I possessed the best possible conceptual propositional knowledge about swimming and had the best possible imaginary pictures of swimming (and could hence pass any quiz on the subject with the greatest success), I still might not be able to swim. Even if the pool were right in front of me, I would not know what to do if I were asked to jump into the water and swim. Obviously, both learning to do something successfully and practicing or exploiting practical skills and competencies entails learning by doing. That kind of learning cannot be replaced by any lecture hall theory, be it ever so complete and perfect.

Learning by doing is what knowing-how is about, for each instance of knowing-how is knowledge of practice and action that is embodied in the practices, actions, skills, and capabilities themselves—that is, in practice itself. It shows up only when successfully executed. So knowing-how does not mean a certain type of pre-existing knowledge that is poured into actions as though into containers or that must crystallize in them. That image equates the practices, actions, skills, and capabilities with initially empty forms of knowledge that pre-existing knowledge-how would require in order to manifest itself as a knowing-how. This erroneous image would completely miss the performative character of practice and thus of knowing-how itself.

I also call attention to a second, equally misleading picture. Knowing-how as skills, capabilities, adroitness, and habitual customs, each of which constitutes its own particular practice, cannot be understood and analyzed according to the model of beliefs, nor, hence, as the classical model of knowledge as "justified true belief". Why not? The answer is simply that beliefs can obviously play an important role in knowing-how, yet the knowing-how understood as skill and ability is not about either beliefs or the conditions of theoretical truth; it is about the conditions of practical success and satisfaction. Every knowing-how is tied to conditions of satisfaction (to success or failure in practice), not to conditions of truth (which one must necessarily connect to linguistic propositional judgments). Hence, the modeling of knowing-how does not have to be based primarily on beliefs but rather on practical skills, capabilities, and adroitness. This readjustment in matters of modeling is crucial to clarifying the relation between knowing-*how* and knowing-*that*.

If beliefs were constitutive and conditional for knowing-how, then one would have to deliver a theory of knowing-how in the terms of belief and the propositional and inferential mechanisms built into beliefs. But no one has yet succeeded in doing so, for the reciprocal effects between beliefs and knowing-how are not of the kind that the belief regarding a practical skill (e. g., swimming, cello-playing, speaking, thinking, or acting) in itself leads to possession of the practical skill and competence and the ability to demonstrate them. On the contrary, close examination shows that beliefs are in many cases based on abilities (in the case of knowing and recognizing, for instance, on abilities to know and recognize). People's beliefs do not come out of the blue, nor have they been instilled by a divine spirit or by evolution as prefabricated, isolated, and individuated beliefs. Beliefs are already past their genesis, and their future still lies ahead of them.

This genealogical dependence of beliefs on abilities is relevant in cases where (as in classical epistemology) beliefs are part of the justification of claims to truth and knowledge. Take, for example, the coherence theory of truth and knowledge. This theory takes beliefs as foundations in a way that connects the truth of a judgment to the coherence of the beliefs informing that judgment. In order for beliefs to do this job, however, one must already possess the epistemic ability to use beliefs to justify and give reasons. And that ability itself cannot simply be a bare belief, for then the threat of infinite regress would arise, and justifications of claims of truth and knowledge could never be well founded. More incisively, the ability to account for and justify something cannot itself be a knowing-that; it must be a knowing-*how*, if one can meaningfully speak of justified and well-founded theoretical knowledge at all.

In this sense even the "logical space of reasons"[8] still depends on a knowing-how that is already presupposed and utilized. Moreover, the justifications and accounts of theoretical claims to truth (and, analogously, of moral and ethical claims to being right) that are derived from the

---

8   Sellars (1956).

practice of reason-giving and reason-taking in the logical space of reasons are linked with the demand to be implemented in further theory-building, in human life practice, or in both. In all these cases the indispensability of knowing-how is eminently conspicuous. For without the necessary application knowledge, even the most elegant theoretical, moral, or ethical justification remains but an empty exercise in intellectual self-reflection. In an ethical account, for instance, the formally most conclusive moral argumentation still offers no guarantee for factually moral ways of living.

In this context it again becomes clear that a satisfactory philosophy of language, of mind, or of action is not possible without recourse to the fundamental function of knowing-how. Without taking the knowing-how dimension into account, one cannot arrive at any comprehensive answer to the question of a life world's and a life practice's *normativity* (i.e., the degree to which it is internally connected with people's speaking, thinking, and acting) and, thus, its ethics. At this juncture, what is likely the deepest seat of knowing-how in life becomes apparent.

Moral (and religious) experiences and questions center on how the individual is supposed to live rightly, on how that person should come to terms with love, jealousy, sickness or death. These are no questions of *theoretical* knowledge that could be answered by a metaphysical (or theological) call from the realm of theoretical propositions. The moral (as well as the religious) person is not to be thought of as someone possessing an arsenal of theoretical moral (and religious) knowledge. If all is well, this person has the practical knowing-how that enables him to manage his life. The knowing-how that pertains to the right way to lead one's life can be regarded as the highest and most demanding form of practical knowing-how. Because other persons always have a bearing on any success that an individual may have in leading his or her life (after all, one cannot do it on one's own), knowing-how can also be seen as the distinguished seat of the *conditio humana*.

Given the analysis of knowing-how and its central position in this article thus far, the question of exactly what type of rule-following characterizes knowing-how practices becomes all the more interesting.

II. Knowing-How as Practice Knowledge and as the Ability to Follow Rules

1. Practice-internal Rule-Following

The rule-following characteristic of knowing-how practices is *internal* to the practices themselves. It cannot be described as a criteria-governed application of external rules, nor as a propositionally conceived knowledge of rules. More specifically, the practice's very inescapability when it comes to knowing-how makes it impossible to conceive the rule-following ability (which this practice embodies) as a mere application or species of knowing-*that* underlying the knowing-*how*. The following four points are highly relevant in this context.

First, successful execution of knowing-how (e. g., how to ride a bicycle) does not require an explicitly conscious intention of the agent. And to keep balance while bicycling, Peter must avoid making that ability depend on either a previous or concurrent, explicitly conscious intention, lest he endanger his balance even before he begins riding. Second, a successfully practiced knowing-how does not require an explicit knowledge of the procedural rules that one must assume are satisfied in the successful practical execution of bicycling or tying a necktie, for instance. To use Wittgenstein's felicitous expression (which he coined to describe actual speaking), one could say that in successful practice of knowing-how people follow the rule "blindly"[9]. Practical rule-following does not depend on preexisting knowledge, a choice, a recognition, or an intuition. It does not even depend on inspiration. Third, successful knowing-how does not require an explicit representation of either the practical knowing-how involved or the practical rules in order for the agent to follow that representation in a second step and engage in the action (e. g., keeping one's balance while riding a bicycle, or executing the movements of a ballerina). Fourth, no explicit knowledge of the other circumstances and contextual dependencies of success is required in successful knowing-how. To ride a bicycle, Peter does not need to know the material peculiarities of the pavement or the anatomical mechanisms of his leg and joint movement.

If one asks how knowing-how is acquired, learned, and taught, the answer in most cases is that it is mainly a result of showing, illustrating,

---

9 Wittgenstein (1980), § 219.

providing examples, practicing, and training. In successful acquiring, learning, and teaching knowing-how, the practice-internal regularity of these executions is absorbed and incorporated. It becomes quasi-organic and organizes experience. For example, one can say that Paul can continue on his own to master the practice and technique of riding a bicycle; that he knows how to ride a bicycle, tie a necktie, provide an argument or proof, or deal with Claudia. Such skills and capabilities need to be learned and practiced. Adroitness does not simply come from nowhere, not even in theory, much less in practice. The acquisition and development of practical skills of knowing-how consist in mastering the practice and technique in question and thereby building up the required skills, activating them, exploiting them, and employing them efficiently. If someone succeeds at playing the cello or providing a proof, he or she has every reason to be happy about it, not least because the action is not the mere application of a knowing-*that* and of a theoretical (and criteria-based) rule knowledge but rather a nonreductive practical skill and practice-internal ability to follow rules.

The theoretical groundlessness of the practice executions themselves need not trouble anyone as long as the practice runs smoothly. Only a metaphysician of the "ultimate grounds" would need to be concerned in light of this thought. The nonmetaphysical facet of the practice-internal ability of rule-following is rather the fact that being practically and pragmatically established regarding successful knowing-how practice provides all the certainty one could reasonably expect and affords everything needed for the successful exercise of one's skills, capabilities, and competencies. To demand any more evidence than the practical success itself would be self-destructive.

2. *Action and Rule*

The various practical processes differ in character, but in none of them do things occur without any regulation. They all exhibit the internal connection between practices and rules, between actions and rules. Yet how is this connection to be understood? And where do criteria and propositional knowledge come in? Perhaps the example of language, more precisely competence in using language and signs, can clarify these questions and the limits on the role that propositional knowledge plays in knowing-how.[10]

To what extent is rule-following in actual speaking (and in other practices such as bicycling, tying a necktie, cello-playing) dependent on or independent of propositional knowledge of these rules? If Peter is unable to respond to a question by spelling out the rule and the propositional knowledge that he followed in speaking, bicycling, or cello-playing, for example, must I then assume that he cannot speak, ride a bicycle, or play the cello, although I just heard him speak, saw him ride a bicycle, and heard him play cello? I am not concerned merely with the situation in which Peter happens to be tired and thus cannot articulate what is asked of him, though he would be able to do so after a double espresso. The situation I mean is much graver. It is the irritating point that the *practice-internal* ability to follow rules escapes articulation in its own peculiar way. Indeed, the more I strive to articulate it by way of propositions, the more elusive it becomes.[11] I would first like to detail this scenario by drawing on some of Wittgenstein's ideas about following rules in language as a practical ability acquired through training and practice beginning early in life. Then I would like to expand on these analyses of rule-following in language, extending them into the region of rule-following in what we generally regard as knowing-how practices.

At first it seems attractive to conceive of the relation between the "expression of a rule" (e. g., a directional road sign, as in Wittgenstein's example[12]) and "my actions" by stating that it is determined by explanatory interpretation (and propositional interpretation, or knowledge-that) regarding what the rule says about *how* I am supposed to respond to the road sign (i. e., what direction I have to take). But as Wittgenstein rightly notes, there are many equally legitimate interpretations (and, I may add, many propositionally formulatable knowing-that sentences) that are consistent with the expression of the rule. One such interpretation might be *not* to go in the direction indicated by the road sign's arrow but rather in the opposite direction, or even down the signpost and into the ground.

---

10 Chapter 3 in Abel (forthcoming 2012) will treat this subject.
11 The relevance of nonpropositional forms of knowledge is a constant subject in the work of Hogrebe (1992, 2006).
12 Wittgenstein (1980), § 198.

The answer to a knowing-how question (e.g., "Do you know how the directional road sign works?") can indeed lead to a propositional answer (e.g., "I know that the sign points in the direction shown by the arrow" and "I know that we must take the direction in which the arrow points"). But this possibility does not mean that the orientational function of the directional sign depends on a that-proposition. It is actually the other way around: Only because the directional road sign is grounded in known customs does it become the orienting sign that it is in practice.

This example shows that one must differentiate between two cases, neither of which can be conceived of as dependent on propositional interpretation and propositional knowledge-that. The first is that in which one is not yet competent in, say, communicating through language and signs or riding a bicycle. Merely claiming that a linguistic or practical (and propositionally constituted) competence is innate or presupposed does not help. And saying that the demonstration of competence in language and signs (and in bicycle riding) is based on the interpretation of a theoretical rule (or, analogously, on propositional knowledge of bike-riding) would lead to a regress of interpretations-*that* and of propositions-*that*. This regress could be ended only by an intellectual leap through which the infinite chain of propositions was itself brought to a final propositional termination. Yet that tactic would be linguistic, intellectual, and propositional dogmatism, which does not occur when people continue their practices fluently.

The second case is that in which one has already acquired competence in using language and signs (or, say, riding a bicycle). The profound insight that Wittgenstein offers with his example of the directional road sign is that, even *after* the successful acquisition of competence in using language and signs, fluent speaking and understanding in a language (or smooth bicycling) is not a propositionally formulated or even formulatable theoretical knowledge-*that*. The issue is rather one of a basic practice knowledge, an ability, a practical skill, an adroitness, an understanding about practices—in a word: a knowing-how.

This reasoning makes it clear that each factual action, or practice, is *not* brought into accord with the rule through an explanatory interpretation-that and a propositional knowledge-that. Wittgenstein rightly draws the conclusion that one can grasp a rule *without* resorting to explanatory interpretation.[13] Analogously, and with particular regard to

---

13 Wittgenstein (1980), § 201.

the other, nonlinguistic knowing-how practices, I put it more sharply by stating that in matters of learning and engaging in a practice there is a kind of rule-following that cannot be regarded as the comprehension and application of a propositionally formulatable rule but must rather be understood as an entirely practice-internal ability to follow rules.

A doubting Thomas might well agree with Wittgenstein and object that the expression of a rule cannot regulate its own application and implementation. Now, if the focus is placed on the practice-internal following of rules, the question would be whether the rule *does* regulate its own implementation and thus whether I would have to override Wittgenstein's fundamental insight. The answer is no. The proposed diagnosis about rule-following also applies to practice-internal rules. But how is that validity to be understood?

To answer this question, I introduce a terminological difference between "rule" and "regularity". By regularity I mean practice-internal rule-following in the sense of the regularity of the executions inherent in this practice itself. The confusing aspect is that practicing something (e.g., playing cello or riding a bicycle) yields the regularities that the executions internally follow as executions. By contrast, I use the word "rule" to mean that guideline which is necessary, say, in a language community for linguistically correct usage of the language and binding, say, for the linguistic grammar of attributive sentences (such as "Peter knows how to ride a bicycle").

There is a genealogical relation between rule and regularity. The successful application of a rule (which is external, propositionally formulatable, and criteria dependent) rests on the rule's compliance or fitting interplay with regularity. At the level of practice-internal executions, the main concern is with those interpretation- and proposition-free regularities that are internally connected with the factual execution of one's practices and skills. Successful knowing-how praxis internally instantiates and exemplifies those regularities that are proper to it as a successful practice-internal ability to follow rules. Simple examples are successful bicycling and fluent speaking, thinking, and acting.

Hence, the success of a propositional rule knowledge-*that* ultimately depends on the practice-internal ability to follow regularities. But that dependence also means that the rule-propositionalists cannot be correct in proclaiming a systematic priority of knowing-*that* over knowing-*how*. In this context I also emphasize Wittgenstein's important insight that practices of speaking, thinking, acting, and behaving are not always completely limited everywhere by rules. This conclusion in no way implies inability to distinguish between the right and the wrong use of a word or between what is and what is not the ability to ride a bicycle. But the limits of a word's are not cast in granite. Rather, we humans are the ones who must draw those boundaries, and we do so quite successfully in practice. We would say that Peter can ride a bicycle if he is able to do so by steering the handlebars with his feet and moving the pedals with his hands. At the circus this feat would likely reap applause as an artistic bicycling skill. But if he were to shoulder the bicycle and move about on his hands so that the bicycle's rear wheel rolled on the ground, we might well hesitate to say that this action might still be called "riding a bicycle". And what if Peter stubbornly defied every usual description of bicycling and asserted that he was indeed "riding a bicycle" exactly as meant by the standard expression "ride a bicycle" in the ascriptive sentence, "Peter knows how to ride a bicycle"? Well-rehearsed practices tend to convey a reliable understanding of what it does and does not mean to be able to ride a bicycle or to ride it only in an unusual way.

As for speaking, acting, and the other nonlinguistic practices, Wittgenstein showed that following a rule is not something that only *one* person could do *once* in his or her life.[14] One might even say that "following a rule" is a somewhat legal matter. With reference to the justification for using a word (e.g., *same*) Wittgenstein says that "someone else can teach me" that, in a given context, "same" is the "right" word.[15] This is true not only for successful speaking and, hence, not only for interpersonal communication but also for the internal rule-following ability in all of one's practices beside, before, and outside language.

But what exactly is one to make of this idea? Two points are important. First, in order for knowing-how to be acquired, repeated rule-following and regular action and practice must occur. If Peter should succeed only once (and perhaps by pure accident) at what is known as bike-riding, people would not likely speak of his feat as the ability to follow rules. Second, two or more persons must in principle be able to execute the action in order to speak of and identify it as bicycle riding in the first place. For following rules is a mode of action shared with other persons, and in this sense a *public* mode of action, skill, and competence. When a person accidentally succeeds once at tying a necktie yet fails in every

---

14 Wittgenstein (1980), § 199.
15 Wittgenstein (1980), § 378.

further attempt, people would not assert that he is able to tie a necktie. A rule-following action must be executed repeatedly to count as successful rule-following. This requirement is analytically inherent in every talk of a "rule" and of "regularity." Without such regularity, practical skills and competencies do not count as learned or successfully taught.

If the aforementioned conditions of knowing how to follow rules are met, and if one is dealing with, say, Peter's practical skill at riding a bicycle, then special attention has to be drawn to the following four facets of practical skills and competencies. (a) They cannot be analyzed or demonstrated through the linguistic syntax and semantics of the propositional attributive sentences assigned to them. That approach would constitute a linguistic fallacy. (b) They cannot be analyzed or demonstrated by recourse to mental images. That approach would constitute a mental fallacy. (c) "Fit" (or "nonfit") between the ascriptive sentences and the factual praxis (i. e., of linguistically and propositionally formulatable rule knowledge and practice-based, internal knowing how to follow rules) is not about either isomorphy or the insertion of propositional content into the mechanisms of praxis (e.g., bicycling). (d) The actual executions of an action are not an explicit external demonstration of an implicit inner praxis knowledge. Rather, the generation and layering of practical knowing-how operate entirely through the internal ability to follow rules in the sense discussed above. This knowing how to follow rules is presupposed in every example of linguistic, propositional knowledge both as requisite competence in using language and signs and as appropriate application knowledge, not the other way around.

3. Practical Execution Skills and Conceptual Knowledge

At the level of the mind's operations and of explicit speaking, thinking, and acting, everyone is familiar with the processes of linguistic, conceptual, and action-related discrimination, individuation, connection, delineation, generalization, elimination, comparison, inclusion, preferencing, and classification. Regarding the skills and competencies entailed by successful knowing-how praxis, I call attention to the pre-theoretical and pre-propositional analogue of the aforementioned operations related to understanding, language, and action. Actions and perceptions at this level, and thus in knowing-how, cannot simply be isolated from each other. They work together holistically, so the following remarks refer to practical skills, sensory perception, and their mutual interpenetrations.

In sensory perception and everyday behavior people encounter processes of pre-conceptual, pre-linguistic, pre-theoretical, pre-propositional (e. g., sensoriphenomenal) discrimination, individuation, connection, delineation, elimination, inclusion, preferencing, comparison, ordering, and sensoripractical classification. Sensoriperceptual and practice-internal patterns, scenarios, schemata, and contents are both actively used and passively experienced. It may be that a person passively experiences these things when simply looking around or carrying out a practice (e. g., bicycling) automatically, that is, without any intervention from explicit understanding or rules, while still obviously doing, seeing, discriminating, and sensoriphenomenally individuating a great many things. One can differentiate, find shades of color, or competently ride a bicycle in this manner without needing explicit knowledge of grammar and other rules.

Such things touch on the fundamental question of the relation between the practical (as well as sensorial) execution skills and the forms of explicitly conceptual knowledge. I propose now to take the perspective developed above—namely, that the level of sensory, perceptual, and practical executions of a knowing-how praxis is a sort of pre-theoretical analogue of the activities of theoretical understanding—and recast it as a version of the relation between practical skills and conceptual knowledge.

The sensoriperceptual and practical skills of a knowing-how praxis are not simply mere analogues in a world other than that of concepts, language, propositions, or, in a nutshell, conceptual knowledge in the sense of a knowing-*that*. They can be regarded as genuine and primordial achievements of organization. They prefigure relation of human beings to the world, to other persons, and to themselves long before the conceptual organization of this triangular relation began to be made explicit by, say, rule formulations, rule knowledge, conceptual classifications, theories, and evaluations. If I were to stick to the image of the aforementioned analogy, I would find myself confronted with the difficulty of having to explain how these two analogous areas are connected and in what way they might be bridged. The metaphor of bridging a gap, though, would be unsatisfactory in this context. For factually sensoricognitive executions are not about bridging gaps. Rather, the praxis of actual perception, speech, thought, and action obviously functions in such a way that the individual components working within are fused together and interpenetrate holistically from the very outset.

Against this background I would like to argue for another model, one based on a continuity and genealogy of the explicitly conceptual and linguistic propositional knowledge in the sphere of practical and sensoriperceptual discrimination and individuation. These basal mechanisms and practical abilities can also be considered the foundation for higher order mechanisms: "forming concepts", "having conceptual abilities", "being able to formulate rules", "possessing conceptual knowledge", and "having conceptual understanding". The sensorial and practical abilities involved in discrimination and the other basic operations of the human being's orientation to the world are epistemically relevant; They have the power to generate knowledge. As these components develop, they become manifest as higher level formations, such as rule-formulating and concept-forming competencies, each with its own proper form that cannot simply be reduced to sensorial and practical matters. These higher order mechanisms do essential work as conceptual knowledge for one's relation to and understanding of the world, other persons, and oneself. And the point, in my opinion, is that the practical and sensoriperceptual competencies have knowledge-generating and world-orienting functions *by virtue* of their practical and sensoriperceptual character.

I do *not* presuppose that practical and sensoriperceptual skills include quasi-dormant, but principally finished, theories and epistemics that eventually become ever more explicit and finally begin to lead their own lives. Rather, the challenge consists in showing that both the practical and the sensoriperceptual abilities are epistemically relevant, knowledge-generating, and experience-organizing elements. "Practical and perceptual (e.g., visual) thinking" would be a heading for this endeavor. In brief, considerably more is meant than merely the image of sensoriperceptual input or that of practical, technical ability as a prerequisite to conceptual knowledge. For this claim pertains to the cognitive and epistemic power of sensoriperceptual and practical abilities themselves. This message is the crucial thing. With respect to the connection between perception, action, and thought, the issue is what one can call "visual and practical thinking". The issue is not that sensoriperceptual and practical skills—perceptual and practical knowing-how—be seen merely as secondary illustrations and, at best, as versions of a more basally conceived domain of conceptual knowledge (as intellectualists and propositionalists never grow weary of asserting).

At the same time I emphasize that the epistemic relevance and knowledge-generating power of the sensoriperceptual and practical abilities is located within a holistic and internal interplay of perception, action, and cognition. This image does not amount to reductionism to the biology of the human being's visual system and physical capabilities. From the outset it is accentuated that the conceptual knowledge stemming from the knowledge-inducing power of the sensoriperceptual and practical component develops its own genuine logic, one that cannot be subjected to biological, physical, or a computer-based reduction.

Does this constellation have a common basis from which one might nonreductionistically conceive both the pragmatic genealogy of conceptual knowledge and the interpenetrations of perceptual, practical, and conceptual knowledge? This question must be answered because it is no longer possible to be concerned with the alternative position of reductionistically tracing conceptual knowledge back to sensoripractical skills, or vice versa. A unified theory of perception, cognition, and action can be achieved only as a holistic web and no longer in the isolated strands of theories of perception, cognition, and action.[16] I believe a possible common basis emerges as soon as one takes seriously the obvious insight that all conceptual, perceptual, and practical knowledge occurs and is performed by virtue and by means of sign- and interpretation processes.

In a general philosophy of signs and interpretation, an attempt is made to develop the continuous spectrum of abilities and knowledge—ranging from the sensoriperceptual and practical to the conceptual—on the basis of the different systems and functions of signs and interpretation.[17] Conceptual and linguistic (as well as gestural, auditory, olfactory, and haptic) processes take place by way of signs and interpretations. I would like to expand this view to the field of perceptual and practical knowing-how skills, of which one could also say that they take place in the use and comprehension of signs and interpretations. This agenda admittedly necessitates a detailed explanation that cannot be provided in this article. For now, I identify only three aspects:

---

16 This matter will be addressed in more detail in Abel (forthcoming 2012, chap. 4: "Unified Theory of Knowledge and Action"). See also Abel (1999), chap. 13.
17 For a thorough explication of this approach and on what follows in this article, see Abel (1989; 1995; 1999; 2004; 2010a).

1. With respect to concepts and conceptual knowledge in the narrow sense of the term, the dependence upon signs and interpretations is obvious, as is the fact that the processes they entail take place *in* and *via* signs and interpretations. To use Peirce's famous statement, there is no thinking without signs, and I add that there is no thinking without interpretations. To assume the existence of thought and conceptual knowledge *without* signs and interpretations would make no sense. For one would then have to know already what thought and knowledge is without signs and interpretations. To have and use terms and concepts and to have conceptual abilities at one's disposal can be regarded as a particular way of using signs and interpretations and of possessing the appropriate competencies relating to language, signs, and interpretation.
2. The sensoriperceptual and practical processes can also be described methodologically as constructs of signs and interpretation. The moment one describes processes retrospectively and prospectively, distinguishing their profiles and constituents, reporting about them, or communicating them, one is building constructs of signs and interpretation in order to discriminate, individuate, describe, communicate, and evaluate.
3. The direct executions of sensoriperceptual and practical abilities can be understood as executions within a world of signs and interpretations. They can be conceived as factual executions of signs and interpretations (including perceptual and practical course corrections). Their character as signs and interpretations is just as palpable with perceptual processes as with actions.[18] This statement could easily apply to the other practical skills as well.

If such a web of processes involving signs and interpretation seems plausible in these three ways, then it is also clear what it means to regard these processes as the common basis for the entire spectrum of a nonreductionist and pragmatic genealogy of conceptual and linguistic propositional knowledge drawn from perceptual and practical knowing. The challenge and essential philosophical task in this respect can easily be formulated: The processes of perceptual and practical knowledge would have to be conceived of and spelled out as different processes for using signs and interpreting them.

---

18 From cognitive perception psychology, cf. in this respect especially Rock (1984). On action see Lenk (1978).

With this background in mind, one may also see that the sensoriperceptual patterns, scenarios, schemes, and content of perceptual and practical knowing will be transferred into the semantic logic of language and understanding as soon as the following two things occur: (a) when the elementary acquisition of the abilities and competencies operating in the perceptual and in the practical field develops into higher level abilities and competencies and then encompasses explicit rule formulations (a process that occurs quickly with children) and (b) when the sensoriperceptual patterns, scenarios, schemes, and contents become attributable to other persons, communicated, reported, classified, and evaluated by an individual from either the first-person or an observer perspective.

As for the profile of knowing-how as a practical skill, one usually overlooked nuance is crucial: the difference between (a) the knowledge of *how* to follow a rule and (b) the formulatable knowledge about *what* one does when following the rule and about the retrospective statement of what rule one has followed. Anyone unable to recognize this difference will also be unable to appreciate the peculiar nature of rule-following as a practical skill in the sense discussed in this article. Without this distinction, it is scarcely possible to see, as rightly emphasized by Wittgenstein,[19] that knowing-how is an ability, a way of acting, a "technique" that functions "without reasons".[20] I add that it functions without propositional reasons and without previously accessible and linguistically formulatable propositional knowledge. As soon as the practices have been acquired and habitualized, this practical competence functions on its own, as a matter of course. It is these nonpropositional practical matters of course that make up and underlie the fluent functioning and success of practical, epistemically relevant skills, capabilities, customs, and competencies. Knowing-how praxis is *not* an object of logical semantics. It is the former that makes the latter possible.

As noted above, knowing-how praxis does not function as a logical or causal effect that occurs when propositional knowledge is applied to praxis (e. g., successful bicycling). If knowing-how praxis *did* function in that manner, it would be self-destructively intellectualistic and in a way paradoxical, for it would both presuppose and deny the knowing-how that is the competence of using and understanding language and signs. Furthermore, it would obscure all moderate versions of propositional knowledge that are obviously to be encountered in successful know-

---

19   Wittgenstein (1980), § 199; § 232.
20   Wittgenstein (1980), § 211.

ing-how. For when closely examined, every knowing-how praxis proves to be a complex, holistic web of interpenetrations involving many different forms and practices of knowing. And one of these components is propositional knowledge.

Translation from German by Hadi Nasir Faizi and David R. Antal.

References

Abel (1989): Günter Abel, "Interpretations-Welten", in: *Philosophisches Jahrbuch* 96, 1–19.
Abel (1994): Günter Abel, "Was ist Interpretationsphilosophie?", in: J. Simon (ed.), *Zeichen und Interpretation I*, Frankfurt/Main, 6–35.
Abel (1995): Günter Abel, *Interpretationswelten. Gegenwartsphilosophie jenseits von Essentialismus und Relativismus*, 2nd edition, Frankfurt/Main.
Abel (1999): Günter Abel, *Sprache, Zeichen, Interpretation*, Frankfurt/Main.
Abel (2004): Günter Abel, *Zeichen der Wirklichkeit*, Frankfurt/Main.
Abel (2007): Günter Abel, "Forms of Knowledge: Problems, Projects, Perspectives", in: P. Meusburger (Series ed.); P. Meusburger/M. Welker/E. Wunder (Volumes eds.), *Knowledge and Space: Vol. 1. Clashes of Knowledge*, Dordrecht, 11–33.
Abel (2010a): Günter Abel, "Knowing-How. Eine scheinbar unergründliche Wissensform", in: J. Bromand/G. Kreis (eds.), *Was sich nicht sagen lässt. Das Nicht-Begriffliche in Wissenschaft, Kunst und Religion*, Berlin, 319–340.
Abel (2010b): Günter Abel, *La filosofia dei segi e dell'interpretazione*, Neapel.
Abel (2011): Günter Abel, "Knowledge Research: Extending and Revising Epistemology", in: G. Abel/J. Conant (eds.), *Berlin Studies in Knowledge Research*, vol. 1, *Rethinking Epistemology*, Berlin/New York.
Abel (forthcoming 2012): Günter Abel, *Die Logik praktischer Fähigkeiten*, Berlin/New York.
Hogrebe (1992): Wolfram Hogrebe, *Metaphysik und Mantik. Die Deutungsnatur des Menschen*, Frankfurt/Main.
Hogrebe (2006): Wolfram Hogrebe, *Echo des Nichtwissens*, Berlin.
Lenk (1978): Hans Lenk, "Handlung als Interpretationskonstrukt", in: H. Lenk (ed.), *Handlungstheorien interdisziplinär*, vol. II, Munich, 279–350.
Lewis (1990): David Lewis, "What Experience Teaches", in: W. G. Lycan (ed.), *Mind and Cognition*, Oxford, 499–518.
Marr (1982): David Marr, *Vision: A Computational Investigation into the Human Representation and Processing of Visual Information*, San Francisco.
Nemirow (2007): Laurence Nemirow, "So This Is What It's Like. A Defense of the Ability Hypothesis," in: Torin Alter/Sven Walter (eds.), *Phenomenal Concepts and Phenomenal Knowledge. New Essays on Consciousness and Physicalism*, Oxford, 32–51.
Rock (1984): Irvin Rock, *Perception*, New York.

Sellars (1956): Wilfrid Sellars, "Empiricism and the Philosophy of Mind", in: H. Feigl/M. Scriven (eds.), *Minnesota Studies in the Philosophy of Science*, vol. 1: *The Foundations of Science and the Concepts of Psychology and Psychoanalysis*, Minnesota, 253–329.

Stanley/Williamson (2001): Jason Stanley/Timothy Williamson, "Knowing How", in: *The Journal of Philosophy*, 411–444.

Wittgenstein (1980): Ludwig Wittgenstein, *Philosophische Untersuchungen*, Schriften 1, Frankfurt/Main.

Knowledge-How, Linguistic Intellectualism, and Ryle's Return

David Löwenstein

1 Introduction

How should we understand knowledge-how – knowledge how to do something? And how is it related to knowledge-that – knowledge that something is the case?[1] In this paper, I will discuss a very important and influential aspect of this question, namely the claim – dubbed 'Intellectualism' by Gilbert Ryle – that knowledge-how can be reduced to knowledge-that.[2] Recently, Jason Stanley and Timothy Williamson have tried to establish Intellectualism with the aid of linguistic considerations.[3] This project – Linguistic Intellectualism – will be criticized on three levels. First, I will reconstruct and object to Stanley and Williamson's positive argument in favour of Intellectualism (section 2). Second, I will assess their view of the relationship between knowledge-how and practical ability and argue that their stance is not well-motivated (section 3). Third, I will discuss their criticism of Ryle's objection against Intellectualism. After distinguishing between different versions of Ryle's argument, I will show that its strongest version is both immune to the objection by Stanley and Williamson and a decisive argument against their own theory (section 4). Given that Intellectualism fails for these three reasons, I finally draw on a broader reading of Ryle in order to develop the beginnings of a positive account of knowledge-how and its relationship to knowledge-that (section 5).

---

1 It should be briefly noted that not every use of "knows that" indicates knowledge-that and not every use of "knows how" indicates knowledge-how. For example, "She knows that person" does not indicate knowledge-that, and "He knows how long the journey takes" does not indicate knowledge-how. For various other uses of "knows how" which do not indicate knowledge-how, compare Bengson/Moffet/Wright (2009, 389).
2 Ryle (1945, 1949).
3 Stanley/Williamson (2001).

2 Linguistic Intellectualism

2.1 The Argument from Linguistics

In the words of Gilbert Ryle, champions of Intellectualism hold that "the primary exercise of minds consists in finding the answers to questions".[4] Stanley and Williamson fit this bill precisely. Their argument in favour of Intellectualism relies on the idea that knowledge-how consists in knowing the answer to a question, namely the question which is syntactically 'embedded' in the sentence attributing knowledge-how.[5] For example, if Gregor knows how to ride a bicycle, linguists tell us that the expression 'how to ride a bicycle' is an embedded version of a question like "How can one ride a bicycle?" Then, to say that Gregor knows how to ride a bicycle is just to say that Gregor knows an answer to such a question, that he knows that such-and-such would be a way for him to ride a bicycle. Since this knowledge is knowledge-that, Stanley and Williamson conclude that knowledge-how is a species of knowledge-that.

It is crucial to note that this argument begins with an account not of knowledge-how, but of *ascriptions* of knowledge-how. These, the claim goes, are best understood in terms of embedded questions. The reason is simple:

> Our view of ascriptions of knowledge-how is very straightforward. It is just that the standard linguistic account of the syntax and semantics of embedded questions is correct.[6]

I will not give a full account of the linguistic theories Stanley and Williamson cite in order to get their argument going.[7] However, let me label the linguistic theory they rely on the Karttunen Account – in honor of their central point of reference, an article by Lauri Karttunen[8] – and indicate briefly that its core idea is a unified explanation of the semantics of 'to know' followed by an interrogative particle:

---

4   Ryle (1949), 27.
5   Stanley/Williamson (2001).
6   Ibid. 431.
7   Cf. Ibid. 417–432.
8   Karttunen (1977).

Hannah knows where to find a nickel.
Hannah knows whom to call for help in a fire.
Hannah knows why to vote for Gore.[9]

All of these are accounted for in terms of knowledge-that as an answer to an embedded question: Hannah knows where to find a nickel just in case she knows, for some place x, that x is a place where to find a nickel. This is an answer to the question "Where to find a nickel?" By the same token, Hannah knows why to vote for Gore just in case she knows, for some reason r, that r is a reason why to vote for Gore. This is an answer to the question "Why vote for Gore?"

Stanley and Williamson merely add that this theory of knowledge-*wh* – knowledge-where, knowledge-whom, and so on – can be extended in order to include a further interrogative particle: "how". Thus, what they derive from the Karttunen Account is that ["Hannah knows how to ride a bicycle."] is true if and only if, for some contextually relevant way w which is a way for Hannah to ride a bicycle, Hannah knows that w is a way for her to ride a bicycle.[10]

Generally speaking, they hold that "S knows how to F" is true if and only if, for some contextually relevant way w which is a way for S to F, S knows that w is a way for them to F.[11] This is obviously a claim about the truth conditions of "S knows how to F", but Stanley and Williamson go on to infer a claim about knowledge-how and knowledge-that, Intellectualism. I will call this argument the Argument from Linguistics. This is how it works in detail:

1 Linguistics determines that "S knows how to F" is true if and only if S knows an answer to the question "How to F?"

---

9   Examples from Stanley/Williamson (2001), 417 f.
10 Stanley/Williamson (2001), 426.
11 Sometimes it is true that somebody knows how to do something, but it may be impossible to specify a way to do so because the activity is too complex. David Wiggins (2005) has proposed several such examples and even argued that in such cases, we have little reason "to believe that there is some simple propositional knowable that spells out the whole set of complete procedures which would somehow comprise and exhaust" a person's knowledge-how (Wiggins 2005, 271). I sympathize with this worry, but I will nevertheless grant the existence and knowability of such propositions for the sake of Stanley and Williamson's argument.

2 Linguistics determines that S knows an answer to the question "How to F?" if and only if, for some contextually relevant way w which is a way for S to F, S knows that w is a way for them to F.

3 Thus, linguistics determines that "S knows how to F" is true if and only if, for some contextually relevant way w which is a way for S to F, S knows that w is a way for them to F.

4 If Linguistics determines that "S has the property P" is true if and only if S has the property Q, then P is Q.

5 Knowledge how to F is, for some contextually relevant way w, knowledge that w is a way to F.

6 Thus, knowledge-how is a species of knowledge-that if and only if knowledge how to F is, for some φ, knowledge that $\varphi(F)$.

7 Thus, knowledge-how is a species of knowledge-that.

The first part of this argument, premises 1 and 2 and their consequence 3, are what Stanley and Williamson derive from the Karttunen Account. It is therefore possible to reject their argument simply by rejecting that theory. However, Stanley and Williamson are correct when they point out that the Karttunen Account is a standard theory in formal semantics. Of course, this does not mean that everybody has to accept it, but it would be better to have good reasons not to do so, reasons independent from the question of knowledge-how.

One such independent reason to reject the Karttunen Account would be a better rival theory from the literature within linguistics. One such rival has been proposed by Manfred Krifka,[12] and Laura Michaelis explicity shows how an even further linguistic account bears on the philosophical problem of knowledge-how.[13] A further option is to deny that knowledge-how can be understood in terms of knowledge-wh, or – with Jonathan Schaffer – to deny that knowledge-wh can be understood in terms of knowledge-that.[14] Finally, as opposed to rejecting the Karttunen Account in general, one might argue specifically against the first two premises of the Argument from Linguistics, such as Daniele Sgaravatti and Elia Zardini,[15] who object to premise 1, and Rowland Stout[16] who objects to premise 2.[17]

---

12 Krifka (2001).
13 Michaelis (forthcoming).
14 Schaffer (2007).
15 Sgaravatti/Zardini (2008).

However viable and interesting these dialectical options are, I will not discuss them here. My strategy will be to show that – independently of the outcome of these debates at the intersection of linguistics and the philosophy of language – the Argument from Linguistics fails. It fails because it is not clear that linguistics can do philosophical work in the way Stanley and Williamson assume. Their bridge from the analysis of language to metaphysical claims is premise 4. As far as I can see, they do not even explicitly formulate this claim, but they evidently rely on it.[18] I will provide two indepenedet arguments for the conclusion that this bridge is unstable. We should reject premise 4 and with it the Argument from Linguistics.

Before getting started, let me make two remarks. First, by arguing that *this* bridge from language to metaphysics is unstable, I do not reject *every* such bridge. I agree that much of philosophy has to start with an analysis of the way we think and talk. Given that premise 4 turns out to be a problematic connection between language and metaphysics, we should still look out for better ones.

---

16   Stout (2010).
17   Both of these enterprises rely heavily on the distinction between what does and what does not qualify as an answer to a question in a strict sense. I cannot discuss this issue in the present context, but on a standard view of the matter, both seem to fail. *Sgaravatti and Zardini* claim that one can know an answer to the question "How to square the circle?" – the *only* correct answer "In no way!" – without thereby knowing how to square the circle. But they acknowledge that a question of the form "How can one F?" typically carries the presupposition that there is a way to F. Thus, "In no way!" cannot count as an answer in the strict sense. Compare: When asked "Have you stopped beating your wife?", one can deny the question's presupposition, but only "Yes" and "No" count as answers in a strict sense. By contrast, *Stout* argues that one might know *of* an answer to a question that it is true without thereby knowing an answer *to* that question. He thinks that both "What does 3 + 5 make?" and "What added to 5 makes 8?" can be answered by citing the fact that 3 + 5 makes 8. However, the answers to these questions are "8" and "3", respectively. One can know these answers in virtue of the fact that 3 + 5 makes 8, and one can even say "3 + 5 makes 8" in response to them. But that fact is not *itself* an answer. "8" and "3" are the answers, even if this is conveyed in the statement "3 + 5 makes 8". After all, one can also know that "3" is the answer to "What added to 5 makes 8?" in virtue of a different fact, the fact that 8−5 makes 3, and one can convey this answer by saying "8−5 makes 3". In any case, it is not clear at all whether such a case can be constructed for knowledge-how.
18   Cf., for example Stanley/Williamson (2001), 411 f.

Second, it could be argued in defense of Stanley & Williamson that while premise 4 might indeed be problematic, the instance needed for their argument might nevertheless be true. That is, we might simply replace 4 with:

4★ If Linguistics determines that "S knows how to F" is true if and only if, for some contextually relevant way w which is a way for S to F, S knows that w is a way for them to F, then knowledge how to F is, for some contextually relevant way w, knowledge that w is a way to F.

But this defense begs the question. If 4 is implausible, the burden of proof about particular instances of this scheme – such as 4★ – is on those *defending* them, not on those rejecting them. In other words, unless we learn what should be special about knowledge-how and the expression "to know how to", we can reject the Argument from Linguistics by rejecting 4.

2.2 Language understated

I have promised two arguments against Stanley and Williamson's bridge from language to metaphysics. The first of these has already been developed nicely by Ian Rumfitt.[19] He argues that if the Argument from Linguistics is sound, so are corresponding arguments about languages other than English. And if metaphysical claims can be inferred from claims about *some* language, these claims should be consistent with what *other* languages suggest. In short, if Stanley and Williamson urge us to take language seriously, we cannot take only *one* language seriously. They understate language.

This shows that the Argument from Linguistics is specific to English. In particular, the first step of the argument should be corrected. It turns out that we do not arrive at 3, but at:

3★ Linguistics determines that "S knows how to F" is true *in English* if and only if, for some contextually relevant way w which is a way for S to F, S knows that w is a way for them to F.

But how can we now use 4 in order to derive 5?

4 If Linguistics determines that "S has the property P" is true if and only if S has the property Q, then P is Q.

---

19 Rumfitt (2003).

3★ concerns the truth-conditions of English ascriptions of knowledge-how whereas 4 concerns *all* ascriptions of knowledge-how. Accordingly, Rumfitt points out that this step of the argument will be undermined if we find examples of ascriptions of knowledge-how which differ from those in English. In particular, the argument fails if we find a sentence "such that the best semantic theory for the language to which it belongs will construe its knowledge-verb as expressing (in that sentential context) a relation between a person and an activity."[20] Without looking out for such sentences, it would be premature to infer a metaphysical thesis – such as Intellectualism – from linguistic data. And "the quest for such examples cannot be confined to English sentences. This is because the metaphysical thesis concerns the nature of knowledge-how, not the semantics of 'knows how'."[21] In short, it is possible to derive 5 from 3★ and 4 *only if* the linguistic evidence across languages is univocal.

Given the vast number and diversity of languages, it should not be surprising that there is evidence to the contrary. This is even aggravated by the fact that French, a language very closely related to English, provides such counterexamples. Consider sentences involving the expression 'savoir faire', for example "Il sait nager." Again bracketing the exact linguistic subtleties, there is a crucial difference between this sentence and English sentences involving 'to know how': "Il sait nager" is not analyzed in terms of embedded questions. Therefore, it is impossible to apply the Karttunen Account and infer that this sentence attributes knowledge-that.[22]

A natural defense on behalf of Stanley and Williamson is to claim that the 'linguistic deep structure' even of prima facie counterexamples like this still turns out to conform to the analysis they have given for English. Ascriptions of knowledge-how in other languages might also involve embedded questions – even if there is no interrogative particle involved at all.[23] But this seems to beg the question. Why should we accept such a globalization of the Karttunen Account? Stanley and Williamson could try to justify this conjecture with a further conjecture, the idea that "the uses of 'know' in ['Hannah knows how to ride a bicycle'] and ['Hannah knows that penguins waddle'] are translated by the

---

20   Ibid. 160.
21   Ibid.
22   Cf. Rumfitt (2003), 160 f.
23   Jason Stanley (2011) claims that this is the case.

same word" in all natural languages.[24] However plausible such a line of argument from lexical uniformity to syntactic deep structure may be, we can yet again make the unsurprising discovery that some languages use different words in order to translate these two uses of 'to know'. In most cases, German fits this bill,[25] but in any case, Rumfitt shows that Russian is an absolutely clear case in point.[26] Thus, this line of defense is blocked by the linguistic data.

I conclude that Rumfitt is right: Taking language seriously requires taking langua*ges* seriously. And then, the Argument from Linguistics fails because premise 4 turns out to be false. It cannot be true that if Linguistics determines that "S has the property P" is true if and only if S has the property Q, then P actually *is* Q. Instances of "S has the property P" in different languages have different truth-conditions. And it would be absurd to hold that *all* of these are necessarily instantiated whenever *any* instance of "S has the property P" is true, regardless of the language it is formulated in.

2.3 Language overstated

The above argument relies on the idea that Stanley and Williamson do not take language seriously enough. However, there is a complementary reaction to their argument: Why should linguistics bear on metaphysics in the first place? Alva Noë has suggested that the Argument from Linguistics is an instance of "good old-fashioned Oxford philosophy (GOOP)",[27] which is "methodologically backward".[28] According to him, there is no reason to infer facts about knowledge from facts about 'to know'. Stanley and Williamson simply overstate language.

So far, this worry is far too general. But it relies on more than an intuitive unease with a certain style of philosophy. While Noë goes on to criticize mainly how Stanley and Williamson treat knowledge-

---

24 Stanley/Williamson (2001), 237.
25 In German, there are three verbs corresponding to the three uses of 'to know' philosophers have found most important. Knowledge by acquaintance – as in "I know her" – is expressed by 'kennen', knowledge-that is expressed by 'wissen' and knowledge-how is expressed by 'können'. However, instead of 'können', one sometimes also uses 'wissen wie', which is similar to 'to know how'.
26 Cf. Rumfitt (2003), 164.
27 Noë (2005), 279.
28 Ibid. 290.

how and abilities (compare section 3), I think that there is an independent argument for the conclusion that the Argument from Linguistics overstates language.

I have already indicated that the Karttunen Account is praised, among other things, because it offers a unified explanation of the expression 'to know' followed by various interrogative particles including 'how'. But in philosophical discussions, there is one such construction which has received considerable interest, namely: "Tom knows what it is like to be a bat." Crucially, the Karttunen Account treats 'knows what it is like to' along the very same lines.[29] It implies that Tom knows what it is like to be a bat just in case he knows that something is the case. In line with Stanley and Williamson's analysis of knowledge-how, the most natural candidate is this: Tom knows what it is like to be a bat just in case he knows, for some quality of experience q, that q is what it is like to be a bat.

I think that these considerations provide a further reason to reject Stanley and Williamson's bridge from linguistics to metaphysics:

4   If Linguistics determines that "S has the property P" is true if and only if S has the property Q, then P is Q.

If the Karttunen Account is true, this claim seems to be false. For even if ascriptions of knowledge-what-it-is-like are true just in case some knowledge-that about qualia can also truly be ascribed, it does not follow that knowledge-what-it-is-like therefore *is* knowledge-that about qualia. Rather than knowledge *about* qualia, knowledge-what-it-is-like essentially involves phenomenal *acquaintance with* something, say, being a bat. Even if this were coinstantiated with knowledge-that, how could it actually *be a species* of knowledge-that?

It should be noted that some philosophers explain the difference between knowledge-what-it-is-like and knowledge-that by claiming that knowledge-what-it-is-like is a form of knowledge-how – very roughly, knowledge how to imagine the experience in question.[30] Of course, this

---

29 I will not go into detail here, but linguists have confirmed that this is correct.
30 The so-called Knowledge Argument against physicalism – formulated most prominently by Nagel (1974) and Jackson (1982, 1986) – has been criticized on these grounds by Levin (1986), Nemirow (1990) and Mellor (1993). This dialectic has partly motivated a renewed interest in knowledge-how and Intellectualism; compare, for example, Stanley/Williamson (2001, 442 ff.) and Snowdon (2003, 26 ff.). Compare Alter (2001) and Nida-Rümelin (2009) for

view presupposes the falsity of Intellectualism since knowledge-what-it-is-like, understood in terms of knowledge-how, only differs from knowledge-that if knowledge-how differs from knowledge-that. Thus, in criticizing the Argument from Linguistics on the basis of a notion of knowledge-what-it-is-like that differs from knowledge-that, I have to reject this view on pain of committing a *petitio principii*. As already indicated, I think that knowledge-what-it-is-like is best understood in terms of the notion of acquaintance and I see no need to understand acquaintance in terms of knowledge-how. But I cannot discuss this issue here in more detail.

My argument about knowledge-what-it-is-like is a reductio of the conjunction of premise 4 and the Karttunen Account. Thus, it could also be used in order to attack the latter rather than the former. But I will not take sides on the Karttunen Account in this paper. My argument only targets Stanley and Williamson's bridge from language to metaphysics and remains neutral on the linguistic question. One reason why I think that this is a better way to take the present argument is that there are parallel problems at the intersection of formal semantics and the philosophy of language. In particular, I think that modality is a phenomenon that should lead us to the same conclusion. Even if the best linguistic account of some expressions analyzes them in terms of possible worlds, it does not follow that possible worlds are more fundamental than modalities and that modalities actually *are* constellations of possible worlds. Given linguistic theory, there is still room for debate about metaphysics.

Let me briefly point out a further complication for Stanley and Williamson. The kind of knowledge-that they take to be identical with knowledge-how involves ways of doing things. But what are these? Stanley and Williamson write:

> We believe that any successful account of natural language must postulate entities such as ways. But we shall not have much more of substance to say about the metaphysics of ways in this paper.[31]

By analogy, it seems like they are committed to the claim that any successful account of natural language must postulate entities such as qualia. For just like ways of doing things are part of the kind of knowledge-that

---

further discussion, especially on the question if the response relies essentially on the notion of know-how rather than the notion of ability.

31 Stanley/Williamson (2001), 427.

to which knowledge-how is reduced, qualia are part of the kind of knowledge-that to which knowledge-what-it-is-like is reduced.[32] Again, we are presented with the claim that a metaphysical question – "Are there qualia at all?" – is decided by linguistic theory. Of course, one might try to avoid this problem by looking for a different analysis of knowledge-what-it-is-like as knowledge-that which does not involve qualia. But even if such an analysis is possible, it merely solves this further complication. It still remains incredible that knowledge-what-it-is-like actually is knowledge-that.[33]

I conclude that Stanley and Williamson's bridge from linguistics to metaphysics does not hold. We have good reason to reject premise 4 and thereby the Argument from Linguistics.

3 Intellectualism and ability

Having cast some doubt on Stanley and Williamson's Argument from Linguistics, let me now go on to cast doubt on its conclusion. In particular, I will discuss what Stanley and Williamson say about the relationship between knowledge-how and practical ability (section 3.1) and show that this view is unfounded (section 3.2).

3.1 From abilities to practical modes of presentation

If knowledge-how is merely knowledge that such-and-such is a way to do something, where does the ability to actually do so come in? Stanley and Williamson answer: "Nowhere, and why should it?":

> It is simply false, however, that ascriptions of knowledge-how ascribe abilities. [...] [A]scriptions of knowledge-how do not even entail ascriptions of the corresponding abilities. For example, a ski instructor may know how to perform a certain complex stunt without being able to perform it herself.

---

32 Of course, even if qualia exist, the logical space for accounting for them will remain large. For example, they may be ontologically grounded in other entities such as brain-states.
33 In conversation, Jason Stanley has expressed his readiness to bite these bullets. While this issue leads to a more thorough discussion of phenomenal knowledge, my reaction is: So much the worse for Linguistic Intellectualism.

Similarly, a master pianist who loses both her arms in a tragic car accident still knows how to play the piano. But she has lost her ability to do so.[34]

Does this mean that it is simply a mistake to think that there is a conceptual connection between my knowledge-how and my actions? Let us assume for a moment that knowledge-how has indeed little to do with ability. Still, Stanley and Williamson see for themselves that there are prima facie counterexamples to their theory:

> Suppose that the way in which John is riding his bicycle is in fact a way for Hannah to ride a bicycle. So, where the demonstrative 'that way' denotes John's way of riding a bicycle, (28) seems true:
> (28) Hannah knows that that way is a way for her to ride a bicycle.
> Relative to this context, however:
> (29) Hannah$_i$ knows [how PRO$_i$ to ride a bicycle].
> seems false.[35]

What Hannah lacks is a connection between her knowledge and *her* actions rather than John's. Stanley and Williamson agree. However, they think that what is missing is not Hannah's ability to ride a bicycle, but something concerning her knowledge-that about John's way of riding a bicycle. In order to account for this missing element, they amend their linguistic account of the truth-conditions of "S knows how to F" with some philosophy of language and claim the following:

> "S knows how to F" is true if and only if, for some contextually relevant way w which is a way for S to F, S knows that w is a way for them to F, and S entertains w under a practical mode of presentation.[36]

Accordingly, what Hannah lacks is a practical mode of presentation of John's way of riding a bicycle. She entertains this way in a purely demonstrative mode of presentation and therefore lacks knowledge-how.

But what are practical modes of presentation of ways of doing things? Stanley and Williamson rely substantively on this concept, and unless they spell out in more detail what such modes of presentation might be, their attempt of accomodating the intuitive connection between knowledge-how and action is incomplete. Even worse, enter-

---

34 Stanley/Williamson (2001), 416.
35 Ibid. 429 f.
36 Cf. Ibid. 430. I will omit the question whether modes of presentation are part of pragmatics rather than semantics. Stanley and Williamson are right: Their account can accomodate this, too. Further, let me note that the addition of modes of presentation changes the content of parts of the Argument from Linguistics, but that this does not bear on the discussion above.

taining some way w under a practical mode of presentation might come down to knowing how to instantiate it – Stanley and Williamson's account would then be circular.[37] Alternatively, entertaining some way w under a practical mode of presentation might be having the ability to instantiate that way, contrary to their explicit denial of a connection between knowledge-how and ability.[38]

However, Stanley and Williamson try to avoid these consequences by leaving the exact nature of practical modes of presentation for another occasion. What matters, they claim, is that there are such things, never mind what exactly they are. They argue by analogy:

> Suppose that John is looking in a mirror, which he mistakenly believes to be a window. Seeing a man whose pants are on fire, and not recognizing that man as himself, John forms the demonstrative belief that that man is on fire. [...] [R]elative to this envisaged context, (26) is true and (27) false:
> (26) John believes that that man has burning pants.
> (27) John believes that he himself has burning pants.[39]

It is typically assumed that (26) and (27) both picture John as believing in the truth of one and the same proposition, that he believes, of himself, that he has burning pants. In (26), John believes, of *the person he happens to be*, that that person has burning pants. In (27), John believes, of himself *as himself*, that he has burning pants. Canonically, this is explained by appeal to the mode of presentation under which John entertains that belief about himself: The first case involves a demonstrative mode of presentation and the second case a first-personal mode of presentation.

Now, Stanley and Williamson grant that it may be very difficult to characterize exactly both what first-personal and what practical modes of presentation are. But they compare (26) and (27) with their examples (28) and (29) which are quoted on the previous page.

> In both cases, however, one can provide an existence proof for such modes of presentation. If, as is assumed in much of philosophy of language, there is a sound argument from (26) and (27) to the existence of first-personal guises of propositions, then there is a sound argument from (28) and (29) to the existence of practical guises of propositions.

Alva Noë has criticized this analogy as "plainly circular" because we have "no independent reason to believe that the complement clauses

---

37 Cf. Koethe (2002).
38 Cf. Rosefeldt (2004) and Jung/Newen (2010).
39 Stanley/Williamson (2001), 428.

in (28) and (29) express the same proposition."⁴⁰ But this is mistaken since the first part of the Argument from Linguistics provides such an independent reason. One may disagree with this argument, but Stanley and Williamson do not commit a dialectical mistake.

This concludes Stanley and Williamson's attempt of accomodating the intuitive connection between knowledge-how and action. They argue that there are such things as practical modes of presentation of ways of doing things and claim that these are independent from being able to engage in those ways of doing things. How such modes of presentation should be understood, however, remains an open question.

3.2 Abilities reestablished

It has turned out that Stanley and Williamson's commitment to practical modes of presentation of ways of doing things is not without its problems. However, it is a consequence of two ideas they explicitly endorse, the Argument from Linguistics on the one hand, and the claim that knowledge-how is independent from ability on the other. Given this background, assuming such modes of presentation is a bullet they simply have to bite. Accordingly, there are two independently sufficient ways to avoid such a commitment. Above, I have already criticized the Argument from Linguistics. Now, I will cast serious doubt on their view of the relationship between knowledge-how and ability.

Like Stanley and Williamson, Paul Snowdon also thinks that knowledge how to F is independent from the ability to F.[41] In order to support this claim, these authors rely on examples like the following:[42]

Skiing   A ski instructor knows how to perform a complex stunt. Still, he is not able to do so himself.

Piano   A piano player loses her arms. She still knows how to play the piano, but has lost her ability to do so.

---

40 Noë (2005), 288.
41 Snowdon (2003).
42 Skiing and Piano are taken from Stanley/Williamson (2001), 416, the others from Snowdon (2003), 8 f. Snowdon also cites three further cases, but I think that these can be accounted for along the lines of the cases I discuss. Namely, Snowdon's cases "(b)" and "(d)" parallel Piano and his case "(e)" parallels Etiquette.

Pudding   A cook knows how to make Christmas pudding. If the world's supply of sugar is obliterated, he still knows how to do so, but has lost his ability to do so.

Etiquette   Susan knows how to address the queen correctly, but is unable to do so because she gets too nervous in the queen's presence and develops a speech impediment.

I agree that these cases show that there is *some* sense in which one may have knowledge how to do something without having the ability to do so. However, they eventually fail to support the claim that knowledge-how is independent from ability. In order to bring out this point, I will have to offer better redescriptions of these alleged counterexamples.[43]

I take it that three of the four cases can be redescribed following a simple strategy: The person in question does not only have knowledge how to do something, but also has the ability to do so, which, for some reason or another, is blocked from being executed.[44]

Piano   The piano player still has the ability to play the piano, but without her arms she cannot execute it. Her ability is blocked by a bodily impediment.

Pudding   The cook still has the ability to prepare Christmas pudding, but without sugar he cannot execute it. His ability is blocked by an external impediment.

Etiquette   Susan has the ability to address the queen correctly, but because of her nervous condition she cannot execute it. Her ability is blocked by a psychological, possibly a neurological impediment.

These redescriptions are perfectly intelligible because the notion of an ability is tied to the notion of possible successful action, given some preconditions. If these preconditions are absent, and the action in question therefore cannot be performed, there is no need to infer that there is no ability in the first place.[45] But what if the impediments in question are so

---

43 One might criticize this by claiming that my redescriptions are biased. Bengson et al. (2009) have tried to support the rival claim that knowledge-how and ability are independent by engaging in a statistical study of people's intuitive verdicts about these and cognate cases. Bracketing how plausible experimental philosophy is in general, this study in particular is flawed in several respects, as shown by Jung/Newen (2010).

44 Cf. Noë (2005).

45 Cf. Hawley (2003). Of course, abilities cannot be understood in such a way that too many impediments are compatible with their existence. For example, it would be false to say that I have the ability to beat every chess grand master,

severe that the abilities are not only temporarily, but *forever* blocked from being executed? For example, having lost her arms, the piano player will never be able to play again. If so, how can we continue to believe that she has the ability to do so?

This is a fair question, but it is not the only one. It has a sibling, namely: How can we continue to believe that she knows how to do so? What the alleged counterexamples would have to show is that these questions have to be answered independently. But they fail to establish this. Rather, it is possible – and, I would say, very plausible – to claim that the question whether or not the ability to play the piano can be retained even if both arms are lost has to be answered in tandem with the question whether or not knowledge how to do so can be retained under these conditions. Either both are retained or none.[46] Then, the most natural position is that both the knowledge-how and the ability to play the piano are lost. However, both may be able to persist in the way part of that person's brain works and what information is stored there. When these features of her brain are gradually lost, so are both the ability and the knowledge-how in question.[47]

This leaves one last case in support of the view that knowledge-how and ability are independent:

Skiing A ski instructor knows how to perform a complex stunt. Still, he is not able to do so himself.

I am not alone in thinking that this case is misdescribed even more profoundly.[48] The idea that this ski instructor knows how to perform a stunt simply relies on the fact that he is able to teach others how to perform that stunt. But the knowledge-how *that* implies it is not knowledge how to *perform* the stunt, but knowledge how to *teach others* how to perform

---

which happens to be blocked because of the limits of my intelligence. I simply do not have that ability. There is a threshold for what may count as a blocked ability and what cannot sensibly be called an ability at all.

46 Let me note two things at this point. First, this account is also available to Stanley and Williamson. The acquaintance with a way of doing something under a practical mode of presentation may very well fade if it is not used in action. Thus, even if knowledge-how is understood along the lines of Linguistic Intellectualism, it might still be linked to ability. Second, this connection between knowledge-how and ability leaves entirely open whether or not some knowledge-that related to the capacities in question might survive their loss. I will come back to this in section 5.2.
47 Cf. Jung/Newen (2010), 117.
48 Cf. Noë (2005).

the stunt. It is a commonplace truth that knowledge how to teach how to do something does not imply knowledge how to do it. Some teachers know how to do what they teach, others do not. Maybe there are activities one can only know how to teach if one knows how to perform them oneself. Performing a ski jump is not one of those, but maybe philosophizing and conducting an orchestra are. But this still does not show that knowing how to perform and knowing how to teach how to perform are the same thing.

I conclude that the alleged independence of knowledge-how from ability has not been established by any of the examples cited by Stanley and Williamson and Snowdon. Even though I have not positively shown why knowledge-how and ability are connected,[49] there is no reason to detach them.[50] I will come back to this connection in section 5.

4 Ryle's objection

I have argued that Stanley and Williamson fail to establish Intellectualism (section 2) and that they fail to establish the claim that knowledge-how is independent from practical abilities (section 3). In this section, I will turn to Gilbert Ryle's influential stance on knowledge-how. He writes:

> Philosophers have not done justice to the distinction which is quite familiar to all of us between knowing that something is the case and knowing how

---

49 Those who support this view include Carr (1979, 1981) and Katzoff (1984). Often, they rely on possible successful action as a crucial connection between ability and knowledge-how. Above, I have subscribed to possible success as an ingredient of the notion of ability, but I will not continue to explore these questions in my own discussion of knowledge-how. Katherine Hawley (2003) has proposed an interesting analysis of this issue.

50 The claim that knowledge-how is a form of ability implies that animals pose a further threat to Linguistic Intellectualism. For if some abilities of animals can be classified as knowledge-how, this theory implies that they possess knowledge-that. But given knowledge-how in animals, it should remain an open question whether or not they have propositional knowledge, too. Stanley and Williamson think that we ascribe knowledge-that to animals as happily as knowledge-how (2001, 438 f.). But I take it that most of us would credit, say, some dogs with knowledge how to catch a frisbee, but have trouble conceiving of those dogs as knowing that such-and-such is a way for them to catch a frisbee (cf. Rosefeldt 2004, Noë 2005 and Jung/Newen 2010). However, I will bracket animal cases in this context.

> to do things. In their theories of knowledge they concentrate on the discovery of truths or facts, and they either ignore the discovery of ways and methods of doing things or else they try to reduce it to the discovery of facts. [...] I want to turn the tables and prove that knowledge-how cannot be defined in terms of knowledge-that and further, that the concept of knowledge-how is a concept logically prior to the concept of knowledge-that.[51]

I will argue that Stanley and Williamson's reconstruction of Ryle's argument misses a crucial point. I distinguish between different versions of Ryle's argument and show how what I take to be the strongest version is both immune to the objection by Stanley and Williamson and a decisive argument against their own version of Intellectualism. Thus, next to my above arguments against the motivation of Linguistic Intellectualism, Ryle's objection provides a clear-cut argument showing directly that this view is mistaken.

4.1 Stanley and Williamson's Ryle

Gilbert Ryle writes:

> The crucial objection to the intellectualist legend is this. The consideration of propositions is itself an operation the execution of which can be more or less intelligent, less or more stupid. But if, for any operation to be intelligently executed, a prior theoretical operation had first to be performed and performed intelligently, it would be a logical impossibility for anyone ever to break into the circle.[52]

Here is how Stanley and Williamson construe this reasoning:

> Ryle's argument has two premises:
> (1) If one Fs, one employs knowledge how to F.
> (2) If one employs knowledge that p, one contemplates the proposition that p.[53]

> If knowledge-how is a species of knowledge-that, the content of knowledge how to F is, for some φ, the proposition that $\varphi(F)$. So, the assumption for reductio is:
> RA: knowledge how to F is knowledge that $\varphi(F)$.[54]

---

51 Ryle (1945), 4 f.
52 Ryle (1949), 31.
53 Stanley/Williamson (2001), 413.
54 Ibid. 414.

The idea is that, given (1) and (2), RA implies that "doing anything would require contemplating an infinite number of propositions of ever-increasing complexity."[55] But since nobody should be credited with the ability to do that and many people in fact do employ knowledge-how, RA is rejected. However, Stanley and Williamson think that

> Ryle's argument does not get off the ground. There is no uniform reading of the two premises in Ryle's argument on which both are true; the argument is unsound.[56]

The problem is that premise (1) has to be restricted to intentional actions, while contemplating propositions, as mentioned in premise (2), is not an intentional action. As for premise (1), there are many things we do without knowing how to do them. Stanley and Williamson present convincing examples: digesting food or winning a fair lottery.[57] Thus, if Ryle's argument is to be valid, premise (2) will also have to be read as concerning an intentional action of contemplating.

Let me make this correction explicit and add two premises which have already been mentioned (2 and 5 below). Given these changes, this is a full statement of how Stanley and Williamson understand Ryle:

1 If one intentionally Fs, one employs knowledge how to F.
2 Knowledge-how is a species of knowledge-that if and only if knowledge how to F is, for some φ, knowledge that $\varphi(F)$.
3 If one employs knowledge that p, one intentionally contemplates the proposition that p.

---

4 Thus, if knowledge-how is a species of knowledge-that, to intentionally F requires contemplating an infinite number of propositions of ever-increasing complexity.
5 To intentionally F does not require that.

---

6 Thus, knowledge-how is not a species of knowledge-that.

Let me call this argument the Contemplation Regress. This reconstruction makes clear how the vicious regress arises. By 1, intentional action requires knowledge-how. Assuming the doctrine that knowledge-how is a species of knowledge-that, 2 requires that such knowledge-how is propositional. By 3, employing such knowledge requires contemplating

---

55 Ibid.
56 Ibid. 416.
57 Ibid. 414 f.

a proposition. Since this is an intentional action, by 1, it requires a further bit of knowledge-how. This, by 2, consists in a further bit of knowledge-that, the employment of which, by 3, requires contemplating a further, more complex proposition, and so on ad infinitum. Thus, premises 1–3 imply 4, which allows for the use of 5 in order to reject the doctrine that knowledge-how is a species of knowledge-that.

Where do Stanley and Williamson disagree with Ryle? They point out that the argument depends on premise 3, what I would like to call the Contemplation Requirement, and assert that this is "straightforwardly false".[58] If contemplating a proposition is an intentional action, "it is simply false that manifestations of knowledge-that must be accompanied by distinct actions of contemplating propositions".[59] If we say that the contemplation of a known proposition is in some sense required in order to employ knowledge-that, this contemplation should not be regarded as an intentional action.

Stanley and Williamson support this view with a counterexample due to Carl Ginet:[60]

> I exercise (or manifest) my knowledge *that* one can get the door open by turning the knob and pushing it (as well as my knowledge *that* there is a door there) by performing that operation quite automatically as I leave the room; and I may do this, of course, without formulating (in my mind or out loud) that proposition or any other relevant proposition.[61]

This is indeed suited at least to call the Contemplation Requirement into question. For my present purposes, I will therefore grant that the Contemplation Regress should be rejected.[62]

However, Stanley and Williamson miss a crucial part of Ryle's argument. Intellectualism, he writes, is committed to the view that to employ knowledge-that is

> always to do two things; namely, to consider certain appropriate propositions, or prescriptions, and to put into practice what these propositions or prescriptions enjoin. It is to do a bit of theory and then to do a bit of practice. [...] I shall argue that the intellectualist legend is false and that when

---

58 Stanley/Williamson (2001), 415.
59 Ibid.
60 Ibid.
61 Ginet (1975), 7.
62 It should nevertheless be noted that this counterexample conflates the contemplation of propositions with their *conscious* contemplation.

we describe a performance as intelligent, this does not entail the double operation of considering and executing.[63]

Of this 'double operation' of considering and executing, Stanley and Williamson have addressed only half. They have argued that considering propositions, understood as an intentional action, cannot be required for employing knowledge-that. However, they have left the "putting into practice" of these propositions out of the picture. This is puzzling, since they themselves quote Ryle as follows:[64]

> I largely rely on variations of one argument. I argue that the prevailing doctrine leads to vicious regresses, and these in two directions. (1) If the intelligence exhibited in any act, practical or theoretical, is to be credited to the occurrence of some ulterior act of intelligently considering regulative propositions, no intelligent act, practical or otherwise, could ever begin [...]. (2) If a deed, to be intelligent, has to be guided by the consideration of a regulative proposition, the gap between that consideration and the practical application of the regulation has to be bridged by some go-between process which cannot by the pre-supposed definition itself be an exercise of intelligence and cannot, by definition, be the resultant deed.[65]

Thus, Ryle can give away the argument sketched after "(1)" in this passage – the Contemplation Regress – and fall back on a second regress argument supporting the same conclusion: the one sketched after "(2)".[66] This argument can be presented as follows:

1★ If one intentionally Fs, one employs knowledge how to F.
2★ Knowledge-how is a species of knowledge-that if and only if knowledge how to F is, for some φ, knowledge that $\varphi(F)$.
3★ If one employs knowledge that p, one intentionally applies the proposition that p to the case at hand.

4★ Thus, if knowledge-how is a species of knowledge-that, to intentionally F requires applying an infinite number of propositions of

---

63 Ryle (1949), 30.
64 Cf. Stanley/Williamson (2001), 412.
65 Ryle (1945), 2.
66 Why have Stanley and Williamson overlooked this? In the part both they and I have omitted from the above quotation, Ryle mentions that the first regress "is the turn of the argument that I chiefly use" (1945, 2). Also, they quote only this passage from Ryle's Presidential Address on *Knowing How and Knowing That* (1945) and otherwise rely exclusively on Ryle's later discussion of knowledge-how in *The Concept of Mind* (1949), where the second argument plays a very minor role.

ever-increasing complexity to an infinite number of cases of ever-increasing complexity.

5★ To intentionally F does not require that.

6★ Thus, knowledge-how is not a species of knowledge-that.

I will call this argument the Application Regress. Obviously, it closely parallels the Contemplation Regress. Among other things, 1★, 2★ and 6★ are identical with 1, 2 and 6, respectively. Also, the inference from 1★-3★ to 4★ can be understood along the same lines as the corresponding inference in the first regress argument.

However, as my labels already indicate, the nature of the regress has changed (4★ and 5★). While the Contemplation Regress rejects Intellectualism on the grounds that it requires *contemplating* an infinite number of propositions, the Application Regress does so on the grounds that it requires *applying* these propositions to an infinite number of *cases*. Ryle himself explicitly states this problem. Speaking of the "go-between application-process" as construed by Intellectualists, he says:

> Consistency requires, therefore, that this schizophrenic broker must again be subdivided into one bit which contemplates but does not execute, one which executes but does not contemplate and a third which reconciles these irreconcilables. And so on for ever.[67]

> [I]t requires intelligence not only to discover truths, but also to apply them, and knowing how to apply truths cannot, without setting up an infinite process, be reduced to knowledge of some extra bridge-truths.[68]

Obviously, this difference relies on a different premise as the trigger of the regress, namely 3★, which I would like to call the Application Requirement. Let me evaluate the plausibility of this requirement with the aid of Stanley and Williamson's own example.[69]

I have granted that my knowledge that one can get the door open by turning the knob and pushing it does not have to be contemplated in order for me to be able to leave the room. However, there is clearly some sense in which I need to *apply* this knowledge in order do so. Given that I know that one can get the door open by turning the knob and pushing it, I must judge what specific action I need to perform in order to do so. This will turn on my knowledge of the location of the

---

67 Ryle (1945), 3.
68 Ibid. 5.
69 Stanley/Williamson (2001), 415, and Ginet (1975), 7.

door and how I can reach it. But, again, without applying this knowledge, it is not clear how it helps me actually leave the room.

John Koethe has suggested that an objection along these lines is "similar in spirit to Ryle's"[70] and claimed that it eventually defeats Intellectualism. I agree that Ryle can be read as making this argument. However, Stanley and Williamson are free to object against the Application Regress in the very same way as they have objected against the Contemplation Regress. They can simply deny that the application of propositions to cases is an intentional action: Even though employing knowledge-that *does* mean applying this knowledge to a case, such an application is not an *intentional* action. Just like one can walk intentionally without *intentionally* engaging in several sub-actions of muscle contraction, one can employ knowledge-that without *intentionally* engaging in the sub-action of applying it. Thus, both the Contemplation Regress and the Application Regress eventually fail.

4.2 Correctness

I have discussed how Stanley and Williamson understand Ryle and how they can answer both the Contemplation Regress, which they explicitly discuss, and the Application Regress, which they fail to address. In both cases, the problem is that if employing knowledge-that requires some further action, it is plausible to deny that it has to be an intentional action.

However, I think we should shift the issue from a problem about *intentional* action to a problem about *correct* action. This is both closer to Ryle's original ideas and more plausible independently.[71] And it leads to a third and final regress argument against Intellectualism.

This third argument can be understood as an adaptation of the Application Regress. Its core insight is that we should look not at acting *intentionally* and *intentional* application of knowledge-that, but at acting *correctly* and *correct* application of knowledge-that. Accordingly, I will call this argument the Correctness Regress. Here is how it works in detail:

---

70 Koethe (2002), 328.
71 Charles Wallis (2008) discusses extensively why conscious intent does not play an important role for knowledge-how, whether Intellectualism is true or not.

1' If one correctly Fs, one employs knowledge how to F.
2' Knowledge-how is a species of knowledge-that if and only if knowledge how to F is, for some φ, knowledge that $\varphi(F)$.
3' If one employs knowledge that p, one correctly applies the proposition that p to the case at hand.

4' Thus, if knowledge-how is a species of knowledge-that, to correctly F requires correctly applying an infinite number of propositions of ever-increasing complexity to an infinite number of cases of ever-increasing complexity.
5' To correctly F does not require that.

6' Thus, knowledge-how is not a species of knowledge-that.

I do not think that Gilbert Ryle does a very good job at distinguishing the Application Regress from the Correctness Regress.[72] Much of what he says naturally leads to the idea that knowledge is supposed to be applied intentionally and thereby to the Application Regress. All things considered, however, I hold that the Correctness Regress fits in more smoothly with Ryle's overall thinking about knowledge and action, and that it brings out the full force of his objection to Intellectualism.

The core fact which leads me to this conclusion is that Ryle hardly ever speaks of "intentional" action. Rather, he repeatedly states that he is interested in "operations [that are] intelligently executed".[73] Such 'exercises of intelligence' are picked out in terms of the attributes we can attach to them. They are actions which can be called 'witty', 'stupid', 'intelligent', 'smart', 'dull', 'attentive' and so forth.[74] In other words, they can be evaluated according to their rationality, simplicity, originality and the like – that is, in the light of *standards of intelligent conduct*. And according to these standards, actions can be better or worse, correct or incorrect.

These passages show that it is well justified to ascribe premise 1' to Ryle. Also, premise 3' is well supported by Ryle's texts. He explicitly writes that "whatever "applying" may be, it *is* a proper exercise of intelligence"[75] and that somebody who has learned maxims of playing

---

72 And neither do many of his commentators. For example, the presentations of Ryle's argument by Jennifer Hornsby (2005, 113 ff.) and David Wiggins (2005, 268 f. and 273) can be read in either way.
73 Ryle (1949), 31.
74 Cf. Ryle (1945), 1 f., and Ryle (1949), 26.
75 Ryle (1945), 3.

chess well "might still play chess stupidly, that is, be unable intelligently to apply the maxims".[76] Thus, the Correctness Regress expresses best what Ryle was up to all things considered: In order to apply knowledge-that, never mind whether or not this is an intentional action, one has to apply it *correctly*. And to do something correctly requires knowledge how to do so.

Let me remark that I do not want to claim that whether somebody acts correctly is independent from the question whether she acts intentionally. But I do claim that Ryle's argument can be formulated without bothering too much about this question. What is at issue is not – as in the first two regress arguments – the agent's inner life, her intentions and how she acts upon them. Rather, we are concerned with the explanation of doing something well or correctly, which transcends this inner life and includes essentially intersubjective standards.[77]

I think that this is an argument Stanley and Williamson cannot resist. After all, they are themselves committed to the claim that intersubjective standards play a role in ascriptions of knowledge-how. They write:

> Consider now:
> (19) Hannah knows how PRO to ride a bicycle.
> In such an example, we should expect the embedded question to have four interpretive possibilities, corresponding to (20a-d):
> (20a) Hannah knows how she ought to ride a bicycle.
> (20b) Hannah knows how one ought to ride a bicycle.
> (20c) Hannah knows how she could ride a bicycle.
> (20d) Hannah knows how one could ride a bicycle.[78]

(20a) and (20b) show that knowledge-how concerns doing something how it ought to be done – correctly. And (20b) and (20d) show that this is something which is not specific to a single person – it is intersubjective. However, Stanley and Williamson go on:

---

76 Ibid. 5.
77 A further remark: Ryle would probably add a second Correctness Regress, which relies on the claim that to apply knowledge-that requires correctly *contemplating* a proposition *before* correctly applying it (compare the passage quoted on page 284, as well as Ryle 1945, 2 ff.). But I do not see exactly how a proposition can be contemplated in an incorrect way, if this does not mean that it is not contemplated at all because what is actually contemplated is a different proposition. However, this complication is independent from the Correctness Regress as I have stated it.
78 Stanley/Williamson (2001), 424 f.

The interpretations given in (20a) and (20b) quite obviously seem to attribute some kind of propositional knowledge to Hannah, so they are not the interpretations underlying the thesis that knowledge-how is not a species of knowledge-that.[79]

Of course, these interpretations do not immediately show why Intellectualism is false. But they do play a role in showing that. By granting a role for intersubjective standards of correctness in knowledge-how, Stanley and Williamson have effectively granted premise 1' of the Correctness Regress. They think that "[i]t is rather interpretations such as (20c) and (20d) that seem to be at issue in philosophical discussions of knowledge-how" and that "(20c) [is] the paradigm reading of (19), on which we shall focus in the rest of this discussion".[80] But this is a mistake. Once we have seen that the different readings of ascriptions of knowledge-how support premise 1', the Correctness Regress is on its way.

This argument shows that Linguistic Intellectualism is false *qua* Intellectualism. Still, let me take the time and spell out the argument as applied to Stanley and Williamson's account.

Suppose that Hannah is riding her bicycle, which is something she does properly, or correctly, and that she thereby knows how to ride a bicycle. If Linguistic Intellectualism is true, her knowledge how to ride a bicycle boils down to her knowledge that, say, sitting in the saddle and pedaling is a way for her to ride a bicycle. Given that she correctly employs this knowledge in riding a bicycle, she knows how to employ her knowledge that sitting in the saddle and pedaling is a way for her to ride a bicycle. Given Linguistic Intellectualism, this knowledge-how again boils down to her knowledge that, say, placing herself on the saddle and letting her muscle memory do the rest is a way for her to correctly employ her knowledge that sitting in the saddle and pedaling is a way for her to ride a bicycle. But again, this knowledge needs to be applied.

Generally speaking, Linguistic Intellectualism leads to the result that to do something correctly (to F correctly) requires knowledge that w is a way to F, which requires knowledge that w' is a way to correctly employ knowledge that w is a way to F, which in turn requires knowledge that w★ is a way to correctly employ knowledge that w' is a way to correctly employ knowledge that w is a way to F, and so on ad infinitum.

---

79 Ibid. 425.
80 Ibid.

It is natural to wonder whether Stanley and Williamson can simply bite this bullet. The idea is that there is nothing wrong with the claim that knowing how to ride a bicycle involves knowing that an infinite number of propositions is true because there are other cases where such infinite propositional knowledge is accepted much more naturally. However plausible, it might be argued that some people's mathematical knowledge includes knowledge of an infinite number of true propositions. Unfortunately, however, even if there are such cases, this reply does not suffice to block the Correctness Regress. In order to reject 5', the premise in question, one would have to show not only that people may indeed have infinite propositional knowledge, but also that correct action requires the correct application of infinite propositional knowledge.

This, I take it, is a bullet nobody should be prepared to bite. Even if, say, my own mathematical knowledge were to include knowledge of an infinite number of true propositions, it would still be false that I rely on this knowledge when I solve equations or prove theorems. The direction of explanation would be exactly the other way around. My solving equations correctly and proving theorems correctly would make it plausible to attribute such infinite propositional knowledge to me – if such an attribution is plausible in the first place.

5 Knowledge-how and methodological knowledge

I have argued that the Correctness Regress is Ryle's strongest weapon against Intellectualism and the most plausible statement of his argument. In this last part of my paper, I would like to indicate briefly how Ryle draws on this insight and even suggests a more adequate account of knowledge-how and one specific form of knowledge-that: methodological knowledge.

But let me begin by remarking that the Correctness Regress does not entail this. As I use this term, methodological knowledge is a specific form of knowledge-that: knowledge that such-and-such is a way (or procedure or method) to F. This is just the kind of knowledge-that Stanley & Williamson have in mind. However, the Correctness Regress is neutral on the question whether or not any knowledge-that, let alone methodological knowledge, plays a role when an actor exercises knowledge-how. The only claim the argument entails is that *if* knowledge-that is involved *at all*, it cannot be *everything*. At least *some* knowledge-how is needed, as well.

Given this insight, one may even go on to claim that a distinction with such consequences should be abandoned and that both knowledge-that and knowledge-how should eventually be understood in terms of abilities.[81] By contrast, I will maintain this distinction and draw on Ryle's own further comments on knowledge-how and one of its paradigm cases in order to propose a positive account of knowledge-how its relation to methodological knowledge.[82]

5.1 Ryle on rules and knowledge-how

In the Correctness Regress, Ryle talks about knowledge-how in one of its paradigmatic roles: the explanation of correct action. Given this, he seems to suggest that *knowledge-how is an ability to do something according to intersubjective stardards of correctness*. But what are these?

Ryle explicitly draws a connection between knowledge-how and one kind of intersubjective standard of correctness: *rules*. He writes: "Knowing a rule is knowledge how."[83] And he also holds that the converse is true. When we credit people with knowing how to do something, he writes:

> Part of what is meant is that, when they perform these operations, they tend to perform them well, i. e. correctly or efficiently or successfully. Their performances come up to certain standards, or satisfy criteria.[84]

One of Ryle's prime examples of knowledge-how is knowledge how to draw inferences. He cites Lewis Carroll's tortoise,[85] who fails to grasp the inference in a modus ponens argument on the basis of an explicit statement of the corresponding rule of inference.[86] I take it that this

---

81   For example, Stephen Hetherington (2006, 2008) argues along these lines.
82   Spelling out the distinction between methodological knowledge and knowledge-how is a key problem in the current debate; compare, for example, Bengson/Moffett (2007), Williams (2008), Lihoreau (2008), and Fantl (2008). But this question is often framed in terms of a distinction between readings of ascriptions of knowledge-how which entail abilities and those which do not; compare footnote 91.
83   Ryle (1945), 7.
84   Ryle (1949), 29.
85   Carroll (1895).
86   Cf. Ryle (1945), 6 f.

well-known argument is simply an instance of the Correctness Regress: To correctly infer 'q' from 'p' requires knowledge how to do so. But if this knowledge consists in nothing but knowledge that the conditional '*if p, then q*' is true, that statement needs to be applied to 'p' — and *correctly* so. Thus, the question how to correctly infer 'q' from 'p' is transformed into the question how to correctly infer 'q' from 'p' and '*if p, then q*'. But this question raises the same problem and calls for a further premise to be added — if 'p' and '*if p, then q*', then 'q' — and so on ad infinitum.

Ryle expands on this particular instance of the Correctness Regress in his essay "*If*", "*So*", *and* "*Because*",[87] which has been published shortly after his works on knowledge-how. Here, he uses an analogy in order to spell out how he understands the notion of correct application.

> The Argument "Today is Monday, so tomorrow is Tuesday" is an application of "if today is Monday, tomorrow is Tuesday"; and it is in this notion of application that lies the answer to our question [...].[88]

> Knowing "*if p, then q*" is, then, rather like being in the possession of a railway ticket. It is having a licence or warrant to make a journey from London to Oxford.[89]

Since the ability to draw inferences is one of Ryle's own examples of knowledge-how, it is natural to wonder if this analogy carries over to knowledge-how in general.

On the one hand, we have the argument "Today is Monday, so tomorrow is Tuesday" and the statement "If today is Monday, tomorrow is Tuesday", and on the other hand we have Hannah's riding a bicycle correctly and — what? I propose that the missing element might be something like Stanley and Williamson's proposal as a definiens of knowledge-how. It might be Hannah's methodological knowledge that doing such-and-such would be a way to ride a bicycle.

For now, I would like to bracket the exact form of this methodological knowledge and rely on an intuitive understanding of this notion. Methodological knowledge is knowledge how something is done — knowledge that such-and-such is a way to do it. Then, Ryle's extended analogy can be spelled out as follows:

---

87   Ryle (1950).
88   Ibid. 328.
89   Ibid. 329.

1. I can draw the inference from "Today is Monday" to "Tomorrow is Tuesday" with or without the conditional statement "If today is Monday, tomorrow is Tuesday". But knowing and applying this statement allows me to *state explicitly* what I am doing in drawing the inference and to *justify* that I am doing it *correctly*.
2. Hannah can be able to ride a bicycle correctly with or without the methodological knowledge that doing such-and-such is a way to ride a bicycle. But having and applying this methodological knowledge allows her to *state explicitly* what she is doing in riding a bicycle and to *justify* that she is doing it *correctly*.

Of course, the most obvious and probably best way for Hannah to justify that she knows how to ride a bicycle is simply to demonstrate this by riding a bicycle. But we cannot rely on such practical demonstrations as a justification for knowledge-how in every case. For example, it is much more convenient for me to justify my knowledge how to extinguish a fire by saying what I would do in order to do so – by citing methodological knowledge – than by actually extinguishing a statistically significant number of fires.

Ryle's extended analogy suggests that to apply methodological knowledge about how to F is to state explicitly what one does in F-ing and to justify that one is able to F correctly. Given the Correctness Regress, and contra Stanley and Williamson, this cannot be identical with knowledge-how. But how exactly should we think of their relationship? In the next and final section of this paper, I will provide a preliminary answer to this question.

5.2 Explicating knowledge-how

I think that methodological knowledge is an interesting and often crucial kind of knowledge, and that it underlies our correct performances in many cases. One sometimes knows how to do something partly because one has methodological knowledge about it – that is, because one knows how it is done. But it is equally possible to know how something is done without knowing how to do it. That is, methodological knowledge is neither sufficient nor necessary for knowledge-how.

For example, I know that forcing my opponent in a game of chess to trade pieces is a way for me to maintain the upper hand. Partly because of this, I know how to maintain the upper hand. But, crucially, my methodological knowledge is not sufficient for my knowledge how to do this. It only translates into knowledge how to maintain the upper hand in virtue of my knowledge how to do what to do in order to do so. It is only in virtue of my knowledge how to force my opponent to trade pieces that my knowledge what to do in order to maintain the upper hand translates into my knowledge how to do so.

Let me put this point more abstractly: Sometimes S knows how to F in virtue of S's methodological knowledge about F, that is, in virtue of S's knowledge that w is a way for them to F. But this is true only in cases where S *also* knows how to *instantiate* w.

This also explains why it is possible for me to know how something is done without knowing how to do it. That was my second claim: Methodological knowledge does not imply knowledge-how. I might know that forcing my opponent to trade pieces is a way for me to maintain the upper hand, but fail to know how to do so. If I do not know how to force my opponent to trade pieces, I probably do not know how to maintain the upper hand. At the very least, I do not know how to do so in virtue of my methodological knowledge about forcing a trade of pieces. I might know other ways of maintaining the upper hand, but this is independent from the methodological knowledge in question.

The same phenomenon underlies the Skiing case discussed above.[90] A ski instructor who knows how to teach others how to perform a complex stunt, but is unable to perform it himself, does know *something* about performing that stunt. But what he possesses is methodological knowledge rather than knowledge-how.[91] He knows that doing such-and-such is a way to perform the stunt, and he does not know how to perform the stunt himself precisely because he cannot *instantiate* that way of performing the stunt. Still, he can employ his methodological knowledge about performing the stunt in teaching others how to do

---

90 Cf. section 3.2 on pages 280 ff.
91 It might be argued that sentences of the form "S knows how to F" are ambiguous between methodological knowledge and knowledge-how, which would explain why some are tempted to agree that the ski instructor knows how to perform the stunt in *some* sense; for discussion, compare Stanley and Williamson (2001), Rumfitt (2003), and Rosefeldt (2004), among others. However, I think that once the distinction between proper knowledge-how and methodological knowledge is clarified, "S knows how to F" can be seen to attribute knowledge-how, while methodological knowledge is attributed by "S knows how F-ing is done" or "S knows what to do in order to F". On a related issue, compare footnote 43.

so. Other things equal, more methodological knowledge makes for better teaching.

Given that I claim that methodological knowledge is neither necessary nor sufficient for knowledge-how, one might wonder why methodological knowledge should be of any interest with respect to knowledge-how. This point about teaching already shows one important connection: In many if not all cases, it is partly in virtue of a teacher's methodological knowledge about an activity F that she is able to teach others how to F.

We can also make a corresponding point about learning: If a student wants to learn how to F, a very important way to do so is to seek methodological knowledge about that activity. In particular, such a student will look for methodological knowledge which involves ways or methods of doing things she already knows how to instantiate. If she is successful, she will have learned how to F because she knows that w is a way to F and because she can instantiate w.

The Rylean considerations I discussed above even entail a further important aspect of methodological knowledge. The extended analogy I have proposed suggests that to apply methodological knowledge about how to F is to state explicity what one does in F-ing and to justify that one knows how to F correctly. We are now in a position to unpack this idea. First, I can claim that doing such-and-such is a way to extinguish a fire and thereby *specify* what extinguishing a fire amounts to (or can amount to). Second, I can use this claim in order to *justify* that I know how to extinguish a fire. Just like above, this justification will be successful only if I know how to instantiate the way to extinguish a fire I have cited. Third, however, methodological knowledge is also crucial for the fact that knowledge-how is what underlies the 'exercises of our intelligence' we can evaluate in the light of intersubjective standards. Methodological knowledge is crucial here because it lets us *understand* and *discuss* which of some candidate actions count as doing something correctly.

As a simple example, card games can be played correctly or incorrectly. There are rules governing which cards can be played when and by whom. But many traditional card games come in regional variants. It is therefore a crucial competence of players of card games that they can explicitly discuss what counts as playing the game correctly. Is playing such a card at such a point correct or not? Is my way of setting up the rules better or yours? We can make parallel observations for other instances of knowledge-how. It is important not only to be able and know how to solve an equation, but also to be able to discuss what counts as a way of doing so correctly – say, which methods are appropriate. It is important not only to be able and know how to falsify a theory, but also to be able to discuss what counts as a way of doing so correctly – say, which experiment is the right one.

This phenomenon can also be found in the case of conditionals, as the Rylean analogy from the last section indicates. If I can use conditionals, I can say that, wonder whether and discuss if certain inferences are correct ones. Generally speaking, if I understand methodological knowledge, I can say that, wonder whether and discuss if doing such-and-such qualifies as doing something correctly. I can talk about that practice in terms of its intersubjective standards of correctness.

Taken together, the role of methodological knowledge I have described is one of *explicating knowledge-how*. Methodological knowledge can be used to *say* what doing something amounts to, which could otherwise merely be *shown* by doing it. And it can be used to talk about what does or should count as doing something *correctly*. Methodological knowledge lets us become self-conscious about our knowledge-how – that is, about the things we do according to intersubjective standards of correctness.

Of course, this is merely a preliminary account of knowledge-how, methodological knowledge and their relationship. I think that such a Rylean view on these notions is very promising,[92] but I will not be able to say more about this in the present context.[93]

---

[92] One merit of such a Rylean perspective is that it brings out how knowledge-how is connected to other important issues in the vicinity. The best example for this strength is that the relationship between knowledge-how and the problem of rule-following, which is neglected almost entirely in the current debate, comes back into view. Ryle himself writes that exercises of knowledge-how satisfy criteria, but that "this is not enough. […] To be intelligent is not merely to satisfy criteria, but to apply them; to regulate one's actions and not merely to be well-regulated." (Ryle 1949, 29). This thought plays a prominent role in Ludwig Wittgenstein's *Philosophical Investigations* (1953) and in the discussion he has sparked. Arguably, Wittgenstein himself even endorses an argument along the lines of the Correctness Regress when he shows that we arrive at a "paradox" if we fail to appreciate "that there is a way of grasping a rule which is *not* an *interpretation*" (1953, § 201). However, I will have to leave an adequate assessment of this issue for another occasion.

[93] I think that it would be interesting to attempt to spell out such an account of the role of methodological knowledge in the specification and justification of knowledge-how in terms of Robert Brandom's notion of making normative

6 Conclusion

I have offered a thorough criticism of Stanley and Williamson's attempt to establish Intellectualism against the canonical criticism of Ryle. I have argued that their positive argument in favour of this view is unsound and that their view of the relationship between knowledge-how and practical abilities begs the question. Then, I have pointed out a crucial blind spot in their reading of Ryle's arguments and shown how this eventually leads to a fatal objection against their own version of Intellectualism.

Finally, I have drawn on a broader reading of Ryle in order to develop what might once be a full-fledged account of knowledge-how and the species of knowledge-that I call methodological knowledge. I think that an account along these lines would enrich the debate sparked by Stanley and Williamson's article. It has been neglected that the Correctness Regress is Ryle's strongest weapon against Intellectualism and that Ryle himself says more about knowledge-how by saying more about one of his prime examples of knowledge-how, drawing inferences. A more fully worked-out Rylean account will hopefully become an interesting contender in the current debate.[94]

References

Alter (2001): Torin Alter, "Know-How, Ability and the Ability Hypothesis", in: *Theoria* 67, 229–239.
Bengson/Moffett (2007): John Bengson/Marc Moffett, "Know-how and concept possession", in: *Philosophical Studies* 136, 31–57.
Bengson/Moffett/Wright (2009): John Bengson/Marc Moffett/Jennifer C. Wright, "The folk on knowing-how", in: *Philosophical Studies* 142, 387–401.

---

practices explicit (1994, 2008). But this is only one possibility among several and nothing I have said in this paper depends on more specifically Brandomian commitments.

94 I am grateful to the faculty and participants of the Second Graduate International Summer School in Cognitive Sciences and Semantics 2010 at the University of Latvia and to the participants of a Colloquium at Freie Universität Berlin for stimulating discussions and helpful input on earlier versions of parts of this paper. Special thanks for rigorous and insightful feedback on the entire paper are due to Holm Tetens, Stefan Tolksdorf, Ellen Frildand, David Lauer, Jan Janzen and Anna Wehofsits.

Brandom (1994): Robert Brandom, *Making It Explicit. Reason, Representing, and Discursive Commitment*, Cambridge.
Brandom (2008): Robert Brandom, *Between Saying and Doing. Towards an Analytic Pragmatism*, Oxford.
Carr (1979): David Carr, "The Logic of Knowing How and Ability", in: *Mind* 88, 394–409.
Carr (1981): David Carr, "Knowledge in Practice", in: *American Philosophical Quarterly* 18, 53–61.
Carroll (1895): Lewis Carroll, "What the Tortoise said to Achilles", in: *Mind* 4, 278–280.
Fantl (2008): Jeremy Fantl, "Knowing-How and Knowing-That", in: *Philosophy Compass* 3, 451–470.
Ginet (1975): Carl Ginet, *Knowledge, Perception, and Memory*, Dodrecht.
Hawley (2003): Katherine Hawley, "Success and Knowledge-How", in: *American Philosophical Quarterly* 40, 19–31.
Hetherington (2006): Stephen Hetherington, "How to Know (that Knowledge-that is Knowledge-how)", in: S. Hetherington (ed.), *Epistemology Futures*, Oxford, 71–94.
Hetherington (2008): Stephen Hetherington, "Knowing-That, Knowing-How, and Knowing Philosophically", in: *Grazer Philosophische Studien* 77, 307–324.
Hornsby (2005): Jennifer Hornsby, "Semantic Knowledge and Practical Knowledge", in: *Proceedings of the Aristotelian Society. Supplementary Volume* 79, 107–130.
Jackson (1982): Frank Jackson, "Epiphenomenal Qualia", in: *The Philosophical Quarterly* 32, 127–136.
Jackson (1986): Frank Jackson, "What Mary Didn't Know", in: *The Journal of Philosophy* 83, 291–295.
Jung/Newen (2010): Eva-Maria Jung/Albert Newen, "Knowledge and abilities: The need for a new understanding of knowing-how", in: *Phenomenology and Cognitive Science* 9, 113–131.
Karttunen (1977): Lauri Karttunen, "Syntax and Semantics of Questions", in: *Linguistics and Philosophy* 1, 3–44.
Katzoff (1984): Charlotte Katzoff, "Knowing How", in: *Southern Journal of Philosophy* 22, 61–69.
Koethe (2002): John Koethe, "Stanley and Williamson on Knowing How", in: *The Journal of Philosophy* 99, 325–328.
Krifka (2001): Manfred Krifka, "For a Structured Meaning Account of Questions and Answers", in: C. Fery/ W. Sternefeld (eds.), *Audiatur Vox Sapientiae. A Festschrift for Arnim von Stechow*, Berlin, 287–319.
Levin (1986): Janet Levin, "Could Love Be Like a Heatwave? Physicalism and the Subjective Character of Experience", in: *Philosophical Studies* 49, 245–261.
Lihoreau (2008): Franck Lihoreau, "Knowledge-How and Ability", in: *Grazer Philosophische Studien* 77, 263–305.
Mellor (1993): D. Hugh Mellor, "Nothing Like Experience", in: *Proceedings of the Aristotelian Society* 93, 1–16.

Michaelis (forthcoming): Laura Michaelis, *Knowledge Ascription by Grammatical Construction*, in: J. Bengson/M. Moffett (eds.), *Knowing How: Essays on Knowledge, Mind, and Action*, Oxford.

Nagel (1974): Thomas Nagel, "What is it Like to be a Bat?", in: *Philosophical Review* 83, 435–450.

Nemirow (1990): Laurence Nemirow, "Physicalism and the Cognitive Role of Acquaintance", in: W. G. Lycan (ed.), *Mind and cognition. A reader*, Cambridge, 490–499.

Nida-Rümelin (2009): Martine Nida-Rümelin; "Qualia: The Knowledge Argument", in: E. Zalta (ed.) *The Stanford Encyclopedia of Philosophy*, http://plato.stanford.edu/entries/qualia-knowledge/.

Noë (2005): Alva Noë, "Against intellectualism", in: *Analysis* 65, 278–290.

Rosefeldt (2004): Tobias Rosefeldt, "Is Knowing-how Simply a Case of Knowing-that?", in: *Philosophical Investigations* 27, 370–379.

Rumfitt (2003): Ian Rumfitt, "Savoir Faire", in: *The Journal of Philosophy* 100, 158–166.

Ryle (1945): Gilbert Ryle, "Knowing How and Knowing That", in: *Proceedings of the Aristotelian Society* 46, 1–16.

Ryle (1949): Gilbert Ryle, *The Concept of Mind*, Harmondsworth.

Ryle (1950): Gilbert Ryle, "If," "So," and "Because", in: M. Black (ed.), *Philosophical Analysis*, Ithaca, 323–340.

Schaffer (2007): Jonathan Schaffer, "Knowing the Answer", in: *Philosophy and Phenomenological Research* 75, 383–403.

Sgaravatti/Zardini (2008): Daniele Sgaravatti/Elia Zardini, "Knowing How to Establish Intellectualism", in: *Grazer Philosophische Studien* 77, 217–261.

Snowdon (2003): Paul Snowdon, "Knowing How and Knowing That: A Distinction Reconsidered", in: *Proceedings of the Aristotelian Society* 105, 1–25.

Stanley (2011): Jason Stanley, "Knowing (How)", in: *Noûs* 45, 207–238.

Stanley/Williamson (2001): Jason Stanley/Timothy Williamson, "Knowing How", in: *The Journal of Philosophy* 98, 411–444.

Stout (2010): Rowland Stout, "What You Know When You Know an Answer to a Question", in: *Noûs* 44, 392–402.

Wallis (2008): Charles Wallis, "Consciousness, context, and know-how", in: *Synthese* 160, 123–153.

Wiggins (2005): David Wiggins, "Knowing How To and Knowing That", in: H.-J. Glock/J. Hyman (eds.), *Wittgenstein and Analytic Philosophy: Essays for P. M. S. Hacker*, Oxford, 263–277.

Williams (2008): John N. Williams, "Propositional knowledge and know-how", in: *Synthese* 165, 107–125.

Wittgenstein (1953): Ludwig Wittgenstein, *Philosophical Investigations*, Oxford.

Chapter Two
Knowledge in Situations: Contexts and Contrasts

Part One: Contextualism

Two Varieties of Knowledge
Gerhard Ernst

1. Introduction

One word can have quite different translations in different contexts. The Latin word "animus", for example, can mean "heart", "soul" or "courage" (and a couple of other things) depending on how it is used. This rather trite phenomenon draws our attention to something not altogether trivial: If one and the same word has to be translated differently in different contexts, it is quite plausible to assume that the word does not mean exactly the same in these different contexts. One could say that in this case the word is ambiguous. If "animus", for example, means "soul" as well as "courage" one might say that it simply has two different meanings. But I don't think that this is the best way to put it since then too many words would come out as ambiguous. Almost all words have more or less different translations when used in different contexts. So, almost all words show these "variations of meaning", as I want to call them.

These variations mostly go unnoticed in our own language. But they are there nonetheless. Consider the word "case", for example: Does it mean exactly the same in the following phrases: "a good case for complaint", "a case in point", "a leading case", "a case of conscience"? No. A good case for complaint is a good opportunity for complaint, a case in point is an apt example, a leading case is a precedent, a case of conscience is a question of conscience. And ask yourself whether it is a conceptual truth that cases are things which can or cannot be adjourned. Cases of conscience and cases in point can neither be adjourned nor fail to be adjourned. Is the word ambiguous then? It is, if you think of "brief case" or "cigarette case", but it is certainly not ambiguous in the phrases I mentioned.[1] The word "case" simply shows variations of meaning, as so many words do. And a consequence of this is that slightly different linguistic rules apply to one and the same

---

1 It is important to note that these phrases, though idiomatic, are not idioms.

word when used in different contexts. It is a conceptual truth that cases are things which can or cannot be adjourned – when you consider some contexts of use of the word "case". But it doesn't make sense to speak of adjourned cases in other contexts. Variations of meaning are nothing to be surprised about. They are rather to be expected. Our language is a very flexible tool.

The main thesis I want to argue for in this paper concerns variations of meaning of a whole sentence, a sentence epistemologists are very much interested in: "*S* knows that *p*".[2] As I want to show, there are at least two very important variations of meaning of this sentence and, therefore, two different varieties of knowledge,[3] which are not properly distinguished in the project known as the analysis of knowledge. And this doesn't go unpunished. In my opinion, the project comes to grief precisely because it does not take account of these two slightly different meanings of "*S* knows that *p*". My paper is structured as follows. In the first two sections I want to describe the two varieties of knowledge I have in mind. As it turns out, the way to become aware of them is to pay attention to the – different kinds of – practical interests we take in knowledge. In the subsequent section I want to give part of a defence of my account of knowledge against the most obvious objection, and in the last part of my paper I will try to indicate some of the benefits of adopting that account. In this paper, I want to present one of the main ideas of a book-length investigation of mine, and so I have to skip many details.[4] But I hope at least to say enough to show that my account is worth objecting to.

---

2 I am only interested in personal propositional knowledge in this paper (not in impersonal knowledge, knowledge by acquaintance or non-propositional knowledge). So, a more explicit title of my paper would be "Two varieties of personal propositional knowledge".

3 In my opinion, analysing knowledge *basically* is the same as analysing our concept of knowledge. And analysing our concept of knowledge *basically* is the same as analysing the uses of "to know". Although I can't argue for this claim within the confines of the present paper, I hope not too much opposition results from the fact that I will proceed as if it were true.

4 Cf. Ernst (2002).

2. Knowledge for the ignoramus

When we try to analyse knowledge, the usual procedure is to start with more or less far-fetched examples. This is familiar from the somewhat tedious debate following Gettier's paper. But also important recent publications, like Jason Stanley's *Knowledge and Practical Interests* and Keith DeRose's *The Case for Contextualism* start with the description of examples and our supposedly untutored reactions to them.[5] This is a good thing because, at least in my opinion, epistemology is concerned with conceptual clarification. And this clarification can only be brought to pass by clarifying the use of words. Therefore, the authority to appeal to in epistemology is the linguistic intuition of the competent speaker. Nevertheless, the usual appeal to examples is less than fully satisfactory because many authors seem to live on a one-sided diet of scenarios. If you want to understand knowledge, and especially if you want to find out whether there are different varieties of it, you have to consider all the uses of "*S* knows that *p*". How can we go about doing this?

I think the right way to proceed is to begin with a reflection on what the sentence is good for. Words are like tools, as ordinary language philosophers used to say. What kind of tool, then, is "*S* knows that *p*"? In which situations do we really use it? Or, to put it differently, which practical interests does it serve? This is a question few philosophers have tried to answer in a systematic way, most notably Oswald Hanfling. In what follows I am going to build on a variant of his classification of the different situations in which we ascribe knowledge in order to describe the two variations of meaning I want to highlight.[6]

In the first class of situations in which we use "*S* knows that *p*" the one who ascribes the knowledge that *p* doesn't (at first) take himself to know whether *p*. Let's call the practical interests which guide us in this kind of situation the *interests of the ignoramus*. In the other class of situations the one who ascribes the knowledge that *p* takes himself to know that *p* already. Let's call his interests the *interests of the knower*. In this section I am going to discuss the first class of situations in more detail. I will come to the situations in which we use "*S* knows that *p*" with the interests of the knower in the next section.

---

5   Cf. Stanley (2005), 3 ff., and De Rose (2009), 1 f.
6   Cf. Oswald Hanfling (1985), 40–56. A rather similar classification of situations is also given by Clarke. Cf. Clarke (1990), 188 ff.

Why is someone who doesn't take himself to possess knowledge interested in knowledge? Why is the question whether S knows whether p of any importance to him? Usually the main reason will be that he himself wants to know whether or not p. A typical use of "to know" in this situation is in sentences like these: "Jason, do you know what time it is?", "Does anyone know?", "Ah, Tim knows what time it is."[7] When we speak about knowledge in situations like these we are looking for *a good informant* and the sentence "S knows that p" serves in these situations, as Edward Craig has put it, as a means to "flag approved sources of information".[8] Therefore, I take it, the first variation of meaning of "S knows that p" is given thus:[9] S knows that p just in case S is a good informant concerning the fact that p. Hence, in order to say more about knowledge in these situations we should turn to the concept of a good informant.

A good informant is able to tell me what I want to know. Therefore he must have a belief concerning the matter in question and that belief has to be true – someone without a belief can't *tell* me the facts,[10] and someone with a false belief can't tell me the *facts*. But there is more to a good informant than this. A person is a good informant for me only if I am ready to believe what he tells me. He should therefore be able to dispel the doubts I have concerning what he says. He has to be able to rule out the alternatives I take into account, and the usual way to do this is to give reasons. Of course, I might know that someone is reliable from some independent source (or I might simply believe that he is) and then I don't have any doubts concerning what he says and I don't take any alternatives into account. In this case he doesn't need reasons to be a good informant. But if I don't believe that someone is a reliable source of information (either from some inde-

---

7 As long as we don't possess the piece of knowledge we are asking for, in the majority of cases we use sentences like "S knows whether/when/why ..." (instead of "S knows that p") in order to ascribe knowledge. Still, we are interested in personal propositional knowledge. So, nothing of importance changes for the analysis of knowledge.

8 Cf. Craig (1999), 11. The idea that the concept of knowledge is needed when we are looking for good informants is the basic idea of his book.

9 For a defence of this thesis I refer the reader to Craig's book.

10 The belief-condition is plausible at this point but it might not be strictly necessary. Whether *knowing* always implies believing I discuss elsewhere. Cf. Ernst (2002), 69–78.

pendent source or because he can give appropriate reasons) he is no source of information for me at all because I don't believe him.[11]

At this point we have to notice that the concept of a good informant is ultimately a relational concept. Not everyone in need of information is bothered by the same doubts. People looking for information differ in what they already know and in how important the relevant information is for them. (This is *one* place where different practical interests play a role in the analysis of knowledge.) Therefore, not everyone takes the same alternatives to a given answer into account. Hence, someone who is a good informant for me need not be a good informant for you. He may be able to dispel my doubts but not yours. And if I believe that someone acquired his belief in a reliable manner but you don't he is a good informant for me but not for you (given, of course, that his belief is true).

So, in the end, we can't decide whether someone is a good informant without specifying *for whom* or, as we might say, from what point of view he is supposed to be a good informant. The doubts someone has (the alternatives she takes seriously) define a point of view which has to be taken into account when answering the question whether someone is a good informant or not. There is no independent fact of the matter about being a good informant. But to know something, we just said, is (in certain situations) to be a good informant. Therefore we should expect to find that (sometimes) there is no independent fact of the matter about knowledge. Is this plausible?

In order to show that it is, let us consider a familiar example from the Gettier-tradition.[12] John sees Tom Grabit, a man he knows, taking a book in the library, hiding it under his jacket, and leaving the library. He comes to believe that Grabit stole a book, which is in fact what has happened. He doesn't know, however, that Tom's father tells everyone who cares to listen that Tom has a kleptomaniac twin brother. But Mr. Grabit is an inhabitant of a mental asylum: The evil ways of Tom, who has no twin brother, have driven him insane. In this situation we say that John knows that Tom stole the book because the evidence which suggests that he might have been wrong is misleading. This example is used to show that a special set of necessary and sufficient con-

---

11 Is there even more to a good informant? Is it not a necessary condition that he must be *willing* to provide the information I want to have? We can get around this, I presume, by focusing on *potential* informants.
12 Cf. Lehrer (1990), 139.

ditions is inadequate.[13] That, however, is not the point I want to make. Rather, I want to ask whether the example is as clear-cut as it is usually taken to be.

That appearances are deceptive is suggested by Robert Fogelin's version of the Grabit story.[14] He asks whether we would still be willing to ascribe knowledge to John if we were to imagine ourselves to be engaged in an actual enquiry. Let's take ourselves at first to know about Mr. Grabit's testimony, but not that it is due to his insanity. At this stage we would not say that John knows that Tom stole the book because he is not in the position to rule out the alternative that a twin brother of Tom took the book. Later on we find out about Mr. Grabit's sad condition and we come to believe that John is right after all. But would we now ascribe knowledge to him even though he doesn't know anything about Mr. Grabit's statement nor about his mental illness? Probably we wouldn't because John is not in the position to rule out the twin alternative, although we are. Fogelin takes this to show that the Grabit example is not a clear-cut case of knowledge – contrary to what has been taken for granted.

What are we to make of this? Who is right, those who take the Grabit example as a case of knowledge or those who take it as a case of ignorance? I think the answer has to be: both and neither. Concerning this example we simply can adopt two different points of view. Considered from one point of view John knows that Tom stole the book, while considered from another he doesn't. There is no fact of the matter about whether John knows independently from the point of view we take. Asking whether Tom *really* knows in this situation is like asking whether Big Ben really is on the right hand side of the river Thames.

Of course, this is exactly what we should expect if "S knows that p" is used to flag approved sources of information. John is a good informant concerning the question who stole the book for someone who knows that Mr. Grabit's testimony is irrelevant. But John is not a good informant for someone who is in doubt about whether there is a twin brother

---

13 The definition attacked is: S knows that p iff (i) S believes that p, (ii) p is the case, (iii) S is justified in believing that p, and (iv) S would still be justified in believing that p when given further information. Cf. Klein (1971), 475. In the Grabit example John knows even though he wouldn't be justified in believing what he believes if we would tell him about Mr. Grabit's testimony but not about him being insane. So the definition entails a condition which isn't necessary.

14 Fogelin (1994), 37 ff.

of Tom or not. We are inclined to take the former point of view if we are told about Mr. Grabit's condition from the beginning. But we are inclined to take the latter point of view in Fogelin's variant.[15]

This analysis of situations in which we speak about knowledge to flag good informants, in my opinion, explains the attraction of contextualism. According to the contextualist the sentence "S knows that p" contains something like to an indexical element.[16] And I think he is right concerning the situations considered so far. When we say "S knows that p" here, we say something like "S is a good informant with respect to the fact that p *for me*" (or sometimes maybe "*for you/him/her/us/them*"). And someone might be a good informant for me at the shopping mall when I ask about the time but not for the sceptic who is in doubt about whether he is a brain in a vat. I am not going to argue for any specific contextualist analysis of knowledge in this paper.[17] But however the details, I think the contextualist is on the right track concerning the variety of knowledge under consideration so far.

Let me add a last remark about knowledge and good informants. Why, you might ask, is this indexicality of "S knows that p" hardly visible in our ordinary discourse? I think, two things can be said: First of all, contextualists have given examples in which we can see the context-sensitivity of the sentence "S knows that p". Think about the well-known bank cases in which we are ready to ascribe or to deny knowledge from different points of view.[18] And the two variants of the Grabit example I have just given also constitute a case in point. The second thing to notice is that the relativity of knowledge to a point of view is hardly visible in our daily life because there is a privileged point of view: our own. Normally, when we are looking for good informants, we are looking for good informants for me or for us. And as long as we all take the same point of view the relativity vanishes – just like in the case of left and right when we all look in the same direction. And I suspect that if normally we would all look in the same direction even the context-sensitivity of the words "left" and "right" would not be so salient any more.

---

15 Even though we finally learn that the testimony of Tom's father is irrelevant it isn't John we learn it from.
16 For a detailed recent defence of contextualism cf. De Rose (2009).
17 But cf. Ernst (2005), 159–178, where, as the title promises, I argue for a fairly radical form of contextualism.
18 Cf. again De Rose (2009), 1 f.

My main claim is that there are variations of meaning of "*S* knows that *p*", and, therefore, varieties of (personal proposition) knowledge. In order to have a handy label, let's call the variety of knowledge considered so far the *perspective variety of knowledge*.

3. Knowledge for the knower

Philosophers engaged in the project of analysing knowledge have been, for a long time, preoccupied with situations in which we use "*S* knows that *p*" in order to flag good informants (although, for the most part, they did not acknowledge the fact). But this leads to a one-sided diet of examples. In fact, we are not only interested in knowledge when we are looking for good informants. That is, we are not only interested in the question whether someone knows whether or not *p* when we don't know whether *p* or not ourselves. Consider the following situations.

I've heard the soccer results on the radio and I ask Eric: "Do you know who won the championship?" What I am interested in here is not a good informant but rather someone for whom I can be a good informant. I want to tell Eric who won the championship, and I want to know whether he knows or not in order to decide whether there is any point in telling him. I want to surprise him, maybe to banter with him. Or consider the situation of a husband cheating on his wife. He would, naturally enough, like to know whether his wife knows about it. Not in order to get the information from her, but to know whether he managed to keep it from her. If she doesn't know about the affair he might carry it on, otherwise probably a different action is called for. Or take the situation in which a judge wants to know whether the accused person knew or didn't know that his wife was in danger. Whether that person will be punished for not helping his wife depends on that question.[19]

The practical interests we have in these situations can be called the *interests of the knower*. We take ourselves to know that *p*, and we want to know whether *S* also knows that *p* in order to decide whether we can be informants for *S*, whether we managed to keep the information from *S*, and also in order to understand and maybe evaluate the actions of *S*. The person is not seen as a good informant but as an *information-receiver*

---

19 These examples are adopted from Hanfling (1985).

or as an *agent* here. When we want to find out which analysis of "S knows that *p*" is adequate for these kinds of situations we have to ask ourselves what we are interested in when we ask "Does Eric know the soccer results?", "Does Helen know about Susan?", "Did Mr. Smith know that Mrs. Smith couldn't swim?" – I think the clear answer in all these cases is: We want to know whether the subjects were aware of the relevant facts. Being aware of a fact, in these cases, amounts to knowledge.

But what is "being aware of a fact"? Obviously, there are two sides to this, a subjective and an objective side, as it were. Whether you are aware of a fact or not depends on how the world is, and on how you consider it to be. A natural way to put this is to say that being aware of a fact amounts to having a true belief. And, I submit, this is indeed the right analysis of knowledge in the situations determined by the interests of the knower.[20] Here, a person knows that *p* if and only if she has the true belief that *p*. In this kind of situations we are not interested in whether the knowing (or not knowing) person is in the position to rule out any alternatives to what she believes. Whether I can tell Eric something interesting, whether the husband has to be careful, and whether the accused person will be punished depends on whether they (Eric, the wife, the accused person) have true beliefs or not. The relativity of the perspective variety of knowledge simply drops out. Therefore, I want to call knowledge as true belief the *objective variety of knowledge*.

To block some misunderstandings form the very beginning: The word "belief" is not innocuous in the context of an analysis of knowledge as is well known from the literature.[21] Therefore, I want to stress two points. First, you can only ascribe beliefs to someone on the presupposition that she is minimally rational. A lucky guess cannot, by its very nature, lead to a belief. You can hold beliefs, even very firm ones, without adequate evidence. But you cannot hold beliefs on the basis of nothing. The superstitious person maybe believes that the black cat indicates bad luck (which it doesn't) and therefore believes that she is doomed. The gambler who firmly believes that red is next takes himself to possess a sixth sense etc. If there is really nothing to back up a belief we would not talk about a belief but rather about a hunch, a foreboding, an intuition or whatever. Therefore, cases of merely true belief are *eo ipso* al-

---

20 The same conclusion is drawn by Clarke. Cf. Clarke (1990), 189.
21 For a discussion cf., for example, Ernst (2002), 69–78.

ways cases in which a person is minimally rational.[22] Secondly, the kind of belief which constitutes awareness of a fact need not only be true but also firm enough. When is a belief firm enough for knowledge? That's not at all easy to say. A good indication for someone to have the relevant kind of belief is that the person is willing to claim knowledge for herself. But even this criterion is not fool-prove. A student in an examination might be reluctant to claim knowledge because he is scared. That doesn't mean that he doesn't know the answer or that his belief isn't firm enough. We can see this from his relevant behaviour in other situations. Feeling sure in a situation is neither necessary nor sufficient for believing or knowing. Believing and knowing are linked to dispositions; they are not occurrences.

I think that it is paramount for the understanding of knowledge to take notice of the situations in which we have the interest of the knower. In fact, most of the times when we talk about knowledge, we take this practical interest in it. That is because in order to obtain information we often do not need to ask for knowledge. We are usually in the position to ask, for example, "Tim, what time is it?" instead of asking who knows what time it is first. For quite a long time the situations in which we use "to know" with the interest of the knower have been ignored. But recently much interest has been taken in the connection between knowledge and action.[23] And the relevant situations are indeed contained in the class of situations under consideration in this section. The judge, for example, wants to evaluate the action of the husband of the drowned woman. And he therefore wants to know whether the husband knew that she couldn't swim. If he knew he should have acted on the basis of this knowledge. I think the analysis of knowledge John Hyman proposed about ten years ago is very appropriate here: "knowledge is the ability to do things, or refrain from doing things, or believe, or want, or doubt things, for reasons that are facts".[24] If the husband knew that the wife couldn't swim, this fact could have been his reason to help her. I think the analysis of Hyman is adequate for the situations at hand, and, I would add, it is compatible with a true belief account. The fact that p can be Herbert's reason for doing

---

22 I think this staves off an objection Christoph Jäger recently put forward against true belief accounts of knowledge. Cf. Jäger (2009), 19–40.
23 Cf., f.e., Stanley (2005), and Fantl/McGrath (2009).
24 Cf. Hyman (1999), 441.

something if and only if he is aware of it, i. e. if he truly and firmly believes that *p*.

Hyman and others who see a connection between knowledge and action don't agree. Jason Stanley, for example, adheres to the principle that one ought to act on what one knows.[25] But according to him one certainly shouldn't act on all things one truly believes. It would take a paper of its own to argue against this and similar positions but let me, at least, indicate why I think that true belief is an adequate analysis of knowledge here. Consider the following example.[26]

Herbert firmly believes that Pegasus, a horse, will win the next race. He bets all his money, and he wins (because Pegasus wins). At home, his wife complains: "How could you bet all your money on a horse? That was totally irresponsible because you didn't know that this particular horse would win." If Herbert would have known that Pegasus would win he would have acted responsibly. He didn't act responsibly, so he didn't know although he had a true belief. Therefore, knowledge is not true belief. – Well, I think there are two things to be taken into account here. The first is, as already mentioned, that it is problematic, to say the least, to credit Herbert with a belief in this case. He might have had a hunch or a premonition but is it intelligible to ascribe a firm belief to a person in this situation? I don't think so. But even if we suppose that we can ascribe a full-blown and firm enough belief to Herbert: Is it true that it was irresponsible for him to bet all the money on Pegasus? In a sense it was, because Herbert should not have acquired the belief that Pegasus would win in the first place. But given that he really had this firm belief: Wouldn't it then have been irresponsible *not* to bet? What else can we demand of someone than to act on the basis of his firm beliefs? If Herbert would not have betted his money on Pegasus, this, certainly, would have been a case of weakness of the will. And akrasia is a form of practical irrationality. So, I don't accept that it was irresponsible for Herbert to bet all his money without qualification. It was irrational to form the belief that Pegasus would win, but once formed it was *not* irrational to act on this belief.

Philosophers in the Gettier-tradition have been preoccupied with situations in which we look for informants when we ask for knowledge. Some recent epistemologists focus mainly on situations in which we

---

25 Cf. Stanley (2005), 9, 98, 114, 115, 119.
26 Thanks to John Hyman for putting this example to me. A slightly different version was already included in Hyman (1999), 447.

want to understand and evaluate agents when we talk about knowledge. I think that we also have to keep in mind the situations in which we want to know whether we are potential informants for others but most of all: We have to remember that *"S knows that p"* is used for *all* these purposes. When we use this sentence we are guided by quite different practical interests. While we want to know something *from S* when we ask about his knowledge with the interest of the ignoramus, we want to know something *about S* when we ask with the interests of the knower. While we judge *S* as a potential informant in the first kind of situations, we judge *S* as a potential receiver of information or as an agent in the second kind of situations. In each class of situations slightly different linguistic rules apply. According to my account of knowledge the most important rules are captured in the two definitions I indicated. In other words: there are two variations of meaning of *"S knows that p"*. Sometimes *"S knows that p"* means *"S is a good informant concerning the fact that p"* which, in turn, can be analysed in a contextualist manner; sometimes *"S knows that p"* means *"S is aware of the fact that p"* which, in turn, means *"S has the true belief that p"*. Hence, there are two kinds of knowledge: a perspective and an objective variety. – Probably, not everyone is convinced. Therefore, I now want to turn to what I take to be the most pressing objection against this account of knowledge.

4. Mixed cases

Even if we are willing to accept that in the situations guided by the interest of the knower we are only interested in true beliefs when asking for knowledge, it might be objected that we *tacitly* assume that further conditions are met even if we are not directly interested in them. The argument for this is that, allegedly, we withdraw our ascriptions of knowledge as soon as we find out that the relevant subject had *merely* true beliefs. But is this true?

I think it is true that we withdraw our ascriptions of knowledge as soon as we find out that the relevant subjects only made lucky guesses. But this is due to the fact already mentioned that lucky guesses don't give us beliefs, and certainly not the firm beliefs we need for knowledge.[27] We can be informants for someone who made a lucky guess:

---

27 This point is forcefully made by Sartwell (1991), 157–165.

Obviously we can inform the person that his guess was lucky. And someone who made a lucky guess will act and is justified to act differently than someone who knows. By contrast, for someone who has an appropriately firm belief – a belief which would lead him to claim knowledge – we cannot be informants and he will also act and is justified to act exactly like someone who knows. So, lucky guess examples are not a problem for my account of knowledge.

The cases which are most problematic, once again, are Gettier-style examples, in which the relevant subjects most certainly do have true beliefs but in which we nevertheless don't ascribe knowledge. Take the following familiar one:[28] Barney cruises around in the countryside. Looking out of the window of his car he sees a barn and thereby comes to believe that he has just passed a barn, which in fact he has. But Barney doesn't know that many fake-barns, that is mere barn facades, have been placed (for whatever reasons) in the vicinity. By luck Barney came across the only real barn within miles. (And he would not have been able to distinguish a real barn from a fake-barn.)

We would deny that Barney knows that there is a barn. But it can hardly be denied that he has acquired a (firm enough) true belief. If Barney didn't come to have a full-blown belief about a barn by looking out of his car window, nobody ever will come to have a full-blown belief. So this seems to be a genuine counterexample to the claim that knowledge is true belief. Confronted with Gettier-style examples and other cases of true belief arrived at by unreliable means[29] we normally would deny that the subject has knowledge though she has a true belief.

This clearly rules out the possibility of analysing knowledge as true belief in all contexts. But then, Gettier-examples aren't considered with the interests of the knower in mind. We don't judge the persons in these examples as receivers of information or as agents. Nothing in the examples points in that direction. We are rather concerned with the credentials of the relevant subjects and that's a typical feature of situations in which we judge someone as an informant. So, in telling the example we switch to the other variety of knowledge which, indeed, is different from true belief.

---

28 Cf. Goldman (1976), 771–791.
29 For brevity's sake I'll omit this addition in what follows. Nevertheless, the argument I am about to give holds equally for all cases of true belief arrived at by unreliable means.

But now, it seems, I am begging the question. It seems to be unfair to my opponent to say: Look, whenever we want more than true belief for knowledge, this merely shows that we have switched to a context in which we are not guided by the interests of the knower any longer. I am really inclined to say something like this, so how are we to decide whether the objection or my thesis – that nothing but true belief is at stake in the situations guided by the interests of the knower – is sound? I propose to use what I want to call the *modification strategy*:

We start with an alleged counterexample to my claim, in this case a Gettier-example. Then we go on to modify the example in a way which makes it easier to see it from the point of view of someone who has the interests of the knower while leaving the "Gettier-structure" unchanged – that is, we do not change the reasons of the person or the way in which she acquires her true belief. If my thesis is correct we should expect that in so modifying the example our intuition to deny that the person has knowledge will become weaker and the intuition to ascribe knowledge will become stronger. The more we adopt the perspective of someone judging the person as a potential receiver of information or as an agent, the more we are willing to ascribe knowledge in spite of the fact that the person doesn't meet the demands on a good informant. If, on the other hand, the objection is sound, our intuition has to remain *totally* unchanged. The point of the objection is that a necessary condition for knowledge isn't satisfied in the Gettier-examples and therefore no adornment should lure us into ascribing knowledge. Compare the case of a false belief. Whatever we add to an example in which someone has got a false belief, we will never ascribe knowledge. So if a necessary condition isn't met there's no way to make us change our mind about ascribing knowledge. There's not even a way to make us uncertain about the matter. Hanfling provided a type of example which suits my purpose.[30] Similar to his modification of one of Gettier's original examples I am going to give two modifications of the Barney scenario.

First modification: While spending my holidays in the Scottish Highlands I stumble across a gold mine and, naturally enough, I want to buy the piece of land where the gold mine is located. The piece of land (and the gold mine) is well marked by a lonely barn in the middle

---

30 Cf. Hanfling (2003), 262 f., and Hanfling (1985), 52 f. Hanfling argues (in the latter) for the thesis that the whole project of trying to find a definition of knowledge in terms of necessary and sufficient conditions is flawed. I don't follow him in this, although I think that it is impossible to find a *single* definition.

of nowhere. Unfortunately, I am a bit short of cash, so I am eager to keep my discovery a secret for as long as it takes me to raise funds. But somehow my rich arch-enemy Barney finds out about the mine under the barn and he sets out to find the piece of land so easily detectable by the only barn within miles. I can't prevent him from searching for the barn, but as the locals are my friends I can bring them to place fake-barns all around. And now, as usual, Barney cruises around, takes a look out of his car window, sees a barn (unfortunately the real barn and not one of the many fake-barns), and draws the conclusion that this is where the gold mine is.

Would we still be willing to say that Barney doesn't know that he has passed a barn and that he doesn't know which piece of land to buy? Or would we rather say that he now knows, though only by (bad) luck. Obviously we can't say: "Barney still doesn't know where the lonely barn is (and therefore which piece of land to buy)." Because, if he didn't know, my efforts to keep the location of the gold mine a secret would have been successful – and obviously they were in vain. Barney doesn't need an informant any longer; we can't surprise him by telling him where the barn (and the gold mine) is and so on. So, for all intends and purposes Barney knows that there is barn.

Second modification: Let's assume that Barney is a child (and therefore not allowed to pass the barn by car). He takes a walk through the countryside and sees, as usual, the real barn. Now a heavy rain comes down. But instead of taking shelter in the barn Barney prefers to jump up and down in the falling rain, becomes soaking wet, and catches a cold. Later on his mother is angry with him because he didn't go into the barn. Could Barney find an excuse in the following way: "I can't be blamed for not going into the barn because I didn't know at the time that I had passed a barn." – Barney later learned about the fake-barns in the vicinity – "And since I didn't know that I had passed a barn, I didn't know where to take shelter." But his mother seems to be right in reproaching him. So wouldn't we be willing to say that in a sense Barney knew very well where to go? Obviously, the fact that there was a barn could have been Barneys reason to run to it and take shelter. He was well aware of the fact that there was a barn. Again, for all intends and purposes Barney knew that there was a barn.

Hanfling takes examples like these as clear-cut cases of knowledge. He would claim that we would say something false if we denied that Barney has got knowledge. But for my modification strategy to be successful I don't need such a strong claim. The only thing I need is that the two cases aren't clear-cut cases of ignorance. Because, for the objection against my position to succeed that would have to be the case. No adornment of an example where necessary conditions aren't satisfied can lure us into ascribing knowledge. And in the two modifications it can hardly be denied that we are at least uncertain what to say. In a sense Barney doesn't know that he has passed a barn. But then, in another sense he does. And that's exactly what we should expect in cases where two variations of meaning get into conflict with each other!

Of course, the modification strategy works both ways. We could also start with one of my examples in which we see someone as a receiver of information or as an agent and therefore accept his true belief as knowledge. Then we add features which focus our attention on his being a bad informant. (We only have to make his belief the result of an unreliable method.) And we will end up with examples very similar to the two modifications of the Barney example I have just given. Again we will be uncertain what to say. That there are actually two different varieties of knowledge at issue is in my opinion the best explanation for our ambiguous reaction to such examples.

At this point someone (especially a philosopher) might be tempted to argue as follows: "Our unguided reaction to such examples may indeed be ambiguous. Nevertheless, *strictly speaking* the examples are cases of ignorance." I think that this objection is beside the point. I don't want to deny that one might say that the examples are cases of ignorance and if you want to call this "speaking strictly", there is no need for me to object. My point is that we also might say that the examples are cases of knowledge. And even if this doesn't amount to "speaking strictly", it still shows that there must be a second meaning of "S knows that p".

Another objection might be that Barney has a *justified* true belief, not only a true belief. I took these examples in order to make sure that we are really talking about the right kind of true belief not only about lucky guesses, hunches etc. But I think that the examples work nearly as well for unjustified true belief. They are more unrealistic then, because normally people do not form their beliefs in a wildly irrational manner. But even if they do: As long as their true beliefs are as firm as in the case of Barney, I am inclined to say that for all intends and purposes they know – from the point of view of the knower that is. But even if I had to admit that some sort of rationality condition is necessary in addition to true belief in these cases we would still have two different varieties of knowledge (since having an internally justified true belief is not enough for being a good informant). And that is what I am arguing for.

5. Some results

Let me, finally, at least indicate what the benefit of adopting my account of knowledge is. Our investigation into the practical interests we have in knowledge led us, I submit, to distinguish two varieties of knowledge. In its objective variety knowledge should be analysed as true belief. When we share the interests of the knower this variety is at issue. In these situations we ascribe knowledge to express insights like "If he doesn't know that p yet, I may surprise him with the information that p" or "He couldn't help because he didn't know what to do" or "What the mind doesn't know the heart doesn't grieve". Here knowledge is something which is independent of the special perspective of the person ascribing knowledge. Or to put it differently: Everyone who shares the interests of the knower has got the same point of view. It cannot (and must not) be possible in these situations that someone knows from one point of view and doesn't know from another. A perspective concept of knowledge wouldn't work as a means to capture what we are interested in in these situations. Either Eric knows already who won the match or he doesn't. If he doesn't know it, I can surprise him, if he does, I can't. It makes no more sense to say that he knows from one point of view but not from another than to say that he will be surprised from one point of view but not from another. Whether he will be surprised depends only on what he believes and on how the world happens to be. We believe that it is as much a fact about Eric that he knows that p as it is a fact about him that he is surprised. So, in many situations the sentence "S knows that p" can be used to describe an independent matter of fact and then its truth does not depend on the special point of view of the one using it. These situations are the source of our intuition that there has to be an independent fact of the matter about knowledge. And this intuition is arguably at the root of most anti-contextualist arguments.[31]

---

31 Cf., for example, the arguments against contextualism based on belief (about knowledge) reports. De Rose (2009), 161–170, and arguments based on the "semantic blindness"-allegation in general.

It would be a mistake, though, to conclude that whether someone knows something or not is *always* independent of the point of view of the one ascribing knowledge. In many situations "*S* knows that *p*" is used to flag good informants, that is, people from whom we can get the information we need. This time it is the perspective variety of knowledge that suits our purpose. If we look for an informant we want someone who can give relevant information *to us*. We are not concerned with an independent fact of the matter about knowledge (knowledge *in itself*) but in knowledge *for us*. And we can only obtain information from someone who is in the position to dispel our doubts. These situations, I think, are the source of our intuition that knowledge is more than simply true belief.

When considering examples in philosophy, somehow or other we have to judge them *by analogy* to common situations. We have no independent intuitions concerning philosophical examples. Therefore, it is important to understand by analogy to which common situations we interpret examples in philosophy. I think the key to understanding the examples in the Gettier-tradition is to appreciate that we judge them by analogy to those common situations in which we are looking for an informant.[32] Nothing in these examples suggests adopting the point of view of the knower. Instead, we are concerned with circumstances in which we would be interested when in the position of the ignoramus. Therefore, we judge the persons in these examples as potential informants, which means that we ignore the fact that we know already that they are right in what they believe.

Given this insight, it becomes intelligible why we react to the examples in the way we do. Take the (original) example of Barney. He wouldn't be a good informant for us if we knew what the example tells us but not that he actually has a true belief. The example suggests taking the fake-barn alternative into account and Barney is not in the position to rule that alternative out – therefore he doesn't know (from that point of view). In the Grabit examples things become more complicated. In the original version John would be a good informant because we know from the beginning that the testimony of Tom's father is irrelevant and that therefore we don't have to take the twin-alternative into account. Hence, we are inclined to ascribe

---

[32] A similar thought is behind Craig's investigation, although he rejects the search for a definition of knowledge in terms of necessary and sufficient conditions. Cf. Craig (1999).

knowledge. In Fogelin's version, on the other hand, we are explicitly asked to adopt the point of view of someone who doesn't know that Tom's father is demented but who knows about his statement, and who does therefore take the twin-alternative into account. And, of course, from this point of view John wouldn't be a good informant any more. If we come to know about the mental illness of the father later on, it isn't John we learn it from, and therefore we don't consider him to be a good informant even with the benefit of hindsight.

This provides at least the beginnings of an explanation for our intuitions about the examples in the Gettier tradition.[33] In these examples the important question is not whether the epistemic performance of the persons in question is adequate from an objective point of view – there's no such thing (for this purpose) – but whether it is adequate from the point of view we adopt. It depends on the example what specific point of view we are inclined to adopt, that is, which alternatives we are inclined to take into account. Some examples very clearly suggest taking certain alternatives seriously (and therefore they suggest a special point of view), others are more indeterminate (and therefore it is easy to switch form one point of view to another). Therefore, we sometimes have clear intuitions while sometimes it is easy to adopt different points of view.

Even our reaction to the modifications of the Barney example I discussed in the last section becomes intelligible as soon as we are aware of the fact that there are two varieties of knowledge: If we see Barney only as a potential receiver of information or as an agent we want to ascribe knowledge. (Then the objective variety of knowledge is at issue.) If, on the other hand, we see him only as a potential informant for someone taking the fake-barn alternative into account we want to deny that he knows. (Then the perspective variety of knowledge is at issue.) As the modifications contain elements which liken them to both normal situations we are uncertain what to say.

If we keep in mind that there are two quite different common uses of "S knows that p" from which we draw our intuitions, it becomes clear why the analysis of knowledge was bound to get into trouble. Following the intuitions we form in the situations in which we have the

---

33 In fact, a full explanation can be given on that basis. But in order to defend this claim I would have to describe which specific contextualist analysis of the perspective variety of knowledge I propose. Cf. Ernst (2005), 159–178, and Ernst (2002), 114–146.

objective variety of knowledge in mind we expect that there *has to be* an analysis of knowledge according to which the answer to the question whether someone knows something is independent of the one ascribing knowledge. Following the intuitions we form in the situations in which we have the perspective variety of knowledge in mind we expect that the question whether someone knows something is not simply the question whether someone has got a true belief or not. But when we try to determine *what* else is required we can't avoid taking the point of view of the one ascribing knowledge into account. What is necessary for knowledge depends on the alternatives taken into account by him. Therefore we *cannot* determine what is necessary independently of the special point of view of the one ascribing knowledge. So some uses of "*S* knows that *p*" force us to take the point of view of the one ascribing knowledge into account, others force us to exclude it from the analysis. That is the reason why it isn't possible to find *one* analysis which fits *all* examples. Insofar as knowledge is independent of the point of view of the person ascribing knowledge it is to be analysed as true belief. And insofar as it cannot be analysed as true belief it is dependent on the point of view of the one ascribing knowledge. The project of analysing knowledge comes to grief because it tries to do justice to the genuine intuition that there has to be an independent fact of the matter about knowledge and the likewise genuine intuition that knowledge is more than true belief at the same time. But that's impossible. It should be clear by now why those objecting to a contexualist analysis of knowledge are as right as those objecting to the true belief account. No analysis gives the whole truth about knowledge – but half of it.[34]

References

Clarke, (1990): David S. Clarke Jr., "Two Uses of 'Know'", in: *Analysis* 50, 188–190.

Craig (1999): Edward Craig, *Knowledge and the State of Nature. An Essay in Conceptual Synthesis,* Oxford.

---

34 For very helpful discussions on the topic of this paper I would like to thank Erich Ammereller, Edward Craig, Eugen Fischer, Oswald Hanfling, John Hyman, Richard King, Ulises Moulines, Stephan Sellmaier, Wilhelm Vossenkuhl, and Ralph Walker. I have presented versions of this paper on various occasions, and I am very grateful for the sympathetic criticism I received from my audiences.

De Rose (2009): Keith De Rose, *The Case for Contextualism*, Oxford.
Ernst (2002): Gerhard Ernst, *Das Problem des Wissens*, Paderborn.
Ernst (2005): Gerhard Ernst, "Radikaler Kontextualismus", in: *Zeitschrift für philosophische Forschung* 59, 159–178.
Fogelin (1994): Robert Fogelin, *Pyrrhonian Reflections on Knowledge and Justification*, New York/Oxford.
Fantl/McGrath (2009): Jeremy Fantl/Matthew McGrath, *Knowledge in an Uncertain World*, Oxford.
Goldman (1976): Alvin Goldman, "Discrimination and Perceptual Knowledge", in: *Journal of Philosophy* 73, 771–791.
Hanfling (1985): Oswald Hanfling, "A Situational Account of Knowledge", in: *The Monist* 68, 40–56.
Hanfling (2003): Oswald Hanfling, "A Gettier Drama", in: *Analysis* 68, 262–263.
Hyman (1999): John Hyman, "How Knowledge Works", in: *Philosophical Quarterly* 197, 433–451.
Jäger (2009): Christoph Jäger, "Why To Believe Weakly in Weak Knowledge: Goldman On Knowledge as Mere True Belief", in: *Grazer Philosophische Studien* 79, 19–40.
Klein (1971): Peter Klein, "A Proposed Definition of Propositional Knowledge", in: *Journal of Philosophy* 68, 471–482.
Lehrer (1990): Keith Lehrer, *Theory of Knowledge*, London.
Sartwell (1991): Crispin Sartwell, "Knowledge Is Merely True Belief", in: *American Philosophical Quarterly* 28, 157–165.
Stanley (2005): Jason Stanley, *Knowledge and Practical Interests*, Oxford.

Nonindexical Contextualism – an Explication and Defense[1]

Nikola Kompa

1. Some examples

The conversational contextualist's starting point is the observation that sometimes we are inclined to attribute knowledge to a given person under certain circumstances but not under others – even given that the person's evidential situation is the same throughout. (When I speak of contextualism in what follows I should be understood as speaking of conversational contextualism.) Contextualist examples such as Keith DeRose's bank-case or Stewart Cohen's airport-case are commonly adduced to illustrate the point.[2] In DeRose's bank-case a speaker self-ascribes knowledge so that the putative knower's context and the attributors' context get easily mixed up. Consider therefore – to begin with –, the following modified version of the case.[3]

Case A1: It is Saturday morning. Susan and Tom go shopping. In the grocer's shop lots of people are waiting in line at the counter. Susan and Tom decide to come back in the afternoon. Susan wonders whether the shop will be open in the afternoon. That is not a particularly pressing problem, though, for if the shop were closed in the afternoon they could equally well buy the things they need on Monday morning. While discussing what to do, a friend, Sarah, calls. Susan asks her whether she knows if the shop will be open in the afternoon. Sarah tells her that she has been to the shop on Saturday afternoon two weeks ago and so knows that it will be open. Susan informs Tom: "Sarah knows that it is open on Saturday afternoon."

---

1 I am indebted to more people than I am able to list here. My greatest debts for comments and critique are due to Stephen Schiffer, Sebastian Schmoranzer, Jason Stanley, and Stewart Cohen.
2 See DeRose (1992), 913; Cohen (2000), 95.
3 Taken with slight modifications from Kompa (2002), 81; cf. also Stanley (2005), 3 ff.

Case B1: Same as in case A; except that this time Susan and Tom are going to give a party that evening. And they still have to buy some very important things for the party. Susan wonders as before whether the shop will be open. Tom replies as before. Again, Sarah calls, and she tells Susan that she has been to the shop Saturday afternoon two weeks ago. But this time Susan also mentions the possibility that the shop might have changed its opening hours – something Sarah cannot rule out. Susan and Tom conclude: "Sarah doesn't know that the shop is open Saturday afternoon." They decide to join the line.

And here is another example due to David Annis.[4]

Case A2: We are sitting in a coffee house and are talking about medical issues, bragging about our lay medical knowledge. In particular, we would like to find out whether Tom, a non-medically trained person, knows that polio is caused by a virus. We ask him and he tells us that he remembers having read it in an apothecary leaflet. Given the circumstances, that might be enough for us to attribute the said knowledge to him.

Case B2: Now suppose the context is an examination for the M.D. degree. Here we expect a lot more. If Tom simply said what he said before "we would take him to be very deficient in knowledge."[5] We would probably say that he does not know that polio is caused by a virus – irrespective of the fact that Tom's evidential situation, his respective beliefs, reasons etc., are exactly the same as before.

Finally, consider the following example, taken (again with slight modifications) from John Turri.[6]

Case A3: Lara, Ann and Tom have just left the house to place a letter in the mailbox at the corner. Ann and Lara ask Tom, who was the last to leave the house, whether the door is locked. Tom says: "Yes, it is locked. I remember turning the key and feeling it click." Given the circumstances, Ann and Lara do not hesitate to say of Tom that he knows that the door is locked.

Case B3: But suppose Lara, Ann and Tom have just left the house to go on vacation. Moreover, although the neighborhood is fairly safe just recently there have been a couple of burglaries. Pulling out of the driveway, Ann and Lara ask Tom whether the door is locked. Tom replies as above. Lara reminds him of those burglaries and how bad it would be if

---

4   Annis (1978), 215.
5   Ibid.
6   Turri (2010), 88.

they found their home ransacked on their return. And she continues "It's rare, but sometimes the bolt hits the strike plate in such a way that it clicks but doesn't lock. So … I ask again: Is it locked?"[7] Tom, though still confident, goes back to check. Given these circumstances, Ann and Lara deny that Tom knows that the door is locked – until he has checked, that is.

2. The idea

These cases aren't particularly far-fetched; rather, they are familiar, everyday cases. The contextualist takes cases such as these as evidence for the following contextualist *Basic Claim*:

> [BC] It is possible that there are two conversational contexts C_A and C_B such that an utterance of "X knows that P", made in context C_A, is true[8] while an utterance of the very same sentence, made in context C_B, is false, although both utterances are about the same person and the same state of affairs P, and the putative knower's evidential situation is also taken to be the same in both cases.

The contextualist takes these examples to show that it is possible that a given knowledge attribution is true as uttered in one context while the corresponding knowledge denial is true as uttered in another context owing to epistemic as well as non-epistemic differences between the attributors' conversational contexts – differences about what is at stake, which error possibilities came up and should be taken seriously, the purpose of the conversation etc. The relevant contexts are the attributors' conversational contexts, not the putative knowers' context.[9] Whether or not A's utterance of "X knows that P" is true depends not on X's but rather on A's interests, purposes etc.

Let us take a closer look at what changes from the A-cases to the B-cases in the above examples and how the changes affect the truth-values of the knowledge attributions in question. The B-cases are more demanding in certain respects. Stronger requirements are imposed on the would-be-knower; more is at stake. In case B1 and B3, it is partic-

---

7   Turri (2010), 88.
8   The idea of an utterance's being true *simpliciter* will be subject to further qualifications below.
9   Those who hold that the putative knower's context calls the shots are sometimes called subject-sensitive invariantists; for a more detailed exposition see e.g. Fantl/McGrath (2002), Hawthorne (2004), Stanley (2005).

ularly important to those attributing (or denying) knowledge that P really is the case. They need be able to rely on the putative knower as their informant. Also, the possibility of error is made more salient in case B1 and B3. In case B2 it is particularly important to the examiners that the examinee really knows that P. He is going to be a doctor, and they need to make sure that he is going to do his job well.

How is that supposed to affect the truth-value of a knowledge attribution? Contextualists disagree over the details of the mechanisms involved. Roughly, though, the idea is something like this. Contextual factors such as the attributors' interests and concerns, the purpose or point of the conversation, their reasons for taking certain error possibilities more seriously than others, their intentions and shared background assumptions etc. help setting a certain *standard* for knowledge, the standard someone has to live up to in order to count as someone who knows relative to the (attributors') context at hand. The context-sensitivity of knowledge attributions is, accordingly, a complex kind of sensitivity to interests, purposes, concerns etc. Moreover, due to the workings of these factors the standard can be raised or lowered, as the case may be. If it is raised, the would-be-knower has to be in a better "epistemic position" than before if he is still to count as someone who knows. He needs to be able to answer more queries, provide better reasons, cite better evidence and more reliable sources, rule out more objections etc.

Many contextualists think that these mechanisms also help to cope with the skeptic for they are commonly motivated by two concerns. On the one hand, they seek to give an account of our everyday practice of attributing knowledge which respects our intuitions about the truth-values of everyday knowledge attributions, i.e., an account according to which many of the attributions we ordinarily take to be true come out true. On the other hand, they want to do justice to skeptical worries. They want to take them seriously and not simply dismiss them as irrelevant. So in contexts, they say, where skeptical scenarios of perfect illusion are being discussed, the standards for knowledge tend to rise. We can attribute knowledge to others only if they are able to rule these skeptical scenarios out – something they cannot do, presumably. Therefore, they do not have knowledge relative to these contexts. In ordinary contexts, on the other hand, standards for knowledge may be not quite as high. It takes less to count as someone who knows in these contexts. Accordingly, we can attribute knowledge relative to these contexts.

Now let us not go into the question of whether the contextualist maneuver is successful or not. It needs emphasizing, though, that a contextualist is not committed to the view that there are exactly two standards of knowledge: *Low* (everyday) and *High* (skeptical), for even within non-skeptical contexts standards of knowledge tend to vary to a considerable extent – as the examples adduced above were meant to illustrate.[10] The plausibility of contextualism does not solely depend on how successfully it deals with the skeptical problem. (Although it would speak in its favor if it were able to provide a solution to the skeptical problem, I guess.)

3. Contextualism – epistemic or semantic?

The basic contextualist claim is a claim about knowledge attributions. Does that make it a purely semantic claim, a claim about truth-conditions of knowledge attributions and their semantic content? Some say so.[11] Nonetheless, epistemic contextualism should not be *reduced* to a semantic claim. (The context-sensitivity involved might not even be a semantic phenomenon in the strict sense of the term – see below.) It is not *just* a semantic claim. It has ample epistemological significance, too.

Knowledge is – the contextualist might say (not everyone agrees that this is also what he *should* say, I guess) – not an intrinsic state of a person, let alone pace Timothy Williamson a certain state of mind. It is not something someone has, not something he or she possesses independently of any knowledge attribution. Instead, knowledge is said to be in the eye of the beholder (or attributor), as Crispin Wright aptly puts it.[12] The question of whether someone *really* has knowledge, independently of any knowledge attribution, is not a sensible question. There is no particular set of beliefs (reasons) or sense impressions (evidence) someone has to have in order to be a knower. There is, in other words, no internal state of a person that marks him as a knower. Whether someone has knowledge (is a knower) is, so to speak, determined externally – relative to the attributors' interests, purposes etc. Just as there

---

10 There may not even be a single scale along which standards vary but rather a multi-dimensional ‚variation space'. In any case, more needs to be said about how the attributer's context fixes a particular standard.
11 Cf., e.g., Rysiew (2009), section 2.
12 Wright (2005), 237.

is no particular set of qualities something has to possess for it to be interesting; no thing is interesting in itself. It is interesting only for someone – relative to someone's interests, concerns, assumptions etc.

And the contextualist might elaborate the point further along the following lines. Knowledge, he might add, is attributed to someone in order to indicate his special epistemic status. The word "know" is, in Michael Williams' terms, an honorific term.[13] Consequently, a contextualist will be inclined to agree with David Henderson that the following should be an uncontroversial point: the concept of knowledge "is used to certify epistemic agents as good sources for an understood audience. Attributions of (and denials of) knowledge are used in a kind of epistemic gate keeping for communities with which the attributor and interlocutors are associated."[14]

More fully, if we say that someone knows that P then our use of the word "know" indicates that she is to be treated as an authority, as a potential informant, as someone to rely on when it comes to the question of whether P or not. And although other accounts of knowledge can accommodate these points, too, the contextualist account seems particularly suited to that purpose. Because whether we want to rely on someone's claim that P seems to depend on what is at stake; on our interests, intentions, and purposes; on which alternatives to P we have reasons to take seriously etc. And these factors vary with context. So, whether someone is to be treated as an authority, as a potential informant, varies accordingly. In other words, we call someone a knower if she answers to our epistemic needs. Knowledge is something that gets attributed in light of certain interests, concerns, assumptions etc. That is a substantive epistemological claim; and it helps explain the context-sensitivity at issue. If the function of knowledge attributions is as specified, then we should expect uses of "know" to be sensitive to the attributors' interests, concerns etc. Nonetheless, more needs to be said about the alleged context-sensitivity.

---

13 Williams (2001), 11.
14 Henderson (2009), 119 f.; also, as Gerhard Ernst has pointed out, different interests might guide our uses of the word "know"; cf., e.g., Ernst (2009), 131–134.

4. Indexicality and hidden syntactic structure

Various attempts have been made at explicating the context-sensitivity at issue. More specifically, the basic contextualist claim has been amended by various semantic claims. Some have claimed, for instance, that the context-sensitivity of the word "know" has to be modeled on the case of indexicals. Keith DeRose, e.g., makes a proposal to that effect.[15] He is thereby reacting to certain problems the contextualist seems to face. A well-rehearsed point in the literature by now is that contextualism seems to make us say awkward things. Consider the following dialogue, adapted from Palle Yourgrau:[16]

A: Do you know where your car is parked?
B: Yes, it is parked in its usual spot.
A: But can you rule out that it has been stolen?
B: No, I can't.
A: But then you have to admit that you didn't know that it is parked in its usual spot when I asked you a moment ago.
B: No, I *did* know *then* that it is parked there. But after your question, I no longer know.

The last line of the dialogue doesn't sound like a sensible thing to say. But isn't that exactly what speaker B should say if contextualism were true? The DeRosean contextualist might reply that B should rather say something like this: "The proposition I expressed before when I uttered 'I know that my car is at place x' is true, and so is the proposition I expressed when I said just now 'I don't know that my car is at place x'. It's is just that in *this* context I cannot express a true proposition by uttering what I uttered before." But then, does that sound like a sensible thing to say?

Suppose Ann in context C_A says something true in uttering "Tim doesn't know that P", while Bob in context C_B says something true in uttering "Tim knows that P". Suppose further that Ann considers Bob's knowledge attribution and that she is well aware of the low standards operative in Bob's context. It looks as if Ann said something true were she to say:

---

15 Cf. also, e.g., Cohen (1999).
16 Cf. Yourgrau (1983), 295.

[1] Bob says something true in uttering "Tim knows that P" but Tim doesn't know that P.[17,18]

Sentence [1] sounds odd. But it should not sound odd if "know" were context-sensitive, as the contextualist says it is. DeRose diagnoses a fallacy in cases such as these: the fallacy of semantic descent. Accordingly, he suggests that the real commitments of contextualism have to be couched in meta-linguistic terms.[19] DeRose's point is that one cannot simply go from a meta-linguistic statement such as "A's utterance of 'X knows that P' is true" to the object-language statement "X knows that P". It is not legitimate to apply a disquotational principle across-the-board, he claims. And the analogy is with indexical expressions such as *I* or *here*. In these cases, too, one cannot validly infer from "A's utterance of 'John is here' is true" that "John is here" is true.

The problem with this diagnosis is that the indexical account of *know* is itself fraught with problems.[20] As Stephen Schiffer, Wayne Davis and others have convincingly argued, it is highly questionable whether the word "know" is an indexical.[21] Stephen Schiffer, for instance, has emphasized that the indexical solution to skeptical puzzles involves a very implausible error theory. We are taken in by skeptical arguments simply because we are mistaken about which propositions the arguments' premises and conclusions express. Moreover, the error theory is in tension with the indexical semantics since we are usually not confused about which propositions indexical utterances express.[22] In other words, a proponent of the indexical account of "know" owes us an explanation of why competent speakers can easily be made to see the context-sensitivity of genuine indexicals but fail to see any alleged context-sensitivity of the word "know". Indexicals wear their

---

17 Cf. Kompa (2002), 18.
18 Does Ann herself have to know that P relative to the raised standard? Well if not, then someone subscribing to the knowledge norm of assertion will claim that she cannot assert that Bob says something true (cf. Stanley 2005, 54 fn. 5). So let us simply suppose, in order to keep matters as simple as possible, that she knows that P even relative to the more demanding standard.
19 Cf. DeRose (2000), 102–105.
20 That is not to say, though, that any of the other views on the market fare any better in this respect; see e.g. footnote 27.
21 Cf. Schiffer (1996) and Davis (2004, 2005 and 2007).
22 Cf. Schiffer (1996), 325.

context-sensitivity on their sleeves; the word "know" obviously doesn't.[23]

Others have tried to alternatively model the context-sensitivity of the word "know" not on the case of indexicals but on the case of predicative uses of comparative adjectives such as "tall", "rich" or "flat". The idea would be that there is *hidden syntactic structure* in knowledge attributions, too. Just as the logical form of "Joe is tall" is – arguably – something like "Joe is tall for a sixth-grader", so the logical form of "X knows that P" is something like "X knows that P relative to standard S". Yet on first glance this doesn't seem to be a very promising move either as it doesn't square well with the linguistic data. For example, as Jason Stanley has pointed out, predicative uses of comparative adjectives can be modified, as in "he is very rich". But "know" cannot be thus modified. Also, we can say something like "six feet tall" or "42 years old" but there is no natural measure phrase with "know". And, most strikingly, there is a comparative form of all the comparative adjectives (hence their name). We can say something like "richer than", "flatter than", "taller than", etc. But there is no comparative form of "know".[24] A contextualist need not be overly impressed by these data, though, as he might point out that grammatical differences between "know" and gradable adjectives do not seem particularly relevant to the question of whether a given expression is context-sensitive or not.[25] Alternatively, he might suggest a different analogy by assimilating "I know that P" not to sentences such as "He is tall" or "She is rich" but to sentences such as "It is raining". Just as a speaker is, by uttering the latter sentence implicitly referring to a certain place, a speaker who utters "X knows that P" is implicitly referring to a certain epistemic standard, or so the contextualist might claim. (But then, again, the reference can be easily made explicit in the former case but not in the latter.)

---

23 Wayne Davis speaks, very aptly, of semantic blindness in these cases. He defends a pragmatic account of the data, based on the idea that we often use expressions of our language loosely. So "S knows that P" is, according to Davis, "commonly used loosely to implicate 'S is close enough to knowing that p for contextually indicated purposes.'" (Davis 2007, 395.)
24 Cf. Stanley (2004 and 2005).
25 He might go so far as to claim that even semantic differences between "know" and comparative adjectives would fail to proof "know" not to be context-sensitive as the context-sensitivity of "know" need not be a semantic phenomenon at all, thereby dismissing the indexical as well as the hidden-structure account of knowledge attributions. I am going to pursue that line of thought – see below.

Yet there is still another problem for the indexical as well as the hidden-syntactic-structure account that has drawn much attention recently: the problem of (lost) disagreement. If "know" were an indexical or required a hidden argument place in logical form, then speaker A who is employing demanding standards and therefore *denies* that X knows that P and speaker B who is employing relaxed standards and *claims* that X knows that P do not really disagree. For A doesn't deny what B asserts. A expresses something like the following proposition: *X doesn't know that P relative to high standards* (or on the indexical account: *X doesn't know$_A$ that P* – where "know$_A$" is the knowledge relation denoted by A's use of the word "know"). While B expresses something like the following proposition: *X knows that P relative to low standards* (or, again: *X knows$_B$ that P*).[26] So if "know" were an indexical or required a hidden argument place in logical form, then the disagreement between A and B would be only apparent.[27] But that is not what we want to say on an intuitive basis, at least not in all cases.

Let us try to pinpoint the underlying problem. The problem is that content has to meet two incompatible demands. On the one hand, content is supposed to be what speakers say and what hearers take speakers to have said. Yet in the case of knowledge attributions, speakers will not have the impression of having said something about epistemic standards nor about their own concept of knowledge. If we want to respect competent speakers' intuitions about what has been said we have to render the content of knowledge attributions homophonically. That is also

---

26 As Richard Feldman points out: "It is *always* possible to explain the conflicting inclinations we have in these cases by appeal to context dependence or ambiguity: […] Similarly, whenever people seem to disagree, it is possible to say that there is no real disagreement, but that they are asserting and denying different propositions." (Feldman 2001, 72.) And he goes on to claim that there are many cases, for example cases of a moral controversy, in which "a contextualist solution to our wavering intuitions" (ibid. 73) is not plausible at all. So the question is whether the explanation for our "wavering intuitions" regarding knowledge attributions is to be modeled on cases of moral controversy or rather on those cases where we aptly appeal to context-sensitivity.

27 This is a problem for relativist views, too. If what I say when uttering P is true relative to my standards while what you say when uttering non-P is true relative to your standards, we are not really disagreeing either – or so it seems. For I may well agree with you that what you say is true relative to your standard just as you may agree with me that what I say is true relative to my standard. Nonetheless, there is room for disagreement – more on this in section 6.

necessary in order to capture speakers' intuitions concerning disagreement.

But then, on the other hand, content is supposed to be complete, truth-apt without any further relativization. Both the indexical and the hidden-structure contextualist work with the classical syntactico-semantic notion of content.[28] Content is the result of semantically interpreting syntactic structure; it is complete and truth-apt; not in need of any further specification or relativization.[29] In accordance with the Kaplanian framework, context is needed only to supply the denotations to indexicals and demonstratives. And the truth-value of the content (or proposition) expressed is the result of evaluating content at circumstances of evaluation.[30][31] If content depicts or represents things as they stand in those circumstances, it is true; otherwise it is false. But one might wonder whether any content could be true or false as it stands, complete in the required sense? Isn't it speakers that *interpret* something as true or false – in light of certain purposes and assumptions? Take a picture of something. Could there be a complete picture – a picture that is true or false as it stands? Could its content be complete, true or false *simpliciter*? Similarly, as Anne Bezuidenhout puts it:

> There is no sentence that we can produce that can settle all questions about how some original sentence is to be understood, since language doesn't function that way. It is not self-interpreting.[32]

In a nutshell, then, the problem the indexical and the hidden-structure account are subject to is this: Content is supposed to be complete; in order to make it so it gets distorted beyond recognition. Content is

---

28 A certain commitment to what Emma Borg calls *Formalism* – 'the idea that there is an entirely formal (i.e. syntactic) route to semantic content' (cf. Borg 2007, 355) – is commonly made.

29 A content or proposition that is said to be complete and truth-apt in this sense should, presumably, be specifiable by means of a sentence that exhibits contextual *in*dependence: "a sentence whose truth value stays fixed through time and from speaker to speaker" (Quine 1960, 193); a sentence (statement) whose "truth value is uniquely determined independently of any speaker and context of utterance" (Mühlhölzer 1988, 192).

30 Cf. Kaplan (1989), 501.

31 According to Kaplan a "context is a package of whatever parameters are needed to determine referent, and thus content, of the directly referential expressions of the language" (Kaplan 1989, 591). A circumstance, on the other hand, "will usually include a possible state or history of the world, a time, and perhaps other features as well." (Kaplan 1989, 502).

32 Bezuidenhout (2002), 113.

also supposed to be what speakers and hearers recognize as what has been said. Yet there does not seem to be a notion of content fit to serve both purposes.

5. Nonindexical contextualism

Given the problems the indexical and the hidden-syntactic-structure account face it might be worthwhile to search for alternatives. Various proposals have been made; which proposal one favors depends on what notion of content one prefers and how one thinks of the relation between content and truth. Much *en vogue* nowadays are various forms of (moderate or radical) relativism.[33] The relativist holds, as his name suggests, that truth is relative. That in itself is neither a particularly interesting nor a particularly contested claim. It is widely acknowledged, e.g., that sentences (at least some of them) are true only relative to a context and, maybe, a language (depending on how one prefers to individuate sentences). Things get more interesting, though, if one takes – as is common among relativists – contents or propositions to be the bearers of truth and falsity and claim that their truth (or falsity) is relative to something else. What, then, is the truth-value of a proposition relative to? According to a much discussed and well elaborated conception of relativism – due to John MacFarlane – the truth-value of a proposition is relative to and varies with certain parameters of the *context of assessment*:[34]

> The notion of a context of assessment may be unfamiliar, but it is readily intelligible. Just as a context of use is a situation in which a sentence might be *used*, so a context of assessment is a situation in which a (past, present, or future, actual or merely possible) use of a sentence might be *assessed* for truth or falsity.[35]

Yet the view I would like to further explicate and defend is closest to (though not exactly the same as) what John MacFarlane calls *nonindexical contextualism*.[36]

---

33 See Kölbel (2008) for an overview.
34 Cf. MacFarlane (2005 and 2009).
35 MacFarlane (2005), 217.
36 Cf. MacFarlane (2005, 2007, and 2009).

According to MacFarlane, the nonindexical contextualist holds that the word "know" is context-sensitive but not indexical.[37] This is not to suggest that the word "know", although not an indexical, nonetheless takes on different semantic values in different contexts. Rather, the point of nonindexical contextualism is, as MacFarlane emphasizes, that no alleged reference to an epistemic standard is part of the proposition expressed by a knowledge claim. What a speaker says (i.e. the proposition he expresses) when he utters a sentence of the form "X knows that P" is just that X knows that P – nothing more and nothing less. Yet whether what he thereby says is true or false depends, according to MacFarlane's rendering of nonindexical contextualism, on the *circumstances of evaluation* determined by the *context of utterance*. He draws on David Kaplan's distinction between contexts of utterance and circumstances of evaluation. David Lewis distinguishes in a similar vein between a context and an index. And index is an n-tuple of features of context – features that may be relevant to truth. He defines the two-place relation of a sentence's being true at a context as follows:

> Let us say that sentence s is true at context c iff s is true at c at the index of the context c.[38]

This way of putting the point nicely highlights the two distinct roles context is supposed to play: It has to supply the denotations to indexical terms in sentence s. It also provides features on which the truth of the whole sentence may depend, such as, arguably, an epistemic standard. For, as Lewis emphasized, indices have exactly those features of context "that are packed into them as coordinates, and no others."[39] Accordingly, an utterance of "X knows that P" in context c would be true, according to nonindexical contextualism, if the proposition thereby expressed were true when evaluated relative to circumstances (w, e), where w is the world of c and e is the epistemic standard operative in c.[40]

Adopting this proposal would allow us to keep the semantics of the word "know" simple in that no reference to a standard of knowledge (or any such thing) is part of the proposition expressed in knowledge ascriptions. Nor are different properties (or relations or whatever the referent of the word "know" may be on the indexical account) referred

---

37 Cf. MacFarlane (2009), 236 f.
38 Lewis (1980), 31.
39 Ibid. 30.
40 Cf. MacFarlane (2009), 237.

to by different uses of the word "know". For all that, whether we correctly attribute knowledge to someone or not is sensitive to contextual factors; there are cases in which a speaker with certain interests, purposes, and intentions can truly assert that person X knows that P while another speaker with different interests etc. can truly assert that X doesn't know that P. Consequently, the context-sensitivity does affect truth-value; that is the contextualist claim.[41]

The problems the indexical and the hidden-structure account face attest to the fact that the word "know" exhibits a rather subtle form of context-sensitivity. It is worth noting, though, that subtle as it may be, speakers are nonetheless aware of varying contextual requirements concerning the application of the word "know". If they weren't, the contextualist stories couldn't even be told. The contextualist examples would never have attracted any attention at all if speakers weren't sensitive to varying contextual requirements in the cases depicted. Trivially, a bar room chat imposes another standard of knowledge than a hearing in a court of law. Speakers know that – even if they are in no position to explicate their knowledge (a common phenomenon). Standards of knowledge are invoked here for explanatory purposes. Yet they need not be part of semantics to serve that purpose. For it is true that when a speaker makes a knowledge claim of the form "X knows that P", he will not have the impression of having said something about epistemic standards or having referred to his own, private property of knowledge. And maybe that is so because he did not say anything about epistemic standards nor refer to his own, private property of knowledge by his use of the word "know".

So the proposal is relativist in that it keeps content syntactically and semantically simple; no opaque indexicality or hidden syntactic structure is postulated. It is contextualist in that it takes the factors on which truth depends to be provided by the context in which the sentence in question is used.[42] More needs to be said on both counts.

---

41 This intimately relates to a debate in philosophy of language about the extent and manner in which semantic and pragmatic processes interact in linguistic interpretation. One of the proposals at issue is what has come to be called truth-conditional pragmatics (cf., e.g., Bezuidenhout 2002, Carston 2002, and Recanati 2004).

42 MacFarlane is explicit about this: "[...] nonindexical contextualism differs from relativism [...] in taking the epistemic standard parameter to be initialized by the context of use, rather than the context of assessment. For this reason, it may be attracitive to those who find the notion of assessment-relative truth too

But first, let me emphasize that this kind of dependence is a widespread phenomenon. It comes in different degrees of obviousness, though. For example, whether something can truly be said to be circular, hexagonal or flat depends on how much laxity is permissible. Given such and such contextual requirements, only something close to being perfectly circular can be truly described as such. Given other requirements, anything of roughly circular form will do. Also, whether something can be said to be interesting, helpful, good, new, exciting, legitimate, reliable, worthwhile, evident, etc. depends on the participants' standards, purposes, background assumptions etc. Of course, one could again postulate hidden-syntactic structure – attested, one might claim, by the fact that some of these expressions can be used to express two-place relations. But then again, they don't have to be so used. And to suggest that nonetheless there is always a second argument place in logical form that needs to be contextually filled in is to make syntax and semantics unnecessarily opaque. Moreover, the contextualist point generalizes even further as whether something can be said to be green, or round, or a game of baseball (or what have you) depends on the participants' interests, intentions, concerns etc. as well.[43] We call something reliable, someone interesting or someone a knower in the light of certain interests and goals, to a particular purpose, and against the background of certain assumptions. And when we interpret these utterances and evaluate them as true or false, we interpret and evaluate them in the light of these interests, purposes, and assumptions. All these factors vary with context.

6. Truth and content

Yet how exactly do we evaluate content relative to certain circumstances (of evaluation)? Also, more needs to be said about the notion of content in play and about its relation to truth. Let us take the second point first. What notion of content are we working with here? As Crispin

---

much to swallow." (MacFarlane 2009, 237). Also, I am granting MacFarlane's point that if someone else assesses a given claim made in another context he may well apply different criteria of assessment than the ones that were operative when the claim was made. But I am interested in the question of how a given utterance is understood and evaluated *in the context in which it was made*.

43 Cf., e.g., Bezuidenhout (2002), 106, Moravcsik (1998), 35, or Travis (1997), 89.

Wright has pointed out, we are working with a non-representational notion of content; for given that propositional truth is relative, what representational content could a particular proposition P still possess? "For what state of affairs might we think of P as representing?"[44] Unless one is willing to countenance relative states of affairs – states of affairs that hold only relative to something else, the point seems well taken.

But maybe that is as it should be. Maybe we are not always – even when making sincere assertion – representing the world as being a certain way. As Mark Richards puts it: "My statement, that Mary is rich, is as much an invitation to look at things in a certain way, as it is a representation of how things are."[45]

The idea, of course, is not new; it is very close to what David Lewis called "accommodation".[46] The idea of accommodation will, I think, help us better understand what it is to evaluate content relative to a circumstance (of evaluation). Let a speaker, call him Tom, utter a given sentence. The utterance will provide a hearer with all kinds of phonetic, morphological, syntactic, semantic and contextual information. The hearer will then begin to interpret the sentence by availing himself of whatever information he can get a hold on. And he will, commonly, try to interpret the speaker charitably. Suppose Tom said: "John is tall. And Mary is rich". (Not a very sensible utterance, presumably; but let us put that aside, for the moment.) Isn't Tom thereby suggesting to his audience that "tall" and "rich" are to be so understood in their shared context – i.e. given their shared interest and assumptions, the purpose or point of the conversation etc. – that John falls under the term "tall" and Mary under the term "rich"? And if he gets away with it, isn't what he thereby said – given that they are all well-informed (not mistaken about John's height and Mary's wealth, that is), competent and reasonable – not true simply due to the fact that well-informed, competent, and reasonable speakers have agreed to take it to be true in light of their interests, purposes etc.? Nonetheless, they are not thereby presenting it as an undeniable fact – true once and for all – that John is tall and Mary rich. For those very same speakers may well agree in another context that John is not tall (talking now about NBA players) and Mary not rich (talking now about Bill Gates and people of that ilk). So let us think – contrary to commonly held opinion – of assertion not as

---

44 Wright (2008), 168.
45 Richards (2004), 226.
46 Cf. Lewis (1979).

aspiring (at least not on all cases) to say something *eternally and objectively true* but to bring about a certain understanding; make one's audience view things a certain way, count certain things as being a certain way, for present purposes.

But, again, Tom does not *say* that John is tall given such and such interests. Nor does he say anything about certain standards. That is the nonindexicalist point. He just says that John is tall. That is the content of his utterance. Yet there is no one way for the world to be to make that content true. There are many ways – relative to different interests, purposes, etc. Relative truth simply reflects the fact that in different contexts different interests, concerns, purposes etc. guide us; and that we therefore accommodate differently. But that does not mean that anything goes, that truth is arbitrary and totally up to us. For our interests etc. are not arbitrary either.

Consequently, if someone who is party to the conversation disagrees, he may do so for various reasons. He might have different interests etc. He would agree to count Mary as rich if such and such were their interests. But he does not think these are or should be their interests. Also, he may be mistaken about what the other participants' interests are. Or he may think that they should not count Mary as rich, e. g. – even given their interests, purposes etc.; maybe he has a different concept of wealth. (Is there something like the right concept?) Yet he may also know something the others do not know; maybe he knows more about Mary's income and assets than they do. So there is ample room for disagreement – be it factual, conceptual or normative.

To sum up, the idea is that if a speaker, call her Ann, utters, e. g., the sentence "Tom knows that birds fly" she thereby says that Tom knows that birds fly. The participants in the conversation will evaluate what Ann has said relative to certain circumstances, more specifically relative to circumstances comprising the epistemic standard determined by their context. The standard in turn is determined by the participants' interests, concerns, purposes etc. Consequently, whether Ann said something true or not will depend on these things, too.

Still, one might wonder what a non-representational content or proposition could possibly be? Talk of propositions might misleadingly suggest that there is a content in the traditional sense that just waits to be evaluated. For those who are uneasy with the idea of non-representational content, there is an alternative way of looking at things that requires a more radical departure from semantic orthodoxy. For one might claim that content itself allows for accommodation, can be construed differently, if need be; is open to contextual negotiation – an idea pretty much *en vogue* in cognitive linguistics for quite some time now.[47] More specifically, one might take the pervasive context sensitivity of natural language to show that the contextually relevant meaning or content of a word or sentence is not a ready-made entity but has to be constructed or negotiated in context. According to Robyn Carston, for instance, often in linguistic interpretation "an ad hoc concept is constructed and functions as a constituent of what is explicitly communicated".[48]

One might even venture to suggest that we go one step further even and do without meanings (in the traditional sense) altogether. Words, one might say, encode semantic information; yet the information itself doesn't amount to something like a full-fletched meaning or content. At best, it provides us with something like a proto-content or default interpretation. Words provide semantic information about former, paradigmatic uses of the expressions, about admissible default interpretations, about the thing denoted by the expression etc. (You won't know the meaning of the word "table" unless you know something about tables.) And that is all there is to meaning in the semantic sense. The information is the starting point for pragmatic inferences that result in a contextually specified understanding and evaluation of the sentence in question.[49] A pragmatic inference is a defeasible inference; something like an inference to the best interpretation. And this is where the idea of accommodation comes into play again. If you say "Mary is rich", then your interlocutors will, if cooperative, understand "rich" in such a way that Mary counts as rich – thereby making your utterance true in the context at hand. In so doing, they will be taking the participants' shared interests, the purpose or point of the conversation, certain background assumptions etc. into account in order to pragmatically infer the contextually relevant understanding and evaluation of what you said.

7. *Summing up*

Epistemic contextualism rests on the idea that knowledge attributions are context-sensitive. The truth-value of a given knowledge attributions may vary with variations in the context of attribution. Knowledge is

---

47 Cf. e.g. Croft/Cruse (2004).
48 Carston (2002), 357.
49 Cf., e.g., Recanati (2004), 146 ff. and Croft/Cruse (2004), 97 ff.

something that we – given our interests, concerns etc. – attribute to someone in order to indicate his special epistemic status.

The context-sensitivity at issue is commonly modeled on the case either of indexicals or of gradable adjectives in predicative use. But since both suggestions are problematic I tried to develop an alternative account that is very close to what MacFarlane calls nonindexical contextualism. It seeks to explain the context-sensitivity of knowledge attributions as a pragmatic phenomenon in that it takes the semantic content of (or the semantic information provided by) knowledge attributions not to vary from context to context.

Nonetheless, knowledge attributions may vary in truth-value relative to different circumstances of evaluation – due to the mechanisms of pragmatic interpretation and accommodation. They have to be evaluated in the light of certain interest, concerns etc. Their truth is, therefore, relative to *circumstances of evaluation*; circumstances which comprise an epistemic standard that is in turn determined by the participants' interests, concerns, purposes etc.

References

Annis (1978): David Annis, "A Contextualist Theory of Epistemic Justification", in: *American Philosophical Quarterly* 15, 213–219.
Bezuidenhout (2002): Anne Bezuidenhout, "Truth-Conditional Pragmatics", in: *Philosophical Perspectives* 16, 105–134.
Borg (2007): Emma Borg, "Minimalism versus Contextualism in Semantics", in: G. Preyer/G. Peter (eds.), *Context-Sensitivity and Semantic Minimalism: New Essays on Semantics and Pragmatics*, Oxford, 339–359.
Carston (2002): Robyn Carston, *Thoughts and Utterances: The Pragmatics of Explicit Communication*, Oxford.
Cohen (1999): Stewart Cohen, "Contextualism, Skepticism, and the Structure of Reasons", in: J. E. Tomberlin (ed.), in: *Philosophical Perspectives* 13, *Epistemology*, Oxford, 57–89.
Cohen (2000): Stewart Cohen, "Contextualism and Skepticism", in: *Philosophical Issues* 10, 94–107.
Croft/Cruse (2004): William Croft/Alan D. Cruse, *Cognitive Linguistics*, Cambridge.
Davis (2007): Wayne A. Davis, "Knowledge claims and context: loose use", in: *Philosophical Studies* 132, 395–438.
Davis (2004): Wayne A.. Davis, "Are knowledge claims indexical?", in: *Erkenntnis* 61, 257–281.
Davis (2005): Wayne A. Davis, "Contextualist theories of knowledge", in: *Acta Analytica* 20, 29–42.

DeRose (1992): Keith DeRose, "Contextualism and Knowledge Attributions", in: *Philosophy and Phenomenological Research* 52, 913–929.
DeRose (2000): Keith DeRose, "Now you know it, now you don't", in: *Proceedings of the Twentieth World Congress of Philosophy, Volume 5*, Ohio.
Ernst (2009): Gerhard Ernst, *Einführung in die Erkenntnistheorie*, Darmstadt.
Fantl & McGrath (2002): Jeremy Fantl & Matt McGrath, "Evidence, Pragmatics, and Justification", in: *The Philosophical Review* 111, 67–94.
Kölbel (2008): Max Kölbel, "Introduction: Motivations for Relativism", in: M. García-Carpintero/M. Kölbel (eds.), *Relative Truth*, Oxford, 1–38.
Feldman (2001): Richard Feldman, "Skeptical Problems, Contextualist Solutions", in: *Philosophical Studies* 103, 61–85.
Hawthorne (2004): John Hawthorne, *Knowledge and Lotteries*, Oxford.
Henderson (2009): David Henderson, "Motivated Contextualism", in: *Philosophical Studies* 142, 119–131.
Kaplan (1989): David Kaplan, "Demonstratives. An Essay on the Semantics, Logic, Metaphysics, and Epistemology of Demonstratives and Other Indexicals", in: J. Almog/J. Perry/H. Wettstein (eds.), *Themes from Kaplan*. Oxford, 481–563.
Kompa (2002): Nikola Kompa, "The Context Sensitivity of Knowledge Attributions", in: *Grazer Philosophische Studien* 64, 1–18.
Lewis (1979): David Lewis, "Scorekeeping in a Language Game", in: *Journal of Philosophical Logic* 8, 339–359.
Lewis (1980): David Lewis, "Index, Context, and Content", in: S. Kangar/S. Öhman (eds.), *Philosophy and Grammar*, Dordrecht.
MacFarlane (2005): John MacFarlane, "The Assessment Sensitivity of Knowledge Attributions", in: T. S. Gendler/J. Hawthorne (eds.), *Oxford Studies in Epistemology*, Oxford, 197–233.
MacFarlane (2007): John MacFarlane, "Semantic Minimalism and Nonindexical Contextualism" in: G. Preyer & G. Peter (eds.), *Context-Sensitivity and Semantic Minimalism: New Essays on Semantics and Pragmatics*, Oxford, 240–250.
MacFarlane (2009): John MacFarlane, "Nonindexical Contextualism", in: *Synthese* 166, 231–250.
Moravcsik (1998): Julius M. Moravcsik, *Meaning, Creativity, and the Partial Inscrutabilty of the Human Mind*, Stanford.
Mühlhölzer (1988): Felix Mühlhölzer, "On Objectivity", in: *Erkenntnis* 28, 185–230.
Quine (1960): Willard Van Orman Quine, *Word and Object*, Cambridge.
Récanati (2004): François Récanati, *Literal Meaning*, Cambridge.
Richards (2004): Mark Richards, "Contextualism and Relativism", in: *Philosophical Studies* 119, 215–242.
Rysiew (2009): Patrick Rysiew, "Epistemic Contextualism", in: E. N. Zalta (ed.), *The Stanford Encyclopedia of Philosophy (Spring 2009 Edition)*, URL = <http://plato.stanford.edu/archives/spr2009/entries/contextualism-epistemology/>.
Schiffer (1996): Stephen Schiffer, "Contextualist Solutions to Scepticism", in: *Proceedings of the Aristotelian Society* 96, 317–333.

Stanley (2004): Jason Stanley, "On the Linguistic Basis for Contextualism", in: *Philosophical Studies* 119, 119–146.
Stanley (2005): Jason Stanley, *Knowledge and Practical Interests*, Oxford.
Travis (1997): Charles Travis, "Pragmatics", in: B. Hale/C. Wright (eds.), *A Companion to the Philosophy of Language*, Oxford, 87–107.
Turri (2010): John Turri, "Epistemic Invariantism and Speech Act Contextualism", in: *The Philosophical Review* 119(1), 77–95.
Williams (2001): Michael Williams, *Problems of Knowledge*, Oxford.
Wright (2005): Crispin Wright, "Contextualism and Scepticism: Even-Handedness, Factivity and Surreptitiously Raising Standards", in: *The Philosophical Quarterly* 55, 236–262.
Wright (2008): Crispin Wright, "Relativism about Truth itself: Haphazard Thoughts about the very idea", in: M. García-Carpintero/M. Kölbel (eds.), *Relative Truth*, Oxford, 157–185.
Yourgrau (1983): Palle Yourgrau, "Knowledge and Relevant Alternatives", in: *Synthese* 55, 175–190.

Part Two:
Contrastivism

What is Contrastivism?

Jonathan Schaffer

> To know that x is A is to know that x is A within a framework of relevant alternatives, B, C, and D. This set of contrasts (…) serve to define what it is that is known (…).[1]

What is contrastivism? Contrastivism is a view about the *structure* of the knowledge relation. It is a view concerning the number of places in the knowledge relation, and what fits in these places. The orthodox view is that knowledge is a two-place relation, with one place fit for a subject and another place fit for a proposition. The contrastive view is that knowledge is a three-place relation, with an additional place fit for a contrast proposition, in addition to the place fit for a subject and the place fit for a proposition. In short: instead of the orthodox two-place Ksp structure ('s knows that p'), the contrastivist posits the three-place Kspq structure ('s knows that p rather than q').

Perhaps there are additional places in the knowledge relation, fit for neither the subject, nor the known proposition, nor a contrast. For instance, perhaps there is a place fit for the situation at issue. Whether or not there is such a place is neutral as between the orthodox view and the contrastive view. So an even more neutral construal of contrastivism would involve saying that the orthodox view posits a certain *baseline* number of places in the knowledge relation, with no place fit for anything like a contrast proposition; while the contrastive view posits an *additional* place in the knowledge relation, fit for a contrast proposition. For definiteness I will continue to speak of the orthodox view in terms of two-place Ksp relations, and of the contrastive view in terms of three-place Kspq relations, but the relevant aspect is the posit of the additional q place for a contrast proposition. What exactly q gets added to is by and large an orthogonal matter.

Why accept contrastivism? There are a number of potential motivations for thinking that the knowledge relation has an additional contrast argument. The contrastivist of course needs to provide some motivation for her deviation from orthodoxy, but there is no one particular moti-

---

[1] Dretske (1970), 1022.

vation that any contrastivist must endorse. But just to exhibit one natural motivation, consider a given normal subject Ann in a given situation of seeing a goldfinch in the garden, and ask whether Ann knows that there is a goldfinch in the garden. The contrastivist will say, *it depends on the contrast:* Ann might well know that there is a goldfinch in the garden rather than a raven, but yet fail to know that there is a goldfinch in the garden rather than a canary. And so it seems that specifying the subject and the proposition (and the situation at issue) is still insufficient to settle whether the knowledge relation holds. One must also specify the contrast.

So much for what contrastivism is, and what sort of motivations there are for it. But it is equally important to explain what contrastivism is *not*. First, contrastivism is not a view about how to analyze the K relation. The contrastivist is committed to the claim that the K relation has a contrast argument, but is not committed to any particular analysis of her contrast-supplemented relation Kspq. For instance, she might regard K as a primitive relation, or offer some sort of tracking account of contrastive knowledge.[2] That said, it is perhaps most natural for the contrastivist to work with something like a classical relevant alternatives conception of knowledge, on which knowledge requires (*inter alia*) the elimination of the relevant alternatives.[3] The contrast place q can then be understood as the place fit for the disjunction of the relevant alternatives, and contrastivism becomes the natural metaphysics of the relevant alternatives view. For instance, to return to the example above of Ann and the goldfinch, it might be that Ann has the ability to eliminate the alternative of the bird being a raven but lacks the ability to eliminate the alternative of the bird being a canary. Her abilities and disabilities would then explain why she knows that there is a goldfinch in the garden rather than a raven, yet fails to know that there is a goldfinch in the garden rather than a canary.

Second, contrastivism is not a view about the semantics of 'know.' The contrastivist could, for instance, even think that 'know' semantically expresses a two-place non-contrastive relation, but hold out for con-

---

2 See Yablo (*manuscript*) for a version of contrastivism that works with a tracking requirement.
3 The classical relevant alternatives conception of knowledge traces back at least to Austin (1946). See Lewis (1996) for a contextualist version of this approach.

ceptual revision.[4] Or she might think that 'know' in English functions as an indexical expressing different epistemic relations $K\star_1$, $K\star_2$, ... in different contexts, with each $K\star_n$ relation corresponding to a different value for q in the $Kspq$ relation. But the contrastivist might also claim that 'know' directly expresses her ternary contrastive $Kspq$ relation (this is the line I take). In defending this view, the contrastivist might appeal to ordinary language knowledge ascriptions with articulated "rather than"-phrases and to knowledge ascriptions with interrogative complements (compare: 'Ann knows whether there is a goldfinch or a raven in the garden' and 'Ann knows whether there is a goldfinch or a canary in the garden'). She will hold that in ordinary language knowledge ascriptions with no overt contrast phrase ('Ann knows that there is a goldfinch in the garden'), context supplies a value for some sort of covert semantic material, perhaps via the question under discussion.

As the last paragraph should bring out, the relation between contrastivism and contextualism is a complicated matter, and I would now say that these two doctrines are best regarded as independent views of distinct subject matters. Contrastivism is a view about the metaphysical structure of the knowledge relation, whereas contextualism is a view (or perhaps a family of views) about the semantics of the word 'know.' And so one can be a contrastivist but not a contextualist, for instance by thinking that 'know' invariantly denotes a binary relation, but holding out for conceptual revision. And likewise one can be a contextualist but not a contrastivist, for instance by thinking that 'know' variantly denotes a plurality of binary relations.[5] My own preferred view is both contrastivist and contextualist. Or at least it is contextualist in respect of positing a third semantic argument position projected by 'know' which is evaluated by context when left implicit. My view is invariantist in respect of treating 'know' as invariantly denoting the one and only ternary K relation.

The underlying issues involving contrastivism concern the structure of the knowledge relation. There are of course further structures beyond

---

4 I take this to be the view of Morton & Karjalainen (2003) as well as Sinnott-Armstrong (2004).
5 Moreover the variation might not involve anything to do with contrasts. The contextualist who is not a contrastivist might think that the variation involves some other factor, such as the degree of evidential support one needs to count as sufficiently justified. See Cohen (1988) for an articulation of such a view, and Schaffer (2005) for some further relevant discussion.

the binary and contrastive forms to consider, and there is the underlying deep question as to what factors are relevant to determining the structure of any given relation. In the end, discussion of contrastivism should be taken as an opportunity to go beyond simply *assuming* that knowledge is a binary relation, and to articulate *reasons* for imputing a given structure to the knowledge relation, whatever that structure might be.

References

Austin (1946): John Langshaw Austin, "Other Minds", in: *Proceedings of the Aristotelian Society* 20, 149–87.
Cohen (1988): Stewart Cohen, "How to be a Fallibilist", in: *Philosophical Perspectives* 2, 91–123.
Dretske (1970): Fred Dretske, "Epistemic Operators", in: *Journal of Philosophy* 67, 1007–23.
Lewis (1996): David Lewis, "Elusive Knowledge", in: *Australasian Journal of Philosophy* 74, 549–67.
Morton/Karjalainen (2003): Adam Morton/Antti Karjalainen, "Contrastive Knowledge", in: *Philosophical Explorations* 6, 74–89.
Schaffer (2005): Jonathan Schaffer, "What Shifts? Thresholds, Standards, or Alternatives?" in: Preyers/Peters (eds.), *Contextualism in Philosophy: Knowledge, Meaning, and Truth*, Oxford, 115–130.
Sinnott-Armstrong (2004): Walter Sinnott-Armstrong, *Pyrrhonian Skepticism*, Oxford.
Yablo (manuscript*)*: Steve Yablo, "Knowing about Things", (manuscript).

Contrastive Knowledge*

Jonathan Schaffer

> I know a hawk from a handsaw
> (Hamlet)

Does G. E. Moore know that he has hands? *Yes,* says the dogmatist: Moore's hands are right before his eyes. *No,* says the skeptic: for all Moore knows he could be a brain-in-a-vat. *Yes* and *no,* says the contrastivist: *yes,* Moore knows that he has hands rather than stumps; but *no,* Moore does not know that he has hands rather than vat-images of hands.

The dogmatist and the skeptic suppose that knowledge is a *binary, categorical* relation: *s* knows that *p*. The contrastivist says that knowledge is a *ternary, contrastive* relation: *s* knows that *p* rather than *q*.

I propose to develop the contrastive account of knowledge. Such an account requires five stages of development. One needs to report the *use* of knowledge ascriptions (§1), limn the *structure* of the knowledge relation (§2), show how the ascriptions *express* the relation (§3), analyze or otherwise *illuminate* the relation (§4), and resolve outstanding *paradoxes* (§5). On route, I will compare the contrastive account to *binary* accounts. Once home, I will compare contrastivism to *contextualism* (§6).

The view that emerges links knowledge to *inquiry* and to *discrimination*. There is no such thing as inquiring into *p*, unless one specifies: *as opposed to what?* There is no such thing as discriminating that *p*, unless one adds: *from what?* And likewise I will argue that there is no such thing as knowing that *p*, unless one clarifies: *rather than what?*

1. Use

The first stage of an account of knowledge is to report the *use* of knowledge ascriptions. What are knowledge ascriptions *for?* I propose:

---

* Originally published in *Oxford Studies in Epistemology* 1 (2005), pp. 235–271. Reprinted by permission of the publisher, Oxford University Press.

(1) Knowledge ascriptions certify that the subject is able to answer the question.

I will now clarify, argue for, and address objections to (1).

Clarifications

"Knowledge ascriptions" in (1) refers to tokens containing "knows" in the *informational sense*. In the terms of Gilbert Ryle, (1) covers "knows that", not "knows how".[1] More accurately, (1) covers "knows" in the sense of *savoir* not *connaître* (French), and in the sense of *wissen* not *kennen* (German).

"Certify" describes the act performed by the ascriber. In the terms of J. L. Austin, such certification constitutes the *illocutionary force* of the utterance.[2] In the terms of Robert Brandom, such certification consists in the conferral of an *entitlement* ("You may answer the question"), with subsequent *commitment* to endorsing the answer ("Whatever you say").[3]

"Able to answer" denotes an *epistemic capacity*. It is epistemic in that one may guess rightly without having the requisite ability (just as a blind throw may find the target). It is a capacity insofar as one need not actually speak or otherwise exercise the ability in order to possess it.

"The question" denotes the *options* relevant in the context of ascription. The question need not be explicitly posed, but it is always recoverable from context, since a context may be modeled as "the set of possible worlds recognized by the speakers to be the 'live options' relevant to the conversation".[4]

By way of illustration, imagine that Holmes and Watson are investigating who stole the sapphire. Here the live options might be: {Black stole the sapphire, Scarlet stole the sapphire, Mustard stole the sapphire}.

---

1   Ryle (1949). Though Ryle's "knows that"/"knows how" distinction does not mark the informational/acquaintance distinction accurately. First, Ryle's distinction misses other forms of knowledge ascription, such as "knows who", "knows what", and "knows where", which are informational. Second, Ryle's distinction obscures the fact that "knows how" is informational, as evident in "I know how turtles reproduce", and Monty Python's explanation of how to play the flute: "Well you blow in one end and move your fingers up and down the outside." See Stanley/Williamson (2001) for further discussion.
2   Austin (1962).
3   Brandom (1994).
4   Stalnaker (1999a), 84 f.

Now imagine that Holmes finds Black's fingerprints on the lock. So Watson reports, "Holmes knows who stole the sapphire." What Watson is *doing* with this speech act, according to (1), is giving his stamp of approval to Holmes, for selecting who stole the sapphire. Watson is identifying someone able to answer the question. He is fingering an answerer.

Arguments

First, (1) *fits our practice*. In the case of Holmes and Watson, one expects Watson to report that Holmes knows who stole the sapphire, only when Holmes is able to answer the question. Or consider our practice of testing students. The professor attributes knowledge to the students on the basis of which questions they are able to answer ("Let's see what you know"). Or consider our practice of fielding questions. One may say "I know" or "Ask Pam, she knows". One fingers an answerer.

Second, (1) serves our goal of *scoring inquiry*. Our ultimate epistemic goal is truth, and our method for seeking truth is inquiry.[5] So it is apt for knowledge ascriptions to be directed to questions, to gauge the progress of inquiry. In this vein, Christopher Hookway remarks: "The central focus of epistemic evaluation is ... the activity of inquiry ... When we conduct an inquiry, ... we attempt to formulate questions and to answer them correctly".[6]

Third, (1) *explains the other proposals in the literature*. For instance, according to Ludwig Wittgenstein, knowledge ascriptions serve to indicate when "one is ready to give compelling grounds".[7] While according to Edward Craig, the role of the knowledge ascription is "to flag approved sources of information".[8]

Wittgenstein's and Craig's proposals must be *relativized to questions*. If one is inquiring into *who* stole the sapphire, then the evidence of Black's fingerprints on the lock might constitute compelling grounds for "Black stole the sapphire", and the detective might count as an approved source of that information. But if one is inquiring into *what* Black stole, then the

---

5   The *Peircean* (following Peirce 1877) may rephrase the argument of the main text as: "Our ultimate epistemic interest is the fixation of belief. Our method for fixing belief is inquiry." The same directedness to answers would be called for.
6   Hookway (1996), 7.
7   Wittgenstein (1969), §243; also §§50, 483–5.
8   Craig (1990), 11.

evidence of his fingerprints might not constitute compelling grounds for "Black stole the sapphire", and the detective might not count as an approved source. The fingerprints may help identify who did the stealing, but they may not help establish what was stolen. In an inquiry into *what* Black stole, the owner's testimony that there was a sapphire in the safe might constitute compelling grounds for "Black stole the sapphire", and the owner might count as an approved source of that information. The owner's testimony may help identify what was stolen, but it may not help identify who stole it. While if one is inquiring into *how* Black obtained the sapphire (or *why* he stole it, etc.) then different evidential factors come to the fore. In short, what counts as compelling grounds, and who counts as an approved source, depends on which question is at issue.

Now (1) clarifies Wittgenstein's and Craig's proposals, by imposing the needed relativization to a question. And (1) *explains what is right* about these proposals, suitably relativized. What counts as compelling grounds relative to a question is just what counts as a basis for an answer. Who counts as an approved source relative to a question is just who is able to provide an answer.[9]

Objections

First, one might object that (1) is *overly intellectual* in its focus on answers. We routinely ascribe knowledge to *animals* (and infants, etc.), though they cannot answer questions or participate in inquiry. Thus, the objection concludes, (1) misconstrues our practice.

In reply, animals may be thought to have the *ability* to answer, which is all that (1) requires. That is, animals may have the *cognitive basis* by which the answer is reached, though they lack the means to express it. Thus Fido might know who feeds him, though he cannot express the answer save through his affections.[10]

---

9 A further example: John Greco addresses the "what are we doing?" question by identifying: "an important illocutionary force of knowledge attributions: namely, that when we credit knowledge to someone we mean to give the person credit for getting things right" (2002, 111). What suffices for 'getting things right' is just what suffices for selecting the right answer.

10 Our intuitions to ascribe knowledge to animals seem to sway with our inclinations to ascribe them the concepts involved. For instance, our inclination to say, "Fido knows where he buried the bone", seems to sway with our inclination to

Second, one might object that (1) is *socially disruptive* in its relativity to questions. We *traffic* in knowledge ascriptions, without tracking questions. For instance, if Watson tells Lestrade, "Holmes knows that Black stole the sapphire", then Lestrade may repeat Watson's words to Scotland Yard, in a different context with a different question on the table. Thus, the objection concludes, (1) undermines our practice.

In reply, trafficking in knowledge ascription must be regarded as a *risky act,* which is all that (1) entails. The careless trafficker may wind up doing something inappropriate. Imagine that, while Holmes and Watson were pursuing the question of who stole the sapphire, Lestrade and Scotland Yard were stuck on the question of whether what was stolen was a sapphire or a paste imitation. If Lestrade now repeats Watson's words to Scotland Yard, then Lestrade would have acted inappropriately, by representing Holmes *as if* he had tested the sapphire.

There is nothing special about knowledge ascriptions here. We traffic in *assertions* generally, while recognizing that repeating any assertion out of context is risky. Misunderstandings may arise when the originator and the repeater are in *conversational disequilibrium*. That is, if the originator and repeater have different presuppositions, then their assertions may be identical in word but not in deed. We redress misunderstandings if they count.

The ultimate test of (1), of course, is whether it coheres with a successful epistemology. I will argue (§2) that (1) calls for a contrastive view of knowledge. Whether this counts as a further argument for (1), or an objection to it, is left to the reader's judgment.

2. Structure

The second stage of an account of knowledge is to limn the *structure* of the knowledge relation. What is its *form?* I propose:

(2) The knowledge relation has the ternary, contrastive structure: $Kspq$.

---

say that Fido possesses the concepts *bury* and *bone*. Thus, to the extent that we are willing to ascribe knowledge to animals, we are committed to their possessing the concepts that would form the cognitive basis for answering.

Here K is the knowledge relation, s is the subject, p is the proposition selected, and q *is* the proposition rejected.[11] Kspq may thus be rendered as: s knows that p rather than q.

Objection

One might object that (2) is *implausibly radical* in contravening the widespread assumption that knowledge has the binary form: Ksp. Have so many epistemologists been *wrong?*[12] Thus, the objection concludes, (2) deserves to be met with a blank stare, or at least with steeply arched brows.

In reply, it is unclear *why* the assumption of binarity is so widespread. For what it is worth, I have found no explicit arguments for binarity in the literature. Perhaps binarity is assumed because it reflects the *surface form* of knowledge ascriptions. After all, some knowledge ascriptions look binary: "I know that I parked the car on Elm." But surface form is *equivocal*. There are interrogative ascriptions that do not look binary: "I know where I parked the car." And there are declarative ascriptions that look explicitly contrastive: "I know that I parked the car on Elm rather than Main". In any case, surface form can mislead.

Perhaps binarity is assumed because it reflects the *intuitive adicity* of knowledge. But adicity is not so easily intuited. Our intuitive judgments merely provide evidence as to the acceptability of utterances.[13] Anything more is *theory*.

Perhaps binarity is assumed because it is required to solve *theoretical problems*. But which? What have accounts of Ksp produced but problems? *What if contrastivity works better?*

---

11 The proposition q may be glossed as the disjunction of the 'relevant alternatives'. As such, two constraints on q are needed: (i) q must be non-empty, and (ii) p and all the disjuncts of q must be pairwise exclusive.

12 Some exceptions: Fred Dretske flirts with the contrastive view: "To know that x is A is to know that x is A within a framework of relevant alternatives, B, C, and D. This set of contrasts... serve to define what it is that is known" (1970, 1022). Bredo Johnsen describes the intuitive content of knowledge ascriptions as contrastive: "what is known is always a contrastive proposition to the effect that P-rather-than-any-other-member-of-category-C is true" (2001, 401), though he makes this point in service of *skepticism*. And Adam Morton and Anti Karjalainen (2003), as well as Walter Sinnot-Armstrong (2004), uphold contrastivism, though as a *revisionary* proposal.

13 Chomsky (1977).

Arguments

First, (2) *fits* (1) by logging the question. That is, the contrastive structure K*spq* records the information about which question was asked, and so is the right form for the job of fingering who is able to answer.

To begin with, the ability to answer is *question-relative*. Some questions are harder to answer than others. The ability to answer *p* to the question on the table does *not* entail the ability to answer *p* to all other questions in the field. Anyone who has devised an exam will recognize this—add a trick option, and the question will be harder. Compare:

(Q1) Is there a *goldfinch* in the garden, or a *raven*?
(Q2) Is there a *goldfinch* in the garden, or a *canary*?
(Q3) Is there a goldfinch in the *garden,* or at the *neighbor's*?

All can be answered by p: there is a goldfinch in the garden. But the ability to answer Q1 does not entail the ability to answer Q2 or Q3. Q1 is an easy question. While to answer Q2 one might need an ornithologist, and to answer Q3 one might need the homeowner. So fingering answerers requires logging the question, because the abilities to answer Q1-Q3 are different abilities.

Logging the question requires recording the alternatives. All well-formed questions are multiple-choice questions. As James Higginbotham writes, "An *abstract question* [is] a nonempty *partition* II of the possible states of nature into *cells*".[14] These cells are the semantic image of a (possibly infinite) *multiple-choice slate*.[15]

The contrastive structure K*spq* logs the question, by recording the alternatives. Here $\{p, q\}$ conforms to the multiple-choice slate—*p* corresponds to the selected answer and *q* to the disjunction of the rejected alternatives. Thus one who knows that *p:* there is a goldfinch in the garden, rather than *q1:* there is a raven in the garden, is able to answer Q1. While one who knows that *p* rather than *q2:* there is a canary in the garden, can answer Q2. And one who knows that *p* rather than *q3:* there is a goldfinch at the neighbor's, can answer Q3. Thus differences at *q* correspond to different abilities to answer different questions. Contrast-relative

---

14 Higginbotham (1993), 196.
15 The association of questions with multiple-choice slates is known as *Hamblin's dictum* (Hamblin 1958), and is implemented in Nuel Belnap and Thomas Steel's (1976) erotetic logic, and maintained in the leading linguistic treatments of interrogatives, such as that by Jeroen Groenendijk and Martin Stokhof (1997).

knowledge is question-relative knowledge, and so befits our question-relative usage.

The second argument for (2) is that contrastivity *models inquiry* by measuring progress. Inquiry is the engine of knowledge (§1), and it is driven by a question-and-answer process.[16] Drawing on Jaakko Hintikka, inquiry may be modeled as a cooperative game played between Questioner and Answerer, represented by a sequence of question-and-answer pairs $<< Q_1, A_1 >, < Q_2, A_2 >, ..., < Q_n, A_n >>$.[17] Progress in inquiry is movement through the sequence, so answers make for progress. Suppose the chemist is identifying a sample of potassium (K), via the following line of inquiry: $<<$ Q1: What element is the sample?, A1: Potassium$>$, $<$ Q2: Is the sample ionized?, A2: No$>>$. To answer Q1, the chemist might run experiments (putting the question to nature) that test for atomic mass. To answer Q2, the chemist might run experiments that test for charge or reactivity (K and K^+ have nearly the same atomic mass, but while K is neutral and reactive, K^+ is positive and inert).[18]

The contrastive structure measures progress, because q measures which stage of inquiry has been concluded. The chemist progresses from ignorance through knowledge that the sample is K rather than some other element: $Kspq_1$; and then knowledge that the sample is K rather than K^+: $Kspq_2$. The epistemic state that corresponds to no progress is: $\sim Kspq_1$ & $\sim Kspq_2$; partial progress is: $Kspq_1$ & $\sim Kspq_2$; and complete progress is: $Kspq_1$ & $Kspq_2$. In general, progress can be pictured in terms of finding actuality in *widening regions* of logical space. To find w_a from amongst worlds w_1-w_m is to know that $\{w_a\}$ rather than $\{w_1, w_2, ..., w_m\}$. To make further progress is to find w_a from amongst worlds w_1-w_n $(n > m)$, which is to know that $\{w_a\}$ rather than $\{w_1, w_2, ..., w_m, ...,$

---

16 This is the *Deweyian view* of inquiry: "Inquiry and questioning, up to a certain point, are synonymous terms." (1933, 105). See also Levi (1984), in which expansion of a belief corpus is directed by an ultimate partition over a set of possible answers to a question. For an application to scientific progress, see Kleiner (1988). As Matti Sintonen comments in this regard: "If there is a philosophy of a working scientist it certainly is the idea that inquiry is a search for questions and answers." (1997, 234).
17 Hintikka (1975a) and (1981).
18 Note that the entire inquiry is framed within certain presuppositions. At no point, for instance, does the chemist test the option: *the sample is but a dream*. If one looks at dichotomous keys, for instance, one never finds an entry for *pinch yourself*.

w_n}.[19] Thus differences at q correspond to different stages of inquiry. Contrast-relative knowledge is progress-relative knowledge, and so befits the structure of inquiry.

The third argument for (2) is that contrastivity *fits perception*, which is basically a discriminatory ability. Thus the psychophysicist S. S. Stevens remarks: "When we attempt to reduce complex operations to simpler and simpler ones, we find in the end that discrimination or differential response is the fundamental operation. Discrimination is prerequisite even to the operation of denoting or 'pointing to,'".[20] The discriminatory powers of perception are codified in Weber's Law, which states that just noticeable differences are well-described by: $\Delta S/S = K$. In words: the size of a just noticeable difference in stimulation S is a constant proportion K of the existing stimulus. For instance, in normal humans, just noticeable differences in tonal frequency are well-described by $K = .0025$ (at least for the central portion of the human range). Thus if the existing stimulus S is 1000 Hz, then differences of ± 2.5 Hz will be just noticeable.

The contrastive structure fits perceptual discrimination, by logging both the reported stimulus: p, and what the stimulus was discriminated from: q. Suppose that a normal human subject Norm hears a tone of S1 = 1000 Hz. Norm can discriminate S1 from a tone of S2 = 1005 Hz, but cannot discriminate S1 from S3 = 1001 Hz. Then he knows that p: the tone is 1000 Hz, rather than $q1$: the tone is 1005 Hz. But he does not know that p: the tone is 1000 Hz, rather than $q2$: the tone is 1001 Hz. In general, for a stimulus S and a perceiver whose just noticeable difference for such stimuli is $K = x$, this perceiver can know that he is perceiving S rather than any difference in S greater than or equal to KS, and cannot know that he is perceiving S rather than any lesser difference. Thus differences at q correspond to what the

---

19 On this view of progress, progress essentially consists in *replacing presupposition with evidence*. When the subject is able to answer Q1 and hence able to find w_a from amongst worlds w_1-w_m, the remainder of logical space is simply presupposed away. When the subject progresses through Q2 and is able to find w_a from amongst worlds w_1— w_n ($n > m$), less is presupposed away and more is ruled out by evidence. The (ideal) limit of inquiry would consist in finding w_a from amongst all of logical space, which would be a full grasp of truth by evidence. Thus movement towards the limit consists in finding w_a from amongst widening spheres of logical space, which would be a greater grasp of truth by evidence, and a lesser need for presupposition. Of course, at each stage short of the limit, assumptions remain. But that does *not* mean that there had been no progress—not all assumptions are equal.

20 Quoted by Watson (1973), 278.

percept is being discriminated from. Contrast-relative knowledge is discrimination-relative knowledge, and so befits the nature of perception.

In the remaining sections I will add three more arguments for (2), namely that (2) is the best fit for decoding knowledge ascriptions (§3), illuminating the knowledge relation (§4), and resolving the closure paradox (§5).

Comparison

The ultimate test of contrastivity is how it compares to binarity.[21] How does Kspq compare to Ksp?

I suspect that Ksp induces systematic problems for lack of a contrast slot. Nothing in the Ksp relation logs the queried alternatives, the stage of inquiry, or the discriminatory task. So there is no natural fit to fingering answerers, modeling inquiry, and measuring perception. Consider the subject who enjoys *merely partial success*. For instance, consider the subject who can answer, "Goldfinch or raven?" but not, "Goldfinch or canary?".[22] Given binarity, he must either know that the bird is a goldfinch, or not (I leave it to the dogmatist and skeptic to dispute which). But if the subject knows, then his inability to answer, "Goldfinch or canary?" seems inexplicable. With a minimum of logical acumen, he ought to be able to apply his alleged knowledge to answer this further question. So partial success would explode into total victory. Whereas if the subject does not know that the bird is a goldfinch, then his ability to answer, "Goldfinch or raven?" seems inexplicable. He ought not to be able to answer where he is allegedly ignorant. So partial success would collapse into total defeat. Ksp seems too impoverished to provide a stable account of partial success in answering, inquiry, and discrimination.[23]

My aim is to develop a contrastive view, not to refute the binary view in all its forms. *That* would be a Herculean task. Perhaps the binary the-

---

21 Why not let knowledge come in *both* binary and contrastive forms? Because (i) this would require an ambiguity in "knows" that the evidence does not support, (ii) I will argue (§3) that the contrastive form fits all of our knowledge ascriptions, and (iii) I will suggest (§5) that the binary form is paradoxical.

22 Or, to borrow a case from Dretske (1970), consider the zoo-goer who can answer, "Zebra or mule?", but not, "Zebra or cleverly painted mule?".

23 Perhaps the *contextualist* has a way to model partial success, in terms of the *plurality* of binary K$_x$ relations they postulate as the range of semantic values for "knows". Here there is the added structure of a subscript to K. For further discussion of contextualism, see §6.

orist can find some devious strategy to model partial success. But I think it fair to conclude, at the least, that (2) provides *the more natural fit* to the contrast-relative tasks of answering, inquiry, and discrimination.

3. Encoding

The third stage of an account of knowledge is to show how knowledge ascriptions *express* the knowledge relation. What is the *code?* I propose:

(3) Knowledge ascriptions encode Kspq, by encoding relations to questions.

I will now defend (3) by exhibiting three main surface forms of knowledge ascription, and showing the mechanisms for question-relativity encoded in each.

Surfaces

There are three main types of knowledge ascription (in the informational sense of "knows": §1), which may be distinguished syntactically: (i) interrogative ascriptions, which employ a *wh*-headed complement phrase, such as: "I know what time it is", (ii) noun ascriptions, which employ a noun (determiner) phrase, such as: "I know the time",[24] and (iii) declarative ascriptions, which employ a *that*-headed complement phrase, such as: "I know that it is midnight". An account of encoding is responsible for every type of ascription.

---

24 Noun ascriptions can express either the informational or practical sense of "knows" (§1). Here are three tests for whether a given noun ascription is informational or practical. First, only the practical sense supports comparatives: compare ?"I know the time very well" and ?"I know the time better than I know Ben", with "I know Ann very well" and "I know Ann better than I know Ben". Second, only the practical sense supports "but not as such" constructions: compare ?"I know the time but not as such" to "I know Ann but not as such". Third, only the informational sense entails knowledge-*wh*: "I know the time" entails "I know what the time is", but "I know Ann" does not entail "I know what Ann is" (nor does it entail "I know who she is" or "I know where she is", etc.).

Epistemologists, however, have focused nearly exclusively on declarative ascriptions.[25] Interrogative and noun ascriptions are typically ignored, or else hastily fitted to the Procrustean bed of Ksp. Why the focus on declarative ascriptions? These seem relatively rare in natural language, especially when compared to interrogative ascriptions. So why the focus on such an unrepresentative sample? Perhaps the widespread focus on declarative ascriptions is due to the widespread assumption that knowledge is a binary relation (§2). Perhaps here is a case where theory dictates observation: "Our theoretical presuppositions about the natural order tell us what to expect".[26] In any case, it must not be *presumed* that declarative ascriptions are more fundamental. Perhaps it is the interrogative ascriptions that are more fundamental, in the sense that it is they that wear their logical forms closer to their surfaces.

Mechanisms

Starting with interrogative ascriptions (perhaps the most frequent in natural language), these embed *questions*. Questions present contrasts (§2). The mechanism of question-relativity is thus on the surface, in the *wh*-clause. So, for instance, if one says, "I know who stole the bicycle", then the embedded question "who stole the bicycle" presents a set of alternatives, such as: {Mary stole the bicycle, Peter stole the bicycle, Paul stole the bicycle}.[27] Here p is the selected answer, and q is the disjunction of the rejected alternatives. So if it was Mary who stole the bicycle, then to know who stole the bicycle is to know that p: Mary stole the bicycle, rather than q: Peter stole the bicycle or Paul stole the bicycle. In this vein, Higginbotham says: "Mary knows who John saw"

---

25 Some exceptions: Hintikka (1975b) distinguishes the full spectrum of knowledge ascriptions, yet he classifies all the others as departures from the "knows that" form. And Lewis (1982), Boer/Lycan (1986), and Stanley/Williamson (2001) discuss (respectively) "knows whether", "knows who", and "knows how". Yet even here Stanley and Williamson contrast "question-embedding uses of 'know' and *normal* clausal-complement uses of 'know' " (Stanley/Williamson 2001, 421; italics added), and all of these philosophers attempt to reduce knowledge-*wh* to knowledge that p. The exceptions prove the rule.

26 Laudan (1977), 15.

27 The set of alternatives is determined by (i) the contextually determined domain of quantification, and (ii) the matrix: x is a bicycle thief. So if the individuals in the domain are Mary, Peter, and Paul, then the set of queried alternatives is: {Mary stole the bicycle, Peter stole the bicycle, Paul stole the bicycle}.

should be interpreted as: "Mary knows the (or an) answer to the question who John saw".[28]

Here are three tests that confirm the question-relative treatment of interrogative ascriptions. First, differences at q can *affect truth-values*. For instance, suppose that Joe glances at George W. Bush speaking on television, and compare the following knowledge claims:

(I1) Joe knows whether Bush or Janet Jackson is the speaker.
(I2) Joe knows whether Bush or Will Ferrell is the speaker.[29]

Intuitively, I1 may be true but I2 false. Joe can discriminate Bush from Jackson, but perhaps only First Lady Laura Bush can discriminate Bush from Ferrell. In other words, Joe is able to answer whether Bush or Jackson is the speaker (this is an easy question—Joe knows the answer to *that*), but Joe cannot answer whether Bush or Ferrell is the speaker (this is a hard question—Joe can only *guess*). The difference in truth-value between I1 and I2 is not due to a difference in s or in p—the subject is Joe and the true answer p is: Bush is the speaker. So the difference must lie elsewhere. The difference is at q, between $q1$: Jackson is the speaker, and $q2$: Ferrell is the speaker. The question is what is differentiating the truth-value.

To take another example (from §2), suppose that Ann sees a goldfinch in the garden, and compare the following claims:

(I3) Ann knows whether there is a goldfinch or a raven in the garden.
(I4) Ann knows whether there is a goldfinch or a canary in the garden.
(I5) Ann knows whether there is a goldfinch in the garden or at the neighbor's.

Intuitively, I3-I5 may differ in truth-value. I3 is a relatively easy item of knowledge. While I4 is harder, requiring some ornithology. And I5 is incommensurable, requiring some sense of the landscape. The difference in truth-value between I3-I5 is not due to a difference in s or in p—the subject is Ann and the true answer p is: there is a goldfinch in the garden. So the difference must lie elsewhere. The difference is at q, between $q3$: there is a raven in the garden, $q4$: there is a canary in the garden, and $q5$: there is a goldfinch at the neighbor's. The question is what is differentiating the truth-value.

---

28 Higginbotham (1993), 205.
29 Background information: Janet Jackson is a pop diva who would be quite hard to confuse with Bush, while Will Ferrell is a skilled Bush impersonator.

A second confirmation for the question-relative treatment of interrogative ascriptions comes from *existential generalization*. If I know who stole the bicycle, then it follows that there is a question (namely, the question of who stole the bicycle) that I know the answer to. Likewise if I know what time it is, then it follows that there is a question (the question of what time it is) that I know the answer to. The question is what is being generalized on.

A third confirmation comes from *substitution*. If I know when Napoleon was born, and if the question of when Napoleon was born is a historical question, then it follows that I know the answer to a historical question. Likewise if I know why the sky looks blue, and if the question of why the sky looks blue is a scientific question, then it follows that I know the answer to a scientific question. The question is what is being substituted for.[30]

Turning to noun ascriptions, these are at least semantically equivalent to interrogative ascriptions. Thus, for instance, "I know the time" is semantically equivalent to "I know what time it is", and "I know the murderer" (in the informational sense) is semantically equivalent to "I know who the murderer is".[31] The mechanism of question-relativity is thus present in the interpretation of the noun phrase. So if it is noon, then to know the time is that it is to know that p: the time is noon, rather than q: the time is 1p.m. or 2p.m. or... or 11a.m. And if the murderer is Oswald, then to know the murderer is to know that p: Oswald is the murderer, rather than q: Castro is the murderer or the CIA is the murderer.

The question-relative treatment of noun ascriptions is confirmed by the same three tests as with interrogative ascriptions. First, differences at q can affect truth-value. For instance, suppose that, in context $c1$, the domain of quantification is {Bush, Jackson}, so that the question of who the speaker is denotes: {Bush is the speaker, Jackson is the speaker}. While in $c2$, the domain of quantification is {Bush, Ferrell}, so that the question of who the speaker is denotes: {Bush is the speaker, Ferrell is the speaker}. Then consider the utterance type:

(Nl) Joe knows the speaker.

---

30 For further discussion of interrogative ascriptions, see Schaffer n.d.
31 Thus Heim (1979) refers to this as the *concealed question* use of noun phrases, saying: "As we naturally understand the sentence ["John knows Bill's telephone number"] we could paraphrase it as "John knows what Bill's telephone number is".

Intuitively, a token of Nl may be true if uttered in $c1$, but false if uttered in $c2$. After all, Joe knows whether Bush or Jackson is the speaker—which is what N1 is semantically equivalent to in $c1$. But Joe does not know whether Bush or Ferrell is the speaker—which is what Nl is semantically equivalent to in $c2$. There is no difference in s or p here—the subject is Joe and the true answer p is: Bush is the speaker. So the difference in truth-value must lie elsewhere. The difference is at q, between $q1$: Jackson is the speaker, and $q2$: Ferrell is the speaker. The question is what is differentiating the truth-value.

A second confirmation for the question-relative treatment of noun ascriptions comes from *existential generalization*. If I know the time, then it follows that there is a question (namely, the question of what time it is) that I know the answer to. Likewise if I know the murderer, then it follows that there is a question (the question of who the murderer is) that I know the answer to. The question is what is being generalized on.

A third confirmation comes from *substitution*. If I know the date Napoleon was born, and if the question of when Napoleon was born is a historical question, then it follows that I know the answer to a historical question. Likewise if I know the reason the sky looks blue, and if the question of why the sky looks blue is a scientific question, then it follows that I know the answer to a scientific question. The question is what is being substituted for.

Moving finally to declarative ascriptions (perhaps the rarest form in natural language), these inherit their contrasts from *context*. A context is an implicit question. According to Stalnaker, a context may be represented by a set of possible worlds, "which includes all the situations among which speakers intend to distinguish with their speech acts".[32] This set is "the set of possible worlds recognized by the speakers to be the 'live options' relevant to the conversation".[33] Thus a context is a set of options (§1). A set of options is the slate of a question (§2). So if one says, "I know that Mary stole the bicycle", in a context in which the identity of the bicycle thief is in question, then the value of p is: that Mary stole the bicycle, and q is: that some other suspect stole the bicycle. If one says this in a context in which Mary's behavior toward the bicycle is in question, then the value of p is: that Mary stole the bicycle, and q is: that Mary acted in some other way towards the bicycle. While if

---

32 Stalnaker (1999b), 99.
33 Stalnaker (1999a), 84 f.

one says this in a context in which the nature of Mary's contraband is in question, then the value of p is: that Mary stole the bicycle, and q is: that Mary stole some other loot. In general, context provides the default source of contrasts.

The question-relative treatment of declarative ascriptions is confirmed by the same three tests as with interrogative and noun ascriptions. First, differences at q can affect truth-value. For instance, suppose that the context set for $c1$ is: {Bush is the speaker, Jackson is the speaker}. While the context set for $c2$ is: {Bush is the speaker, Ferrell is the speaker}. Then consider the utterance type:

(D1) Joe knows that Bush is the speaker.

Intuitively, a token of Dl may be true if uttered in $c1$, but false if uttered in $c2$. After all, if one is wondering whether the speaker is Bush or Jackson—which is the implicit question of $c1$—then one would do well to ask Joe. But if one is wondering whether the speaker is Bush or Ferrell—which is the implicit question of $c2$—then Joe is not the one to ask. There is no difference in s or p here—the subject is Joe and the true answer p is: Bush is the speaker. So the difference in truth-value must lie elsewhere. The difference is at q, between $q1$: Jackson is the speaker, and $q2$: Ferrell is the speaker. The question is what is differentiating the truth-value.

To take the example of the goldfinch in the garden, suppose that the context set for $c1$ is: {there is a goldfinch in the garden, there is a raven in the garden), the context set for $c2$ is: {there is a goldfinch in the garden, there is a canary in the garden}, and for $c3$ is: {there is a goldfinch in the garden, there is a goldfinch at the neighbor's}. Then consider the utterance type:

(D2) Ann knows that there is a goldfinch in the garden.

Intuitively, what it takes for a token of D2 to be true differs among $c1$, $c2$, and $c3$. In other words, if one is wondering whether there is a goldfinch or a raven in the garden—which is the implicit question of $c1$—then one might ask virtually anyone. While if one is wondering whether there is a goldfinch or a canary in the garden—which is the implicit question of $c2$—then one might need to ask the ornithologist. And if one is wondering whether there is a goldfinch in the garden or at the neighbor's—which is the implicit question of $c3$—then one might need to ask the homeowner. There is no difference at s or p, only at q. The question is what is differentiating the truth-value.[34]

A second confirmation for the question-relative treatment of declarative ascriptions comes from *existential generalization*. If I know that the time is noon, then it follows that there is a question (namely, the question of what time it is) that I know the answer to. Likewise if I know that Oswald is the murderer, then it follows that there is a question (here, the question of who is the murderer) that I know the answer to. The question is what is being generalized on.

A third confirmation comes from *substitution*. If I know that Napoleon was born in 1769, and if the question of when Napoleon was born is a historical question, then it follows that I know the answer to a historical question. Likewise if I know that the sky looks blue because of Rayleigh scattering (blue's short wavelength causes it to get scattered far more than the longer wavelength colors), then it follows that I know the answer to a scientific question. The question is what is being substituted for.

Here are four additional arguments for the question-relativity of declarative ascriptions. The first additional argument is that declarative ascriptions should *fit the pattern* of knowledge ascriptions generally. Since interrogative and noun ascriptions are question-relative (and since "knows" is not ambiguous here), declarative ascriptions should be expected to be question-relative too.

A second additional argument comes from *focus*. As Dretske recognized, focus is semantically efficacious in declarative ascriptions:

> Someone claiming to know that Clyde sold his typewriter to Alex is not (necessarily) claiming the same thing as one who claims to know that Clyde sold his typewriter to Alex... A person who knows that Clyde sold his typewriter to Alex must be able to rale out the possibility that

---

34 John Hawthorne suggests that the question-sensitivity of our intuitions here may be explained away, on grounds that "the very asking of a question may provide one with new evidence regarding the subject matter" (Hawthorne 2004, 78). The idea is that Ann has different evidence in contexts $c1$, $c2$, and $c3$, concerning which question was asked of her. *But* this assumes that (i) Ann fields the question, and (ii) Ann trusts the questioner to select the likely options. Ann need not field the question. She might not be privy to the conversation at all. Others might be discussing what she knows. (This situation might arise when one is deciding who to ask—one tries to figure out *in advance* which third party knows the answer.) In any case, Ann need not trust the questioner to select the likely options. She might just play along. (Anyone who has questioned students will recognize this situation.)

he *gave* it to him, or that he loaned it to him ... But he needs only a nominal justification, if he needs any justification at all, for thinking it was Alex to whom he sold it.[35]

Following David Sanford[36], one can model the effect of focus by sets of relevant alternatives, as follows:

$$\text{I know that} \left\{\begin{array}{c}\text{Mary}\\ \text{Peter}\\ \text{Paul}\end{array}\right\} \left\{\begin{array}{c}\text{stole}\\ \text{begged}\\ \text{borrowed}\end{array}\right\} \text{the} \left\{\begin{array}{c}\text{bicycle}\\ \text{unicycle}\\ \text{tricycle}\end{array}\right\}$$

Thus if one says, "I know that *Mary* stole the bicycle", then the value of p is: that Mary stole the bicycle, and q is: that Peter or Paul stole the bicycle. If one says, "I know that Mary *stole* the bicycle", then the value of p is: that Mary stole the bicycle, and q is: that Mary begged or borrowed the bicycle. While if one says, "I know that Mary stole the *bicycle*", then the value of p is: that Mary stole the bicycle, and q is: that Mary stole the unicycle or the tricycle. The semantic efficacy of focus is thus explained: differences in focus determine differences in the proposition expressed. Focus is a mechanism of contrastivity.[37] Where focus is semantically effective, it is because contrasts are semantically operative.

A third additional argument comes from the *binding* test. Suppose that Sally has aced her exam. Here one might boast on her behalf: "On every question, Sally knew the answer." This has a natural reading on which it is semantically equivalent to: "On the first question, Sally knew the answer *to that question*; on the second question, Sally knew the answer *to that question*; etc." Here the quantifier is binding q.[38]

A fourth and final additional argument comes from *explicit contrasts*. One can directly articulate the contrasts with "rather than"-clauses. For instance, if one says, "I know that there is a goldfinch in the garden rath-

---

35 Dretske (1981), 373.
36 Sanford (1991).
37 Thus Rooth (1992) proposes the *alternative semantics* approach to focus, on which focus adds a semantic marker whose value is a contextually determined set of alternatives. So "I know that *Mary* stole the bicycle" gets semantically interpreted as [... that [Mary]$_F$ stole ...], where [Mary]$_F$ induces a dual interpretation, one of which is Mary, and the other of which are the other suspects.
38 The binding test is due to Barbara Partee (1989), and is used extensively by Stanley, who maintains: "[B]ound readings within a clause are due to the existence of a variable binding operator standing in a certain structural relationship to a co-indexed variable in that clause" (Stanley 2000, 412).

er than a raven", then the value of p is: there is a goldfinch in the garden, and q is: there is a raven in the garden. While if one says, "I know that there is a goldfinch in the garden rather than a canary", then the value of p is: there is a goldfinch in the garden, and q is: there is a canary in the garden. Whereas if one says, "I know that there is a goldfinch in the garden rather than at the neighbor's", then the value of p is: there is a goldfinch in the garden, and q is: there is a goldfinch at the neighbor's. The "rather than"-clause is a mechanism of contrastivity. It explicitly articulates q.

The binary surface form of declarative ascriptions may thus be misleading. There are many *precedents* for misleading surfaces. For instance, "Ann prefers chocolate" looks to have the binary form: s prefers x. But it should be obvious on reflection that there must be an implicit contrast (to vanilla? to double chocolate chip? to peace on earth?), which is what Ann prefers chocolate *to*. To take another example, "Rayleigh scattering explains why the sky looks blue" looks to have the binary form: C explains E. But it has been argued that there must be an implicit contrast (rather than red? rather than violet?), which is what Rayleigh scattering makes a difference to.[39] Or consider, "I asked Ann where she was going. Ann answered that she was going to the bar." The second sentence looks to have the binary form: s answered that p. But it should be obvious on reflection that answering is question-relative.

The binary surface form of declarative ascriptions may have misled Moore. When Moore declared, "I know that I have hands", perhaps he was misusing the language. Thus Wittgenstein writes: "[C]an one enumerate what one knows (like Moore)? Straight off like that, I believe not.—For otherwise the expression 'I know' gets misused".[40] Wittgenstein suggests that Moore must have "been thinking of something else in the interim and is now saying out loud some sentence in

---

39 Background information: Rayleigh scattering explains why the sky looks blue rather than red, because blue's short wavelength causes it to get scattered around ten times more than longer wavelength colors like red. But Rayleigh scattering does not explain why the sky looks blue rather than violet. In fact, since violet is an even shorter wavelength than blue, Rayleigh scattering predicts that the sky should look violet. What explains why the sky looks blue rather than violet is that our visual system is relatively insensitive to violet. Contrastive views of explanation are defended by van Fraassen (1980), Garfinkel (1981), and Lipton (1991), *inter alia*.
40 Wittgenstein (1969), §6.

his train of thought".[41] Perhaps the preceding train of thought functions to generate a contrast-setting question.[42]

The audience can accommodate Moore by charitably imputing an easy question. For instance, on hearing, "I know that I have hands", one might glance to see whether Moore has hands or stumps. Or one might look a bit closer, to see whether he has hands or prostheses. (What *does* one look for?) Perhaps this is why Moorean declarations seem undeniable, yet empty.

Comparison

How does (3) compare to a binary view of encoding? That is, what are the prospects for interpreting various types of knowledge ascription as expressing K*sp*?

I suspect that binary views face systematic problems with respect to all types of knowledge ascription. (Here I continue to focus on *invariantist* binary views, postponing discussion of contextualism until §6.) Consider the interrogative ascription: "Ann knows whether there is a goldfinch or a raven in the garden." The natural way to chop this ascription to fit the Procrustean bed of K*sp*, is to treat *p* as: there is a goldfinch in the garden. In general, the natural way to fit interrogative ascriptions into the binary mold is to treat them as expressing K*sp*, where *p* is the true answer to the question posed by the *wh*-clause.[43]

---

41 Wittgenstein (1969), §465; also §§350, 423, 553.

42 Revealingly, Moore himself uses focused and overtly contrastive ascriptions in key passages. He begins his "A Defence of Common Sense" with the focused ascription that he knows "that there exists at present a living human body which is *my* body" (Moore (1959a), 33). And he begins "Certainty" by listing his convictions in contrastive format: "I am at present, as you all can see, in a room and not in the open air; I am standing up, and not either sitting or lying down; I have clothes on, and am not absolutely naked; I am speaking in a fairly loud voice, and am not either singing or whispering or keeping quite silent;" (Moore (1959b), 227). Perhaps it is here that Moore captures the content of common sense knowledge.

43 Thus Higginbotham proposes the rule: "know $(x,^\wedge \pi) \leftrightarrow (\exists p)$ (know(x,p) & p answers π)" (Higginbotham (1996), 381). Instances of this rule are implicit in Hintikka's treatment of "knows who", Lewis's treatment of "knows whether", and Stanley and Williamson's treatment of "knows how". Thus, for Hintikka, "*a* knows who *b* is" is analyzed as: $(\exists x)$ *a* knows that $(b = x)$ (Hintikka (1975b), 4). For Lewis, "Holmes knows whether… if and only if he knows the true one of the alternatives presented by the 'whether'-clause, whichever one that is"

The binary treatment of interrogative ascriptions, though, is counterintuitive. It implies that "Ann knows whether there is a goldfinch or a raven in the garden", "Ann knows whether there is a goldfinch or a canary in the garden", and "Ann knows whether there is a goldfinch in the garden or at the neighbor's" all express the same proposition. (Or at least, that all have the same truth conditions). When intuitively these can differ in truth-value.[44]

My aim is to develop a contrastive view, not to refute binary views. Perhaps the binary theorist can find some devious strategy to encode interrogative ascriptions (similar issues arise with respect to the other types of ascription). But I would suggest, at this point, that (3) supplies *the more natural code* for the full range of question-relative knowledge ascriptions.

4. Knowledge

The fourth stage of an account of knowledge is to analyze or otherwise *illuminate* the relation. What is *knowledge*? I propose:

(4) Kspq iff: (i) p, (ii) s has proof that p rather than q, and (iii) s is certain that p rather than q, on the basis of (ii).

I should emphasize from the outset that (4) is the least important and least promising part of the contrastive view. It is the least important insofar as Kspq is compatible with virtually any analysis of knowledge

---

(Lewis (1982), 194). And for Stanley and Williamson, "Hannah knows how to ride a bicycle" is "true if and only if, for some contextually relevant way w which is a way for Hannah to ride a bicycle, Hannah knows that w is a way for her to ride a bicycle". From which they conclude: "Thus, to say that someone knows how to F is always to ascribe them knowledge-that" (Stanley/Williamson (2001), 426).

44 A less natural possibility is to transform p into a big conditional. Here "Ann knows whether there is a goldfinch or a raven in the garden" is to be transformed (somehow) into: "Ann knows that if (there is a goldfinch or a raven in the garden), then there is a goldfinch in the garden." But this gives the wrong truth-value *when all the options are false*. For instance, "Moore knows whether he has tentacles or flippers" seems false, since Moore has neither tentacles nor flippers. But the 'corresponding' conditional is: Km ((p∨q) ⊃ p), where p is: that Moore has tentacles, and a is: that Moore has flippers. And this knowledge claim is *true* (or at least the binary theorist should think it true), since Moore should know that the antecedent of the conditional is false, and Moore knows that conditionals with false antecedents are true.

(even none at all). And it is the least promising insofar as the history of philosophical analyses suggests that counterexamples are inevitable. Thus (4) is merely intended as a *useful gloss*.

Clarifications

Overall, (4) is a contrastive implementation of the contextualist idea that knowledge is the elimination of relevant alternatives.[45]

Piecewise, the first condition is the *truth* condition. (Note that since p and q are mutually exclusive, p's truth implies q's falsity.)

The second condition is a contrastive interpretation of *justification*. It is a form of *restricted infallibilism* about evidence. It is infallibilist insofar as it requires proof, which is conclusive evidence, evidence that could not possibly obtain without p being true. But it is restricted insofar as the space of possibilities open to disproof is restricted to: $\{p\} \cup \{q\}$[46].

The third condition is a contrastive interpretation of *belief* (plus a provision that belief and justification must be appropriately related via *basing*[47]). It is a form of *restricted indubitabilism* about belief. It is indubitabilist insofar as it requires certainty, which is an absence of any doubt that p is true. But it is restricted insofar as the space of possibilities open to doubt is restricted to: $\{p\} \cup \{q\}$.

Arguments

First, (4) fits (1) by *comprising the ability to answer*. That is, the analysis in (4) is the right form for the task of fingering answerers as per (1), because to meet (4) *is* to be an answerer. In this way, (4) implements Hector-

---

[45] Austin (1946); Dretske (1981); Lewis (1996); Ram Neta (2002).
[46] I have not said what *evidence* consists in, nor whether the notion can be reduced. Though what I say is compatible with Lewis's (1996) conception of one's evidence as one's total experience. Lewis defines *elimination* as follows: possibility p is eliminated for s (at t) iff p is inconsistent with s's total experience e (at t). S has conclusive evidence that p rather than q, on this interpretation, iff q is eliminated for s. (Notice that the actuality possibility cannot be eliminated; thus p, if true, is ineliminable.)
[47] Basing is a hybrid of *causation* and *rationality*: one's proof must be a rationalizing, non- deviant cause of one's certainty. For further discussion of basing see Korcz (2000).

Neri Castañeda's idea that, "knowledge involves essentially the non-doxastic component of a power to answer a question".[48]

The first condition, the truth condition, is required to fit (1). That is, being able to select the truth is a necessary condition on being able to answer the question. Questions with no true alternatives involve false *presuppositions*,[49] and ought to be rejected rather than answered.

The second condition, the contrastive justification condition, is also required to fit (1)—having proof for p rather than q is a necessary condition on being able to answer: $p \vee q$? As long as one's evidence is compatible with multiple queried alternatives, the inquiry cannot be concluded. This comports with the methodological insight of Sherlock Holmes: "It is an old maxim of mine that when you have excluded the impossible, whatever remains, however improbable, must be the truth" *(The Adventure of the Beryl Coronet)*.

The third condition, the contrastive belief condition, is also required to fit (1)—being certain that p rather than q is a necessary condition on being able to answer: $p \vee q$? As long as one is in doubt, the inquiry is still open. This comports with the Peircean view of doubt as the irritant that spurs inquiry. (The basing relation is required as well: if one's certainty is not based on the proof, then the inquiry has not been closed on proper grounds.)

Perhaps meeting all three conditions is still insufficient for being able to answer. But what could be lacking? Imagine taking a multiple choice exam, having proof that all but one answer is wrong, and being certain of the true answer on this basis. What could be lacking, as far as knowing the answer?

The second argument for (4) is that it resolves numerous problem cases in the literature, including *lottery cases* and *Gettier cases*, via restricted infallibilism. Lottery cases beg for infallibilism; the ticket holder does not know in advance that her ticket will lose rather than win, no matter how long the odds, because her evidence remains fallible—she might be wrong, she might win, she does not know that she will lose. Gettier cases also beg for infallibilism: the passerby who sees a clock stopped twenty-four hours ago on 3p.m. does not know that it is now 3p.m. rather than 4p.m., despite some evidence for a true belief, because his evidence remains fallible—he might be wrong, the clock might be

---

48 Castañeda (1980), 194.
49 Question Q presupposes proposition p iff p is entailed by all answers to Q (Belnap and Steel 1976).

off, he does not know what time it is. Here the fallibility of the connection between evidence and truth is what opens up the possibility of a merely accidental correlation.[50] (Such an infallibilism does not induce skepticism, since the infallibilism is restricted. Knowledge is still possible, when the alternatives in q are eliminable.)

Objections

First, (4) faces *the problem of the giveaway question*. The giveaway question arises when p and q are both dubious hypotheses for s, p is luckily true, and q is easily eliminable. For instance, suppose that Poirot can prove that it was Mayerling who was murdered, but has no evidence that it was Darrow who did the deed. Then, on (4), Poirot can count as knowing that Darrow killed Mayerling rather than that Darrow killed Japp. Yet intuitively, it might seem that Poirot knows nothing of the sort—he need not even know who Darrow is.

In reply, perhaps Poirot does know that Darrow killed Mayerling rather than Japp. After all, if Poirot were to engage the question, "Did Darrow kill *Mayerling*, or *Japp?*", he would be able to answer properly—he can eliminate all but one option. Poirot would pass the test. This is an epistemic achievement. The knowledge claim marks this achievement. It distinguishes Poirot's epistemic standing from that of Poirot's sidekick Hastings, who does not even know who was murdered. Poirot at least knows that it was *Mayerling* rather than *Japp* who Darrow murdered.[51] Or try: Poirot knows whether Darrow killed *Mayerling* or *Japp*.

A second reply (which I reserve as backup) would be to add a further condition to (4). The most natural addition would require some sort of *positive evidence for* p. This would entail that Poirot does not know that Darrow murdered Mayerling rather than Japp, on grounds that Poirot lacks evidence for the proposition that Darrow killed Mayerling. Here there is room to explore a mixture of fallibilism and infallibilism, on which s must have infallible evidence that p rather

---

50 For further discussion of the restricted infallibilist solution to lottery and Gettier cases, see Lewis (1996), Cohen (1998a), and Heller (1999).

51 In this vein, Johnsen imagines that Milan Kundera might just happen to be in Ventimiglia, and claims that he (Johnsen) would at least know that Kundera is in Ventimiglia rather than *Johnsen's office* (2001, 405).

than q, plus fallible evidence that p. I leave this for further exploration.[52] As indicated above, I am merely aiming for a useful gloss here.

Second, one might object that (4) *induces skepticism*. The contrastivist promises to resist skepticism, by allowing Moore to know that he has hands rather than stumps. But, the objection runs, (4) does not allow for this, since there are stump-possibilities that Moore cannot eliminate, such as possibilities in which Moore has stumps but is dreaming of hands, or has stumpy arms stapled onto his envatted brain. Thus, the objection concludes, (4) disallows knowledge.

In reply, there are possibilities that Moore can eliminate, which is what (4) requires for knowledge. Here it will help to leave the shifty 'that'-clauses of English behind, and speak directly of the worlds they denote. There are plenty of worlds that Moore can eliminate, including worlds in which he veridically perceives his stumps. And there are plenty of worlds that Moore cannot eliminate, including actuality and its skeptical variants. In general, for any subject s and true proposition p, s will have a *discriminatory range* R over p, where R is the union of those $\sim p$-worlds which s is able to discriminate from actuality. For all nonempty subsets $R-$ of R, s is in a position to know that p rather than that $R-$ obtains. Whereas for all nonempty subsets $S-$ of the complement of R, $\sim KspS-$ holds.

So does Moore know that he has hands rather than stumps? *Yes*, in a sense. What Moore knows can be more fully described as follows: he knows that he has hands rather than *stumps that are apparent*. Or more fully: Moore knows that he has hands rather than *stumps that he would veridically perceive*. Fuller descriptions are always available. Which worlds these descriptions denote is contextually variable. Thus, strictly speaking, what follows from (4) is that "Moore knows that he has hands rather than that he has stumps" is *true* in contexts in which "that he has stumps" denotes worlds within Moore's discriminatory range R. The context-invariant truth is of the form: Moore knows $\{w_a\}$ rather than $\{w_1, w_2, \ldots, w_m\}$.

---

52 Dretske (1981), expresses some ambivalence on this point, saying that the subject, "needs only a nominal justification, if he needs any justification at all" for the non-contrasted aspect of the knowledge claim, 373.

Comparison

How does (4) compare to various binary views of knowledge? If the task is to provide a finite, non-circular, and intuitively fitting set of necessary and sufficient conditions, all views may prove equally hopeless. If the task is merely to provide a useful gloss of a relation (a decent approximation), perhaps (4) proves best.

The advantage of (4), shared only by some versions of contextualism, is the ability to steer between, "the rock of fallibilism and the whirlpool of skepticism",[53] by implementing a restricted infallibilism. This is an advantage insofar as fallibilism is *implausible, arbitrary,* and *lottery-wracked*. Fallibilism is implausible insofar as it licenses the breathtaking conjunction: "I might be wrong, though I still know." Fallibilism is arbitrary insofar as any line of evidence (or shading of a penumbra) below 1 is arbitrary. Fallibilism is lottery-wracked insofar as any line below 1 will be exceeded by evidence that, in a suitably large lottery, a given ticket is a loser. Implementing a restricted infallibilism is also an advantage insofar as unrestricted infallibilism is *skeptical*. These points are all controversial, and I cannot defend them here. This is left to the reader's judgment. But I would suggest, for these reasons, that (4) offers the *more illuminating gloss* of knowledge, rivaled only by contextualism.

5. Skepticism

The fifth and final stage of an account of knowledge is to resolve outstanding *paradoxes*. How does contrastive knowledge *help?* I propose:

(5) Contrastive knowledge resolves the closure paradox.

Paradox

The closure paradox is typically formulated in binary terms, as follows:
(C1) Moore knows that he has hands.
(C2) Moore doesn't know that he is not a brain-in-a-vat.

---

53 Lewis (1996), 221.

(C3) If Moore doesn't know that he is not a brain-in-a-vat, then he doesn't know that he has hands.[54]

These premises are individually plausible, but conjointly contradictory.

There are four main replies to the closure paradox from within a binary framework: the *skeptic* denies C1, the *dogmatist* denies C2, the *denier of closure* denies C3, and the *contextualist* denies that C2 and C3 entail the falsity of C1 (by maintaining that the denotation of "knows" shifts, rendering the argument equivocal). These positions have been extensively debated.[55] So I will simply state what I find objectionable about each position, to set the stage for the contrastive solution.

I object to skepticism and dogmatism on two parallel counts. First, the denials of C1 and C2 strike me as *absurd*. At least, some explanation is needed of their plausibility. Second, skepticism and dogmatism *collapse distinctions*.[56] Suppose that Student, Assistant, and Professor are visiting the zebras at the zoo. Student is remarkably ignorant, and can't even discern a zebra from a mule; Assistant can discern a zebra from a mule by its stripes, but cannot discern a zebra from a cleverly painted mule; Professor can discern a zebra even from a cleverly painted mule by anatomical features that no mere paint job can disguise. The skeptic confuses Student with Assistant, denying that either knows that the beast is a zebra, since neither can eliminate the painted mule hypothesis. The dogmatist confuses Assistant with Professor, maintaining that both know that the beast is a zebra, since both can eliminate the unpainted mule hypothesis. Both skepticism and dogmatism thereby distort partial knowledge.[57]

---

54 This formulation is found in DeRose (1995) and Schiffer (1996), *inter alia*. See Unger (1975) for arguments that this is the *root* skeptical argument. See Brueckner (1994), Cohen (1998b), and Vogel (n.d.) for further discussion of how closure relates other skeptical concerns such as underdetermination.

55 For a defense of skepticism, see Unger (1975); for a defense of dogmatism, see Klein (1981), Sosa (1999), and Pryor (2000); for a defense of the denial of closure, see Dretske (1971) and Nozick (1981); for a defense of contextualism, see Stine (1976), Cohen (1988) and (1999), DeRose (1995), Lewis (1996), and Neta (2002).

56 Heller (1999) levels this criticism at the skeptic: "[Skeptical] standards fail to draw the distinctions that are important to us. Even though neither my wife nor I can rule out the possibility of an evil genius deceiving us about where the leftovers are, she is in a better epistemic position than I am", 119.

57 Though see Schaffer (2004b) for a defense of the skeptic from these objections. Overall, I would rate skepticism the second-best option.

I object to the denial of closure on two counts. First, the denial of C3 seems *absurd,* at least without some explanation of its plausibility. Second, denying closure *collapses inferences.* Surely deduction transmits knowledge. How could it not, given that our ultimate epistemic interest is truth, and deduction preserves truth? How could it not, given that mathematical proof is deductive and mathematical proof yields knowledge? Pending a replacement for C3, the anti-closure view cripples knowledge.[58]

I object to contextualist solutions on four counts. First, the compatibility of C1 and C2 seems *absurd,* at least without some explanation of the appearance of incompatibility.[59]

Second, the way that C1 and C2 are rendered compatible is *overly concessionary* to both skepticism and dogmatism. For the contextualist concedes that dogmatism holds in the courtroom, so that there one can count as knowing that one is not a brain-in-a-vat. But surely one can never know so much. And the contextualist concedes that skepticism holds in the classroom, so that there one cannot count as knowing that one has hands. But surely one can never know so little. Thus the contextualist is stuck with the implausibilities of both views, and their subsequent conflations. In any given context, the contextualist must either confuse Student with Assistant, or Assistant with Professor. In no context can the contextualist successfully distinguish all three.

Third, the contextualist machinery turns our knowledge attributions *manic*. The contextualist swings from highs of dogmatism to lows of skepticism, at the mere drop of a skeptical scenario. Surely our dispositions to ascribe knowledge are more stable.[60]

Fourth, contextualism renders "knows" too shifty to score inquiry consistently (§2). Scoring inquiry requires being able to evaluate how a subject performs through a sequence of questions. This requires having epistemic vocabulary that can keep a consistent score through a range of contexts. But "knows" as the contextualist conceives it cannot keep a consistent score, because "knows" as the contextualist conceives it is continually warped by the present context.

---

58 See Williamson (2000) for a defense of closure based on the idea that "deduction is a way of extending one's knowledge", 117. For extended discussion see Hawthorne (2004), 31–50.
59 As Schiffer (1996) notes in a criticism of the contextualist solution, "If that's the solution, what the hell was the *problem"*, 329.
60 Johnsen (2001), 395; see also Dretske (1991), 192; Feldman (1999), 106.

Resolution

The contrastivist rejects the closure paradox as formulated, since C1–C3 all concern binary knowledge. I will now argue, on behalf of (5), that contrastivism (i) dissolves the paradox, (ii) explains the plausibility of its premises, and (iii) answers all the objections leveled above at the other approaches.

Contrastivism dissolves the paradox by revealing how ordinary knowledge and skeptical doubt are compatible: they concern different contrasts. Moore knows that he has hands rather than stumps. Moore does not know that he has hands rather than vat-images of hands. In interrogative terms, Moore knows whether he has hands or stumps, but does not know whether he has hands or vat-images of hands. In general, for any subject s and proposition p, s is in position to know that p rather than q for any proposition q within s's discriminatory range (§4). Whereas for any q that extends beyond s's discriminatory range, ~$Kspq$.

Some of the inferential relations that hold between contrastive knowledge states can be adduced from the notion of discriminatory range. A valid schema will preserve discrimination of truth. It will preserve the elimination of all-but-p. Here are two valid schemas:

Expand-p: if $p_1 \to p_2$ then $Ksp_1q \to Ksp_2q$[61]
Contract-q: if $q_2 \to q_1$ then $Kspq_1 \to Kspq_2$

And here are four *in*valid schemas, which do not preserve discrimination of truth:

★Contract-p: if $p_2 \to p_1$ then $Ksp_1q \to Ksp_2q$
★Expand-q: if $q_1 \to q_2$ then $Kspq_1 \to Kspq_2$
★Replace-p: $Ksp_1q \to Ksp_2q$
★Replace-q: $Kspq_1 \to Kspq_2$

Since Replace-q is invalid, one cannot use the fact that Moore knows that he has hands rather than stumps to infer that Moore knows that

---

61 These schemas are only valid as *idealizations*. Expand-p, for instance, needs limitation to prevent the p-worlds from *swallowing* q. Contrastivity needs to be preserved under p-expansion. So a more accurate statement of Expand-p would be: if $p_1 \to p_2$ and $p_2 \cap q = \emptyset$, then $Ksp_1q \to Ksp_2q$. Expand-p should also be restricted to cases of competent deduction (here I am following Williamson 2000). So an even more accurate statement of Expand-p would be: if (i) $p_1 \to p_2$, (ii) $p_2 \cap q = \emptyset$, (iii) s competently deduces p_2 from p_1, and (iv) s comes to be certain that p_2 rather than q on the basis of (iii), then $Ksp_1q \to Ksp_2q$. These details won't matter for what follows.

he has hands rather than vat-images of hands. The fact that the vat possibility lies outside Moore's discriminatory range does not entail that the stumps possibility does too.

Ordinary knowledge concerns discriminations in a limited range. Skeptical doubts reveal the limits of that range. Since the existence of possibilities outside one's discriminatory range does not imply the absence of any possibilities inside that range, skeptical doubts do not imply any absence of ordinary knowledge. Thus ordinary knowledge and skeptical doubt are compatible. Paradox dissolved.

Why then are the premises of the paradox so plausible? The contrastivist explanation is that (i) we charitably accommodate binary knowledge ascriptions by imputing a question (§3), and (ii) the natural questions for C1-C3 in fact generate contrastive truths. Starting with C1, the natural question would concern whether Moore has hands or is some sort of amputee. Indeed, the only implicit questions for C1 that would generate falsity would be those concerning skeptical scenarios, supplying of which would be both unnatural and unaccommodating. In the case of C2, the implicit question that leaps out concerns whether Moore is handed or envatted. Since Moore cannot discriminate between these alternatives, we naturally assent to C2, And finally in the case of C3, we naturally interpret it as embedded in an inquiry that concerns whether Moore is handed or envatted. So we naturally think of C3 as saying: if Moore does not know that he's not a brain-in-a-vat rather than a brain-in-a-vat, then he doesn't know that he's a hand-owner rather than a brain-in-a-vat. This has the form: $\sim Ksp_1 \sim p_1 \rightarrow \sim Ksp_2 \sim p_1$, where $p_2 \rightarrow p_1$ (hands entails not-vatted). This is a valid inference, as it is an instance of the contrapositive of Expand-p.

Putting this together, the contrastive reformulation of closure is:

(C1') Moore knows that he has hands rather than stumps.
(C2') Moore does not know that he is handed rather than envatted.
(C3') If Moore doesn't know that he's not envatted rather than envatted, then he doesn't know that he's handed rather than envatted.[62]

To put the reformulation in interrogative terms:

---

62 This is the reformulation that preserves the truth of each premise. Alternatively the paradox could be reformulated so as to preserve the incompatibility of the premises via: C3'*: If Moore doesn't know that he's handed rather than envatted, then he doesn't know that he has hands rather than stumps. But C3'* is false—just because "Hands or vat-images of hands?" falls beyond Moore's discriminatory range does not imply that "Hands or stumps?" does too.

(C1") Moore knows whether he has hands or stumps.
(C2") Moore does not know whether he has hands or is envatted.
(C3") If Moore does not know whether he is non-envatted or envatted, then he doesn't know whether he is handed or envatted.

Each premise is true. There is no paradox. The plausibility of each of C1–C3 is due to our naturally processing them as something like C1'–C3' (equivalently: C1"–C3") respectively.

Contrastivism, finally, answers all the objections leveled above against skepticism, dogmatism, the denial of closure, and contextualism. With respect to skepticism and dogmatism, contrastivism explains the plausibility of C1 and C2, as per the previous paragraph. And contrastivism captures the distinctions that skepticism and dogmatism collapse. Student does not know that the beast is a zebra rather than a mule. Assistant knows that the beast is a zebra rather than a mule, but does not know that the beast is a zebra rather than a painted mule. Professor knows that the beast is a zebra rather than a mule, and that the beast is a zebra rather than a painted mule. What distinguishes these characters is their discriminatory ranges.

With respect to the denial of closure, contrastivism explains the plausibility of C3, as above. And contrastivism captures the inferences that the denier of closure disallows, via Expand-p and Contract-q. In particular, Expand-p preserves the sense in which deductive proof is knowledge-transmitting.

With respect to contextualism, the contrastivist can explain the apparent incompatibility of C1 and C2 as due to neglect of the covert contrast variable. And covert variables can induce confusion among competent speakers. The compatibility of C1' and C2' allows the contrastivist to avoid conceding dogmatism in one context and skepticism in another, as the contextualist must. Ordinary knowledge and skeptical doubt do not need to be cordoned off into separate contexts. They coexist in both the courtroom and the classroom. Moore always knows that he has hands rather than stumps, and never knows that he has hands rather than vat-images of hands. The context-invariance of C1' and C2' provides the stability that contextualism precludes. The invocation of skeptical possibilities does not change which discriminations s can make one whit. Thus one can track s's discriminatory range through a sequence of questions, and thereby properly keep score of inquiry.

Comparison

Contrastivism reveals that the closure paradox is *an artifact of binarity*. Contrastivism provides the following recipe for binary paradoxes. First, find an easy question that s can successfully answer by p. This will generate a context in which *"s knows that p"* encodes a true proposition: $Kspq_1$. Treat this as binary knowledge: Ksp. Second, find a hard question that s cannot answer involving p. This will generate a context in which *"s knows that p"* encodes a false proposition: $Kspq_2$. Treat this as binary ignorance: $\sim Ksp$. Third, conjoin and tremble. Skeptical scenarios merely help provide hard questions for the second step ("Or has she just dreamt the whole episode?")

For all we philosophers might fret over skepticism, ordinary inquiries never shipwreck on skeptical possibilities. No court case has ever been dismissed due to the closure paradox ("Your Honor, that witness knows nothing!"). Ordinary inquiries succeed because ordinary questions are restricted. *The wile of the skeptic is to shift the question.* Thus resolving the closure paradox requires rendering knowledge in a structure that logs the question: the contrastive structure.

6. Contextualism

Epistemic contrastivism is cousin to the family of *epistemic contextualisms*. It might prove useful, by way of epilogue, to clarify the relations.[63]

Contextualisms feature three main family traits, which I label *indexicalism, relevantism,* and *equivocationism*. Indexicalism is the thesis that "knows" functions like an indexical in having a stable character but a context-dependent content. Relevantism is the thesis that what one knows is determined by a set of relevant alternatives. Equivocationism is the thesis that the closure paradox involves an equivocation between the contents of "knows" generated by the first two premises (§5).[64] To

---

63 See Schaffer (2004a) for a more extended discussion of these issues.
64 While more recent contextualisms (such as DeRose 1995; Lewis 1996) exhibit indexicalism, relevantism, and equivocationism together, these traits are independent. Indexicalism does not entail relevantism, since the context-dependence of "knows" might turn on something other than relevance, such as the degree of justification required by the stakes. Cohen (1988) is perhaps best read this way. And indexicalism does not entail equivocationism, since, for instance, "knows" might not be variable enough for skeptical doubts. DeRose

clarify the relations between contrastivism and the family of contextualisms, it will prove most helpful to compare contrastivism to indexicalism, relevantism, and equivocationism directly, as separate positions.

Indexicalism

Contrastivism and indexicalism are similar in the following way. On both theories, a binary knowledge ascription may be true in one context, and false in another.

But contrastivism and indexicalism differ in two main ways. First, the mechanism of context-dependence is different. With indexicalism, it is the content of the relation denoted by "knows" that is contextually shifty. With contrastivism, it is the value of the contrast relatum q that is shifty. Thus indexicalism, but not contrastivism, is committed to the postulation of context-dependence without representation in logical form.[65]

Second, the extent of context-dependence is different. With indexicalism, since it is the occurrence of the term "knows" that induces shiftiness, every knowledge ascription must be shifty. With contrastivism, since it is the value of q that is shifty in binary ascriptions, interrogative, noun, and overtly contrastive ascriptions must be relatively stable, since these at least partially fix the value of q. This seems intuitively correct: "Moore knows that he has hands" seems shiftier than "Moore knows that he has hands rather than stumps". Further, this stable form of

---

(1995) allows though does not endorse this position. Relevantism does not entail indexicalism, since relevance might be determined purely in terms of s's objective situation, with no reference to the context of utterance. Dretske (1991) and Hawthorne (2004) endorse this view. And relevantism does not entail equivocationism, since, for instance, skeptical possibilities might never be relevant. Austin (1946) takes this line. Equivocationism, finally, does not entail either indexicalism or relevantism, since the equivocation might be due to polysemy (with neither sense indexicalized or involving a relevance function). Malcolm's (1952) distinction between the "strong" and "weak" senses of "knows" might serve as a prototype for such a view.

65 Stanley (2000) argues that it is implausible to postulate context-dependence that is unrepresented in logical form, except for the cases of the obvious indexicals, demonstratives, and pronouns. Stanley's argument applies against indexicalism but not contrastivism. There are plenty of precedents (including "prefers" and "explains", §3) for verbs with additional contrast slots, while there seem to be no precedents for verbs that are indexicalized.

knowledge ascription is required by the scorekeeping function of knowledge (§5).

Relevantism

Contrastivism and relevantism are similar in the following way. On both theories, whether one knows is calculated with reference to a set of alternatives.

But contrastivism and relevantism differ in two main ways. First, what one knows is different. With relevantism, by eliminating the relevant alternatives, one knows that p. With contrastivism, one knows that p rather than q. The relevantist is still in the grip of binarity.

Second, the alternatives are generated in different ways. With relevantism, the alternatives are generated by a relevance function. With contrastivism, the alternatives are generated by an explicit or implicit question (§3). But what is 'relevance'? By far the best account of relevance is to be found in Lewis.[66] But Lewis's account is subject to counterexamples.[67] Worse, it is (i) *imprecise,* (ii) *epistemically tailored,*[68] and (iii) *ad hoc* in certain respects (such as why resemblance with respect to evidence is non-salient). The contrastivist mechanisms (§3), on the other hand, are (i) *precise,* (ii) *linguistically general* mechanisms, and their application is (iii) *motivated* by the role of knowledge in inquiry.

Equivocationism

Contrastivism and equivocationism are similar in the following way. On both theories, ordinary knowledge and skeptical doubts are compatible.

But contrastivism offers a better solution to the closure paradox in four main ways (§5): (i) contrastivism provides a better explanation of

---

[66] Lewis's (1996) account may be the only serious account of relevance. Dretske (1981, 373–377) makes a number of programmatic remarks, but otherwise one finds little of substance on this topic in the entire literature. Not for nothing does Sosa warn that relevantism "will remain unacceptably occult" (1986, 585). See also Vogel (1999).

[67] See Vogel (1999).

[68] Lewis begins by invoking the linguistic mechanism of *quantifier domain restriction.* This much is linguistically general. But then most of Lewis's subsequent rules of ignoring are epistemically tailored.

the apparent incompatibility of ordinary knowledge and skeptical doubt; (ii) contrastivism avoids conceding dogmatism in some contexts and skepticism in the others, by allowing ordinary knowledge and skeptical doubts to be compatible *in the same context:* "Moore knows whether he has hands or stumps; but he does not know whether he has hands or vat- images of hands"; (iii) contrastivism avoids manic swings from dogmatism to skepticism thereby; and (iv) contrastivism allows "knows" to serve its inquiry-scoring function, since one can keep a consistent score through a range of contexts. Assistant can successfully answer the question: "Zebra or [normal] mule?" After it emerges that Assistant cannot answer the question: "Zebra or painted mule?", one can still report Assistant's previous success: "At least he knows whether the beast is a zebra or a normal mule."[69]

References

Austin (1946): John Langshaw Austin, "Other Minds", in: *Proceedings of the Aristotelian Society* 20, 149–87.
Austin (1962): John Langshaw Austin, *How to Do Things with Words*, Cambridge.
Belnap a. Steel (1976): Nuel Belnap a. Thomas Steel, *The Logic of Questions and Answers*, New Haven.
Boër a. Lycan (1986): Steven Boër a. William Lycan, *Knowing Who*, Cambridge.
Brandom (1994): Robert Brandom, *Making it Explicit*, Cambridge.
Brueckner (1994): Anthony Brueckner, "The Structure of the Skeptical Argument", in: *Philosophy and Phenomenological Research* 54, 827–835.
Castañeda (1980): Hector-Neri Castañeda, "The Theory of Questions, Epistemic Powers, and the Indexical Theory of Knowledge", in: P. French/T. Uehling, Jr./H. Wettstein (eds.), *Midwest Studies in Philosophy vol. V: Studies in Epistemology*, Minneapolis, 193–238.
Chomsky (1977): Noam Chomsky, *Essays on Forms and Interpretation*, Amsterdam.
Cohen (1988): Stewart Cohen, "How to be a Fallibilist", in: *Philosophical Perspectives* 2, 91–123.

---

[69] Thanks to Kent Bach, Martijn Blaauw, Thomas Blackson, John Collins, Fred Dretske, Tamar Gendler, Ed Gettier, John Hawthorne, Mark Heller, Michael Huemer, Bredo Johnsen, Antti Karjalainen, David Lewis, Adam Morton, Roald Nashi, Ram Neta, Barbara Partee, Walter Sinnott-Armstrong, Jonathan Vogel, Brian Weatherson, and audiences at the Bellingham Summer Philosophy Conference, the Pacific APA, the University of Colorado, and the University of Florida.

Cohen (1998a): Stewart Cohen, "Contextualist Solutions to Epistemological Problems: Scepticism, Gettier, and the Lottery", in: *Australasian Journal of Philosophy* 76, 289–306.
Cohen (1998b): Stewart Cohen, "Two Kinds of Skeptical Argument", *Philosophy and Phenomenological Research* 52, 143–159.
Cohen (1999): Stewart Cohen, "Contextualism, Skepticism, and the Structure of Reasons", in: *Philosophical Perspectives* 13, 57–89.
Craig (1990): Edward Craig, *Knowledge and the State of Nature: An Essay in Conceptual Synthesis*, Oxford.
DeRose (1995): Keith DeRose, "Solving the Skeptical Problem", in: *Philosophical Review* 104, 1–52.
Dewey (1938): John Dewey, *Logic: The Theory of Inquiry*, New York.
Dretske (1970): Fred Dretske, "Epistemic Operators", in: *Journal of Philosophy* 67, 1007–1023.
Dretske (1981): Fred Dretske, "The Pragmatic Dimension of Knowledge", in: *Philosophical Studies* 40, 363–378.
Dretske (1991): Fred Dretske, "Knowledge: Sanford and Cohen", in: B. McLaughlin (ed.), *Dretske and his Critics*, Oxford, 185–196.
Feldman (1999): Richard Feldman, "Contextualism and Skepticism", in: *Philosophical Perspectives* 13, 91–114.
Garfinkel (1981): Alan Garfinkel, *Forms of Explanation: Rethinking the Questions in Social Theory*, New Haven.
Greco (2002): John Greco, "Knowledge as Credit for True Belief", in: L. Zagzebski/M. DePaul (eds.), *Intellectual Virtue: Perspectives from Ethics and Epistemology*, Oxford, 111–134.
Groenendijk a. Stokhof (1997): Jeroen Groenendijk a. Martin Stokhof, "Questions", in: J. F. A. K. van Benthem/A. G. B. ter Meulen (eds.), *Handbook of Logic and Language*, Amsterdam, 1055–1124.
Hamblin (1958): Charles L. Hamblin, "Questions", in: *Australasian Journal of Philosophy* 36, 159–168.
Hawthorne (2004): John Hawthorne, *Knowledge and Lotteries*, Oxford.
Heim (1979): Irene Heim, "Concealed Questions", in: R. Bäuerle/U. Egli/A. von Stechow (eds.), *Semantics from Different Points of View*, Berlin, 51–60.
Heller (1999): Mark Heller, "Contextualism and Anti-Luck Epistemology", in: *Philosophical Perspectives* 13, 115–129.
Higginbotham (1993): James Higginbotham, "Interrogatives", in: K. Hale/S. J. Keyser (eds.), *The View from Building 20: Essays in Honor of Sylvain Bromberger*, Cambridge, 195–228.
Higginbotham (1996): James Higginbotham, "The Semantics of Questions", in: S. Lappin (ed.), *The Handbook of Contemporary Semantic Theory*, Oxford, 361–383.
Hintikka (1975a): Jaakko Hintikka, "Answers to Questions", in: *The Intensions of Intentionally and Other New Models for Modalities*, Dordrecht, 137–158.
Hintikka (1975b): Jaakko Hintikka, "Different Constructions in Terms of the Basic Epistemological Verbs: A Survey of Some Problems and Proposals", in: *The Intensions of Intentionality and Other New Models for Modalities*, Dordrecht, 1–25.

Hintikka (1981): Jaakko Hintikka, "On the Logic of an Interrogative Model of Scientific Inquiry", in: *Synthese* 47, 69–84.
Hookway (1996): Christopher Hookway, "Questions of Context", in: *Proceedings of the Aristotelian Society* 96, 1–16.
Johnsen (2001): Bredo Johnsen, "Contextualist Swords, Skeptical Plowshares", in: *Philosophy and Phenomenological Research* 62, 385–406.
Klein (1981): Peter Klein, *Certainty: A Refutation of Skepticism*, Minneapolis.
Kleiner (1988): Scott Kleiner, "Erotetic Logic and Scientific Inquiry", in: *Synthese* 74, 19–46.
Korcz (2000): Keith A. Korcz, "The Causal-Doxastic Theory of the Basing Relation", in: *Canadian Journal of Philosophy* 30, 525–550.
Laudan (1977): Larry Laudan, *Progress and its Problems: Towards a Theory of Scientific Growth*, Berkeley.
Levi (1984): Isaac Levi, "Abduction and Demands for Information", in: *Decisions and Revisions: Philosophical Essays on Knowledge and Value*, Cambridge.
Lewis (1979): David Lewis, "Scorekeeping in a Language Game", in: *Journal of Philosophical Logic* 8, 339–359.
Lewis (1982): David Lewis, "Whether Report", in: T. Pauli (ed.), *Philosophical Essays Dedicated to Lennart Aqvist on his Fiftieth Birthday*, Uppsala, 194–206.
Lewis (1996): David Lewis, "Elusive Knowledge", in: *Australasian Journal of Philosophy* 74, 549–67.
Lipton (1991): Peter Lipton, *Inference to the Best Explanation*, New York.
Malcolm (1952): Norman Malcolm, "Knowledge and Belief", in: *Mind* 51, 178–189.
Moore (1959a): George Edward Moore, "A Defence of Common Sense", in: *Philosophical Papers*, London, 32–59.
Moore (1959b): George Edward Moore, "Certainty", in: *Philosophical Papers*, London, 227–251.
Morton a. Karjalainen (2003): Adam Morton a. Antti Karjalainen, "Contrastive Knowledge", in: *Philosophical Explorations* 6, 74–89.
Neta (2002): Ram Neta, "S Knows that p", in: *Noûs* 36, 663–81.
Nozick (1981): Robert Nozick, *Philosophical Explanations*, Cambridge.
Partee (1989): Barbara Partee, "Binding Implicit Variables in Quantified Contexts", in: *Proceedings of the Chicago Linguistics Society* 25, Chicago, 342–365.
Peirce (1877): Charles Sanders Peirce, "The Fixation of Belief", in: *Popular Science Monthly* 12, 1–15.
Pryor (2000): James Pryor, "The Skeptic and the Dogmatist", in: *Noûs* 34, 517–549.
Rooth (1992): Mats Rooth, "A Theory of Focus Interpretation", in: *Natural Language Semantics* 1, 75–116.
Ryle (1949): Gilbert Ryle, *The Concept of Mind*, Chicago.
Sanford (1991): David Sanford, "Proper Knowledge", in: B. McLaughlin (ed.), *Dretske and his Critics*, Oxford, 38–51.
Schaffer (2004a): Jonathan Schaffer, "From Contextualism to Contrastivism", in: *Philosophical Studies* 119, 73–103.
Schaffer (2004b): Jonathan Schaffer, "Skepticism, Contextualism, and Discrimination", in: *Philosophy and Phenomenological Research* 69, 138–155.

Schaffer (n.d.): Jonathan Schaffer, "Knowing the Answer", unpublished typescript.
Schiffer (1996): Stephen Schiffer, "Contextualist Solutions to Scepticism", in: *Proceedings of the Aristotelian Society* 96, 317–333.
Sinnott-Armstrong (2004): Walter Sinnott-Armstrong, *Pyrrhonian Skepticism*, Oxford.
Sintonen (1997): Matti Sintonen, "Explanation: The Fifth Decade", in: M. Sintonen (ed.), *Knowledge and Inquiry: Essays on Jaakko Hintikka's Epistemology and Philosophy of Science*, Amsterdam, 225–38.
Sosa (1986): Ernest Sosa, "On Knowledge and Context", in: *Journal of Philosophy* 83, 584–585.
Sosa (1999): Ernest Sosa, "How to Defeat Opposition to Moore", in: *Philosophical Perspectives* 13, 141–153.
Stalnaker (1999a): Robert Stalnaker, "Assertion", in: *Context and Content*, Oxford, 78–95.
Stalnaker (1999b): Robert Stalnaker, "On the Representation of Context", in: *Context and Content*, Oxford, 96–113.
Stanley (2000): Jason Stanley, "Context and Logical Form", in: *Linguistics and Philosophy* 23, 391–434.
Stanley a. Williamson (2001): Jason Stanley a. Timothy Williamson, "Knowing How", in: *Journal of Philosophy* 98, 411–44.
Stine (1976): G. C. Stine, "Skepticism, Relevant Alternatives, and Deductive Closure", in: *Philosophical Studies* 29, 249–261.
Unger (1975): Peter Unger, *Ignorance: A Case for Scepticism*, Oxford.
Van Fraassen (1980): Bas van Fraassen, *The Scientific Image*, Oxford.
Vogel (1999): Jonathan Vogel, "The New Relevant Alternatives Theory", in: *Philosophical Perspectives* 13, 155–180.
Vogel (n.d.): Jonathan Vogel, "Varieties of Skepticism", unpublished typescript.
Watson (1973): Charles S. Watson, "Psychophysics", in: B. B. Wolman (ed.), *Handbook of General Psychology*, Englewood Cliffs, NJ, 275–306.
Williamson (2000): Timothy Williamson, *Knowledge and its Limits*, Oxford.
Wittgenstein (1969): Ludwig Wittgenstein, *On Certainty*, in: G. E. M. Anscombe/G. H. von Wright (eds.), Oxford.

Contrastivism rather than Something Else? – On the Limits of Epistemic Contrastivism*

Peter Baumann

One of the most recent trends in epistemology is contrastivism.[1] It can be characterized as the thesis that knowledge is a ternary relation between a subject, a known proposition and a contrast proposition (which is incompatible with the known proposition, and which can consist of a conjunction of propositions).[2] According to contrastivism, knowledge attributions have the form "S knows that p, rather than q" (where "rather than q" is, of course, not part of what is claimed to be known here). Here is an example. Jack is eating cheddar cheese which he is able to distinguish from marmalade but not from gruyère cheese. Hence, he might know that he is eating cheddar cheese rather than marmalade but he does not know and is not in a position to know that he is eating cheddar rather than gruyère. Like contextualism, contrastivism has interesting things to say about epistemic scepticism. Jack might not be able to rule out that he is being deceived by a Cartesian demon into thinking that he is eating cheddar; hence, he cannot know that he is eating cheddar rather than just suffering from Cartesian cheddar illusions. However, he can still know that he is eating cheddar rather than marmalade. Contrastivism is close not just to epistemic contextualism[3] but also to relevant alternatives theories of knowledge (or justification).[4] In contrast, however, to relevant alternatives accounts, contrastivism assumes that knowledge is ternary. And in contrast to contextualism, contrastivism is not wedded to (but could be combined

---

* Originally published in *Erkenntnis* 69 (2008), pp. 189–200. Reprinted by permission oft he publisher, Springer.
1 See Sinnott-Armstrong (2004), Schaffer (2005a), Karjalainen/Morton (2003), Johnson (2001) and Blaauw (2004); an early precursor can be found in Dretske (1972); s. also a short passage in Swinburne (2001), 34.
2 Contrastivism about knowledge can easily be combined with an analoguous contrastivism about justification.
3 See, e.g., DeRose (1999).
4 See, e.g., Dretske (1970).

with) the idea that the truth conditions of knowledge attributions can vary with the attributor's contexts. Contrastivism as explained above is neutral with respect to contextualism: It implies neither contextualist theses nor their negations. One could call any non-contextualist version of contrastivism "pure contrastivism"[5] and any contextualist version of it "hybrid (contextualist) contrastivism". Some of the problems raised below might find a solution if contrastivism is combinded with contextualism. – In the following I will raise several critical concerns for contrastivism (and include an appendix on contrastivism about beliefs). They point at limitations and necessary modifications of contrastivism and are arranged in the order of increasing weight.

1. Non-contrastive Knowledge

There are many cases which seem to strongly support a contrastivist account of knowledge.[6] Perhaps the best case for contrastivism is perceptual knowledge based on discriminatory abilities. Jack can distinguish between dogs and cats but not between dogs and wolves. He sees a dog in front of him (under normal conditions) and thus comes to know that there is a dog in front of him. According to the contrastivist, "Jack knows that there is a dog in front of him" is elliptical for something like "Jack knows that there is a dog in front of him rather than a cat." One of the greatest advantages of contrastivism is that it can account for the lack of knowledge in cases like Jack's inability to tell dogs from wolves: "Jack does not know that there is a dog in front of him rather than a wolf" is also true, according to the contrastivist. A binary view of knowledge has problems accounting for our opposing tendencies to attribute and deny knowledge that there is a dog to Jack; contrastivism easily resolves the puzzle. The application to the problem of epistemological scepticism is also tempting: Jack can know that it is a dog rather than a cat but he may not know that it is a dog rather than a dog-hallucination brought about by Descartes' evil demon. Contrastivism can, like contextualism, account for both our sceptical and our anti-sceptical views and tendencies.

Crucial to all this is the idea that a subject might know that p with respect to some but not all potential contrast propositions. To be sure,

---

5   See, e.g., for this view Sinnott-Armstrong (2004).
6   See, e.g., Schaffer (2005a).

the contrastivist does not need to deny the possibility of cases where a subject knows some proposition with respect to all possible contrast propositions. But this would be an extreme case. Contrastivism makes its point when analyzing normal cases where a subject knows that p rather than q but does not know that p rather than r (see above). If that were not the case, contrastivism would lose its point and attractiveness.[7] This leads to the following plausibility constraint for any contrastivist analysis of knowledge of a certain type (perception, memory, etc.):

> (Specificity) A contrastivist analysis of knowledge of a certain type is plausible only if there are, for a given subject S, a lot of triples of propositions p, q and r such that S knows that p rather than q but S does not know p rather than r (where "knows" refers to knowledge of that type).

This condition is vague in so far as it does not indicate a minimal number of such triples of propositions for some person and type of knowledge. However, we do not need to be more specific here. It is already clear that only some but not all types of knowledge meet the specificity-condition: perception for instance. However, other types of knowledge don't meet it.

Take knowledge of obvious mathematical truths, like the simple one that 2+2=4. Does anyone who knows that know it in contrast to something else? In contrast to what, then? To *2+2=5* (Or *2+2=-7?* Or *3+3=4?* Or *12x12=1212?*)? There simply does not seem to be a plausible contrast proposition around. The problem is that (Specificity) does not seem to hold for this kind of knowledge. It is hard to imagine, for instance, how there could be two numbers x and y (not equal to 4) such that S knows that 2+2=4 rather than 2+2=x but that S does not know that 2+2=4 rather than 2+2=y. It would be very interesting to find someone who, e.g., knows that 2+2=4 rather than 2+2=40 but who does not know that 2+2=4 rather than 2+2=5 ("too close!"). It would be very hard to make sense of such a subject or even to attribute knowledge to her in the first place. It seems that whoever knows that 2+2=4 knows this rather than 2+2=z, for any z not equal to 4.[8]

---

7   See, e.g., Schaffer (2005a), sec.2; Schaffer (2005b).
8   To be sure, few, if any, subjects are able to grasp all possible contrast propositions to a given, known proposition. For instance, someone might understand that 2+2=5 but not understand that 2+2=1/4, due to a lack of understanding of fractions (thanks to a referee here). However, that there is such a difference between "accessible" (for the subject) contrast propositions and non-accessible contrast propositions does not at all support the claim that knowledge is con-

The contrastivist might reply here that this is still compatible with his view: S knows that p rather than not-p (or rather than any alternative). This, however, is perhaps compatible with the letter but certainly not with the spirit of contrastivism. The prize for this kind of manoeuvre is the rejection of (Specificity) and trivialization. Nobody would deny that one can talk like that but this way of talking would be like an additional wheel spinning in the void. We might as well go back to the binary view of knowledge.

The point above is not restricted to mathematical knowledge. Similar things can be said about basic forms of logical knowledge. To be sure, there are very difficult questions in mathematics or logic with respect to which it might make sense to say that someone knew at a time that this formula is valid rather than that one. However, this manœuvre won't work for basic and simple cases like knowledge that if p then p, or that everything is identical with itself (what would be the contrast here?). I will not repeat the argument from specificity here but rather shortly mention another case, namely linguistic or conceptual knowledge. What would be a plausible contrast proposition for knowledge that vixen are female foxes? One can suspect that at least some of the classical candidates for apriority create this kind of trouble for contrastivism because they don't meet (Specificity).

All this suggests that not all knowledge is contrastive. More cautiously: Nobody so far has shown (and it does not seem likely) that all types of knowledge admit of contrastivist analyses. To put it more positively: It seems that contrastivism is most plausible and probably only plausible with respect to a particular kind of knowledge: knowledge of propositions which involves the use of discriminatory cognitive abilities. The use of such abilities need not be restricted to one's external environment: Discrimination is also needed when it comes, for instance, to the identification of a particular emotion as sympathy rather than pity. So, why not explicitly restrict contrastivism to cases of discriminatory knowledge?

One might, however, want to propose more radical consequences.[9] Starting with the assumption that

---

trastive in the first place or that contrast propositions or a subset of them play the role the contrastivist thinks they play. Similar things hold in the case of contrast proposition which either lack a truth value or are false for non-mathematical reasons, like, e.g., "2+2=Julius Caesar".

9   Thanks to a referee here.

(A) If some kinds of knowledge are contrastive, then all kinds of knowledge are contrastive.

One could argue that since some kinds of knowledge (e.g., knowledge based on discriminatory abilities) are contrastive all kinds of knowledge are contrastive. However, given the above point about mathematics, things would rather cut the other way around: Since not all kinds of knowledge are contrastive, none are. This conclusion would, of course, be very bad for the contrastivist. However, since I do not see any good reason to accept (A)[10], I would rather propose to restrict contrastivist analyses of knowledge in the way indicated above.

2. Restricted Relata

The third relatum of contrastivism is a contrast proposition. But why should only contrast propositions be able to fill the third argument place?

Take the following example. Mary is a meteorologist. On her way to work she runs into a friend who asks her whether it will be raining later that day. Both can clearly see dark rain clouds coming up. Mary replies that she hasn't been to the weather lab yet but that she would certainly expect rain later that day. Let us assume that it does indeed rain later that day. In an ordinary context it then seems true to say of Mary that she knows that it is going to rain later that day. One hour later, however, a colleague at the weather lab asks her whether she already knew whether it was going to rain later that day. Not having finished the usual checks required for the daily weather report, she denies that. In a meteorological context it seems false to say of Mary that she knows that it is going to rain later that day.

How should one analyse this in terms of contrast propositions? To be sure, Mary might know that it is going to rain rather than snow but not know that it is going to rain rather than drizzle. But that is beside the point of our example: What varies in the example above is not the contrast proposition but something else: standards relevant in partic-

---

10 There are all kinds of differences between the kinds of epistemic states we call "knowledge": e.g., some kinds of "knowledge" preserve information (memory), others involve the acquisition of new information (perception). Why shouldn't there be some kinds of the epistemic states we call "knowledge" which are contrastive while others aren't?

ular contexts (meteorological contexts, non-work contexts, etc.).[11] One can account for all this by proposing that knowledge is a ternary relation between a subject, a known proposition and, third, something out of a bunch of entities: contrast propositions, context-specific epistemic standards, practical interests (how important is it to get it right?), etc.[12] This is, I think, still compatible with the contrastivist spirit even if not with its letter as it has been developed so far. It would be compatible with the spirit of contrastivism if one were to generalize the account and open the third argument slot up for many different kinds of things, or, at least, for more things than just contrast propositions. At the same time, contrastivism would lose some of its simplicity and elegance.

3. More Relativization

In the last section I proposed to broaden contrastivism with respect to admissible kinds of third relata while in the first section I proposed to restrict it with respect to kinds of knowledge. Now, I am going to argue that the contrastivist should accept a further condition on the

---

11 To be sure, Mary might know that it is going to rain rather than drizzle only given lab standards but she might know that it is going to rain rather than snow also given lay standards. The point above, however, is a different one: that she might know that p (it is going to rain), rather than q (it is not going to rain) according to some standards (relevant in non-work contexts) but not according to some other standards (relevant in lab contexts). Hence, there is more to take into account for the evaluation of knowledge attributions than contrast propositions. S. Baumann (2008a).

12 The third argument slot would take n-tuples of entities of different kinds (standards, interests, contrasts, etc.) as its argument. The number of entities might vary from case to case: sometimes only a contrast proposition, sometimes only a standard, sometimes both, etc. An alternative way to go about would be to admit n additional argument places (where the value of "n" can, of course, vary; see above). This difference does not matter here. – To indicate what kinds of entities could go into the third slot would be a follow-up task for the contrastivist; I cannot go any deeper into that here. Suffice it to say that, again, there is no threat of theoretical disunity if one admits that the third argument slot has a disjunctive form. If there were such a threat and if knowledge could therefore not be "disjunctive" in the way indicated, then the argument in this section would be even more critical for contrastivism because it would suggest that contrastivism has unacceptable implications (that it cannot account for the unity of knowledge).

knowledge-relation, a further relativization. Here is what I have in mind.

Consider Sue who cannot distinguish between a terrier and a dachshund even though she clearly sees a difference between a terrier and a cat as well as between a dachshund and a cat. She also sees a difference between a dachshund and a labrador or between a terrier and a collie; it is just the small dogs which give her epistemic trouble. According to the standard contrastivist view, Sue might well know on one occasion that there is a dachshund in front of her rather than a cat and she might also know on another occasion that there is a terrier in front of her rather than a cat – even though she cannot tell dachshunds from terriers and thus cannot know whether there is a dachshund in front of her rather than a terrier. This, however, sounds abominable and incorrect. It seems false to say that she knows out of the contrast class [dachshund; cat] that there is a dachshund.

What is wrong with such attributions of knowledge? Here is a first rough idea which will have to be developed and modified step by step. Consider Sue, again, who cannot (under any circumstances) distinguish between a dachshund and a terrier. To say that Sue knows that there is a dachshund rather than a cat seems to imply that she can identify dachshunds as such (at least in contrast to, say, terriers) and refer to dachshunds as such. It seems to imply that she also knows that there is a dachshund rather than a terrier. If she does not know the latter, then it would rather be correct to say something like "She knows that there is a small dog rather than a cat" but not "She knows that there is a dachshund rather than a cat."

This suggests that there is a further condition concerning the propositions involved in the knowledge relation. Suppose S cannot distinguish between Fs and Gs (e.g., dogs and wolves). Then there are pairs of propositions p containing F ("F-propositions"; e.g., There is a dog) and r containing G ("G-propositions": e.g., There is a wolf) such that

> replacing *F* by *G* at one or more places in *p* gives us *r* and S does not know that p rather than r, and only because S cannot distinguish between Fs and Gs.[13]

---

13 This excludes cases like the following: S does not know that Fa rather than Ga, where "F" stands for "x is a dog and Goldbach's conjecture is true" and "G" for "x is a cat and Goldbach's conjecture is true".

Let us call each member of such a pair of propositions a "defeating proposition" of the other member of the pair. We can now generalize the point made above in a very preliminary way:

> (Distinguish-a) If someone knows that p rather than q, then there is no defeating proposition r for p.

In our case above, Sue cannot distinguish between dachshunds and terriers and thus does not know that there is a dachshund in front of her rather than a terrier; thus she does not know that there is a dachshund in front of her rather than a cat. There is a defeating proposition (that there is a terrier).

What we can still say about Sue is this:

> (1) Sue knows that there is a dachshund or another kind of small dog rather than a cat.

For reasons analogous to the ones above, we also have to introduce a further condition concerning the contrast proposition. Suppose Sue cannot distinguish (under any circumstances) between cats and mountain lions. We should then say something like this about her:

> (2) Sue knows that there is a dachshund or another kind of small dog in front of her rather than a cat or another four-legged furry animal indistinguishable from it.

We thus have to add a complement to (Distinguish-a) relating to the contrast proposition instead of the known proposition. Since the contrast proposition is not known, we have to add a slightly different kind of condition here.

Suppose that S cannot distinguish between Hs and Ks (e.g., cats and mountain lions). Then there are pairs of contrast propositions q containing H ("H-propositions"; e.g., *There is a cat*) and s containing K ("K-propositions": e.g., *There is a mountain lion*) such that

> replacing H by K at one or more places in q gives us s and

> S cannot tell whether q or s, and only because S cannot distinguish between Hs and Ks.

Let us call each member of such a pair of propositions an "undermining proposition" of the other member of the pair. Again, we can say in a very preliminary way:

> (Distinguish-b) If someone knows that p rather than q, then there is no undermining proposition s for q.

If Sue cannot distinguish between cats and mountain lions and thus cannot tell whether there is a cat or a mountain lion in front of her, then she does not know that there is a dog in front of her rather than a cat. There is an undermining proposition (that it is a mountain lion).

Putting (Distinguish-a) and (Distinguish-b) together, we get

> (Distinguish★) If S knows that p rather than q, then there are no defeating propositions r for p and no undermining propositions s for q.[14]

There is, however, a huge fly in the ointment: What if r is a sceptical hypothesis?[15] By the very nature of a sceptical hypothesis, we can in principle not distinguish between an ordinary scenario (p) and a sceptical one (r). The contrastivist wants to say that we don't know that p rather than r. Given (Distinguish★), we would then have to accept that we don't know that p rather than q – for any ordinary propositions p and q. This is unacceptable to the contrastivist. An analogous point can be made about the contrast proposition and some sceptical undermining proposition. What then can the contrastivist do about this?

Insofar as (Distinguish★) seems to go into the right direction, we should not give it up but rather introduce a further restriction. Not only do we have to think about potentially defeating or undermining propositions (r, s) but also about what to admit into the group of potentially defeating or undermining propositions. In a sceptical "mood" we admit sceptical propositions into this group, in a non-sceptical mood we don't. What belongs into the classes (|R, |S) of potentially defeating or undermining propositions can vary from situation to situation. Knowledge is relative not just to contrast propositions or classes thereof but also to classes of potentially defeating or undermining propositions. This does not only concern traditional sceptical propositions but all kinds of propositions the subject cannot rule out. Hence, we have to modify (Distinguish★) in the following way:

> (Distinguish) If S knows that p rather than q, then the classes of potentially defeating or undermining propositions are restricted in such a way that

---

14 Since this is not a definition of "knowledge", there is no bad infinite regress looming here. – One could also put the point like this: If there is such a proposition r or s, then the correct knowledge ascription has the form of "S knows that (p or r) rather than q" or "S knows that p rather than (q or s)" or "S knows that (p or r) rather than (q or s)".

15 This includes traditional sceptical hypotheses like the evil demon-hypothesis as well as more ordinary hypotheses, like the hypothesis that it is not real cheddar one is eating but something that just looks and smells like it.

there are no defeating propositions r for p and no undermining propositions s for q.

This condition thus forces the contrastivist to also relativize to |R and |S, not just to contrast propositions.[16] That this further relativization is quite valuable and important becomes clearer if we look at cases. Consider Sue, again, who cannot tell dachshunds from terriers but can tell them from labradors and collies. Contrast her with Jack who is unable to tell any kind of dog from any other kind. Both can tell dogs from cats. Suppose they are both confronted with a terrier. We might, given normal circumstances, be entitled to say about both that they know there is a terrier in front of them rather than a cat. However, while "Jack knows that there is a terrier rather than a cat" is true only if "It is a labrador" is excluded from |R, "Sue knows that there is a terrier rather than a cat" is still true if "It is a labrador" is included in |R (but not if, say, "It is a dachshund" is included). And if "It is a labrador" is included in |R both in Sue's and in Jack's case, then it is true to say of Sue but false to say of Jack that they know that there is a terrier in front of them rather than a cat. Hence, the further relativization to the classes |R (and |S in Sue's and in Jack's case is needed for a full explanation of the truth conditions of the corresponding knowledge attributions.[17]

What determines |R and |S? It is tempting to give a contextualist answer here. In that case, contrastivism would have to be combined with contextualism. This also goes some way towards explaining the initial phenomenon: that it seems false to attribute knowledge to Sue that there is a dachshund in front of her rather than a cat. If "There is a terrier" is included in |R, then Sue violates (Distinguish) and the corresponding knowledge attribution is false. What if only "There is a dachshund" is included in |R? Isn't it then correct to say that she knows that there is a dachshund rather than a cat? Yes, but in many if not most or all contexts we would not want to restrict |R in this way. In these contexts, such a restriction seems inadmissible; the context puts a constraint

---

[16] |R and |S are not included in the set of contrast propositions. Suppose Sue knows that there is a dog rather than a cat. There is just one contrast proposition, namely that there is a cat. The propositions that there is a dachshund or that there is a mountain lion belong to |R and |S respectively.

[17] Given that |R is not empty, all this also amounts to a holistic condition for knowledge: In order to know that p rather than q, S also needs to know that p rather than r (for a number of instantiations of "r").

on admissible restrictions of |R (similar things hold of |S, of course). In most normal contexts we would not be willing to restrict |R in such a way that, say, "Sue knows there is a dachshund born in 2002 and from North-East Switzerland rather than a cat" comes out true. This is not to say that there could never be any contexts where we would make this restriction. The Swiss association of dachshund owners might test their member's expertise at their annual meeting by asking them to determine age and origin of the dachshunds at the meeting. And some members might be able to tell whether a given dachshund was born in 2002 or some other year, etc.

Finally, a worry: Doesn't (Distinguish) clash with (Specificity) (sec. 1)? Doesn't the latter allow for something the former excludes, namely that S knows that p rather than q while not knowing that p rather than r? No. When we say that S knows that p rather than q, we are excluding any proposition like *r* from |R. However, we are not thereby denying that there are such propositions (like *r*) – whose existence is demanded by (Specificity). The appearance of a clash between (Distinguish) and (Specifity) might well be due to not explicitly relativizing to the restricted class |R.

The contrastivist can stick to the ternary analysis of knowledge but will have to add the further relativization to classes of defeating and undermining propositions in order to keep her view plausible. The prize to pay for this is a remarkable loss of simplicity (and elegance).[18] Apart from that, the contrastivist will have to explain why some choices of such classes seem inadmissible. A contextualist story seems needed here. This would make contrastivism "impure."

4. Conclusion

Contrastivism is, I have argued, plausible only for certain types of knowledge (section 1); it has a narrower scope than its proponents seem to expect. Furthermore, the third relatum of the knowledge relation cannot be restricted to contrast propositions (section 2); acknowl-

---

18 Perhaps there is also a loss of fit with the empirical data concerning ordinary ways of talking and thinking about knowledge. However, the two additional relativizations result from theoretical constraints within contrastivism (see above). If a lack of fit with certain kinds of data results and if that is a problem, then all the worse for contrastivism.

edging this makes contrastivism lose some of its characteristic profile. Apart from that, additional relativization and contextual constraints concerning admissible propositions complicate the picture considerably (section 3).[19] To be sure, not even in conjunction do these points "refute" contrastivism. However, they point at limitations of the theory and at certain prizes it has to pay if it wants to retain plausibility.

Appendix: Contrastive Beliefs?

What about contrastivism about beliefs?[20] If belief is contrastive, then perhaps knowledge derives its contrastive nature from belief?[21] The thesis would be that belief, too, is a ternary relation between a subject, a believed proposition and a contrast proposition. Sentences of the form "S believes that p" would be elliptical for sentences of the form "S believes that p rather than q" (where "rather than q" is, of course, not part of the content of the belief). Sue might believe that she is seeing a dog rather than that she is seeing a cat but she might not believe that she is seeing a dog rather than that she is seeing a wolf. Is this unorthodox view about the nature of belief plausible?

Let us start with the uncontroversial idea that an acceptable account of belief must allow for an account of the truth conditions of beliefs. If one thinks of beliefs in the usual way – as a dyadic relation between a

---

[19] Some authors (s. Hawthorne (2004), 29; Stanley (2005), 9) hold that acceptable practical reasoning requires knowledge of its premises. Whatever the connection between knowledge and practical reasoning should turn out to be, if there is one at all, then contrastivists about knowledge will also have to tell a corresponding contrastivist story about practical reasoning (s. Sinnott-Armstrong (2004), (2006)). This project, however, is problematic for reasons I cannot go into here (but s. Baumann (2008b) for related problems concerning moral reasoning).

[20] Schaffer (2005), sec. 4 seems to assume that belief is contrastive; however, in personal communication he has denied this. Swinburne (2001), 34, very shortly remarks that belief is contrastive but does not go into details. Much more detailed is Blaauw (2004), ch.6, and recently Morton/Karjalainen (2008), 278–279).

[21] I am not assuming the false principle here that if F is L and F is necessary for G, then G is L. If knowledge should inherit its contrastive nature from belief, then the inheritance would have to be based on something else than the mere fact that belief is necessary for knowledge.

person and a proposition –, then it is easy to give truth conditions for beliefs. It works according to the following schema:

The belief that p is true iff p.

There is a principle at work here which is analogous to disquotation principles for sentences: Skip "the belief that" on the left side of "is true iff" and you get the right hand side of the bi-conditional (assuming that the meta-language contains the object-language).

How does this work in the case of contrastive belief? One might think of something like the following schema:

The belief that p rather than q is true iff p rather than q.

A principle resembling the above "disquotation" principle has been used but now with a weird result: We don't understand what kind of condition that is and what the right-hand side of the conditional means. What does it mean to say that "p rather than q"? One way to go would be to extend contrastivism to truth. Truth would be contrastive insofar as truth conditions (for sentences, beliefs, etc.) are themselves contrastive. I wouldn't choose this option: It is hard if not impossible to make any sense of this idea. Apart from all that, "rather than q" is not part of the content of the belief and for that reason one might not want to include it in the "disquotation".

Perhaps we need to modify the disquotation principle for contrastive belief in the following way:

The belief that p rather than q is true iff p.

But this also leads to several problems: The belief that p rather than q would have the same truth conditions as the belief that p rather than r.[22] The belief that the book is red rather than blue would have the same truth conditions as the belief that the book is red rather than yellow. How could these two beliefs have the same truth conditions if they are substantially different beliefs? I am not suggesting that truth conditions alone individuate beliefs. Rather, I am suggesting that quite different beliefs should not be expected to share their truth conditions.

There is also another problem. It seems possible that S has two beliefs:

The belief that p rather than q

---

[22] Thanks to Robin Cameron here.

and

The belief that q rather than r,

such that "p" and "q" cannot, of course, both be true.
Here is an example:

Fred believes that Jack stole the bike (p) rather than Jill stole the bike (q),

But it is also the case that

Fred believes that Jill stole the bike (q) rather than Jill stole the car (r).

Let us assume here that only one theft has occurred. What would be the truth conditions of these two beliefs according to the modified disquotation principle? The first belief is true iff p whereas the second belief is true iff q. So far, so good, one might say. But rather, so far so bad: p and q cannot both be true because q is a contrast proposition for p. On the other hand, the two beliefs do not seem contradictory or mutually inconsistent. But how can their truth conditions then be mutually incompatible?

The overall conclusion is clear: Even if you are a contrastivist about knowledge you shouldn't be a contrastivist about belief.

References

Baumann (2008a): Peter Baumann, "Contextualism and the Factivity Problem", in: *Philosophy and Phenomenological Research*, 580–602.
Baumann (2008b): Peter Baumann, "Some Problems for Moral Contrastivism. Comments on Sinnott-Armstrong", in: *Philosophical Quarterly*, forthcoming.
Blaauw (2004): Martijn Blaauw, *Contrastivism: Reconciling Skeptical Doubt with Ordinary Knowledge*, Ms.
DeRose (1999): Keith DeRose, "Contextualism: An Explanation and Defense", in: J. Greco/E. Sosa (eds.), *The Blackwell Guide to Epistemology*, Oxford, 187–205.
Dretske (1970): Fred Dretske, "Epistemic Operators", in: *Journal of Philosophy* 67, 1007–1022.
Dretske (1972): Fred Dretske, "Contrastive Statements", in: *Philosophical Review* 81, 411–437.
Hawthorne (2004): John Hawthorne, *Knowledge and Lotteries*, Oxford.
Johnson (2001): Bredo C. Johnson, "Contextualist Swords, Skeptical plowshares", in: *Philosophy and Phenomenological Research* 62, 385–406.
Karjalainen/Morton (2003): Antti Karjalainen/Adam Morton, "Contrastive Knowledge", in: *Philosophical Explorations* 6(2), 74–89.

Morton a. Karjalainen (2008): Adam Morton a. Antti Karjalainen, "Contrastivity and Indistinguishability", in: *Social Epistemology* 22, 271–280.
Schaffer (2005a): Jonathan Schaffer, "Contrastive Knowledge", in: T. S. Gendler/J. Hawthorne (eds.), *Oxford Studies in Epistemology* vol.1, 235–271.
Schaffer (2005b): Jonathan Schaffer, "What Shifts? Thresholds, Standards, or Alternatives?", in: G. Preyer/G. Peter (eds.), *Contextualism in Philosophy, Knowledge, Meaning, and Truth*, Oxford, 115–130.
Sinnott-Armstrong (2004): Walter Sinnott-Armstrong, "Classy Pyrrhonism", in: W. Sinnott-Armstrong (ed.), *Pyrrhonian Skepticism*, Oxford, 188–207.
Sinnott-Armstrong (2006): Walter Sinnott-Armstrong, *Moral Skepticisms*, Oxford.
Stanley (2005): Jason Stanley, *Knowledge and Practical Interests*, Oxford.
Swinburne (2001): Richard Swinburne, *Epistemic Justification*, Oxford.

Contrastive Knowledge: Reply to Baumann

Jonathan Schaffer

Baumann raises three main concerns for epistemic contrastivism[1]. These lead him to a more complicated re-conception of knowledge, involving varying numbers of argument places for varying sorts of arguments. I will argue that these complications are unneeded. The more elegant and uniform contrastive treatment can resolve all of Baumann's concerns in a straightforward way.

1. Is there non-contrastive knowledge as well?

Baumann grants that the contrastive approach is plausible for perceptual knowledge, but questions whether it is equally plausible for mathematical knowledge. So he asks: "Why shouldn't there be some kinds of knowledge which are contrastive while others aren't?"[2] I offer two replies: (i) contrastivism is equally plausible for mathematical knowledge, and (ii) if some knowledge is ternary then knowledge is a ternary relation, and so all knowledge must be ternary.[3]

1.1 Contrastivism is equally plausible for mathematical knowledge

Baumann considers the proposition that $2 + 2 = 4$, and suggests that if someone knows this, then there "does not seem to be a plausible contrast proposition around."[4] But consider the following three people:

> Ann is a young child who has only mastered the numbers 1–9 so far, and just a bit of addition. If you ask Ann what is $2 + 2$, and allow her to choose between the numbers 1–9, she will get the answer. But if you allow her to

---

1 Baumann (2008a).
2 Baumann (2008a), 192, fn. 4.
3 Schaffer (2005a), 243, fn. 11.
4 Baumann (2008a), 191.

choose between the numbers 1–20, she will get confused, and no longer know the answer.

Ben is a teenager who has mastered the natural number system, and can add any natural numbers. But he has yet to master the negative numbers. If you ask Ben what is 2 + 2, and allow him to choose among the natural numbers, he will get the answer. But if you allow him to choose with negative numbers in the mix as well, he will get confused, and no longer know the answer.

Claire is an adult professor of mathematics. If you ask her what is 2 + 2, and allow her to choose among any numbers whatsoever, she will get the answer. But she has never really thought about the philosophical issues arising with mathematical ontology. If you allow her to consider the radically skeptical idea that 2 + 2 = 4 is literally false because there are no numbers, but is only true according to the fiction of mathematics, she will be flummoxed, and no longer know the answer.

I think there are plausible contrast propositions available for Ann, Ben, and Claire. Ann knows that 2 + 2 = 4 rather than 5, she knows that 2 + 2 = 4 rather than 6, and indeed she knows that 2 + 2 = 4 rather than any other number between 1–10. But she does not know 2 + 2 = 4 rather than 11, or rather than 1000, etc. Ben knows everything that Ann knows, plus he knows that 2 + 2 = 4 rather than 11, and rather than 1000, and indeed rather than any other natural number. But he does not know that 2 + 2 = 4 rather than -4, or rather than -11, etc. Claire knows everything that Ben knows, plus she knows 2 + 2 = 4 rather than -4, and rather than -11, and indeed rather than any other number whatsoever. But she does not know that 2 + 2 = 4 rather than nothing at all because strictly speaking there are no numbers.[5]

The 2 + 2 example may be misleading just because the answer is so obvious. Consider a slightly more complicated example, such as 27 * 513 * -1. If you ask me whether 27 * 513 * -1 is -13851 or 13851, I can answer that question in a flash, just by seeing that the multiplication by -1 will yield a negative number. But if you ask me whether 27 * 510 * -1 is -13851 or -13951, I can't immediately answer that question. So I might well know that 27 * 513 * -1 is -13851 rather than 13851, without yet knowing that 27 * 513 * -1 is -13851 rather than -13951. And note that the issue here is not a lack of understanding of any of the con-

---

[5] Baumann (2008a), 191, fn. 2 briefly considers a similar suggestion, that someone might know that 2 + 2 = 4 rather than 5, but not know that 2 + 2 = 4 rather than 1/4, "due to a lack of understanding of fractions". But I am afraid that I simply do not understand Baumann's response.

cepts involved. It is just that it is harder to rule out some alternatives (such as -13951) than others (such as 13851).

Perhaps there are problems lurking for contrastivism with respect to mathematical knowledge, but I must conclude that Baumann has not revealed any problems. For all that he has shown, contrastivism seems applicable to mathematical knowledge in a straightforward way.[6]

1.2 If perceptual knowledge is ternary then mathematical knowledge must be ternary

Baumann grants—at least for the sake of the argument—that perceptual knowledge is contrastive, but still maintains that mathematical knowledge is binary. I think this conflicts with the truism that perceptual and mathematical knowledge are both *knowledge*. If there is a single relation K, then we need only ask, *how many arguments does K have?* Does it have just two arguments (subject and proposition), or does it have a third (contrast) argument? If the perceptual case teaches us that K is a ternary relation, then instances of K arising in the mathematical case must also be ternary—otherwise it is just not K anymore.

Baumann considers the claim: "(A) If some kinds of knowledge are contrastive, then all kinds of knowledge are contrastive"[7], but merely says that he does "not see any good reason to accept (A)", adding in a footnote that there "are all kinds of differences between kinds of knowledge"[8]. I think this is way too quick. Here is why (A) is plausible:

1. Perceptual and mathematical knowledge are both instances of a single relation K

---

6   Indeed, Baumann (2008b), 582, while spelling out his own contextualist view, says: "A contextualist who finds herself in a mathematics classroom might deny that a certain lay mathematician knows that Fermat's last theorem is true. At the same time, however, the contextualist has to accept that in a lay context it is true to say that our lay mathematician knows that Fermat's theorem is true, given that he has heard about Wiles' proof in the news." One would have thought that the same principle should apply to the 2+2=4 case as to Fermat's Last Theorem. In both cases, one can know the proposition in question via testimony, as long as there is no relevant alternative that raises, e.g, unresolved doubts about the accuracy of the testimony.
7   Baumann (2008a), 192.
8   Baumann (2008a), 192, fn. 2.

To think otherwise would be to posit an extremely implausible ambiguity in the term "know", and would go against Baumann's own admission that these are all "kinds of knowledge".

2. If any relation is ternary in some of its instances, then it is a ternary relation, and thereby ternary in all of its instances

Premise 2 is just a truism about the nature of relations, which can perhaps most easily be grasped by thinking of a relation *in extension,* as a set of ordered *n*-tuples. A binary relation is thus thought of as a set of ordered pairs, and a ternary relation as a set of ordered triples. If you find a relation that has in its extension an ordered triple, then it must be a ternary relation. And so:

3. So if the K relation is ternary in some of its instances, then it is a ternary relation, and thereby ternary in all of its instances

And so if perceptual knowledge is ternary, then mathematical knowledge is ternary too.

Of course the argument 1–3 is reversible. If a relation is binary in any of its instances, then it is thereby binary in all of its instances. (In general, a relation has an adicity.) Baumann notes the prospect of reversal: "[G]iven the above point about mathematics, things would rather cut the other way around: Since not all kinds of knowledge are contrastive, none are."[9] But there is a key asymmetry which I think Baumann has missed. I argued, and Baumann granted, that contrasts are *needed* to understand perceptual knowledge. To reverse the argument, Baumann would need to argue that binarity is *needed* to understand mathematical knowledge. But the most he has even tried to argue for is the much weaker claim that the contrast slot is not useful here, on grounds that if there were no need to be specific about the contrast, "contrastivism would lose its point and attractiveness"[10]. So while the argument 1–3 is in principle reversible, Baumann himself has not yet done nearly enough to reverse it.

Overall I would conclude that Baumann has not established any problem for contrastivism with respect to mathematical knowledge. And I would suggest that the more elegant and uniform contrastive treatment should be preferred over Baumann's disunified disjunctive approach. By my lights, the critic of contrastivism should either defend the

---

9 Baumann (2008a), 192.
10 Baumann (2008a), 192.

orthodox view that knowledge is binary, or at least aim for a unified alternative.

2. Should the third slot be opened to standards and other arguments?

Baumann also suggests—at least for cases of perceptual knowledge that he grants involve additional argument slots—allowing a range of arguments to fill the third slot, including not just contrasts, but also standards and practical interests: "[W]hy should only contrast propositions be able to fill the third argument place?"[11] I offer two replies: (i) Baumann's motivating case of Mary the meteorologist is easily handled by contrasts, and (ii) if some knowledge is contrastive then knowledge must be a contrastive relation, and so all knowledge must be contrastive.

2.1 Contrastivism can account for Mary the metereologist

Baumann gives the example of Mary the meteorologist, who sees the dark clouds in the morning sky and casually tells her friend that it will rain later that day (it will), but who refrains from such a claim when she arrives at the weather lab until she has conducted further checks. Baumann thinks that this is a case where "Mary knows that it will rain later that day" is true in the context of her casual discussion with her friend, but false in the context of the weather lab. I agree. He then asks: "How should one analyse this in terms of contrast propositions?" and with virtually no further discussion concludes: "What varies in the example above is not the contrast proposition but something else: standards relevant in particular contexts."[12]

This is way too quick. Indeed I think it is relatively simple to handle the case with contrasts. Perhaps the easiest way forward is to start describing which worlds Mary can rule out and which she cannot, and recover the contrasts in this way. So let $w1$-$w3$ be as follows:

$w1$: The sky is clear and it will not rain later that day
$w2$: The sky is cloudy but it will still not rain later that day, as further checks at the weather lab will reveal

---

11 Baumann (2008a), 192.
12 Baumann (2008a), 193.

w3: The sky is cloudy but it will still not rain later that day, which further checks at the weather lab will not reveal

(Think of the clouds as a weak indicator of rain, and think of the further checks at the weather lab as a strong but still imperfect indicator. Think of *w1* as the sort of world in which the clouds properly indicate, think of *w2* as the sort of world in which the clouds do not properly indicate but the weather lab checks do properly indicate, and think of *w3* as the sort of world in which neither the clouds nor the weather lab checks properly indicate.) When Mary sees the dark clouds in the morning and (using the weak indicator) casually tells her friend that it will rain later that day, Mary is in a position to rule out worlds like *w1*, but not to rule out worlds like *w2* or *w3*. After she has conducted further checks (adding the strong indicator), she will be in a position to rule out worlds like *w1* and *w2*, but still not to rule out worlds like *w3*. This is her underlying epistemic situation.

It remains to describe the underlying epistemic situation in contrastive terms. Let *q1* be the proposition associated with the set of worlds like *w1*, and let *q2* be the proposition associated with the set of worlds like *w2*. Then what Mary knows all along is that it will rain later today, rather than *q1*. And what she does not yet know—until she has conducted the further checks—is that it will rain later today, rather than *q2*. (And what she will never get to know is that it will rain later today, rather than *q3*—where *q3* is the proposition associated with the set of worlds like *w3*.) We only need to add the plausible assumption that *q1* is the relevant contrast proposition in the context of Mary's casual discussion with her friend, and that *q2* is the relevant contrast proposition in the context of the weather lab, and the contrastive account handles Mary the metereologist exactly as Baumann demanded. Or at least, if there is any real problem lurking for contrastivism, Baumann has not yet established it.

Indeed I think that turning away from contrasts and invoking standards only makes matters harder. For it is plausible enough that, in the context of Mary's casual discussion with her friend, the clouds are presupposed to be properly indicative of rain, while in the context of the weather lab such a claim is not presupposed. But why think there is such a thing as a single epistemic standard in each context? Perhaps in the context of Mary's casual discussion with her friend, claims about politics receive heavy scrutiny, while in the weather lab everyone is happy to presuppose various political views. Which context has the 'high standard' now, and which has the 'low standard'? The invocation of standards is, in my view, at best an oversimplification for the question of what range of contrasts are generally in play.[13]

2.2 If some knowledge is contrastive, then all knowledge is contrastive

If knowledge is sometimes a relation between a subject, a proposition, and a contrast, then it is in the nature of knowledge to be a contrastive relation, and so all knowledge must be contrastive.[14] Asking why we can't sometimes have a contrast argument and sometimes a standard argument is, to my mind, akin to asking, given that belief is just a binary relation between a subject and a proposition, why not open the second argument place for a standard (or for furniture, while we are at it)? Belief is not—we are supposing—just a binary relation, it is a binary relation between entities of a certain type (a subject and a proposition). A binary relation between a subject and a piece of furniture (e.g. the sitting relation that holds between me and this chair) is simply a different relation.

Baumann does consider the charge that opening up the third argument to all sorts of things would undermine the unity of knowledge, and replies that "there is no threat of theoretical disunity if one admits that the third argument slot has a disjunctive form"[15]. But I simply do not understand how going disjunctive does anything to avert disunity. Rather a mere disjunction seems the very mark of disunity. Consider what the conditions will be for knowledge, if the third slot can take various different sorts of entities:

K$sp\_$ iff

(i) the blank is filled by a contrast propostion, and ... [*insert account of contrastive knowledge here*]

13　Cf. Schaffer (2005b) for further arguments against the invocation of standards, and in favor of contrasts as a unified source of contextual variability in knowledge ascriptions. Though Baumann never says what he means by "standards", so it is possible that my arguments do not apply to his view.

14　In §1.2 I argued that if some knowledge is ternary, then all knowledge is ternary. This section makes the further claim that if the third argument is a contrast in some instances of knowledge, then it is a contrast in all instances of knowledge.

15　Baumann (2008a), 193, fn. 6.

(ii) the blank is filled by an epistemic standard, and ... [*insert account of standard-relative knowledge here*]
(iii) the blank is filled by practical interests, and... [*insert account of interest-relative knowledge here*]
(iv) ...

Actually things are even less unified for Baumann, since he allows that there are also knowledge relations with two, three, four, and more argument places[16]. So it will look more like:

$Ksp\_\_\_\_$ ... iff

(i) none of the blanks are filled, and ... [*insert account of binary knowledge here*]
(ii) the first blank is filled by a contrast proposition, none of the remaining blanks are filled, and ... [*insert account of contrastive knowledge here*]
(iii) the first blank is filled by an epistemic standard, none of the remaining blanks are filled, and ... [*insert account of standard-relative knowledge here*]
(iv) the first blank is filed by practical interests, none of the remaining blanks are filled, and ... [*insert account of interest-relative knowledge here*]
(v) ...
(vi) the first blank is filled by a contrast proposition, the second blank is filled by an epistemic standard, none of the remaining blanks are filled, and ... [*insert account of contrastive and standard-relative knowledge here*]
(vii) the first blank is filled by a contrast proposition, the second blank is filled by practical interests, none of the remaining blanks are filled, and ...[*insert account of contrastive and interest-relative knowledge here*]
(viii) ...
(ix) the first blank is filled by a contrast proposition, the second blank is filled by an epistemic standard, the third blank is filled by practical interests, none of the remaining blanks are filled, and ... [*insert account of contrastive, standard-relative, and interest-relative knowledge here*]
(x) ...

---

16 Baumann (2008a), 193, fn. 6.

If ever there was a disunified and inelegant approach, here it is. And merely disjoining all these conditions seems of little help. Again, the contrastivist is offering an elegant and uniform picture of a single ternary relation, receiving a single unified account. Surely this is preferable.[17]

3. Should we worry about 'defeating' and 'undermining' possibilities?

Baumann finally suggests—at least for those cases of knowledge that he would allow involve a contrastive relation—that a fourth argument needs to be added, to handle what he calls 'defeating' and 'undermining' possibilities. He concludes that adding such a fourth argument would be bad news for the contrastivist, since: "The [price] to pay for this is a remarkable loss of simplicity (and elegance)"[18]. I find this charge astounding given Baumann's own massively disjunctive position, but will let this pass. I offer two more substantive replies: (i) Baumann's motivating case of Sue at the zoo is not compelling, and (ii) The case of Sue at the zoo can be accommodated within a ternary, contrastive theory, should this be desired. Though it will pay to first spell out Baumann's worry in more detail.

---

17 It may be that Baumann no longer holds this massively disjunctive view. Or at least, when spelling out his own positive contextualist view elsewhere, he (2008b), 589 claims to "take 'knowledge' as referring not to a binary but to a ternary relation between a person, a proposition, and a standard (or whatever else is responsible for the context-dependency)." Here he is halfway to contrastivism. Contrastivism just adds the specific claim that what is responsible for the context dependency is (not a standard but) a contrast. Baumann notes that at this point he is in agreement with me about ternicity, but without further elaboration adds (2008b), 589, fn. 20: "I do not want to endorse Schaffer's 'contrastivism' here, though." At this point the *only* remaining difference Baumann's more considered view and my own is whether what is responsible for context dependence is a standard or a contrast. I would just add that I defend the use of contrasts over standards in some detail in Schaffer (2005b), which arguments Baumann does not consider.
18 Baumann (2008a), 197.

3.1 What Baumann is worried about

Baumann introduces us to Sue, who has a hard time distinguishing between small dogs like dachshunds and terriers, but has no trouble distinguishing a small dog from a cat. Sue sees a dachshund, and—by contrastivist lights—is in a position to know that the beast is a dachshund rather than a cat, but not that the beast is a dachshund rather than a terrier. Then she sees a terrier, and—again by contrastivist lights—is in a position to know that the beast is a terrier rather than a cat, but not that the beast is a terrier rather than a dachshund. All this sounds reasonable enough to me, but according to Baumann it is "abominable and incorrect"[19], since: "It seems false to say that [Sue] knows out of the contrast class [dachshund; cat] that there is a dachshund.

Baumann then adds that an analogous issue arises on the contrast side of the ledger. Imagine that Sue also cannot tell a cat from a mountain lion. Then he thinks it false to say that Sue knows that the beast is a dog rather than a cat—at most what is true is that Sue knows that the beast is a dog rather than either a cat or a mountain lion.

He takes all this to suggest that we add the following condition for knowledge:

> (Distinguish★) If S knows that p rather than q, then there are no defeating propositions r for p and no undermining propositions s for q.

(Where a 'defeating' proposition r is an alternative to p that s cannot rule out, and an 'undermining proposition' s is an alternative to q that s cannot rule out.) To my mind this move is completely misguided, especially for someone who (like Baumann) has already endorsed a contrastivist treatment of perceptual knowledge. For *Distinguish*★ effectively requires s to eliminate every single alternative to p, whether or not that alternative is relevant. *Distinguish*★ effectively takes us back to Unger's skeptical idea that knowledge requires that elimination of every possible alternative[20].

Baumann then notices that there is "a huge fly in the ointment"[21] with skeptical hypotheses, and suggests that the contrastivist should invoke context to restrict the range of 'defeating' and 'undermining' propositions in play, as per:

---

19 Baumann (2008a), 194.
20 Cf. Unger (1975).
21 Baumann (2008a), 195.

(Distinguish) If S knows that p rather than q, then the classes of potentially defeating or undermining propositions are restricted in such a way that there are no defeating propositions r for p and no undermining propositions s for q.[22]

Distinguish is effectively a standard version of contextualist relevant alternatives theory. Effectively Baumann has undone all the work of contrastivity via the fully skeptical *Distinguish**, and then tried to recover epistemic sanity through the contextualist approach found in *Distinguish*.

Indeed I would have thought that Baumann should, by his own lights, reject *Distinguish*. *Distinguish* licenses—in certain contexts—the very claim about Sue that Baumann had earlier disparaged as "abominable and incorrect". If we are in a context in which the beast's being a dachshund is the only relevant small dog possibility, then "Sue knows that the beast is a dachshund rather than a cat" will come out true.[23]

3.2 Is there a worry with Sue at the zoo?

I do not wish to quibble over intuitions, but I must say that nothing here sounds "abominable and incorrect" to me. Consider Sue on the first occasion when there is a dachshund in front of her, and consider the question: "Is the beast a dachshund or a cat?" Clearly Sue can get the right answer, and clearly she can do so in an epistemically proper way (on the basis of her evidence, without any guessing). So I think it is plausible to say that she does know the answer to the question— she knows whether the beast is a dachshund or a cat. And that is just to say that she knows that the beast is a dachshund rather than a cat. Now consider Sue on the second occasion when there is a terrier in front of her, and consider the question "Is the beast a terrier or a cat?" Again Sue can get the right answer, in a proper way. So likewise I think it is plausible to say that she does know the answer to the ques-

---

22 Baumann (2008a), 196.
23 Baumann (2008a), 196 sees the worry: "What if only 'There is a dachshund' is included in |R? Isn't it then correct to say that she knows that there is a dachshund rather than a cat?" But his (2008a), 196 response seems non-responsive: "Yes but in many if not most or all contexts we would not want to restrict |R in this way." Why does it matter if in many contexts we do not restrict the relevant alternatives in this way? Isn't Baumann's theory still delivering a verdict he had previously pronounced "abominable and incorrect" in the contexts where we do restrict the relevant alternatives in this way?

tion—she knows whether the beast is a terrier or a cat. And that is just to say that she knows that the beast is a terrier rather than a cat. I think this is all perfectly fine. Baumann offers nothing to buttress his intuitions, so I do not think he has established any problem for contrastivism.

If there is a problem here, I think it is what I had earlier called *the problem of the giveaway question*[24]. Consider Sue's brother Tom, who cannot tell any small animals apart whatsoever, but at least can tell that the beast in front of him (which happens to be a terrier) is not an elephant. Does Tom know that the beast is a terrier rather than an elephant? Alternatively, given that the beast is in fact a terrier, does Tom know whether the beast is a terrier or an elephant? Some have the intuition that Tom does not know that the beast is a terrier rather than an elephant, because Tom lacks positive evidence for the beast being a terrier, having only negative evidence against the alternative that the beast is an elephant.

But I am not convinced. Consider the following parallel example, given by Johnsen[25]. Imagine that—unbeknownst to Tom—Milan Kundera is now in Ventimiglia. Might Tom at least know that Kundera is in Ventimiglia rather than *sitting on Tom's lap*? My intuitions line up with Johnsen's. Tom is at least in a position to know this. I don't mean to insist that this is the right verdict, only that it is not obviously wrong.

3.3 If there is a worry, can it be resolved within a contrastive theory?

If your intuitions are like mine, you won't think that there is any real problem arising for contrastivism with Sue at the zoo. But if your intuitions are like Baumann's, there are still at least three modifications you might consider to the account I offer of contrastive knowledge, all of which would preserve the elegant and uniform K*spq* structure, while providing a better fit for your intuitions.

First, the contrastivist might seek to expand the contrast argument *q*, by allowing that there can be more to the contrast argument than is made explicit in the "rather than" clause. One plausible implementation of this idea is to treat the contrast argument as disjoining the material explicit in the "rather than" clause with contextually implicit material. Then Baumann's claim "Sue knows that the beast is a dachshund rather

---

24 Schaffer (2005a), 257.
25 Cf. Johnsen (2001), 405.

than a cat"—expressed in a context in which the beast's being a terrier has evidently been made relevant—will require K <Sue, that the beast is a dachshund, that the beast is a cat or a terrier>. And since by hypothesis Sue cannot tell a dachshund from a terrier, the contrastivist will thereby get the result Baumann demands: the claim will be false. Likewise "Sue knows that the beast is a dog rather than a cat"—expressed in a context in which the beast's being a mountain lion has evidently been made relevant—will require K <Sue, that the beast is a dog, that the beast is a cat or a mountain lion>. So the mountain lion possibility will come into play after all.[26] And likewise Johnsen's claim "Tom knows that Kundera is in Ventimiglia rather than sitting on Tom's lap"—expressed in a context in which locales all over the world are evidently relevant—will require K <Tom, that Kundera is in Ventimiglia, that Kundera is on Tom's lap or in any other locale>. This too will be false.[27]

Second, and relatedly, the contrastivist might achieve the same effect, not by expanding the contrast argument but instead by expanding what knowledge requires. The idea is to say that the subject must not only eliminate the contrast but must also eliminate further possibilities in some (perhaps contextually variable) halo surrounding the contrast. This is a second strategy for getting a wider range of error possibilities into play, differing from the first only in the details of implementation.

Third, the contrastivist might require more from the subject, evidentially speaking, than just eliminating the contrast. The contrastivist might additionally require some level of positive evidence in favor of the known proposition p[28]. Then for Tom to know that Kundera is in Ventimiglia rather than on his lap, Tom would not merely have to eliminate the prospect that Kundera is on his lap, Tom would also

---

26 This has the result that the original claim ("Sue knows that the beast is a dog rather than a cat") comes out true, which strikes me as the right result.

27 Baumann ultimately suggests—albeit for different reasons—that the contrastivist appeal to contextual factors to resolve these cases. Thus he (2008a), 197 concludes the section with: "A contextualist story seems needed here. This would make contrastivism 'impure'." I am afraid I simply have no idea what the problem is. The contrastivist all along appealed to contextual factors to set the contrast for simple binary knowledge ascriptions like "Moore knows that he has hands". So if the only price of resolving Baumann's worries is to include a contextualist aspect, this is a price the contrastivist has already paid in full.

28 Cf. Schaffer (2005a), 258.

need some positive evidence for thinking that Kundera was actually in Ventimiglia—which he by hypothesis lacks.

Overall, it is essential to separate the general contrastivist idea that knowledge is a ternary relation with a contrast argument, from any more specific account of what contrastive knowledge would consist in. Consider the following foolish argument against the idea that knowledge is a binary relation: the account of binary knowledge as justified true belief fails, therefore knowledge is not a binary relation. The argument from the failure of a specific account of contrastive knowledge to the denial of contrastivism would be equally foolish. The preceding three ideas illustrate that there are a wide range of options open to the contrastivist, with respect to Sue at the zoo. The critic of contrastivism should seek an *in principle* problem for any account with a contrastive form.

I conclude that Baumann has not yet established any problem for contrastivism, on this or any other point. I do not mean to suggest that contrastivism is problem-free, but only to encourage the critic of contrastivism to push further.[29]

References

Baumann (2008a): Peter Baumann, "Contrastivism Rather than Something Else? On the Limits of Epistemic Contrastivism", in: *Erkenntnis* 69, 189–200.

Baumann (2008b): Peter Baumann, "Contextualism and the Factivity Problem", in: *Philosophy and Phenomenological Research* 76, 580–602.

Johnsen (2001): Bredo Johnsen, "Contextualist Swords, Skeptical Plowshares", in: *Philosophy and Phenomenological Research* 62, 385–406.

Schaffer (2005a): Jonathan Schaffer, "Contrastive Knowledge", in: *Oxford Studies in Epistemology* 1, 235–71.

Schaffer (2005b): Jonathan Schaffer, "What Shifts, Thresholds, Standards, or Alternatives?", in: Preyer/Peter (eds.) *Contextualism in Philosophy*, Oxford, 115–30.

Unger (1975): Peter Unger, *Ignorance: A Case for Scepticism*, Oxford.

---

29 Thanks to Peter Baumann for helpful discussion.

PS: Response to Schaffer's Reply

Peter Baumann

Jonathan Schaffer makes several interesting replies (see above in this volume) to my 2008a (see the preceding paper). Many thanks! Schaffer aptly defends his own elegant and sophisticated version of contrastivism. In the end, I am not convinced that he is right (though I would put some things differently now, but these are all minor points). In the following I will respond to Schaffer's reply. I will be brief and directly comment upon Schaffer's reply without much of a recapitulation of what he is saying. I will also leave out some less important details and disagreements between us.

1. Contrastive Mathematical Knowledge?

Schaffer presents three cases which are supposed to show that there are cases of contrastive mathematical knowledge.[1] One important trait of all these cases – which Schaffer does not mention – is that they all deal with contrast propositions beyond the grasp of the subject. This is an important characteristic of these cases because the intuition that there is contrastive knowledge in these cases loses a lot if not all of its appeal if we drop the assumption that some of the contrast propositions are beyond the grasp of the subject. But aren't there always propositions which are beyond the grasp of the subject, especially in mathematics? Sure, but what Schaffer needs here is the stronger claim that there are always (in every context) ungraspable (for the subject) propositions included in the set of contrast propositions. This, however, is implausible and has not been argued for by Schaffer.

Furthermore, it seems uncontroversial that while a subject can know that a given proposition is true she cannot know that proposition without understanding or being able to grasp the proposition. If one construes "knowledge" along contrastive ideas, then it seems very plausible to say that the contrast propositions also have to be graspable by the sub-

---

1 See Schaffer (2011), sec. 1.1.

ject. Otherwise, we would have to accept knowledge attributions like the following one "Jack, a four year old kid, knows that there is a dog in front of him rather than a canis lupus" even if Jack has no clue what words like "canis lupus" (or even "wolf") mean. I should add here, though, that I am not sure how seriously one can take such linguistic intuitions in the case of rather unusual contrastive constructions involving the verb "to know".[23]

2. Unity of Knowledge?

Schaffer stresses[4] that if perceptual knowledge is ternary then mathematical knowledge must be ternary, too: They are both knowledge. Given that I do hold, according to Schaffer, that perceptual knowledge is ternary I should also hold that mathematical knowledge is ternary. But I don't.

First, I did not mean to commit myself in 2008a to contrastivism about perceptual knowledge[5] neither did I try to refute it. Rather, I wanted to be as charitable as possible to contrastivism and simply not as-

---

2   Schaffer (Schaffer (2011), fn.1) says that he does not understand a remark in fn.2 of my 2008a; I hope the remarks above also help with that. – Schaffer's third case raises tricky and controversial questions about ontology. Even if one accepts the legitimacy of the philosophical doubt whether there "really" are numbers, it is not clear where that would lead us here. Schaffer remarks about his third case: "But she does not know that $2 + 2 = 4$ rather than nothing at all because strictly speaking there are no numbers." (Schaffer (2011). I am really not sure what this could mean. Does the subject not know that $2 + 2 = 4$ rather than $2 + 2 = $ nothing at all? But what would that mean? Or does the subject not know that $2 + 2 = 4$ rather than nothing at all? But "nothing at all" does not express a proposition. Perhaps Schaffer wants to express the idea that, according to some, mathematical propositions lack truth values. But then this kind of case won't help Schaffer – given that knowledge is factive – to establish that there are cases of contrastive knowledge. – A holist about belief might suggest that at least in Schaffer's first two cases and certainly in the first case one should doubt whether the subject has any mathematical knowledge, given how impoverished her understanding of the whole system of mathematics is. I don't want to endorse this objection here but just mention it.
3   Schaffer does not go into my remarks about the non-contrastive nature of logical knowledge or of linguistic and conceptual knowledge (see Baumann (2008a), 191–2). It is not obvious what Schaffer could say about these cases.
4   See Schaffer (2011), sec.1.2.
5   Against Schaffer (2011).

sume that perceptual knowledge is not contrastive.[6] I wanted to see where one gets from a charitable starting point; what Schaffer calls "Baumann's disunified disjunctive approach"[7] is not my own approach but rather what one ends up with, according to me, if one wants to be a contrastivist.

Second, even if one accepted contrastive knowledge attributions in some cases, this would not entail that the contrastive aspect cannot be eliminated and the contrastive attribution replaced by an equivalent non-contrastive one. Contrastivist aspects of knowledge-attributions might only express superficial features of some knowledge-sentences.

Third, and more importantly, it is not obvious whether knowledge really has the kind of unity Schaffer thinks it has. Why should one not be a pluralist about "knowledge" in the sense of holding the following view: Some of what we call "knowledge" is a ternary relation but some might not be a ternary relation?[8] I am not defending pluralism here but simply want to state that it is not off the table. A view like Wittgenstein's family resemblance view of (some) concepts can – whether one agrees with it or not (I don't) – inspire the thought that the relations which we call "knowledge" might differ in adicity.[9] Why not? Such a view is not out of the question. Does contrastivism have to imply anything concerning the unity of knowledge? I think contrastivists should not make their case depend too much on such controversial general claims.[10]

Schaffer later[11] makes a parallel point about contrastivity: If some knowledge is contrastive, then all knowledge is contrastive. The remarks just made apply here too, *mutatis mutandis*.[12]

---

6 Hence, I have no business arguing from the binarity of mathematical knowledge to the binarity of all knowledge (see Schaffer (2011).
7 Schaffer (2011).
8 My fn.4 in Baumann (2008a) is, as Schaffer correctly points out (Schaffer (2011), misleading; it should have been formulated in terms of "what we call 'knowledge'".
9 Wittgenstein did not comment upon the formal characteristics of a given concept, like the concept of a game. However, this disanalogy does not matter here where "inspiration" is the issue.
10 Schaffer remarks that "surely" a unified account "is preferable" (Schaffer (2011). Sure, but not if there are good reasons to think there is no unity of the kind Schaffer assumes there is.
11 See Schaffer (2011), sec. 2.2.
12 I don't see how Schaffer can say that an account with more than 3 argument places is "even less unified" (Schaffer (2011) than an account with a disjunctive

3. Mary: Standards or Contrasts?

I also disagree with Schaffer about Mary, the meteorologist: Variability of what I call "standards" is not just variability of sets of contrast propositions. Schaffer says about Mary before she gets to the lab: "Mary is in a position to rule out worlds like $w1$, but not to rule out worlds like $w2$ or $w3$."[13] Later and after checks in the lab, he continues, "she will be in a position to rule out worlds like $w1$ and $w2$, but still not to rule out worlds like $w3$." Mary's epistemic situation has changed relevantly by doing the checks in the lab – she is acquiring more or better evidence. But what should we say about her before the checks? Can she rule out $w2$ ("The sky is cloudy but it will still not rain later that day, as further checks at the weather lab will reveal")? Suppose her evidence is evidence of a significant probabilistic relation between these kinds of clouds and rain later (P(rain/clouds)=3/4). Suppose Mary says to her friend outside the lab: "I have seen these clouds many times and I know that they bring rain in three out of four cases; I don't need the lab to tell you that. So, cancel the picnic!" Can Mary rule out $w2$? It depends on whether a probability of .75 for a proposition is high enough for ruling out some incompatible proposition. Mary's collaborators in the lab might say "No, sorry, .75 is not good enough" while Mary's friend outside the lab might say "yes, sure, no prob". In other words, what varies with the context is not just the set of relevant contrast propositions but also the standards for what counts as "ruling out". Perhaps Schaffer can think of a way to put the latter in terms of the former but I must confess that I don't see how that could be done. Some contextualists (DeRose, for instance) do indeed explain difference of epistemic standards in terms of the different sets of possible alternatives the subjects is expected to rule out. But I don't see any reason why one should restrict oneself to this view. The Mary-example suggests that there is more going on than just the expansion and contraction of contrast sets.[14]

---

third slot. Given that the 3rd, 4th etc. argument places need not be ordered (why should they?), both ways of representing the additional complexity only seem to amount to notational differences.

13 Schaffer (2011), sec.2.1.

14 Schaffer quotes (Schaffer (2011), fn.2) a passage from my 2008b where I seem to admit that at least some mathematical knowledge is contrastive. I don't see this at all, given that the quoted passage concerns contextually variable standards and not contrast propositions. – I agree with Schaffer that one should not assume that there is always only one standard for each context. But neither do I see

4. Further Relativization?

In sec.3 of his reply, Schaffer deals with my argument that the contrastivist should also take the relativity to sets of defeating and undermining possibilities into account.[15] Again, I won't recapitulate here much of what I said and what Schaffer said I said. Let me rather comment upon what I take to be Schaffer's main reply in sec.3.2. In my example, Sue is confronted with a dachshund which she cannot distinguish from a terrier while she can distinguish it from a cat. I argued that it is abominable and incorrect to say that Sue "knows that the beast is a dachshund rather than a cat". Schaffer brings in the question "Is the beast a dachshund or a cat?"[16] and continues: "(...) it is plausible to say that she does know the answer to the question – she knows whether the beast is a dachshund or a cat."[17] I don't agree. Sure, if we assume that Sue has been explicitly asked "Is this a dachshund or a cat?", then it would be reasonable for her to assume that by asking this question the questioner conveys (by implicature, for instance) the information that it is either a dachshund or a cat. So, the asking of the question gives Sue more information (given that she can trust the questioner as a source of information). Under these circumstances, she does know that the beast is a dachshund and not (rather than) a cat. The point, however, is that it is still as odd as before to say this if we don't include the asking of such an explicit question in the scenario. The scenarios I discussed in 2008a did not include this addition. I think therefore that the motivation for introducing an additional complexity and adding a relativity to defeating or undermining propositions remains strong.

---

how that is relevant here nor do I think that I am committed to such an "oversimplification" (see Schaffer (2011).

15 In his sec.3.1 Schaffer criticizes my introduction of (Distinguish*) as "misguided" (Schaffer (2011)) and points to the tension between this principle and the later (Distinguish). I think he is simply misunderstanding the role of (Distinguish*) here: As I say in 2008a, 194–6, (Distinguish*) is not something I want to defend but merely a stepping stone on the way to a more adequate principle, namely (Distinguish). – On fn.6 Schaffer asks why it matters that in many contexts we do not restrict the set of defeating propositions |R in a certain way (only including "There is a dachshund")? Well, it matters because in those contexts the subject could not be said to know that there is a dachshund rather than a cat. And this point motivates the introduction of |R in the first place.

16 Schaffer (2011).
17 Schaffer (2011).

Schaffer ends[18] with some very interesting proposals for the modification of his contrastivist account, in the hope or expectation that such modifications might dispel the worries that motivated my introduction of defeating and undermining propositions in the first place. I am not quite sure how happy Schaffer himself would be with these kinds of modifications. The first one seems to introduce the kind of disunity Schaffer wants to avoid by allowing for disjunctive (endlessly disjunctive?) contrast propositions. The second proposal goes into the same direction by adding further requirements for knowledge. All this is fine with me but I don't see this as a theoretical alternative to the relativization I propose: It makes the same point in a different way.

Similar things hold for Schaffer's third proposed modification – requiring "some level of positive evidence in favor of the known proposition p"[19]. In addition, this proposal should be worrisome for the contrastivist: Don't evidentialist accounts of knowledge bring the risk to make the contrastivist element obsolete?

5. Conclusion

Towards the end, Schaffer remarks: "The argument from the failure of a specific account of contrastive knowledge, to the denial of contrastivism, would be … foolish."[20] I agree. But who wouldn't?[21] In the end, Schaffer and I agree on many things but we also disagree on some important things: on the scope and necessary complexity of the view. Schaffer holds that contrastivism is universal and simple while I hold that it is restricted and quite complex. At some points, our "intuitions" seem to diverge[22] but I hope our disagreement does not just boil down to divergent inclinations to say this or rather that under such and such circumstances.

---

18 See Schaffer (2011), sec.3.3.
19 Schaffer (2011).
20 Schaffer (2011).
21 On, fn.8 Schaffer states that he has no idea why making contrastivism "impure" by adding contextualist elements should be a problem. Well, the problem is that "pure contrastivism" (Baumann (2008a), 190) would be incomplete without the addition of contextualist elements. Schaffer might be a contextualist contrastivist already but others aren't: Sinnott-Armstrong, for instance, is a non-contextualist contrastivist (s. Sinnott-Armstrong (2004)).
22 See sec.3.2, 3.3.

References

Baumann (2008a): Peter Baumann, "Contextualism and the Factivity Problem", in: *Philosophy and Phenomenological Research*, 580–602.

Schaffer (2011): Jonathan Schaffer, "Contrastive Knowledge: Reply to Baumann", in: S. Tolksdorf (ed.), *Conceptions of Knowledge*, Berlin/New York.

Sinnott-Armstrong (2004): Walter Sinnott-Armstrong, "Classy Pyrrhonism", in: W. Sinnott-Arnstrong (ed.), *Pyrrhonian Skepticism*, Oxford, 188–207.

Chapter Three
*Challenging Justification –
The Nature and Structure of Justification*

Verantwortlichkeit und Verlässlichkeit*[1]

Michael Williams

1. Ich werde zwei erkenntnistheoretische Ansätze diskutieren, den Responsibilismus und den Reliabilismus. Obwohl beide wesentliche Einsichten in unsere Begriffe von Wissen und Rechtfertigung gewinnen, werden sie häufig als fundamentale Gegensätze betrachtet, was nicht überrascht, da sich die Philosophen die Zähne daran ausbeißen, sie unter einen Hut zu bringen. Wie dieses Problem entsteht und wie es zu lösen ist, sind die zentralen Fragen dieses Artikels.

Der Responsibilismus (unter dessen Begriff ich auch einige, wenngleich nicht alle Fassungen der „Tugendtheorie" subsumiere) geht von einem deontologischen Ansatz zu Wissen und Rechtfertigung aus. Philosophen, die sich zu dieser Schule zählen, betonen die Bedeutung von „Verantwortlichkeit" in einem zweifachen Sinne. Wir sind für das, was wir glauben, verantwortlich im Sinne von *rechenschaftspflichtig*. Der Gegenbegriff zu „verantwortlich" ist hier *nicht verantwortlich*. Aber um gerechtfertigt zu sein, das zu glauben, was wir glauben, müssen wir mit unseren Überzeugungen auf eine epistemisch verantwortliche Weise umgehen. Der Gegenbegriff zu „verantwortlich" ist hier *unverantwortlich*. Diese beiden Arten der Verantwortlichkeit sind auf offenkundige Weise miteinander verknüpft: Wir sind für unsere Überzeugungen genau deshalb rechenschaftspflichtig, weil wir die Pflicht haben, mit ihnen angemessen umzugehen. Responsibilisten zufolge schließen Wissen und Rechtfertigung die Einhaltung angemessener Maßstäbe epistemischen Verhaltens ein, wobei sich die Einhaltung dieser Maßstäbe nicht auf regelkonformes Verhalten beschränkt, sondern beinhaltet, dass man diese

---

* Originally published in *Philosophical Papers* 37 (2008), pp. 1–26. Reprinted and translated by permission of the publisher, Taylor & Francis.

1 Eine Fassung dieses Artikels wurde auf dem Symposium „Expanding Epistemology" des Treffens der APA Pacific Division im März 2009 vorgetragen. Die anderen Teilnehmer des Symposiums waren Guy Axtell, Robert Brandom und Miranda Fricker. Eine etwas andere Fassung wurde bei einer Konferenz zur Philosophie Keith Lehrers im Juni 2007 in Porto Alegre, Brasilien, vorgestellt. Ich danke den anderen Teilnehmern und vor allem meinen Kommentatoren Ted Poston und Thomas Senor.

Regeln *anerkennt* oder sich nach ihnen *richtet*. (Kantisch gesprochen erfordert epistemische Verantwortlichkeit mehr als ein Handeln *in Übereinstimmung mit* einer Regel: Es erfordert ein Handeln *um einer* Regel *willen*.)

Diese Betonung eines bewussten Umgangs mit Überzeugungen hat bedeutsame Konsequenzen. Erstens erfordert er, dass man weiß, was es mit den eigenen Überzeugungen auf sich hat. Gerechtfertigt sein schließt also ein, dass man weiß (oder eine gerechtfertige Meinung darüber hat), weshalb man etwas glaubt. Oder es beinhaltet zumindest, dass man *in der Lage* ist, dies zu wissen. Eine Konsequenz davon ist, dass gerechtfertigt sein wesentlich damit verknüpft ist, die eigenen Überzeugungen rechtfertigen zu können, indem man *Gründe für sie gibt*. Deshalb geht man im Allgemeinen davon aus, dass responsibilistische Ansätze in der Erkenntnistheorie „internalistischer" Natur sind. So charakterisiert, zieht der Internalismus keinen *Subjektivismus* nach sich: Gründe und Belege betreffen nicht nur das, was „in uns" vorgeht. Es ist jedoch nicht zu leugnen, dass ein großer Teil der traditionellen Erkenntnistheorie eine Tendenz zum Subjektivismus hatte, und dieser Tatsache müssen wir Rechnung tragen.

Die traditionellen Erkenntnistheorien waren überwiegend responsibilistisch und deshalb in ihrer theoretischen Orientierung internalistisch. Aber seit etwa 1960 trat der Reliabilismus als eine starke Gegenbewegung zu dieser Tradition hervor. Dem Reliabilismus zufolge ergibt eine wahre Überzeugung Wissen, wenn sie durch das Wirken eines hinreichend zuverlässigen kognitiven Prozesses erworben und aufrechterhalten wurde. Solche Ansätze zur Erklärung von Wissen werden manchmal für nichtrechtfertigend gehalten. Das ist zutreffend, wenn wir Rechtfertigung als etwas ansehen, das wesentlich mit der Fähigkeit der Begründung verbunden ist. Wenn wir eine gerechtfertigte Überzeugung aber als eine Überzeugung auffassen, die auf eine bestimmte Weise „epistemisch angemessen" ist, können wir die Frage, worin epistemische Angemessenheit besteht, offenlassen. Reliabilisten werden sagen, dass die epistemische Angemessenheit einer Überzeugung davon abhängig ist, dass die Prozesse, die sie hervorbringen und erhalten, *de facto* zuverlässig sind, aber nicht davon, dass der Glaubende diese Zuverlässigkeit erkennt oder von seiner Fähigkeit, *irgendwelche* Gründe zu geben. Einem radikalen Reliabilisten zufolge erfordert Wissen, dass p, nicht einmal, *dass man in der Lage ist*, zu wissen, woher man weiß.

Obwohl reliabilistische Auffassungen bereits in der Spätantike vorweggenommen wurden, darf ihre Wiederbelebung in jüngster Zeit als eine Revolution in der Erkenntnistheorie gelten. Verschiedene Faktoren machen den Reliabilismus für zeitgenössische Erkenntnistheoretiker attraktiv. Zwei dieser Faktoren sind für die Belange dieses Artikels jedoch besonders wichtig.

Erstens liefert der Reliabilismus eine Erklärung dafür, warum wir an Wissen und Rechtfertigung interessiert sind, unter anderem an Rechtfertigung, die die spezielle Form der Begründung von Überzeugungen aufweist. Um mit den sich ständig verändernden Umständen in der uns umgebenden Welt zurechtzukommen, müssen wir wahre Überzeugungen ausbilden und Irrtümer vermeiden. Rechtfertigende, im Sinne von (in Bezug auf Wahrheit) verlässliche Methoden, sind die Mittel zu diesem Zweck. Wenn wir uns bei der Bildung unserer Überzeugungen von empirischen Belegen leiten lassen, dann handelt es sich um einen *speziellen Fall* einer wahrheitsdienlichen Methode, nicht um ein wesentliches Merkmal von Wissen. Zweitens erscheinen jene traditionellen Erkenntnistheoretiker, die großen Wert darauf legen, dass wir für unsere Überzeugungen Gründe haben, hyperintellektuell. Selbst bei Menschen scheint ein Großteil des Wissens aus dem unreflektierten Gebrauch elementarer kognitiver Vermögen zu kommen, zum Beispiel aus der Wahrnehmung. Diese Vermögen liefern auch dann Wissen, wenn man sie nicht besonders gut versteht. Wie das Beispiel des Wissens von Tieren zeigt, müssen sie überhaupt nicht verstanden werden. Dies führt zu einer zentralen Schwierigkeit für den Responsibilismus, dass nämlich Glauben im Allgemeinen etwas Unwillkürliches ist. Glauben ist nicht etwas, wofür wir uns entscheiden: Es *geschieht* einfach. Wenn dem aber so ist, dann ist der Responsibilist auf dem Holzweg, wenn er Glauben als eine Handlung (oder vielleicht als eine Art von Handlung) auffasst, mit dem Ergebnis, dass seine deontologische Redeweise völlig deplaziert ist.[2]

Viele Philosophen betrachten Wahrheitsdienlichkeit als Kennzeichen *epistemischer* Rechtfertigung. Eine Überzeugung, die in pragmatischer Hinsicht nützlich ist oder ein gutes Licht auf den Charakter der Person wirft, mag eine Art von Rechtfertigung besitzen, aber sie besitzt keine epistemische Rechtfertigung. Falls ein Responsibilist dies akzeptiert,

---

2   Ein dritter Grund für die Popularität des Reliabilismus ist, dass er gut zu den naturalistischen Neigungen eines Großteils der heutigen anglophonen Philosophen passt. Reliabilisten glauben gewöhnlich, dass Wissen seiner Art nach bei Menschen und Tieren gleich ist. Der Reliabilismus erlaubt uns also, Wissen als „natürliches Phänomen" anzusehen. Zur Verteidigung der Vorstellung von Wissen als einem natürlichen Phänomen vgl. Kornblith (2002). Ich diskutiere Kornbliths erkenntnistheoretische Ansichten in Schantz (2005).

übernimmt er automatisch die Verpflichtung, Verantwortlichkeit mit Verlässlichkeit zu verbinden. Reliabilisten werden jedoch die Auffassung vertreten, sie würden dadurch, dass sie eine wesentliche Verbindung zwischen Wissen und der Rechtfertigung durch Gründe leugneten, von einer entsprechenden Verpflichtung entbunden. Das ist der Schachzug, gegen den ich mich wehren möchte. Denn wenn man ihn macht, verliert man den wesentlich *normativen* Charakter aus den Augen, den die Begriffe epistemischer Bewertung haben, zumindest dann, wenn wir sie auf uns selbst anwenden. Es ist unbestreitbar, dass wir von einander Rechenschaft für unsere Überzeugungen verlangen, ganz ähnlich, wie wir das für unsere Handlungen tun. Tiere, die wir von dieser Verantwortung ausnehmen, sind ebenso wenig epistemische Subjekte, wie sie moralische Subjekte sind. Zweitens ist ein gewisses Maß an epistemischem Selbstverstehen ein offenkundiges und wichtiges Element menschlichen Wissens. Wenn wir davon abstrahieren, ist das, was uns noch bleibt, ein sehr viel ärmeres Phänomen, als wir dachten.[3] Als eine Theorie *menschlichen* Wissens greift der Reliabilismus deutlich zu kurz.

Ich neige dazu, die Rede vom „Wissen der Tiere" gewissermaßen als eine *façon de parler* zu betrachten. Aber vielleicht möchten wir sagen, dass es auch im Fall des Menschen zwei Arten von Wissen gibt: eine primitive Art von Wissen, die wir mit den Tieren teilen, und eine höher entwickelte Art von Wissen, die sich über dem primitiven Fundament erhebt. Wenn wir diese zweiteilige Konzeption vertreten, können wir sagen, dass Reliabilisten und Responsibilisten über unterschiedliche Dinge reden. Aber da sie uns keine einheitliche Theorie menschlichen Wissens liefert, sollte eine solche Strategie der Zweiteilung nur als letzter Ausweg betrachtet werden. Um menschliches Wissen in seinem spezifischen Charakter zu verstehen, und das auf einheitliche Weise, müssen wir Verlässlichkeit mit Verantwortlichkeit verknüpfen.

Es ist jedoch nicht offensichtlich, wie dies zu bewerkstelligen ist. Eine rein verbale Verknüpfung reicht hierfür jedenfalls nicht aus. Betrachten wir etwa Linda Zagzebskis Version einer Tugendtheorie des Wissens.[4] Zagzebski sagt, ein Akt sei genau dann ein Akt der Tugend *A*, wenn

> er aus der motivationalen Komponente von A hervorgeht, ein Akt ist, den Personen mit der Tugend A typischerweise unter diesen Umständen voll-

---

3 Ernest Sosa zufolge wurde der Reliabilismus in der Antike von Galen vorweggenommen, und er wurde zu dieser Zeit dafür kritisiert, dass er menschliches Wissen auf ein Glauben reduziert, das „zufällig" wahr ist. Vgl. Sosa (1997a), 231 f.
4 Zagzebski (1999), 92–116.

ziehen, und mit Erfolg den Zweck der Tugend A verwirklicht, weil er die Eigenschaften eines solchen Akts hat.[5]

Wissen definiert sie dann als „Überzeugung, die aus Akten intellektueller Tugend hervorgeht".[6] Da der Zweck intellektueller Tugend Wahrheit ist, folgt aus dieser Definition eine begriffliche Verbindung zwischen Tugend und Verlässlichkeit. Zagzebski beeilt sich jedoch, darauf hinzuweisen, dass ihre Definition damit vereinbar ist, dass es verschiedene Sinne gibt, in denen Wissen gut ist. Während nämlich gewöhnliche Wahrnehmungs- und Erinnerungsfähigkeiten nahezu natürliche Tugenden sind, wie etwa Stärke, scheint Wissen ein „erhabener Zustand" zu sein, der in einem „nahezu moralischen" Sinne gut ist.[7] Was die Definition angeht, könnte es also zwei Arten von Wissen geben. Damit erkennt man auf eine andere Weise auch das Problem, den Responsibilismus mit reliabilistischen Einsichten zu versöhnen.

Eine ideale Lösung des Problems bestünde darin, Verantwortlichkeit mit Verlässlichkeit zu versöhnen, indem man sich zunächst die paradigmatischen Beispiele der Externalisten, z.B. das des gewöhnlichen Wahrnehmungswissens, vornimmt. Das ist die Strategie, die ich verfolgen will. Diese Strategie sieht sich jedoch mit zwei eng verknüpften Hindernissen konfrontiert. Das erste Hindernis besteht darin, dass man leicht der Versuchung erliegt, sich von dem, was epistemisch verantwortungsvolles Glauben verlangt, eine übertriebene Vorstellung zu machen. Der erste Schritt ist also, eine vernünftigere Vorstellung zu präsentieren und zu motivieren. (In diesem Punkt stimme ich erneut mit Zagzebski überein.) Das zweite Hindernis stellt sich in Form von bestimmten traditionellen skeptischen Bedenken, die, wenn wir sie kritiklos hinnehmen, es unmöglich machen, Verantwortlichkeit mit Verlässlichkeit auf eine angemessen allgemeine Weise zu verbinden. Der zweite Schritt besteht also darin, dafür zu argumentieren, dass man diese Bedenken legitimerweise umgehen kann. Ich werde die Auffassung vertreten, dass wir diese beiden Schritte genau deshalb tun können, weil die allzu anspruchsvolle Vorstellung von epistemischer Verantwortung und die traditionellen skeptischen Probleme eine gemeinsame Wurzel in einer falschen Auffassung der Struktur epistemischer Rechtfertigung haben.

2. Ich werde zunächst ein Beispiel für einen extremen epistemischen Internalismus untersuchen: die von Roderick Chisholm in seinem 1963

---
5   Ebd. 108.
6   Ebd. 109.
7   Ebd. 109.

erschienenen Aufsatz „Theory of Knowledge in America" präsentierte Erkenntnistheorie.[8] In diesem Aufsatz verfolgt Chisholm, der wohl einflussreichste Erkenntnistheoretiker seiner Generation, zwei Hauptziele. Das erste Ziel ist, die Notwendigkeit genuin theoretischer Bemühungen in der Epistemologie gegen die Kritik zu verteidigen, die von Philosophen der „Ordinary Language" vorgebracht wurde, dahingehend, dass die traditionellen erkenntnistheoretischen und vor allem die skeptischen Fragestellungen auf Missverständnissen beruhen. Das zweite Ziel ist, den Fundamentalismus gegen seinen kohärentistischen Konkurrenten in Schutz zu nehmen. Die Art und Weise, in der Chisholm seine Ziele verfolgt, spiegelt eine ganz bestimmte Konzeption der Erkenntnistheorie wider:

(i) Chisholm geht davon aus, dass Wissen eine Art von gerechtfertigter wahrer Überzeugung ist. Obwohl er in seiner Diskussion vorwiegend von Wissen spricht, liegt sein Hauptaugenmerk auf dem Problem der Rechtfertigung.

(ii) Chisholm setzt voraus, dass Rechtfertigung einen normativen, und zwar einen deontologischen Aspekt aufweist. Die Erkenntnistheorie ziele darauf ab, „epistemische Prinzipien" zu formulieren, die epistemisch angemessenes Glauben in derselben Weise leiten, wie moralische Prinzipien moralisch verantwortliches Handeln leiten. Gleichzeitig beruhe epistemische Rechtfertigung auf Wahrheitsdienlichkeit, der das Befolgen epistemischer Prinzipien folglich förderlich sein müsse.

(iii) Chisholms Prinzipien sind Prinzipien der Evidenz. Gegen die Vertreter einer kohärentistischen Theorie der Rechtfertigung macht er geltend, dass es selbstbeglaubigende *(self-evidencing)* fundamentale Überzeugungen geben müsse, die auf *apriorische* Weise mit den von ihnen gestützten nicht-fundamentalen Überzeugungen verknüpft seien. Chisholms Prinzipien identifizieren also die elementar evidenten Überzeugungen, die wir aus unseren grundlegenden Informationsquellen wie der Wahrnehmung gewinnen, sowie die Rechtfertigungsbeziehungen, in denen diese Überzeugungen zu solchen stehen, die nicht elementar evident sind. Auf diese Weise ist die Verbindung zwischen Verantwortlichkeit und Verlässlichkeit gesichert. Chisholms Erkenntnistheorie ist also mit dem ausdrücklichen Anspruch entworfen, Verantwortlichkeit mit Verlässlichkeit zu verknüpfen. Aber die Art und Weise, wie er diese Verknüpfung herstellt, geht mit einer Auffassung von Wissen und Rechtfertigung einher, die auf kompromisslose Weise internalistisch,

---

8 Der Aufsatz ist wiederabgedruckt als Kapitel 10 in Chisholm (1982).

evidentialistisch und aprioristisch ist. Seine Theorie liefert ein paradigmatisches Beispiel für jene Art von fundamentalistischer Erkenntnistheorie, die Wilfried Sellars zufolge auf dem Mythos des Gegebenen beruht.[9] Wenn eine solche hyperintellektualistische Auffassung von Wissen dann noch durch den Responsibilismus verstärkt wirkt, ist es kein Wunder, dass so viele Philosophen Reliabilisten sind.

Der Responsibilismus trägt jedoch nicht allein die Verantwortung für das Entstehen der von Chisholm vertretenen Sichtweise. Chisholms Auffassung von Rechtfertigung ist vielmehr tief in seinem Verständnis des Ziels der Erkenntnistheorie verwurzelt. Der Erkenntnistheoretiker befasst sich nicht mit der Rechtfertigung spezifischer Überzeugungen, sondern mit der Rechtfertigung von Überzeugungen, insofern sie unter sehr *allgemeine* Kategorien fallen: zum Beispiel Überzeugungen über die Außenwelt, Überzeugungen die Vergangenheit betreffend oder religiöse Überzeugungen. Da die Überzeugungen, die unter diese Kategorien fallen, unterschiedliche Quellen zu haben scheinen – Wahrnehmung, Erinnerung, Offenbarung und bzw. oder religiöse Erfahrung – kann man die Aufgabe der Erkenntnistheorie auch darin sehen, die Zuverlässigkeit dieser typischen Quellen der Erkenntnis zu untersuchen und zu bewerten. Da es jedoch zumindest vorstellbar ist, dass diese Quellen nicht zuverlässig sind, so dass wir in keiner dieser allgemeinen Kategorien, denen die Aufmerksamkeit der Erkenntnistheoretiker gilt, über Wissen verfügen, heißt dies nichts anderes, als dass dem Skeptizismus die Hauptsorge der Erkenntnistheorie gilt. Chisholms Auffassung von Rechtfertigung ist so, wie sie ist, weil sie die Verbindung zwischen Verantwortlichkeit und Verlässlichkeit als unproblematisch erweisen soll, und zwar *im Zusammenhang einer ernst genommenen Bedrohung durch einen allgemeinen und radikalen Skeptizismus*. Der Wunsch, dem Skeptizismus entschieden entgegenzutreten, ist die Quelle für den Hyperintellektualismus, den wir in weiten Bereichen der traditionellen Erkenntnistheorie vorfinden.

3. Ich möchte nun der Vermutung, dass der Skeptizismus die Quelle unseres Problems ist, eine Alternative gegenüberstellen. In einer scharfsinnigen Analyse hat Alvin Goldman, der Begründer des modernen Reliabilismus, die traditionelle Vorliebe für Internalismus und Evidentialismus auf eine, wie er sie nennt, „regulativ-deontologische" (RD) Konzeption von Rechtfertigung zurückgeführt.[10] Wie Goldman sagt, sei

---

9 Sellars (1999).
10 Goldman (2002), 3 ff.

es eines der traditionellen Ziele der Erkenntnistheorie gewesen, „den Geist zu leiten oder zu lenken", ein Ziel, das der Titel von Descartes' „Regeln zur Leitung des Geistes" zum Ausdruck bringt.[11] Goldman führt weiter aus, dass die Auffassung von Rechtfertigung als Regulativ häufig mit einer deontologischen Auffassung verknüpft worden sei, wonach eine gerechtfertigte Überzeugung eine Überzeugung ist, die durch ein intellektuell verantwortliches Verhalten hervorgebracht und aufrechterhalten wird. Die Verbindung von regulativer und deontologischer Konzeption lege Philosophen die Annahme nahe, dass epistemische Verantwortlichkeit das Befolgen geeigneter Regeln für die Bildung von Überzeugungen erfordere. Geleitet werden kann man jedoch nur von etwas, das einem bewusst ist. Die Befolgung dieser Regeln wird also darin bestehen, dass die eigenen Überzeugungen auf die richtige Weise gemäß der empirischen Belege, die man hat, gebildet werden. Die RD-Konzeption von Rechtfertigung bildet die Grundlage von Internalismus und Evidentialismus, wie man sie so häufig in der traditionellen Erkenntnistheorie antrifft. Goldman räumt zwar ein, dass die deontologische Auffassung von Rechtfertigung nicht unbedingt an die Idee der Lenkung gebunden sei. Aber ohne diese Verbindung, so behauptet er, liefere sie keine Stütze für den Internalismus.

Interessanterweise findet sich Goldmans Diagnose bereits in Sellars' Aufsatz „Der Empirismus und die Philosophie des Geistes" vorgebildet. Ebenso wie Goldman behauptet auch Sellars, dass eine bestimmte Auffassung der Lenkung durch Regeln uns dem Mythos des Gegebenen anheimgebe. Aber anders als Goldman hält er an einem im Wesentlichen internalistischen und deontologischen Ansatz zur Rechtfertigung fest. Aus der Sicht von Sellars ist eine Überzeugung ihrem Wesen nach etwas, das als Grund dienen kann und wofür man Gründe fordern darf.[12] Glauben ist „gesättigt mit Sollen" („fraught with ought"). Des Weiteren besteht Sellars darauf, dass sich das Befolgen einer Regel nicht darauf beschränkt, in Übereinstimmung mit ihr zu handeln. Deshalb kann Sellars auch nicht gegen die RD-Konzeption als solche Einwände haben, sondern bloß gegen eine bestimmte Version dieser Auffassung.

Sellars diskutiert die RD-Konzeption von Rechtfertigung in seiner Darstellung, wie ein fundamentalistischer Empirismus dazu bewogen wird, sich dem Mythos des Gegebenen zu verschreiben. Sellars setzt an,

---

11 Ebd.
12 Sellars (1999).

indem er zwei bindende Annahmen des traditionellen Fundamentalismus hervorhebt. Sie lauten:

> ... dass es eine Ebene einzelner Tatsachen gibt, ja geben *muss*, wobei gilt: (a) Jede hierzu gehörige Tatsache kann nicht nur auf nicht-inferentielle Weise gewusst werden. Sie setzt darüber hinaus auch kein weiteres Wissen voraus, ganz egal ob es sich dabei um ein Wissen einzelner Tatsachen oder um ein Wissen allgemeiner Wahrheiten handelt. (b) Das nicht-inferentielle Wissen von Tatsachen, die auf diese Ebene gehören, bildet die letzte Berufungsinstanz aller faktischen Behauptungen – besonderer und allgemeiner über die Welt.[13]

Ein solch grundlegendes Wissen findet seinen Ausdruck in Beobachtungsberichten. Das Wort „Bericht" wird hier in einem technischen Sinne verwendet. Dem gewöhnlichen Sprachgebrauch zufolge ist Berichten eine *Handlung*: Jemand berichtet jemandem etwas. Für den traditionellen Empiristen muss „Berichten" nicht mehr bedeuten als *in foro interno* festzustellen „Das ist grün", wenn man einem grünen Gegenstand gegenübersteht.[14]

Elementare Beobachtungsberichte müssen sowohl Autorität besitzen als auch voraussetzungslos sein. Wenn es ihnen an Autorität mangelt, dann können sie anderen Überzeugungen nicht als Rechtfertigungsgrund dienen. Ja, wenn sie Evidenz für weitere, nicht-elementare Überzeugungen liefern sollen, wie es sich die Fundamentalisten erhoffen, muss ihre Autorität *anerkannt* werden. Aber ihre Rolle als *letzte* Quellen der Evidenz bedeutet, dass ihre Autorität nicht von weiteren Voraussetzungen abhängig sein darf und also nicht von unserer Erkenntnis, dass wir verlässlich berichten, ableitbar sein kann. Um dem fundamentalistischen Bild treu zu bleiben, müssen alle allgemeinen Überzeugungen, einschließlich jener über unsere kognitiven Fähigkeiten, ihre Glaubwürdigkeit aus der Evidenz herleiten, die die elementaren Berichte liefern. Woher kommt aber dann die Autorität dieser elementaren Berichte?

Die Antwort der Empiristen lautet, dass die elementaren Beobachtungsberichte, wie etwa „Dies (hier, jetzt) ist grün", ihre Autorität einer bestimmten Art von *semantischen Regeln* verdanken, die wir bei ihrer Formulierung befolgen. Diese Regeln sehen in etwa folgendermaßen aus:

> *Regel für „dies"*: man sage/denke „dies", während man die Aufmerksamkeit auf ein Objekt/einen Bereich im eigenen Gesichtsfeld richtet (geistig darauf

---

[13] Ebd. 59.
[14] Ebd. 72 f.

zeigt).

Regel für (den berichtenden Gebrauch) von „grün": man sage/denke „ ... ist grün" nur dann, wenn das Objekt, auf das man die Aufmerksamkeit richtet, sichtbar grün ist (erscheint).

Wenn man diese Regeln achtsam befolgt, garantieren sie, dass ein Bericht, der in einem Vorkommnis von „Dies ist grün" besteht, nicht falsch sein beziehungsweise höchstens ein „verbaler" Irrtum sein kann. Wie Sellars bemerkt, bringt uns diese Theorie elementarer Berichte dazu

> dass wir der unverblümtesten Form von Gegebenheit direkt ins Auge blicken ... Man wird zur Annahme einer Ebene von autoritativen nichtsprachlichen Episoden („Bewusstseine") verpflichtet, deren Autorität sich auf einen Überbau *sprachlicher Handlungen* überträgt, vorausgesetzt, die dabei vorkommenden Ausdrücke werden angemessen *verwendet*.[15]

Das ist genau das Bild, das wir bei Chisholm finden, der glaubt, dass elementare Aussagen im Lichte unseres Bewusstseins „selbstpräsentierender" geistiger Zustände gerechtfertigt sind. Es ist ein auf die Spitze getriebener Internalismus.[16] Die Reliabilisten tun das Richtige, wenn sie ihn zurückweisen.

Wo läuft hier etwas schief? Sellars Analyse liefert hier eine subtilere Diagnose als Goldman. Sellars identifiziert *vier* unterschiedliche bindende Annahmen:

1. Rechtfertigung ist eine Sache der Befolgung normativer Regeln.
2. Das Befolgen einer Regel „im eigentlichen Sinne des Wortes" besteht nicht allein darin, mit der Regel *übereinzustimmen*, sondern (in einem bestimmten Sinne) *im Lichte* der Regel *zu handeln*.
3. Obwohl das „Berichten" in dem technischen Sinne nicht mehr erfordert als das Formulieren eines sprachlich kodierten Gedanken, bleibt das Berichten eine *Handlung*.
4. Normative Regeln, die Handlungen leiten, weisen die Form von Imperativen auf: „Unter Umständen U tue H".[17]

---

15 Ebd. 63.
16 Sellars hat mehrere Gründe zu glauben, dass die Berufung auf das Gegebene fehlgeleitet sein muss. Der wichtigste ist folgender: Es kann nicht sein, dass uns etwas grün zu sein scheint, wenn wir nicht den Begriff *grün* haben. Aber um den Begriff *grün* zu erwerben, müssen wir den Gebrauch des Wortes „grün" meistern (oder seine funktionale Entsprechung in einer anderen Sprache). Wir können uns folglich nicht auf ein vorsprachliches Bewusstsein berufen, um den Gebrauch des Wortes zu erklären. In dieser Hinsicht ist die RD-Konzeption unhaltbar. Vgl. 32 ff.
17 Vgl. die „drei Anmerkungen" von Sellars, 62.

Wenn 1–4 gegeben sind, ist Gegebenheit in ihrer unverblümtesten Form unvermeidlich, denn um eine Regel für das Berichten zu befolgen, muss man sich bereits *bewusst sein*, dass man sich in der entsprechenden Situation für eine Äußerung z.B. von „grün" befindet. Während 1–4 jedoch zu dem extremen mentalistischen Internalismus des Geleitetwerdens durch selbstpräsentierende Zustände führen, *sind nur 1 und 2 von wesentlicher Bedeutung für eine robuste deontologische Konzeption von Rechtfertigung.*

Radikale Reliabilisten empfehlen natürlich, dass man 1 und 2 aufgibt. *De-facto*-Verlässlichkeit als hinreichend für Rechtfertigung anzusehen (beziehungsweise für Wissen, wenn man geeignete Bedingungen hinzufügt), bedeutet nichts anderes als zu sagen, dass „epistemische Regeln" nichts anderes sein müssen als Regularitäten, mit denen wir übereinstimmen. Sie müssen keine Normen sein, die wir achten. Aber angesichts Sellars' Analyse des Wegs zum Mythos des Gegebenen kann der Responsibilist entgegnen, dass es nicht notwendig ist, das normative Kind mit dem mentalistischen Bade auszuschütten. Denn während 1 und 2 ein gewisses Maß an epistemischem Selbstbewusstsein erfordern, ziehen sie nicht notwendigerweise den mentalistischen bzw. evidentialistischen Internalismus nach sich, den wir bei Philosophen wie Chisholm finden.

An dieser Stelle müssen wir auf jenen Einwand gegen den Responsibilismus eingehen, der von Anfang an am wirkungsvollsten erschien: dass die deontologische Redeweise auf Überzeugungen nicht anwendbar ist, da Glauben nicht etwas ist, das wir zu einem bestimmten Zweck tun. Sellars, der dieses Problem antizipierte, lädt uns dazu ein, zwischen *Handlungen* und *Akten* zu unterscheiden.[18] *Handlungen* werden zu einem bestimmten Zweck vollzogen: Sie sind etwas, in Bezug worauf man sinnvoll fragen kann „Warum hast du das getan?" oder „Was hast du vor?".[19] *Akte* hingegen sind Aktualisierungen eines Vermögens. Nun gibt es gewiss geistige Handlungen, z.B. Überlegungen anstellen oder sich den Kopf zerbrechen, um sich einen Namen in Erinnerung zu rufen. Aber Sehen – als eine Form der Erkenntnis – ist ein geistiger Akt und keine Handlung. Zu sehen, etwa dass ein Hase im Garten ist, erfordert die Aktualisierung eines ausgebildeten Erkenntnisvermögens. Dies bedeutet, dass Sehen nicht zu der Art von Dingen gehört, die man „zu einem

---

18 Sellars (1968). Vgl. vor allem 73 ff.
19 Die Antwort könnte lauten: „Ich habe keinen Grund: Ich habe bloß Lust darauf." Es geht nicht darum, dass wir immer aus Gründen handeln, sondern darum, dass es immer sinnvoll ist, nach Gründen zu fragen. Vgl. Vogler (2002), Kap. 2.

bestimmten Zweck tut". Soweit hat der Reliabilist Recht: Eine Menge von gewöhnlichem Wissen beruht auf der unbewussten Ausübung elementarer kognitiver Fähigkeiten. Der Reliabilist verkennt jedoch, dass Akte genauso wie Handlungen normativen Regeln unterliegen können. Gewiss, die entsprechenden normativen Regeln können zunächst nicht die Form von Imperativen aufweisen: Sie können nicht das sein, was Sellars „Sollte-Tun"-Regeln („ought-to-do") nennt. Aber daraus sollten wir den Schluss ziehen, dass nicht alle Regeln Sollte-Tun-Regeln sind.

Es gibt Gründe zu glauben, dass nicht alle Regeln – epistemische oder semantische – Sollte-Tun-Regeln sein *können*. Wie Sellars erkannte, müssen Regeln ab einem gewissen Punkt „blind" befolgt werden, wie Wittgenstein sagt. Wir können diese Einsicht jedoch akzeptieren, ohne Regelfolgen insgesamt auf bloßes Übereinstimmen mit Regeln zu reduzieren. Hierfür müssen wir eine weitere Art von normativer Regel identifizieren, die Sellars „Sollte-Sein" („ought-to-be") nennt. Regeln dieser Art setzen Bedingungen für die Richtigkeit von Akten. Damit ich beispielsweise sehe und nicht nur glaube zu sehen, dass da ein Hase im Garten ist, *müssen* allerlei Bedingungen erfüllt sein. Einige dieser Bedingungen betreffen mich: Ich muss bei klarem Verstande sein, aufmerksam und in der Lage zu erkennen, was vor sich geht, und so weiter. Andere betreffen den Gegenstand und die Situation: Das Tier muss ein Hase sein und darf kein ausgestopftes Tier sein, die Lichtverhältnisse müssen gut genug sein, dass man die Gestalt des schwarzen Flecks mitten auf dem Rasen erkennen kann, und so weiter. Wären diese Bedingungen nicht erfüllt, wäre ich nicht in der Lage zu sehen, dass da ein Hase im Garten ist.

Wie können Sollte-Sein-Forderungen genuin normativer Natur sein? Genauer gesagt, was haben sie mit der Lenkung unserer Überzeugungen zu tun? Die Antwort lautet, dass solche Regeln als *Regeln der Kritik* fungieren. Wenn es Grund gibt zu glauben, dass eine oder mehrere der Sollte-Sein-Bedingungen nicht erfüllt sind, wird meine Berechtigung zu glauben, was ich zu sehen glaubte, in Frage gestellt. Das wiederum bedeutet, dass es Dinge gibt, die ich tun oder nicht tun sollte: Ich sollte mich nicht weiter auf etwas verlassen, was eine Falschinformation sein könnte; Ich sollte (wenn ich kann) herausfinden, ob die Umstände so beschaffen waren, wie ich dachte. Auf diese Weise sind Sollte-Tun-Regeln wesentlich mit dem verknüpft, was sein sollte. Der entscheidende Punkt ist: Obwohl Wahrnehmungswissen nicht dadurch *entsteht*, dass man bewusst prozeduralen Regeln folgt, *unterliegt* eine wahrnehmungsbasierte Überzeugungsberechtigung ihrem Wesen nach *der Bewertung* durch anerkannte Maßstäbe und *zieht* epistemische Verpflichtungen *nach sich*. Mehr an „Internalismus" ist für eine deontologische Konzeption von Rechtfertigung nicht erforderlich.

Die Unterscheidung zweier Arten von Regeln ist in einem – wie Robert Brandom es nennt – „Vorschuss-und-Anfechtungs"-Modell von Rechtfertigung zu Hause.[20] (Die Idee, wenn auch nicht der Name, kann man bei Austin, Wittgenstein und Gilbert Harman finden.) Nach diesem Modell können wir gerechtfertigt sein zu glauben, dass p – berechtigt anzunehmen, dass p, für die Zwecke der Schlussfolgerung und des Handeln – *ohne etwas Besonderes* getan zu haben, um diese Berechtigung zu verdienen. Der Verweis auf „etwas Besonderes" ist wichtig. Eine solche Vorschussberechtigung wird nur anerkannten epistemischen Subjekten eingeräumt. Den Status eines epistemischen Subjekts, wie auch den eines moralischen Akteurs, erwirbt man durch Übung und Erziehung.

Bei ausreichend geübten Subjekten – und ihren Erkenntnisfähigkeiten entsprechend – ist die Wahrnehmung eine Quelle der Vorschussberechtigung (von Überzeugungen). Ja, sie ist sogar die Quelle des Anspruchs auf nicht-inferentielles Wissen. Da sie aber „Sollte-Sein"-Regeln unterliegt, ist eine solche Vorschussberechtigung mit der Verpflichtung verbunden, die entsprechende Überzeugung gegebenenfalls zu verteidigen. Wenn begründete Fragen bezüglich meiner Kompetenz auftauchen oder bezüglich der Umstände, unter denen ich dachte, dies oder jenes zu sehen, erlischt meine Berechtigung, bis diese Fragen beantwortet sind. Auf diese Weise bestimmt das Ineinandergreifen von epistemischen Normen des Sollte-Sein- mit denen des Sollte-Tun-Typs die Parameter epistemisch verantwortlichen Glaubens. Obwohl nicht alles gerechtfertigte Glauben aus dem bewussten Befolgen von Sollte-Tun-Regeln resultiert, modifizieren wir auf diese Weise das System unserer Überzeugungen im Lichte anerkannter epistemischer Maßstäbe. Wir können also zu dem Schluss kommen, dass nichts daran falsch ist, eine responsibilistische Konzeption von Rechtfertigung als eine *regulativ*-deontologische Konzeption aufzufassen, solange wir „Geleitetwerden" nicht ausschließlich im Sinne eines bewussten Befolgens von Sollte-Tun-Regeln verstehen.

Gemäß seinem Wunsch, dem Skeptiker entschieden entgegenzutreten, übernimmt Chisholm eine RD-Konzeption von Wissen und Rechtfertigung und baut darin eine andere Struktur epistemischer Berechtigung ein: das Modell vorheriger Begründung („Prior Grounding

---

20 Brandom (2000), 265 ff.

Modell"). Ein integraler Bestandteil dieses Modells ist eine Konzeption von Rechtfertigung als *positiver Autorisierung*, und zwar ohne Einschränkung. Ihr zufolge gibt es keine Ansprüche, die man sich nicht dadurch verdient, dass man bestimmte Schritte in Übereinstimmung mit entsprechenden Regeln vollzieht. Wie wir gesehen haben, führt diese Auffassung zu einer übermäßig anspruchsvollen Konzeption epistemisch verantwortlichen Glaubens. Das Vorschuss-und-Anfechtungsmodell reduziert die Last epistemischer Verantwortung dagegen erheblich. Wenn man den Status eines epistemischen Subjekts erst einmal erlangt hat, kann man vernünftigerweise vieles als selbstverständlich voraussetzen, solange es keine guten Gründe gibt, dies nicht zu tun. Epistemische Verantwortlichkeit erfordert die nötige Vorsicht und Aufmerksamkeit. Aber wie Zagzebski betont, fordern Tugenden wie Achtsamkeit und Gründlichkeit nicht „ein Maß an intellektueller Gewissenhaftigkeit, das an Verfolgungswahn grenzt".[21] Ich würde sagen: nicht nur fordern sie dies nicht, sondern sie schließen es aus.

4. Obwohl die Unterscheidung zweier Arten von Regeln natürlicherweise in dem Vorschuss-und-Anfechtungsmodell von Rechtfertigung zuhause ist, vermittelt Sellars allerdings den Eindruck, als sei er versucht, einen eher traditionellen Kohärentismus zu vertreten. Die Quelle dieser Versuchung ist nicht schwer zu finden. Sellars akzeptiert die anspruchsvolle internalistische Forderung, dass *der Berichtende* selbst die Autorität seiner Wahrnehmungsberichte *anerkennen* muss. Er glaubt, dies beinhalte, dass der Berichtende nicht nur mit einem verlässlichen Erkenntnisvermögen ausgestattet ist, sondern auch *um seine Verlässlichkeit wissen* muss. Ja, er glaubt, dieses Verlässlichkeitswissen sei von wesentlicher Bedeutung für die Autorität des Berichtenden. Aber wenn die Aufgabe von Verlässlichkeitswissen unter anderem die ist, bestimmte Ansprüche, etwas wahrzunehmen, zu autorisieren, und wenn daraus folgen soll, das bestimmte Wahrnehmungsüberzeugungen und Überzeugungen bezüglich der Verlässlichkeit unseres Wahrnehmungsvermögens sich gegenseitig stützen, dann landen wir bei einer Kohärenztheorie der Rechtfertigung. Dann streiten wir mit Chisholm erneut auf der Grundlage von dessen theoretischen Voraussetzungen.

Obwohl oberflächlich betrachtet plausibel, ist dieser Gedankengang fragwürdig. Das Wissen, dass man im Hinblick auf einfache Erkenntnisvermögen zuverlässig ist, ist im Allgemeinen nicht in der Lage, eine Rolle bei der Rechtfertigung konkreter wahrnehmungsbasierter Wis-

---

21 Vgl. Zagzebski (1999), 110.

sensansprüche zu spielen. Ich weiß, dass auf dem Tisch ein Buch liegt, weil ich es dort liegen sehe. Unter besonderen Umständen kann ich mich in so einfachen Fragen wie dieser irren. Aber normalerweise ist solch ein einfaches Wahrnehmungsurteil so gewiss wie ein Urteil nur sein kann und wird nicht gewisser durch allgemeine Erwägungen bezüglich meiner Wahrnehmungsfähigkeiten. Die Vorstellung, dass es feste Rechtfertigungsbeziehungen zwischen verschiedenen „Formen" des Wissens gibt, ist, wie ich schon lange behaupte, an sich fragwürdig, und es ist dies auch dann, wenn die Beziehungen gegenseitig sein sollen. Worauf man sich bei Rechtfertigungen berufen kann, variiert mit dem Kontext.[22] Um zu wissen, was in meinem Umfeld passiert, verlasse ich mich auf die Wahrnehmung. Aber ich kann mein Wissen darüber, was in meinem Umfeld passiert, auch dafür gebrauchen, dass ich meine Augen teste.

Trotzdem, glaube ich, beharrt Sellars zu Recht darauf, dass wir Überzeugungen bezüglich unserer Verlässlichkeit als Wahrnehmende haben, und er hat auch Recht, wenn er diese Tatsache als relevant ansieht für unsere Autorität als Berichterstatter über dass, was um uns vorgeht. Die Frage ist, warum Verlässlichkeitswissen von wesentlicher Bedeutung ist, wenn man von einem Vorschuss-und-Anfechtungsmodell ausgeht.

Nach dem Vorschuss-und-Anfechtungsmodell ist nichts falsch an der Vorstellung, dass es äußere Bedingungen gibt, die uns autorisieren. Was allein zählt, ist, dass man eine Vorschussberechtigung dafür hat, anzunehmen, dass diese Bedingungen erfüllt sind. Eine solche Annahme muss nicht *bewusst vermerkt werden*, denn sie kommt einer Erlaubnis gleich, bestimmte Möglichkeiten zu ignorieren: einer Erlaubnis, sie nicht in Betracht zu ziehen, und zwar gleichgültig ob sie uns in den Sinn kommen oder nicht.[23] Wenn die Frage aufkommt, ob diese Annahmen erfüllt sind, kann man sie anführen und verteidigen. Dennoch gibt es Gründe dafür, nicht alle Sollte-Sein-Bedingungen, die irgendwie für die Autorität einer Vorschussberechtigung relevant sind, so aufzufassen, als brächten sie (im Allgemeinen) direkt die Rechtfertigung ins Spiel. Der Besitz von Dispositionen zu verlässlicher Berichterstattung, die für meinen Status als epistemisches Subjekt überhaupt erforderlich sind, ist eine *befähigende* und nicht eine rechtfertigende Bedingung für Wahrnehmungswissen. Wie James Pryor bemerkt, mag meine Rechtfertigung dafür, den Satz des Pythagoras zu glauben, sich daraus ergeben, dass ich einen Beweis gelesen

---

22 Mehr zur kontextuellen Veränderbarkeit epistemischer Maßstäbe in Williams (2001), Kap. 14.
23 Hier folge ich Lewis (1996), 549–67.

und verstanden habe. Um den Beweis zu verstehen, muss ich die Sprache verstehen, in der er abgefasst ist, z. B. Englisch. Aber dass ich Englisch verstehe, würden wir normalerweise nicht als Teil meiner Rechtfertigung ansehen.[24] Es ist vielmehr eine Hintergrundbedingung dafür, dass ich in der Lage bin, eine unbestimmte Menge gerechtfertigter Überzeugungen zu erwerben. Warum aber, wenn die Verlässlichkeit der Wahrnehmung so aufzufassen ist, sollten wir dann überhaupt auf Verlässlichkeits*wissen* pochen?

Ernest Sosa glaubt, dass Sellars einen Fehler mache, ganz allgemein darauf zu beharren.[25] Sosa zufolge ist das Wissen von den eigenen kognitiven Fähigkeiten charakteristisch für einen speziellen und hochentwickelten Typus von Wissen: menschliches Wissen. Es gibt einen anderen Typus von Wissen, nämlich das Wissen von Tieren, der nicht mehr als De-facto-Verlässlichkeit erfordert. Ausgehend von diesem Wissen können wir fortschreiten zu einem Bild von uns selbst und unserer Welt, das das Erkennen unserer Verlässlichkeit als Sammler von Informationen über die Welt berücksichtigt. Das ist die Art von Zweiteilungsstrategie, die wir meines Erachtens vermeiden sollten.

Interessanterweise teilt Robert Brandom, einer der größten Bewunderer von Sellars, Sosas Bedenken gegenüber Sellars' Beharren auf Verlässlichkeitswissen als allgemeiner Bedingung für eine wahrnehmungsbasierte Berechtigung für Überzeugungen. Brandom glaubt, dass dieses Beharren auf Verlässlichkeitswissen Folgendes impliziert: „Damit demjenigen, der Bericht erstattet, Wissen zugeschrieben wird, muss er in der Lage sein, eine Rechtfertigung der fraglichen Überzeugung in Form eines Schlusses zu geben." Sellars „befürwortet" also „einen erkenntnistheoretischen Internalismus, der ihn in Widerspruch bringt zu dem reliabilistischen Externalismus jüngeren Datums."[26] Brandom bezweifelt, dass Sellars auf einer so starken Form des Internalismus beharren muss. Wenn einem Wahrnehmungsbericht Berechtigung zuerkannt wird, mag es sein, dass *irgendjemand* den „Schluss auf die Verlässlichkeit" billigen muss: Aber warum muss dies immer der Berichtende sein? Brandom legt Sellars eine Reihe rhetorischer Fragen vor:

---

24 Pryor (2004), 354.
25 Sosa (1997b), 275–86. Ich antworte auf Sosas Kritik an Sellars in Williams (2003), 91–112. Sosas Erwiderungen auf meinen Beitrag finden sich im selben Band.
26 Sellars (1997), mit einer Einleitung von Richard Rorty und einem Study Guide von Robert Brandom, 158.

Warum reicht es nicht, dass der Wissen *Zuschreibende* dem Schluss von der reaktiven Disposition des Berichtenden, den Begriff *rot* nicht-inferentiell zu gebrauchen, zu dem Urteil, dass der Gegenstand (wahrscheinlich) rot ist, beipflichtet?[27]

Brandom meint, es gebe hierfür keinen Grund.

Nach Ansicht von Brandom folgt aus seiner Kritik an Sellars, dass wir die „Gründungseinsicht" des Reliabilismus akzeptieren sollten,

> dass wahre Überzeugungen zumindest in einigen Fällen auf echtes Wissen hinauslaufen können, auch wenn die Rechtfertigungsbedingung nicht erfüllt wurde (in dem Sinne, dass der Wissenskandidat nicht in der Lage ist, geeignete Rechtfertigungsbedingungen hervorzubringen). Dazu muss allerdings sichergestellt sein, dass sich die Überzeugungen aus der Ausübung von Fähigkeiten ergaben, die ihrerseits *verlässliche* Produzenten von wahren Überzeugungen in den Umständen sind, in denen sie faktisch ausgeübt werden.[28]

Dies ist jedoch ein stark eingeschränktes Zugeständnis an den Externalismus. Die Bezugnahme auf „einige Fälle" ist hier von entscheidender Bedeutung. Brandom glaubt nicht, dass Wissen (oder gerechtfertigte Überzeugung) *ganz allgemein* eine Sache von bloßer Verlässlichkeit sein kann. Tatsächlich glaubt er nicht, dass Wissen *jemals* eine Sache *bloßer* Verlässlichkeit sei. Nach Brandoms Auffassung haben Wesen, die keine Gründe vorbringen können, überhaupt keine Überzeugungen, geschweige denn Überzeugungen, die gerechtfertigt sind oder Wissen gleichkommen. Gleichzeitig widerspricht er der Sellarschen Ansicht, dass eine wahrnehmungsbasierte Berechtigung *in allen Fällen* auf Verlässlichkeitswissen beruht, d.h. auf der Fähigkeit des Wissenden, auf Aufforderung Gründe zu geben. Er bringt das Beispiel einer Expertin für klassische mittelamerikanische Keramik vor, die toltekische von aztekischen Tonscherben durch bloße Inaugenscheinnahme unterscheiden kann und die dadurch zu der Überzeugung kommt, dass einiger dieser Scherben toltekisch und andere aztekisch sind. Gleichzeitig kann sie sich bei der Rechtfertigung ihrer Überzeugung nicht auf irgendwelche unterscheidenden Merkmale der Bruchstücke berufen und betrachtet deshalb die Meinungen, die sie sich gebildet hat, mit größtem Misstrauen. Obwohl sie selbst sich nicht als eine verlässliche nichtinferentielle Berichterstatterin über klassische mittelamerikanischer Keramik betrachtet, so Brandom, sind *wir* nichtsdestotrotz völlig berechtigt, sie als eine solche

---

27 Ebd. 159.
28 Brandom (2001), 127.

anzusehen. Die Gründungseinsicht des Reliabilismus verweist also auf den *sozial-perspektivischen* Charakter von Wissenszuschreibungen. Aus einer externen Perspektive können *wir* sie (gemessen an reliabilistischen Maßstäben) als sachkundig betrachten, obwohl sie sich aus ihrer internen Perspektive selbst nicht so sieht. Natürlich können *wir* unsere Wissenszuschreibung auch dadurch *rechtfertigen*, dass wir auf ihre Verlässlichkeit hinweisen, die sie selbst nicht anerkennt. Auf seine eigene Weise verfolgt auch Brandom eine Strategie der Zweiteilung. Gewiss, er möchte nicht sagen, dass es zwei Arten von Wissen gibt. Er behauptet vielmehr, dass es zwei Perspektiven gibt, von denen aus Wissenszuschreibungen gemacht werden, von denen *eine* Wissenszuschreibungen entspricht, wie Externalisten sie verstehen.

Ich finde Brandoms Beispiel nicht überzeugend. Erstens ist es nämlich fraglich, ob die Keramikexpertin wirklich *glaubt*, was ihr ihre spontanen Reaktionen nahe legen. Brandom zufolge misst sie diesen „kein großes Gewicht " bei.[29] Da P zu glauben nach Brandoms Ansicht in der Disposition besteht, sich bei Schlussfolgerungen und Handlungen auf P zu verlassen, sollte ihn die Frage, ob es sich hier überhaupt um eine Überzeugung handelt, mehr beunruhigen, als dies augenscheinlich der Fall ist. Brandom behauptet, die Expertin bestehe auf Belegen, die ihr spontanes Urteil bestätigen, womit er zu erkennen gibt, dass sie nur die *Neigung* zu glauben hat, die sie ignorieren will. Aber was sollen wir denken, wenn sie wiederholt herausgefunden hat, dass ihre spontanen Reaktionen durch systematische Untersuchungen bestätigt werden? Dann ist sie mit den von Brandom auch diskutierten Küken-Geschlechtsbestimmern vergleichbar, die Küken in weibliche und männliche sortieren können, aber nicht in der Lage sind zu sagen, wie sie das machen; und wie Brandom richtig erkennt, wenn man nicht in der Lage ist zu sagen, wie man etwas macht, ist das nicht dasselbe, wie wenn man keinen Grund hat, den eigenen Fähigkeiten zu trauen. Schließlich ist da immer noch der Verlässlichkeitsschluss.

Brandom ist sich dieser Bedenken wohl bewusst: die Fälle, die die Gründungseinsicht stützen, so gibt er bereitwillig zu, seien unvermeidlich „feingesponnen und speziell".[30] Ich stimme ihm zu: Sie sind zu feingesponnen und speziell, als dass sie die Gründungseinsicht stützen könnten.

Es gibt einen wichtigen Unterschied zwischen dem Fall eines Erkenntnisvermögens, von dem Brandom bei seiner Verteidigung der

---

29 Ibid. 129.
30 Ibid. 134.

Gründungseinsicht Gebrauch macht („aztekisch"), und der Art von Fällen, die Sellars interessieren („rot"). Es ist sehr viel leichter, sich vorzustellen, dass man bei Fällen der ersteren Art bezüglich der eigenen spontanen Reaktionen unsicher ist als bei letzteren. Was hieße es denn, im Hinblick auf die eigene Fähigkeit, rote Gegenstände zu erkennen, unsicher zu sein, wenn man einmal von einer Behinderung, von der man weiß, wie etwa Farbenblindheit, absieht? Sellars kann erwidern, dass er nicht an spezialisierte Erkenntnisvermögen gedacht hat, bei denen wir tatsächlich von unsicheren aber verlässlichen Berichterstattern als Melder Gebrauch machen könnten, sondern an *elementare* Erkenntnisvermögen. Sellars behauptet, dass jemand, der bezüglich dieser Fähigkeiten nicht in der Lage ist, auf Verlässlichkeit zu schließen, nicht an dem Spiel teilnehmen würde, in dem man Gründe gibt und nach Gründen fragt, so wie es der Besitz genuiner begrifflicher Fähigkeiten erfordert. Eine solche „Person" *wäre tatsächlich* ein *Melder* und nicht nur jemand, der in besonderen Fällen als ein solcher betrachtet werden könnte. Selbst wenn ich zu Unrecht behaupte, dass diejenigen Fälle, die vermeintlich die Gründungseinsicht des Reliabilismus bestätigen, zu feingesponnen und speziell sind, folgt hieraus, dass wir immer noch *einen sehr umfangreichen* Bedarf an Verlässlichkeitswissen haben. Wenn diese Einsicht nur durch die Betrachtung von Fällen bestätigt werden kann, die feingesponnen und speziell sind, hat man uns noch keinen Grund für die Annahme geliefert, dass sie auch für (die Mehrheit der) Fälle gilt, die weder das eine noch das andere sind. Wir benötigen immer noch eine Erklärung für die Rolle des Verlässlichkeitswissens, die nicht von einer Zweiteilung ausgeht.

Um unser Problem zu lösen, müssen wir gründlich darüber nachdenken, was daraus folgt, dass Sollte-Sein-Regeln Regeln der Kritik sind, die einen Bereich potentiell berechtigter Anfechtungen einer Vorschussberechtigung festlegen. Diese Auffassung von Sollte-Sein-Regeln erlaubt uns, eine wesentliche Rolle für das Verlässlichkeitswissen zu erkennen, die sich von der allgemeinen Rolle der Autorisierung, die es angeblich in Schlüssen auf die Verlässlichkeit spielt, unterscheidet. Was das Verlässlichkeitswissen angeht, so ist es wirklich von größter Bedeutung, dass wir die *Grenzen unserer Verlässlichkeit* erkennen, denn um in der Lage zu sein, legitime Anfechtungen zu erkennen und auf sie zu reagieren, müssen wir uns darüber im Klaren sein, wie wir uns irren können. *In besonderen Fällen* können wir Anfechtungen abwehren, indem wir uns auf unsere allgemeine Verlässlichkeit berufen. Es ist von wesentlicher Bedeutung, dass Verlässlichkeitswissen, da es auf Sollte-Sein-Bedingungen bezogen ist, mehr mit Anfechtungen und der Reaktion auf

Anfechtungen zu tun hat als mit positiver Autorisierung. Der Fehler von Sellars – oder möglicherweise der Fehler seiner Interpreten – ist es, der Rolle allgemeiner Autorisierung von Schlüssen auf die Verlässlichkeit ein zu großes Gewicht beizumessen. Vom Standpunkt der Generierung legitimer Anfechtungen aus spielt es jedoch keine Rolle, ob eine Sollte-Sein-Regel, die unserer Vermutung nach verletzt worden sein könnte, eine autorisierende oder eine ermöglichende Bedingung betrifft. Wir müssen auf jeden Fall wissen, wie die Dinge liegen sollten und wie es geschehen kann, dass sie nicht so liegen. Im Falle von Wahrnehmungswissen erfordert dies ausgiebige Kenntnis unserer Verlässlichkeit und ihrer Grenzen.

Ich habe mich Sellars darin angeschlossen, von zwei Arten von Regeln zu sprechen. Diese Überlegungen zur wesentlich negativen Bedeutung von Verlässlichkeitswissen weist jedoch darauf hin, dass die Rede von Regeln in diesem Zusammenhang mit einer gewissen Vorsicht aufgenommen werden muss.[31] Unsere Anerkennung einer Sollte-Sein-„Regel" besteht in erster Linie in unserer Disposition, die Ausnahmen zur Kenntnis zu nehmen und angemessen auf sie zu reagieren. In der Tat wird der *Inhalt* solcher Regeln, soweit wir ihn explizieren können, weitgehend von den Einschränkungen unserer Verlässlichkeit getragen. Verlässlich sind wir unter „normalen" Umständen: was aber „normal" ist, wird durch das bestimmt, was es nicht ist. In dieser Hinsicht verhält es sich bei

---

31 Wittgenstein trifft den Nagel auf den Kopf:
   25. Auch darin, „dass hier eine Hand ist", kann man sich irren. Nur unter bestimmten Umständen nicht. – „Auch in einer Rechnung kann man sich irren – nur unter gewissen Umständen nicht."
   26. Aber kann man aus einer *Regel* ersehen, unter welchen Umständen ein Irrtum in der Verwendung der Rechenregeln logisch ausgeschlossen ist?
   Was nützt uns so eine Regel? Könnten wir uns bei ihrer Anwendung nicht wieder irren?
   27. Wollte man aber dafür etwas Regelartiges angeben, so würde darin der Ausdruck „unter normalen Umständen" vorkommen. Und die normalen Umstände erkennt man, aber man kann sie nicht genau beschreiben. Eher noch eine Reihe von abnormalen.
   34. Wem man das Rechnen beibringt, wird dem auch beigebracht, er könne sich auf eine Rechnung des Lehrers verlassen? Aber einmal müssten doch diese Erklärungen ein Ende haben. Wird ihm auch beigebracht, er könne sich auf seine Sinne verlassen – weil man ihm allerdings in manchen Fällen sagt, man könne sich in dem und dem besonderen Fall *nicht* auf sie verlassen? –
   Regel und Ausnahme.
   Wittgenstein (1989), ÜG: *Über Gewißheit*, 124 ff.

„normal" wie bei „real". Was die Schlüsselbegriffe für Sollte-Sein-Regeln angeht, so folgt die Semantik der Spur der Erkenntnistheorie.

5. Bis jetzt ging es mir darum zu zeigen, wie Verlässlichkeitserwägungen in eine weitgehend reliabilistische Auffassung von Rechtfertigung integriert werden sollten. Der Schlüssel hierfür, so habe ich argumentiert, liegt darin zu erkennen, dass sich Rechtfertigung nach einer Vorschuss- und Anfechtungsstruktur richtet. Ich habe jedoch zu Beginn gesagt, dass das Problem der Verknüpfung von Verantwortlichkeit und Verlässlichkeit im Zusammenhang des Versuchs einer Antwort auf den allgemeinen Skeptizismus eine besondere Schwierigkeit aufweist. Ja, ich habe die Neigung, von der epistemischen Verantwortung zu viel zu verlangen, auf die Überzeugung zurückgeführt, dass eine Erkenntnistheorie dem Skeptizismus entschieden entgegentreten müsse. Eine vollständige Verteidigung einer bescheideneren Auffassung epistemischer Verantwortung bedarf dementsprechend eines Mittels der *Abwendung* der skeptischen Herausforderung. Eine Untersuchung der Frage, was ein Responsibilist zum Skeptizismus sagen sollte, wird die von mir vertretene regulativ-deontologische Auffassung deutlicher vor Augen führen.

Als wesentlichen ersten Schritt müssen wir zwei Formen des Skeptizismus unterscheiden, die agrippinische und die cartesianische.[32] Sie bedürfen einer etwas unterschiedlichen Handhabung.

Die agrippinische Skepsis ergibt sich aus der Art und Weise, wie uns Ansprüche auf Wissen oder gerechtfertigte Überzeugungen mit der Drohung eines infiniten Regresses konfrontieren. Wenn ich behaupte etwas zu wissen oder gerechtfertigterweise zu glauben, kann mich der Skeptiker auffordern, mich zu rechtfertigen. Was auch immer ich sage, er wird seine Frage wiederholen: Warum sagst Du das? Wenn ich den Prozess, Gründe für Gründe geben, nicht zu einem Ende bringen kann, bin ich anscheinend in die Falle eines infiniten Regresses geraten. Aber wie soll ich diesen Prozess stoppen? Wenn ich mich irgendwann weigere, eine Antwort zu geben, wird der Skeptiker sagen, dass ich bloß eine Annahme mache; und wenn ich mich dabei wieder finde, eine Antwort zu wiederholen, die ich schon gegeben hatte, wird er mich beschuldigen, dass ich zirkulär argumentiere. Regress, Annahme, Zirkularität: Das ist Agrippas Trilemma.

Der cartesische Skeptizismus funktioniert ganz anders. Kartesische Argumente spielen mit skeptischen Szenarien: zum Beispiel dass ich das Opfer eines bösen Betrügers bin oder ein Hirn im Tank. Die Sorge ist

---

32 Zur Verteidigung dieser Klassifikation vgl. Williams (2001), Kap. 5.

hier, dass meine Erfahrung genauso sein könnte, wie sie ist, auch wenn die Welt tatsächlich ganz anders ist, als sie mir erscheint (wenn es überhaupt eine Welt gibt, in einem Sinne, den ich vortheoretisch verstehen würde). Meine Erfahrung, also alles, was mir jemals gegeben sein wird, scheint unzureichend, um zu bestimmen, wie die Wirklichkeit beschaffen ist. In der Tat scheint sie im Hinblick auf meine gewöhnlichen Überzeugungen und verschiedene skeptische Alternativen *neutral* zu sein. Der cartesische Skeptizismus richtet sich auf eine Reihe von *Unterbestimmtheits*problemen.

Die Vorschuss-und-Anfechtungskonzeption von Rechtfertigung liefert ganz offensichtlich eine Antwort auf agrippinische Bedenken. Vom Standpunkt der Vorschuss-und-Anfechtungskonzeption ist die Gefahr eines infiniten Regresses eine Illusion. Die Gefahr scheint nur deshalb aufzutauchen, weil der Skeptiker eine unbeschränkte Lizenz erhält, Gründe einzufordern. Das heißt, der Schein eines Regresses wird durch eine extreme und unplausible Asymmetrie zwischen dem Behauptenden und dem Herausforder erzeugt. Das Vorschuss-und-Anfechtungsmodell setzt keine solche Asymmetrie voraus. Ebenso wie die Berechtigung manchmal, aber nicht immer, erworben werden muss, so muss auch das Recht der Anfechtung manchmal, aber nicht immer, erworben werden.

Dies zeigt sich besonders klar im Fall wahrnehmungsbasierter Berechtigung, bei dem sich legitime Anfechtungen sich auf vermutete Verletzungen spezifischer Sollte-Sein-Bedingungen beziehen. Die Stellung der Frage „Woher weißt du das?" oder „Warum glaubst du das?" reicht nicht aus, eine Sollte-Tun-Bedingung zu aktivieren. In vielen solchen Fällen könnte und sollte man auf solche Fragen mit den Gegenfragen beantworten „Weshalb glaubst du, ich könnte mich irren? An welchen Irrtum denkst du?". Wenn diese Fragen unbeantwortet bleiben, so liegt auch keine konkrete – und vielleicht auch keine verständliche – Anfechtung vor. Nur dann, wenn eine konkrete Anfechtung vorliegt, liegt auch etwas Bestimmtes vor, dem man entgegentreten muss. Zugegeben, Erwiderungen auf legitime Anfechtungen können eventuell selbst wieder infrage gestellt werden, so dass der Prozess von Anfechtung und Erwiderung keinen festen Schlusspunkt hat. Aber damit wird nur die Offenheit der Untersuchung anerkannt und nicht die Tür zu einem infiniten Regress der Rechtfertigung geöffnet.

Die Asymmetrie zwischen dem Behauptenden und dem Herausforderer wurzelt in dem konkurrierenden Modell von Rechtfertigung, auf das ich im Zusammenhang mit Chisholm angespielt habe: das Modell vorheriger Begründung. Dieses Modell beinhaltet die uneingeschränkte

Forderung, dass es bei jeder Rechtfertigung auch eine spezifische (und tatsächlich anerkannte) positive Autorisierung geben muss.[33] Da man durch die bloße Tatsache, dass man sich als wissend darstellt, implizit einen Anspruch auf eine solche Autorisierung erhebt, ist es vollkommen vernünftig, wenn der Skeptiker verlangt, dass man die Quelle der eigenen Berechtigung offen legt. Der Skeptiker hat das Recht zu dieser anscheinend unmotivierten Anfechtung jedoch nur, wenn wir ein Modell epistemischer Berechtigung annehmen, das ihm dieses Recht *gibt*.

Dem Modell vorheriger Begründung zufolge gibt es keine Berechtigung, die man sich nicht eigens durch eine Art von bewusster und verdienstvoller Leistung erwirbt. Was nichtbasale Überzeugungen angeht, so erfordert die verdienstvolle Leistung, dass man Belege für sie hat und angemessenen Gebrauch von ihnen macht. Was basale Überzeugungen angeht, so erwirbt man sich epistemische Autorität dadurch, dass man sie auf eine prozedural korrekte Weise gewinnt. Wenn wir darauf beharren, dass jede gerechtfertigte Überzeugung einer bestimmten Art von spezifischer positiver Autorisierung bedarf, gelangen wir unvermeidlich zu der Annahme, dass die Ausbildung einer basalen Überzeugung – die Erstattung eines basalen Berichts – eine Handlung ist, die bestimmten Sollte-Tun-Normen unterliegt. Wenn dies richtig ist, dann ist die Konzeption von Rechtfertigung, welche für den extremen Internalismus verantwortlich ist, den wir bei Philosophen wie Chisholm finden, *auch* die Triebfeder des agrippinischen Skeptizismus. Ja, in dem sie letzteren antreibt, drängt sie zu ersterem. Verständlicherweise provoziert dieser extreme Internalismus bei Goldman und anderen eine kritische Reaktion. Wie wir aber gesehen haben, kann die regulativ-deontologische Konzeption vom Modell vorheriger Begründung getrennt werden.

Nachdem ich aufgezeigt habe, wie die Vorschuss-und-Anfechtungskonzeption von Rechtfertigung mit dem agrippinischen Argument umgeht, möchte ich ganz kurz auf den cartesischen Skeptizismus eingehen, insbesondere auf die Skepsis bezüglich unseres Wissens die Außenwelt betreffend. Diese Form des Skeptizismus stellt für mich ein dringliches Problem dar, zumal ich für eine Konzeption von Rechtfertigung argumentiere, die uns von Anfang an einen Standort in dieser Welt

---

33 Zu den genaueren Details vgl. Williams (2001), Kap. 13. Zu der Verbindung zwischen dem Vorschuss-und-Anfechtungsmodell und der kontextuellen Veränderbarkeit vgl. wiederum Kap. 14. Vgl. auch meinen Aufsatz „Skepticism" in *The Blackwell Guide to Epistemology*.

gibt. Versetzt mich das nicht in eine dürftige Position, was meine Auseinandersetzung mit dem Außenwelt-Skeptizismus angeht?

Eine detaillierte Antwort auf diese Herausforderung kann ich hier nicht vorbringen. Ich kann jedoch eine generelle Strategie vorschlagen. Das responsibilistische Modell von Rechtfertigung muss ergänzt werden durch eine *diagnostische Erklärung*, wie der Außenwelt-Skeptizismus entsteht. Insbesondere muss der Responsibilist Argumente dafür liefern, dass der Außenwelt-Skeptizismus kein naives oder bloß intuitives Problem darstellt, sondern das künstliche Ergebnis verzichtbarer theoretischer Festlegungen ist. Idealerweise würde es sich dabei um Festlegungen handeln, deren Vermeidbarkeit zeigen würde, dass eine responsibilistische Erkenntnistheorie haltbar ist. Die responsibilistische Konzeption von Rechtfertigung würde also den Schlüssel zu einer befriedigenden Diagnose liefern.

Ich glaube, dass die Aussichten für die Verwirklichung einer solchen Strategie ausgezeichnet sind. Wie ich an anderer Stelle ausführlich gezeigt habe, sollte uns allein schon die Kategorie „Überzeugungen die Außenwelt betreffend" verdächtig sein.[34] Dieser Kategorie fehlt es an ausgewiesener theoretischer Seriosität, da sie sich auf die Gesamtheit der Natur- und Sozialwissenschaften erstreckt so wie auch auf die gänzlich heterogene Masse alltäglicher Informationen. „Überzeugungen die Außenwelt betreffend" ist vergleichbar mit „Dinge, die an einem Mittwoch passieren". Niemand erwartet eine einheitliche Theorie von an Mittwochen stattfindenden Ereignissen. Vortheoretisch gesehen gibt es genauso wenig einen Grund für die Erwartung einer einheitlichen Erklärung des Wissens über die Außenwelt.

Warum ist die Frage des Skeptikers anscheinend nicht fehlgeleitet? Die Antwort lautet, dass die Kategorie „Überzeugungen die Außenwelt betreffend" ein gewisses Maß an theoretischer Seriosität gewinnt, *wenn man von einer bestimmten Theorie der Erkenntnis ausgeht*. Glaubt man, dass alle Überzeugungen bezüglich der Außenwelt auf der Basis der Erfahrung gerechtfertigt sind – wobei das wie auch immer verstandene Haben einer Wahrnehmungserfahrung hinter dem Wissen über die uns umgebende Welt zurückbleibt – so kann man natürlich fragen, ob die Erfahrung diese Funktion erfüllen kann. Wenn wir diesem Rückzug jedoch widerstehen, können wir das Problem vermeiden, das die Rückkehr von einer solchen Flucht aufwerfen würde.

---

34 Das ist die zentrale Behauptung von Williams (1992), Kap. 3.

Der Antrieb für den Rückzug auf eine Erfahrungsbasis für Überzeugungen bezüglich der Außenwelt ist das agrippinische Problem, das uns anscheinend dazu zwingt, einen natürlichen Schlusspunkt für die Kette von Rechtfertigungen ausfindig zu machen. Da diese Basis an sich betrachtet sicher ist, wird sie unvermeidlich schmal sein. Ich ziehe aber eine radikale Lehre aus dieser Überlegung. Meiner Ansicht nach *konstituiert* die durch den traditionellen Empirismus erzwungene epistemische Trennlinie zwischen der „Erfahrung" und dem Wissen bezüglich der Welt dieses Wissen als einen Gegenstand theoretischer Untersuchung. Wenn das richtig ist, dann verschreibt man sich einer seltsamen Metaphysik, die ich „epistemologischen Realismus" nenne, sobald man das Problem akzeptiert. Nach dieser Ansicht fallen alle Überzeugungen unter natürliche epistemische Arten und stehen zueinander in natürlichen Beziehungen epistemischer Priorität. Diese angebliche „Struktur empirischen Wissens" ist unveränderlich und liegt allen *lokalen* Praktiken epistemischer Bewertung zugrunde. Sie ist ein unveränderliches Merkmal der *condition humaine*.

Das Vorschuss-und-Anfechtungsmodell von Rechtfertigung lädt uns ein, diese Dinge in einem ganz anderen Licht zu sehen. In einem gegebenen historischen Kontext bricht die Rechtfertigung mit einer Vorschussberechtigung ab. Eine solche Vorschussberechtigung konstituiert keine theoretisch zugängliche Art von Überzeugung. Folglich zwingt uns das Vorschuss-und-Anfechtungsmodell nichts auf, was der empiristischen Kluft zwischen der Erfahrung und den Überzeugungen bezüglich der Welt gleichen würde. Vertreter dieses Modells brauchen und sollten nicht das Wissen bezüglich der Welt als Gegenstand der Erkenntnistheorie anerkennen.[35]

Diese Bemerkungen liefern nicht mehr als einen Hinweis darauf, wo ein Argument gesucht werden sollte. Aber wenn ich damit Recht habe, dass das Problem der Außenwelt auf dem extremen Internalismus beruht, den wir auf das Modell vorheriger Begründung zurückgeführt haben, folgt daraus, dass die regulativ-deontologische Konzeption von Rechtfertigung, die das Vorschuss-und-Anfechtungsmodell beinhaltet, Antworten auf den agrippinischen und den cartesischen Skeptizismus liefern kann. Im letzteren Falle gelingt ihr dies aber mehr dadurch, dass sie zeigt, wie wir legitimerweise skeptische Probleme beiseitelegen können, als

---

35 Vgl. Williams (1992), Kap. 2. Die Ansicht, dass der Außenweltsskeptizismus nicht von seinen fundamentalistischen Prämissen abtrennbar ist, habe ich bereits in Williams (1977) vertreten.

durch eine direkte Lösung dieser Probleme. Aber wenn erst einmal der Außenwelt-Skeptizismus ad acta gelegt ist, dann können wir Verantwortung mit Verlässlichkeit versöhnen, was eine befriedigende Erkenntnistheorie tun sollte.[36]

References

Brandom (2000): Robert Brandom, *Expressive Vernunft*, Frankfurt/Main.
Brandom (2001): Robert Brandom, *Begründen und Begreifen*, Frankfurt/Main.
Chisholm (1963): Roderick Chisholm, *Theory of Knowledge in America*.
Chisholm (1982): Roderick Chisholm, *The Foundations of Knowing*, Minneapolis.
Goldman (2002): Alvin Goldman, „Internalism Exposed", in: A. Goldman, *Pathways To Knowledge*, Oxford.
Kornblith (2002): Hilary Kornblith, *Knowledge and Its Place in Nature*, Oxford.
Lewis (1996): David Lewis, „Elusive Knowledge", in: *Australasian Journal of Philosophy* 74, 549–67.
Pryor (2004): James Pryor, „What's Wrong With Moore's Argument?", in: *Philosophical Issues* 14 (2004).
Sellars (1968): Wilfrid Sellars, *Science and Metaphysics*, London.
Sellars (1999): Wilfrid Sellars, *Der Empirismus und die Philosophie des Geistes*, Paderborn.
Sellars (1997): Wilfrid Sellars, *Empiricism and the Philosophy of Mind*, Cambridge.
Sosa (1997a): Ernest Sosa, ‚How To Resolve The Pyrrhonian Problematic: A Lesson From Descartes', in: *Philosophical Studies* 85, 229–249.
Sosa (1997b): Ernest Sosa, „Mythology of the Given", in: *History of Philosophical Quarterly*, vol. 14, 275–86.
Vogler (2002): Candace Vogler, *Reasonably Vicious*, Cambridge.
Williams (1977): Michael Williams, *Groundless Belief*, Oxford.
Williams (1992): Michael Williams, *Unnatural Doubts*, Oxford.
Williams (2001): Michael Williams, *Problems of Knowledge*, Oxford.
Williams (2003): Michael Williams, „Mythology of the Given: Sosa, Sellars and the Task of Epistemology", in: *Aristotelian Society*, Supplementary Volume LXXVII, 91–112.
Williams (2005): Michael Willams, „Knowledge a Natural Phenomenon?", in: R. Schantz (ed.), *The Externalist Challenge*, Amsterdam.
Wittgenstein (1989): Ludwig Wittgenstein, *Über Gewißheit*, Frankfurt/Main.
Zagzebski (1999): Linda Zagzebski, „What Is Knowledge?', in: J. Greco/E. Sosa (eds.), *The Blackwell Guide to Epistemology*, Oxford, 92–116.

---

[36] Aus dem Englischen übersetzt von Erich Ammereller.

Justification, Deontology, and Voluntary Control

Matthias Steup

In contemporary epistemology, it is widely rejected that epistemic justification—the kind of justification traditionally considered a necessary condition of knowledge—is by nature deontological.[1] I shall present a brief outline of the deontological account of justification (epistemic deontology, for short) and then discuss the two arguments on which its rejection is based.

Deontological Justification Defined

According to epistemic deontology, the concept of justification is to be defined in terms that belong to the family of deontic locutions such as *obligation, prohibition,* or *permission,* each of which can in turn be defined in terms of an *ought*. To say that φ-ing is obligatory means that one ought to φ, to say that φ-ing is prohibited means that one ought not φ, and to say that φ-ing is permitted means that it's not the case that one ought not φ. Taking a justified belief to be a permissible belief, let us define justification as follows:

$J_d 1$ S is justified in believing that p $=_{df}$ It is not the case that S ought to refrain from believing that p.[2]

---

1   Trusting the reader will not need to be constantly reminded of what kind of justification this paper is about, I will henceforth omit the qualifier *epistemic*, except for contexts in which adding it is called for to distinguish epistemic from other kinds of justification.
2   An alternative would be to take justified belief to be obligatory belief. But this does not adequately capture the meaning of the word *justification*. William Alston puts the point aptly when he says the following about the justification of an action: "To say the action was justified does not imply that it was required or obligatory, only that its negation was not required or obligatory. This holds true whether we are thinking of moral, legal, institutional, or prudential justification of actions." Alston adds: "The most natural way of construing the justification of beliefs is in parallel fashion." See Alston (1989), 125 f.

Compare J_d1 with an alternative definition, suggested by William Alston's claim that deontological justification is most centrally freedom from blameworthiness:[3]

J_d2 S is justified in believing that p $=_{df}$ It is not the case that, in believing that p, S is blameworthy.

Whether J_d1 and J_d2 are equivalent depends on how we understand the notion of blameworthiness. Let's distinguish between a weak and a strong sense of the notion:

B_w S is blameworthy for φ-ing $=_{df}$ S ought not φ.
B_s S is blameworthy for φ-ing $=_{df}$ S does deserve to be blamed for φ-ing.

If the word 'blameworthy' in J_d2 is understood in the sense of B_w, J_d2 is equivalent to J_d1; if the word is understood in the sense of B_s, J_d2 is not equivalent to J_d1. In fact, in that case, J_d2 yields an account of justified belief that should be rejected.

Suppose we understand *being justified in φ-ing* as *not deserving to be blamed for φ-ing*. This understanding distorts what the concept of justification ordinarily means. The distortion is due to the fact that when one's φ-ing constitutes a rule infraction but one has an *excuse* for φ-ing, then one does not deserve to be blamed for φ-ing. Hence, if we define *being justified* as freedom from blameworthiness in the strong sense, we get the following result: whenever an agent has an excuse for φ-ing, the agent's φ-ing is justified. This is a bad result since having an excuse is not a condition that gives one justification for φ-ing.

Suppose Sam didn't pay his rent on time because at the end of a vacation a volcano eruption delayed his flight back home by a week. The unforeseeable delay gives Sam an excuse, but not a justification, for not paying his rent on time. The sort of thing giving him justification would be, for example, his landlord's permission to pay his rent on the 15th instead of the 1st. The same point applies to beliefs. A severe headache, sleep deprivation, or detrimental side-effects of a drug might give us an excuse for believing something silly. Such conditions, however, do not give us justification for the silly belief. Hence, if J_d2 is construed in terms of B_s, the result will be a defective account of justified belief.

---

3   In his classic "Concepts of Epistemic Justification, Alston says "J_d is, most centrally, a concept of freedom from blameworthiness, a concept of being 'in the clear' so far as one's intellectual obligations are concerned." See Alston (1989), 89.

Note that there is no inconsistency in classifying an action or a belief as blameworthy in the weak sense while not being blameworthy in the strong sense. Sam's not paying his rent on time was unjustified or blameworthy in the sense that Sam didn't do what he ought to have done, namely pay his rent on time. But since he had an excuse, it would be unfair to blame him for this omission. Likewise, if due to the side-effects of a drug you believe something silly, you hold an unjustified or blameworthy belief in the sense that you believe something that you ought not believe. Saying this is entirely compatible with the concession that, since you have an excuse, we shouldn't blame you for this belief.

To sum up: If we understand J_d2 in terms of B_w, then J_d1 and J_d2 are equivalent. In that case, nothing substantial rides on which definition we employ. If, however, we understand J_d2 in the sense of B_s, the result will be an ill-conceived notion of justification. Deontological justification, then, should not be defined in terms of the strong sense of the concept of blameworthiness.

Epistemic and Non-Epistemic Justification

Next, we need to consider how the *epistemic* ought differs from the ought of prudence and morality. The definiens in J_d1 should not be taken to mean: "It is not the case that S *prudentially* ought to refrain from believing that p." Nor should it be taken to mean: "It is not the case that S *morally* ought to refrain from believing that p." Rather, the definiens of D_j1 must be understood this way: "It is not the case that S *epistemically* ought to refrain from believing that p." The *epistemic* ought differs from the *ought* of prudence and the ought of morality, and thus the definiens of D_j1 implies nothing with regard to the question of what S ought to believe prudentially or morally. Exactly how, though, does the epistemic ought differ from the ought of prudence or morality?

Let us approach the question this way: Advocates of epistemic deontology would say that what one epistemically ought or ought not believe is a function, not of one's moral or prudential reasons, but of one's epistemic reasons.[4] How, though, do epistemic reasons differ from

---

4 Since one's reason are one's evidence, epistemic deontology thus understood is a version of evidentialism, according to which whether what one believes is jus-

moral or prudential reasons? The standard approach to answering this question is to invoke the truth goal. Exactly how the truth goal is to be invoked is not an easy matter to settle.[5] Bracketing difficult issues that would lead us astray in the present context, I will just say the following: Epistemic reasons are the kind of reasons that are relevant when we aim at the goal of believing a proposition p only if p is true, and thus are the kind of reasons that confer probability or likelihood of truth on our beliefs. In this regard, epistemic reasons differ from moral or prudential reasons, for neither of the latter kind of reasons confers probability on our beliefs, or makes our beliefs likely.

Why Favor Deontological Justification?

Not all normativity is deontological. We can, for example, evaluate agents with regard to their physical suitability for certain athletic activities. We might say that with regard to height and weight, Al is suited better than Ben for playing basket ball, whereas Ben is better suited than Al for the sport of wrestling. Making such judgments does not entail anything deontological. It does not entail that Al had an obligation to acquire fitness for the game of basket ball, or that it was permissible for Ben to have physical characteristic making him suitable for the game of wrestling.

Likewise, some epistemologists favor evaluating an agent's performance as a believer in a fashion that is analogous to the way we evaluate an agent's suitability for a certain kind of sport.[6] According to this non-deontological approach, we might want to evaluate one belief as justified and another as unjustified because we think that the first, but not the second, serves the pursuit of truth, without intending this evaluation to imply that one is permitted or even obliged to hold the first but not the second belief. What motivates such a non-deontological approach to justification are, primarily, two arguments:

---

tified is determined by one, and only one, thing: one's evidence. Cf. Conee and Feldman (2004).
5   For an illuminating discussion of the relevant issues, see David (2001).
6   Cf. Alston (1989), 96 f.

The Argument from Lacking Truth Conduciveness
Deontological justification is epistemologically irrelevant because it is not truth-conducive.[7]

The Argument from Doxastic Involuntarism
Beliefs are unsuitable for deontological evaluation because we lack voluntary control over them.[8]

I will discuss these arguments in due course. For now, suppose deontologists have the resources for an effective rebuttal of them. This rebuttal, by itself, does not explain why one might, *to begin with*, favor the deontological over the non-deontological approach. What, then, is the primary motivation recommending the deontological understanding for justification?

In a nutshell, the answer is that deontologists view belief formation as a form of agency. A person's physical characteristics, such as her height, hair color, or eye color fall outside the scope of agency. From the deontological point of view, beliefs do not. Believing *is* a form of agency, and thus we bear responsibility for our beliefs just as much as we bear responsibility for our actions. Just as there are things we ought to do and ought not do, there are propositions we ought to believe and others we ought not believe.

A secondary motivation for endorsing a deontological understanding of epistemic justification arises from the fact that deontological evaluation of our doxastic conduct is deeply entrenched in our ordinary linguistic practices. When someone states a belief we consider irrational, we might say 'You shouldn't believe this.' Similarly, when someone refuses to believe what we consider being supported by excellent evidence, we might easily say 'You ought to believe it.' There would be nothing linguistically infelicitous about saying such things. If those who reject epistemic deontology were right, then we would need an error theory: a theory explaining how it can be that, in our ordinary practices of evaluating each other's performance as believers, we employ a framework that is fundamentally mistaken inasmuch as it takes belief to be something it isn't, namely a form of agency. Advocates of epistemic deontology enjoy the theoretical advantage of not having to supply an error theory of that kind.

---

7   Cf. Alston (1989), 95, 145 f.
8   Cf. Alston (1989), 95, 119–136.

The Argument From Lacking Truth-Conduciveness

According to the first of the two primary anti-deontological arguments mentioned above, deontological justification is not truth-conducive and thus fails to be *epistemic* justification, the kind of justification that is relevant in epistemology. To establish this point, Alston describes two situations in which a subject enjoys deontological justification for a belief without having reasons in support of the belief that confer likelihood on it.[9] I will discuss only the first of Alston's two examples, since what I will say about it can easily be applied to the second as well. Alston's first example presents us with a culturally isolated tribe. Suppose members of this tribe base a belief about the outcome of a battle on reading the entrails of a dead animal. What these entrails reveal, according to the tribe's experts on predicting the future in this fashion, is that they will win the battle. Let's use 'W' to refer to this belief. Alston's argument can be summed up as follows:

(1) Deontological justification is essentially freedom from blameworthiness.
(2) In believing W, the tribe members are free from blameworthiness. (Since they are culturally isolated and thus have never been exposed to criticism of their cognitive practices, they do not deserve to be blamed for believing W.)

Therefore:

(3) The tribe members have deontological justification for believing W.
(4) Epistemic justification for believing W requires possessing a reason that confers likelihood on W.
(5) The tribe members do not possess a reason that confers likelihood on W. (Their only reason for W is a proposition about what the dead animal's entrails say, and that reason does not confer likelihood on believing W.)

Therefore:

(6) The deontological justification the tribe members have for believing W is not epistemic justification.

Above, I argued that we must distinguish between a strong and a weak sense of 'blameworthiness':

B_w S is blameworthy for doing x $=_{df}$ S ought not do x.

---

9 See Alston (1989), 95.

B_s S is blameworthy for doing x $=_{df}$ S ought to be blamed for doing x.

If we understand 'blameworthiness' in the strong sense, then the first premise is false. If we understand 'blameworthiness' in the weak sense, then the second premise is false.

Suppose we understand the first premise in the strong sense of 'blameworthiness'. As I argued above, we then get the implausible consequence that, whenever a subject has an excuse for a silly belief, her silly belief is justified. But what justifies a belief is one's evidence, not the kind of conditions that give one an excuse for believing something silly.[10] Hence a B_s construal of first premise must be rejected.

Now suppose we understand the first premise in the weak sense of blameworthiness. In that case, we should judge that the tribe members' belief is blameworthy, a belief they ought not hold, for the belief is based on not probability-conferring reasons but the unreliable method of interpreting the entrails of a dead animal. In making this judgment, we need not also judge that the tribe members ought to be blamed for believing W. Rather, even though we think they ought not believe W and are blameworthy for believing W in that sense, we could easily agree with Alston that, due to their long-standing customs and traditions, firmly in place due to cultural isolation, the people of this tribe ought not to be blamed for believing W. There is no inconsistency involved at all in making these two judgments.[11] Hence, given a B_w reading of the first premise, the second premise of Alston's argument must be rejected.

Doxastic Involuntarism and the Datum Supporting It

Next, I turn to an examination of the other primary objection to epistemic deontology, the Argument from Doxastic Involuntarism. Doxastic involuntarism is the view that beliefs – or more generally, our dox-

---

10 Externalists would of course say that it's not one's evidence but some external condition such as reliability that justifies one's beliefs. But, I take it, they would agree that conditions providing an excuse are not among the conditions that justify our beliefs.

11 About an earlier response of mine to his cultural isolation case (see Steup 1988), Alston says "I think that Steup is displaying an insensitivity to cultural differences." s. Alston (1989), 146. The response offered here, it seems to me, is not a proper target for the charge of cultural insensitivity.

astic attitudes such as belief, disbelief, and suspension of judgment – differ from actions in the following respect: Whereas we have voluntary control over what we do, we lack voluntary control over what we believe. According to the Argument from Doxastic Involuntarism, introduced to the epistemological literature by William Alston, the significance of doxastic involuntarism lies in its incompatibility with epistemic deontology. If indeed beliefs differ from actions in being beyond our control, then belief is not a form of agency and thus unsuitable for deontological evaluation. More formally, the argument may be stated as follows:

(1) If our doxastic attitudes are suitable for deontological evaluation, then we have voluntary control over them.

(2) We do not have voluntary control over our doxastic attitudes.

Therefore:

(3) Our doxastic attitudes are unsuitable for deontological evaluation.

Sharon Ryan rejects both premises of this argument.[12] The first premise raises certainly interesting and difficult issues. Since an evaluation of it is beyond the scope of this paper, I will focus just on the second premise only. I will begin by reviewing why this premise enjoys a good deal of initial plausibility and then proceed to argue that there are good reasons to reject it.

Alston's defense of the second premise is based on examples: You cannot now believe that the United States is still a colony of Great Britain.[13] When you see and feel that it is raining, you cannot refrain from believing that it is raining.[14] Such examples generalize to what I will call the 'datum' in support of doxastic involuntarism: You cannot believe what in light of your evidence is clearly false, and you cannot refrain from believing what in light of your evidence is clearly true. In addition, there is a third category: propositions that, given your evidence, are neither clearly false nor clearly true. Propositions of this kind are such that you can neither believe nor disbelieve them. I will use the following three propositions to illustrate the datum to which Alston appeals:

H   I have hands.
W   I have wings.
D   The number of ducks is even.

---

12 See Ryan (2003).
13 See Alston (1989), 122.
14 See Alston (1989), 129.

Given my evidence, H is clearly true and W is clearly false. Hence I cannot believe W and cannot refrain from believing H. D, in light of my evidence, is neither clearly true nor clearly false. Hence I can neither believe D nor disbelieve D, which is to say that I cannot refrain from suspending judgment about D. The vast majority of our doxastic attitudes falls into one of these three categories and hence would appear to be beyond our control. In a nutshell, then, Alston's datum can be expressed thus: Given our evidence, we cannot believe otherwise. In light of this datum, it would seem that the second premise is true.

The Two Ingredients of Voluntary Control

To assess whether the datum really succeeds in establishing the truth of doxastic involuntarism, we must take note of the fact that voluntary control involves two aspects: executional and volitional control. Suppose you are in an auditorium listening to a lecture. If you have control over your whereabouts, then it must be the case that, if you choose to stay, you will not be forcibly removed from the premises, and if you choose to leave, you will not be prevented from doing so by locked doors. We may define this kind of control as follows:

Executional Control
One has voluntary control over φ-ing $\rightarrow$ If one decides to do φ, one can φ, and if one decides to refrain from φ-ing, one can refrain from φ-ing.

If you can no longer stand listening to an excruciatingly boring lecture and decide to leave, then being tied with ropes to your seat, experiencing sudden paralysis of your legs, or encountering locked doors stand in the way of executing your decision, thus robbing you of executional control over whether to leave or not. Similarly, if the lecture is fascinating and you want to continue listening to it, but security personal forcibly removes you from the auditorium, then you cannot execute your choice to remain in the lecture hall. In that case you no longer enjoy executional control over whether to stay or not.

Here are two further examples of executional control failure:

Paralyzed Peter
Due to a stroke, Peter encounters sudden paralysis of his right arm. He wants to raise it to reach for his coffee, but his arm won't move.

> *Twitching Tom*
> His eye lid twitches. Tom is trying hard to stop his eye lid from twitching, but with no success.

Peter and Tom are suffering from executional control failure. Hence Peter doesn't have voluntary control over the behavior of his arm, and Twitching Tom does not have voluntary control over the behavior of his eye lid. Executional control failure, however, is not the only way in which one can be prevented from enjoying voluntary control. Consider two further examples:

> *Agoraphobic Al*
> His friends are taking a walk in the park, but Al can't join them because he suffers from agoraphobia, an excessive and irrational fear of wide, open places. Due to his mental illness, he cannot decide to do an unnerving thing as going to the park.

> *Mysophobic Mel*
> Although Mel has perfectly clean hands, he just washed and then disinfected them for the 67th time since he got up in the morning. He did this because he suffers from mysophobia, an excessive and irrational fear of germs and contamination. Due to his mental illness, he decides, up to 100 times a day, to wash and disinfect his hands.

The problem Al and Mel encounter is not that of being unable to do what one has decided to do, that is, that of being unable to execute one's decision. It's not the case that Al doesn't take a walk in the park because each time he tries to do that muscle spasm prevent him from doing it, or civil unrest on the streets would make leaving one's house unwise. Rather, Al's problem is that, due to his mental illness, he cannot decide to take a walk in the park. Similarly, the reason why Mel is washing his hands is not that he is forced at gunpoint to do so, or that a series of muscular convulsions miraculously results in an episode of undesired hand washing. Rather, due to his mental illness, Mel cannot help but decide to wash his hands once again. Al and Mel, then, suffer from a loss of *volitional* control – control over one's decisions and choices – which we may be defined as follows:

> *Volitional Control*
> One has voluntary control over φ-ing $\rightarrow$ One can decide to do φ and one can decide to refrain from φ-ing.

To sum up, voluntary control breaks down into two parts: the ability to execute one's will, and control over one's will itself. Each of them is a necessary condition of voluntary control.

Why We Can't Believe Otherwise

Let us return to Alston's datum, our inability to believe otherwise given the evidence we have. Is this inability due to control failure of the executional or the volitional kind? Let us consider my inability to believe that I have wings.

Given my evidence – I see and feel that there are no wings that are attached to my body – I am forced to disbelieve the proposition that I have wings. Now, am I forced to disbelieve this proposition

(a) because I cannot decide to believe a crazy thing like that

or

(b) because, upon deciding to believe such a crazy thing, I cannot execute my decision?

Here are four reasons for thinking that (a) is correct. First, in our personal experience, typically we are not familiar with episodes in which we resolved to believe or disbelieve something and then find ourselves unable to execute that choice. Although such cases are not impossible, they are quite rare.[15]

Second, under normal circumstances, it is easy to execute one's doxastic choices. It's even easier than turning the light on or off. On the way to the light switch, one might fall and break one's neck. Other people might try to prevent one from flipping the switch. No such risks are involved in executing a doxastic decision. The kind of thing that might block a doxastic volition to believe p are an emotional aversion to p or a deep commitment involving the rejection of p. However, executional control failure due to such phenomena is rare.

Third, supposing I could somehow decide to believe I have wings, why should my evidence, having thus far pitifully failed to prevent me from being irrational, finally spring into action and block my endeavor when it comes to putting the crazy belief into my belief box? This would be a rather strange and mystifying explanation of my inability to believe that I have wings.

---

15 Consider a subject who, having been brought up in a devout family, takes at college a course in the Philosophy of Religion and, upon studying the problem of evil, decides that the God he used to believe in does not exist. In a case like this, it is easily imaginable that the theistic belief 'sticks', that it does not easily go even though the subject is trying to get rid of it.

Fourth, doxastic and practical irrationality are similar. Suppose that, listening to a philosophy talk in which the speaker advocates a view with which you strongly disagree, you consider taking off a shoe and throwing it at the speaker. Suppose further that you couldn't do an impolite and irrational thing like that. What explains your inability? Would it be

(a) because you can't *decide* to do it

or

(b) because you are unable to *execute* the decision to do it? (We might imagine that, knowing your deed will meet with public disapproval, you get so nervous that you find yourself unable to take off a shoe.)

Again neglecting rare and unusual cases, it seems obvious that (a) is the correct answer. In general terms, the point is that, if your inability to make a bad *practical* decision explains why you can't perform an obviously irrational *act*, then we have confirmation for thinking that your inability to make a bad *epistemic* decision explains why you cannot acquire an obviously irrational *belief*.

These reasons apply with equal force to the other examples illustrating Alston's datum. We cannot refrain from believing that we have hands, and we can neither believe nor disbelieve that the number of ducks is even because, given our evidence, we cannot make the decisions required for adopting these doxastic attitudes. What explains the datum, then, is that our evidence makes it difficult, if not psychologically impossible, for us to decide in favor of attitudes that clearly conflict with it.[16]

Compatibilism and Incompatibilism about Volitional Control

We now have an improved understanding of Alston's datum. The reason why we cannot deliberately believe contrary to what our evidence dictates is that we cannot *decide* to adopt doxastic attitudes that are clearly inconsistent with our evidence. Does this datum support doxastic involuntarism in any straightforward fashion? To discuss this question, we

---

16 H. H. Price appears to express agreement with this point when he writes: "If you are in a reasonable frame of mind, you cannot help preferring the proposition which the evidence favors, much as you may wish you could." See Price (1954), 16.

must briefly consider the issue of free will and determinism. Compatibilists and incompatibilists agree that one has voluntary control over φ-ing only if one has executional control over φ-ing. For example, they would agree that, if I want to leave but the doors are locked, I don't have control over my whereabouts. What libertarians and compatibilists do disagree about is what it takes to have volitional control. Here is a brief statement of each view:

Incompatibilism
Volitional control requires the ability to decide otherwise under the very same circumstances. This requirement is satisfied only in the absence of causal determination. In a deterministic world, control over our decisions and choices is impossible.

Compatibilism
Control over our decisions and choices is possible even in a deterministic world. Volitional control does not require the ability to decide otherwise under the very same circumstances. What it requires is not the absence of causal determination but rather causal determination *of the right kind*.

The point of compatibilism is to allow for free decisions, or control over one's will, in a deterministic world. Compatibilists secure this result by insisting that, when we want to assess whether an agent's decision was under her control or not, what is relevant is not *whether* the decision was caused, but rather *how* it was caused.[17] What matters is whether it was caused in a way that enables or prevents control. Let us say that a control-enabling causal history is a *good* causal history, whereas a control-preventing one is a *bad* causal history. Obviously, a lot of work needs to go into developing the details of an account of how to discriminate between good and bad causal histories. Here, there is no need to review the array of options available for developing these details. Instead, I will consider just one prominent approach, according to which the difference between a good and a bad causal history is constituted by the presence of absence of reason responsiveness.[18]

The basic idea of this reason responsiveness approach can be illustrated as follows. Suppose you decide to wash your hands. Suppose further the following is true of you: (i) you made this decision because your hands are dirty; (ii) you would also have decided to wash your hands if you were about to prepare a meal in your kitchen, or if you

---

17 For a useful introduction to the compatibilist literature, see McKenna (2009).
18 See Fischer and Ravizza (1998). For alternative approaches, see, for example, Frankfurt (1971) and Strawson (1962).

just dispensed an insecticide to deal with an ant problem in your house; (iii) you would not have decided to wash your hands if since the last time you washed them nothing happened to make them dirty or contaminate them with contagious agents. In that case, your decision exhibits reason responsiveness, which entitles us to judge that it was under your control. Mysophobic Mel, in contrast, doesn't satisfy the requirement of reason responsiveness. His recurring decisions to wash his hands, being rooted in mental illness, do not display the kind of sensitivity to one's reasons that voluntary control requires. Mel's hand washing decisions, therefore, are not under his control.

Compare Mel's decision to wash his hands with your decision to wash your hands. Your decision is no less causally determined than Mel's. In the circumstances prevailing at the moment the decision is made, neither you nor Mel could have decided otherwise. That, according to reason responsiveness compatibilism, is irrelevant to the question of whether the decisions are voluntary. What matters is that, unlike Mel's, your decision in favor of hand washing instantiates responsiveness to the relevant range of reasons and thus counts as voluntary.

Generalizing, we may say that, according to the reason-responsiveness approach, voluntary control arises from the sensitivity of an agent's actions to the agent's practical reasons.[19] Henceforth, I will use the term *compatibilism* to refer to the reason responsiveness version. There are, of course, other versions of compatibilism. The line of reasoning I am going to advance could easily be adjusted to these alternative versions.[20]

---

19 Developing a detailed account of reason responsiveness is a challenging project. One pitfall to avoid is the consequence that irrational conduct—which constitutes some sort of failure to be responsive to *good* reasons—is invariably involuntary. Surely irrational behavior is not always involuntary. How the reason-responsiveness approach can meet this desideratum is not instantly obvious. See Bayer (2010).

20 Cf. Steup (2000) and (2008).

The Compatibilist Case for Doxastic Voluntarism

Suppose you are committed to both compatibilism and doxastic involuntarism.[21] To test the consistency of your view, let's focus on your belief that you have hands. The question is whether this belief is under your voluntary control. As an advocate of doxastic involuntarism, you would say that it is not. But this answer would appear to be in conflict with your endorsement of compatibilism. Surely your belief that you have hands has a good causal history. It originates in visual and tactile perception, which are excellent sources of cognition. And we can easily see that your belief exhibits reason responsiveness. It is not true of you that you stick compulsively to the belief that you have hands no matter what your reasons are. If you were presented with visual and tactile perceptions indicating the loss of your hands, you would no longer believe that you have hands. Suppose, however, you wish to stick to your dual commitment. You wish to abandon neither compatibilism nor doxastic involuntarism. In that case, you would have to argue, implausibly, that your belief that you have hands has a bad causal history: that, being rooted in mental illness or similarly bad causes, is not the result of a reason-responsive process of belief formation.

Note that Alston's datum is representative of belief formation in general. The vast majority of our doxastic attitudes are locked into place by our evidence. Given our evidence, it is not possible for us to adopt alternate doxastic attitudes. Hence, if you take Alston's datum to establish general doxastic involuntariness, and you endorse compatibilism, you need to bite a particularly unbecoming bullet, namely the consequence that the vast majority of our doxastic attitudes have a bad causal history. You would then have to view our doxastic attitudes as the products of processes rooted in bad causes such as mental illness, addiction, manipulation, brain washing, hypnosis, etc. This line of reasoning would be exceedingly implausible, amounting to a *reductio* of your dual commitment.

If compatibilists wish to avoid this *reductio*, they need to abandon doxastic involuntarism. Under normal circumstances, one's belief that one has hands is an instance of reason responsiveness and thus has a good causal history. If one's evidence were inconsistent with hand pos-

---

21 It would be interesting to examine what follows about belief control if we adopt an incompatibilist account of volitional control, but I won't do so here. For some discussion of this, see Steup (2000).

session, we wouldn't believe we have hands. Compatibilists, then, should say that our belief that we have hands is a belief that's under our voluntary control. Analogous reasoning applies to the vast majority of our beliefs, having their causal origin in perception, memory, introspection, and reasoning. Such beliefs have a good causal history. Compatibilists should say that they are under our voluntary control.

The Argument from Intentionality

There is a move compatibilists can make to avoid the consequence of having to embrace doxastic voluntarism. They can make intentionality a necessary condition of voluntary control and argue that beliefs don't satisfy this condition. This argument can be stated as follows:

(1) For any doxastic attitude α, if α is under one's voluntary control, then α is adopted intentionally.
(2) Doxastic attitudes are never adopted intentionally.

Therefore:

(3) For any doxastic attitude α, α is not under one's voluntary control.[22]

Initially it seems true that one's φ-ing is under one's voluntary control only if it is intentional. Consider the behavior of Twitching Tom's eye lid. Its twitching is not under Tom's voluntary control and it is not intentional. Compare this with a normal episode of washing one's hands, which is both under one's voluntary control and intentional. Generalizing, it would seem that behavior over which one has voluntary control is intentional action, whereas behavior over which one fails to have voluntary control, such sneezing, slipping on ice, facial tics and the like, do not fall under the category of intentional action. The first premise, then, seems plausible.

In light of Alston's datum, the second premise seems plausible as well. Your belief that you have hands did not come about because you decided and henceforth intended to believe that you have hands.

---

22 Bennet (1990), Feldman (2001), and Nottelmann (2006) all argue that intentionally held belief is impossible. For a discussion of my (2008) response to the argument, see Booth (2009). For an interesting response to the Argument from Intentionality, one that is different from the one I pursue here, see Weatherson (2008), 547. For a useful summary of literature on intentionality, see Setiya (2010).

Rather, it would seem the belief is an automatic response to your evidence. This point generalizes. It seems that our beliefs are nearly always a causal response to various inputs, some of them good, others bad. So intentions don't seem to play a role in belief production.

Contrary to initial appearance, the first premise is false. Further below, I will argue that the second premise is false as well. For now, let us focus on premise (1). While it is certainly true that frequently when we act, we are carrying out some intention or other, it is also true that a lot of what we do is done *without* antecedently formed intentions. Here are some examples: shifting from 2nd to 3rd gear while driving to work, turning the doorknob or pressing the door handle down while opening a door, and unscrewing the cap of your toothpaste before brushing your teeth. Actions like these are habitual, automatic responses that we perform without thinking about them. They are part of sequences that don't involve a prior intention for each step of the sequence. Yet such actions are not involuntary. Gear shifting, doorknob turning and unscrewing of caps are not behaviors over which we lack voluntary control. So the first premise is false.

Two Kinds of Intentionality

In response to my appeal to automatic actions, advocates of doxastic involuntarism could try to recover a kind of intentionality that automatic actions instantiate but doxastic attitudes do not. For example, involuntarists could employ Searle's distinction between *prior intention* and *intention in action*.[23] About the items on my list of automatic actions, Searle would say that, while they are not examples of carrying out prior intentions, they are nevertheless examples of intentionality because each of them has an intention in action. Advocates of involuntarism could argue that, while there is such a thing as intention in action without prior intention, as exhibited by automatic actions, there is no such

---

23 See Searle (1983), 84 ff. In his (2008), although as an opponent of doxastic involuntarism he agrees with quite a bit of what I say in my (2000) and (2008), Weatherson argues that, contrary to what I am claiming, automatic actions are intentional after all. He does not, however, distinguish between prior intention and intentions in action. If what he has in mind is the latter, then I would agree with him that automatic actions are intentional in the second, weaker, sense of intentionality.

thing as *intentionality in belief*. Beliefs, therefore, do not exhibit any kind of intentionality.

Exactly what phenomenon is picked out by the term *intention in action*? Searle offers an interesting explanation of the difference between behavior where an intention in action is present and behavior where it is not present. The difference, Searle suggests, lies in the *experience of acting*.[24] In so-called 'Penfield Cases', an experimenter manipulates a subject's brain so as to make the subject's arm go up. When the subject is afterwards asked whether he raised his arm, the typical answer is: "I didn't do that; you did." The subject can assert this with complete assurance because, in a Penfield-type arm movement, the experience of acting is missing. This is different when one raises one's arm automatically, say so as to catch a ball. The same applies to the examples on my list of automatic actions. When we shift gears, turn a doorknob, or unscrew the cap from the toothpaste, it certainly does not feel as if an external power is controlling our physical movements. Rather, in each of these cases, there is an experience of acting.

I do find Searle's explanation of what an intention in action is helpful. However, if the intentionality of automatic actions is indeed to be equated with the experience of acting, or, in more general terms, the *experience of agency*, then it will remain mysterious why beliefs should fail to exhibit an analogous kind of intentionality. To argue that beliefs do not instantiate the experience of agency is to equate belief formation with the arm movement in Penfield cases, or with Tom's twitching eye lid, or with the behavior of Peter's paralyzed arm. But the claim that the phenomenology of belief is like the phenomenology of these kinds of involuntary behavior is exceedingly implausible. The involuntary behaviors just mentioned lack what typically characterizes our beliefs: reason responsiveness. When we form and drop beliefs, we respond to our evidence and are *aware* of being responsive to our evidence. Since we are aware of our ability to believe differently as our evidence changes, there is associated with belief an experience of agency that is also characteristic of automatic actions.

To sum up: Given that compatibilists conceive of voluntary control by distinguishing between good and bad causes, it follows that doxastic attitudes are under our voluntary control whenever the process by which they are formed exhibits reason responsiveness. In response, involuntarists can argue that behavior is under our voluntary control

---

24 See Weatherson (2008), 88 f.

only to the extent it can be described as carrying out an intention. This move runs afoul of the fact that automatic actions are voluntary but cannot be so described. Attempting to handle the problem automatic actions pose, involuntarists might argue that such actions exhibit a kind of intentionality that doxastic attitudes lack. However, if that kind of intentionality is to be identified with Searle's intention in action, i.e., with an experience of acting or agency, then this maneuver fails, for beliefs exhibit such intentionality no less than automatic actions do.

Intentionally Held Belief

As an alternative to claiming that there is a kind of intentionality that automatic actions have and beliefs do not, involuntarists could argue that voluntarily performed actions need not be intentional, but they need to be such that, *in principle*, they can be performed intentionally. Each of the examples I mentioned above—gear shifting, doorknob turning, the unscrewing of the toothpaste cap—can be done by way of carrying out an antecedently formed intention. It's just that typically we do these things automatically, without having to dwell on them in advance. Doxastic attitudes, in contrast, cannot be adopted intentionally at all. In response to this modified argument from intentionality, the appeal to automatic actions in not effective. However, the modified argument fails if doxastic attitudes *can* be adopted intentionally. Next, I will argue that it is indeed possible to acquire a belief intentionally.

Here is a case in which I believe something because I intended to believe it. Suppose that, having returned from a trip and taken a shuttle to the airport parking garage, I am now where I thought I left my car. To my surprise, it is no longer there. I wonder whether it has been stolen. There is of course the possibility that I don't accurately remember where I parked it. So I retrieve the paper slip which states the exact location of the parking spot I had chosen at the outset of my trip. According to the slip, I am at the right spot. Considering my evidence – the absence of my car and the parking slip – I conclude that my car was stolen. Since I do not suffer from a mental illness or a brain lesion preventing me from acquiring this belief, I encounter no problem executing my decision. Upon deciding to believe it, I instantly believe it. This, I submit, is a case in which I decided to believe that my car was stolen, and in which my belief is intentionally held. In believing that my car was stolen, I carry out the intention to believe this. Cases like this show that the second premise of the Argument from Intentionality is false as well.

This conclusion might be resisted because, in typical cases, a decision is momentary but the resulting intention persists. Suppose, after working in the garden, I decide to wash my hands because I want to prepare a meal. While I am on my way to the sink, a friend calls me on the phone. After the phone call is over, I finally wash my hands. My decision has been executed, and my intention has been carried out. Involuntarists might take this example to show that, by way of φ-ing, one carries out an intention to φ only if the following condition is met: after the decision to φ has been made, there is a temporal interval, beginning with the time of the decision and ending with the time of the decision's execution, during which there is an intention to φ that has not yet been carried out. The process leading to my belief that my car has stolen does not meet this condition, for the decision to believe this and the acquisition of the belief are simultaneous or are at least perceived as simultaneous. Hence in believing that my car was stolen, I do not carry out any intention.

However, a temporal interval as described above is not a necessary feature of forming an intention and then carrying it out. Suppose I decide to blink. If there is a temporal gap between my decision and the movement of my eye lid, it is too small for me to perceive it. In my experience, it seems that the decision and its execution are simultaneous. Nevertheless, it is correct to say that I intended to blink, and that by moving my eyelid down and up I carried this intention out.[25] It's not the case, therefore, that φ-ing intentionally always involves an interval during which one's intention has not yet been carried out. Hence the demand for such an interval is not a good objection to my claim that I intentionally acquire the belief that my car was stolen.

The features of the car theft example can be summed up as follows:

(i) Wondering whether p is true, I suspend judgment about p.
(ii) I consider my reasons for and against p.
(iii) Concluding that I have good reasons for taking p to be true, I decide to believe p.

---

25 One might hesitate to refer to blinking as an action. It might be better classified by calling it an instance of 'intentional bodily behavior'. Note, however, that if by blinking I give someone a signal, we would be less hesitant to call it an action.

(iv) My attitude of suspending judgment about p is replaced by that of believing p.
(v) I believe p because I conclude that I have reasons for taking p to be true, and the causal relation between my decision to believe p and S's believing p is non-deviant.[26]

These conditions, I submit, are sufficient for intentionally acquiring a belief. Suppose I decide to *do* something in an analogous fashion:

(a) I wonder whether I should φ.
(b) I consider my reasons for and against φ-ing.
(c) Concluding that I have good reason to φ, I decide to φ.
(d) I no longer wonder whether to φ but commence φ-ing.
(e) I am φ-ing because I decided to φ, and the causal relation between my decision to φ and my φ-ing is non-deviant.[27]

The degree of similarity between the belief case and the action case is striking. It is difficult to see why, if (a)-(e) are sufficient for φ-ing intentionally, (i)-(v) should not be sufficient for intentionally believing p.

One might wonder why so many authors are convinced that it is impossible to hold a belief intentionally. The answer, it seems to me, is that these authors think only of intentions as responses to practical reasons, overlooking the possibility that an intention to believe might be a response, not to practical reasons, but to epistemic reasons. It is this attitude that motivates the next argument I will discuss.

---

26 The non-deviancy clause is needed because there are possible cases in which S's decision to believe p causes S's belief that p, but not in the right way. Deviant causation is well known when it comes to the relation between the intention to φ and an agent's actual φ-ing. Suppose Ben intends to kill his uncle. While driving, he is thinking about how to get the job done. Being unnerved by his thoughts, Ben loses control over his car and runs over a pedestrian, killing him. The pedestrian happens to be Ben's uncle. So Ben intended to kill his uncle, his killing his uncle was caused by his intention to kill his uncle, yet his killing his uncle is not an intentional action. See Searle (1983), 82. Similarly, suppose a Harry Frankfurt-type counterfactual intervener – Dr. No – monitors my thought processes. Dr. No's plan is to prevent me from ever believing anything intentionally. Upon noticing that I decided to believe p, Dr. No uses his ray gun to cancel out any causal effect of my decision, but then causes me to believe p anyhow. In this case, mediated through Dr. No's intervention, I believe p because I decided to believe p, but I do not believe p intentionally.
27 See the previous note.

The Monetary Incentive Argument

Advocates of involuntarism have one option left to block the compatibilist case for doxastic voluntarism. They could concede that my belief that my car was stolen does exhibit a kind of intentionality – call it *epistemic intentionality* – but that that kind of intentionality isn't the right kind needed for voluntary control. What voluntary control requires is *practical intentionality*, which is the kind of intentionality resulting from decisions that respond to practical reasons. The test whether φ-ing is something over which one has voluntary control is to ask oneself whether one can φ in response to a monetary reward. Thus the question at hand is: Is it possible to acquire a doxastic attitude in response to a monetary reward? I would agree that the answer to this question is 'no'. Belief formation responds to our evidence (or sometimes what we mistakenly take to be our evidence), but never responds to monetary rewards (perhaps neglecting rare cases).

The Monetary Incentive Argument can be stated as follows:

(1) If one has voluntary control over φ-ing, then one can φ in response to a monetary reward.
(2) One cannot adopt a doxastic attitude in response to a monetary reward.

Therefore:

(3) One does not have voluntary control over one's doxastic attitudes.[28]

The first premise of this argument is false. I conclude this paper by stating five reasons for rejecting it:

(i) *The Moral Fiber Argument:* Jones is an American GI fighting the Germans in the last stages of WW II. In battle, he deliberately and intentionally kills an enemy soldier whose name is Schmidt. A man of strong moral fiber, it would have been impossible for Jones to kill Schmidt in response to a monetary incentive. The first premise implies that Jones's killing Schmidt was not under Jones's voluntary control. To avoid this implausible outcome, the first premise must be rejected.

(ii) *The St. Francis Argument.* Actions can be performed in response to *prudential* and in response to *moral* reasons. Suppose St. Francis performs a good deed in response to a moral reason. He could not have performed this deed in response to a monetary incentive. The 1st prem-

---

28 For deployment of this argument, see Bennett (1990) and Chrisman (2008).

ise has the implausible consequence that St. Francis's good deed was involuntary.

(iii) *The Argument from Arbitrariness*: Actions can be performed in responsiveness to moral or prudential reasons. According to the monetary incentive argument, φ-ing in response to a moral reason is voluntary only if the agent could also φ in response to a prudential reason. But assigning priority to prudential over moral reasons is arbitrary. To avoid such arbitrariness, involuntarists could enlarge the scope of the first premise by replacing the appeal to monetary incentives with an appeal to *practical* reasons, understood broadly enough to include both prudential and moral reasons. But then we may wonder why, when it comes to beliefs, assigning priority to practical over epistemic reasons isn't just as arbitrary as assigning priority to prudential over moral reasons. If we aim at a general account of voluntary control that avoids arbitrary favoritism of one kind of reason over another, then we must reject the first premise.

(iv) *The Kinds of Control Argument*: Since one can be responsive to one kind of reason without, at the same time, being responsive to another kind of reason, it makes sense to distinguish between as many kinds of voluntary control as there are kinds of reasons to which we might or might not be responsive. Let us distinguish between three: Prudential control, moral control, and epistemic control. Suppose St. Francis φ-s, and, while his φ-ing is an indication of responsiveness to moral reasons, it does not involve any responsiveness to prudential reasons. The first premise yields the simplistic and implausible result that his φ-ing was not under his control at all. A better approach is to say that, when St. Francis φ-s, he has moral but not prudential control over φ-ing. Since St. Francis has moral control over his φ-ing, it would be bizarre to deny that he bears responsibility for φ-ing and can be given credit for it. When it comes to control over beliefs, an analogous treatment is called for. In believing that you have hands, you are responsive to epistemic reasons but not to practical reasons. Though you do not have practical control over the belief, you enjoy epistemic control. It would be equally bizarre to deny that you bear responsibility for it, and that you can be given credit for believing in accord with your evidence.

(v) *The Missing Argument Argument*: According to the first premise of the Monetary Incentive Argument, responsiveness to practical reasons is a necessary condition of voluntary control over both actions and beliefs. In light of (i)—(iv), we may conclude that this premise is not self-evident. Since it is not self-evident, unless the premise is defended with a good argument, it is unacceptably *ad hoc*. Alas, thus far I have not seen any argument in its support at all.[29]

References

Alston (1989): William Alston, *Epistemic Justification. Essays in the Theory of Knowledge*, Ithaca.
Bayer (2010): Ben Bayer, *The Elusiveness of Doxastic Compatibilism*, Forthcoming.
Bennett (1990): Jonathan Bennett, "Why Is Belief Involuntary?", in: *Analysis* 50, 87–107.
Booth (2009): Anthony Booth, "Compatibilism and Free Belief", in: *Philosophical Papers* 38, 1–12.
Chrisman (2008): Matthew Chrisman, "Ought to Believe", in: *The Journal of Philosophy* 105, 346–70.
Conee/Feldman (2004): Earl Conee/Richard Feldman, *Evidentialism. Essays in Epistemology*, Oxford.
David (2001): Marian David, "Truth as the Epistemic Goal", in: M. Steup (ed.), *Knowledge, Truth, and Duty*, Oxford, 151–169.
Feldman (2001): Richard Feldman, "Voluntary Belief and Epistemic Evaluation.", in: M. Steup (ed.), *Knowledge, Truth, and Duty*, Oxford, 77–92.
Fischer/Ravizza (1998): John Martin Fischer/Mark Ravizza, *Responsibility and Control*, Cambridge.
Frankfurt (1971): Harry Frankfurt, "Freedom of the Will and the Concept of a Person", in: *The Journal of Philosophy* 68, 5–20.
McKenna (2009): Michael McKenna, "Compatibilism", in: *Stanford Encyclopedia of Philosophy* (http://plato.standford.edu/entries/compatibilism).
Nottelmann (2006): Nikolaj Nottelmann, "The Analogy Argument for Doxastic Voluntarism", in: *Philosophical Studies* 131, 559–82.
Price (1954): Henri Haberley Price, "Belief and the Will", in: *Proceedings of the Aristotelian Society*, Supplementary Volume 28, 1–26.
Ryan (2003): Sharon Ryan, "Doxastic Compatibilism and the Ethics of Belief", in: *Philosophical Studies* 114, 47–79.
Searle (1983): John Searle, *Intentionality*, Cambridge.
Setiya (2010): Kieran Setiya, "Intention", in: *Stanford Encyclopedia of Philosophy* (http://plato.standford.edu/entries/compatibilism).
Steup (1988): Matthias Steup, "The Deontic Conception of Justification", in: *Philosophical Studies* 53, 65–84.
Steup (2000): Matthias Steup, "Doxastic Voluntarism and Epistemic Deontology", in: *Acta Analytica* 15, 25–56.
Steup (2001): Matthias Steup (ed.), *Knowledge, Truth, and Duty*, Oxford.

---

[29] For helpful comments or discussion, I wish to thank Mylan Engel, Richard Fumerton, Adam Leite, Bruce Russell, and Stefan Tolksdorf.

Steup (2008): Matthias Steup, "Doxastic Freedom", in: *Synthese* 161, 375–92.
Strawson (1962): Peter Frederick Strawson, "Freedom and Resentment", in: *Proceedings of the British Academy* 48, 1–25.
Weatherson (2008): Brian Weatherson, "Deontology and Descartes's Demon", in: *The Journal of Philosophy* 105, 540–69.

Infinitism and the Epistemic Regress Problem[1]
Peter D. Klein

Introduction

The purpose of this paper is to show that infinitism is the correct solution to the epistemic regress problem. The paper has four steps.

First, I will make some preliminary comments about the nature of the regress problem in order to make clear what exactly the perceived problem is.

Second, I will discuss a seemingly natural presumption underlying the way in which the regress problem was originally understood by the Pyrrhonians and Aristoteleans. The result of that discussion is that the Pyrrhonian skeptical response to the regress problem is the appropriate one given that presumption. More specifically, if a belief must, itself, be fully justified in order for it to confer full justification on another belief for which it is the offered reason, then no belief is fully justified. By "fully justified" I mean to be referring to the justification condition in the traditional analysis of knowledge.[2] More about that later.

Third, I will discuss two ways in which the presumption can and has been challenged. The first challenge arises from various forms of the reliabilist account of justification including what I call 'austere reliabilism'

---

1 This paper is a re-working of a paper originally published as "Infinitism," *Routledge Companion to Epistemology*, (see Klein 2011a). In some places entire paragraphs or series of paragraphs are lifted from that paper. I have elaborated some of the arguments in that paper and have amended others. In addition, this paper uses some of the ideas and material in other papers of mine referred to in the "References." I will note those specific places.
2 I take knowledge to be true, fully justified belief plus a defeasibility condition. I have developed a defeasibility account of knowledge elsewhere (see Klein 1971, 2004), but the issues here do not concern the defeasibility condition. I mention that because the title of this volume concerns conceptions of knowledge and I am here only concerned with one of the necessary conditions. I do not want to leave the impression that fully justified, true belief is knowledge; the full justification must also be not-defeated in order for the belief to rise to the level of knowledge.

as well as various forms of reliabilism that I call 'embellished reliabilism.' I will argue that as long as one feature of austere reliabilism is maintained by embellished reliabilism, the normative issues raised by the regress argument have not been successfully addressed. The second challenge originates with contemporary coherentism and infinitism. I will argue that contemporary coherentism is not a viable response. That leaves infinitism as the only viable, non-skeptical response.

Fourth, I will describe infinitism, point to some of its advantages, and show that the primary objections to it miss the mark.

1. Preliminary Comments

Infinitism, along with coherentism and foundationalism, is a view about the structure of reasons and reasoning that is designed to provide a solution to the epistemic regress problem. Where "fully justified" means the property that satisfies the justification condition in the analysis of knowledge, the regress problem is whether reasoning can contribute in a significant way to a belief being fully justified. More specifically, the problem can be put this way: Suppose that in answer to a legitimate question concerning the basis on which we believe some proposition, b, we give a reason, r1. Then, we are asked, again legitimately, for our reason for holding r1, and we provide the reason, r2. Then, we are asked, again legitimately, for our reason for r2, and we give r3. Now, either this process could go on indefinitely, which seems to suggest that nothing has been gained by providing a reason because there is always another one needed; or if some reason repeats, it seems that we have argued in a circle and no such reasoning could provide a good basis for accepting b; or if at some point there is no further reason, it seems that the stopping point is arbitrarily held because there is no reasonable basis for holding it. The problem is that, contrary to strong pre-theoretical intuitions, there seems to be no point in giving reasons for our beliefs. We seem to be no better off epistemically after giving reasons for our beliefs than we were before giving the reasons.

Of course, Pyrrhonian Skeptics would welcome such a result. For it struck them that reasoning could not help to settle matters.[3] But for the purposes of this essay, I will assume that if one of the three ways to address the problem (infinitism, coherentism, foundationalism) can explain

---

3   I have dealt with this in more detail in Klein (2011b).

how reasoning can contribute to a belief being fully justified, that solution is preferable to skepticism since it tends to validate our pre-theoretical intuitions.

Infinitism holds that the solution to the regress problem is that there is no reason that can be given for any belief which is so privileged that it is immune to further interrogation and, thus, the branching tree of reasons does not terminate in a so-called basic proposition. In addition, although contemporary coherentism shares some features in common with infinitism, full justification does not emerge in the fashion described by the coherence theorist. The key to understanding infinitism is to recognize that if justifying a belief by giving a reason can contribute significantly to a belief being fully justified, then the regress problem has been solved because there is a good explanation of the way in which reasoning can make us epistemically better off.

2. The Traditional Problem

Aristotle gave this gloss of the regress problem in the *Metaphysics*:

> There are ... some who raise a difficulty by asking, who is to be the judge of the healthy man, and in general who is likely to judge rightly on each class of questions. But such inquiries are like puzzling over the question whether we are now asleep or awake. And all such questions have the same meaning. These people demand that a reason shall be given for everything; for they seek a starting point, and they seek to get this by demonstration, while it is obvious from their actions that they have no such conviction. But their mistake is what we have stated it to be; they seek a reason for things for which no reason can be given; for the starting point of demonstration is not demonstration.[4]

Even though Aristotle is speaking about "demonstration," which refers to a specific form of reasoning that employs syllogisms whose premissess are "first principles," the claim here is that reasoning, in general, reaches an end because there are some privileged stopping points "for which no reason can be given" because "the starting point of demonstration is not demonstration." No reason needs to be given because reasoning presupposes something not inferred – namely the premisses that provide the basis for the reasoning.

---

4   Aristotle, *Met.*, 1011a2–14.

Here is a redacted paragraph about the regress argument from William Alston's *Epistemic Justification* that illustrates the foundationalist's basic claim, namely, that a belief is justified by reasoning only if the reasoning ends in a basic, immediately justified belief:

> The argument [for foundationalism] is that the original belief [the one that requires justification] will be mediately justified only if every branch [of the justificatory tree] ... terminates in an immediately justified belief... I do not claim that this argument [the regress argument for foundationalism] is conclusive; I believe it is open to objection in ways I will not be able to go into here. But I do feel that it gives stronger support to foundationalism than any other regress argument.[5]

I will give my own statement of the regress argument for foundationalism below. Here my point is merely that the regress argument is an important tool, if not the most important tool, used to motivate foundationalism.

Foundationalism was proposed as a solution to the classical statement of the regress argument as presented by Sextus Empiricus who used it to provide a *reductio* of the claim that reasoning could provide a way to settle disputed propositions:

> The later Skeptics hand down Five Modes leading to suspension, namely these: the first based on discrepancy, the second on the regress *ad infinitum*, the third on relativity, the fourth on hypothesis, the fifth on circular reasoning. That based on discrepancy leads us to find that with regard to the object presented there has arisen both amongst ordinary people and amongst the philosophers an interminable conflict because of which we are unable either to choose a thing or reject it, and so fall back on suspension. The Mode based upon regress *ad infinitum* is that whereby we assert that the thing adduced as a proof of the matter proposed needs a further proof, and this again another, and so on *ad infinitum*, so that the consequence is suspension [of assent], as we possess no starting-point for our argument. The Mode based upon relativity ... is that whereby the object has such or such an appearance in relation to the subject judging and to the concomitant percepts, but as to its real nature we suspend judgment. We have the Mode based upon hypothesis when the Dogmatists, being forced to recede *ad infinitum*, take as their starting-point something which they do not establish but claim to assume as granted simply and without demonstration. The Mode of circular reasoning is the form used when the proof itself which ought to establish the matter of inquiry requires confirmation derived from the matter; in this case, being unable to assume either in order to establish the other, we suspend judgement about both.[6]

---

5   Alston (1989), 54 f.
6   Empiricus *PH* I, 166–169.

There are five modes mentioned in the passage from Sextus Empiricus. The modes of relativity and discrepancy are crucial to understanding the *reductio* put forth by Sextus because those modes are designed to show that neither a judgment based solely on how things appear nor a judgment based upon what we collectively hold to be true (either qua "philosophers", i.e., experts, or qua "ordinary" persons) is so privileged that it does not need to be supported by further reasoning. There will always be a basis for an initial challenge to such judgments and, if they are to be answered effectively, reasoning will have to adjudicate disagreements. Considerations similar to those motivating the modes of relativity and discrepancy form part of the motivation for infinitism and will be discussed later.

The foundationalist's answer to the skeptical conclusion is that there must be some basic propositions that need not be justified by further reasoning because, to put it bluntly, reasoning cannot create epistemic justification, it can only transfer it from the premises to the conclusion. From the foundationalist's perspective, the problem is typically not *whether* there are fully justified beliefs; the problem is, rather, *how* fully justified beliefs arise and how full justification is transferred.

This is clear, for example, from Aristotle's dismissive attitude towards skepticism manifested in the quotation above, and even more clearly in the *Posterior Analytics* in which he begins by arguing that *if* some knowledge is the result of demonstration, then some knowledge must not be the result of demonstration. For either the series of demonstrations terminates or it doesn't. It must terminate, because "one cannot traverse an infinite series."[7] But if it terminates, it cannot terminate in another proposition that requires a demonstration because the conclusion would not be "properly" known because it "rests on the mere supposition that the premisses are true."[8]

There is another logically possible structure of reasoning, namely circular reasoning, that Aristotle considers and rejects because the premisses in a demonstration must be "prior to and better known than the conclusion" and "the same things cannot be simultaneously both prior and posterior to one another."[9] Thus, *if* there is demonstrative knowledge, then there must be non-demonstrative knowledge. He never takes the sceptical possibility seriously and says that his "own doc-

---

7   Aristotle, *An. Post.* 72b10.
8   Aristotle, *An. Post.* 72b14.
9   Aristotle, *An. Post.* 72b25–28.

trine is that not all knowledge is demonstrative; on the contrary, knowledge of the immediate premisses is independent of demonstration."[10,11]

Near the end of the *Posterior Analytics* he provides a sketch of how such knowledge reliably originates with sensation and ends with rational insight. The details of Aristotle's proto-reliabilist sketch are not important at this point, although I will return to it and a general discussion of reliabilism in the next section. What is important here is to present the regress argument for foundationalism that underlies both traditional and contemporary foundationalism.

The regress argument for foundationalism

1. Reasoning in support of a belief can have only three structures: it is finite and has a beginning point, it is circular, or it is infinite.
2. Circular reasoning is not acceptable because a belief would have to be epistemically prior to itself.
3. Reasoning infinite in length could not be carried out by humans.
4. Thus, if there is knowledge that results from reasoning, the reasoning must be finite in length.
5. The beginning points of the reasoning must be known (otherwise it would be mere supposition.)
6. Thus, if there is knowledge that results from reasoning, there must be some beliefs that are known by some process other than reasoning.

The conclusion is the basic claim made by the foundationalist, namely, if there is some knowledge that is the result of reasoning, some knowledge is not the result of reasoning. Note the hypothetical nature of the conclusion. Although most foundationalists eschew skepticism, a foundationalist need not hold that there is knowledge based upon reasoning in any specific area, or even in general. There can be and have been skeptical foundationalists: Hume, for example.[12] There can be non-skeptical foundationalists: Locke and Descartes, for example.

---

10 Aristotle, *An. Post.* 72b18.
11 This paragraph is slightly revised from Klein (2007a), 2 f.
12 Hume, of course, appealed to custom and habit as providing a basis for knowledge of matters of fact. Thus, he was not a skeptic about knowledge of matters of fact. He was, however, a skeptic about knowledge of matters of fact *based upon reasoning*.

I think it is fair to say that there is one core presupposition underlying the foundationalist "solution" to the regress problem:

Inheritance Principle: Reasoning cannot originate *any* form of justification but merely transmits justification from one belief to another.

The difficulty with foundationalism, according to the Pyrrhonians, is that although Aristotle might be right that in practice we do not push for reasons beyond those that are taken for granted by all of the participants in a discussion, that kind of contextualist agreement does not indicate the presence of basic beliefs whose truth cannot be challeneged. Indeed, the Pyrrhonians would remind the foundationalists that this is where the modes of relativity and discrepancy come into play. The objects of perception and the objects of mutually agreed upon opinion can be subjected to interrogation. The fact that they are typically not challenged is not a good reason for thinking that they cannot legitimately be challenged. That's not to say that reasons for holding such beliefs can't be located. Typically foundationalists will have reasons for thinking that the so-called basic propositions are true. Rather it is to say that the so-called basic beliefs are not privileged in the way required by foundationalism.

In the next section, I will give some reasons for thinking that the Pyrrhonians were right in thinking that the so-called foundational beliefs are not immune to further interrogation, and thus, the appeal to foundational propositions will not provide the basis for a solution to the regress problem. For now, let us merely assume something that I will argue for later, namely, that the so-called foundational beliefs are like all other beliefs in that there are legitimate questions that can be raised about their truth and once those questions are raised, the so-called foundational beliefs require reasons in order to be fully justified.

It is important to note that the Inheritance Principle is telling against infinitism and circular reasoning, if both views were to accept the principle. If reasoning cannot originate any aspect of epistemic justification, then neither infinitism nor the circular form of coherentism can explain how justification arises in the first place.

To see that, let us begin with infinitism. If the Inheritance Principle were correct, each step in the potentially infinite reasoning process would inherit whatever justification it has from the previous step in the reasoning process. So, the infinitist's account of justification cannot provide an explanation of how justification arises in the first place.

Here's how one contemporary foundationalist, Carl Ginet, puts this point:

> A more important, deeper problem for infinitism is this: Inference cannot *originate* justification, it can only transfer it from premises to conclusion. And so it cannot be that, there actually occurs justification, it is all inferential.[13]

Another contemporary foundationalist, Jonathan Dancy, makes a similar point:[14]

> Suppose that all justification is inferential. When we justify belief A by appeal to belief B and C, we have not yet shown A to be justified. We have only shown that it is justified if B and C are. Justification by inference is conditional justification only; A's justification is conditional upon the justification of B and C. But if all justification is conditional in this sense, then nothing can be shown to be actually non-conditionally justified.[15]

Similarly, if the Inheritance Principle were correct, circular reasoning can only transmit some features of justification from one belief to another and no account of the origin of those features of justification would have been provided. Consider the analogy of basketball players standing in a circle and passing the ball to each other. Once the ball is there, it is clear how it can be passed from one player to another. But the question is this: How did it get there in the first place?

The upshot, from the Pyrrhonian point of view, is withholding beliefs. To them, what looked like a good argument for foundationalism actually provides a basis for a skeptical attitude towards beliefs if one grants that contextually basic propositions do not, thereby, gain full epistemic justification.

3. Responses to the Skeptic's Use of the Regress Argument

Aristotle was not content with the contextualist response mentioned in the previous section. In the *Posterior Analytics* he provides the sketch of another type of response, namely one designed to provide a basis for thinking that some basic beliefs arise by a process that is reliable. Here is a somewhat redacted and interpolated quotation that remains true

---

13 Ginet (2005), 148.
14 Ginet correctly points out that at one time I did not fully understand the point Dancy was making. (Ginet 2001, 148.)
15 Dancy (1985), 55.

to the basic Aristotelean view. I have indicated exact quotes with double quotation marks:

> In order for us to acquire the basic propositions "we must possess a capacity of some sort" which is "a characteristic of all animals, for they all possess a congenital discriminative capacity which is called sense-perception. But though sense perception is innate in all animals, in some the sense-impression comes to persist, in others, it does not." In those animals in which sense perception persists, there "comes to be what we call memory, and out of frequently repeated memories of the same thing develop experience ... [and] from experience ... originate the skill of the craftsman and the knowledge of the man of science".[16]

The essence of this proposal is what I call 'austere reliabilism' which holds that if the process that produces a given belief does so reliably and does not take other beliefs as inputs, then such a belief is fully justified and, ceteris paribus, it rises to the level of knowledge. Here is a relatively recent example (at least as compared to Aristotle's discussion!) discussed by A. J. Ayer:

> Suppose that someone were consistently successful in predicting events of a certain kind, events, let us say, which are not ordinarily thought to be predictable, like the results of a lottery. If his run of successes were sufficiently impressive, we might very well come to say that he knew which number would win, even though he did not reach this conclusion by any rational method ... We might say that he knew it by intuition, but this would be to assert that he did know it but that we did not know how.[17]

Ayer goes on to say that in cases like this one in which there are no "recognized criteria for deciding when one has the right to be sure... we are left free to decide" whether the verb "to know" applies.[18] Austere reliabilists would "decide" that this is a case of knowledge.

I think such a "decision" simply ignores the normative intuition that a belief for which we have reasons is more fully justified than a belief produced by the same process for which we don't have reasons. Of two successful lottery-winner predictors, the one who can provide a basis for believing that he is correct is better justified in his predictions than the one who cannot. Imagine that the first person has checked every time whether his predictions are true and can offer the track record as a reason for believing his current prediction is true compared to a second person who has never checked to see whether he is right.

---

16 Aristotle, *An. Post.* 99b33–100a8.
17 Ayer (1956), 32–33.
18 Ayer (1956), 34.

The first person might be deemed to have knowledge, but the second one is surely epistemically better off simply because he has reasons for his beliefs.

'Embellished reliabilism' does not adhere strictly to the Inheritance Principle mentioned above because it allows that reasoning can produce either a new type of epistemic justification or augment the amount of epistemic justification. Nevertheless, embellished reliabilism, like austere reliabilism, holds that some beliefs, namely so-called basic beliefs, have a type of epistemic justification that rises to the level of knowledge merely because of the truth conducive way in which the belief was produced. But embellished reliabilism holds that once the so-called basic beliefs or those inferred from them become members of a set of beliefs that have been subjected to careful self-reflection – including reflection about the reliability of our (or, in a Cartesian mode, my) epistemic capacities – a different characteristic of full justification can emerge. Here is a passage from Ernest Sosa that makes that very point:

> Admittedly, there is a sense in which even a supermarket door "knows" when someone approaches, and in which a heating system "knows" when the temperature in a room rises above a certain setting. Such is "servo-mechanic" knowledge. And there is an immense variety of animal knowledge, instinctive or learned, which facilitates survival and flourishing in an astonishingly rich diversity of modes and environments. Human knowledge is on a higher plane of sophistication, however, precisely because of its enhanced coherence and comprehensiveness and its capacity to satisfy self-reflective curiosity. Pure reliabilism is questionable as an adequate epistemology for such knowledge.[19]

I share Sosa's view about the importance of what is distinctive about human knowledge, as opposed to servo-mechanical knowledge. We find it important to have reasons for our beliefs whenever those beliefs are challenged. There might be some sort of knowledge that arises whenever the process which produces the belief is appropriately and sufficiently reliable, but what is distinctive about human knowledge is the importance of reasoning in making a belief fully justified.[20]

---

19 Sosa (1991), 95.

20 I do not mean to be claiming that only humans offer reasons for beliefs and find it important to do so. Maybe other entities, of which we are as yet unaware, do that. But if they do, then they, too, acknowledge this normative imperative that is not captured or acknowledged by austere reliabilism. I should also mention that although I agree with Sosa that there is an important distinction between what he calls pure reliabilism (which I think parallels what I mean by "austere

Consider how a belief can become justified. On the one hand, austere reliabilists think of a belief being justified in virtue of the process that produces the belief. And surely it can be granted that one characteristic of a fully justified belief depends upon the type of process that produced it. But just as surely, by giving reasons for our beliefs *we justify* the beliefs. We make them justified by giving reasons. "To justify" is factive in the same sense that "to rectify," "to clarify," and "to codify" are factive. If we justify a belief, the belief is justified. If we rectify a situation, the situation is rectified, etc. In this sense of "justified," processes don't justify beliefs, people do.

Our fully justified beliefs share one feature in common with some of the representational states of animals and other entities that possess servo-mechanical knowledge. They are produced by a reliable process, i.e., a process that results in accurate representations sufficiently often. But what is distinctive about adult human justified beliefs is that they gain one important feature of fully justified beliefs because *we justify* them. Thus, there are at least two distinct properties that fully justified beliefs have: (i) they are reliably produced and (ii) they are made justified by the reasons we use to support them. I use "fully justified" to refer to beliefs that have at least those two properties. There might be other properties that such beliefs have, but for our purposes it is sufficient to note these two in order to (i) clarify the normative intuitions motivating the regress problem, (ii) show the inadequacy of the foundationalist and contemporary coherentist responses, and (iii) explain the infinitist solution to the regress problem.

However, it is not my purpose here to examine either austere or embellished reliabilism in detail because, although the latter recognizes the normative imperative to provide reasons for at least some of our beliefs in order to fully justify them, both forms fail to fully recognize the fundamental intuition informing the regress – namely that *no* belief can

---

reliabilism") and normative characterizations of justification, his contrast term, i.e., "self reflective knowledge," is not parallel to the way in which I would draw the distinction. I think the views that contrast with austere reliabilism are ones that stress the significance of the act of justifying beliefs in developing an account of fully justified beliefs, but I don't think justifying beliefs always requires engaging in the more ambitious project of developing a more comprehensive, coherent and self-reflective set of beliefs. Although in some cases justifying a belief might involve that noble goal, justifying a belief merely requires providing reasons for its being true.

reach the status of being fully justified for S if S has no reasons for believing it.

Now, if it is correct that no belief can be fully justified for S if S does not justify it, and if reasoning cannot be circular (and I take it that Aristotle and the Pyrrhonians were right about the fact that circular reasoning cannot increase the degree of justification of the target belief), then infinitism is the only solution to the regress argument.

To see that, consider any proposed ending belief in the regress, call it "E". One can ask the self-reflective thinker the following question: In virtue of *what* is E an epistemically proper ending point? If no answer is forthcoming, then it clearly appears arbitrary (as the Pyrrhonians would say) to believe E without a reason. Up to that point reasons were needed. Why should the regress end at E rather than at some earlier step or at some possible later step?

Suppose the answer is that E is the appropriate ending belief in virtue of E's having some foundational property, F. Then, the next question becomes: Does E's possessing F make it more likely that E is true than it would be if E did not possess F?

It seems clear that there is a normative imperative to produce an answer which, if correct, would provide some good evidence for believing that possessing F is truth-conducive. Consider what I have called elsewhere a "Wednesday Foundationalist" – a foundationalist who holds that any belief arising on Wednesday has the austere form of justification.[21] Of course, no one is such a foundationalist because there is absolutely no reason to believe that Wednesday-beliefs are any better than, say, Friday or Sunday-beliefs.

Foundationalists pick F-properties that are truth-conducive. For example, Aristotle's description of the process by which we reach the first principles was designed to show that the process was truth conducive. There are arguments that are designed to show that evolution would have favored truth-conducive perceptual and rational modalities, so those modalities if "properly" functioning in the appropriate environment would produce truths. There are arguments to the effect that if we believe that we are in some kinds of mental states, then we are. For example, if we believe that we are in pain, then we are in pain. There are arguments to the effect that if we have a reddish-seeming sense impression, then if we are aware of no infelicitous circumstances, it is likely that there is a reddish something. There are arguments with

---

21 Klein (2007a), 15.

the conclusion that 'clarity and distinction' is the test of truth, etc. My point is not that any of those arguments are sound or that they are unsound; rather my point is that foundationalists will pick F-properties for which they think such arguments can be formulated. By doing so, they have tacitly acknowledged that the regress does not stop with the assertion of E or the assertion that E has property F.

Once the question is asked and understood about whether E's possessing F is truth conducive, there are four possible responses available to some person, S: It can be ignored, or "yes," or "no," or "I don't know." I take it that ignoring the question is to fail to grasp the normative imperative underlying the regress argument, and both the "no" and the "I don't know" answers preclude S from using E to justify further beliefs. Although E might have the type of justification that austere reliabilism attributes to it, it cannot be used by S to fully justify another belief because S thinks either that there is no reason to think E is true because it possesses F or S remains agnostic about that. In either case, S could not employ E to justify another belief. In other words, E cannot be used by S in the way that foundationalism requires.

This argument against foundationalism works against the current forms of emergent coherentism as well – and that form is the only initially plausible form of coherentism. The other form – what I call transference coherentism – was probably never held since it takes individual propositions to be the primary bearers of justification and embraces circular reasoning by accepting the inheritance principle. As mentioned above, that logically possible but completely unsatisfying view was well disposed of by Aristotle and the Pyrrhonians.

Emergent coherentism is best exemplified by BonJour.[22] In this view, it is *sets* of propositions that are the primary bearers of justification. All propositions in the appropriate kind of coherent set are justified simply in virtue of being members of that set. Thus, justification is not transferred from one proposition to another – rather justification emerges as a result of the mutual support provided by the propositions in the set.

As Ernest Sosa has pointed out, this form of coherentism shares a formal structure with foundationalism.[23] Using the terminology I am employing, the emergent coherentist takes the foundational property F to be *E's being a member of a set of propositions that is coherent* (and perhaps

---

22 BonJour (1985), 87–110.
23 Sosa (1980).

has other features as well). In other words, emergent coherentism can be seen as one-step foundationalism because all propositions in the coherent set have some degree of prima facie justification. Perhaps some are relatively "more foundational" than others because they are more important to the coherence of the set. But they all have some prima facie justification in virtue of being members of the appropriate kind of set.

For the sake of the argument, let us suppose that some characteristic of full justification could emerge this way (as opposed to the way in which the austere and embellished reliabilists think prima facie justification emerges). My point remains that the regress does not stop with a belief that is immune to questioning because once F is so identified by the coherentist, the question arises about whether E's being a member of a coherent set is truth-conducive. Perhaps some characteristic of full justification emerges as the coherentists claim, but because no belief is immune to interrogation and the reasons for believing the proposition cannot contain the proposition itself, the central claim of infinitism has been granted, namely that there is no privileged belief that is immune to further interrogation.

Now it could be objected 1) that this very general argument for infinitism conflates the important distinction between a belief itself *being* fully justified with the meta-belief that the belief is fully justified and 2) that knowledge only requires that the belief be fully justified.[24]

In order to answer that objection, it is important to distinguish two senses of "belief" and the concomitant two senses in which a belief is justified. In one sense, "belief" refers to the propositional content of a belief-state as in "that belief is true" or "her belief was implied by what she said earlier." In the other sense, "belief" can refer to the belief-state as in "she had that belief for many years" or "her belief was caused by a reliable process." The concomitant distinction regarding justified belief is between the proposition being justified, i.e., propositional justification, and the believing (i.e., the state of believing) being justified, i.e., doxastic justification. The distinction was first introduced by Roderick Firth.[25]

The level-confusion objection is appropriate with regard to propositional justification. There is a clear distinction between a proposition, say p, being justified and the meta-proposition 'p is justified' being jus-

---

24 See Alston (1976).
25 Firth (1978).

tified, and any argument that conflated the distinction is built upon a pun. I am willing to grant that in order for the proposition, p, to be justified for a person, it is not required that 'p is justified' is justified for the person.

The regress argument, at base, is concerned with whether there is any form of reasoning that S can deploy to fully justify a belief – in order for it to become knowledge (if the other necessary and jointly sufficient conditions obtain). Thus, it is crucial to keep in mind that the 'justification' condition in knowledge does not refer to propositional justification; rather it is S's *believing* that must be fully justified. A *proposition*, p, could be fully justified (and true), but fail to be known if either S failed to believe that p or S believed p for the wrong reasons, i.e., reasons that did not provide for propositional justification. What is required for knowledge is that S's believing that p be justified.

Once the question is raised concerning whether E's possessing F makes it more likely that E is true than it would be if E did not possess F, it is S's entitlement to continue to believe that p that is being questioned. If S is not able to defend the "yes" answer to the question given above, some adjustment of S's entitlement to believe E and every belief that justificationally depends upon E is called for. It is not required that S gives up E because E might possess the kind of epistemic justification that austere reliabilism would attribute to it and, as Ayer would say, S has some sort of right to believe E, but those views that recognize the importance of having reasons for our beliefs when their epistemic credentials are challenged (i.e., embellished reliabilism, coherentism, and infinitism) would require some recalibration of our entitlement to continue believing that p.

In other words, it should be clear that the normative force of the regress applies primarily to the requirement that S's believing be fully justified; and answering the "meta-question" whether E's possessing F makes it more likely that E is true is directly relevant to determining whether S's believing that E is fully justified. It is only austere reliabilists who will not grant this point. For them, the belief that p is fully epistemically justified (i.e., it satisfies the justification condition of knowledge) just in case it is produced by an appropriate process. As mentioned above, the normative force behind the regress argument is that having reasons for believing a proposition adds an important feature of full justification. The regress is only problematic when it is seen from the standpoint of normative epistemology in which knowledge is taken to be the most highly prized form of true belief – where, of course, it is the belief-state that is prized, not the propositional content.[26]

4. Infinitism

Recall the Inheritance Principle that motivated foundationalism. That principle seemed intuitively plausible and it clearly rules out infinitism as a solution to the regress problem. For even if we had infinite time to produce reasons, it remains mysterious, if not downright impossible, that some belief could ever be fully justified because reasoning cannot originate justification. Coupled with the fact that compared to an infinitely enduring being, we live less than a nanosecond, the upshot seems to be that the Pyrrhonians were right after all. Suspension of belief is the only warranted attitude.

The answer to this worry and the key to understanding infinitism is that the Inheritance Principle is false, even though it motivates foundationalism and seems plausible at first glance fails. The principle fails to recognize that there are at least two important characteristics of a fully justified belief. As I have granted, one characteristic is acquired by a belief in virtue of the causal process that brought it about, but the other characteristic is acquired by a belief when we justify it by providing reasons for believing it. Providing reasons for a belief contributes significantly to its full justification. Thus, although there is one characteristic of a fully justified belief that does not originate from reasoning, another characteristic of a fully justified belief does originate from reasoning. Hence, the Inheritance Principle is false.

Put another way: A reason, r, for a belief, b, can be used by S to provide b with a type of justification that r, as yet, does not possess because no reason for r has yet been given by S. So, in spite of it sounding odd to our well conditioned foundationalist ears, b could be known without r being known because b could be fully justified without r being fully justified.

The infinitist will take the belief that p to be doxastically fully justified for S only if S has justified the belief that p by providing "enough" reasons. We could say that S is certain that p, i.e., *completely* doxastically fully justified, only if every reason in a limitless path of reasons were provided. But since it takes some time to discover and offer reasons,

---

26 Plato (1997), *Meno* 97a–98b.

even though a *proposition* might be completely justified (if there is a suitable endless path of reasons), no *belief* could ever be completely doxastically fully justified. Thus, nothing is ever completely settled in the sense that it is beyond further interrogation, but S can fully justify a belief by providing adequate reasons for believing it, assuming the belief also has the appropriate causal pedigree. How far forward in providing reasons S needs to go seems to me to be a matter of the pragmatic features of the epistemic context – just as which beliefs are being questioned or which can be taken as reasons is at least partially contextually determined.[27]

Responses to some objections to infinitism

Infinitism has seemed to many people to be so implausible that it has not even been a serious contender with foundationalism or coherentism for a solution to the regress problem. Usually, the objections are not clearly articulated because the view seems so initially implausible. I hope the previous sections have provided infinitism with enough initial credibility so that considering some of the objections has become worthwhile.

1. The finite mind objection

Aristotle correctly observed that beings with a finite mind cannot traverse an infinitely long inference path. And that seemed to stop infinitism in its tracks. But infinitism – or at least the kind that makes proper use of the distinction between propositional and doxastic justification, and the distinction between the two very different characteristics of a doxastically fully justified belief – does not require that an infinite set of reasons be produced in order for a belief to rise to the level of the most highly prized form of true belief. Knowledge requires being able to provide enough reasons for our believing to be fully justified, it does not require us to provide an infinite number of reasons.

What constitutes "enough" reasons requires careful elaboration and I have not done that here. Such an elaboration would include a discussion of the role of the contextual considerations that make further questioning either necessary because a legitimate question has been raised or frivolous because the amount of added warrant that further investigation

---

27 See Klein (2005a,b); (2007a,b); and Fantl (2003).

would produce is minuscule. Those issues are beyond the scope of this essay.

2. The no-starting point objection

The Pyrrhonians said that the process of reasoning endorsed by infinitism could not succeed in justifying a belief sufficiently for us to adopt it because "we possess no starting-point for our argument." That objection has an intuitive tug if one adopted the Inheritance Principle – and at first glance that principle seemed correct. But I hope I have dispelled its intuitive appeal by showing how reasoning can produce a new type of justification that is not inherited from the offered reason.

3. Skepticism

Some philosophers have argued that knowledge entails certainty, where certainty includes at least having finally settled the matter. And they would point out that infinitism makes that kind of certainty impossible and, thus, infinitism leads to skepticism. There are two replies to this objection.

First, as I mentioned earlier, there are both skeptical and non-skeptical forms of foundationalism. There would be skeptical forms of coherentism if no belief set held by creatures like us could be sufficiently coherent to satisfy the requirements of knowledge. In a similar vein, there certainly could be skeptical forms of infinitism that held that the normative requirements of justification simply cannot be fulfilled. But, although the fact that a theory of justification leads to skepticism might provide a basis for looking more carefully at whether the theory is correct, that fact, alone, does not strike me as a sufficient reason for rejecting the theory. Skepticism is a logically possible view.

Second, the form of infinitism that I am defending does not lead to skepticism. It is a form of fallibilism that eschews certainty, where certainty is construed as requiring that the degree of epistemic justification necessary for knowledge makes the belief immune to further interrogation. Indeed, I think the form of infinitism articulated here can explain why certainty is taken to be both a relative notion as when we say that one belief is more certain than another and an absolute notion as when we say that a belief is certain only if there is no belief that is more certain. It can also explain why absolute certainty cannot be obtained because any belief can always be made a little more certain by producing more reasons along the path of reasons while at the same time it can explain how a belief can be certain enough to rise to the level required by knowledge.[28]

4. Infinitism really endorses a form of arbitrary foundationalism

It has been claimed that 1) infinitism is really a form of an unjustified (arbitrary) foundationalist view and 2) that a "bad" reason, r, could justify a belief, b.[29] That it is not foundationalism should be clear because it eschews the central claim of foundationalism, namely, that there are some beliefs immune to further interrogation.

The answer to 2) is more complex. There are several distinct factors that could make a reason "bad" for believing b: i) A reason, r, could be "bad" because it was not formed in a reliable manner. Such a bad reason could not transfer the kind of warrant required by the austere reliabilist to b by reasoning, and consequently, neither b nor r would be knowledge – even according to the infinitist. In other words, the infinitist can embrace the reliabilists' basic insight that a belief must be properly caused in order to be knowledge. ii) A reason, r, could be "bad" because there is *no* further reason for it. But note that in such a case, r couldn't have been formed reliably because being so formed is a reason for thinking it is true. Hence, what was said with regard to (i) applies here as well. iii) A reason, r, could be "bad" because S does not have available an answer to the question as to why she believes that r is likely to be true. In such a case, although b has gained some justification because r was produced as a reason for believing b, some recalibration of b's degree of justification is warranted. That strikes me as just what a theory of justification should dictate. We are epistemically better off by possessing r as a reason for b than we would be if we had no reason for believing b, but we are not completely in the epistemic clear. If it is sufficiently important that believing b be fully justified to a greater degree – we have more work to do. iv) A reason, r, could be "bad" because it is false or there is a defeater of the reason for r. If it is false, there is a defeater of the inference from the "bad" reason (namely, ~r). Infinitism, per se, is an account of only the justification condition in knowledge; an infinitist, like me, can include a no-defeater condition in the necessary conditions for knowledge.

---

28 See Klein (2005c).
29 See Bergmann (2007) for the objection and Klein (2007b) for a response.

5. Conclusion

I have argued that (i) neither foundationalism nor coherentism can provide a solution to the epistemic regress problem and (ii) there is a form of infinitism that provides a solution to the regress problem by explaining how reasoning can increase the epistemic worth of a belief, and (iii) the objections to infinitism can be answered successfully.

(i) Neither foundationalism nor coherentism can explain how reasoning can increase the epistemic worth of a belief because each supposes that there are some prima facie fully justified beliefs whose full justification does not depend upon other beliefs being justified. I argued that there are no such prima facie fully justified beliefs because their full justification depends upon their being reasons for believing that whatever property makes them prima facie justified also makes them likely to be true.

(ii) The form of infinitism that was developed and defended holds that reasoning can generate some important characteristics of a fully justified belief, where "fully justified belief" refers to the type of justification required for what is distinctively adult human knowledge. That form of infinitism necessitated jettisoning a cherished epistemic principle that required that in order for a belief to acquire some positive epistemic status it could do so only if that positive status was inherited from another belief that already possessed that status. I argued that the Inheritance Principle failed to take into account that the act of justifying a belief gives it a positive epistemic status that the reason might not yet enjoy. Hence reasoning can increase the epistemic status of a belief. It does not only transfer the epistemic status.

(iii) I have considered what I think are the best objections to various forms of infinitism and argued that those objections miss the mark because they mischaracterize what infinitism is committed to. No doubt there are other objections that have not been dealt with here or have yet to be formulated.[30] New objections will develop because infinitism is a view that has only recently been taken with enough seriousness to be explored carefully. When those objections arise, new reasons will have to be found to strengthen the case for infinitism. But that is, as it should be.

---

30 Some additional objections are discussed in Klein (1999), (2005a,b), and (2007a,b).

References

Alston (1976): William P. Alston, "Two types of Foundationalism", in: *Journal of Philosophy* 73, 165–185.
Alston (1989): William P. Alston, *Epistemic Justification*, Ithaca.
Aristotle, all citations are to Richard McKeon (1941): *The Basic Works of Aristotle*, New York.
Ayer (1956): Alfred J. Ayer, *The Problem of Knowledge,* New York.
Bergmann (2007): Michael Bergmann, "Is Klein an Infinitist about Doxastic Justification?", in: *Philosophical Studies* 134.1, 19–24.
BonJour (1985): Laurence BonJour, *The Structure of Empirical Knowledge,* Cambridge.
Dancy (1985): Jonathan Dancy, *Introduction to Contemporary Epistemology*, Oxford.
Empiricus, S., all citations are to Bury, R.G. (1976), *Outlines of Pyrrhonism*, Cambridge.
Fantl (2003): Jeremy Fantl, "Modest Infinitism," in: *Canadian Journal of Philosophy* 33:4, 537–562.
Firth (1978): Roderick Firth, "Are Epistemic Concepts Reducible to Ethical Concepts?", in: A. Goldman/J. Kim (eds.), *Values and Morals*, Dordrecht.
Ginet (2005): Carl Ginet, "Infinitism is not the Solution to the Regress Problem", in: M. Steup/E. Sosa (eds.), *Contemporary Debates in Epistemology,* Malden, 140–149.
Klein (1971): Peter D. Klein, "A Proposed Definition of Propositional Knowledge", in: *Journal of Philosophy* 67 (16), 471–482.
Klein (1999): Peter D. Klein, "Human Knowledge and the Infinite Regress of Reasons," in: J. Tomberlin (ed.), *Philosophical Perspectives* 13, 297–325.
Klein (2004): Peter D. Klein, "Knowledge is True, Non-defeated Justified Belief", in: S. Luper (ed.), *Essential Knowledge*, 124–135.
Klein (2005a): Peter D. Klein, "Infinitism Is the Solution to the Epistemic Regress Problem", in: M. Steup/E. Sosa (eds.), *Contemporary Debates in Philosophy*, 131–140.
Klein (2005b): Peter D. Klein, "Reply to Ginet,", in: M. Steup/E. Sosa (eds.), *Contemporary Debates in Epistemology*, 149–152.
Klein (2005c): Peter D. Klein, "Infinitism's Take on Justification, Knowledge, Certainty and Skepticism", in: *Perspectives in Contemporary Epistemology*, (a special edition of *Veritas*), 50.4, 153–172.
Klein (2007a): Peter D. Klein, "Human Knowledge and the Infinite Progress of Reasoning", in: *Philosophical Studies* 134:1, 1–17.
Klein (2007b): Peter D. Klein, "How to be an Infinitist about Doxastic Justification", in: *Philosophical Studies* 134.1, 25–29.
Klein (2011a): Peter D. Klein, "Infinitism", in: S. Bernecker/D. Pritchard (eds.), *Routledge Companion to Epistemology*, 245–256.
Klein (2011b): Peter D. Klein, "Epistemic Justification and the Limits of Pyrrhonism", in: D. Machuca (ed.), a collection on Pyrrhonism edited by Springer, forthcoming.
Plato (1997): Plato, *Complete Works*, J. Copper (ed.), Hackett.

Sosa (1980): Ernest Sosa, "The Raft and the Pyramid: Coherence versus Foundations in the Theory of Knowledge", in: *Midwest Studies In Philosophy* 5:1, 3–26.
Sosa (1991): Ernest Sosa, *Knowledge in Perspective*, Cambridge.

Das einfache Argument*

Steven Luper

Wenn man sagt, dass Wissen unter bekannter logischer Implikation geschlossen ist, dann sagt man, dass das folgende Prinzip (möglicherweise unter Berücksichtigung gewisser Einschränkungen) richtig ist:

> K: Wenn das Subjekt S weiß, *dass p* und es zudem glaubt, *dass q*, weil S weiß, dass p q impliziert, dann weiß S, *dass q*.

Dieses Prinzip K, dass Wissen unter bekannter logischer Implikation geschlossen ist (kurz: Geschlossenheitsprinzip), wurde auf der Basis von Fällen, wie den folgenden, in Frage gestellt.

> *Der Tisch-Fall*: Ted befindet sich in einem ganz normalen Haus, in dem gute Sichtbedingungen herrschen und glaubt, *dass sein Tisch rot ist* (kurz: *dass rot*), allein weil er seinen Tisch und dessen Farbe sieht; zudem glaubt er, *dass es falsch ist, dass sein Tisch weiß ist* und dieser von einem roten Licht beleuchtet wird (kurz: *dass nicht-weiß*), weil *dass nicht-weiß* aus *dass rot* folgt.[1]

> *Der Auto-Fall*: Sam hat sein Auto unter typischen (nicht-Gettierartigen) Umständen geparkt und glaubt, dass sein Auto draußen steht, weil er es dort geparkt hat (kurz: *dass Auto*); er glaubt zudem, dass er nicht bloß träumt, dass sein Auto draußen steht (kurz: *nicht-(nicht-Auto und träumen)*), weil es aus *dass Auto* folgt.[2]

In Anbetracht der Stärke der epistemischen Position, in der Ted sich hinsichtlich der Proposition *dass rot* befindet, scheint Ted zu wissen, *dass rot*; ebenso stark scheint Sams epistemische Position hinsichtlich der Proposition *dass Auto* zu sein. Tatsächlich erscheint sie so stark, dass er *dass Auto* zu wissen scheint. Für Ted aber mag es zu *einfach* erscheinen, *dass nicht-weiß* zu wissen, indem er dies aus *dass rot* deduziert, was er aufgrund seiner Wahrnehmung glaubt; und in Anbetracht der epistemischen Position, in der sich Sam befindet, mag es für ihn zu *einfach* erscheinen, *dass nicht-(nicht-Auto und träumen)* zu wissen, indem er es aus *dass Auto* deduziert. Trotz der offensichtlich intuitiven Anziehungskraft, die von K

---

* Originally published in *Acta Analytica* 22 (2007), pp. 321–331. Reprinted and translated by permission of the publisher, Springer.
1 Cohen (2002).
2 Harman u. Sherman (2004).

ausgeht, stehen diese Eindrücke im Widerspruch zu K. Diese und ähnliche Beispiele (die wir als die *schwierigen Fälle* bezeichnen können) illustrieren ein interessantes Problem, nämlich dass die folgenden drei Behauptungen im Widerspruch zueinander stehen, obwohl jede für sich überzeugend erscheint.

1. Teds epistemische Position ist stark genug für ihn, um *dass rot* zu wissen.
2. Ted kann nicht, *dass nicht-weiß* auf der Basis von *dass rot* wissen.
3. Unter angemessener Einschränkung ist das epistemische Geschlossenheitsprinzip wahr.

Andere Beispiele (die später diskutiert werden) illustrieren, wie uns unsere Intuition nahelegen kann, unsere epistemische Position sei stark genug für uns, um Dinge wissen zu können, die uns aber nicht dazu befähigen, weitere Dinge wissen zu können, selbst wenn Erstere überzeugende induktive Untermauerungen für Folgende mitgeliefert haben. Stewart Cohen[3] hat dieses dreifache Aufeinanderprallen von Intuitionen das Problem des einfachen Wissens genannt.

Eine skeptische Reaktion auf dieses Problem wäre 2 und 3 zu akzeptieren und 1 abzulehnen. Diejenigen, die hoffen den Skeptizismus umgehen zu können, scheinen zwei Optionen zu haben.

Gemäß des *schwierigen Arguments* besteht die beste Reaktion darin, K abzulehnen und zu behaupten, dass, auch wenn Ted und Sam wissen, *dass rot* und *dass Auto*, sie weder *dass nicht-weiß* noch *dass nicht-(nicht-Auto* und *träumen)* wissen. Eine zweite Reaktion besteht darin, unabhängig von dem bestehenden Eindruck zu sagen, dass sowohl Ted, *dass nicht-weiß* als auch Sam, *dass nicht-(nicht-Auto und träumen)* wissen. Hier lehnen wir die Annahme ab, dass in den schwierigen Fällen auf zu einfache Art und Weise *dass nicht-weiß* und *dass nicht-(nicht-Auto* und *träumen)* gewusst wird. Dies soll das *einfache Argument* genannt werden. Es könnte aber noch eine dritte Alternative geben. Eventuell können wir die Möglichkeit eliminieren, aufgrund einer Überzeugung auf zu einfache Art und Weise zu einer weiteren Überzeugung zu gelangen, indem wir die Bedingungen unseres Wissens hinsichtlich der ersten etwas verschärfen, aber nicht so stark, dass man sich den Gefahren skeptischer Konsequenzen aussetzt und ohne K aufzugeben. Mit diesem Ansatz behaupten wir, der Grund dafür, warum es für Ted zu einfach ist, *dass nicht-weiß* zu wissen, indem er es aus *dass rot* deduziert, liege darin, dass er, *dass rot* von Anfang an überhaupt

---

3 Cohen (2002).

nicht weiß; das Gleiche gilt für Sam. Wir behaupten, dass die epistemische Position, in der Ted sich hinsichtlich *dass rot* befindet, nicht hinreichend für das Haben von Wissen ist. Sie ist deswegen nicht hinreichend, weil er nicht allein dadurch, dass ihm sein Tisch rot erscheint wissen kann, *dass rot*. Er kann seine epistemische Position aber leicht genug verbessern, um *dass rot* wissen zu können. Was also gebraucht wird, ist eine ausreichend starke Analyse von Wissen, die die Möglichkeit des einfachen Arguments im Keim erstickt. Sie darf aber nicht so stark sein, dass sie verhindert, dass Menschen Dinge durch den Gebrauch ihrer Sinne wissen können. Zugegebenermaßen bietet dies Boden für den Skeptiker. Wenn wir aber dadurch einfaches Wissen meiden und gleichzeitig K beibehalten können, lohnt es sich vielleicht diesen Preis zu zahlen. Ich werde diese Herangehensweise das *umgekehrte Argument* (*the reverse argument*) nennen.

In diesem Aufsatz gehe ich zwei Aufgaben an. In Teil 1 werde ich das schwierige Argument nicht weiter in Betracht ziehen, sondern eine aktuelle Version des umgekehrten Arguments kritisieren. Ich behaupte, dass die umgekehrte Herangehensweise an das Problem des einfachen Wissens letztlich zurück zum Skeptizismus führt. Im zweiten Teil kritisiere ich eine Version des schwierigen Arguments. Meine Kritikpunkte dienen der Unterstützung des einfachen Arguments, indem sie seine Alternativen ankratzt. Dennoch führen alle drei Argumente zu problematischen Konsequenzen. Ich denke, dass es am einfachsten ist, mit diesen problematischen Konsequenzen des einfachen Arguments zu leben.

Die umgekehrte Strategie

Wenn wir annehmen, Wissen könne in der Art und Weise analysiert werden, wie es der Theoretiker erwartet, der die umgekehrte Strategie vertritt (d. h., dass wir eine Analyse finden können, die das einfache Argument im Keim erstickt, ohne K abzulehnen und ohne dass wesentliche skeptische Konsequenzen auftreten), dann wird es möglich sein, jede Analyse zu kritisieren, die Vorkommnisse von einfachem Wissen zulässt. So z. B. solche, wie die von Ted, der in dem Tisch-Fall weiß, *dass nicht-weiß*. Ein erfolgreiches umgekehrtes Argument, das sich gegen eine Analyse richtet, muss jedoch mehr leisten, als zu zeigen, dass diese Analyse einfaches Wissen toleriert. Denn es ist möglich, dass *keine* plausible Erklärung den Erwartungen des Theoretikers entspricht, der das umgekehrte Argument vertritt und es ist müßig, einer Theorie auf der Grundlage zu widersprechen, dass ihr nicht gelingt, was keiner plausiblen

Theorie gelingen kann. Ich werde dafür argumentieren, dass die von mir in Betracht gezogene umgekehrte Strategie die Erwartungen der Strategen, die diese vertreten, selbst nicht erfüllt. Dann werde ich darauf hinweisen (aber nicht vorführen), dass ihr Scheitern unvermeidlich war, weil jede ausreichend starke Erklärung, der es gelingt, das einfache Argument zu vermeiden, so stark ist, dass sie zu unplausiblen skeptischen Konsequenzen führt. Das Ergebnis ist klar: Die Verträglichkeit mit einfachem Wissen stellt keinen Grund für die Ablehnung einer Theorie dar.

Ich werde eine Version des umgekehrten Arguments betrachten, die von Richard Fumerton[4] und Jonathan Vogel[5] gegen verschiedene reliabilistische Analysen des Wissens eingesetzt wurde. Sie lehnen das Zuverlässigkeitsprinzip, den Reliabilismus, ab, weil er ein Argumentationsmuster zulässt, welches Vogel '*Bootstrapping*'[6] nennt, und *Bootstrapping* generiert Wissen auf zu einfache Art und Weise. Vogel bietet das folgende Beispiel an: Roxanne „glaubt vorbehaltlos, was ihre Tankanzeige angibt. Dabei weiß sie nicht, dass ihre Tankanzeige überhaupt zuverlässig ist. ... Wenn die Tankanzeige auf 'F' steht, dann glaubt sie in diesem Fall, dass der Tank voll ist. Zudem glaubt sie in diesem Fall, dass die Tankanzeige auf 'F' steht."[7] Indem sie beides miteinander kombiniert, glaubt sie, dass die Tankanzeige in diesem Fall auf 'F' steht und dass 'F' wahr ist. Diese letzte Proposition impliziert, dass die Angabe der Tankanzeige in diesem Fall genau zutrifft. Roxanne wiederholt ihr Inferenzmuster immer wieder und schlussfolgert per Induktion, dass die Tankanzeige zuverlässig ist. Vogel behauptet, der Reliabilismus impliziert bei jedem dieser Schritte, Roxanne wisse, dass ihre Überzeugungen wahr sind. Er impliziert, Roxanne könne wissen, dass die Angaben ihrer Tankanzeige zutreffend sind, da ein zuverlässiger Prozess darauf hinweist, nämlich die Angaben der Tankanzeige selbst. Und angenommen induktive Schlussfolgerungen sind zuverlässig, so folgt daraus, sie könne nun verschiedene derartige Überzeugungen zusammensetzen und so wissen, dass ihre Tankanzeige zuverlässig ist. Da Roxannes Vorgehensweise des *Bootstrappings* zwei-

---

4 Fumerton (1995).
5 Vogel (2000).
6 Bootstrapping könnte man etwa mit zirkulärer Selbstbestätigung gleichsetzen. Der Begriff verweist sinnbildlich auf eines der Abenteuer des Lügenbarons Münchhausen, der berichtet hat, dass er sich selbst an seinen Schnürsenkeln aus dem Sumpf gezogen hat. Anm.d.Ü.
7 Vogel (2000), 614.

felhaft ist, vom Reliabilismus jedoch zugelassen wird, sollten wir den Reliabilismus ablehnen.

Vogels Beispiel ist fehlerhaft. Auf die Zuverlässigkeit einer Tankanzeige wird nicht allein dadurch zuverlässig hingewiesen, dass sie in einigen Situationen den korrekten Wert angibt, ganz gleich wie oft sich diese Gelegenheiten häufen. Noch sind derartige Tankanzeigen die Basis für eine offenkundig starke induktive Schlussfolgerung – d.h. eine die imstande ist, Wissen zu generieren. Vielleicht zeigt die Nadel der Tankanzeige meines Autos, das über Jahre hinweg nicht in Gebrauch war, immer auf 'Leer'. In dieser Zeit habe ich den Tankanzeiger zwei Mal am Tag überprüft und er hat jedes Mal 'Leer' angezeigt. Meine Auswahl an angezeigten Werten ist in diesem Fall einfach nicht repräsentativ. Nur die wiederholten richtigen Werte der Tankanzeige in auffällig verschiedenen Arten von Situationen könnten auch zuverlässig auf die Zuverlässigkeit der Tankanzeige hinweisen und die Basis für eine induktive Schlussfolgerung bilden, die uns in die Lage versetzt, über das Wissen zu verfügen, dass die Tankanzeige zuverlässig ist.

Um Vogel auszuhelfen, können wir sein Beispiel etwas abändern. Das veränderte Beispiel beginnt genau wie das Original: Roxanne glaubt, *dass p,* weil ihre Tankanzeige, die zuverlässig ist, *dass p* angibt. Sie sammelt viele ähnliche Überzeugungen, die sie aufgrund der Angaben ihrer Tankanzeige erlangt hat. Sie fügt die Prämisse hinzu, dass die Anzeigen in auffällig verschiedenen Situationen abgelesen wurden. Daraufhin schließt sie, per Induktion, dass ihre Tankanzeige zuverlässig ist.

Bis auf Weiteres sei angenommen, dass Argumentationen, die *Bootstrapping* beinhalten, fehlerhaft sind und dass der Reliabilismus Wissen toleriert, das durch *Bootstrapping* zustande gekommen ist. Wir haben gesagt, dass dies nur dann ein Schlag gegen den Reliabilismus ist, wenn es einen plausiblen Weg gibt, Wissen auszuschließen, welches durch *Bootstrapping* zustande gekommen ist. Gibt es einen solchen Weg?

Vogel denkt, es gibt ihn. Er möchte die traditionelle Ansicht wiederaufleben lassen, nach der Wissen Rechtfertigung impliziert. Demzufolge kann Roxanne nur dann aufgrund der Angabe ihres Tankanzeigers wissen, ihr Tank enthalte so und so viel Benzin, wenn sie aufgrund von Rechtfertigungen glaubt, ihre Tankanzeige gebe den Benzinstand zuverlässig an. Was sie braucht, ist einen „unabhängigen Grund, um glauben zu können, dass die Position der Nadel auf ihrer Tankanzeige auf zuverlässige Weise mit der Menge Benzin korreliert, die sich im Tank befindet."[8] Da sie bereits von Anfang an einen solchen Grund zur Verfügung haben muss, kann sie nicht durch *Bootstrapping* zu ihrem Wissen gelangen. Nun zu einigen Vorbehalten gegenüber Vogels Vorschlag.

Wie Cohen verzeichnet, ist 'einfaches Wissen' nicht nur auf Fälle von *Bootstrapping* beschränkt. Wenn es für Roxanne zu einfach ist, zu wissen, dass ihre Tankanzeige zuverlässig ist, dann liefert der Tisch-Fall ein weiteres Beispiel, in dem Wissen zu 'einfach' ist. Die Annahme, dass Wissen in dem Tisch-Fall als 'einfaches' gilt, führt dazu, dass Vogel einen Weg benötigt, dieses auszuschließen.

Vogel würde sich folgendermaßen dazu äußern: die Sache ist insofern falsch gelaufen, als dass Ted über keine gerechtfertigte Überzeugungen verfügt, dass seine Wissensquelle, die aus seiner Farbwahrnehmung besteht, zuverlässig ist. Daher weiß er nicht, dass sie zuverlässig ist. Passen wir das Beispiel entsprechend an. Angenommen Ted glaubt, dass seine Sehkraft generell zuverlässig ist und dass diese Überzeugung gerechtfertigt ist. Leider scheint es so als wenn Ted, selbst unter diesen Umständen, auf zu einfache Weise zu dem Wissen gelangt, *dass nicht-weiß*. Das angepasste Beispiel wird nicht dadurch unproblematisch, dass Ted über eine gerechtfertigte Überzeugung in Bezug auf die Zuverlässigkeit seines Sehvermögens verfügt.

Warum scheint Teds Wissen immer noch zu 'einfach'? Eben weil Teds Fähigkeit, *dass rot* zu wissen von der Wahrheit von *dass nicht-weiß* abhängt. Insofern scheint es verdächtig zirkulär, dass Ted über das Wissen der Proposition *dass nicht-weiß* verfügt, indem er diese aus *dass rot* deduziert. Dieser Eindruck wird nicht durch die Annahme eliminiert, dass Ted eine gerechtfertigte Überzeugung darüber hat, dass seine Farbwahrnehmung auf generelle Art und Weise zuverlässig ist.

Der Punkt kann deutlicher gemacht werden, wenn wir zwischen zwei Arten unterscheiden, auf die unsere Farbwahrnehmung zuverlässig sein kann. Auch wenn unsere Farbwahrnehmung *generell* zuverlässig ist, gibt es Umstände, in denen sie nutzlos ist, und Teds Wissen, dass sein Tisch rot ist, hängt davon ab, dass er sich nicht in derartigen Umständen befindet. Zum Beispiel funktioniert unsere Farbwahrnehmung unter nicht standardmäßigen Lichtverhältnissen nicht gut, etwa wenn ein weißer Tisch von einem roten Licht beleuchtet wird. Es gibt eine Art von Zuverlässigkeit, die ihr in Lichtverhältnissen fehlt, welche nicht dem Standard entsprechen; sie bringt aber nur dann Wissen hervor, wenn sie über diese Art von Zuverlässigkeit verfügt. Der Einfachheit halber werde

---

8 Vogel (2000), 622.

ich sagen, ihr fehlt *spezifische Zuverlässigkeit*. Von Feinheiten abgesehen, ist eine Quelle dann auf generelle Art und Weise zuverlässig, wenn die durch sie bekräftigten Überzeugungen im Gebrauch einer großen Vielzahl von tatsächlichen Umständen wahr wären. Während eine Quelle auf spezifische Art und Weise zuverlässig ist, wenn die durch sie bekräftigten Überzeugungen im Gebrauch spezifischer Umstände, wie die, die wir oben genannt haben, wahr wären. Spezifische Zuverlässigkeit ist notwendig für Wissen.⁹ Das ist das Fazit des Aufsatzes von Gettier. Die generelle Zuverlässigkeit von Teds Sehvermögen hing nicht von dem Umstand ab (oder unterstützte nicht), *dass nicht-weiß*. Die spezifische Zuverlässigkeit von Teds Sehvermögen hingegen *hing* von dem Umstand ab, *dass nicht-weiß*. Demzufolge beseitigt die Annahme, dass das Sehvermögen generell zuverlässig ist, nicht den Anschein von Zirkularität, von dem Teds Wissen, *dass nicht-weiß*, zu dem er auf der Basis von *dass rot* gelangt ist, betroffen ist.

(Möglicherweise würde Vogel hierauf mit folgender Behauptung reagieren: Damit Ted *dass rot* wissen kann, muss er wissen und d. h. die gerechtfertigte Überzeugung haben, dass seine Farbwahrnehmung auf *spezifische* Weise zuverlässig ist. Wie ich jedoch weiter unten aufzeigen werde, führt dieser Weg zum Skeptizismus.)

Vogels umgekehrte Strategie war nicht erfolgreich; er hat uns nicht mit einem überzeugenden Verfahren ausgestattet, mit dem einfaches Wissen im Keim erstickt werden kann. Zum Teil liegt dieser Fehlschlag an der Tatsache, dass er das Problem des einfachen Wissens unterschätzt hat. Im Folgenden werde ich versuchen, ihr wesentliches Merkmal zu charakterisieren. Wenn ich Recht habe, können wir die Möglichkeit einfachen Wissens nicht ausschließen, ohne entweder die Geschlossenheit aufzugeben oder eine Analyse mit inakzeptablen skeptischen Konsequenzen anzunehmen. In der Annahme, dass keine dieser Alternativen akzeptabel ist, können wir den Schluss ziehen, dass Wissen manchmal eben tatsächlich einfach *ist*.

Warum also scheint es kontraintuitiv zu sagen, Ted und Roxanne wissen, dass die Dinge, die sie glauben, wahr sind? Ich schlage vor, die beste Erklärung dreht sich um die Tatsache, dass diese Fälle Argumentationen zu beinhalten scheinen, bei denen von einer Proposition auf etwas geschlossen wird, auf das diese Proposition selbst *gegründet* ist (*grounds*) und zwar im folgenden Sinne: *dass p gründet auf (grounds) dass g für die Person S*, in dem Falle, in dem die Wahrheit von *dass g* für das Wissen

---

9 Vgl. Luper (1987b).

von *dass p* für S entscheidend ist. Es ist anzunehmen, dass solche Argumentationen pseudo-zirkulär sind.[10] Es erscheint kontraintuitiv zu behaupten, Wissen könne wesentlich von pseudo-zirkulären Folgerungen abhängen, was es in den Fällen von Ted und Roxanne aber tun würde. Insofern wäre es kontraintuitiv, Ted und Roxanne Wissen zuzuschreiben. (Um die Möglichkeit zuzulassen, etwas aufgrund verschiedener Quellen glauben zu können, sollten wir die Erklärung folgendermaßen formulieren: Das Wissen, dass eine Überzeugung wahr ist, verlangt, wenigstens über eine Quelle zu verfügen, die keine pseudo-zirkuläre Argumentationen beinhaltet, doch Teds und Roxannes Überzeugungen beruhen auf keiner derartigen Quelle. Im Interesse der Einfachheit werde ich diese alternative Erklärung nicht weiter verfolgen.)

Meine Erklärung bezieht sich auf Wahrheiten, die für unser Wissen von etwas 'entscheidend' ('instrumental to') sind. Ich wähle diese zugegebenermaßen vage Terminologie bewusst, so dass meine Erklärung nicht die Wahrheit einer bestimmten Theorie des Wissens voraussetzen wird. Verschiedene Theoretiker werden verschiedene Ansichten darüber haben, wann die Wahrheit einer Proposition für das, was wir wissen, entscheidend ist. Zur Veranschaulichung gilt es die folgenden Aspekte des Tisch-Falls zu betrachten, welche meines Erachtens ziemlich unumstritten sind. Teds Wissensquelle ist grob gesehen sein visueller Wahrnehmungsprozess. Aufgrund dieses Prozesses weiß Ted Dinge nur dann, wenn die Umstände, unter denen er stattfindet, so sind, dass Teds Sehvermögen hinreichend zuverlässig ist. Dass es hinreichend zuverlässig ist, hängt von der Wahrheit verschiedener Propositionen ab; für Ted ist jede dieser Propositionen entscheidend, um durch seine Quelle zu Wissen von etwas zu gelangen. Ein Beispiel ist die Proposition, dass es falsch ist, dass Teds Tisch weiß ist und dieser von einem roten Licht beleuchtet wird. Unser Wissen *dass p* gründet (grounds) auf der Proposition *dass g,* wenn die erforderliche Zuverlässigkeit der Quelle von *dass p* an der Wahrheit von *dass g* hängt. Kommen wir nun zu Propositionen, die Argumentationen zu Nichte machen, die für jemandes Überzeugung *dass p* wesentlich sind (ohne dabei eine falsche Überzeugung zu rechtfertigen): Die Negation einer jeden solchen Proposition ist entscheidend für das Wissen, *dass p*, welches aufgrund dieser Argumentation zustande kommt.

Ich kenne keine klarere allgemeine Analyse der Propositionen, auf denen Wissen gründet. Die möglichen Analysen, die einem einfallen,

---

10 Vgl. Luper (2005); Luper (2006).

scheinen fehlerhaft. Angenommen wir sagen zum Beispiel, dass *p für die Person S* auf g gründet, wenn gilt:

(S weiß, *dass p*) impliziert *dass g*.

Aber ich weiß, *dass Fische im Wasser leben* (kurz: *dass Fische*), und mein Wissen, *dass Fische* impliziert jedes der vielen Dinge, welche auch die Tatsache, *dass Fische* selbst impliziert, etwa dass Fische entweder im Wasser leben oder „dass mir der Mond wie eine Pizza erscheint" (the moon hits my eye like a pizza pie). Dennoch spielen wenige – sicherlich nicht alle – dieser Propositionen eine Rolle in Bezug auf mein Wissen, *dass Fische*.

Eine bessere Analyse besagt, dass *für die Person S dass p* auf g gründet, wenn gilt:

(S weiß, *dass p*) impliziert (oder impliziert vielleicht: materialiter) *dass g*, aber *dass p* impliziert nicht *dass g*.

Diese Analyse schließt jedoch Propositionen aus, die aus den schwierigen Fällen zu folgen scheinen. Zum Beispiel wird das Wissen von Sam, *dass nicht-(nicht-Auto und Träumen)*, welches er auf der Basis von *dass Auto* hat, von vielen Theoretikern, wie etwa von Harman, als zu einfach aufgefasst, obwohl das Letztere doch das Erste impliziert.

Oder sollten wir sagen, Sams Wissen, dass *dass Auto* gilt gründe auf *dass nicht-träumen* und nicht auf *dass nicht-(nicht-Auto und träumen)*? Wir könnten sagen, das Erstere (wie dass mein Gehirn keine vorgefertigten Erfahrungen hat) sei die Negation einer skeptischen *Kern*hypothese und das Letztere (etwa dass ich kein losgelöstes Gehirn bin, das sich *auf dem weit entlegenen Planeten Crouton* befindet und vorgefertigte Erfahrungen hat) die Negation einer trivialen Konsequenz dieser Hypothese. Vielleicht gründet Sams Wissen, dass *dass Auto* gilt auf der Falschheit der skeptischen Kernhypothese, aber nicht auf *dass nicht-(nicht-Auto und träumen)*. Wir haben schon gesagt, eine Proposition könne auch dann eine Rolle in unserem Wissen spielen, wenn einige ihrer Konsequenzen dies nicht tun. Angenommen wir sagen, dass, während unser Wissen auf der Falschheit skeptischer Kernhypothesen gründet, es nicht auf der Falschheit der trivialen Konsequenzen dieser Hypothesen gründen kann. Wenn eine derartige Kernthese gilt, können wir die Behauptung, es sei zu einfach für Sam, *dass nicht-(nicht-Auto und träumen)* zu wissen, als eine Illusion fallen lassen. Die Illusion rührt von dem Scheitern zu erkennen her, dass diese Proposition nicht wirklich entscheidend für Sams Wissen, *dass Auto* ist. *Dass nicht-(nicht-Auto und träumen)* allein auf der Basis des eigenen Wissens, dass *dass Auto* gilt, zu wissen, ist nicht problematischer als aufgrund des Wissens, dass ich zwei Hände habe, zu wissen, dass ich wenigstens eine Hand habe. Außerdem können wir sagen, weder der Tisch- noch der Auto-Fall stellen eine Bedrohung für K dar. In Anbetracht von K sollte sich Ted in einer Position befinden, in der er weiß, *dass nicht-weiß*, wenn er weiß, *dass rot* und Sam sollte sich daran machen zu dem Wissen zu gelangen, *dass nicht-(nicht-Auto und träumen)*, wenn er weiß, *dass Auto*, aber das stellt kein Problem dar, wenn die jeweils Letztgenannten nicht auf den Erstgenannten gründen. Für Ted mag es nicht möglich sein, über das Wissen zu verfügen, dass sein Tisch nicht von einem roten Licht beleuchtet wird, auch wenn er weiß, *dass rot*. Und für Sam mag es nicht möglich sein, über das Wissen zu verfügen, dass er nicht träumt, auch wenn er weiß, *dass Auto*, denn (unter anderem) gründen die jeweils Letztgenannten auf den Erstgenannten, was jedoch völlig vereinbar mit K ist.[11] Ich vermute, dass die meisten Theoretiker die Kernthese nicht akzeptieren und werde mich im Folgenden auch nicht weiter auf sie berufen.

Die schwierigen Fälle werden für diejenigen problematisch sein, die denken, eine Proposition könne nicht auf der Basis von etwas gewusst werden, das eben auf dieser Proposition gründet (und die die Kernthese ablehnen). In Vogels Beispiel handelt es sich um das *Bootstrapping*, das pseudozirkulär ist. Die Wahrheit einer Überzeugung kann nur dann gewusst werden, wenn ihre Quelle generell zuverlässig ist. Die angegebenen Werte von Roxannes Tankanzeige ermöglichen es ihr nur dann etwas zu wissen, wenn diese Angaben zuverlässig sind. Wenn also diese Dinge (die ihr ihre Tankanzeige angibt) ihre Gründe dafür sind, an die Zuverlässigkeit ihre Tankanzeige zu glauben, dann ist ihre Argumentation pseudozirkulär.

Wenn wir K akzeptieren und sowohl den Skeptizismus als auch die Kernthese ablehnen, werden wir Pseudozirkularität wohl tolerieren müssen.[12] Um Pseudozirkularität auf vereinbare Weise mit K auszuschließen, müssen wir so etwas wie die folgende *Unabhängigkeitsbedingung* akzeptieren:

> Wenn S weiß, *dass k,* und wenn die Proposition *dass g* entscheidend für das Wissen von *k* für S ist, dann weiß S, *dass g,* und dass *k* nicht entscheidend für ihr Wissen von *g* ist.

---

11 Siehe die Gegenüberstellung von K mit dem Prinzip Moores in Luper (2007).
12 Vgl. Van Cleve (2003).

Entsprechend gilt:

> Wenn für S *dass k* auf der Proposition *dass g* gründet, dann weiß S, *dass g,* und *dass g* gründet für S nicht auf *dass k*.

Die Unabhängigkeitsbedingung lässt pseudozirkuläre Quellen des Wissens nicht mehr gelten: In Anbetracht der Unabhängigkeitsbedingung ist es nicht möglich, auf der Basis eines Teils von Wissen etwas über das zu erfahren, auf dem eben dieser Teil des Wissens gründet. Die Unabhängigkeitsbedingung steht zudem im Einklang mit dem Geschlossenheitsprinzip: Jede Folgerung eines Teils des Wissens *dass k* muss unabhängig von *dass k* gewusst werden, wenn *dass k* auf ihm gründet. Es kann jedoch aufgrund von *dass k* gewusst werden, wenn *dass k* nicht auf ihm gründet.

Warum sollte man nicht anstelle der Unabhängigkeitsbedingung ein schwächeres Prinzip annehmen, welches uns erlaubt, über das Wissen einer Proposition *dass k* zu verfügen, ohne dafür die unabhängige Wahrheit von irgendeinem *dass g,* auf dem *dass k* gründet, wissen zu müssen, so lange *dass k* nicht impliziert, *dass g*. Das folgende Prinzip ist genau in diesem Sinne schwächer:

> Wenn für S *dass k* auf der Proposition *dass g* gründet und *dass k dass g* impliziert, dann weiß S, *dass g,* und *dass g* gründet für S nicht auf *dass k*.

Dies, d.h. die Folge-Unabhängigkeitsbedingung, schließt gleich ihrem Vorgänger aus, für Ted folge aus der Tatsache, dass sein Tisch rot erscheint, das Wissen, es sei falsch, dass sein Tisch weiß ist und dieser von einem roten Licht beleuchtet wird. Dennoch lässt die Folge-Unabhängigkeitsbedingung zu, dass Ted weiß, sein Tisch ist rot, ohne dass er unabhängig davon wissen muss, dass dieser nicht von einem roten Licht beleuchtet wird, obwohl das Vorangegangene auf dem Letzteren gründet (grounds), denn dass der Tisch rot ist, impliziert nicht, dass er nicht von einem roten Licht beleuchtet wird. Indes ist es schwer zu verstehen, was für die Ausnahmen spricht, die durch die Folge-Unabhängigkeitsbedingung zugelassen werden: Wenn das Wissen, dass sein Tisch rot ist, von Ted ein davon unabhängiges Wissen erfordert, dass der Tisch nicht weiß und von einem roten Licht beleuchtet wird, warum sollte es dann nicht auch sein davon unabhängiges Wissen erfordern, dass er nicht von einem roten Licht beleuchtet wird? (Wenn wir sagen würden, dass Teds Wissen, *dass rot* nur auf einem dieser beiden Fällen gründe, wäre es, wie oben angemerkt, plausibler, die Option zu wählen, dass der Tisch nicht von einem roten Licht beleuchtet wird, als die falsche Auffassung, dass der Tisch weiß ist und von einem roten Licht beleuchtet wird.)

Ich habe festgestellt, die Unabhängigkeitsbedingung erlaubt es uns gleichzeitig Pseudozirkularität auszuschließen und Geschlossenheit beizubehalten. Wenn wir uns darauf stützen, dass die Unabhängigkeitsbedingung die Geschlossenheit mit dem Ausschluss der Pseudozirkularität in Einklang bringt, müssen wir bedauerlicherweise einen Preis dafür bezahlen: nämlich dass gewöhnliche Fälle von Wissen dem Skeptizismus ausgesetzt sind.

Dies verhält sich aus folgenden Gründen so: Die Unabhängigkeitsbedingung verlangt, dass Ted für das Wissen, dass sein Tisch rot ist, wissen muss, dass sein Sehvermögen auf spezifische Weise zuverlässig ist und dass keine der Umstände gelten, in denen es nicht auf spezifische Weise zuverlässig ist. Sie verlangt zudem, dass er diese Dinge auf eine Art und Weise weiß, die unabhängig von jeglichem Wissen ist, welches ihm sein Sehvermögen mit deren Hilfe vermittelt, wie etwa sein Wissen, dass sein Tisch rot ist. Das bedeutet aber, Ted weiß nicht, dass sein Tisch rot ist, da er eben *nicht* versucht *hat*, die vielen Möglichkeiten auszusortieren, die die spezifische Zuverlässigkeit seines Sehvermögens untergraben könnten. Zum Beispiel hat er nicht versucht, festzustellen, ob er etwa optische Halluzinationen hat, in denen Tische vorkommen. (In dem Tisch-Fall ist Ted zu dem Schluss gekommen, es sei falsch, dass sein Tisch weiß ist und dieser von einem roten Licht beleuchtet wird, aber er hat nicht versucht dies unabhängig von seinem Wissen festzustellen, dass der Tisch rot ist.) Betrachten wir nun Sam. Um *dass nicht-(nicht-Auto und träumen)* festzustellen, muss Sam entweder *dass Auto* oder *dass nicht-träumen* feststellen. Um dies zu tun, ohne sich dabei auf *dass Auto* zu stützen, muss er *dass nicht-träumen* feststellen. Das hat er aber nicht einmal versucht. Also weiß er nicht, *dass Auto*. Dennoch würden auf jedermanns Liste gewöhnlicher Fälle von Wissen Teds Überzeugung *dass rot* und Sams Überzeugung *dass Auto* vorkommen. Und so lässt sich ebenso wie bei Ted und Sam bei den meisten von uns in der Regel nicht davon sprechen, dass wir über Wissen gewöhnlicher empirischer Wahrheiten verfügen, denn wir versuchen, solche Möglichkeiten, wie z. B. *dass nicht-träumen*, nicht auszuschließen.

Dass die meisten von uns in der Regel nicht über gewöhnliche empirische Wahrheiten verfügen, ist eine extrem kontraintuitive skeptische Konsequenz. Es könnte natürlich noch schlimmer stehen. Es könnte sich herausstellen, dass wir derartige Wahrheiten gar *nicht* wissen *können*. Und tatsächlich könnte es sein, dass die Unabhängigkeitsbedingung dazu führt, dass wir über kein Wissen von normalen empirischen Wahrheiten verfügen. Faktisch verlangt die Unabhängigkeitsbedingung jede Wissensquelle zu überprüfen, und zwar in dem Sinne, dass wir herausfinden müssen, ob sie auf spezifische Weise zuverlässig ist und ob die Wahrheiten gelten, von der diese Zuverlässigkeit abhängt. Müssen alle mutmaßlichen Wissensquellen überprüft werden, damit sie uns überhaupt Wissen vermitteln können, dann stellt sich die Frage, wie wir zu dem Wissen gelangen, auf welche Art und Weise diese Überprüfungen selbst durchzuführen sind? Hier stehen wir dem standardmäßigen skeptischen Trilemma gegenüber. Unsere Bemühungen, unsere Quellen zu überprüfen, werden mit Annahmen beginnen, deren Wahrheit wir nicht kennen oder die in einen infiniten Regress führen oder sie werden irgendeine Art von Zirkularität beinhalten, die von der Unabhängigkeitsbedingung abgelehnt werden. Es gilt zu bedenken, dass allen fünf Sinnen spezifische Zuverlässigkeit fehlt, wenn gewisse skeptische Hypothesen gelten, wie z.B. wenn wir unter einer komplexen Menge von Halluzinationen leiden, die sich auf alle unsere Sinne auswirkt. In Anbetracht der Unabhängigkeitsbedingung ist es uns nicht möglich, mittels unseres visuellen Wissens zu verifizieren, ob unser visueller Sinn nicht von diesen Halluzinationen untergraben wird. Noch können wir taktiles Wissen als Bestätigung dafür verwenden, dass unser Tastsinn nicht von diesen Halluzinationen untergraben wird. Können wir visuelles Wissen als Verifikation dafür verwenden, dass sie nicht unseren *Tast*sinn untergraben, und den Tastsinn als Verifikation dafür, dass sie nicht unser Sehvermögen untergraben? Allem Anschein nach nicht. Um über visuelles Wissen zu verfügen, dürfen wir nicht unter Halluzinationen leiden. Wenn wir unser visuelles Wissen verwenden, um etwas zu verifizieren, das wiederum bestätigt, dass wir nicht unter Halluzinationen leiden, verletzen wir die Unabhängigkeitsbedingung.

Das schwierige Argument und Lotterieartige Propositionen

Umgekehrte Argumente, wie z.B. das in dem vorigen Abschnitt verworfene, sind erst vor relativ kurzer Zeit im Rahmen von Veröffentlichungen in Erscheinung getreten, die epistemische Fragestellungen betreffen. Schwierige Argumente waren zuerst Teil der dort stattfindenden Auseinandersetzungen. Eine Version des schwierigen Arguments ist äußerst bekannt[13]: Angenommen eine Proposition ist dann und nur dann *flüchtig (elusive)*, wenn unsere Erfahrungen auch dann die gleichen bleiben würden, wenn die Proposition falsch ist. Zum Beispiel: *dass nicht-weiß* ist

---
13 Nozick (1981); Dretske (1970); Dretske (2003); Dretske (2005).

wahr und Ted hat bestimmte Erfahrungen, die er auch dann noch haben würde, wenn *dass weiß* wahr wäre. Laut des Arguments der Flüchtigkeit (argument from elusiveness) scheitern wir darin, wissen zu können, ob flüchtige Propositionen wahr sind, selbst wenn wir von ihnen überzeugt sind, weil sie von uns bekannten Dingen impliziert werden. Daher sollten wir K ablehnen. Mittlerweile ist das Argument der Flüchtigkeit viel kritisiert worden und ich werde es nicht weiter behandeln. Stattdessen werde ich eine Version des schwierigen Arguments berücksichtigen, die versucht, Lotterie-Propositionen und lotterieartige Propositionen gegen das Prinzip der Geschlossenheit ins Feld zu führen.

Der Standardfall einer *Lotterie*-Proposition besteht in der Proposition *dass nicht-gewinnen*. Das Los in meiner Hand – eines von den zehn Millionen, das von der heute Abend endenden Staatslotterie ausgestellt wurde – ist kein Gewinn. Was charakteristisch für diese Propositionen ist, ist dass sie normalerweise nur auf der Basis ihrer hohen Wahrscheinlichkeit vertretbar sind. Um z. B. meine Behauptung zu stützen, dass mein Los eine Niete ist, würde ich normalerweise die Tatsache anführen, dass die Wahrscheinlichkeit dafür sehr hoch ist, wenn auch geringer als 1. Wie Jonathan Vogel[14] und andere Theoretiker angemerkt haben, ähneln Propositionen, die selbst nicht wirklich von Lotterien handeln, trotzdem Lotterie-Propositionen insofern ihnen eine Wahrscheinlichkeit von weniger als 1 zugeschrieben werden kann. Ich schlage vor, diese Propositionen als lotterieartig zu bezeichnen. Zum Beispiel: dass mein Auto nicht gestohlen und südlich der Grenze gebracht wurde (kurz: *dass nicht-gestohlen*), erscheint in Anbetracht der Statistiken bezüglich gestohlener Autos in den USA lotterieartig. In Bezug auf diese Statistiken ist die Wahrscheinlichkeit von *dass nicht-gestohlen* geringer als 1, selbst wenn sie dabei recht hoch ist.

Lotterie-Propositionen können nicht allein aufgrund dessen gewusst werden, dass ihre Wahrheit höchst wahrscheinlich ist.[15] Darauf zu bestehen, dass sie auf dieser Basis gewusst werden können, ruft den Geist von Kyburgs Lotterie-Paradox[16] hervor. Es ist zudem zu beachten, dass es nicht akzeptabel ist, in dem epistemischen Sinn von 'könnte' sowohl „Ich weiß, *dass p*" und „*dass p* könnte falsch sein" zu sagen. Dennoch könnte jede Lotterie-Proposition im epistemischen Sinne falsch sein.

---

14 Vogel (1990).
15 Vgl. Harman (1968).
16 Siehe Kyburg (1961).

Wie mehrere Theoretiker bemerkt haben, können wir Paradoxien vermeiden und erklären, warum wir normalerweise nicht im Stande sind, über das Wissen von Lotterie-Propositionen zu verfügen. Dies können wir tun, indem wir sagen, unser Wissen *dass p* setze unsere Überzeugung *dass p* aufgrund von etwas voraus, das die Wahrheit von *p festlegt*. Diese Auffassung von Wissen findet sich in unterschiedlichen aber nah verwandten Formulierungen wieder: Dretske[17] behauptete, dass Wissen einen zwingenden Grund dafür verlangt, warum wir das, was wir glauben für wahr halten; David Armstrong behauptete „knowledge requires a belief-state which *ensures* truth" („Wissen erfordert einen Glaubens-Zustand, der Wahrheit *garantiert*)[18] und Sherman und Harman behaupten „one knows only if one believes as one does because of something that settles the truth of that belief." („Man weiß nur etwas, wenn man es so glaubt, wie man es aufgrund von etwas tut, dass die Wahrheit dieses Glaubens festlegt")[19]. Befürworter der Analyse des Wissens[20], die auf sicheren Anzeichen beruht, werden auch sagen, dass wir Dinge nur dann wissen, wenn wir sie auf die Art und Weise glauben, wie wir es eben tun, nämlich auf der Basis von dem, was deren Wahrheit festlegt. Laut dieser Analyse wissen wir nur *dass p*, wenn wir *dass p* auf der Basis eines Ereignisses oder Tatbestandes R, der sicher die Wahrheit von *dass p* anzeigt, glauben, d. h. in dem Fall, in dem R nur dann die Wahrheit von *dass p* sicher anzeigt, wenn der folgende irreale Konditionalsatz wahr ist:

dass p würde gelten, wenn R gilt.

Laut jedem dieser Ansätze scheitern wir darin, Dinge, Lotterie-Propositionen inbegriffen, zu wissen, wenn unsere alleinige Basis für unseren Glauben an sie aus ihrer hohen Wahrscheinlichkeit besteht.

Vermutlich liegt es daran, dass wir einfach nicht über das Wissen von Lotterie-Propositionen verfügen, weshalb einige Theoretiker sie für 'schwierig' erachten. Dass sie schwierig sind, stellt jedoch kaum eine große Gefahr für K dar, denn es ist nicht offensichtlich, dass es alltägliche Wissensansprüche gibt, die echte Lotterie-Propositionen implizieren. Es gilt die Proposition *dass nicht-kaufen* zu betrachten: ich werde morgen keine 10-Millionen-Dollar-Villa an der Französischen Riviera kaufen, da es mir an den Mitteln dafür fehlt und an dem Konditional: wenn *gewinnen*,

---

17 Dretske (1971).
18 Armstrong (1973), 187.
19 Sherman u. Harman (2004), 492.
20 Siehe z. B. Luper (1984); Luper (2003a); Sosa (2000).

dann *kaufen*. Z.B.: Ich werde morgen die Villa kaufen, wenn ich heute Abend bei der Staatslotterie gewinne. Wenn *dass nicht-kaufen* und wenn *gewinnen,* dann *kaufen* zu den Dingen gehören, die ich weiß, steht K unter Druck, denn sie implizieren *dass nicht-gewinnen,* so dass es in Anbetracht von K ein Leichtes für mich ist, *dass nicht-gewinnen* zu wissen. Genauer gesagt, steht nicht K, sondern eher das folgende stärkere Prinzip unter Druck.

GK: Wenn S über das Wissen mehrerer Propositionen verfügt und dabei glaubt, *dass p,* weil S weiß, dass diese *p* implizieren, dann weiß S, dass *p*.

Doch ist der Befürworter von GK gut aufgestellt, um dafür zu argumentieren, dass ich *dass nicht-kaufen* nicht weiß. Ein Grund dafür, warum mir dies nicht gelingt, liegt genau darin, dass die Wahrheit dieser Proposition zum Teil davon abhängt, ob ich die Lotterie gewinnen werde und ich weiß einfach nicht, ob dies passieren wird oder nicht.[21]

Allerdings scheitert diese Strategie, wenn man sie auf die weiter gefasste Gruppe lotterieartiger Propositionen anwendet. Es ist relativ unumstritten, dass ich weiß, dass mein Ford 100, Baujahr 1969, unten in meiner Garage steht (kurz: *dass Ford*). Aber *dass Ford* impliziert die lotterieartige Proposition *dass nicht-gestohlen,* so dass in Anbetracht von K das Letztgenannte auf einfache Art und Weise gewusst werden kann. Und Befürworter von K können nicht glaubhaft reagieren, indem sie leugnen, dass ich weiß, *dass Ford*. Zu viele der Propositionen, die wir ganz offensichtlich wissen, implizieren lotterieartige Propositionen.

Eine bessere Strategie besteht in der Betonung, echte Lotterie-Propositionen seien normalerweise nur aufgrund dessen vertretbar, dass ihre Wahrheit höchstwahrscheinlich ist. Hingegen können lotterieartige Propositionen auf der Basis von Dingen vertretbar sein, die ihre Wahrheit festlegen. Während lotterieartige Propositionen auf der Basis von Dingen basieren *können,* die wahrscheinlich sind, kann deren Wahrheit nicht auf der Basis solcher Dinge gewusst werden. Aber sie können auch aufgrund von etwas, das ihre Wahrheit festlegt, geglaubt werden und insofern können sie gewusst werden. Meine Überzeugung *dass nicht-gestohlen,* basiert nicht auf Kriminalitätsstatistiken; wenn sie das tun würde, würde ich nicht wissen, dass sie wahr ist, denn auf dieser Grundlage wäre meine Überzeugung bestenfalls höchstwahrscheinlich. Eine besonders herausragende Rolle unter meinen Gründen spielt meine Beobachtung *O*: Ich

---

21 Vgl. Harman (1986), 71.

habe meinen Ford gerade erst unten geparkt. Es wäre nicht wahr, dass O festlegt, dass *dass nicht-gestohlen* in Gettierartigen Situationen gilt; z. B. würde O seinen Zweck nicht erfüllen, wenn in meiner Gegend Auto-Diebe am Werke wären, wenn ich einen Sohn hätte, der mit seinen eigenen Autoschlüsseln, ohne dass ich es weiß, im Begriff ist, mit dem Auto loszufahren und so weiter. Aber unter normalen Umständen legt O fest, *dass nicht-gestohlen* und dass *dass Ford* gilt.

Wir können eine ähnliche Schlussfolgerung in Bezug auf echte Lotterie-Propositionen ziehen. Es kann nicht gewusst werden, dass sie wahr sind, wenn sie allein aufgrund ihrer hohen Wahrscheinlichkeit geglaubt werden. Aber in ungewöhnlichen Umständen kann gewusst werden, dass sie wahr sind. Um über das Wissen zu verfügen, *dass nicht-gewinnen*, müsste ich wissen, dass mein Los eine Fälschung ist oder dass die Lotterie zu meinem Nachteil manipuliert wurde oder ähnliches. Wenn S glaubt, dass *p*, weil S sieht (weiß), dass es von etwas impliziert wird, dass S weiß, dann schlage ich vor, dass es sich bei *dass p* um *gesichertes Wissen* handelt. Bei lotterieartigen Propositionen handelt es sich selten um gesichertes Wissen, aber wenn es gesichert ist, dann weiß man, dass sie wahr sind.[22]

(Eine kürzere Version dieses Aufsatzes wurde auf der Bled Conference on Epistemology, 28. Mai – 2. Juni 2007, vorgetragen. Ich danke den Teilnehmern, meinem Kollegen Curtis Brown und den anonymen Gutachtern für ihre Kommentare.)

References

Armstrong (1973): David M. Armstrong, *Belief, Truth and Knowledge*, Cambridge.
Cohen (2002): Stewart Cohen, „Basic Knowledge and the Problem of Easy Knowledge", in: *Philosophy and Phenomenological Research* 65.2, 309–329.
Cohen (2005): Stewart Cohen, „Why Basic Knowledge is Easy Knowledge", in: *Philosophy and Phenomenological Research* 75.2, 417–30.
Dretske (1970): Fred Dretske, „Epistemic Operators", in: *Journal of Philosophy* 67, 1007–1023.
Dretske (2003): Fred Dretske, „Skepticism: What Perception Teaches", in: Luper (2003b).
Dretske (2005): Fred Dretske, „Is Knowledge Closed Under Known Entailment?", in: Steup (2005).

---

22 Translated from English by Ute Feldmann.

Fumerton (1995): Richard A. Fumerton, *Metaepistemology and Skepticism*, Lanham/MD.
Harman, (1968): Gilbert Harman, „Knowledge, Inference and Explanation", in: *American Philosophical Quarterly* 5, 164–73.
Harman (1986): Gilbert Harman, *Change In View*, Cambridge.
Harman/Sherman (2004): Gilbert Harman/Brett Sherman, „Knowledge, Assumptions, Lotteries", in: *Philosophical Issues* 14, 492–500.
Hawthorne (2006): John Hawthorne, *Knowledge and Lotteries*, Oxford.
Kyburg (1961): Henry Kyburg, 'Conjunctivitis', *Probability and the Logic of Rational Belief*, Middletown/Conn.
Luper (1984): Steven Luper, „The Epistemic Predicament: Knowledge, Nozickian Tracking, and Skepticism", in: *Australasian Journal of Philosophy* 62, 26–50.
Luper (1987a): Steven Luper (ed.), *The Possibility of Knowledge: Nozick and His Critics*, Totowa/NJ.
Luper (1987b): Steven Luper, „The Causal Indicator Analysis of Knowledge", in: *Philosophy and Phenomenological Research* 47, 563–587.
Luper (2003a): Steven Luper, „Indiscernability Skepticism", in: Luper (2003b).
Luper (2003b): Steven Luper, *The Skeptics*, S. Luper (ed.), Hampshire.
Luper (2005): Steven Luper, „Epistemic Closure Principle", in: E. N. Zalta (ed.), *Stanford University Encyclopedia of Philosophy*.
Luper (2006): Steven Luper, „Dretske on Knowledge Closure", in: *Australasian Journal of Philosophy* 84.3, 379–394.
Luper (2007): Steven Luper, „Re-Reading G. E. Moore's 'Certainty'", in: *Philosophical Papers* 36.1, 151–163.
Luper (2007): Steven Luper, „The Easy Argument", in: *Acta Analytica* 22, 321–331.
Nozick (1981): Robert Nozick, *Philosophical Explanations*, Cambridge.
Sosa (2000): Ernest Sosa, „Neither Contextualism Nor Skepticism," in: Luper (2003b), 165–182.
Steup/Sosa (2005): Matthias Steup/Ernest Sosa (eds.), *Contemporary Debates in Epistemology*, Malden/MA.
Van Cleve (2003): James Van Cleve, „Is Knowledge Easy—or Impossible? Externalism as the Only Alternative to Skepticism," in: Luper (2003b), 45–61.
Vogel (1990): Jonathan Vogel, „Are There Counterexamples to the Closure Principle?" in: M. Roth/G. Ross (eds.), *Doubting: Contemporary Perspectives on Skepticism*, Dordrecht.
Vogel (2000): Jonathan Vogel, „Reliabilism Leveled", in: *Journal of Philosophy* 97, 602–623.

What Is Transmission Failure?

Anthony Brueckner

Let us say that an *inference* is a psychological process in which a reasoner believes a premise P and on the basis of this belief comes to believe a conclusion C. Following Crispin Wright, let us say that an inference is *cogent* iff (i) P entails C, and (ii) S's warrant for P *transmits across the entailment from P to C*.[1] Some inferences exhibit *Transmission Success* (hereafter *TS*)—these are the cogent inferences—while others satisfy (i) and yet exhibit *Transmission Failure* (hereafter *TF*). What exactly is TF? In a recent paper, Nicholas Silins raises some worries about how to coherently characterize TF in a way which makes it plausible to suppose that TF exists.[2] I want to elaborate on Silins's worries and to offer the TF proponent a way of dissolving the worries.

Let us begin by considering two alleged examples of TF, Soccer and Zebra. In Soccer, my warrant for my premise P=*The man just kicked a goal* is my experience of seeing the man kick a soccer ball into the net as the crowd goes wild. My conclusion C is *There is a game of soccer in progress*. In Zebra, my warrant for my premise P=*The animal is a zebra* is my experience of seeing an animal that looks just like a zebra, and my conclusion C is *The animal is not a cleverly disguised mule*. Both cases exhibit TF, according to Wright.

In order to be clear about what TF is supposed to consist in, says Silins, we must pay close attention to an oft-noted distinction regarding warrant. Silins has us distinguish between (a) S having a warrant *for believing P* (where this entails that S believes P and that this belief is a warranted belief), and S having a warrant *to believe P* (where this does not entail that S believes P; if S does not believe P, it is nevertheless true that *were* S to come to believe P on the basis of his warrant to believe P, S would then come to have a warrant *for believing P*, holding all else that is epistemically relevant fixed). This distinction is sometimes

---

1   Cf. e.g. Wright (2003).
2   Cf. Silins (2005).

characterized as the distinction between *doxastic warrant* and *propositional warrant*.[3]

According to Silins's reconstruction of TF theorists such as Wright, in both Soccer and Zebra, there is a certain requirement that must be satisfied if S's alleged warrant for his premise indeed has the power to warrant his belief of the premise. The requirement is that S must have an *independent warrant* to believe his conclusion C. Without such a *warrant to believe* in place, S's alleged warrant for his premise in Soccer and Zebra will fail to provide a genuine *warrant for believing* the pertinent premise. The following *Independence Requirement* holds in Soccer and Zebra:

(IR) If S's alleged warrant for his premise P indeed provides a genuine warrant for S's believing P, then S has an independent warrant to believe his conclusion C.

The holding of IR in Soccer and Zebra, according to Silins's reconstruction, is thought to engender TF in these cases.

Before moving on to discuss the nature of TF, it is natural to ask: what is meant by *independent warrant* in IR? It turns out that Silins's criticisms of the notion of TF do not turn upon any settled understanding of the notion of independent warrant. We can at least say that on one understanding of the notion, S has an independent warrant w to believe his conclusion C iff w includes neither P itself nor S's warrant w' for believing P. In some cases of TF, says Wright, S's independent warrant to believe C will consist in an unearned, default entitlement to believe C.

According to Silins, there are two notions of TF, each corresponding to one of the two notions of warrant distinguished above. Let us look first at S's warrant *to believe* his conclusion C. Suppose that an inference satisfies IR. This suffices for TF in the following sense:

(TF1) S cannot acquire his first warrant *to believe* C on the basis of his reasoning from P to C.

We are to see TF as a kind of limitation on the *warrant-generating* power of an inference. Let us assume that in a given case TF1 holds in virtue of the application of IR to the case. Why would TF1 hold in such a case? Assume that at t, prior to reasoning from P to C, S's belief of P is indeed

---

3   Silins's terminology is ill-chosen, since in the literature one can often find writers using the phrase 'S has justification for believing P' in a way that is compatible with S *failing to believe P*; such writers use the phrase to mean what Silins means by his 'S has justification to believe P'.

warranted: S has warrant *for believing* P. Then by IR, S must have at t an independent warrant *to believe* C. Thus, if at t' S comes to believe C by reasoning from P to C, S will not at t' acquire his *first* warrant *to believe* C. S *already had* such a warrant to believe C at t. So given that IR applies to Soccer and Zebra, these cases exhibit TF1.

In order to see the problem for explicating TF as TF1, we must first note that Wright endorses a Closure principle for warrant which implies that if S has warrant to believe P, then S also has warrant to believe C, given that P entails C.[4] Wright holds that cases of TF do not contravene Closure but rather presuppose Closure. For example, given the application of IR to Soccer and Zebra, S's alleged warrant for his premise in the cases succeeds in warranting the premise only if S has an independent warrant for his conclusion. So if S has a warrant to believe P in the cases, then S also has a warrant to believe C.

In light of Wright's endorsement of Closure, let us look at a TS case—a case in which there is Transmission *Success*. Let us suppose that S's inference from P=*I have hands* to C=*Either I have hands or God exists* exhibits TS (or choose some other case from the set of TS cases—there surely must be *some* TS cases!). Suppose that S believes P at t but has not yet considered C. By Closure, S has warrant *to believe* C at t.[5] This TS case exhibits TF1 just as much as do Soccer and Zebra, since in the present case S does not at t' acquire his first warrant to believe C by reasoning at t' from P to C. S already had a warrant to believe C at t, prior to his reasoning process. So TF1 cannot be the correct understanding of what constitutes Transmission *Failure*.

Suppose we look at S's warrant *for believing* C in a TF case and characterize TF in the following way:

(TF2) S cannot acquire his first warrant *for believing* C on the basis of his reasoning from P to C.

Let us again assume that IR applies to a given inference and that the inference therefore exhibits TF. Suppose that S has warrant for believing P at t. Then by IR, S has an independent warrant to believe C at t. Suppose that S does not believe C at t and comes to believe C at t' by rea-

---

4   The Closure principle for *warrant to believe* needs to be restricted to C's that are not necessary truths. Otherwise my having warrant to believe some P would give rise to my having warrant to believe all necessary truths, since all necessary truths are entailed by P.
5   Silins puts this sort of point by saying that given Closure, S *automatically* has warrant to believe C at t, in virtue of believing P at t.

soning from P to C. Then S *will* acquire his first warrant *for believing* C at t'. Thus the TF case in question (in which we supposed IR to be satisfied) will *not* exhibit TF2.[6]

We have been trying to explicate TF. If we understand TF as TF1, we end up with cases of TS exhibiting TF in virtue of satisfying TF1. If we explicate TF as TF2, we end up with cases which supposedly exhibit TF failing to exhibit TF2. So it so far seems difficult to find a coherent formulation of the view that in cases such as Soccer and Zebra, there is a limitation on the warrant-generating power of S's reasoning that merits the appellation *Transmission Failure*.

The problem with TF2 as an explication of TF is that in an IR case in which S believes P at t but does *not* believe C at t, S at t will have warrant to believe C. Thus, when S comes to believe C at t', he will acquire his first warrant for believing C, as in a TS case. But consider a case in which S has warrant for believing P at t and *also* believes C at t, though *not* on the basis of believing the entailing P, and *not* on the basis of any other proposition that is appropriately evidentially related to P, and *not* on the basis of experience, testimony, memory, or rational insight. So S does not at t have a warrant *for believing* C. In a TS version of a case meeting these conditions, S can acquire his first warrant for believing C at t' by seeing the connection between P and C and then reasoning from P to C at t'. In a TF version of a case meeting these conditions, in which IR is satisfied, S will have an independent warrant to believe C at t on the supposition that he has warrant for believing P at t. Before seeing the connection between P and C and then reasoning from P to C at t', S's belief of C at t is *already* a warranted belief in virtue of S's having an independent warrant to believe C at t. S's belief of C *at t* will be a *warranted belief*, i.e., in Silins's terminology, S will *at t* have a warrant *for believing* C. So when S reasons from P to C at t', S cannot acquire his *first* warrant for believing C. S already had such a warrant for believing P at t.

So we can provide the following revised characterization of Transmission Failure:

---

6 Silins does not give this argument. Instead, he considers the interplay between TF2 and a modified version of IR which concerns cases in which S is required to have an independent warrant *for believing* C (as opposed to an independent warrant to believe C) in order for his alleged warrant for believing C to indeed provide a warrant for believing C. Note that both Soccer and Zebra fit the template in the text.

(TF3) If S believes C at t, then S cannot acquire his first warrant for believing C at a later time t' when S reasons from P to C; alternatively, if S does *not* believe C at t, then it is nevertheless true that: *were* S to believe C at t, S then *could not* acquire his first warrant for believing C at a later time t' when S reasons from P to C.

We seem to have found a coherent understanding of what TF, if it indeed exists, consists in. Are there cases of TF—cases exhibiting TF3? This depends on whether there are inferences that satisfy IR. If there are, then these cases will exhibit TF3 and so count as cases of TF. *Which* inferences, if any, satisfy IR is a further question.

References

Wright (2003): Crispin Wright, "Some Reflections on the Acquisition of Warrant by Inference", in: S. Nuccetelli (ed.), *New Essays on Semantic Externalism and Self-Knowledge,* Cambridge, 57–78.

Silins (2005): Nicholas Silins, "Transmission Failure Failure", in: *Philosophical Studies* 126, 71–102.

Chapter Four
*Varieties and Forms of Knowledge:
Animal, Phenomenal,
and Practical Knowledge*

Epistemology and Cognitive Ethology
Hilary Kornblith

Epistemology, as traditionally practiced, has no interest in the scientific study of cognition. While scientific investigations can tell us just how it is that information processing occurs, the philosophical study of knowledge, at least as traditionally pursued, is simply not interested in matters at this level of detail. In Plato's *Theaetetus*, for example, Socrates asks what knowledge is, and Theaetetus responds that it is "geometry and all the sciences you mentioned just now, and then there are the crafts of the cobbler and other workmen. Each and all of these are knowledge and nothing else." Socrates has a short reply to this: "You are generous indeed, my dear Theaetetus–so openhanded that, when you are asked for one simple thing, you offer a whole variety."[1] As Socrates sees it, we, as philosophers, are looking for a unified account of what it is that makes each of these things knowledge; we want to understand the nature of knowledge itself. Theaetetus has not told us anything about what knowledge is; instead, he has given us a mere list, some examples of knowledge, with no unifying account. The problem with Theaetetus's answer to Socrates, at least as philosophers have traditionally seen things, is equally a problem with attempts to bring scientific studies of cognition to bear on epistemological questions. The philosopher seeks an account of the nature of knowledge, and all that scientific investigation can provide us with is a list of different processes which in fact are at work when individuals confront the world.

There are at least two different problems here. The first has to do with the level of abstraction appropriate to each sort of investigation. Just as Theaetetus's answer to Socrates is far more concrete than he is looking for, the scientific study of cognition provides us with a level of detail which is simply irrelevant to philosophical investigations. Neuroscientists, for example, are interested in the physical mechanisms by way of which cognition takes place, but the philosophical study of knowledge has no concern with the details of these mechanisms. If you are interested in what it is that knowledge consists in, it really

---

1   Cf. Plato (1961), 146d.

doesn't matter what the chemical environment is which allows for electrical signals to be transmitted across neuronal synapses. Scientists, on this view, are interested in understanding things about various trees, while philosophers are interested, instead, in understanding things about the forest.

As this analogy should make clear, however, the problem having to do with level of abstraction cannot be the sole reason for rejecting any scientific input to philosophical investigations. In the case of forests and trees, after all, we may all allow that someone may lose sight of the forest by way of studying individual trees. This does not mean, however, that one need know nothing at all about trees in order to understand the forest. Even if a scientific investigation of cognition proceeds at a level of abstraction far different from philosophical investigation, it might be useful to look at the results of scientific investigations—the various accounts of cognitive processes—to see what it is that they have in common. Thus, even if we grant, as we should, that epistemology deals with questions about cognition at a higher level of abstraction than most scientific investigations of cognition, this point alone would hardly make the scientific study of cognition *irrelevant* to the more abstract, philosophical investigation.

There is, however, a second problem. The scientific study of cognition is purely descriptive, it is often claimed, while a philosophical investigation involves normative matters. When cognitive scientists investigate the various processes by which beliefs are formed, they do not stop to evaluate whether these processes are good, bad or indifferent. Cognitive science, as a scientific inquiry, is silent on evaluative questions. Epistemology, on the other hand, is precisely focused on such questions. It does not seek to describe the ways in which beliefs are acquired; instead, it seeks an understanding of how we ought to arrive at our beliefs. For this reason, it has traditionally been held that scientific investigations of cognition are simply irrelevant to epistemological concerns.

Once again, however, the claim of irrelevance is far stronger than anything genuinely supported by the considerations offered. Even if cognitive science were itself silent on normative matters, and even if epistemology were solely involved with normative concerns, this would surely be very far from demonstrating that the discoveries of cognitive science have no bearing on the normative issues to which epistemology is directly addressed. If scientific investigation were to reveal that certain processes of belief acquisition lauded by epistemologists have a striking tendency to produce mistaken beliefs, epistemologists could not plausibly ignore such results and treat them as irrelevant to the evaluation of those very processes. Proper evaluation is not blind to relevant facts.

My own view, which I will defend here, is that cognitive science has a great deal to offer philosophy, and we can make progress in epistemology only if we allow it to be influenced by the scientific study of cognition. In particular, I will argue that we can learn a great deal about the nature of knowledge, and make progress toward achieving the very sort of unified account of knowledge which Socrates sought, by way of work in cognitive ethology.

Now of all the fields in cognitive science to draw on, cognitive ethology might seem to be one of the least promising for delivering epistemological insights. Philosophers have often specifically addressed themselves to the nature of *human* knowledge, and even those philosophers who have not so qualified their target of investigation have often focused on features of knowledge which are, arguably, unique to human beings. The very features of knowledge which spark epistemological interest, it has seemed to many, are ones which we do not share with other animals, and thus, a scientific investigation of cognition in non-human animals will seem to many to be doubly irrelevant to philosophical concerns.

I am mindful of these points, and I recognize that, even among those philosophers who see scientific studies of cognition as relevant to epistemological investigation, the relevance of cognitive ethology has been less than obvious. I will argue, however, that philosophers' traditional emphasis on human knowledge has led epistemologists to view features unique to humans as essential features of knowledge in general, when, in fact, they are no such thing. More surprisingly, I will argue that the manner in which epistemologists have traditionally examined the nature of knowledge has led to an inaccurate account, not just of knowledge in general, but even of human knowledge itself. An examination of work in cognitive ethology thus serves as a useful corrective to the traditional focus of epistemologists on the human case. Or so I shall argue.

I

Philosophers in the analytic tradition have a standard method for approaching the kind of question which Socrates raised about knowledge. If we wish to devise an account of what knowledge is, we need to come up with a set of necessary and sufficient conditions, conditions defining what it is to be a case of knowledge. If someone offers a proposal for such an account, we may test that account by way of considering various hypothetical cases. When we describe a hypothetical case, contemplation of the description will typically prompt an intuition about whether the case described does or does not constitute knowledge. Thus, for example, Edmund Gettier famously described a case in 1963 in which an individual forms a justified, true belief, and yet, virtually everyone contemplating this case had the strong intuition that the case described did not constitute knowledge.[2] Those who thought that knowledge was nothing more than justified, true belief took this to be a counterexample to that account; it showed that something more was required if a belief is to count as knowledge.

George Bealer has described this method—testing proposed analyses against our intuitions about hypothetical cases—as the standard method in philosophy.[3] For better or for worse, I believe that he is right. A great deal of philosophy in the analytic tradition proceeds by way of just this method. It will therefore be useful to begin by saying something about what this method is supposed to achieve, and how it is designed to achieve it.

On one widely held view, the method of appeals to intuition is legitimate because the proper task of philosophy is conceptual analysis. The goal of philosophy is to understand our concepts, and by examining our intuitive response to hypothetical cases, we gain an understanding of the concepts which we implicitly employ in thinking about the world. The epistemologist, on this view, is interested in our concept of knowledge; the ethicist is interested in our concepts of the good and the right; the philosopher of mind is interested in our concept of mind; and so on. As most philosophers who defend this method see it, philosophy is an armchair discipline: unlike scientific investigation, the examination of our concepts does not require that we look at the world, for the world itself is not the target of our investigation; it is our concepts

---

2   Cf. Gettier (1963).
3   Cf. Bealer (1993).

themselves which we seek to understand, and understanding them requires no more than consulting our intuitions.

Alvin Goldman has recently defended an interesting variation on this idea.[4] While Goldman agrees that a central goal of philosophy is the examination of our concepts, he does not see this as an armchair enterprise. While Goldman believes that our intuitive responses to hypothetical cases provide some genuine insight into the nature of our concepts, he does not believe, as more traditional philosophers do, that these intuitions are the only data with which philosophers need concern themselves. Rather, Goldman believes that our intuitions about cases are, for the most part, caused by features of our concepts: this is why they provide a good first pass at conceptual analysis. There are, however, other factors which may play a role in producing intuitive responses to cases, he believes, and teasing apart these complex causal interactions is a task for cognitive science. As Goldman sees it, the task of conceptual analysis is part of the experimental investigation of human cognition. Goldman is optimistic that the upshot of this experimental investigation will largely confirm the results of armchair analysis; although some corrections of armchair results are inevitable, he believes, the conceptual analyses philosophers have arrived at from the armchair are likely to give a fairly accurate idea of the real features of our concepts.

Goldman and more traditional theorists are thus agreed that the targets of philosophical analysis are human concepts; they disagree, somewhat, on how best to gain an understanding of those concepts.

Now Goldman is clearly right that if we wish to gain an understanding of human concepts, we cannot rest content with the armchair investigations which philosophers have traditionally relied upon. Indeed, once we take seriously the idea that philosophers are trying to understand our concepts, the traditional methods which they have used seem horribly ill-suited to the task. Most philosophers, for example, do little more than consult their own intuitions about cases, and make no serious systematic attempts to consult the intuitions of others. Frank Jackson's comments on this point are revealing:

> I am sometimes asked–in a tone that suggests that the question is a major objection–why, if conceptual analysis is concerned to elucidate what governs our classificatory practice, don't I advocate doing serious public opinion polls on people's responses to various cases? My answer is that I do–when it is necessary. Everyone who presents the Gettier cases to a

---

4   Cf. Goldman (1992), (2005), (2007).

class of students is doing their own bit of fieldwork, and we all know the answer they get in the vast majority of cases.[5]

But the ways in which philosophers present hypothetical cases to their classes are simply a mockery of good experimental technique. Responses are typically elicited by way of a show of hands, thereby undermining the possibility of getting independent input from the various participants. There is typically a good deal of setting up, in which other cases are presented, the importance of related concepts is highlighted, and the target concept is, in at least a preliminary manner, distinguished from closely related concepts. This, of course, simply ignores the influence of priming and order effects. Finally, the results are not typically recorded or quantified; they are subjected to no statistical analysis of any kind. If philosophers are, as Jackson sees it, genuinely trying to get at the concepts which most people have, of knowledge, of the mind, and so on, then they are doing an extraordinarily bad job of it. They are, indeed, attempting to engage in psychological research without any responsible methodology. The suggestion that the standard philosophical method can substitute for carefully controlled experiments turns philosophy into social science done badly.

Goldman's approach takes this kind of criticism seriously because it sees the philosophical investigation of our concepts as continuous with experimental work in the cognitive sciences. Ultimately, Goldman believes, any proposed conceptual analysis would need to withstand the empirical tests and standards which are routinely applied in such experimental work. In effect, Goldman is making an empirical bet: on his view, the features of our concepts which are under investigation when we engage in conceptual analysis are so robust that even the very coarse experimental methods of philosophers—namely, consulting our intuitions about hypothetical cases—are sufficient for gaining a roughly accurate picture of the phenomenon. And if this empirical bet is right, Goldman believes, then although the traditional approach to philosophical method needs some fine-tuning, the integrity of traditional philosophical work may thus be assured.

Goldman's approach is, I believe, a substantial improvement on the idea that philosophical method needs no help from cognitive science. At the same time, however, I believe that it remains untenable. If the targets of philosophical analysis are, as Goldman sees it, our concepts, and if

---

5 Cf. Jackson (1998), 36 f.

the ultimate arbiter of the features of our concepts are, as Goldman allows, the carefully controlled experimental work one finds in the cognitive sciences, then it is very unlikely that anything remotely like traditional philosophical analysis will be legitimated.

First, there are the methodological concerns raised earlier. The traditional philosophical method of consulting one's intuitions about cases is an extremely blunt instrument. It does not involve large numbers of cases; indeed, it involves, typically, the intuitions of a single experimental subject. It ignores order effects. It ignores priming considerations. It ignores the fact that the single experimental subject–the philosopher him or herself–typically has views about what the correct conceptual analysis is, and that such views are likely to have a real influence on the intuitions which that subject has about hypothetical cases. Goldman's empirical bet, that the phenomenon under study is so robust that these problems will, in practice, have little effect, seems like a very bad bet even before we begin any experimental work at all.

Second, once we do look at the experimental work in this area, these suspicions are confirmed. Determining the features of our concepts has turned out to be a subtle business, one which calls for careful experimental work, and attention to fine detail. Even a roughly accurate picture of the nature of our concepts is unlikely to be produced by philosophers attending to their intuitions.

But finally, and most important of all, there is a standard form in which philosophical analyses are canonically given–a set of necessary and sufficient conditions of a certain sort–and this standard form makes substantive assumptions about the manner in which concepts are represented. The kinds of analyses which philosophers offer–and which has been the stock and trade of work by Goldman himself–is what psychologists refer to as "the classical view". The concept of knowledge, for example, might be represented in the following way:

S knows that p iff
(1) S believes that p
(2) S is justified in believing that p
(3) p is true

and, as many philosophers hope, a fourth condition to be filled in later. Similarly, someone who wished to give an analysis of the concept of being a bird, again, in this classical form, would offer something like the following:

> B is a bird iff
> (1) B has wings
> (2) B has feathers
> (3) B has a beak

or some such set of conditions, each of which is individually necessary for membership in the category, and, such that the full set of conditions are jointly sufficient for category membership. This is an attractive idea, and a very old one. It has also, however, been thoroughly undermined. As Gregory Murphy says of this view in his recent book on the subject, "To a considerable degree, it has simply ceased to be a serious contender in the psychology of concepts."[6] Current research in this field is exploring a number of different formats in which concepts might be represented, but the classical view–the view presupposed by standard philosophical analysis–is no longer one of them. So if we take seriously the idea that philosophers are trying to analyze our concepts, then we must, as Goldman urges, take seriously the empirical work of psychologists on this very issue. When we do that, however, far from supporting the kinds of results which philosophers have arrived at, as Goldman suggests it might, the best available theories in this field are thoroughly at odds with the kinds of analyses which philosophers have offered.[7]

What has gone wrong here? The problem, as I've suggested, is not that Goldman wishes to take account of empirical work in the cognitive sciences. Goldman is clearly right to criticize those philosophers who see the philosophical enterprise as one of conceptual analysis, yet refuse to take account of the well-established empirical research program which is designed to illuminate the nature of our concepts. The very subject in which these philosophers claim to have a real interest is one which has been a subject of extensive experimental investigation for decades now, and it simply won't do to close one's eyes to the results of those investigations. What I wish to urge, however, is that Goldman and his a priorist opponents are both mistaken in supposing that our concepts are the targets of philosophical analysis. Epistemologists are not, I believe, interested in our concept of knowledge; it is knowledge itself which they are interested in. Philosophers of mind are not interested in our concept of mind; rather, it is the mind itself which they seek to understand. We misunderstand the nature and integrity of the

---

6 Cf. Murphy (2002), 38.
7 Cf. also Stich (1998), 108.

philosophical enterprise if we view it as directed at features of our concepts rather than the phenomena which our concepts are concepts of.[8]

Consider the case of a natural kind: gold, for example. The concept which many individuals have of gold may be inadequate in two importantly different ways. Their concepts may be incomplete, leaving out certain essential features of gold; and their concepts may be inaccurate, building in certain features which gold does not genuinely have. When it comes to natural kinds such as gold, many, indeed most, people are ignorant of its essential features; and many have certain misconceptions of what the stuff really is. Early on in scientific investigations, there is likely to be no one who has a concept of the target of those investigations which is both accurate and complete. Instead, there are certain properties of the target which bring it to our attention—in the case of gold, for example, its characteristic color and heft—and investigators have an ability to recognize at least some samples of the stuff to make it available for further investigation. These initial recognitional abilities are very far from perfect. The samples initially picked out as gold are likely to include some samples which are not gold at all, and some samples of the stuff are likely to be mistakenly passed over. There are thus likely to be both false positives and false negatives when samples are initially collected for further examination. But the initial recognitional ability, while imperfect, must have some rough bead on the object of study. If investigators are accurately to be described as searching after a true understanding of gold, they must have at least some ability, initially, to pick it out.

Once samples are collected, work can be done on finding out what it is that they genuinely have in common. As this investigation proceeds, some of the samples will come to be seen as false positives: they were not, in fact, of the same kind as the majority of others. Further, as a better understanding is reached of what it is that these samples do really have in common, some of the most salient features which attracted the investigators' initial attention will come to be seen as very imperfect indicators of the natural kind. What it is, at bottom, that the majority of the samples have in common may take quite some time to determine. For this very reason, even the best informed investigators may have concepts of their object of study which simply do not do justice to it. Those who are less well informed, of course, are even less likely to have concepts which accurately and completely characterize the kind. Part of the

---

8   Cf. Kornblith (2002), (2006).

goal of science is to develop concepts which are adequate to the phenomena under study. This is an important achievement of scientific investigation; it is not a prerequisite for initiating such investigations.

Now the idea that our natural kind concepts may fail to live up to the real features of those kinds is a commonplace in philosophy. For this very reason, someone who is genuinely interested in the nature of gold, for example, cannot proceed by examining our concept of gold. Examining folk concepts will tell us what ordinary people believe about gold; but it need not tell us a great deal about gold itself. Even the concepts of the most able investigators, as we have seen, may be a product of both their ignorance and their errors. Someone who is genuinely interested in understanding the nature of gold, of course, must look to the world, to gold itself, rather than to our concepts. A study of our concepts is, at best, an indirect and imperfect way of getting at features of natural kinds. More than this, it is only by studying the world itself that we may have any hope whatever of overcoming the inadequacies embedded in the concepts we currently have.

So too, I believe, with any attempt to understand knowledge. Epistemologists seek to understand the nature of knowledge. It won't do, if this is one's goal, to examine folk concepts of knowledge, for they, like folk concepts of gold, are likely to be the product of ignorance and error. It is not just that *folk* concepts are not the target of philosophical investigation, for the proper target here is not anyone's concept of knowledge, but, instead, it is knowledge itself. In what follows, I will attempt to explain how knowledge itself might be an object of study, and, more than that, I hope to show how cognitive ethology may contribute to such an investigation.

II

Knowledge should be viewed as a natural phenomenon. There are lots of instances of it in the world, and if we wish to understand knowledge, we must begin by looking at such instances, just as we begin an investigation of the nature of gold by examining various samples of it. Just as gold has certain salient properties which bring it to our attention and allow us to, at least tentatively, pick it out, there are properties which cases of knowledge have which bring it to our attention, and which, at least initially, allow us to pick it out. We need to examine these instances and try to understand what it is that they have in common.

Knowledge is a sub-species of belief, and while the study of human cognition has made important advances in understanding belief, there is little reason here, if one is interested in belief and its sub-species, to look only at the human case. Cognitive scientists appeal to belief in explaining human behavior because attempts to predict and explain such behavior entirely in terms of lower level categories have inevitably failed. The same, it seems, is true, however, of a good deal of animal behavior, and although there is reason to worry about problems of anthropomorphism, it is now widely accepted that such concerns do not justify a policy of attempting to explain all of animal behavior without adverting to beliefs.

An illustration here will be useful. Consider Daniel Povinelli's work on whether apes have the concept of seeing.[9] It is quite tempting, at least on casual inspection, to ascribe beliefs about what individuals see to chimpanzees. After all, chimpanzees follow eye movements. If one stares into the corner of a chimpanzee's cage at the zoo, the chimp will look into the corner to see what is there. There is an obvious explanation for this phenomenon: the chimpanzee notices that one is looking into the corner; it believes that something there must have attracted one's attention; there must be something in the corner that one sees; the chimp then looks into the corner to see what that might be. This obvious explanation presupposes a great deal of cognitive sophistication on the part of the chimp. In particular, it presupposes that the chimpanzee has the concept of seeing. This not only assumes that chimpanzees have mental states; it presupposes that they have the concept of mental states.

Povinelli has argued that this obvious explanation is not correct, and that this behavior is better explained by attributing far less cognitive sophistication to the chimps. Interestingly, he has shown that chimps fail to behave in certain ways which one would expect if the obvious explanation were correct. Thus, for example, when a chimp is approached with food by two experimenters, one of whom has an opaque bucket over her head, the other of whom has such a bucket held on her shoulder, the chimp does not show a preference for the experimenter who can obviously see it, begging for food equally from each of the two. On the basis of this and a large number of related experiments, Povinelli argues that the explanation which attributes second-order mental states to the chimp–beliefs about the mental states of the experimenters–should be rejected; a lower level explanation is to be preferred.

---

9   Cf. Povinelli/Eddy (1996).

Now I don't wish to get involved in the controversy over whether Povinelli is right about this. There are, I believe, quite difficult issues which need to be resolved before this debate can be settled. Rather, I bring up this controversy because the way in which Povinelli seeks to undermine the obvious explanation of the chimps' behavior is altogether common in the cognitive ethology literature, and it is taken by some as reason for doubting that chimpanzees, and other animals, have any mental states at all. Thus, for example, Sara Shettleworth speaks of:

> a powerful human tendency to anthropomorphize other species that even professional observers of animal behavior cannot always resist. Its power is implicit in the titles of popular books like *When Elephants Weep, The Human Nature of Birds,* and *The Secret Life of Dogs,* and it is not the least among the factors encouraging cognitive ethologists. Understanding the behavior of other people as the expression of underlying beliefs or intentions is part of *folk psychology,* or plain intuitive common sense. Folk psychology is a useful predictor of other people's behavior, and it may have evolved for that reason. Generalizing to other species can be a useful informal way of predicting behavior, too. A tendency to apply folk psychology to animals could be a human adaptation for hunting and evading predators. Indeed, it is very difficult for most beginning students of animal behavior, let alone consumers of popular books, to conceive of the possibility that other species have a completely different way of understanding the world and behaving adaptively than we do. It takes a real leap of imagination to understand, for example, that a rat doesn't find its way home because it 'knows where it is' but because it is unconsciously pushed and pulled by stimuli it encounters along the way.[10]

Now there can be little doubt that Povinelli's suggestions about chimp behavior required the very sort of "leap of imagination" that Shettleworth is speaking of. There is a natural tendency to see chimps as having an understanding of what others see, and Povinelli is right to consider alternative explanations of that behavior, explanations which attribute less cognitive sophistication to chimps than the supposition that they have an understanding of others' mental states. But notice that Shettleworth goes quite a bit further than this. She suggests that the fact that non-human animals often understand the world in ways quite different from humans is reason for thinking that their behavior is not to be explained in terms of beliefs and desires at all.

Now this is certainly not Povinelli's intention. As he makes clear in his work on whether chimps have the concept of seeing, he does not seek to undermine mentalistic explanations of chimp behavior across

---

10 Cf. Shettleworth (1998), 478 f.

the board; rather, he argues only that chimps do not have the concept of mental states. Indeed, the very explanations he offers to explain chimp behavior in his experiments presuppose, as he emphasizes, that they have extensive beliefs about their physical environment. He is merely arguing that they do not have beliefs about mental states.[11]

Notice that Shettleworth rightly points out the importance of recognizing that "other species have a completely different way of understanding the world and behaving adaptively than we do." But this should not lead her to suggest that they do not understand the world at all. And yet, the conclusion that she draws from the fact that rats find their way home in a way different than we do is that "a rat doesn't find its way home because it 'knows where it is'." One might, with equal justification, conclude that if I find my way home without using a map, but you need to use a map to find my house, that you don't find your way to my house on the basis of any knowledge of where you are. That non-human animals sometimes know things in ways different than we do does not entail that they do not know things at all; indeed, of course, quite the opposite is true.

There are important issues at stake in the cognitive ethology literature about the manner in which non-human animals come to form beliefs about their environment, and there is a good deal of controversy as to exactly what the content of their beliefs is. But there is a well established research program which involves attributing beliefs and desires to animals and explains their behavior on the basis of those mental states, and one should not suppose, as Shettleworth does, that this involves any sort of error at all.

While ethologists have spent a good deal of time arguing that the proper explanation of animal behavior requires attributing intentional states such as beliefs and desires to animals, it is interesting to note that, once this move has been made, ethologists begin, almost immediately to speak of animal knowledge. Consider, for example, the following passage from Michael Tomasello and Josep Call's *Primate Cognition*:

> In the physical domain, virtually all species studied have demonstrated a basic knowledge of permanent objects and some of the ways they may be related to one another spatially, quantitatively, and in terms of their perceptual similarities. In the social domain, virtually all species studied have demonstrated a recognition of individual groupmates and a knowledge of some of the important ways they may be related to one another socially

---

11 Cf. esp., Povinelli/Eddy (1996), 16.

and behaviorally. In both domains individuals have demonstrated the ability to use this knowledge to formulate various types of strategies, ranging from efficient foraging and tool use to coalition strategies and social learning, that help them attain goals with respect to such basic adaptive functions as feeding and mating.[12]

One might be tempted to dismiss this talk of animal knowledge as a mere *façon de parler*. After all, while talk of belief is, as these ethologists argue, required for the explanation of animal behavior, it is hard to see why talk of knowledge should be similarly necessary. When it comes to individual behavior, it is by no means obvious that appeals to what the animal knows can explain anything that appeals to what the animal believes cannot. If an ape knows that food is available in a certain location, one might appeal to this knowledge to explain why it is that the ape looks for food there. In cases like this, however, the ape's behavior is equally well explained by the fact that the ape believes that the food may be found in that location. Talk of what the ape knows, while picturesque, seems to serve no explanatory purpose.

I believe this may well be right when it comes to the explanation of individual behavior, but this is not to say that talk of knowledge does no explanatory work. An evolutionary approach to animal cognition seeks to explain, among other things, the presence of various cognitive capacities in individual species. The environment is seen as making certain informational demands on animals, and their cognitive capacities are the product of the selection pressures which complex environments create. A species may have the capacity to pick up information about certain features of its environment, and the ability to pick up such information reliably serves to explain how it is that the species may successfully negotiate that environment. Here, the difference between mere belief and knowledge is crucial. It is not just forming beliefs about the environment willy nilly which is of use to the animal; rather, it is having the capacity to reliably form true beliefs about its environment which is instrumental in the animal's survival. But this is just to say that the category of reliably produced true belief is one which serves important explanatory purposes within an evolutionary explanation of behavior. When ethologists speak of animal knowledge, it seems, this is precisely what it is they are speaking of: reliably formed true belief.

What I want to suggest is that this is precisely what knowledge is. Just as chemists discovered that water is nothing more than H_2O, and

---

12 Cf. Tomasello/Call (1997), 367.

even though no one before the chemical revolution had any idea that this was true, they were referring to H_2O when they used the term 'water' nonetheless; similarly, we have all been talking about reliably produced true belief when we use the term 'knowledge,' even though individual speakers may not have identified knowledge with reliably produced true belief, and even though many individuals have a concept of knowledge which is, in important ways, quite different from this. If we want to understand what knowledge is, we need to look at the phenomenon of knowledge, not our concept of it, just as those who wished to understand what water is had to look at the world and not at anyone's concept of what the world might contain.

III

It is worth comparing this conception of knowledge with some of the proposals which philosophers have made on the basis of conceptual analysis. Many philosophers have argued that self-conscious reflection on the character of our beliefs is a necessary condition for justified belief, and, accordingly, for knowledge as well. Thus, for example, in *The Structure of Empirical Knowledge*[13], Laurence BonJour argued that an individual is justified in holding a belief only if it coheres with his other beliefs. More than this, BonJour insisted that, if an individual is to be justified in holding a belief, he must hold it precisely because he recognizes that it coheres with his other beliefs. Without this requirement, as BonJour argued, an individual might hold a belief for reasons that have nothing to do with its coherence with his other beliefs; indeed, he might be entirely unaware that the belief in question actually coheres with his other beliefs. In such a situation, the resulting belief would not be justified, and thus could not count as a case of knowledge.

This very intuitive requirement, however, led BonJour to make quite extraordinary demands on knowers. It is not just that an individual must be aware that a given belief coheres with his other beliefs. As BonJour rightly pointed out, "...if the fact of coherence is to be accessible to the believer, it follows that he must somehow have an adequate grasp of his total system of beliefs, since it is coherence with this system which is at issue."[14] Moreover, since coherence requires consistency, an individ-

---

13 Cf. BonJour (1985).
14 Cf. BonJour (1985), 102.

ual must determine that his belief is consistent with his total system of beliefs if he is to be justified in holding it, and hence, for the belief to count as knowledge.

Now these two requirements are quite clearly never satisfied by anyone. When I reflect on the beliefs I hold, I am certainly not capable of grasping my total body of beliefs; indeed, at any given time, I am capable of thinking about only the tiniest fraction of my total body of beliefs. And in this respect, I am not unusual. But coherence with a tiny fraction of one's body of beliefs does not, by any means, serve to justify a belief, and thus I can never have any justified beliefs on this account. For that very reason, I can never know anything. The requirement that one know a given belief to be consistent with one's total body of beliefs is similarly unsatisfiable.[15] Determining the consistency of even a small number of propositions can be a computationally cumbersome task; it is computationally intractable to determine the consistency of a body of propositions even a very small fraction of the size of any human body of beliefs.[16] Knowing that a given belief coheres with one's total body of beliefs, even if one could have a grasp of them, would be beyond anyone's reach. So justified belief, and knowledge, on this account, are doubly unattainable.

More recently, BonJour has rejected the coherentist account of justification he offered earlier in favor of foundationalism.[17] He nevertheless retains the requirement that an individual must be reflectively aware of the features which make it reasonable for him to hold a belief if that belief is to count as justified, and therefore, to count as a case of knowledge. This account has the consequence that we are, at best, rarely justified in the beliefs we hold, since we do not often reflect on these features; in virtue of this, we know very little at all, on BonJour's account.

There is something quite natural about the suggestion that some sort of reflection is a prerequisite for knowledge. We often arrive at our beliefs unreflectively, and there can be little doubt that many of these unreflectively arrived at beliefs are unreasonable. We sometimes fail to take account of relevant evidence which we have; we draw hasty conclusions; we are sometimes influenced by what we would like to believe about a matter more than by what we have reason to believe. Reflective individuals, stepping back from their initial inclinations to believe, at

---

15 Cf. Kornblith (1989).
16 Cf. Cherniak (1984).
17 Cf. BonJour (2002).

least momentarily, attempt to evaluate their evidential situation carefully. And there can be little doubt that such reflection may prevent certain errors to which we are otherwise liable. The thought that genuine knowledge requires reflection is motivated, I believe, by the recognition of points such as these. The unreflective agent may be lucky, perhaps, if the processes which produce beliefs in him happen to be reliable. The reflective agent, however, does not trust to luck, but instead takes matters into his own hands, and by reflecting on the quality of his evidence, and forming beliefs which are in accord with that evidence, assures that his beliefs will be as they should. It is for reasons such as these, I believe, that the requirement of reflection may seem to present a necessary condition both for justified belief and for knowledge.

Natural as this perspective is, I believe that it is deeply mistaken. This way of thinking about things is a product of an overly suspicious approach to the kinds of processes by which we unreflectively arrive at our beliefs, together with an overly romantic approach to the character of reflection.

Consider first, the ways in which we arrive at beliefs when we are not being reflective. When Descartes, for example, discusses unreflective belief acquisition, he begins by pointing out that such belief acquisition is fallible; we sometimes make mistakes. Fair enough. From there, he moves on to present the worry of radical skepticism. For all we know, he argues, our beliefs are the product of an evil demon trying to deceive us into thinking that there is a world outside our minds having certain features, when, in fact, no such world exists. If we rely uncritically on our natural inclinations to believe, he argues, we may well be getting an entirely inaccurate picture of what the world is like, or whether, indeed, there is any such world at all. It is this very sort of thought experiment on which epistemologists often rely to motivate the idea that critical reflection is essential if we are to overcome the errors to which we are naturally susceptible.

Evil demons, however, are not, in actual fact, much of a threat. Many of the kinds of processes which produce beliefs in us when we are not being reflective are extremely reliable. Visual perception, for example, while certainly fallible, is extraordinarily reliable in producing beliefs about the world around us. There is a good deal of work on the reliability of our native inferential tendencies as well, and there is a case to be made here for a qualified optimism.[18] I do not mean to sug-

---

18 Cf., e.g., Kornblith (1993), ch. 5.

gest that unreflective belief acquisition is a universally good thing; it isn't. I merely mean to point out that the kind of deep suspicions about unreflective belief which are often used by epistemologists to motivate an account of knowledge which makes reflection essential to it are extremely unrealistic. A careful evaluation of the reliability of unreflectively arrived at belief would surely reveal areas of tremendous accuracy as well as areas in which we show a real susceptibility to error. Those who wish to make reflection a necessary condition for justification and knowledge tend to focus attention on our susceptibility to error here.

The one-sidedly pessimistic account of unreflective belief which is presented by the champions of reflection is accompanied by an overly optimistic approach to the benefits of self-conscious belief acquisition. The fact is, of course, that reflection on the epistemic credentials of our beliefs is not a panacea for the shortcomings of unreflectively acquired belief. Just as our native inferential tendencies run the gamut from extremely reliable to extremely unreliable, the processes by which we reflect on our unreflective processes also range from very reliable to very unreliable. We should not think that the inevitable result of reflective belief acquisition is a more accurate screening of our beliefs. While self-conscious reflection may certainly serve to correct errors in unreflective processes, it may also serve to further entrench errors which those processes create. And just as self-conscious attention to various motor tasks may, at times, serve to interfere with them rather than perfect them, self-conscious scrutiny of the process of belief acquisition may, at times, interfere with the otherwise smooth and accurate workings of various unreflective processes. It would be a mistake to assume that reflectively acquired belief is quite simply, and across the board, more accurate that unreflectively acquired belief.[19]

Reflectively acquired belief is thus not an unalloyed good. It is a good thing when it enhances our reliability, as it sometimes does; and it is a bad thing when it decreases our reliability, as it sometimes does. But this is just to say that an account of knowledge which sees it as reliably produced true belief already says as much about reflection as needs to be said. Just like every other process which influences belief acquisition, the good of reflection is measured by its reliability.

Those philosophers who make reflection a necessary condition for knowledge rule out the possibility of non-human animal knowledge,

---

19 Cf. Kornblith (2002), ch. 4; (manuscript).

but as we have seen, these views do not even provide a reasonable account of the phenomenon of human knowledge. Any account of human knowledge which has the consequence that we have no knowledge at all, or extraordinarily little knowledge, is, in virtue of that very fact, implausible. But the ways in which philosophers have proposed that human knowledge be marked out as a separate kind are all ones which have this consequence.

Not all philosophical accounts of knowledge which are arrived at by way of conceptual analysis are like this. Indeed, the suggestion that knowledge should be identified with reliably produced true belief is one which was made by Alvin Goldman on the basis, as he presents it, of conceptual analysis.[20] So I am in agreement with Goldman on the account of knowledge he offers. But the disagreement I have with him about philosophical method, and about the target of philosophical analysis, remains. Goldman sees his account as a view about the content of our concept of knowledge. I believe it is more plausibly viewed as an account of knowledge itself. Goldman sees the main source of evidence for his view as deriving from our intuitions about hypothetical cases. As I see it, the best evidence for the view lies in the way in which it explains and unifies our understanding of a certain natural phenomenon.

The view of philosophy I wish to defend is thus a thoroughgoing version of naturalism. Philosophical theorizing is continuous with work in the sciences. In the case of epistemology, it is the science of cognitive ethology which throws the clearest light upon our subject matter.

References

Bealer (1993): George Bealer, "The Incoherence of Empiricism", in: S. Wagner/R. Warner (eds.), *Naturalism: A Critical Appraisal*, Notre Dame, 163–196.

Bonjour (1985): Laurence Bonjour, *The Structure of Empirical Knowledge*, Harvard.

Bonjour (1989): Laurence Bonjour, "Replies and Clarifications", in: J. Bender (ed.), *The Current State of the Coherence Theory: Critical Essays on the Epistemic Theories of Keith Lehrer and Laurence BonJour, with Replies*, Dordrecht, 276–292.

---

20 Cf. Goldman (1986).

Bonjour (2002): Laurence Bonjour, *Epistemology: Classic Problems and Contemporary Responses*, Lanham.
Bonjour (2006): Laurence Bonjour, "Kornblith on Knowledge and Epistemology", in: *Philosophical Studies* 127, 317–335.
Cherniak (1984): Christopher Cherniak, "Computational Complexity and the Universal Acceptance of Logic", in: *Journal of Philosophy* 81, 739–758.
Gettier (1963): Edmund l. Gettier, "Is Justified True Belief Knowledge", in: *Analysis* 23, 121–123.
Goldman (1986): Alvin I. Goldman, *Epistemology and Cognition*, Harvard.
Goldman (1992): Alvin I. Goldman, "Psychology and Philosophical Analysis", in: *Liaisons: Philosophy Meets the Cognitive and Social Sciences*, MIT Press, 143–153.
Goldman (2005): Alvin I. Goldman, "Kornblith's Naturalistic Epistemology", in: *Philosophy and Phenomenological Research* LXXI, 403–409.
Goldman (2007): Alvin I. Goldman, "Philosophical Intuitions: Their Target, Their Source, and Their Epistemic Status", in: *Grazer Philosophische Studien*.
Jackson (1998): Frank Jackson, *From Metaphysics to Ethics: A Defence of Conceptual Analysis*, Oxford.
Kornblith (1989): Hilary Kornblith, "The Unattainability of Coherence", in: J. Bender (ed.), *The Current State of the Coherence Theory: Critical Essays on the Epistemic Theories of Keith Lehrer and Laurence BonJour, with Replies*, Dordrecht, 207–214.
Kornblith (1993): Hilary Kornblith, *Inductive Inference and its Natural Ground*, MIT Press.
Kornblith (2002): Hilary Kornblith, *Knowledge and its Place in Nature*, Oxford.
Kornblith (2006): Hilary Kornblith, "Reply to Bermudez and BonJour", in: *Philosophical Studies* 127, 337–349.
Kornblith (2006): Hilary Kornblith, "Appeals to Intuition and the Ambitions of Epistemology", in: S. Hetherington (ed.), *Epistemology Futures*, Oxford.
Kornblith (manuscript): Hilary Kornblith, "What Reflective Endorsement Can't Do", (manuscript).
Korsgaard (1996): Christine Krosgaard, *The Sources of Normativity*, Cambridge.
Kripke (1980): Saul Kripke, *Naming and Necessity*, Harvard.
Murphy (2002): Gregory L. Murphy, *The Big Book of Concepts*, MIT Press.
Plato (1961): Plato, *Plato: The Collected Dialogues*, E. Hamilton/H. Cairns (eds.), Princeton.
Povinelli/Eddy (1996): Daniel Povinelli/Timothy Eddy, "What Young Chimps Know about Seeing", in: *Monographs of the Society for Research in Child Development* 61, 1–152.
Putnam (1975): Hilary Putnam, *Mind, Language and Reality: Philosophical Papers* Vol. 2, Cambridge.
Shettleworth (1998): Sara J. Shettleworth, *Cognition, Evolution, and Behavior*, Oxford.
Smith/Medin (1981): Edward Smith/Douglas Medin, *Categories and Concepts*, Harvard.

Stich (1998): Stephen P. Stich, "Reflective Equilibrium and Cognitive Diversity", in: M. Depaul/ W. Ramsey (eds.), *Rethinking Intuition: The Psychology of Intuition and Its Role in Philosophical Inquiry*, Notre Dame.

Tomasello/Call (1997): Michael Tomasello/Josep Call, *Primate Cognition*, Oxford.

Williamson (2000): Timothy Williamson, *Knowledge and its Limits*, Oxford.

Non-Human Knowledge and Non-Human Agency
Hans-Johann Glock

My project is to compare human and non-human *animals* (henceforth simply animals) with respect to knowledge. More generally, I shall consider the applicability to animals of epistemic concepts like knowledge, belief, perception, etc. These epistemic concepts are intimately connected to what one might call practical concepts— action, agency, intention, reason for acting, etc. For one thing, the most basic function of epistemic concepts is to explain and justify action; for another, the notion of a reason plays a central role in both the epistemic and the practical sphere. Accordingly, my exploration of animal knowledge will be intertwined with a discussion of animal agency. Of course, both epistemic and practical concepts are also connected to mental notions in general, of which they form important sub-classes.

Traditionally, knowledge or cognition is counted among the 'higher' mental faculties, as opposed to conative or emotive ones. In recent years, however, there has also been a tendency in some quarters to dissociate the term 'cognition' from any mental connotations. Ironically, this trend derives from the so-called cognitive revolution. Although they abandoned many of the methodological restrictions of behaviourism, cognitive scientists continued to look askance at mental phenomena like consciousness, which appear to defy scientific investigation because of being irreducibly private. This qualm is based on an untenable, Cartesian conception of the mind, however[1], and I shall assume that epistemic or cognitive phenomena form part of mental phenomena.

Now, there are two opposing stances on animal minds. *Differentialists* maintain that there are crucial qualitative differences separating us from animals; *assimilationists* insist that the differences are merely quantitative and gradual. The most important variant of differentialism is *lingualism*. It denies on *a priori* grounds that animals without a language can have mental capacities at all, or at least 'higher' mental capacities like those required for knowledge and rational agency. This raises the question of whether there are conceptual connections between the posses-

---

1   See e.g. Glock (2001b).

sion of language on the one hand, and the possession of mental capacities in general and cognitive capacities in particular on the other. Because I am interested in these connections, I shall focus on animals *without language*, leaving aside the hotly contested question of whether some animals are capable of acquiring rudimentary symbolic skills. It is not my ambition, however, to tackle all the lingualist objections against crediting animals with mental powers. I have repudiated many of them elsewhere[2], and shall focus here on those connected to knowledge and other epistemic concepts.

I approach these topics from the perspective of recent *revisionionist* ideas in epistemology and theory of action. In my view, these ideas undermine certain forms of differentialism-cum-lingualism, since they remove apparent hurdles to accepting animal knowledge and agency.[3] As regards knowledge, if knowledge is not true justified belief, then animals cannot be excluded on the grounds that they lack the rational faculties that might be prerequisites for being justified. As regards agency, if reasons for action are not subjective mental states but objective features of the subject's environment, then animals may be capable of acting for a reason without possessing demanding types of self-consciousness, viz. awareness of their own mental states. At the same time, the revisionist ideas throw up new challenges to assimilationism, *some of which* I hope to meet. This paper focuses on epistemic concepts. I shall briefly discuss agency at the beginning, however. For epistemic and practical concepts need to be seen in conjunction. And the most important weakness of differentialism is that the basic connections between the two apply to animals no less than humans.

---

2   Glock (2000) and (2010).

3   Another area in which the comparison can yield fruits concerns the role of agency for cognitive states. With much fanfare, Fodor has trumpeted the view that cognitive states like knowledge and belief are independent of and indeed prior to action and conative states like intending or desiring. The animal-human comparison instead favours the loosely-speaking pragmatist view that we should understand mental states in the context of human and non-human practice. At the same time, one ought to resist a tendency among some recent pragmatists, notably Brandom, namely of drawing a distinction between human practice and animal behaviour that is so sharp and categorical as to rules out the possibility of intermediate stages and hence the possibility of providing a genetic (evolutionary) explanation of the emergence of evolved human knowledge and action.

I. Methodological Prolegomena

Knowledge and agency have been proposed as prerogatives of humans, the former in conjunction with thought, the latter under a variety of headings, which include not just action but also *praxis* and volition. Indeed, some authors give the impression that their accounts of knowledge, action or rational action are motivated at least partly by a desire to ensure that they are beyond the of for animals.[4] In some philosophers one also suspects the opposite tendency, namely to explain various notions of agency, in particular, in such a way that they are attainable for animals, because of moral implications. Neither strategy commends itself. If the questions of whether animals can know or act are to have any point, these notions must not be construed *ab initio* so as to imply either a negative or a positive answer. Rather, they should be construed in ways that are plausible or fruitful on independent grounds.

In this context it is not just legitimate but imperative to start out from the ordinary use of 'know' and 'act', as well as their cognates and equivalents in other languages. In pursuing any question of the form 'What is X?' we shall inevitably rely on a *preliminary notion* of X, an idea of what constitutes the topic of our investigation. In our case we presuppose a preliminary understanding of knowledge and agency. This is not a fully-articulated conception, which would have to emerge from the subsequent debates in epistemology or theory of ac-

---

4   Thus Alvarez maintains that the only motivating reasons are facts (e. g. Alvarez 2010, 3, ch. 4). She grants that we can answer the question 'Why are you *V*-ing?' by citing a goal. Yet she resists the suggestion that goals can be motivating reasons on the following grounds: 'If goals were reasons, it would follow that any animal that acts in pursuit of a goal would also act for a reason. But whereas it is fairly uncontroversial that a dog who digs in order to find a bone acts in pursuit of a goal, it is much more controversial to say that the dog acts for a reason: that what motivates the dog to dig is a reason, namely that digging is a means to find the bone, and that the dog acts guided by that reason'. (Alvarez 2010, 98). But the passage up to the colon simply assumes that reasons should not be the sort of things for which animals can act. Yet it is perfectly unexceptional to say that the reason why the dog digs is that it is looking for a bone. And the passage following the colon does not provide an independent argument against such statements. Even if it is problematic to say that the dog is motivated by the fact that digging is a means to find the bone, this gloss of 'the dog has a reason/is guided by a reason' is forced on us only on the very assumption that the argument purports to justify, namely that goals cannot be reasons, since only facts can be reasons. There is nothing amiss with 'The dog has a reason for digging, namely its goal of finding a bone'.

tion, but an initial idea of what those debates are about. Such a pretheoretical understanding is embodied in the established uses of the relevant epistemic and practical terms.

One might object that for philosophical and scientific purposes we need to graduate from ordinary use towards a more specialized one based on more exacting scrutiny of the phenomena. But this is not an objection to my procedure. First, unless the relation between the novel and the established ways of using the pertinent expressions (between the new and the old concepts) is properly understood, the philosophical problems associated with these expressions will merely be swept under the carpet.[5] Secondly, all neologisms and conceptual modifications, those of science included, need to be explained. By pain of regress, this can ultimately be done only in terms of ordinary expressions which are already understood. Finally, the term 'ordinary use' is ambiguous. It may refer either to the *standard* use of a term as opposed to its irregular use in whatever area it is employed, or to its *everyday* as opposed to its specialist or technical use.[6] My starting point is the standard use. Both the explanation of epistemic and practical concepts and claims about their applicability to animals should in the first instance be measured not against philosophical theories, but against the uses of the relevant terms in established and legitimate forms of discourse. In our case, the latter will include everyday parlance; yet they will also include specialized disciplines from the behavioural sciences, the social sciences and jurisprudence.

Now, we freely apply a wide range of epistemic and practical concepts to higher animals and non-linguistic humans. This is not just an indispensible part of everyday life, but also central to disciplines like comparative psychology, cognitive ethology and developmental psychology. This fact provides at least a prima facie reason against explaining these concepts in ways that preclude such applications. A lingualist has the following options for responding to this fact.

First, he can adopt an error theory, maintaining that ordinary folk and scientists are simply mistaken in crediting animals with epistemic and practical properties. Now, it is possible to regard the ascriptions of some epistemic and practical concepts to some species of animals as

---

5   Strawson (1963).
6   Ryle (1953), 301–304.

empirically false.[7] But it is not easy to see how one could regard the ascription of *all* types of epistemic and practical concepts to *all* species of animals as empirically false.

In any event, most lingualists adopt a second line. They often regard such attributions not as false, but as suffering from a more basic defect, namely that of being meaningless, nonsensical or based on a category-mistake.[8] If the concept of thought is such that it precludes application to non-linguistic creatures, nothing could count as evidence that some animals have thoughts. Ascribing thoughts to animals would then make no more sense than ascribing a colour to a number. Yet it remains a mystery how we could be so fundamentally confused about such basic concepts, not just when language is idling, as in philosophical reflection, but also when it is fruitfully employed, as in everyday discourse and progressing empirical sciences.

These days, the harsh charge of nonsense has given way to a third response. Even though some thought ascriptions to animals are neither empirically false nor straightforwardly conceptually incoherent, the story goes, they cannot be taken literally, but must be regarded as figurative, metaphorical or secondary. We are dealing with a possibly useful but ultimately incorrect *façon de parler*. This stance is illustrated by Davidson's reaction to a well-known tale from Norman Malcolm.

> Suppose our dog is chasing the neighbor's cat. The latter runs full tilt toward the oak tree, but suddenly swerves at the last moment and disappears up a nearby maple. The dog doesn't see this maneuver and on arriving at the oak tree he rears up on his hind feet, paws at the trunk as if trying to scale it, and barks excitedly into the branches above. We who observe this whole episode from a window say, "He thinks that the cat went up that oak tree".[9]

Malcolm claims that we would be right to say this, and Davidson acknowledges that it is *prima facie* plausible. Nevertheless, he insists that 'strictly speaking' Malcolm's dog cannot believe anything, because he does not possess a language.[10] An immediate objection to Davidson is this: animals must be capable of having thoughts because we have no better way of explaining and predicting their behavior than by attribut-

---

7   This is the case, for example, when ethologists like Seyfarth and Cheney (1996), 340–343 use observations to deny that vervet monkeys have a "theory of mind", that is, beliefs about the beliefs of conspecifics.
8   E.g. Stoecker (2009), 268; cf. Fisher (1996), 4–8.
9   Malcolm (1972–73), 13.
10 Davidson (2001), 96–100.

ing thoughts to them.¹¹ Indeed, there may not even be a feasible alternative. In that case, such attributions would even satisfy a well-known methodological principle of comparative psychology. According to 'Morgan's canon', we should only attribute higher mental capacities to a creature if this is the *only* explanation of its behavioural capacities.¹²

A fourth and last ditch attempt grants this point, while insisting that some claims that are strictly speaking false are nonetheless indispensible.¹³ But this strategy requires a compelling explanation of how falsehoods can be *indispensible* not just for practical purposes, but also for perfectly respectable scientific disciplines like cognitive ethology. Furthermore, it not only needs to specify what it is about our extant concepts that precludes their literal application to animals, but also to explain why competent speakers are so blissfully ignorant of this inapplicability.

If these four responses indeed fail, one is entitled to hold it against an analysis of certain practical or epistemic concepts if it precludes their application to animals.¹⁴ Of course, there may be good reasons for *modify-*

---

11 See, e.g. Bennett (1976), §§7–8; Fodor (1975), ch. 1.
12 See Morgan (1894), 53 ff.
13 Stoecker (2009), 256, 268.
14 Thus Stoecker proposes that 'actions … are just those of our doings that are due to our ability to align whatever we do to the call of reason, materialized in the call of the social practice' (Stoecker 2009, 267). He rightly infers from this premise that animals cannot act. But surely that conclusion simply counts against the premise. It goes to show that the proposed analysis is extensionally inadequate, and for a variety of reasons. It precludes not just inanimate objects, animals and fictional creatures like Davidson's swampman (see Glock 2003, 262 f.), but also human beings who have not participated in a linguistic social practice—such as feral children. The mere fact that Kaspar Hauser grew up outside of a linguistic community would not lead us to deny that he acted when he fled from captivity; and we have no reason to adopt such a restrictive stance simply because it follows from popular theories advanced by some externalists and communitarians. Finally, Stoecker's argument in defence of his premise is laudable in refusing to treat reasons as subjective mental states. Yet it is faulty in several respects. Let us grant, for the sake of argument, that 'reasons basically are arguments', and that in a reason explanation 'we say that the agent has acted because a particular argument spoke for her acting as she did'. Stoecker next tries to avoid reference to the agent's belief that something indeed speaks for her action by adding the assumption that 'I am wont to do what is arguably the best'. It is unclear how this move can avoid the objection that in error cases reference to the agent's belief is mandatory. Worse still, Stoecker maintains that the only way of explaining why someone is wont to do what is arguably the best is that he has been 'raised in a social communicative practice' (Stoecker 2009, 266). But this is a non-sequitur, since Stoecker does nothing

ing our established epistemic and practical concepts. But this does nothing to salvage the lingualist case. For one thing, it provides no grounds whatever for answering questions like 'Can animals possess knowledge?' and 'Can animals act?' in the negative. For those questions are phrased in the extant, non-modified concepts. For another, assuming the indispensability of epistemic and practical notions that can be applied to animals, such conceptual reform has little to recommend it.

Rather than dismissing our established ways of describing and explaining animal behaviour as false, confused, metaphorical, attenuated, etc., one ought to consider the following option. In their established uses, our epistemic and practical terms have more or less demanding senses. In the less demanding ones they simply do apply to animals period, whereas in the more demanding ones they may not.[15] And at least prima facie, it is more plausible to regard the simple senses as basic rather than secondary or degenerate.

---

to rule out alternative explanations. Finally, intelligent animals are just as wont to do what is arguably the best in the situations facing them as talkative yet thick humans in situations facing them. Even if all of these points could be waived, however, the argument would at best lead to the conclusion that animals cannot act for a reason. There are other bona fide types of action, notably actions that are subject to teleological explanations without being amenable to rational explanations (see Glock 2009, 239–244 and Alvarez 2010, 191–196).

15 My position here has points of overlap with Ernst's discussion of knowledge (2002), which I read only after finishing the first draft of this paper. He does not discuss the question of whether animals can possess knowledge. And instead of distinguishing between more or less demanding senses of ‚know' he distinguishes between a sense in which we ascribe the term from the perspective of someone already in the know, and a sense in which we ascribe it from the perspective of somone who does not and seeks a reliable source of information. But the former sense is less demanding, in that it requires no more than true belief. And Ernst's discussion is grist to my mill in that from the perspective of someone in the know who either needs to decide whether to provide information or to explain behaviour, we have no qualms about distinguishing animals with from those without knowledge. If the dog has already seen the bone I placed in the bowl for its consumption, I don't need to point it out to him. And if Malcolm's dog does not know that the cat went up the maple, that explains why it is barking up the wrong tree.

II. Animal agency

Practical notions like act, action, agency, intentional action, action for a reason illustrate this point. They are notoriously complex and diverse. The only sensible strategy is to distinguish between different senses of the relevant terms, and to consider their applicability to animals. In what follows, I can only provide an exceedingly brief sketch.[16]

The most general question in this area runs: Can animals act? That general question must be answered in the affirmative by those revisionists who accept non-intentional agency, including agency by inanimate objects. If

(1) The wind knocked over the vase

and

(2) The bleach ruined the linen

report agency in this general sense, then so do

(3) The cat knocked over the vase

and

(4) The dog ruined the linen.

At a grammatical level, we apply an active/passive distinction to many kinds of inanimate objects. When it comes to living things, that distinction takes on a new foundation in reality. For here we can distinguish between what an organism does and what happens to it by reference to the organism's *needs*. Thus plants fulfil their needs by growing roots, orienting their leaves, emitting chemical substances to deter predators, etc. By contrast, they are subjected to various things that are neutral to or detrimental to these needs.

When it comes to animals, we encounter not just needs but also *wants* (goals and purposes). And here the aforementioned distinction applies with a vengeance. An animal can be thrown over a fence or trip accidentally, or it can jump over a fence or fall to the floor obeying an order. In the former case, it is not just needs that remain unfulfilled, certain wants desires of the animal are frustrated or thwarted. And such frustration, just like the fulfilment of the wants, is manifest in the animal's behaviour.

It is points like this that underlie a prominent psychological definition, according to which action is simply behaviour directed towards a

---

16 See Glock (2009).

goal.[17] According to a venerable philosophical tradition, by contrast, human agency goes beyond this level. It is behaviour that has been caused by a special kind of mental event, a *volition*. Now, it is far from obvious that one cannot credit animals with volitions in the sense of *decisions*. After all, there are animals that are not just intelligent, but whose bodily demeanour, facial expressions and activities resemble some of ours, notably the great apes. In these, at least, trained observers can easily detect states of indecision. For instance, one can note how characteristic activities are interrupted by obstacles and problems, how these interruptions are followed by inactivity and characteristic displacement activities and gestures (including the proverbial scratching of heads), and how at the end of the behavioural cycle problem solving activity ensues. Nevertheless, the voluntarist tradition in action theory is less accommodating to animal agency than the current orthodoxy.[18] According to that orthodoxy, the most fundamental feature of human agency is that it is intentional. And that in turn is taken to mean that it is subject to intentional explanations—explanations that refer to the agent's reasons—her beliefs, desires, intentions, goals, purposes, etc.

Animal behaviour is subject to intentional explanations, precisely because animals are capable of acting *purposively* or *intentionally*, in pursuit of their own goals. The question that has been hotly disputed recently is whether they are capable of acting *for a reason*. According to orthodoxy reasons are subjective mental states. This implies that acting for a reason requires the capacity to reflect on one's own mental states. That is a high hurdle. For revisionists, by contrast, reasons are objective conditions—facts, states of affairs, etc. In so far as animals have cognitive capacities, they have access to such objective conditions. And in so far as the deliverances of these capacities guide their behaviour, they are capable of acting for reasons. But revisionists of a differentialist inclination balk at that suggestion. For instance, it has been suggested that animals might be said to act for a reason, a.k.a. goal, without having a reason, since they cannot reflect on these reasons. Two assimilationist responses suggest themselves: one is to question the idea that one can have reasons only if one can reflect on these reasons; the other is to argue that animals can reason or reflect on reasons.

---

17 See White (1979), 1.
18 Thus Stoecker (2009), 259 notes that it is more plausible to say that a cat intends to stalk a bird than to say that it has decided to do so.

This is not the place to resolve these issues. For us the crucial point is that the applicability of intentional explanations to animal behaviour implies the same connection between epistemic capacities—in particular perception—knowledge, belief and action that one also finds in humans.

III. Intentional verbs

As is evident from intentional explanations, our epistemic and our practical concepts are intimately linked to intentional verbs. These verbs occur mainly in three sentential forms:

I	A	*V*s (knows/thinks/believes/expects, etc.)	that *p*
II	A	*V*s (intends/plans/means, etc.)	to Φ
III	A	*V*s (loves/desires/thinks about, etc.)	X

According to an orthodoxy going back to Russell, the verbs that can replace '*V*' denote different types of *intentional attitudes*, 'A' the *subject* of these attitudes, and the substitution instances of 'that *p*', 'to Φ' or '*X*' their *contents*. Statements of all three forms can display a hallmark of intentionality, namely that nothing in reality needs to correspond to the (grammatical) direct object: one can believe something which is not the case, intend to do something which never happens, and love someone who does not exist.[19] *Prima facie*, (I) expresses a *propositional attitude*, (II) an *action-oriented attitude*, (III) an *object-oriented attitude*. Nonetheless it is customary to subsume all forms of intentionality under the heading 'propositional attitude'. This is no coincidence. There is a pervasive tendency to regard (I) as basic and to disregard other forms of intentionality, and this by itself gives succour to linguists. For the term 'proposition' carries strong linguistic connotations. In some contexts, it is downright equivalent to 'sentence in the indicative', in others it signifies something expressed by a sentence and (perhaps) designated by a that-clause or more generally a noun-clause (see below).

However, I know of no compelling reduction of action- and object-oriented attitudes to proposition-oriented attitudes.[20] In the absence of

---

19 Some intentional verbs may not display this feature, in particular in type III contexts. For instance, it is a moot question whether one can regret things one has never done or know a person that does not exist.

20 McDowell (1996) *may* be right to reject 'non-conceptual content' if he means to insist that every object we can identify perceptually can somehow be described conceptually. It does not follow, however, that there is a list of *propositions*

such a reduction, it is sheer dogmatism to insist that admiring Nelson Mandela, intending to climb a tree or craving M&Ms are in the final analysis attitudes towards propositions. Of course, the *reasons* people have for admiring Mandela or intending to climb a tree can be expressed through that-clauses. But so can the reasons people have for kicking a ball, and no one would conclude that kicking a ball is therefore anything other than a relation to an object. This removes an obstacle to crediting animals with intentional states. For it would be foolhardy to deny that chimpanzees can intend to climb trees or crave M&Ms, unless one is in thrall to the prejudice that all intentional states must *au fond* be attitudes towards propositions.[21]

---

which captures precisely and completely what I currently perceive—my visual field. Tugendhat (1982), ch. 6 regards the reduction of all intentional states to propositional attitudes as a distinctive trait of analytic philosophy. He defends this stance on the grounds that even those intentional states which are ostensibly directed towards objects, for example loving, pitying or admiring someone, imply propositional attitudes, attitudes the expression of which involves a that-clause. Even though Dorothea Brooke does not exist, I can admire her only if I believe that she exists. And even if I picture Dorothea Brooke to myself as a fictional character, I picture her as existing. But this argument is unconvincing. To be sure, to imagine an apple is not to imagine an apple as non-existing, but neither is it the same as to imagine that there is an apple, which is what Tugendhat needs to establish. Moreover, it is far from obvious that when I imagine Dorothea Brooke, I imagine her as existing rather than as non-existing (provided that either of these options makes sense in the first place). Kenny (1963), chs. V, XI steers a different course to a proximate destination. He maintains that sentences where 'I want' is followed by a direct object (rather than by an infinitive), as in 'I want an X' can often be expanded into sentences of the form 'I want to Φ an X': I want an apple – I want to eat an apple, etc. Furthermore, in reports of what he calls 'affective attitudes' the grammatical object of the attitude takes a different form depending on the verb: either a 'that' clause, or an infinitive (I hope that p, I want to Φ; I prefer to Φ, etc.). Nonetheless, he maintains, they could all be expressed using the construction 'A volits that p', since he thinks of these affective attitudes as taking an attitude to a state of affairs. Although this would leave type (III) intentionality unaffected, it would mean that type (II) cases could be reduced to type (I), and hence to something propositional. But it is far from obvious that intending to do something is tantamount to wanting a certain state of affairs to come about. It certainly doesn't amount simply to voliting that the results of the action come about. And even if statements of the form 'A wants to Φ' could be paraphrased by statements of the form 'A volits that p', it would *not* follow that the propositional construction is more basic. For the possibility of paraphrase cuts both ways, and the infinitive construction is much more readily understood than the propositional one.

21 Glock (2001); Alvarez (2010), 66 f.

Let us nevertheless focus on intentional verbs of type (I), since here the lingualist worry—the 'proposition problem'—remains acute. Consider a belief ascription such as:

(5) Carl thinks that the cat went up that oak tree

On the one hand, there is the *intentional verb* ('believes'), which informs us that Carl believes, rather than, for example, knows or fears that the cat went up the oak tree. On the other hand, there is a noun-clause ('that the cat went up that oak tree'), which informs us of what it is that Carl believes, the content of his belief, and is therefore known as the *content-clause*. Switching to the material mode, there is the kind of intentional state on the one hand, the kind of content on the other. These two parameters are in turn connected to a well-known equivocation in nouns like 'belief', 'hope', 'desire', etc. 'A's belief' can refer either to *what A believes*, namely *that* the sun is out, or to *what A has*, namely the *belief* that the sun is out. What A has, the belief, can be erroneous, sensible, or tentative. But what A believes—e.g. that the sun is out—i.e. the content of her belief, cannot.[22]

The two parameters raise two distinct questions. One is which *intentional states* can be ascribed—what intentional verbs can be applied to animals; another question is which *contents* can be ascribed to them—which that-clauses, singular terms, infinitives or gerunds can follow these intentional verbs.[23] Concerning the second question, Wittgenstein famously maintained that a dog can believe that its master is at the door, but not that its master will return the day after tomorrow. Concerning the first question, he suggested that dogs are incapable of hope, because that particular concept is applied on the basis of behavioural manifesta-

---

22 White (1972), 81 ff.
23 Stoecker (2009), 263 f. maintains that in reason explanations intentional attitudes play second fiddle to the contents. 'Except for the content, it does not matter much, how we specify the type of attitude'. But the difference between believing and knowing does play an enormous role, as we shall see. And so does the difference between *V*-ing because one wants to and *V*-ing because one is obliged to. Finally, there are not just 'pro attitudes'—in Davidson's terminology—but also con attitudes. I can desire, etc., *V*-ing, yet I can also hate, resent, deplore, etc. *V*-ing. It is interesting to note that with respect to negative conative verbs the continuous form comes more natural than the infinitival. While *A* can be said to hate to *V*, this is less natural than to hate *V*-ing, and resent to *V*, deplore to *V* etc. may be ungrammatical. It would be interesting to speculate whether there is a conceptual difference underlying this grammatical one.

tions that are part of a 'complex form of life', that of linguistic humans.[24] At a more general level, one might grant that animals can believe or perceive that p, yet deny that they can think or judge that p, since these are exercises of rational faculties. The next section is devoted to such a general issue, namely the applicability to animals of 'know' and 'believe'.

IV. Knowledge and Belief

Few contemporary differentialists would deny that some animals possess knowledge how, in Ryle's phrase. Intelligent animals know how to do certain things, not just because they are genetically pre-programmed or have been behaviouristically conditioned, but also because they can learn how to do them off their own bats, whether by trial and error or even through foresight and planning. The moot point is whether animals are capable of what Ryle called knowledge that.[25] It is obvious, however, that the knowledge he had in mind is not tied to that particular grammatical construction. To know who, where, when or whether also constitutes what is sometimes known as propositional knowledge— a label that is highly misleading, as we shall see. Accordingly, if a dog knows whether its master is at the door, it also knows that its master is (not) at the door, and mutatis mutandis for knowing who is at the door. If a chimpanzee knows where to find stones suitable for nutcracking, it also knows that such stones are to be found beneath yonder tree. If a scrub jay knows when it has cached a supply of worms, it also knows that the caching occurred so long ago that the worms are no longer edible. And since the antecedents are commonsensical or strongly supported by empirical evidence, why should it be problematic to ascribe propositional knowledge to animals?

The problems, I submit, are largely the product of contestable philosophical ideas about such knowledge. For proponents of orthodox accounts, belief is a necessary but not sufficient condition of knowledge.

---

24 Wittgenstein (1967), 174.
25 That animals possess knowledge how rules out combining a differentialist denial of knowledge that with the currently popular view that all cases of knowledge how can be reduced to knowledge that. An interesting issue remains, however. In the human case knowing how to Φ can be distinguished from the ability to Φ. An old hunter may know how to skin a rabbit while no longer being able to do so. But can this distinction be drawn in the case of animals? Not by reference to an old chimpanzee telling offspring how to crack nuts with a stone

By the same token, the capacity for belief is merely a necessary condition of the capacity for knowledge. This obviously holds for the tripartite conception of knowledge as true justified belief. On such an account, even if animals can believe that p, they could only know that p if they were also justified in that belief. And *if* this in turn requires that they are capable of justifying that belief[26], knowledge is unattainable for non-linguistic creatures.

The tripartite conception never recovered from the counterexamples devised in Gettier's article 'Is justified true belief knowledge?'.[27] Yet the idea that knowledge is a type of belief soldiered on, even among many opponents of the tripartite concept.[28] Given this assumption, knowledge is belief *plus* something (justification, proper warrant, suitable causal connection, etc.), and hence more demanding. The orthodoxy treats knowing as an 'elite suburb of believing'.[29] Following Wittgenstein, Ryle and White, however, some epistemologists have questioned the idea that knowledge is a species of *belief*. Instead, the revisionist story goes, it is a kind of *ability*. Thus Hyman has argued that to know that p just is to be able to believe or do something for the reason that p.[30]

But isn't this from the frying pan into the fire for assimilationists, not to mention their pets? For how can animals believe or do something for a reason, without rational faculties? As indicated in section II, however, it is far from obvious that a creature can only believe or do something for a reason if it is capable of stating those reasons or to reflect on them. Furthermore, if animals are capable of acting for a reason only in an attenuated sense, the same might hold for their capacity to know. Finally, if my methodological prolegomena are correct, then to the extent to which an account of knowledge rules out cognitively controlled and fruitful applications of epistemic concepts to animals, it also stands in need of revision, e.g. in need of being restricted to humans.

To add force to this last point, the next section argues that crediting animals with certain forms of knowledge is not merely legitimate but inevitable, not just but especially if knowledge is a kind of ability. In the following section I shall tackle a radical attack on orthodox accounts

---

26 A substantial if, see Glock (2009).
27 Gettier (1963).
28 E.g. Williamson (2000).
29 Ryle (1974), 5.
30 Hyman (1999).

of knowledge. It questions an assumption that the orthodoxy shares with its more moderate critics, namely that a creature that is incapable of having beliefs must also be incapable of having knowledge. According to Marcus, animals can know things, yet they cannot believe things. It will transpire that this claim is untenable. Furthermore, it is partly based on a failure to question an orthodoxy in the philosophy of mind, namely the aforementioned assumption that intentional verbs signify 'propositional attitudes', relations between a subject and a proposition.

V. Knowledgeable Brutes!

There are countless examples for everyday attributions of knowledge to higher animals. If Malcolm's dog had noticed the cat's change of course and behaved accordingly, we would have no qualms about

(6) The dog knows that the cat is in the maple tree

Cognitive ethology has added a wealth of more astonishing cases.[31] In many of them, there are legitimate disputes over how precisely to describe the animals' achievements.[32] But these concern the question of what precisely the animals know and how they came by that knowledge. That they do have knowledge of certain facts is not in dispute.

There are good reasons for this consensus. First, both everyday and scientific observations demonstrate that animals have cognitive capacities, capacities to gain information. Indeed, some findings clearly indi-

---

31 See Bekoff/Jamieson (1996); Tomasello/Call (1997); Hurley/Nudds (2006). Here is a selection. Chimpanzees know whether there is food in a container, and not just through direct perception. They can pick the baited among two containers, when they hear that another container shaken by the experimenter doesn't emit a characteristic noise. Chimpanzees know whether an experimenter will cooperate or not. They will point to the baited of two containers when dealing with an experimenter that has been cooperative in the past, to the unbaited, when dealing with an experimenter that has in the past appropriated the indicated container. Scrub jays know not just where they have hidden food, but also whether they have been observed doing so. What is more, they know whether food hidden is still edible.
32 Is some kind of disjunctive inference in play the first case? Do the chimpanzees in the second case know what the experimenters intend to do, or only how they will react? Is the astonishingly intelligent behaviour of the scrub jays a manifestation of episodic memory, etc.?

cate that these capacities are not confined to perception. Still, perception by itself suffices to show that animals are capable of gaining knowledge.

It would be absurd to deny that animals are capable of perception. They can learn about their environment by using their sensory organs. However, perceiving that *p* implies *knowing* that *p*, if 'perceiving' is used as a factive verb, as it commonly is in both the human and the animal case. Accordingly, since animals can perceive that *p*, they are capable of knowing that *p*. Lingualists will contest the idea that seeing is knowing. But on what grounds? The most attractive option for them is to argue as follows. Animal perception is confined to perceiving X, i.e. to perceiving objects or events; it does not include perceiving that *p*.[33] This would mean that they are capable only of type III intentionality, not of type I intentionality. But this response is implausible. The perceptually informed reactions of higher animals to their environment can only be explained by a capacity to perceive that *p*. For instance, the dog sees a bone on the table, but it has been trained not to grab anything on the table and hence simply looks on, panting. Yet as soon as the bone is placed on the floor, the dog grabs it. This sequence of events is not explained by the dog simply seeing a bone, a table or the floor, but only by its seeing first *that* the bone is on the table and then that it is on the floor. One might maintain that the problem vanishes if spatial relations like *x being on y* are among the objects that the dog can perceive. However, simply perceiving three distinct objects—bone, table, *x being on y*—does not explain the dog's behaviour. Such an explanation is only in the offing if the dog can also perceive *that* the bone stands in the relation of *being on* to the table at one moment, to the floor at the next. And in that case we are back with perceiving that *p*. Nor can the lingualist defuse the argument by insisting that the dog simply perceives (sees, smells, etc.) *the bone on the table* or *the bone on the floor*. For either the apposition 'on the table' is used restrictively to identify what bone it sees, in which case the dog's seeing the bone on the table goes no further towards explaining its behaviour with respect to the table than its simply seeing a bone. Or it is shorthand for 'being on the table'. But perceiving the bone *being on the table* is perceiving *that the bone is on the table* by another name. Consequently there is no way around the admission that animals can perceive that something is the case, just as we can.[34]

---

33 Thus Dretske, e.g. Dretske (2004) distinguishes between 'seeing things' and 'seeing facts', maintaining that only the latter is conceptual.
34 Glock (2010).

Furthermore, animals display a kind of behavioural response to what they have learnt through perception which is analogous to the human case—a response appropriate to the circumstances. For instance, vervet monkeys react in a characteristic fashion to different predators, and they signal these different predators through distinctive alarm calls.[35] Furthermore, a vervet monkey that has fled from a snake onto a tree knows that it is safe. And we know that it knows because it is no longer agitated and no longer signals danger, instead observing the snake in a detached, impassive fashion.[36]

Finallly, in higher animals we can detect the same nexus between perception, knowledge and action that is crucial to the application of epistemic and practical concepts to humans, especially according to revisionist accounts. Consider the following ingenious example by Marcus, involving his cat Opie.[37]

(7) Opie tries to paw the pantry door open in order to retrieve the treats.
(8) Opie paws the pantry door open because he is retrieving the treats.
(9) Opie paws the pantry door open because he is trying to retrieve the treats.
(10) Opie paws the pantry door open because the treats are in the pantry.

If Opie fails to paw the pantry door open, (8) – (10) are out of order, just as they would be in the human case. If Opie succeeds at pawing the pantry door open, yet the pantry contains no treats, (9) is in order, while (8) and (10) are not. For these explanations require knowledge of facts. The analogy with human knowledge extends to Gettier style cases, at least if these are dealt with along revisionist lines. Suppose Marcus has moved the treats to the shelf above the pantry. The treats then happen to fall behind the shelf and back into the pantry. Opie, not having observed the switch and suffering from a stuffy nose, is unaware of these developments. In that case we might say

(11) Opie paws the door open because the treats are usually in the pantry

or

---

35 Seyfarth/Cheney (1996).
36 See Rundle (1997), 87.
37 Marcus (2011), ch. 3.

(12) Opie paws the door open because he expects the treats to be in the pantry.

But Opie doesn't paw the door open because the treats are in the pantry *full stop*, as in (10). For '[h]is expectation's being met was merely fortuitous'.

VI. *Incredulous Brutes?*

Marcus rightly concludes that animals are capable of knowledge. Turning received wisdom on its head, however, he demurs at granting that they are capable of *belief*. His line of reasoning can be reconstructed to run roughly as follows.

(P_1) Knowledge is a relation between a subject and a fact
(P_2) Animals can be related (in an appropriate fashion) to facts
(C_1) Animals can know things
(P_3) Belief is a relation between a subject and a proposition
(P_4) Animals cannot be related (in an appropriate fashion) to propositions
(C_2) Animals cannot believe things

Although P_1 and P_2 require careful elaboration, we should accept C_1, for the reasons rehearsed in the last section. A rationale for accepting P_4 will emerge in section VIII. Right now I turn to the argument in favour of P_3, which Marcus derives from Vendler. According to both, 'that' clauses are systematically ambiguous between a fact-interpretation, and a proposition-interpretation. 'that p' in 'A believes that p' always refers to a proposition, whereas 'that p' in 'A knows that p' always refers to a fact. This thesis rightly presupposes that facts and propositions are not to be equated, their logical isomorphism notwithstanding. And Vendler brings to light genuine differences between the roles of that-clauses in belief- and know-strings, respectively. Consider

(13) John believes that grass is green.
(14) I know what John believes.
(15) I believe what John believes.

Vendler's thesis is that 'A knows ___' takes facts as objects, whereas 'A believes___' takes propositions as objects. Accordingly, 'what John believes' in (14) cannot refer to *the object* of John's belief—the proposition that grass is green—since the latter is not a fact. And sure enough, (14) does not mean that I know that grass is green. Rather it means that I know *that John believes grass is green*, which is the fact expressed by (13) as a whole. (14) is similar to

(16) I know what he lost.

in which 'what he lost' is a new sentence-nominalization—a 'wh-nominalization'—of 'that he lost a watch'. By contrast, 'what John believes' in (15) refers back to the proposition on display in (13), viz., that grass is green. In this respect, (13) is similar to

(17) I found what he lost.

where 'what he lost' ultimately derives from a relative clause. (15) is tantamount to

(15') I believe that which he believes [namely, that grass is green].

The cases that cause trouble for Vendler's thesis are those employing two verbs, such as

(18) John believes what Mary knows

These mixed cases seem to show that belief and knowledge *can* have the same object. Vendler dismisses (18) as ungrammatical. Yet that dismissal seems theory-driven. In any event, no competent speaker would balk at a slight modification:

(18') John merely believes that p while Mary knows it[38]

Marcus for his part suggests that mixed cases trade on an ambiguity concerning that-p, which is made to do double-duty, to refer to a proposition in the first conjunct, a fact in the second. He assimilates (18') to cases of syllepsis such as

(19) Ron was still off his rocker and his medications.

Yet ordinary speakers would not regard (19) as a syllepsis, a potentially comical crossing of categories. The addition of 'merely' to (18) does not serve to cross a categorial divide—between propositions and facts. It simply indicates that the sentence settles the 'intra-categorial' question of whether what Mary is stated to know is that John believes that p or rather that p.

Finally, the diagnosis of syllepsis is even less plausible for mixed cases involving the same subject, such as

---

[38] Marcus uses the example 'I merely believe what John (truly) knows', which leaves one with a puzzle about how he could be in a position to state that John knows that p yet credit himself with the mere belief that p.

(20) She now knows what she used merely to believe, namely that exercise is good for you.

Consequently, there is no case for holding that 'that'-clauses are categorially ambiguous in the way maintained by Vendler.[39]

Ironically, it is Vendler's claim that what we know is always a fact that runs up against categorial distinctions of standard English.

(21) A knows that p

does not imply

(22) A knows the fact that p (★)

Rather, it implies

(23) It is a fact that p

and arguably—if A possesses the concept of a fact—

(24) A knows that it is a fact that p.

We shall see below that matters stand even worse for the claim that what we believe are always propositions.

VII. Retreat from Knowledge

It transpires that Vendler's logico-grammatical considerations do not rule out ascriptions of beliefs to animals. What is more, there is an obvious problem with the idea that animals are knowers but cannot be believers, namely the problem of accounting for cases of error or mistake. Animals possess cognitive, and in particular perceptual, faculties which, properly exercised, yield knowledge about the environment. As Malcolm's example illustrates, however, they can also exercise these cognitive capacities in inadequate or insufficient manner. In that case, they do not possess knowledge, even though their behaviour is still guided by these faculties.[40] Attribution of belief is in order, because in the case of animals no less than in the case of humans, there is the possibility of epistemic failure as well as success.

Small wonder, then, that even a differentialist like Rundle writes: 'Certainly, we do no violence to language in speaking of *knowledge*

---

[39] See also White (1982), 45–54; Dolby (2007), ch. 1.1.2.
[40] Davidson has famously argued that a creature cannot have a belief without being mistaken, and that this in turn requires possessing the concept of a mistake. The first claim is correct, the second mistaken. See Glock (2000).

[in the case of animals], and, while it is not the most suitable term, "think" has, …, an intelligible role in those cases where we are obliged to retreat from "know". After all, the move from knowledge to thought or belief can hardly be a move to a state which is more problematic *psychologically*, as it were, given that it is made solely on the strength of the failure of a purely external condition'.[41]

The assimilationist needs to clear two obstacles at this stage. First, isn't the idea that in the case of epistemic failure we still have a case of belief a lapse back into the orthodox account of knowledge as belief plus something? The answer is: No! For we must distinguish between the proper analysis of *knowledge* and the question of whether the *capacity for knowledge* can be attributed without the capacity for belief. When A knows that p, it is not a matter of A believing that p plus it being the case that p plus something else. Nonetheless, only a creature that can (merely) believe that p can also know that p, since only such a creature has cognitive capacities that play a role in explaining its behaviour. Indeed, when it comes to explaining behaviour, we do not distinguish between an explanation by reference to knowledge and an explanation by reference to mere belief. One and the same behaviour can be made intelligible by A knowing that p and by A merely believing that p. That Sarah called out the ambulance is rendered intelligible by her believing that she has gone into labour, whether or not she is right.

The second obstacle is to account for animal belief in view of the assumption that belief is a relation between a subject and a proposition. Even Marcus describes the idea that we commit an error in attributing beliefs to animals through statements like (5) as 'charmless'. He thinks that our hands are forced, however, on pain of accepting that animals grasp propositions.

---

41 Rundle (1997), 89 f. To be sure, Rundle also insists that our ascriptions of belief and thought to animals are not a matter of knowledge. 'The dog believes that there is a squirrel in the tree'—'I am prepared to go along with that way of speaking'. But his reason is that there is no internal process of thought which the subject can manifest. It cannot be said that 'something takes place in the creatures head' which might be reportable by a sentence (Rundle 1997, 90, 105). But this is an unduly mentalistic conception of thinking, at odds with the insights of Ryle and oblivious to the array of thoughts that can be displayed in non-linguistic behaviour.

VIII. Propositional Attitudes' and Animal Intentionality

The assumption that stands in the way of animal belief is P_3, namely that belief is a relation between a subject and a proposition. That assumption is part and parcel of the orthodox picture of intentional states as relations between subjects and propositions (a picture that Vendler and Marcus reject for the case of knowledge yet accept for the case of belief). That picture rules out ascriptions of beliefs to animals quite irrespectively of Vendler's logico-grammatical considerations. According to orthodoxy, what a subject believes (the content of A's belief) is a proposition or thought, a complex object of which concepts are the components; thus the thought that dogs bark is a complex object of which the concepts DOG and BARK are parts. By these lights, if A believes that p, then she stands in relations of grasping and accepting to an entity, a proposition, of which concepts are components. Thus orthodoxy presents a relational account of intentional states and a building-block model of propositions.

As mentioned above, the term 'proposition' is closely related to 'sentence', to the ears of philosophers, linguists and laypeople alike. It also suggests a claim or statement that is being proposed or advanced for consideration. An attitude towards a proposition therefore seems to require an understanding of something proposed, claimed or stated. Furthermore, on most accounts, propositions and concepts are not just linguistic but also abstract. Yet animals cannot stand in the appropriate cognitive/semantic relationship to such entities.[42] Finally, on the orthodox view even straightforward propositional contents such as the one attributed in (5) include concepts like that of a cat or of a tree. But there are difficulties in supposing that animals could grasp and hence entertain these concepts.

One way of defusing the proposition problem is associated with Fodor. According to him propositions and concepts are particulars in the heads of individuals—notably sentences or words of a language of thought—rather than abstract entities. And such particulars occur in the brains of animals no less than in those of humans. Even creatures that do not speak a public language partake of the language of thought—provided their behaviour is explicable by reference to intentional states. As I have argued elsewhere, however, that position is untenable. Propositions and concepts cannot be particulars, since they can

---

42 See Glock (2010), 19; Alvarez (2010), 67; Marcus (2011).

be shared between subjects. They are not signs, but what signs express. And the idea of a language of thought falls foul of the fact that a linguistic symbol is something that is used in a potentially conscious way by a subject. The neural processes Fodor has in mind may charitably be interpreted as causal enablers of thought, yet they cannot be symbols of a language.[43]

IX. Nonconceptual Content?!

A more promising response to the proposition problem invokes the idea of 'nonconceptual content'.[44] This response accepts that intentional verbs signify attitudes towards objects of a special kind, namely *contents*; it parts company with lingualism by insisting that in addition to *propositional* contents consisting of concepts (the contents of human thinking) there are also 'proto-propositional' contents consisting of nonconceptual components, e.g. sensory representations (the contents of animal thinking and pre-reflective human perception). Unfortunately, it is unclear how such proto-propositional entities can be contents of thinking as here understood, i.e. contents signified by the noun-clauses in sentences of the form '*A V*s (perceives, believes, knows) that *p*'

Furthermore, this response to the proposition problem in turn leads to a *congruity problem*. The distinction between different types of content seems to count against ascribing one and the same belief to humans and animals. It suggests that a statement of the form

(25) Both Sarah and the dog believe that *p*

is not so much a falsehood as a syllepsis. For 'Sarah believes that *p*' comes out as 'Sarah stands in the relation of believing to the thought that *p*' while 'The dog believes that *p*' comes out as 'The dog stands in the relation of believing to the protothought that *p*'.

Such a conclusion would undermine the anti-lingualist motive for introducing the notion of nonconceptual content. At the same time, it seems to support lingualists like Marcus and McDowell.[45] The latter resists the idea that there is a 'non-conceptual content' common to the perception of humans and animals (though not on account of the

---

43 Glock (2006).
44 E.g. Cussins (1992); Peacocke (1992); Dummett (1993), chs. 12 f.; Bermúdez (2003).
45 McDowell (1996), 50 f., 63 ff.

congruity problem). Instead, McDowell declares, animals are capable only of 'perceptual sensitivity' rather than genuine experience. In a similar though less dogmatic vein, Malcolm suggests that while the dog can "believe" that the cat went up the oak tree, only humans can "have the thought" that it went up the oak tree. Unfortunately, such a position is faced with an unpalatable dilemma. Either it rejects outright the application of intentional verbs terms like 'perceives', 'thinks' or 'knows' to animals, thereby facing the objections marshaled in section I. Or it diagnoses a fundamental ambiguity in applying such verbs to humans and applying them to animals. In that case, the congruity problem once again raises its ugly head.

Irrespective of whether it arises on account of the content-clause or on account of the intentional verb, the idea that there is such an incongruity is at odds with the way in which ascriptions of beliefs to linguistic and non-linguistic creatures interact. (25) is not a syllepsis like 'Both the exam and the chair were hard'. For it gives rise to perfectly legitimate inferences and explanations. Particularly pertinent is that we can explain a common reaction between Sarah and the dog by reference to statements like (25). If both Sarah and the dog suddenly notice that there is a precipice in front of them, for instance, this explains why both stop dead in their tracks.

We should abandon the unwarranted assumption that an ascription of a belief requires cognitive parity between the ascriber and the subject. A certain disparity between the terms used in a belief report and those that could be used by the subject is present even in the linguistic case, without constituting a fundamental incongruity. The terms which occur in the content-clause are in general dictated not so much "by" the creature whose belief we report, but "by" the concerns of speaker and audience. Thus, 'Sarah thinks that the charlatan you introduced me to is about to give her a biscuit' can be in order, whether Sarah is an adult who regards the person in question as a charlatan, one who does not, a child that lacks the concept of a charlatan, or a dog.[46]

---

46 See Rundle (1997), 83.

X. Doing away with propositional attitudes

The travails of both differentialism and nonconceptual assimilationism count in favour of a more radical attack on the orthodox, relational account of intentional states epitomized by the idiom of propositional attitudes. Its popularity notwithstanding, the idea that an intentional state is a relation between a subject and a proposition is problematic.

One set of difficulties concerns the building-block model of contents (whether conceptual or nonconceptual). There are both empirical and conceptual qualms about the idea that entertaining a part of a thought correlates with a definite stage of a more protracted mental or neuro-physiological process—the entertaining of the whole thought. Even if these could be waived, we would only be dealing with stages of thinking a thought, not with stages of thoughts. As regards the latter, the building-block model transposes the part/whole relation from the spatial and temporal sphere to a sphere—that of abstract entities—to which *ex hypothesi* neither spatial nor temporal notions apply. What seems to give sense to talk of parts and wholes in the case of propositions or thoughts is the fact that the linguistic expressions of thoughts—namely sentences—have components—namely words.[47] What is said or thought can be said to have components only to the extent to which its linguistic expressions have components (these components may, for instance, be what *A* explains when she is called upon to explain what she means by a particular utterance).

In the wake of Quine, many philosophers regard propositions as dubious entities. They are not just abstract but intensional, and hence, allegedly, lack criteria of identity. Such philosophers often replace propositions by sentences as the objects of propositional attitudes, thereby committing themselves to lingualism. I am more inclined to challenge an assumption which the orthodox view shares with Quinean extensionalists and most proponents of nonconceptual content, namely that intentional verbs signify relations to either abstract or concrete objects.[48]

---

47 See Kenny (1989), 126 f.
48 Davidson's attitude towards the building block model is ambivalent. On the one hand, he denies that having a thought is to stand in a relation to a proposition, on the other, he sees no alternative to treating belief sentences like (1) as relational (Davidson 2001, 37, 57 ff.). Stoecker (Stoecker 2009, 264) ignores the former aspect in maintaining that for Davidson having an intentional attitude is 'standing in a certain relation to a content'. Davidson's measurement analogy, to which Stoecker refers, is designed precisely to avoid this reification. Stoecker

The idea of propositional attitudes is problematic not just on account of 'propositional' but also on account of 'attitudes'. For the idea that belief is a relation between a subject and an entity amounts to a reification.

Admittedly, noun-clauses like 'that the cat went up the oak tree' or 'what Carl believes' are grammatically speaking the objects of beliefs. But they are *intentional* rather than *object-accusatives*.[49]

(26) Clare Short believes Tony Blair

entails that there is an object x such that Short believes x. In (26) the psychological verb expresses a genuine relation, since here two relata must exist, one to believe, and one to be believed. By contrast,

(27) Short believes that Iraq possesses weapons of mass destruction

does not entail that there is an object x such that Short believes x. Nothing in reality need correspond to the noun-phrases of (5) and (27), since the relevant state of affairs need not exist or obtain.[50]

A building-block theorist will dig his heels in and insist that something must exist, namely a (propositional) content which is a real object, though probably an abstract one. But this 'something' is an object only in a formal, grammatical sense; it is a projection from that-clauses rather than a genuine thing to be encountered beyond space and time or in the heads of individuals.[51] Brentano was right to insist that to believe is to believe something. (27) entails that there is something Short believes. Yet in the first instance this simply means that Short cannot believe any-

---

thinks that some causal explanations do not refer to causes, and uses this to back up the idea that rational explanations are causal even though actions are not events caused by internal states. But his example of explanations referring to quantitative states is awry. It is wrong to claim that the weight and speed of a truck explain why it broke through the guard vails simply because they narrow down the scope of possible causal processes (as in an inference to the best explanation). Rather, the fact that the truck had a certain impulse (which in turn is a function of weight and velocity) explains the fact that it broke through the barrier.

49   White (1972).
50   This is not the only criterion for an object-accusative, since otherwise factive intentional verbs, as in 'A knows that p'–would govern an object accusative. For more on this point and the following argument see Glock (2010a).
51   Pace Quine, 'something' is wider than 'object'. 'Something' is syntactically transcategorial: it can quantify into the positions of singular term, predicate, and sentence. Only in the first case is it equivalent to 'object'. For the complex relations between these expressions, as well as 'exists', 'there is' and 'real', see Glock (2003), ch. 2.

thing unless there is an intelligible answer to the question 'What does Short believe?'. If I say 'I believe that *p*' and this still leaves you in the dark as to what precisely I believe, I can only respond with an *elaboration* of what I have said, rather than with a more accurate *designation* of an object.

Furthermore, the wh-clause 'what Short believes', like 'what Short weighs', incorporates an interrogative rather than a relative pronoun. Thus 'Prescott knows the person Short believes' and 'The person Short believes is Blair' entails 'Prescott knows Blair'. Yet 'Prescott knows what Claire Short believes' and 'What Short believes is that Iraq possesses weapons of mass destruction' does not entail 'Prescott knows that Iraq possesses weapons of mass destruction', if only because one cannot know a falsehood. Similarly, 'Prescott knows what Short weighs' and 'Short weighs 70 kg' do not entail 'Prescott knows 70 kg', since that sentence is ungrammatical. Neither 'what Short weighs' nor 'what Short believes' signify an object to which Short is related. By the same token, believing that *p* is no more a *genuine relation* to an object than weighing *n* kilograms.

It might be objected that there are pertinent contexts in which 'what Short believes' *does* incorporate a relative pronoun. In conjunction with (27)

(28) Prescott believes what Short believes

entails

(29) Prescott believes that Iraq possesses weapons of mass destruction.

But the move to (29) is not underwritten by our knowledge that Short and Prescott are related in the same way to an entity. Instead, it is underwritten by the fact that both share certain properties regarding a particular question, namely the question of whether Iraq possesses weapons of mass destruction. Even in this context, 'what Short believes' is an interrogative clause in a less direct sense, since its content derives from the way in which Short would or could respond to a certain question, or react in certain situations, e. g. when voting on the attack on Iraq in Parliament.

XI. Doing away with propositional attitudes

The building-block model also goes astray in assuming that the alleged object to which subjects of intentional states are related is a proposition. Many intentional verbs cannot be characterised as expressing a relation either to a proposition or to a sentence. It makes no sense to expect, fear, hope or see a sentence or proposition, at least not the same sense as to expect, fear, hope or see that p. And given that what I can expect or see is what you can believe, this difficulty may be contagious. That is to say, it may show that even though it makes sense to believe the proposition that p, believing that p is not the same as believing the *proposition that p*.[52]

One might respond that in its philosophical usage, 'proposition' is a term of art which is exempted from the vagaries of English that rule out locutions like

(30) A fears/expects/hopes/sees the proposition that p.

But this invites the challenge to explain what precisely that technical term means. And because of the illicitness of (30) that challenge cannot be met by stipulating that propositions are simply what we believe, expect, hope, etc.[53]

On the other hand, the denial that what we believe is *always* a proposition seems to imply that in cases in which we *do* believe the proposition that p, we have two beliefs, a belief that p and a belief in the proposition that p. And such duplication seems implausible. This objection can be fended off as follows. To say that A believes the proposition that p is not to ascribe to her a belief in addition to her belief that p. Rather, it is to place her belief that p in a certain context. Believing that p is simply a matter of *believing something to be so*, whereas believing the proposition that p is a matter of *believing something to be true*. In the case of simply believing that p, the focus is on how things are or might be; in the case of believing a proposition that p it is on how they have or might be stated or believed to be. The latter construction is appropriate if something has been stated to be so or if such a statement is at least 'in the air', with that statement then being up for consideration regarding its truth.

---

52 See White (1972); Rundle (2001).
53 See Glock (2011).

XII. Conclusion

As regards the basic epistemic and practical notions discussed here, my arguments favour a middle stance between assimilationism and differentialism-cum-lingualism.

On the one hand, the difference between humans and animals does not lie in the fact that the former can and the latter cannot believe, know or act. Nor does it lie in the fact that the latter can believe, know or act only in an attenuated sense. It lies rather in the fact that we can believe, know and do *more*.

On the other hand, this difference *is* derivative from our distinctive language-using abilities. Something must count as believing, knowing or desiring that *p* rather than that *q*, otherwise such ascriptions are vacuous. This means that intentional states, although they need not actually be expressed, must be capable of being expressed. And only a restricted range of intentional states can be expressed in non-linguistic behaviour.[54]

Furthermore, in this case a difference in quantity transforms into a difference in quality—to use a Marxist figure of thought. This holds at two levels. At the *factual* level, the emergence of language enabled humans to develop techniques and forms of interaction of unprecedented complexity and sophistication. It permitted division of labour and progressive cultural development. And these have set the way humans act, communicate and think—our way of life—fundamentally apart from even the most intelligent and social of animal species. At the *conceptual* level, the logical connections between epistemic and practical concepts are greatly enhanced when they are applied to linguistic creatures. As a result, in applying our epistemic and practical concepts to animals we employ a rich conceptual apparatus in an area in which some of the logical connections which constitute that apparatus do not apply. But attributing knowledge and action to animals is not simply an impoverished application of a rich technique. For that richer technique evolves around a central core of cases in which creatures believe, know, desire and do things on account of their wants and cognitive capacities. These basics of knowledge and action are shared by humans and animals.[55]

---

54 See Glock (1997).
55 For comments and suggestions I am grateful to David Dolby, Frank Esken, Tim Henning and participants in the 2010 conference on Human Agency and Human Knowledge at Peking University. I should also like to express my pro-

References

Alvarez (2010): Maria Alvarez, *Kinds of Reasons*, Oxford.
Bekoff/Jamieson (1996): Marc Bekoff/Dale Jamieson (eds.), *Readings in Animal Psychology*, Cambridge/MA.
Bermudez (2003): José Luis Bermudez, *Thinking without Words*, Oxford.
Cussins (1992): Adrian Cussins, "Content, embodiment and objectivity", in: *Mind* 101, 651–688.
Davidson (2001): Donald Davidson, *Subjective, Intersubjective, Objective*, Oxford.
Dolby (2007): David Dolby, "Propositions, Substitution and Generality", PhD thesis, University of Reading.
Dretske (2004): Fred Dretske, "Seeing, Believing and Knowing", in: R. Schwartz (ed.), *Perception*, Malden, 268–86.
Dummett (1993): Michael Dummet, *Origins of Analytical Philosophy*, London.
Ernst (2002): Gerhard Ernst, *Das Problem des Wissens*, Paderborn.
Fisher (1996): John A. "The Myth of Anthropomorphism", in: Bekoff/Jamieson (1996), 3–16.
Fodor (1975): Jerry Fodor, *The Language of Thought*, New York.
Gettier (1963): Edmund L. Gettier "Is justified true belief knowledge?", in: *Analysis* 23, 121–3.
Glock (2000): Hans-Johann Glock, "Animals, thoughts and concepts", in: *Synthese* 123, 35–64.
Glock (2001a): Hans-Johann Glock, "Intentionality and Language", in: *Language and Communication* 21.2, 105–118.
Glock (2001b): Hans-Johann Glock, "Wittgenstein and Quine: Mind, Language and Behaviour", in:, S. Schroeder (ed.), *Wittgenstein and Contemporary Philosophy of Mind* , Basingstoke, 3–23.
Glock (2006): Hans-Johann Glock, "Concepts: Representations or Abilities?", in: *Content, Consciousness, and Perception*, E. Di Nucci/C. McHugh (eds.), Cambridge, 37–61.
Glock (2009): Hans-Johann Glock, "Can Animals Act for Reasons?", in: *Inquiry* 52, 232–255.
Glock (2010): Hans-Johann Glock, "Can Animals Judge?", in: *Dialectica* 64, 11–34.
Glock (2010a): Hans-Johann Glock, "Concepts, Abilities and Propositions", in: *Grazer Philosophische Studien* 81, 115–34.
Glock (2011): Hans-Johann Glock, "A Coquitivist Approach to Concepts", in: *Grazer Philosophische Studien* 82, 931–63.
Hurley/Nudds (2006): Susan Hurley/Matthew Nudds(eds.), *Rational Animals*, Oxford.
Hyman (1999): John Hyman, "How Knowledge Works", in: *Philosophical Quarterly* 49, 433–51.
Kenny (1963): Anthony J. P. Kenny, *Action, Emotion and Will*, London.
Kenny (1989): Anthony J. P. Kenny, *The Metaphysics of Mind*, Oxford.

---

found gratitude to the organisers of that conference, and to the Hanse-Wissenschaftskolleg Delmenhorst for a research fellowship in 2011.

McDowell (1996): John McDowell, *Mind and World,* Cambridge/Mass.
Malcolm (1972–3): Norman Malcolm, "Thoughtless Brutes", in: *Proceedings and Addresses of the American Philosophical Society* 46.
Marcus (2011): Eric Marcus, *Rational Causation,* Cambridge/MA.
Peacocke (1992): Christopher Peacocke, *A Study of Concepts*, Cambridge/MA.
Rundle (1997): Bede Rundle, *Mind in Action*, Oxford.
Rundle (2001): Bede Rundle, "Objects and Attitudes", in: *Language and Communication* 21, 143–156.
Ryle (1971): Gilbert Ryle, *Collected Papers* vol. II, London.
Ryle (1974): Gilbert Ryle, "Mowgli in Babel", in: *Philosophy* 49, 5–11.
Ryle (1980): Gilbert Ryle, *The Concept of Mind*, London.
Seyfarth/Cheney (1996): Robert Seyfarth and Dorothy Cheney, "Inside the Mind of a Monkey", in: Bekoff/Jamieson (1996), 337–343.
Stoecker (2009): Ralf Stoecker, "Why Animals Can't Act", in: *Inquiry* 52, 255–71.
Tomasello/Call (1997): Michael Tomasello/Josep Call, *Primate Cognition*, Oxford.
Tugendhat (1982): Ernst Tugendhat, *Traditional and Analytic Philosophy*, Cambridge.
Vendler (1972): Zeno Vendler, *Res Cogitans*, Ithaca.
White (1972): Alan White, "What We Believe", in: N. Rescher (ed.), *Studies in the Philosophy of Mind,* Oxford, 69–84.
White (1979): Alan White, "Introduction", in: A. White (ed.), *The Philosophy of Action,* Oxford, 1–18.
White (1982): Alan White, *The Nature of Knowledge*, Totowa.
Williamson (2000): Timothy Williamson, *Knowledge and Its Limits,* Oxford.
Wittgenstein (1958): Ludwig Wittgenstein, *The Blue and Brown Books,* Oxford.
Wittgenstein (1967): Ludwig Wittgenstein, *Philosophical Investigations,* Oxford.

Phänomenales Wissen und der Hintergrund
Claudio Roller

1. Einleitung[1]

In jüngerer Zeit ist in die Debatten in der Philosophie des Geistes ein Typus von Wissen eingeführt worden, der in besonderer Weise an die Erste-Person-Perspektive eines Erfahrungssubjektes gebunden scheint. Das Wissen wird dementsprechend als „subjektives" oder „phänomenales Wissen" bezeichnet. Eine zunächst einleuchtende Überlegung bezüglich des besonderen Status von phänomenalem Wissen lautet: Um z. B. die Farbe „Rot", „den Geschmack einer Honigmelone", „den Klang eines Englischhorns" oder „den Duft von Lavendel" zu kennen, müssen entsprechende Erfahrungen am eigenen Leib vollzogen werden.

Phänomenales Wissen hat in den letzten Jahrzehnten die Aufmerksamkeit von Philosophen vor allem im Zusammenhang der Diskussionen um den Wissenszuwachs von Frank Jacksons Superwissenschaftlerin Mary auf sich gezogen.[2] Ich möchte jedoch gleich vorweg schicken, dass dieser Essay nicht von der Auseinandersetzung um den Physikalismus handeln wird. Ich vertrete die Auffassung, dass phänomenales Wissen unabhängig von ontologischen Fragestellungen einen Untersuchungsgegenstand von eigenem Wert darstellt.[3] Phänomenales Wissen muss

---

1 Ich danke Günter Abel, Sibylle Anderl, Ute Feldmann, Anna Reinacher und Stefan Tolksdorf für hilfreiche Überlegungen und Kommentare zu diesem Text.
2 Vgl. Jackson (1983). Bekanntlich wächst Mary in einem schwarz-weißen Raum auf, hat ein umfassendes physikalisches Wissen über Farben und lernt (dennoch) etwas Neues, wenn sie erstmalig Farben erlebt.
3 Ich folge mit dieser Einstellung Hugh Mellor und Tim Crane, die zwar unterschiedliche Auffassungen in Bezug auf phänomenales Wissen vertreten, aber gemeinsam haben, dass sie die Diskussion in den Rahmen der Frage verorten, ob es subjektive Tatsachen gibt. Wenn sich herausstellen sollte, dass nicht alle Tatsachen objektive Tatsachen sind, so hätte dieser Befund nicht nur Auswirkungen auf den Physikalismus sondern auf jegliche Form von *Bücherwissen*, beispielsweise auch auf einen dualistischen Ansatz, wie eine cartesianische *Theorie des Geistes*. Damit ist ein erster Schritt weg von der Debatte um den Physikalismus geleistet, der dazu führt, phänomenales oder subjektives Wissen als ein

gegenüber anderen Formen von Wissen als besonders grundlegend angenommen werden und ist somit auch für unser menschliches Selbstverständnis zentral.

In meiner Untersuchung des phänomenalen Wissens möchte ich eine Brücke zur Konzeption des Hintergrundes bei John Searle schlagen und dabei Fragen verfolgen, denen eine „Ingenieur-artige" Einstellung zugrunde liegt: Wie wirken phänomenale Komponenten und propositionale Wissensformen zusammen? Wie baut propositionales Wissen, mithin die Rede von Erfüllungs- oder gar Wahrheitsbedingungen auf grundlegenden kognitiven Orientierungsleistungen auf? Oder um es auf eine knappe Formel zu bringen: Wie *funktioniert* unser Wissen und welche Rolle spielt dabei das subjektive Erleben?[4]

Ein reflektiertes philosophisches Vorgehen erfordert, dass man methodische Rechenschaft ablegt. Wenn ich also auf den Ingenieur Bezug nehme und ein generisches Bild entwickle, dann gilt es zugleich kritisch zu überprüfen, ob eine solche Orientierung an Funktionen, Strukturen und Entwicklungslinien für die Philosophie überhaupt geboten ist. Bei aller Vorsicht gegenüber philosophischen *Theorien* und entsprechendem Metaphysikverdacht gegenüber „unerklärten Erklärern" glaube ich, dass es auch in der Philosophie harmlose Aussagen über den Aufbau und das Funktionieren menschlicher Kognition geben kann. Es handelt sich hierbei um ein Philosophieren, das nach den jeweiligen begrifflichen Voraussetzungen bestimmter in Anspruch genommener Konzepte fragt und dabei auch die Genese komplexer Zustände in einem begriffslogi-

---

    eigenständiges Forschungsdesiderat aufzufassen. Vgl. Mellor (1999); Crane (2007).

4 Aus den von mir formulierten Fragen wird bereits deutlich, dass ich einen weiten Wissensbegriff verwende. Dieser Gebrauch hat für alle Philosophen etwas irritierendes, die den Begriff des Wissens in einem traditionellen Sinne auffassen. Wissen ist demnach die begründete und methodischen Überprüfungsverfahren unterliegende Kenntnis eines Sachverhaltes. Von diesem „engen" Wissensbegriff lässt sich jedoch auch ein „weiter" Begriff von Wissen unterscheiden. Vgl. Abel (2004), 320 ff. In einem weiten Sinn gilt Wissen als Bezeichnung für „allgemein verfügbare Orientierungen im Rahmen alltäglicher Handlungs- und Sachzusammenhänge". Diese Orientierungen sind weder mit subjekt-übergreifenden Ansprüchen verbunden noch sind sie zwangsläufig begrifflicher Natur. Jeder Zusammenhang in dem etwas als ein bestimmtes Etwas aufgefasst wird, ist mit einer orientierenden Kraft verbunden. Dieser Umstand ist für mich der Hauptgrund in diesem Aufsatz ebenfalls von einem „phänomenalen Wissen" zu sprechen.

schen Sinn nachzeichnet, indem es begründet darüber Auskunft gibt, welche Prozesse auf anderen aufbauen.

Ich werde so vorgehen, dass ich zunächst anhand des Gedankenexperiments einer Rot-Grün-Blindheit, welche durch einen operativen Eingriff überwunden werden kann, die verschiedenen Konzepte Mellors (Abschnitt 2) und Cranes (Abschnitt 3) bezüglich „phänomenalen Wissens" vorstelle. Auf dem Prüfstand steht dann im Anschluss an die Überlegungen Mellors die Vorstellung, dass phänomenales Wissen mit nicht-propositionalen Fähigkeiten zu identifizieren sei, die eine grundlegende orientierende Kraft für das Subjekt erfüllen.

Die Idee nicht-propositionale Komponenten als Kernstück des phänomenalen Wissens aufzufassen sieht sich u. U. dem Einwand ausgesetzt, eine Spielart des Mythos vom Gegebenen darzustellen. Dieser Kritik werde ich in einem zweiten Schritt nachgehen (Abschnitt 4) und als Reaktion darauf die semantischen Voraussetzungen in den Blick nehmen, die der Debatte um den begrifflichen bzw. nicht-begrifflichen Gehalt der Erfahrung zugrunde liegen. Ich versuche mit dieser Strategie eine in meinen Augen zu eng geführte Diskussion wieder zu erweitern (Abschnitt 5).

Schließlich legt der fundamentale Charakter der Fähigkeiten des Identifizierens und Vorstellens im Zusammenhang mit „phänomenalem Wissen" eine Verbindung zu Searles Konzept des Hintergrundes – der Annahme, es gäbe nicht-repräsentationale geistige Einstellungen oder Fähigkeiten, die repräsentationale Zustände überhaupt erst ermöglichen – nahe. Diesem Zusammenhang gehe ich im letzten Teil meines Aufsatzes nach (Abschnitt 6).

Wenn Hintergrundfähigkeiten selber noch nicht in der gleichen Art und Weise über Erfüllungsbedingungen verfügen wie ein propositionales Wissen, zugleich aber als basale Wissensform auf die Ausprägung des propositionalen Wissens wirken, dann stellt sich die Frage, wie genau das Verhältnis zwischen nicht-propositionalen, nicht-begrifflichen und vorintentionalen geistigen Komponenten auf der einen und propositionalen, begrifflichen und intentionalen kognitiven Bestandteilen auf der anderen Seite zu denken ist. Wird diese Trennung akzeptiert, so versteht sich ein generisches Bild auf die Entwicklung von Erfüllungsbedingungen als ein erster Schritt zu einer Antwort auf diese Frage.

2. Phänomenales Wissen

Um die Konzeption des „phänomenalen Wissens" einzuführen möchte ich ein einfaches Beispiel konstruieren. Stellen wir uns vor, dass es möglich ist, die Rot-Grün-Blindheit einer erwachsenen Person durch einen operativen Eingriff zu beheben. Nach der Operation erwacht der Patient – nennen wir ihn Paul – aus der Narkose und sieht erstmalig einen roten Apfel und eine grüne Birne neben sich auf dem Nachttisch liegen. Vielleicht denkt er sich in diesem Moment „Ah, so sehen also rot und grün aus." Ob Paul dabei die genaue Zuordnung, dass der Apfel rot und die Birne grün ist, bereits kennt oder erst später erlangt, ist für unsere Zwecke nicht weiter relevant. Das, was Paul im geschilderten Fall erwirbt, scheint ein kontextabhängiges „subjektives Wissen" zu sein. Offenkundig lernt er etwas dazu, was er vorher nicht kannte. Es handelt sich um neue Erfahrungen, die am eigenen Leib vollzogen werden müssen.[5]

Wir können ein ganzes Spektrum von Wissensformen unterscheiden, die möglicherweise im Zuge von Pauls epistemischem Fortschritt involviert sind. Paul macht A) Bekanntschaft mit einer spezifischen Erfahrung (knowing by aquaintance) und erweitert B) mit der Differenzerfahrung von rot und grün seine Fähigkeiten zur Farbdiskrimination, seine Fähigkeit der Wiedererkennung und sein Vorstellungsvermögen (knowing-how). Über diese Wissensformen hinaus ist er C) von nun an in der Lage sagen zu können, dass etwas Rotes und nicht etwas Grünes vorliegt (knowing-that). Zwar konnte er auch schon zuvor die Wörter rot und grün richtig verwenden, doch jetzt ist es ihm möglich, die Wörter

---

5   Die Parallele meines Beispiels zu Jacksons Mary liegt auf der Hand. Der Zweck der Geschichte von Paul liegt nicht darin (wie oben bereits beschrieben), einen Einwand gegenüber dem Physikalismus diskutieren zu wollen, sondern phänomenales Wissen als ein eigenständiges Explanandum zu betrachten. Gleichwohl lautet für beide Gedankenexperimente die entscheidende Frage: welcher Art ist das erworbene Wissen? Als Argument gegen den Physikalismus soll das Wissen Marys auf eine Tatsache in der Welt hinweisen, die durch den Zugriff der Physik nicht eingefangen wird. In dieser Linie muss das Wissen propositional sein und darf nicht, wie einige Verteidiger des Physikalismus angenommen haben, als eine Fähigkeit aufgefasst werden. Vgl. L. Nemirow (1990); D. Lewis (1996). Für die Beschäftigung mit dem Fall von Paul spielt dieser Aspekt zwar keine Rolle, doch auch hier tritt die Frage auf, was für eine Form von Wissen dem Lernprozess Pauls zugrunde liegt und wie diese Wissensform mit anderen Formen von Wissen in Verbindung steht. Martine Nida-Rümelin variiert im Zuge ihrer Materialismuskritik das Beispiel von Mary in ähnlicher Weise. Vgl. Nida Rümelin (1993).

in Bezug auf seine eigenen Wahrnehmungen unmittelbar anzuwenden und beispielsweise ohne Nachfrage rote und grüne Äpfel nach ihrer Farbe zu sortieren. Doch welche Wissensform ist für die Beschreibung von Pauls Wissenserwerb die entscheidende?

Hugh Mellor hat in seinem Aufsatz „Nothings like Experience"[6] den Versuch unternommen, unser Wissen in Bezug auf bestimmte Erfahrungen genauer zu untersuchen. Mellor verweist darauf, dass ein offenkundiger Unterschied zwischen dem Wissen um eine Erfahrung und der Erfahrung selber besteht. Ich kann mir die Farbe gelb vorstellen ohne sie just in diesem Moment zu sehen. Vorstellung und tatsächliche Wahrnehmung sind grundsätzlich verschieden, schließlich würde ich mich in einem Restaurant auch nicht mit der Vorstellung eines bestellten Desserts zufrieden geben. Übertragen auf das Beispiel von Paul sind Mellor zufolge mit dem Wissen um die neuen Erfahrungen zwei Fähigkeiten verbunden: 1.) Zum einen ist Paul nach der Operation in der Lage seine neuen Erfahrungen zu (re-)identifizieren. Dabei muss er zunächst auch nicht die richtigen Begriffe anwenden. Es reicht aus, wenn er sich denkt „diesen Farbton kenne ich doch…" 2.) Darüber hinaus gehört zum Wissen um die neuen Erfahrungen von Rot und Grün, dass Paul sich diese neuen Erfahrungen von nun an auch vorstellen kann. Diese Fähigkeit zur Imagination scheint außerdem, so die Auffassung von Mellor, spezifische Korrektheitsbedingungen zu implizieren, d.h. die Vorstellung muss auch zutreffend sein.[7] Mellor optiert im Hinblick auf die oben vorgestellten Wissensformen für Möglichkeit B): Fähigkeiten im Sinne eines Knowing-how bzw. Knowing-how-to.

Zu Beginn meines Aufsatzes habe ich den zunächst intuitiv plausiblen Gedanken vorgestellt, dass die unmittelbare Bekanntschaft mit einer Erfahrung, oder anders ausgedrückt: eine Erfahrung gehabt zu haben, eine notwendige Bedingung für die Fähigkeit ist, sich diese Erfahrung vorzustellen. Tatsächlich gibt es auch gute Gründe für die Gegenthese. Das Beispiel von Musikern, die sich anhand einer Partitur den Klang einer noch nicht aufgeführten Komposition vorstellen können, überzeugt

---

6   Mellor (1992).
7   Ich sehe an dieser Stelle das Problem, dass nicht genau dargelegt werden kann, auf welcher Basis die Korrektheit bestimmt wird. Mellor scheint Identifikationsfähigkeit und Vorstellungsvermögen auf einer vorbegrifflichen Ebene verorten zu wollen. Wie kann unabhängig von einer gemeinsam mit anderen Menschen geteilten Begrifflichkeit von Korrektheit die Rede sein? Ich werde auf Korrektheits- und Erfüllungsbedingungen im weiteren Verlauf noch ausführlich zu sprechen kommen. Hier gebe ich lediglich Mellors Position wieder.

Mellor davon, dass Bekanntschaft keine notwendige Bedingung für die Fähigkeit zur Vorstellung der betreffenden Erfahrung ist, auch wenn Bekanntschaft der normale Weg zu sein scheint, um phänomenales Wissen zu erlangen.[8] Aber ist den Musikern das Werk tatsächlich vollständig unbekannt? In Bezug auf die Gesamtheit des Musikstückes mag es sich so verhalten, doch der geübte Musiker kennt sehr wohl die Bausteine aus denen das Werk aufgebaut ist: Tonarten, Melodielinien, die Klangfarben aller beteiligten Instrumente, den Klang verschiedener Instrumentengruppen innerhalb eines Orchesters und vieles mehr. Neben dieser „Baustein-Hypothese" mit der ich den engen logischen Zusammenhang von Bekanntschaft und Vorstellungsfähigkeit verteidigen möchte, erscheinen mir Ähnlichkeitsrelationen eine entscheidende Rolle für die Praxis der Imaginationsfähigkeiten zu spielen. Wer den Klang einer Oboe kennt, wird sich auch den Klang eines Englischhorns vorstellen können, wenn er oder sie beispielsweise den Hinweis erhält, „es klingt ähnlich wie eine normale Oboe, aber ist eine Quinte tiefer gestimmt".[9] Auch wenn ich noch nie ein Englischhorn gehört habe, kann ich von einer bekannten Vorstellung ausgehen und diese gemäß der Beschreibung etwas abwandeln. Für diesen Akt der Modulation greife ich auf ebenfalls mir bekannte Konzepte wie „tieferer" oder „dunklerer" Klang zurück. Ich habe vielleicht keine genaue Vorstellung, aber zumindest einen Anhaltspunkt, der dazu führt, dass ich über eine vage Vorstellung oder überhaupt eine Vorstellung verfüge.

An dieser Stelle lohnt es sich einen Augenblick inne zu halten und zunächst zu konstatieren, dass wir mit Mellor bei der Annahme nichtbegrifflicher Fähigkeiten gestartet und nun bei Konzepten wie „tief" und „dunkel" gelandet sind.[10] Dies lenkt die Aufmerksamkeit auf unsere Konzeption von Vorstellungen und auf die Frage was im Zuge von Vorstellungsfähigkeiten zu den (Re-)Identifikations-Fähigkeiten hinzutritt. Wenn überhaupt etwas hinzu tritt, dann scheint dies begrifflicher Art zu sein. Doch selbst wenn wir unsere Vorstellungen von Vorstellungen auf begriffliche Komponenten in Verbindung mit einfachen (Re-)

---

8 Vgl. Mellor (1992), 5 f.
9 Die Relation einer Ähnlichkeit ist schwierig zu fassen, da präzisiert werden muss, in welcher Hinsicht eine Ähnlichkeit besteht. Im vorliegenden Falle heißt Ähnlichkeit jedoch nicht viel mehr, als dass von einer Vorstellung ausgegangen und diese dann moduliert wird. Die Rede von Ähnlichkeit erscheint mir vor diesem Hintergrund weniger problematisch.
10 Ich verwende hier ‚Konzepte' und ‚Begriffe' austauschbar. Später werde ich auf Abstufungen im Bereich des Sinnhaften zu sprechen kommen.

Identifikationsfähigkeiten zurückführen würden, änderte dies nichts an der engen Verbindung von Vorstellungsfähigkeit und Bekanntschaft, um die es mir an dieser Stelle geht.

Worauf ich in meinem Musikbeispiel hinaus wollte ist der Punkt, dass es Abstufungen in der Verwandtschaft von Instrumenten gibt, die sich auch auf der Ebene des Vorstellungsvermögens widerspiegeln. Jede Violine hat ihren eigenen charakteristischen Klang.[11] Dennoch erkennen wir in der Regel Violinen als Instrumentengattung und unterscheiden sie von Violas und Celli. Streichinstrumente lassen sich wiederum von Holzblasinstrumenten oder Blechblasinstrumenten abgrenzen.

Die Überlegungen im Bereich der Klänge lassen sich auch auf unser Ausgangsbeispiel der Farben übertragen. Auf der Ebene der Grundfarben haben wir mit einer Frage zu tun, die unter etwas anderen Vorzeichen schon David Hume nachhaltig beschäftigt hat[12]: Kann ich mir eine bestimmte Farbschattierung wie beispielsweise „karminrot" vorstellen, wenn ich sie zuvor noch nicht erlebt habe? Im Rückgriff auf die Modulations-Hypothese können wir sagen, dass ich mich der Erfahrung annähern kann, (der kategoriale Unterschied von Erfahrung und Vorstellung bleibt ohnehin bestehen)[13] indem ich von der Vorstellung einer bekannten Erfahrung – in diesem Falle einer Roterfahrung – ausgehe und diese durch mir bekannte Konzepte wie z.B. „strahlend" oder „heller als kirschrot" anpasse. Die Zusammenhänge von Bekanntschaft und des spezifischen „Sich-vorstellen-könnens" werden auch im Blick auf die Geschichte von Paul deutlich: Vor dessen Operation ist die Vorstellungsfähigkeit im Unterschied zu normalsichtigen Menschen stark eingeschränkt. Hat Paul ein phänomenales Wissen im Sinne Mellors, d.h.

---

11 Die Verhältnisse bezüglich des Klanges eines Instrumentes sind noch sehr viel komplizierter als ich es hier darstelle. So sind die Klänge auch noch von der Spielweise der Musiker abhängig.
12 Hume (1982), 36.
13 Hugh Mellor unterscheidet zwischen primären, aktual gegebenen Erfahrungen und sekundären Erfahrungen, den Vorstellungen von primären Erfahrungen. Mellor (1992), 11 ff. Die Verhältnisse von Identifikationen in aktuell gegebenen Wahrnehmungssituationen (primäre Erfahrung) und Erinnerungen und Vorstellungen (sekundäre Erfahrungen) können nicht als Prozesse des Abgleichens oder Schlussfolgerns beschrieben werden. Ein Konzept, das für eine zutreffende Identifikation einer primären Erfahrung auf sekundäre Erfahrungen rekurriert, liefe auf eine Regress-Problematik hinaus: erfolgt die Identifikation sekundärer Erfahrungen durch tertiäre Erfahrungen? Identifikationen von Erfahrungen und Vorstellungen müssen wir uns stattdessen als Fähigkeiten bzw. eine Praxis denken, die aus sich heraus die Identifikationsleistungen vollbringt.

kann er sich ein Karminrot vorstellen? Paul kann keinerlei Erfahrungen von Rot erinnern. Gleichwohl kennt Paul Farberfahrungen.[14] Er befindet sich, was die Aussicht auf Vorstellbarkeit betrifft, als Farbenblinder in einer besseren Position als eine Person ohne Sehvermögen. Die Ausgangslage ist ebenfalls besser, als wenn er die Aufgabe gestellt bekäme, sich die „echolotartige" Erfahrung einer Fledermaus vorstellen zu müssen – eine Aufgabe die für uns Menschen als Gattung sehr viel schwieriger erscheint. Und dennoch glaube ich, dass Paul keine echte Vorstellung von einem karminrot entwickeln kann, denn die Differenz zu seinem neuen Vorstellungsvermögen in Bezug auf rot und grün ist nach seiner Operation signifikant. Erst wenn die entsprechende Bekanntschaft vorliegt, ist die Vorstellungsfähigkeit so ausgebildet, dass es berechtigt scheint, von einem phänomenalen Wissen zu sprechen. Der Wissenszuwachs ist auf der Ebene einer nun zureichend entwickelten Fähigkeit zur Imagination der Farberfahrungen von rot und grün zu verorten. Der Grundgedanke von Mellors Fähigkeits- oder Knowing-How Hypothese in Bezug auf phänomenales Wissen sollte mit den bisherigen Ausführungen deutlich geworden sein, und meine Erweiterung durch eine Baustein- bzw. Modulierungs-Hypothese soll die stetige Verbindung zum Wissen durch Bekanntschaft unterstreichen. Die Quintessenz von Mellors Ansatz liegt darin, dass Fähigkeiten als Grundpfeiler des phänomenalen Wissens einen anderen Status haben als Formen des propositionalen Wissens, die auf Sachverhalte in der Welt bezogen sind und durch Wahrheitsbedingungen

---

14 Es ist eine offene Frage, ob Farbenblinde (Rot/Grün-Blindheit) unseren normalen Farbraum in einer reduzierten Weise sehen (reduction view), also die Dinge für sie gelb und blau aber nicht rot und grün aussehen, oder ob sie andere Farben sehen und das, was sie sehen mit unserem Farbraum inkommensurabel ist (alien view). Illustrationen, die Normalsichtigen die Farbwelt eines Farbenblinden vorstellen und die sich an vielen Orten im Internet finden, sind Ausdruck der reduction view. Siehe auch Viénot (1995); Brettel u. a. (1997). Da Dichromaten nicht in der Lage sind ein reines Gelb oder ein reines Blau zu sehen, weil die Redeweise von einer reinen Farbe die Möglichkeit der Beimischung eines anderen Farbtons impliziert, ist es vor diesem Hintergrund angemessen, ihre Farberfahrungen nicht als gelb oder blau, sondern als gelblich oder bläulich zu beschreiben. Mit der Überlegung, dass der eingeschränkte Farbraum von Dichromaten auch das Konzept von „gelb" und „blau" zu „gelblich" und „bläulich" verändert, verschmelzen auch reduction und alien view: „Yellownishness is not an *entirely* alien hue – something is yellowish if it is either yellowish-red, or orange, or yellow, or greenish-yellow, or yellowish-green. But it is alien*ish*: normal trichromats never see this hue without seeing more determinate hues like orange and yellow." Byrne u. Hilbert (2007), 32.

beschrieben werden können. Es gibt im Falle von Fähigkeiten keinen Bezug zu einem Sachverhalt. Es gibt somit auch kein Rätsel, warum sich subjektives Erleben und sein „epistemisch gefasster" Zwilling, das phänomenale Wissen, jeglicher Form eines „Bücherwissens" (insbesondere aber unseren objektiven Wissenschaften) entzieht. Es gibt einfach keine Tatsachen, auf die sich das Bücherwissen bzw. die Wissenschaften beziehen könnten. Es sind keine entsprechenden Fakten als Bezugspunkt vorhanden. Erfahrungen und die Fähigkeit zur Vorstellung von Erfahrungen lassen sich nicht durch sprachlich-propositionale Beschreibungen ersetzen. Dieser Umstand ist auch nicht weiter verwunderlich, denn es ist auch nicht die Aufgabe der Sprache Erfahrungen zu ersetzen und genauso besteht auch keine Notwendigkeit, Erfahrungen durch etwas anderes zu eliminieren. Warum auch? Erfahrungen sind ein natürliches Phänomen und sollten der natürliche Ausgangspunkt einer Konzeption des menschlichen Geistes sein. Oder um es mit den Worten von Hugh Mellor auszudrücken: „For even if there is nothing that experiences are like, there is still nothing like experience."[15] Im Rahmen der von mir vorgeschlagenen Baustein- und Modulations-Hypothese ist Bekanntschaft bzw. Erfahrung die Grundlage für die entsprechenden Imaginationsfähigkeiten bzw. das phänomenale Wissen. Es ist mein Anliegen, im Verlauf meines Essays den fundamentalen Charakter der Erfahrung noch stärker zum Ausdruck zu bringen und ein generisches Bild aufeinander aufbauender Wissensformen zu entwickeln. Bekanntschaft und Knowing-How werden im Rahmen dieses Bildes der Ausgangspunkt der Betrachtung sein.

3. Kritik an der Knowing-how Hypothese

Bevor ich jedoch die Überlegungen Mellors als Plattform für das weitere Vorgehen im Aufsatz verwende, möchte ich eine konträre Position im Blick auf phänomenales Wissen vorstellen. Es handelt sich hierbei um eine subtile Kritik der Knowing-How Hypothese Mellors und ich werde darlegen, welche Aspekte der Kritik gerechtfertigt sind und welche Schlüsse aus den vorgestellten Einwänden zu ziehen sind.

Tim Crane vertritt die Gegenthese zur bislang dargestellten Konzeption Mellors. Er optiert in Bezug auf die oben unterschiedenen Wissensformen für die Alternative C), denn seiner Auffassung nach

---
15 Mellor (1992), 15.

handelt es sich bei Pauls neuem Wissen im Kern um ein propositionales Wissen.[16] Als Begründung verweist er auf Pauls Aussage „ah, so sehen also rot und grün aus". Der Indikativ drückt seiner Ansicht nach eine Proposition aus, die in diesem Falle wahr ist.

Schon der Erscheinungsform des Satzes nach sind Cranes Überlegungen sehr plausibel. Auffällig ist jedoch das Auftreten eines Demonstrativpronomens in Pauls Bemerkung – das „so". Man könnte nun die folgende Überlegung anwenden: Zwar passt sich das Demonstrativpronomen in die Form einer Proposition ein, doch ist es selber nur ein Platzhalter für etwas, das sich einem propositionalen Zugriff entzieht. Man möge Paul auffordern sein neues begrifflich-propositionales Wissen doch zu präzisieren: „Was ist es denn, was Du Neues gelernt hast?" Paul: „Na Rot ist halt *so*." Nachfrage: „Was heißt den so?" Paul: „Na *so* halt!" Offenkundig kann Paul sein neues Wissen nicht sprachlich weiter ausführen. Er muss auf seine Erfahrung verweisen.[17]

Crane sieht das auftretende Demonstrativpronomen als unproblematisch an.[18] Er gesteht auch freimütig zu, dass Paul im Moment seiner Wissenserweiterung *auch* neue Fähigkeiten erworben hat. Entscheidend ist für ihn jedoch, dass Paul letztendlich einen Fortschritt im Geflecht seiner Propositionen erlangt. Mit anderen Worten: Paul lernt etwas Neues über die Welt, nämlich die Art und Weise, wie Rot und Grün einem menschlichen Erfahrungssubjekt erscheinen. Für Crane muss es sich hierbei um mehr als eine Fähigkeit handeln, denn dem neuen Wissen können Wahrheitswerte zugewiesen werden. Crane verweist in diesem Zusammenhang darauf, dass wir ausgehend von dem Satz „So sieht Rot aus" weitere Überlegungen im Rahmen eines Bedingungssatzes anstellen können.

„Wenn Rot so aussieht, dann sieht es entweder auch für Hunde so aus oder nicht." [Es] handelt […] sich um einen Bedingungssatz der Form „Wenn *p*,

---

16 Vgl. Crane (2007), 162 ff. Ich übertrage T. Cranes Überlegungen zum Fall von Mary auf das Beispiel von Paul.
17 Propositionen sind in ihrem Wesen sprachlich. Zwar kann eine Proposition durch unterschiedliche (beispielsweise grammatisch verschiedene) Sätze ausgedrückt werden. Dennoch muss es möglich sein, sie sprachlich auszudrücken.
18 „All diese Überlegungen setzen voraus, dass ein Satz mit einem Demonstrativpronomen („so") eine Proposition ausdrücken kann. Diese Annahme ist jedoch harmlos und dürfte von allen Teilnehmern der Debatte akzeptiert werden." Crane (2007), 162.

dann *q*". Die Substitute für *p* und *q* sind Träger von Wahrheitswerten und deshalb mögliche Objekte propositionalen Wissens.[19]

Auch wenn das „so" nicht weiter sprachlich umschrieben werden kann, ist es dennoch möglich, entsprechende Wahrheitswerte zuzuweisen. Das „so" fungiert dabei als ein Platzhalter für eine besondere Erfahrung. Und sobald Erfüllungsbedingungen vorliegen und spezifiziert werden muss, was auf der Seite der Welt einzutreten hat, damit ein geistiger Zustand erfüllt ist, bewegen wir uns im Reich des Propositionalen. Dass eine normalsichtige Person im Unterschied zu Paul vor seiner Operation über die Fähigkeit verfügt, sich Rot und Grün vorstellen zu können – eine Fähigkeit, die auf einer Bekanntschaft mit Rot und Grün fußt, ist für Crane nicht weiter relevant.

> Der springende Punkt besteht ja nicht darin, dass man bestimmte Fähigkeiten erwirbt, wenn man weiß, *wie* etwas ist, sondern darin, dass man dadurch, dass man weiß, wie etwas ist, zugleich auch weiß, *dass bestimmte Dinge der Fall sind*. Das ist das propositionale Wissen, das der Sehende hat und das dem Blinden fehlt, gleichgültig welche Fähigkeiten sonst noch im Spiel sein mögen.[20]

Soweit die zunächst überzeugende Argumentation Cranes, dass es sich beim Wissenszuwachs Pauls um eine Form von propositionalem Wissen handeln muss. Ich glaube, dass die Angelegenheit weniger eindeutig ist, als es auf den ersten Blick den Anschein hat. Zwar gebe ich Crane Recht, dass Pauls Aussage, als Ganze betrachtet, Ausdruck eines propositionalen Wissens ist. Dennoch bleiben an dieser Stelle im Hinblick auf das Beispiel von Paul zumindest zwei Fragen offen:

1. Ist der Bedingungssatz mit der Form „wenn p, dann q" bereits vor Pauls „Bekanntschaft" (dem neuen „phänomenalen" Wissen) gegeben?

und

2. Welche Rolle spielt das, was für Paul wirklich neu ist, für den Bedingungssatz mit der Form „wenn p, dann q"?

Beide Fragen zielen darauf ab, die propositionale Aussage Pauls „so sieht also rot aus" als ein Amalgam zu betrachten. Ich habe den Eindruck, dass in der Bemerkung Pauls verschiedene Wissens-Komponenten vereinigt wurden und dass die Frage nach dem Charakter des neuen Wissens aus

---

19 Crane (2007), 163. Crane folgt an dieser Stelle Überlegungen von Brian Loar. Vgl. Loar (1997).
20 Crane (2007), 165.

diesem Grund differenziert erfolgen sollte. Auch Crane geht – wie wir gesehen haben – davon aus, dass propositionales Wissen und (nicht-propositionale) Fähigkeiten[21] beidermaßen im Falle von Pauls Lernprozess involviert sind. Er beschreibt jedoch nicht das genaue Zusammenwirken dieser propositionalen und nicht-propositionalen Komponenten und legt sich meiner Ansicht nach zu früh darauf fest, die Aussage Pauls als die zentrale Instanz seines Wissenszuwachses zu betrachten und (zutreffend) als propositional zu charakterisieren.

Ich beginne mit der zweiten Frage. Den Bedingungssatz der Form „wenn p, dann q" konnte Paul bereits vor seiner Augenoperation formulieren und mit entsprechenden Erfüllungsbedingungen versehen. Er hatte die direkte Anschauung verschiedener Farben und ihm war klar, dass normalsichtige Menschen in der gleichen Art und Weise über Rot- und Grünwahrnehmungen verfügen. Der Gedanke „wenn Rot für X in einer bestimmten Art und Weise aussieht, dann sieht es vielleicht auch für Y in dieser Art und Weise aus" war ihm bereits vertraut. Man beachte, dass an die Stelle des „so" der Ausdruck „bestimmte Art und Weise" getreten ist. Die Antwort auf die Frage nach dem Bedingungssatz lautet also: der Bedingungssatz ist unabhängig vom neuen Wissen.

Nun zur ersten Frage. Was passiert nach der Augenoperation? An die Stelle der abstrakten „Art und Weise" tritt eine spezifische Erfahrung. Paul macht Bekanntschaft mit der Farbe Rot. Sind damit neue, zusätzliche Wahrheitsbedingungen aufgetreten? Ich glaube, dass die propositionale Form, die Crane bei Paul gegeben sieht, ebenfalls von Pauls epistemischem Zuwachs unabhängig ist. Die grundlegenden Fähigkeiten und Orientierungsleistungen, die Paul zuvor fehlten und die das „Wissen" durch Bekanntschaft ausmachen präsentieren sich nicht von sich heraus im propositionalen Gewande.

Ich stimme Crane zu, dass die Aussage Pauls „so sehen also rot und grün aus", als Proposition auftritt und letztendlich auch ein propositionales Wissen gegeben ist. Allerdings möchte ich auf den Punkt hinaus, dass Pauls Wissenserwerb in erster Linie auf nicht-propositionalen Komponenten beruhen könnte. Obwohl Pauls neue Erfahrungen in dem Sinne einen Gehalt haben müssen, weil sie sich von anderen Erfahrungen unterscheiden, erscheinen sie mir zu fundamental, um Wahrheitsbedingungen auf sie abzubilden. Stattdessen könnte eine Option darin bestehen, von der Existenz nicht-propositionaler Fähigkeiten auszuge-

---

21 Ich setze an diesem Punkt voraus, dass Fähigkeiten nicht als Propositionen angesehen werden können.

hen, welche bereit stehen, um propositionales Wissen herauszubilden. Die Erfahrung wird durch Begriffe und Erfüllungsbedingungen strukturiert, aber sie geht nicht vollständig in Begriffen und Erfüllungsbedingungen auf. Sie muss als die Basis betrachtet werden vor der sich Erfüllungsbedingungen und Begriffe entwickeln können. Auch wenn zugestanden wird, dass in der Aussage „so sieht also rot aus" Fähigkeiten und propositionales Wissen untrennbar miteinander verschmolzen sind, besteht der Kern von Pauls *neuem* Wissen möglicherweise nicht in einer Proposition. Es hat vor diesem Hintergrund den Anschein, dass Mellors Fähigkeitshypothese der Eigenart des Wissenszuwachses bei Paul *eher* gerecht wird.

4. Ein Rückfall in den Mythos vom Gegebenen?

Ich drücke mich bewusst vorsichtig aus, denn die Vorstellung von Fähigkeiten, die keine Proposition ausdrücken und sich sprachlich nicht vollständig erfassen lassen, sieht sich rasch dem Einwand ausgesetzt, eine Variante des Mythos vom Gegebenen zu sein.[22] Problematisch erscheint der Ansatz vor allem dann, wenn die Annahme dieser Fähigkeiten zu einer Konzeption von „nicht-begrifflichen Gehalten" überleitet. Und das aus folgenden Gründen: Wenn Erfahrung als Instanz für Rechtfertigungen und Begründungen zur Verfügung stehen soll, dann muss sie auch, um als Eintrittskarte in das Reich der Gründe zu fungieren, eine begriffliche Strukturierung mit sich bringen. Es kann keine unstrukturierte nicht-begriffliche Erfahrung geben, die für ein System von Überzeugungen von Relevanz sein kann (das so genannte Gegebene). Vor dem Hintergrund dieses Problemszenarios sucht John McDowell einen Ausweg aus dem folgendem Dilemma: Einerseits droht mit der Annahme eines propositionalen und kohärenten Systems von Überzeugungen der Kontakt zur Welt verloren zu gehen. Die Welt kann nicht über das Einfallstor einer nicht-begrifflichen Erfahrung Einfluss auf das inferentielle begriffliche System nehmen und dieses ggf. korrigieren. Anderseits sind alle Versuche eine Wirkung von bloßen (nicht-begrifflichen) Empfindungen auf das Geflecht von Überzeugungen zu konstruieren nichts anderes als ein Rückfall in den Mythos vom Gegebenen. McDowells Auflösung des Dilemmas besteht darin, Erfahrung als immer

---

22 Und wer möchte schon hinter Sellars Kritik am Empirismus zurückfallen? Vgl. Sellars (1999).

schon begrifflich verfasst anzunehmen.²³ Die Erfahrung schiebt sich dabei nicht zwischen Geist und Welt. Wir Menschen lernen mit unserer Erfahrung, ohne den Umweg über innere Repräsentationen, die Welt kennen und diese Welt wird begrifflich gehaltvoll präsentiert, weil sinnliche Wahrnehmung ein Wahrnehmen von etwas als etwas einschließt.

Befürworter eines nichtbegrifflichen Gehalts der Erfahrung haben dem Konzeptionalismus entgegengehalten, dass besonders feine Nuancen („Feinkörnigkeit") in den Farbschattierungen zwar in der Wahrnehmung unterschieden werden können, unsere menschlichen Fähigkeiten der Identifikation und Re-identifikation in Situationen eines zeitlichen Nacheinanders jedoch übersteigen. Gemeint ist damit der folgende empirische Sachverhalt: Wir können einen marginalen Farbunterschied nur dann erkennen, wenn uns die betreffenden Farben zugleich vorgelegt werden. Werden die Farbtöne nacheinander präsentiert, so ist ein Unterschied nicht erfahrbar.²⁴ Dieser Umstand könnte auch als Fingerzeig begriffen werden, dass die „etwas-als-etwas"-Struktur visueller Erfahrung nicht automatisch begrifflich interpretiert werden muss. Möglicherweise gibt es eine Lesart für Strukturierungsleistungen in der Wahrnehmung, bei der nicht auf Begriffe rekuriert werden muss – beispielsweise eine Strukturierung aufgrund von phänomenalen Farbunterschieden. Darüber hinaus wird dem Bestreben dem Mythos vom Gegebenen zu entkommen die Intuition entgegengehalten, dass Begriffe nicht angeboren sind, sondern sich entwickeln. Auf welcher Basis kann der Begriffserwerb erfolgen, wenn die Erfahrung zur Ausübung dieser Rolle nicht mehr zur Verfügung steht, weil sie immer schon begrifflich gedacht werden muss?

In seiner Erwiderung auf das Argument der Feinkörnigkeit hat McDowell auf Demonstrativpronomen verwiesen, wie sie auch in unserem Beispiel von Paul aufgetreten sind. Seiner Ansicht nach „können wir einem Begriff sprachlichen Ausdruck verschaffen, welcher genauso feinkörnig wie die Erfahrung selbst ist, indem wir eine Wendung wie „diese Tönung" äußern, wobei sich das Demonstrativum der Gegenwart des Musters bedient."²⁵ Doch es bestehen gleich mehrere Schwierigkeiten, mit denen Konzeptualisten zu kämpfen haben, wenn sie auf die Rolle der Demonstrativa verweisen um dem Argument von der Feinkörnigkeit der Erfahrung zu begegnen:

---

23 McDowell (1998).
24 Vgl. Raffman (1999).
25 McDowell (1998), 81.

1. Erstens müssen sie sich mit einem Begriff von „begrifflich" begnügen, der nicht mehr die Fähigkeiten der Identifikation und Reidentifikation im Falle zeitlich nacheinander vor Augen geführter Eigenschaften voraussetzt. Dies ist eine Konsequenz aus dem oben beschriebenen empirischen Sachverhalt (die Natur hätte es auch anders einrichten können) unserer „Wahrnehmungsbeschränkung", mehr Farbtöne bei gleichzeitiger Präsentation unterscheiden zu können als in einem Nacheinander identifizieren zu können.

2. Die Individuierung des Gehaltes erfolgt zweitens über die Gegenwart eines Farbmusters, auf die das Demonstrativum verweist. Doch entgegen McDowells Konzeption von Erfahrung, in der die Rezeptivität der Anschauung und die Spontaneität des Verstandes so verschmolzen sind, dass „von Anfang an kein Abstand zwischen den begrifflichen Inhalten, die sich am nächsten zu den Einwirkungen der externen Realität befinden, und diesen Einwirkungen selbst [herrscht]"[26], scheint es im Falle der Farben eine deutliche Trennung zwischen den Demonstrativa wie „so" oder „dieses" und einem Farbmuster zu geben.[27]

3. Schließlich kommen wir zur Thematik des Begriffserwerbs zurück, der für eine konzeptualistische Position, die keinen Abstand zwischen Begriffen und den sinnlichen Einwirkungen einer externen Welt zulassen möchte, auf natürliche Weise ein Problem darstellt. Wenn der Begriffserwerb im Rahmen einer begrifflich-propositionalen Vorstellung von Erfahrung überhaupt thematisiert wird, dann kann dies nur, überspitzt formuliert, in der Form eines großen Gongschlages geschehen, der an einem bestimmten Punkt in der kindlichen Entwicklung einsetzt und auf wundersame Weise kausale Abläufe (Wirkungen einer Welt auf ein

---

26 McDowell (1998), 33.
27 Mit dem Beispiel von Paul habe ich versucht die Vorstellung nahe zu legen, dass Wissen durch Bekanntschaft und ein entsprechendes propositionales Wissen verschiedenen Ebenen zugewiesen werden können. Die Erfüllungsbedingungen des propositionalen Wissens sind – zumindest in diesem Spezialfall – unabhängig von der Fähigkeit, die Paul erwirbt. Das „so" im Ausdruck „so sieht also rot aus" bewegt sich, wenn man so will, auf einer Meta-Ebene. Natürlich können Demonstrativa mit ihrer Funktion, auf einen Referenten zu verweisen, die Aufmerksamkeit eines Betrachters lenken und aus der Fülle eines visuellen Inputs eine Strukturierungsleistung vollbringen. Dazu ist es jedoch erforderlich, dass der Betrachter die Funktionsweise der Demonstrativa beherrscht. Bei Kleinkindern ist das anfänglich noch nicht der Fall (auch wenn Zeigehandlungen zu den sehr frühen und basalen Sprachspielen gehören) und dennoch erscheint es seltsam diesen Kindern absprechen zu wollen, dass sie ihre Erfahrung strukturieren und ihre Aufmerksamkeit auf Farben lenken können.

Sinnessystem) in einem Zug in eine begrifflich strukturierte Erfahrung, ein holistisch geschlossenes Reich der Gründe transformiert. Wer angesichts dieser Schwierigkeiten einen nichtbegrifflichen Gehalt der Erfahrung propagiert, droht wieder in eine gefährliche Nähe zum Mythos vom Gegebenen zu geraten. Ein solcher Rückfall wäre beispielsweise gegeben, wenn man davon ausginge, dass Kleinkinder mit dem Öffnen ihrer Augen „Ideen" oder moderner formuliert „mentale Repräsentationen" erwerben und in einem zweiten Schritt diese inneren Entitäten mit konventionalisierten Etiketten in Verbindung bringen und in den öffentlichen Raum der Sprache überführen. Die Welt wäre ohne Einsatz von Begriffen bereits eingeteilt. Doch wie sollen sich Strukturen in der Mannigfaltigkeit des sinnlichen Inputs einfach so herausbilden? Es besteht eine grundlegende Kluft zwischen dem normativen oder sinnhaften Bereich unserer alltäglichen Welterfahrung und den sinnlichen Reizen als „bloß" naturwissenschaftlich beschreibbaren Abläufen in der Welt.

Die Herausforderung liegt also darin, eine Alternative zum eben grob skizzierten Mentalismus der Ideen oder Repräsentationen auf der einen und dem Konzeptionalismus im Stile McDowells auf der anderen Seite zu finden. Und ein aussichtsreicher Kandidat eines solchen Projektes ist der Verweis auf einfache Sinnzusammenhänge, die zwar noch nicht sprachlicher Art sind, aber sich von bloß kausalen Beschreibungen abheben und eine basale Sphäre des Normativen herausbilden, die als ein kulturelles Fundament für den Erwerb konventioneller Begriffe fungieren kann. Zu denken ist in erster Linie an primitive Handlungsmuster.[28] In letzter Konsequenz nimmt eine genealogische Betrachtung jedoch auch Fähigkeiten in den Blick, die wiederum die Bedingung der Möglichkeit des Erwerbs einfacher Handlungsmuster sind. Das Unterscheiden und Sich-Vorstellen-Können von Farben ist eine solche Fähigkeit, die

---

28 In seinem Projekt eine pragmatisch-genealogische Philosophie der Sprache in Anlehnung an Überlegungen des späten Wittgensteins und des Entwicklungspsychologen Jerome Bruner zu entwickeln, lenkt Stefan Tolksdorf die Aufmerksamkeit auf vorsprachliche Formen des Sinnvollen. Im Kern steht dabei ein erweiterter Handlungsbegriff, der keine propositionalen Wünsche und Überzeugungen auf Seiten des handelnden Subjekts impliziert. „Das Kind *spielt*, d. h., es interagiert zielorientiert mit seiner personalen und nicht-personalen Umwelt. Unter diesen Umständen können wir sagen: Es treten signifikante Anfangs- und Folgesequenzen zwischen Kind und Erwachsenem auf, das Kind interagiert mit den Eltern, es wird so zu einem Teil des *Handlungszusammenhanges, wenngleich wir von propositionalen Zuschreibungen nicht sprechen sollten*. Mit anderen Worten: *Der Raum des Handelns* fällt nicht mit dem *Raum der Gründe* zusammen." Tolksdorf (2011), 121.

sowohl Voraussetzung für einfache Handlungen wie das kindliche Sortieren bunter Bausteine als auch für den Erwerb unserer konventionellen Farbausdrücke ist. Fähigkeiten dieser Art bewegen sich an der Grenze zwischen Abläufen in der Welt und der Sphäre des Normativen. Sie erfüllen Funktionen die für sich betrachtet noch nicht sinnstiftend sind. Werden sie jedoch in Handlungskontexte eingebunden so sind sie Bedingung und Nährboden für die Ausbildung einfacher Sinnstrukturen.

5. Zur Semantik von „Erfahrung ist immer schon begrifflich"

Dass sich in der Auseinandersetzung um den begrifflichen oder möglicherweise auch nicht-begrifflichen Gehalt von Erfahrung zumindest die gemäßigten Positionen der zwei verschiedenen Lager von Konzeptualisten und Mentalisten nicht zwangsläufig ausschließen wird auch deutlich, wenn wir einen Schritt zurück treten und die begrifflichen Voraussetzungen von McDowells Aussage „Erfahrung ist immer schon begrifflich" selber thematisieren. In Frage steht also das von McDowell und anderen Konzeptionalisten in Anspruch genommene Verständnis von ‚*Erfahrung*', ‚*immer schon*' und ‚*begrifflich*'.

I. „*Erfahrung ist immer schon begrifflich.*" Beginnen wir mit dem Erfahrungsbegriff: In der Philosophie steht es uns ein Stück weit frei Termini festzulegen. Entscheidend für die jeweilige Festsetzung sind Zweckgesichtspunkte. Ein solcher Gesichtspunkt könnte darin bestehen, die Rede von Erfahrung mit der Möglichkeit zusammen zu bringen, dass Überzeugungen durch visuelle Erfahrungen gestützt werden können. Ich bin beispielsweise der Überzeugung, dass ein blauer Kugelschreiber vor mir liegt, weil ich diesen Kugelschreiber sehe. Bloße Sinnesdaten oder alle Kausalketten, die irgendwo in meinem visuellen System enden, können meine Annahme über die Welt nicht in der gleichen Weise unterstützen. Es ist mit dieser Einstellung folgerichtig und konsequent, von Erfahrung nur noch zu sprechen, wenn ausgehend von der Erfahrung ein Zusammenhang zum System der Überzeugungen hergestellt werden kann. *So konzipiert* ist Erfahrung immer schon begrifflich (unter dem Vorbehalt, dass wir noch zu klären haben, in welchem Sinne begrifflich verwendet wird…). Es mag aber Kontexte geben in denen wir den Erfahrungsbegriff nicht nur für Zusammenhänge einer Rechtfertigung reservieren.[29]

---

29 Ein philosophischer Zweckgesichtspunkt könnte darin bestehen philosophische Termini auf paradigmatische Kontexte zurückzuführen, in denen wir die Begriffe

II. „Erfahrung ist *immer schon* begrifflich." Auch bezüglich der Formulierung „immer schon" gibt es interpretatorischen Spielraum. Impliziert der Erfahrungsbegriff begrifflich-logisch einen konzeptuellen Zugriff oder ist die menschliche Erfahrung zeitlich betrachtet immer schon begrifflich. In zeitlicher Hinsicht kommen wir entweder mit Begriffen auf die Welt oder haben ab einem bestimmten Punkt (schlagartig? Siehe oben: Kritikpunkt 3.) Erfahrungen. Es liegt auf der Hand, dass sich McDowell in seinem methodischen Selbstverständnis mit dem begrifflich-logischen Zugang identifiziert. Die Analyse begrifflicher Zusammenhänge gilt als das methodische Merkmal der Philosophie. Möglicherweise lassen sich jedoch zwischen der begrifflichen und historischen Zugangsweise auch Zusammenhänge aufweisen. Mit einer genealogischen Perspektive interessieren wir uns für die genetische Überlegung, dass Begriffe und Erfüllungsbedingungen erworben werden. Der Ausdruck ‚Genese' ist hierbei aber nicht in einem geschichtlich-empirischen Sinne zu verstehen. Auch wenn in der philosophischen Tradition bewusst zwischen Genese und Geltung unterschieden wird, so gibt es ein logisches Verständnis von Genese, das eine Entwicklungslinie nachzeichnet, indem es begründet darüber Auskunft gibt, welche Prozesse und Zustände auf anderen (logisch) aufbauen. Die Logik unserer Sprachspiele hängt in diesem Sinne mit den Kontexten zusammen, in denen sie sich entwickelt haben. Ich werde im nächsten Abschnitt versuchen eine genealogische Perspektive hinsichtlich der Erfüllungsbedingungen von Farbbegriffen zu entwickeln.

III. „Erfahrung ist immer schon *begrifflich.*" Schließlich weist auch der Begriff ‚begrifflich' eine Mehrdeutigkeit auf. In einem ersten Sinne handelt es sich bei Begriffen um Strukturierungsleistungen. Eine Erfahrung ist strukturiert, d.h. sie ist abgegrenzt. Sie ist die Erfahrung von etwas, andernfalls hätte ein Erfahrungssubjekt „alles" und somit „nichts". Diese Form von Strukturierung kann jedoch bereits auf einer subpersonalen Ebene eines visuellen Systems erfolgen. Auch die visuellen Zustände von Kleinkindern und höheren Säugetieren hätten im hier verwendeten Paradigma der Kognitionswissenschaften eine Struktur und mithin einen begrifflichen Gehalt.[30] Ein ambitionierterer Begriff von

---

erlernt haben. Eine Klasse paradigmatischer Fälle des Ausdrucks „Erfahrung" weist eine Nähe zu Ausdrücken wie „Bewusstsein", „Erleben" oder „Geist" auf. In diesem Sinne verfügen auch Kleinkinder und höhere Säugetiere im Unterschied zu Tischen, Stühlen und Steinen über Erfahrungen.

30 Vgl. Evans (2002).

‚begrifflich' besteht im Sinne einer „Verwendung konventioneller Ausdrücke". Wenn sich McDowell an einem solchen Konzept von ‚begrifflich' orientiert, dann stellen feinkörnige Farbschattierungen eine echte Herausforderung für seine Konzeptualisierungs-These der Erfahrung dar. McDowells Hinweis auf Demonstrativpronomen ist ein Versuch das Kriterium der Identifikation und Re-Identifikation von Objekten und Eigenschaften zu unterlaufen. Demonstrativa sollen den Job ausführen auch die Farbschattierungen zu verbegrifflichen und damit in das Reich der Gründe zu integrieren. Doch überzeugt diese Strategie? Reicht es aus, die Farbmuster in ein Begriffssystem einzubetten oder müssen sie darüber hinaus auch begrifflich erfasst werden? Für den Zweck, das sinnliche Material für Rechtfertigungszusammenhänge aufzubereiten reichen Demonstrativa aus und unter Verwendung eines durch diesen Zweck angeleiteten Erfahrungsbegriffs gilt nur dasjenige als kognitiv relevant, was für eine Rechtfertigung zur Verfügung steht. Auf der anderen Seite bleibt mit dem Verweis auf die Einbettung der Farbmuster eine Eigenständigkeit der Anschauung bestehen, die gegen den hohen Anspruch einer nicht mehr trennbaren Verzahnung von Anschauung und Begrifflichkeit spricht. Es gilt zu betonen, dass mit dem Hinweis auf Demonstrativpronomen nicht nur Anschauungsmaterial verbegrifflicht, sondern zugleich begriffliche Komponenten versinnlicht werden.[31] Der Spielraum, in welchem Sinne von Erfahrung und Begriff die Rede ist bleibt vor dem Hintergrund der angestellten Überlegungen groß und bietet genügend Platz, um konzeptualistische und „mentalistische" Intuitionen gleichermaßen plausibel zu vertreten. Ein generisch-logisches Bild versucht diesem Umstand Rechnung zu tragen. Innerhalb dieses Bildes kann beispielsweise gefragt werden wie weit der Bereich des Normativen „hinabreicht" und an welchen Strukturen er ansetzt. Dabei werden auch grundlegende Prozesse in den Blick genommen, die Rechtfertigung nicht direkt zum Thema haben gleichwohl aber als Voraussetzung des gesamten menschlichen kognitiven Haushalts anzusehen sind. Gegenüber diesen Phänomenen wäre es aus diesem Grund vorschnell einen pauschalen Vorwurf eines Rückfalls in den Mythos vom Gegebenen zu adressieren.

Das Beispiel Pauls handelt von einer erwachsenen Person, nicht von einem Kleinkind und scheint deshalb zur Verfolgung genealogischer Überlegungen ungeeignet. Doch eine spannende Pointe des Beispiels besteht gerade in der Umkehrung von generisch „normalen" Verhält-

---

31 Vgl. Lauer (2010).

nissen: Vom Subjekt Paul aus betrachtet lag bereits vor der Operation ein zutreffendes kompetentes Sprechen bezüglich der Farben Rot und Grün vor, ohne dass die entsprechenden Erfahrungen gegeben waren. In diesem speziellen Falle sind also sprachliche Ebene und Erfahrungsebene, zumindest wenn wir lediglich das Subjekt betrachten,[32] voneinander getrennt, auch wenn normalerweise das Sprechen über Farben und das Erfahren von Farben zusammen auftreten. Während unter normalen Umständen Kinder das öffentliche Sprachspiel der Farben im Zusammenhang mit Farberfahrungen erlernen, ist im ungewöhnlichen Fall von Paul im Hinblick auf die Farben Rot und Grün zuerst das Sprachspiel da und erst sehr spät treten die entsprechenden Farberfahrungen hinzu. Das Beispiel von Paul weist also zwei Bereiche des Wissens – Bekanntschaft sowie die Fähigkeiten des Identifizierens und Vorstellens auf der einen und das propositionale Wissen auf der anderen Seite – als getrennt voneinander auf, die im Normalfall nicht nur gemeinsam gegeben, sondern aufeinander bezogen sind.

Ich möchte im Folgenden wieder auf die Frage nach dem Status der Erfüllungsbedingungen im Rahmen des Beispiels von Paul zurückkommen. Der Fokus auf Erfüllungsbedingungen wird mir die Gelegenheit geben, Mellors Idee, Fähigkeiten mit dem phänomenalen Wissen zu identifizieren, mit Searles Konzeption des Hintergrundes zusammenzubringen.[33]

6. Searles Hintergrund

Erfüllungsbedingungen nehmen im Rahmen von John Searles philosophischen Überlegungen eine bedeutende Stellung ein. Sie spielen sogar die Hauptrolle in Searles Versuch, das Phänomen der Intentionalität zu

---

32 Zu beachten ist allerdings, dass sich diese Möglichkeit nur auf das Subjekt und nicht auf die Sprachgemeinschaft bezieht. Das kompetente Sprechen über Farben setzt normalsichtige Menschen voraus.

33 Ich hatte weiter oben die Position eines Mentalismus als Gegenposition zum Konzeptionalismus McDowells vorgestellt. Die Vorstellung eine fundamentale Ebene geistiger Zustände, die ihre Intentionalität auf die öffentliche sprachliche Ebene überführt wird gemeinhin mit der Position John Searles verbunden. Obwohl sich in seinem Buch Intentionalität entsprechende Textbelege ohne große Mühe finden lassen, möchte ich im folgenden Abschnitt die Aufmerksamkeit auf Überlegungen Searles lenken, die mit dem Beschreiten eines alternativen Weges abseits von Konzeptionalismus und Mentalismus kompatibel sind. Es handelt sich hierbei vor allem um Searles Konzept des Hintergrundes.

erfassen bzw. die schillernde Rede von Repräsentation auf ein handhabbares Maß herunterzubrechen.

> Eine Überzeugung ist eine Repräsentation – das heißt einfach: sie hat einen propositionalen Gehalt und einen psychischen Modus, ihr propositionaler Gehalt legt eine Menge von Erfüllungsbedingungen (unter gewissen Aspekten) fest, ihr psychischer Modus legt eine Ausrichtung ihres propositionalen Gehalts fest [...] Erfüllungsbedingungen sind diejenigen [...] Bedingungen, die bestehen müssen, damit der Zustand erfüllt sein kann.[34]

Auf den Ausdruck „Repräsentation" ließe sich Searles Auffassung nach durchaus verzichten. Was übrig bliebe ist eine Konstellation, in der immer schon zwei Komponenten involviert sind: die Seite des intentionalen Zustands und die Seite der Welt. Die jeweiligen Erfüllungsbedingungen beziehen diese beiden Komponenten aufeinander und es ist möglich, sie auf beiden Seiten zu verorten. „Der Ausdruck „Erfüllungsbedingungen" hat die geläufige Vorgang/Ergebnis-Mehrdeutigkeit: er kann die *Forderung* bedeuten, wie auch *das, was gefordert ist*."[35] Egal ob wir von Repräsentationen, geistigen Zuständen oder Intentionalität sprechen (oder diese Redeweise aufgeben wollen) – Erfüllungsbedingungen sind stets das zentrale Element dieser Konzepte.

Bemerkenswert an den Ausführungen Searles ist der Umstand, dass er von einem propositionalen Gehalt ausgeht, der die Erfüllungsbedingungen festlegt. Mein Verdacht ist an dieser Stelle, dass es Searle wichtig ist, dass die Erfüllungsbedingungen klar umgrenzt sind. Diese Funktion kann ein Sachverhalt/eine Proposition einnehmen, auf den bzw. die hin ein geistiger Zustand ausgerichtet ist.[36] Darüber hinaus tappen wir in eine Art Propositions- oder Sprach-Falle, wenn wir angeben wollen, worauf beispielsweise ein Wahrnehmungszustand gerichtet ist. Welcher Art die geistigen Gehalte im Falle einer Wahrnehmung sind, bleibt auch im Hinblick auf die Position Searles eine vollkommen offene Frage, zu der ich gleich noch Stellung beziehen werde.

---

34 Searle (1987), 29.
35 Ebd.
36 Für die Ausrichtung und somit die Art und Weise, wie die Erfüllungsbedingungen zu lesen sind (hat sich die Welt z. B. nach dem geistigen Zustand zu richten oder umgekehrt) ist in Searles Ansatz der Modus zuständig. Ich gehe auf dieses Konzept sowie weitere Bestandteile des Searleschen „Apparatus" wie die Verursachungsrichtung oder der Selbstbezug der intentionalen Komponente nicht weiter ein, sondern konzentriere mich auf den Status der Erfüllungsbedingungen.

Bezüglich der Problematik der Festlegung der für einen intentionalen Zustand charakteristischen Erfüllungsbedingungen vertritt Searle einen Holismus: Die Umgrenzung der Erfüllungsbedingungen erfolgt nicht „atomistisch", einzig und allein aus dem aktuell vorliegenden Zustand heraus. Vielmehr werden Erfüllungsbedingungen jeweils aus einem ganzen Geflecht von intentionalen Zuständen – vor allem auch unter Einbeziehung impliziter, also nicht-aktual gegebener Komponenten – zugeschrieben. Das Geflecht der intentionalen Zustände nennt Searle das Netzwerk intentionaler Zustände.

Darüber hinaus unterscheidet er von diesem Netzwerk Komponenten, die einen so fundamentalen Charakter aufweisen, dass es etwas Irritierendes hat, ihnen einen propositionalen Gehalt zuzusprechen. Der Widerstand der Tastatur meines Computers ist beispielsweise konstitutiv für mein Vorhaben einen Text zu schreiben. Gleichwohl erscheint es seltsam, mir eine Überzeugung mit dem Gehalt zuzuschreiben „dass die Tastatur den Bewegungen meiner Finger Widerstand leistet", auch wenn ich sehr verwundert wäre, wenn es sich nicht so verhielte. Die Aussage ist auf einer so grundlegenden Ebene angesiedelt, dass es zweckmäßiger erscheint, von einer „Praxis des Umgangs mit einem Computer" zu sprechen. Searle fasst „Hintergrund"-Phänomene dieser Art als nicht-repräsentationale geistige Fähigkeiten auf, welche die Bedingung der Möglichkeit von Repräsentation sind.

> Nur vor einem Hintergrund von Fähigkeiten, die selbst keine intentionalen Zustände sind, haben intentionale Zustände ihre Erfüllungsbedingungen und sind mithin erst dadurch die Zustände, die sie sind. Um jetzt die intentionalen Zustände haben zu können, die ich habe, muss ich gewisse Arten von Know-How haben: ich muß wissen, wie die Dinge sich verhalten, und ich muß wissen, wie man gewisse Sachen macht.[37]

Neben der Differenzierung in ein Wissen „wie Dinge sind" und „wie man etwas macht" unterscheidet Searle zwischen einem tiefen Hintergrund (Fähigkeiten, die Menschen aufgrund ihrer biologischen Ausstattung haben wie z. B. gehen, essen greifen, wahrnehmen, wieder erkennen und vorintentionale Einstellungen gegenüber der Festigkeit von Dingen) und dem lokalen Hintergrund (Kulturtechniken wie Dosen öffnen, aus Gläsern trinken, inklusive unserer vorintentionalen Einstellung gegenüber Autos, Bügeleisen und Smartphones). Schon diese wenigen Beispiele verdeutlichen Umfang und Vielschichtigkeit des Hintergrunds. Auch der Anknüpfungspunkt zu unserer Debatte zwischen

---

37 Searle (1987), 182.

Mellor und Crane liegt nun auf der Hand: die Fähigkeit der Farbwahrnehmung gehört zum „tiefen Hintergrund" und kann als Vermögen gedeutet werden, intentionalen Zuständen ihre charakteristischen Erfüllungsbedingungen überhaupt erst zu verleihen.

Die Aussagen von Searle sind in vielerlei Hinsichten bemerkenswert. Hintergrundfähigkeiten sind nicht-intentional und das heißt nichts anderes, als dass keine Erfüllungsbedingungen, keine den Fähigkeiten entsprechenden propositionale Gehalte angegeben werden können. Insbesondere in Bezug auf diesen letzten Punkt lohnt es sich, einen Schritt zurück zu treten und sich zu fragen: verhält es sich wirklich so?

Auch basale Fähigkeiten können in ihrer Ausübung daneben gehen („wie man etwas macht") und ebenso grundlegende Einstellungen gegenüber der Welt („wie die Dinge sind") enttäuscht werden. Searle sieht diesen Aspekt deutlich.[38] Gleichwohl trennt er diese Form von fundamental *gelingenden* Handlungsvollzügen und *eingelösten* Erwartungen von den eigentlichen Erfüllungsbedingungen bzw. propositionalen Gehalten ab. Der Gedanke, dass den intentionalen Gehalten immer schon Handlungsvollzüge logisch vorausgehen, die selber nicht mehr auf ihre Erfüllungsbedingungen hin analysiert werden können, stützt sich auch auf ein Regressargument:[39]

Wenn es keinen Hintergrund gäbe, hätten wir nur ein großes Geflecht von intentionalen Zuständen vor Augen. Die Zustände verfügten über Erfüllungsbedingungen und spätestens im Zuge ihrer Beschreibung über semantische Gehalte. Woher sollen Erfüllungsbedingungen und Gehalte kommen? Es ist zwar möglich eine Reihe von Repräsentationen zu verfolgen – und in einem solchen Durchgang durch die Repräsentationen verwiese jede Repräsentation auf eine andere und es entstünde ein unendlicher Regress. Diese Konsequenz wäre aber nicht hinzunehmen, weil sie empirisch unmöglich ist: die intellektuelle Kapazität von Menschen ist nun einmal begrenzt. Semantischer Gehalt bzw. Erfüllungsbedingungen wenden sich nicht von alleine an. Selbst wenn Gehalte als schon gegeben angenommen werden, was soll mit ihnen getan werden? Letzten Endes ist eine Praxis, ein Handlungsvollzug erforderlich, der

---

38 Die Überraschung, die bei mir einträte, wenn meine Computertastatur jetzt plötzlich keinen Widerstand mehr leisten würde wiese Searle zufolge darauf hin, „daß wir es hier mit irgend so etwas wie Erfüllungsbedingungen zu tun haben." Searle (1987), 182.

39 Vgl. Searle (1991), 289 ff.

in seiner Anwendung die Gehalte respektive Erfüllungsbedingungen herausbildet.

Wird dieses Argument akzeptiert, so stellen sich jedoch unmittelbar Anschlussfragen: Wenn die Handlungsvollzüge in den Mittelpunkt der Betrachtung rücken, warum handelt es sich bei den Hintergrundfähigkeiten um nicht-repräsentationale *geistige* Fähigkeiten?

Searles Antwort auf diese Frage speist sich aus der Überzeugung, dass das Funktionieren von intentionalen Zuständen unabhängig von der Frage sein muss, ob unsere Überzeugungen wahr sind.[40] Es wäre jederzeit denkmöglich, dass wir nur Gehirne im Tank sind und die Hintergrundfähigkeiten müssen deshalb unabhängig davon sein wie die Dinge „wirklich" sind. Die Unabhängigkeit von einer externen Welt führt Searle dazu, die Hintergrundfähigkeiten dem „Kopf" zuzuordnen. Sie sind keine Merkmale der Welt unabhängig vom Geist.

Es mag seltsam anmuten, Fähigkeiten wie das Skifahren in den Kopf verpflanzen zu wollen, aber ich glaube, dass die Überlegung Searles weniger eigenartig erscheint, wenn sie lediglich als ein Aufruf aufgefasst wird, die in Frage stehenden Fähigkeiten konsequent aus der Ersten-Person-Perspektive zu betrachten. Der Weltkontakt ist mit dieser Einstellung immer schon gegeben, vollkommen unabhängig von der genealogisch „späten" und nicht zu befriedigenden skeptischen Frage, ob es die Außenwelt wirklich gibt. Dies ist nicht nur meine Lesart von Searle, sondern darüber hinaus meiner Ansicht nach der einzige plausible Beweggrund, eine Konzeption zu vertreten, die den Anstrich eines Mentalismus mit sich führt ohne verhängnisvolle Konsequenzen zu implizieren.

Ich möchte die angestellten Überlegungen nun zur Anwendung bringen und zu meiner angekündigten Skizze eines genealogischen Bildes kommen. Wenn wir annehmen, dass ein Kleinkind über eine bestimmte (nicht-repräsentationale) Hintergrundfähigkeit verfügt, dann ist damit auch gesagt, dass noch keine Erfüllungsbedingungen vorliegen. Die Konzepte von Intentionalität und Repräsentation sind – zumindest bei Searle – sinnlogisch eng miteinander verwoben und fußen auf dem Auftreten von Erfüllungsbedingungen. Das Kleinkind sieht eine Farbe ohne über eine Repräsentation zu verfügen bzw. ohne dass Intentionalität vorliegt.[41] Ist diese Folgerung noch akzeptabel? Ich glaube, dass sie zu-

---

40 Vgl. Searle (1991), 290 ff.
41 Wenn wir die Konzepte von Intentionalität und Repräsentationen nicht so eng zusammenbringen, sondern im Unterschied zu Searles Ansatz auch Hinter-

mindest intellektuell zu verkraften ist, wenn wir uns mit dem Bild anfreunden, dass bestimmte kognitive Fähigkeiten auf anderen aufbauen und sich mithin ein komplexes Gebilde von Erfüllungsbedingungen erst entwickelt. Fred Dretske hat für die Auffassung argumentiert, dass sich Wahrnehmung auch nicht-intentional im Sinne eines „simple seeings" verstehen lässt. Sehen kann für Dretske auch nicht epistemisch erfolgen:

> One can see, hear, or feel a yellow station wagon without knowing what a yellow station wagon is. Seeing a yellow station wagon is like being run over by a yellow station wagon. You don't have to know what hit you in order to get hit. You don't have to know what you see in order to see it.[42]

Diese Sichtweise nach der unsere Sinnesorgane einfach befeuert werden und erste Strukturleistungen auf der Ebene eines subpersonalen visuellen Systems erbracht werden, möchte ich zum Startpunkt einer Entwicklungslinie erklären, die immer komplexer werdende Formen des Sinnvollen herausbildet. Ich möchte sie mit der Einstellung verbinden, den Gehalt der Wahrnehmung konsequent aus der Ersten-Person-Perspektive zu verfolgen und nicht einfach aus der Dritten-Person-Perspektive eines „Kenners" zuzuschreiben. Zwar wird eine öffentliche, mit anderen Menschen geteilte Praxis vorausgesetzt, um überhaupt die Erfüllungsbedingungen „vor mir liegt ein Apfel" entwickeln zu können. Doch ist diese nicht bekannt, dann liegt auch keine entsprechende Repräsentation vor, sondern vielleicht nur die eines „roten runden Dinges", und sind nicht mal die Sprachspiele von „rot" und „rund" und „Ding" bekannt, existiert nicht einmal ein solcher Gehalt. Der Endpunkt dieser Betrachtung sind Fähigkeiten, welche es überhaupt erst ermöglichen, Sprachspiele zu erwerben. Anders ausgedrückt sind diese Fähigkeiten der Startpunkt unseres kognitiven Haushalts. Farbdiskrimination ist eine solche fundamentale Fähigkeit. Wenn sie tatsächlich zum Hintergrund gehört und Paul in seinem fortgeschrittenen Lebensalter genau diese Fähigkeit erwirbt, dann ist sein neues Wissen keines, das mit Erfüllungsbedingungen bzw. einer umfassenden Proposition in Verbindung gebracht werden kann.

Die Anwendung von Searles Konzept des Hintergrundes auf das Beispiel von Paul gibt uns auch einige Hinweise an die Hand, wie geistige Wahrnehmungsgehalte einem logisch-genealogischen Bild zufolge konzipiert werden sollten. Eine erwachsene Person sieht einen roten

---

grundfähigkeiten in das Reich der Intentionalität aufnehmen, dann ist die Wahrnehmung des Kindes sehr wohl intentional.

42 Dretske (2003), 160.

Apfel. Die Wahrnehmung ist begrifflich-propositional verfasst und wir bewegen uns im Reich der Gründe. Doch es gibt noch mehr Formen des Sinnvollen, die nicht mehr als propositional zu charakterisieren sind und dennoch im Rahmen von Wahrnehmungsvorgängen auftreten. Man denke an ein Kleinkind, das Bauklötze ihrer Farbe nach sortiert. Solche einfach gestrickten Handlungsmuster bilden die Plattform um konventionelle Begriffe zu erwerben. Ob wir diese Form des Sinnvollen auch schon als begrifflich auffassen wollen hängt davon ab, wie weit wir unseren Begriff von begrifflich ausdehnen möchten. Endpunkt der Betrachtung sind Fähigkeiten, die solche Handlungen überhaupt erst ermöglichen. Das „simple seeing" Dretskes ist nicht mehr im Raum der Gründe anzusiedeln, es ist nicht einmal intentional, weil keine Erfüllungsbedingungen gegeben sind. Dennoch sind Voraussetzungen gegeben, um Formen des Sinnvollen herauszubilden.

Ich habe Searles Konzept des Hintergrundes in eine genealogische Perspektive integriert, auch wenn Searles philosophisches Selbstverständnis das einer „rein" begrifflich-logischen Analyse ist. Wir setzen bei unserer Erfahrung an und fragen uns in quasi-transzendentaler Einstellung warum sie so ist, wie sie ist. Wir stoßen auf intentionale Zustände als ein natürliches Phänomen und wollen wissen, wie diese Zustände funktionieren, was sie jeweils voraussetzen. In dieser Perspektive kommen wir zur Hypothese vom Hintergrund. Ich bin davon überzeugt, dass die begriffslogische Herangehensweise und die philosophisch- genealogische Herangehensweise nicht nur zu den gleichen Ergebnissen führen sollten, sondern als zwei Seiten einer Medaille – ein und derselben Logik – anzusehen sind.[43]

Zum Schluss möchte ich noch eine Bemerkung zu meiner Rede von verschiedenen Wissensformen und dem Status des phänomenalen Wissens machen. Aufgrund meines „extremen" Beispiels von Paul und der Konzeption einer Stufenfolge des Sinnvollen hat es den Anschein, als wenn ich davon ausginge, dass die von mir so benannten verschiedenen Formen des Wissens, wie das phänomenale Wissen und das propositionale Wissen streng getrennt voneinander auftreten. Doch der Schein trügt und ein solches Bild wäre schlicht falsch. Worauf ich hinaus will ist eine Konzeption eines Zusammenspiels der Wissensformen, für die ich die Metapher einer Drehtür verwenden möchte. Das Bild, das ich im Kopf

---

43 Bei Searle selber finden sich auch Ansätze für eine philosophisch-genealogische Betrachtungsweise. Man beachte z. B. Searles Überlegungen zur Kausalität. Vgl. Searle (1987), 146 ff.

habe, ist das einer Drehtür, die sich bewegt und dabei immer komplexer werdende Verhältnisse in sich aufnimmt.[44] Begriffe strukturieren die Anschauung und die Anschauung wirkt zurück auf die Begriffe. Nach wenigen „Umdrehungen" ist die Erfahrung begrifflich imprägniert und Anschauung und Begrifflichkeit lassen sich nicht mehr voneinander trennen. Die Metapher einer Drehtür hat den Vorteil aus starren „entweder oder" Entgegensetzungen herauszuführen. Die Frage nach dem logischen Vorrang propositionaler oder nicht-propositionaler Komponenten ist allerdings auch bei der Drehtürmetapher nicht automatisch vom Tisch. Die Anschlussfrage lautet: wo befindet sich der Eingang zur Drehtür?

Wenn meine Überlegungen richtig sind, dann befindet sich der Eingang beim phänomenalen Wissen und grundlegenden Fähigkeiten, welche einen Begriffserwerb überhaupt erst ermöglichen. Das Knowinghow (to) hat einen Vorrang vor dem Knowing-that.

References

Abel (2004): Günter Abel, *Zeichen der Wirklichkeit*, Frankfurt/Main.
Brettel et al. (1997): H. Brettel/F. Viénot/J. D. Mollon, „Computerized simulation of colorappearance for dichromats", in: *Journal of the Optical Society of America A. Optics and Image Science* 14, 2647.
Byrne/Hilbert (2010): Alex Byrne/David R. Hilbert, „How Do Things Look to the Color-Blind?", in: J. Cohen/M. Matthen (eds.), *Color Ontology and Color Science*, Cambridge/MA.
Crane (2007): Tim Crane, *Intentionalität als Merkmal des Geistigen*, Frankfurt/Main.
Dretske (2003): Fred Dretske, „The Intentionality of Perception", in: B. Smith (ed.), *John Searle. Contemporary Philosophy in Focus*, Cambridge.
Evans (2002): Gareth Evans, *The Varieties of Reference*, Oxford.
Hume (1982): David Hume, *Eine Untersuchung über den menschlichen Verstand*, Stuttgart.
Jackson (1982): Frank Jackson, „Epiphenomenal qualia", in: *Philosophical Quarterly* 32, 127–136.
Jackson (1986): Frank Jackson, „What Mary didn't know", in: *Journal of Philosophy* 83, 291–295.

---

44 Die Vorstellung der Drehtür übernehme ich von Günter Abel, der in verschiedenen philosophischen Problemzusammenhängen „drehtürartige Verhältnisse" gegeben sieht und dadurch Dichtotomien, welche das philosophische Denken blockieren, zurücklassen möchte. Vgl. Abel (2004).

Lauer (2010): David Lauer, „Erfahrungen der Sprache. Auf dem Weg zu einer Phänomenologie desGehalts mit Wittgenstein, Gadamer und McDowell", in: G. Bertram/R. Celikates (eds.),*Expérience et réflexivité*, Paris (forthcoming).
Lewis (1996): David Lewis, „Elusive Knowledge", in: *Australasian Journal of Philosophy* 74/4, 549–567.
Loar (1996): Brian Loar, „Phenomenal States", in: N. Block/O. Flanagan/G. Güzeldere (eds.),*The Nature of Consciousness*, Cambridge/MA.
McDowell (1998): John McDowell, *Geist und Welt*, Frankfurt/Main.
Mellor (1992): Hugh Mellor, „Nothing Like Experience", in: *Proceedings of the Aristotelian Society* 93 (1992–3), 1–16.
Nemirow (1990): Laurence Nemirow, „Physicalism and the cognitive role of acquaintance", in: W. Lycan (ed.), *Mind and Cognition*, Oxford, 490–499.
Nida-Rümelin (1993): Martine Nida-Rümelin, „Farben und Phänomenales Wissen", in: *Conceptus-Studien* 9, Wien.
Peacocke (1992): David Peacocke, *A Study of Concepts*, Cambridge/MA.
Raffman (1995): Diana Raffman, „Über die Beharrlichkeit der Phänomenologie", in: T. Metzinger (ed.), *Bewusstsein. Beiträge aus der Gegenwartsphilosophie*, Paderborn.
Searle (1987): John Searle, *Intentionalität: Eine Abhandlung zur Philosophie des Geistes*, Frankfurt/Main.
Searle (1991): John Searle, *Response. The Background of Intentionality and Action*, in: E. Lepore/R. Van Gulick(ed.): *John Searle and his Critics*, Cambridge/MA.
Sellars (1999): Wilfrid Sellars, *Der Empirismus und die Philosophie des Geistes*, Paderborn.
Tolksdorf (2011): Stefan Tolksdorf, „Wittgenstein und das Projekt einer pragmatisch-genealogischen Philosophie der Sprache", in: *Wittgenstein-Studien 2* (2011), Berlin/New York, 103–135.
Viénot et al. (1995): F. Viénot/H. Brettel/L. Ott/A. M'Barek/J. Mollon, „What do color-blind people see?", in: *Nature* 376, 127–128.

Rechtliches Wissen

Thomas Gil

Im Folgenden gehe ich von der Einsicht aus, dass Juristen durch den Einsatz ihres Wissens und Könnens in der Lage sind, in der praktischen Wirklichkeit der handelnden und leidenden Menschen etwas zu bewirken, zum Beispiel einzelne Problem- und Konfliktlagen zu identifizieren und zu ihrer Bewältigung beizutragen. Auf der Basis der von ihnen verwendeten Begriffsrahmen sind Juristen in der Tat fähig, Wissen über die praktische Welt zu erwerben und Problemlösungswissen zu erzeugen, um anstehende Konflikte zu schlichten. Wie sie dies tun, ist Thema dieses Beitrags, in dem eine tentative Bestimmung des Begriffs „rechtliches Wissen" angestrebt wird.

1. Praktisches Wissen

In Anlehnung an die von Gilbert Ryle in seiner klassischen Studie über den menschlichen Geist *The Concept of Mind*[1] eingeführte Unterscheidung von „Wissen, dass" und „Wissen, wie" erweist es sich als sinnvoll, drei aufeinander nicht zurückführbare Grundsorten von Wissen prinzipiell zu unterscheiden: das propositionale (Überzeugungen und Meinungen betreffende) Wissen, das praktische Handlungswissen und das Erlebniswissen (das in Sätzen der Form „Ich weiß, was es heißt" oder „Ich weiß, wie es sich anfühlt" oder „Ich weiß, wie es ist", dieses oder jenes zu sein oder zu erleben, zum Ausdruck gebracht wird). Im Folgenden steht das praktische Handlungswissen im Mittelpunkt. Es mag sein, dass traditionelle Bestimmungen des propositionalen Wissens problematisch sind, wenn sie nämlich versuchen, den Begriff des Wissens auf andere Begriffe wie *Überzeugungen* oder *Wahrheit* zurückzuführen, die genauso schwierig oder ungeklärt sind. Es mag auch sein, dass der Begriff des Erlebniswissens vage ist und häufig als Restkategorie verwendet wird. Hier werden nicht die Probleme diskutiert, die mit diesen beiden Begriffen gekoppelt sind. Vielmehr soll es um eine Klärung des praktischen

---

1 Siehe Ryle (1988).

Handlungswissens gehen, des Wissens also, das in praktischen Zusammenhängen generiert und zum Einsatz gebracht wird, wodurch unterschiedliche Funktionen und Leistungen erfüllt bzw. erzielt werden. Diese Klärung ist notwendig, um die von mir vertretene These vorzutragen und zu verteidigen, dass rechtliches Wissen eine Art von praktischem Wissen ist.

Wenn man vom propositionalen oder theoretischen Wissen spricht, tendiert man häufig dazu, es in Verbindung zu einem möglichen Handeln zu bringen. Klassisch ist die Stelle, an der Francis Bacon die Macht der Naturerkenntnis im „Neuen Organon" expliziert und zwar als die Verwandlung des erzielten Ursachenwissens über Naturprozesse in Regelwissen für mögliches Manipulieren von Naturprozessen. Es heißt bei Francis Bacon: „... that which in contemplation is as the cause is in operation as the rule."[2] Theoretisches Wissen wird somit zum Machtwissen, „scientia est potentia", d. h. Wissenschaft ist Handlungsvermögen.

Wenn im Folgenden von praktischem Wissen die Rede ist, ist keineswegs gemeint, dass das praktische Wissen die andere Seite des theoretischen Wissens ist, wie Bacon dies in bezug auf das menschliche Naturwissen behaupten konnte. Für Bacon war Naturerkenntnis Ursachenwissen und Kenntnis der Handlungsregeln für einen möglichen Umgang mit Natur in einem. Das praktische Wissen, um das es hier geht, ist nicht das natürliche Korrelat eines theoretischen Wissens, sondern ein eigenständiges Wissen, ein Wissen *sui generis*. Es setzt zwar häufig theoretisches Wissen voraus. Es kann aber unabhängig von diesem theoretischen Wissen bestimmt und erfasst werden.

Die Einsicht, dass theoretisches Wissen nicht schon praktisches Wissen ist oder (in einer anderen Variante) dass praktisches Wissen mehr als eine weitere Dimension des theoretischen Wissens ist, ist die Einsicht, die bezüglich der Frage, welche Funktion Philosophen in der Politik zukommen sollte, Aristoteles von Platon trennt. Denn, wie Aristoteles gegenüber Platon zu Recht betont, sind in der Politik andere Kompetenzen als im Bereich des Theoretischen erforderlich, so dass der von Platon bejahte Satz, dass die Philosophen regieren sollten bzw. die Regierenden Philosophen werden sollten, seine ursprüngliche Plausibilität verliert. Das Wissen um das Allgemeine (das theoretische Wissen) ist in Tat etwas anderes als das „Wissen, wie" man (Koexistenz-) Rahmen organisiert, die ermöglichen, dass die Verschiedenen, diejenigen also, die

---

2 Siehe Bacon (1960), 39.

unterschiedliche und heterogene Präferenzen und Lebensstile haben, zusammenleben können. Und hierum geht es nämlich in der Politik als besonderer Sphäre des Praktischen.

Das „Wissen, wie" ist tatsächlich anders beschaffen als das theoretische Wissen. Der Chirurg, der gute Operationen durchzuführen weiß, hat andere Kompetenzen als der Anatomie-Dozent, der Vorlesungen über die verschiedenen Organe des menschlichen Körpers und deren Funktionen hält. Der Chirurg hat auch theoretisches, anatomisches Wissen. Aber das Wissen, das ihn als Chirurgen auszeichnet, ist ein praktisches Wissen. Und dieses praktische Wissen ist die Fähigkeit, gewisse Dinge zu tun, im Falle des Chirurgen: die Fähigkeit zu operieren.

Wer ein Instrument spielt, wer Bäume stutzen kann, wer Kreuzknoten zu knüpfen weiß, wer fremde Sprachen gut spricht, wer Witze gut erzählen kann und wer schließlich präzise argumentieren kann, um einige der Beispiele aufzugreifen, die Gilbert Ryle selbst aufzählt, hat praktisches Wissen, das in keinem Lehrbuch enthalten ist. In Lehrbüchern findet man die Harmonielehre und akzeptable Argumentationstheorien, aber nicht die praktischen Kompetenzen, die man braucht, um bestimmte Dinge tun zu können.

Juristen in ihren verschiedenen Rollen und Funktionen haben eine Reihe von Kompetenzen, die ihnen ermöglichen, bestimmte Dinge zu tun. Das Wissen, über das sie verfügen und das für sie charakteristisch ist, ist dementsprechend ein praktisches Wissen. Was dies genau heißt, soll im Folgenden expliziert werden.

2. Funktionen des Rechts

In *Das Recht der Gesellschaft*[3] unterscheidet Niklas Luhmann die Funktion des Rechts von zwei wichtigen Leistungen eines Rechtssystems. Luhmann lehnt es ab, von Funktionen in der Pluralform zu reden, und konzentriert sich auf *die* Funktion des Rechts. Diese bestimmt er als die Ermöglichung von Erwartungssicherheit bzw. die Stabilisierung von normativen Erwartungen.[4]

Eine so eindeutige Bestimmung der Funktion des Rechts setzt eine ebenso eindeutige Identifizierung des Problems voraus, auf das das Recht eine Antwort ist. Das Problem, das durch die Ausdifferenzierung des

---
3 Siehe Luhmann (1995).
4 Vgl. Luhmann (1995), 152 f., 161.

Rechts (d. h. spezifisch rechtlicher Normen) gelöst wird, ist für Luhmann ein Zeitproblem, „das sich in der gesellschaftlichen Kommunikation immer dann stellt, wenn die gerade ablaufende Kommunikation sich nicht selbst genügt (...), sondern sich in zeitlicher Extension ihres Sinnes an Erwartungen orientiert und Erwartungen zum Ausdruck bringt."[5] Mit anderen Worten: Die Funktion des Rechts hat es mit Erwartungen in einer Gesellschaft zu tun, mit der Möglichkeit, Erwartungen zu kommunizieren und in der Kommunikation zur Anerkennung zu bringen. Prägnant ausgedrückt:

> Konkret geht es um die Funktion der Stabilisierung normativer Erwartungen durch Regulierung ihrer zeitlichen, sachlichen und sozialen Generalisierung. Das Recht ermöglicht es, wissen zu können, mit welchen Erwartungen man sozialen Rückhalt findet, und mit welchen nicht.[6]

Von dieser Funktion der Stabilisierung normativer Erwartungen unterscheidet Luhmann zwei wichtige Leistungen des Rechts: die Leistung der Verhaltenssteuerung und die Leistung der Konfliktlösung.[7]

Gleichgültig ob man Luhmanns präzisierte Begrifflichkeit übernimmt oder nicht, erfüllt das Recht, in einem allgemeinen Sinne gesprochen, unterschiedliche Funktionen. In der Gesellschaft entstehende Interessenkonflikte werden durch das Recht im Sinne eines Ausgleichs von Schäden und Vorteilen gelöst. Die Lösung geschieht im Regelfall durch die Aktivierung von Prozeduren bzw. Verfahren (Gerichts-, Verwaltungs- und Gesetzgebungsverfahren), die nach bestimmten Regeln stattzufinden haben. All die an diesen Verfahren Beteiligten argumentieren juristisch. Mittels solcher Argumentationen werden einzelne Problemfälle identifiziert und einer rechtlichen Lösung zugeführt.

3. Juristische Argumentationen

Das Recht als System von Regeln und Normen ermöglicht in der Praxis die Lösung und Bewältigung von Konflikten, die immer dann auftreten, wenn verschiedene Menschen zusammenleben. Die einzelnen Interessen dieser Menschen koinzidieren nicht. Die ihnen zur Verfügung stehenden Ressourcen sind knapp. Eine Einigung stellt sich nicht immer auf natürliche Weise ein, so dass es zu Handlungen kommt, die das Gemein-

---
5   Siehe Luhmann (1995), 125.
6   Siehe Luhmann (1995), 131 f.
7   Vgl. Luhmann (1995), 157.

wesen nicht gutheißen kann. Das praktische Wissen, das Rechtssysteme zur Verfügung stellen bzw. selbst darstellen, besteht konkret darin, durch die Anwendung einer Reihe von Prozeduren eine friedvolle Regelung der entstandenen Konflikte zu ermöglichen. *Rechtliches Wissen* ist Wissen im Sinne eines praktischen Könnens, das sich auf mehreren Ebenen und in sehr unterschiedlichen Bereichen entfaltet. Was Juristen können, ist, einfach ausgedrückt, die Bewältigung einzelner Problemfälle durch deren interpretative Identifizierung als *Fälle von* zu leisten, die sich dann problemlos allgemeinen Rechtssätzen zuordnen lassen bzw. unter diese *subsumieren* lassen. Juristen verhalten sich inferentiell, wenn sie geltendes Recht anwenden, indem sie einzelne Fälle unter allgemeine Gesetze subsumieren. Wie das konkret vonstatten geht, kann man anhand eines von Karl Engisch in seiner *Einführung in das juristische Denken*[8] bemühten Beispiels gut sehen. Das Beispiel exemplifiziert nämlich auf eine sehr einfache Weise die Technik des juristischen Schließens, den juristischen Syllogismus:

> Der Richter stellt nämlich zunächst anhand des Strafgesetzbuchs einen allgemeinen Aussagesatz auf von der Art: „Der Mörder soll nach § 211 StGB mit lebenslanger Freiheitsstrafe bestraft werden." Mit diesem „Obersatz", der ein echtes Sollensurteil im logischen Sinne (...) ist, kombiniert er den ebenso gearteten „Untersatz": „M. ist Mörder", um daraus die Schlussfolgerung (conclusio) zu gewinnen: „M. soll nach § 211 StGB mit lebenslanger Freiheitsstrafe bestraft werden", was wiederum ein Urteil im logischen Sinne ist.[9]

Rein logisch betrachtet, ist die Struktur eines solchen Schließens ganz einfach. Sie lässt sich folgendermaßen wiedergeben: 1. (x) (Tx $\rightarrow$ ORx); 2. Ta; 3. ORa. *x* ist dabei eine Individuenvariable über den Bereich der natürlichen und juristischen Personen. *a* ist eine Individuenkonstante, zum Beispiel ein Eigenname. *T* ist ein beliebig kompliziertes Prädikat, das die Tatbestandsvoraussetzung der Norm als Eigenschaft von Personen zusammenfasst. Und *R* ist ein gleichfalls beliebig kompliziertes Prädikat, welches das, was die betreffende Person zu tun hat bzw. was zu geschehen hat, zum Ausdruck bringt. *O* ist der deontische Operator. Zippelius rekonstruiert das logische Schema des Schlusses folgendermaßen:

> Der Obersatz lautet: „Wenn die Voraussetzungen t1, t2, t3, ... verwirklicht werden, gilt die Rechtsfolge R." Der Untersatz lautet: „Die Voraussetzungen t1, t2, t3, ... werden durch den konkreten Sachverhalt s1, s2, s3, ...

---
8 Vgl. Engisch (1983).
9 Siehe Engisch (1983), 48 f.

verwirklicht." Der Schluss lautet: „Also gilt für den konkreten Sachverhalt s1, s2, s3, ... die Rechtsfolge R."[10]

Bei juristischen Schlussfolgerungen geht es demnach um die Ableitung einer normativen Aussage, eines Urteilssatzes, aus einer Reihe von Prämissen. Eine solche Ableitung nennt man einen *juristischen Syllogismus* oder die *interne Rechtfertigung* einer normativen Aussage bzw. eines rechtlichen Urteils. Die *interne Rechtfertigung* eines rechtlichen Urteils, d.h. die Anwendung des juristischen Syllogismus, ist in den einfachen Fällen problemlos. Anders verhält es sich in komplizierten Fällen, in denen *externe Rechtfertigungen* nötig sind, um die einzelnen Prämissen der Ableitung festzulegen. Wie wird in solchen Fällen argumentiert bzw. wie funktionieren die *externen Rechtfertigungen* von rechtlichen Urteilen? In fünf verschiedenen Schritten versucht man in den komplizierten Fällen zu einem Urteil zu kommen, wobei alle Schritte bis auf den letzten mit Problemen verbunden sind. In schwierigen Fällen muss man erstens das zu lösende Problem identifizieren. Zweitens muss man herausfinden, warum das Problem ein Problem ist. Es geht dann drittens darum, eine hypothetische Lösung des Problems zu finden, die viertens zu begründen ist. Schließlich und fünftens geht es um den problemlosen Übergang von den in den anderen Schritten festgelegten Prämissen zu dem rechtlichen Schlusssatz.

Beim ersten dieser fünf Schritte kann es unterschiedliche Klassen von Problemen geben. Es gibt Relevanzprobleme, die auftauchen, wenn man nicht weiß, welche die Norm ist, die im zu lösenden Fall anzuwenden ist. Zippelius redet von einem „Aufsuchen des einschlägigen Rechtssatzes", das spezifische Kompetenzen erfordert.[11] Außerdem gibt es Probleme der Interpretation, des Beweises und der genaueren Qualifikation. Interpretationsprobleme stellen sich ein, wenn man nicht weiß, wie die anzuwendende Norm genau zu verstehen ist. Beweisprobleme existieren, wenn man nicht weiß, ob ein bestimmter Sachverhalt tatsächlich der Fall gewesen ist bzw. ob etwas faktisch geschehen ist. Qualifikationsprobleme betreffen schließlich die genaue Zuordnung von Sachverhalten oder Momenten von Sachverhalten. Beim zweiten Schritt der externen Rechtfertigung rechtlicher Urteile hat man es entweder mit einem Zuwenig oder aber mit einem Zuviel an Informationen, Daten und Mitteln zu tun. So können Normen beispielsweise so spezifisch sein, dass

---

10 Siehe Zippelius (1971), 99.
11 Siehe Zippelius (1971), 88 ff.

sie den betreffenden Fall nicht decken, bzw. so weit sein und unterschiedlich verstanden werden, dass es dabei zu inkompatiblen Interpretationen kommt.

Beim dritten Schritt kommt man zur Konstruktion einer Lösungshypothese resp. zur hypothetischen Festlegung neuer Prämissen, die dann im vierten Schritt durch die Erarbeitung von Argumenten zu rechtfertigen sind. Die zu erarbeitenden Argumente bei einem Zuwenig an Daten oder Informationen können darin bestehen, dass man *analoge* Schlüsse (in einem weiten Sinne verstanden, der die sogenannten Schlüsse *a pari* oder *a simili*, *a contrario* oder *a fortiori* umfassen würde) zieht. Bei einem Zuviel an Daten und Informationen bestehen häufig die zu erarbeitenden Argumente in der Eliminierung möglicher Interpretationen durch eine *reductio ad absurdum*.

Der fünfte und letzte Schritt ist unproblematisch. Er setzt aber voraus, dass man die Prämissen für den nun leicht zu vollziehenden juristischen Syllogismus in den anderen Schritten festgelegt hat. Wenn dies der Fall ist, lässt sich der Übergang zum Schluss- oder Urteilssatz leicht bewerkstelligen.

All diese Schritte sind nur möglich auf der Basis rechtlichen Wissens als einer Gesamtheit praktischer und argumentativer Kompetenzen, die nötig für die Lösung einzelner Konflikt- und Problemfälle sind. Die konkrete Lösung geschieht immer durch die gekonnte, angemessene, situationsangepasste Anwendung resp. Verwendung der Mittel, die ein bestimmtes Rechtssystem den es gebrauchenden Akteuren zur Verfügung stellt.

Die Reduktion juristischer Argumentationen auf das Schema eines Syllogismus ist ein theoretisch eleganter Griff, der aber nicht immer zu überzeugen vermag. Deswegen gibt es eine Reihe von Autoren, die auf die Vielfalt juristischer Argumentationen verwiesen haben, in denen nicht nur ein Typ von Argumenten (die deduktiven) vorzufinden sei. Zwar dominiert dieser Typ, was MacCormick in seinen Arbeiten zum juristischen Schließen bzw. Argumentieren immer wieder betont.[12] Aber es gibt auch andere Argumenttypen, die in den konkreten juristischen Argumentationen häufig bemüht werden. Dabei handelt es sich im Einzelnen um: indirekte Argumente, Vergleichsargumente (*a fortiori*, *a maiore*, *a minore* Argumente) Analogieargumente, Beispielargumente, Autoritätsargumente usf. Die Frage der Zurückführbarkeit juristischer Argumentationen auf ein einziges Schema soll nicht erörtert werden. Was

---

12 Vgl. z.B. MacCormick (1978).

hier vielmehr interessiert, ist die Tätigkeit des Argumentierens, die die Juristen in so verschiedenen Rollen und Funktionen aufrechterhalten und durch die einzelne Problemfälle bewältigt werden können. Die Praxis der juristischen Argumentation setzt ein Können seitens der juristisch Argumentierenden voraus, das nichts anderes als das rechtlich-praktische Wissen ist.

4. Rechtliches Wissen

Die Praxis der juristischen Argumentation ist eine komplexe Tätigkeit, bei der es nicht nur um die Anwendung inferentieller Schemata und Verfahren geht, sondern auch verschiedene psychologische, sozialpsychologische, kulturelle, sozialpolitische und ökonomische Faktoren involviert sind, die das Tun der Beteiligten beeinflussen. Die sogenannte *Subsumtion*, durch welche typisierten Tatbestandsmerkmalen ein vorliegender Einzelfall, also eine bestimmte Tatsache, subsumiert wird, ist eine logische Operation, die sich formal modellieren lässt. In der Praxis des Subsumierens gibt es immer Auslegungsspielräume, innerhalb derer vertretbare Entscheidungen und Ermessenshandlungen gefällt bzw. vorgenommen werden können. Es gibt deswegen Autoren, die sich weigern, die Subsumtion selbst als logische Operation aufzufassen. So zum Beispiel formuliert Fritjof Haft in seiner *Einführung in das juristische Lernen*:

> (...) man sollte nicht glauben, die normale juristische Arbeit habe viel mit Logik zu tun. Als Jurist hat man es mit Inhaltsproblemen zu tun, die der Logiker sämtlich ausklammert. Bei dem, was gemeinhin juristische Subsumtion heißt, geht es um die Frage, ob ein konkretes Sprachmodell (eine Fallbeschreibung) dem Typus eines abstrakten Sprachmodells (eines Tatbestandsmerkmales) zugesprochen werden kann (muss) oder nicht. Dazu muss man den Tatbestand zum Konkreten hin verdeutlichen, den Fall zum Abstrakten hin generalisieren. Man muss beide einander angleichen, assimilieren, in die „Entsprechung" bringen (...). Das ist kein logischer Vorgang, das ist ein analogischer Vorgang.[13]

Eine solche Sicht ist nicht die allgemein anerkannte Sicht, der man problemlos zustimmen könnte. Sie indiziert aber, dass Juristen, wenn sie argumentieren, nicht durch inferentielle Schemata in eindeutiger Weise festgelegt sind, sondern Freiheitsspielräume haben, in denen ihr Können, aber auch ihre Interessen und ihre sonstigen Bindungen zur Geltung

---

13 Siehe Haft (1991), 150.

kommen bzw. sich bemerkbar machen und maßgebend werden. Solche Freiheitsspielräume entstehen auf allen Ebenen, auf denen Juristen argumentieren.

Im Recht argumentiert man auf drei unterschiedlichen Ebenen. Man argumentiert auf der Ebene der Erzeugung und Festlegung von Normen. Bei der Anwendung geltender Normen auf einzelne Problemfälle argumentiert man ebenfalls. Und schließlich sind Argumentationen in der Rechtsdogmatik nötig, die sich mit generischen Fällen oder Typen von Fällen beschäftigt. Die gängigen juristischen Argumentationslehren konzentrieren sich in der Regel auf die zweite Ebene, auf die Ebene der Anwendung gültiger Normen, und vernachlässigen die beiden anderen Ebenen. Wie dem auch sei, scheint eines zweifellos zu sein: dass es nämlich keinen anderen professionellen Bereich gibt, in dem so viel argumentiert wird. Der Bereich des Rechts (der Rechtserzeugung, der Rechtsanwendung und der Rechtsfixierung) ist ein Argumentationsbereich par excellence.

Argumentierend im Bereich der Rechtsanwendung fassen Juristen Gutachten ab (in denen einzelne Fälle juristisch erörtert und gelöst werden) und fällen Urteile (in denen Ergebnisse von vorhergehenden Argumentationen hingestellt und begründet werden). Der Stil einer rechtsgutachtlichen Fallprüfung lässt sich vom Stil eines Urteils unterscheiden. Während der Konjunktiv (die Möglichkeitsform) die sprachlich adäquate Sprachform für den Gutachtensstil ist (die Ergebnisoffenheit ist ein Wesensmerkmal des juristischen Gutachtens), ist typisch für juristische Urteile die Tatsache, dass eine einzige und endgültige Entscheidung (die Entscheidung des urteilenden Richters) vorangestellt wird, die in nachfolgenden Ausführungen im Einzelnen und schlüssig begründet wird. Die sprachlich adäquate Ausdrucksform eines rechtlichen Urteils ist der Indikativ (die Wirklichkeitsform).

Gutachten und Urteile werden aber nicht in einem luftleeren Raum abgefasst bzw. gefällt. Rechtliche Expertisen als bestimmter Fall rechtlichen Wissens beispielsweise erweisen sich als wichtige Steuerungsmittel im gesellschaftlichen Prozess. Vorhandene Interessen (die Interessen der Klienten) werden in ihnen aufgegriffen und in ein juristisch vorzeigbares Format (in die Sprache von Gerichten) gebracht. Auf die Weise werden Handlungsmöglichkeiten für die Auftraggeber und Klienten geschaffen. Die Expertisen als konkrete Gestalt rechtlichen Wissens werden als Dienstleistungen für den Staat oder aber für private Auftraggeber angeboten. Sie haben einen Preis und zeigen, dass die Wirklichkeit des Rechts und des rechtlichen Wissens keine abstrakte Realität ist, sondern eine in

Macht- und Wirtschaftszusammenhängen eingebettete. Diese Zusammenhänge gehören wesentlich zur Faktizität der Rechtswirklichkeit, in der es Sozialisationseffekte, unsymmetrische Verhältnisse, Honorare und Vormachtstellungen gibt. Dieses interessiert nicht immer den reinen Rechtstheoretiker bzw. Rechtsdogmatiker, sollte aber in einer Reflexion über das Recht als praktisches Wissen genannt werden.

Rechtliches Wissen wäre nach all dem Gesagten ein praktisches Können, das in rechtlich vermittelten Kommunikationsverhältnissen Vieles und Verschiedenes zu tun ermöglicht: u. a. die praxiswirksame Wahrnehmung und Artikulation von Interessen, die Bewältigung einzelner Konfliktfälle sowie die Steuerung und Stabilisierung einer unsicheren, zeitlich erstreckten Kommunikation.

References

Alexy (1983): Robert Alexy, *Theorie der juristischen Argumentation. Die Theorie des rationalen Diskurses als Theorie der juristischen Begründung*, Frankfurt/Main.
Bacon (1960): Francis Bacon, *The New Organon and Related Writings*, London.
Bringewat (2007): Peter Bringewat, *Methodik der juristischen Fallbearbeitung*, Stuttgart.
Engisch (1983): Karl Engisch, *Einführung in das juristische Denken*, Stuttgart.
Gil (2005): Thomas Gil, *Argumentationen. Der kontextbezogene Gebrauch von Argumenten*, Berlin.
Gil (2006): Thomas Gil, *Die Praxis des Wissens*, Hannover.
Haft (1991): Fritjof Haft, *Einführung in das juristische Lernen*, Bielefeld.
Koch/Rüßmann (1982): Hans-Joachim Koch/Helmut Rüßmann, *Juristische Begründungslehre. Eine Einführung in Grundprobleme der Rechtswissenschaft*, München.
Lüderssen (1972): Klaus Lüderssen, *Erfahrung als Rechtsquelle. Abduktion und Falsifikation von Hypothesen im juristischen Entscheidungsprozeß. Eine Fallstudie aus dem Kartellstrafrecht*, Frankfurt/Main.
Luhmann (1995): Niklas Luhmann, *Das Recht der Gesellschaft*, Frankfurt/Main.
MacCormick (1978): Donald Neil MacCormick, *Legal Reasoning and Legal Theory*, Oxford.
Neumann (1986): Ulfrid Neumann, *Juristische Argumentationslehre*, Darmstadt.
Ryle (1988): Gilbert Ryle, *The Concept of Mind*, London.
Somek (2006): Alexander Somek, *Rechtliches Wissen*, Frankfurt/Main.
Zippelius (1971): Reinhold Zipelius, Einführung *in die juristische Methodenlehre*, München.

Chapter Five
Skepticism: Pragmatic Answers?

Wittgensteins Zweifel

Joachim Schulte

1. In Wittgensteins Schriften der frühen und der mittleren Periode wird der Begriff „Zweifel" zwar hin und wieder thematisiert, aber diese Bemerkungen werden eher nebenbei gemacht und führen nicht zu längeren Betrachtungen.[1] Die erste ausführliche Erörterung des Begriffs „Zweifel" findet sich in einem Manuskript vom Oktober 1937.[2] In diesem 1976 von Rush Rhees unter dem Titel „Ursache und Wirkung: Intuitives Erfassen" herausgegebenen Text[3] stehen die ersten Bemerkungen Wittgensteins, in denen er sich eingehend mit dem Begriff des Zweifels auseinandersetzt. Es handelt sich um insgesamt mehr als zwei Dutzend Manuskriptseiten, die er zwischen dem 12. und dem 15. Oktober sowie am 20. und 21. Oktober 1937 niederschrieb.

Diese Bemerkungen, auf die ich gleich näher eingehen werde, enthalten manche Gedanken, die auf spätere, aus den *Philosophischen Untersuchungen* und *Über Gewißheit* bekannte Überlegungen vorausweisen. Gleich die ersten Bemerkungen bringen eine charakteristische These des späten Wittgenstein zum Ausdruck:

---

1 Siehe MSS 108, 185; 110, 31. Wichtige Bemerkungen finden sich in dem 1936 entstandenen MS 152. Sie wurden dann in die UF der PhU übernommen. (PhU §§84–87, vgl. unten Anm. 8. Eine Liste der Abkürzungen findet sich am Schluß dieses Artikels. Die verschiedenen Fassungen der PhU [Urfassung, Frühfassung usw.] sind abgedruckt in der Kritisch-genetischen Ausgabe, Frankfurt a. M., 2001, hg. von Joachim Schulte in Zusammenarbeit mit Heikki Nyman, Eike v. Savigny und Georg Henrik von Wright.)
2 Zu diesem Zeitpunkt wohnte Wittgenstein in seiner norwegischen Hütte. Dort arbeitete er (mit Unterbrechungen) seit August des vorigen Jahres. Die Manuskriptfassung der ersten 188 §§ der späteren PhU lag bereits vor, vielleicht auch die erste Maschinenschrift dieses Teils. Jetzt beschäftigte er sich mit der Fortsetzung dieser Schrift, das heißt er arbeitete an einem Text, den wir in seiner spätesten Fassung als ersten Teil der *Bemerkungen über die Grundlagen der Mathematik* kennen (bzw. als FF II). Die Manuskripte dieser Zeit enthalten allerdings nicht nur Bemerkungen über Fragen der Philosophie der Mathematik, sondern beispielsweise auch eine umfangreiche Auseinandersetzung mit den Begriffen „Ursache", „Wirkung" und „intuitives Erfassen".
3 Rhees (1976), abgedruckt in James Klagge u. Alfred Nordmann (Hg.) (1993).

> Die Grundform unseres Spiels muß eine sein, in der es den Zweifel nicht gibt. – Woher diese Sicherheit? Es kann doch nicht eine historische sein. ›Die Grundform des Spiels kann den Zweifel nicht enthalten.‹ Wir *stellen* uns da vor allem eine Grundform *vor*; eine Möglichkeit, und zwar eine *sehr wichtige* Möglichkeit. (Die wichtige Möglichkeit verwechseln wir ja sehr oft mit geschichtlicher Wahrheit.)[4]

Wie man sieht, ist der Begriff des Spiels (oder Sprachspiels) in diesem Zusammenhang von zentraler Bedeutung. In erster Linie geht es hier um das Sprachspiel – bzw. die Sprachspiele – in denen von Ursache und Wirkung die Rede ist. Die Beispiele zeigen jedoch, dass viele Aspekte der menschlichen Erkenntnis angesprochen werden.

„Sprachspiel" ist bekanntlich ein Grundbegriff von Wittgensteins Spätphilosophie (der in diesem Zusammenhang freilich nicht besprochen werden kann). Wir sollten uns jedoch fragen, was es mit der auffälligen Rede von einer „Grundform" des Spiels auf sich hat.[5] Dieses Wort „Grundform" kommt in Wittgensteins Gesamtnachlass nur sechs Mal vor: ein Mal in einem frühen Tagebuch von 1915[6], vier Mal in dem hier vorgestellten Text von 1937 und zum letzten Mal in einem Manuskripteintrag vom 5. April 1951, der in *Über Gewißheit* als §473 abgedruckt ist.

Die Stelle aus dem frühen Tagebuch, an der es um Komplexität und Satzsinn geht, können wir hier außer Acht lassen. Aber den Gebrauch des Wortes in den späteren Texten sollten wir uns genau anschauen. An den eben zitierten Stellen wird gesagt, dass die Grundform des Spiels keinen Zweifel enthalten kann. Die Sicherheit, dass es sich so verhält, kommt im Gebrauch der modalen Formulierungen „muß" und „kann nicht" zum Ausdruck. Aber woher rührt diese Sicherheit? Wir haben ja keine unmittelbare Kenntnis von einer solchen Grundform. Das heißt: Wir sind

---

4   PhO, 376.
5   Vgl. den Gebrauch des Wortes „Grundstellung" in einer Bemerkung früherer Fassungen der PhU: „Man kann, das ›taught us‹ [=tortoise] betreffend, sagen: ein Verbum hat für uns eine *Grundstellung* (wie man bei Turnübungen sagt) und dann verschiedene Stellungen, verschiedenen Verrichtungen gemäß. Eine beliebige *dieser* Stellungen zur Bezeichnung dessen nehmen, der (z.B.) *lehrt*, ist so, als nähme man für das Standbild eines Menschen irgend *eine* Stellung, in der er sich auch einmal befinden kann. Die Grundstellung, könnte man sagen, repräsentiert den Menschen und der Infinitiv das Verbum. Es hätte für uns nicht das Komische des Substantivs ›taught us‹, wenn man statt dessen den Infinitiv des Verbums zur Bezeichnung des Lehrers verwendet hätte. …" (Krit.-gen. Ed., 518–9, Anm. 6.) Das Wortspiel *tortoise/taught us* stammt aus Lewis Carrolls (1895), 278–280.
6   MS 102:18.6.15.

nicht durch Erfahrung mit Sprachspielen vertraut, in denen die Äußerung des Zweifels ausgeschlossen, und zwar von vornherein ausgeschlossen ist.

2. Wie Wittgenstein sagt: Die Sicherheit ist nicht „historisch" begründet. Vielmehr ist es so, dass wir uns eine Grundform *vorstellen*, eine Grundform *ohne* Zweifel. Das, was wir uns da vorstellen, braucht nie Wirklichkeit gewesen zu sein. Es ist eine Möglichkeit – eine *wichtige* Möglichkeit, sagt Wittgenstein nachdrücklich. Und wichtige Möglichkeiten verwechseln wir leicht mit historischer Wirklichkeit, wie er anmerkt. Dieser Hinweis ist eine Warnung: Wir sollen auf der Hut sein und uns darüber klar werden, welche Bewandtnis es mit dem Vorstellen wichtiger Möglichkeiten hat.

Wir können sicher sein, dass das Vorstellen möglicher Situationen im Hinblick auf einen bestimmten Zweck betrachtet wird. Wittgenstein will begriffliche oder, wie er sagt, „grammatische" Zusammenhänge erkunden. Aber inwiefern kann uns die Vorstellungskraft, die Phantasie, dabei helfen? Unsere Sprache schreibt uns nicht vor, was wir uns vorstellen können oder dürfen. Es gibt keine grammatischen Regeln, keine sprachlichen Konventionen, durch die festgelegt wäre, was in unserer Vorstellungswelt passieren kann.

Hier muss man verstehen, welches die Stoßrichtung des Redens von Vorstellungen ist. Es mag zwar sein, dass sich beim Hören, Lesen oder Aussprechen bestimmter Ausdrücke diese oder jene Vorstellungen aufdrängen. Das mag dann ein interessantes Faktum sein, das seinerseits Licht auf begriffliche Überlegungen werfen kann. Darum geht es hier aber nicht. Was Wittgenstein vorschwebt, ist ein bewusster Einsatz unseres Vorstellungsvermögens, um bestimmte Facetten relevanter Begriffe zu veranschaulichen.

„Veranschaulichen" heißt nicht: etwas herausfinden. Wittgenstein wehrt sich dagegen, das Wort „Gedankenexperiment" zur Kennzeichnung seines typischen Vorgehens zu verwenden.[7] Experimente werden unternommen, um herauszufinden, was unter bestimmten Bedingungen geschieht, wenn man dies oder jenes tut. Wer das Experiment durchführt, handelt also, um zu sehen, was sich dabei ergibt. Auf die Vorstellung übertragen, hieße das zum Beispiel: Man stellt sich eine bestimmte Person vor und wartet ab, was einem dabei in den Sinn kommt.

---

[7] Siehe MSS 107, 284; 111, 138; PhGr, 109, 155.

Das ist nicht Wittgensteins Verfahren. Er vergleicht sein Vorgehen mit mathematischen Prozeduren. In einer späten Bemerkung[8] schreibt er: „Ich mache scheinbar ›Gedankenexperimente‹. Nun, es sind eben keine Experimente. Viel eher Rechnungen."[9] Und das heißt, auf die Vorstellung übertragen, dass man sich bemüht, nach Regeln Bilder zu erzeugen, die eine Ausgangsgegebenheit – etwa eine Gleichung oder eine graphische Darstellung – durch Exemplifizierung veranschaulichen. Ein Beispiel wäre die regelgemäße Variation eines gegebenen Musters, insbesondere dann, wenn es sich um die Aufgabe handelt, durch entwickelnde Variation von einem Ausgangsmuster zu einem Zielmuster zu gelangen.[10]

3. Diesen Gedanken wollen wir nun auf die Untersuchung des Begriffs „Zweifel" anwenden. Zunächst betrachten wir gegebene Sprachspiele, um einige Binsenweisheiten zu sammeln, die auf sie zutreffen. Im Lichte dieser Binsenweisheiten tun wir sodann den zweiten Schritt und versuchen – durch entwickelnde Variation – Situationen zu konstruieren, aus denen die wirkliche hätte hervorgehen *können*. Dabei werden wir feststellen, dass einige mögliche Situationen plausibel wirken, während andere überhaupt nicht einleuchten.

Zu den Binsenweisheiten, die Wittgenstein sammelt, gehören die folgenden: In unseren Sprachspielen werden Wörter geäußert, die in einem regelmäßigen Zusammenhang mit unseren Handlungen stehen. Wenn Zweifel aufkommen, stellen sie „ein retardierendes Moment" dar; der Zweifel ist, „sehr wesentlich, eine Ausnahme von der Regel".[11] Ferner hat der Zweifel Gründe; und dies sind Gründe, „ein eingefahrenes Geleise zu verlassen".[12]

Wenn man diese Bedingungen mit anderen Möglichkeiten als den uns geläufigen umgibt, wird sich zeigen, dass unsere Welt „ganz, ganz anders" erscheint. Malen wir uns etwa aus, ein Kind, das die Anfangsgründe der Muttersprache und damit die Grundelemente praktischer

---

8 LS §519.
9 Vgl. „Ich glaube, ich treibe eine Art Mathematik ohne Zeichen/Notation/. Richtiger: ich tue, was auch Mathematiker tun; ich mache ähnliche Gedankenbewegungen; aber sie finden nicht in einer Rechnungsart ihre Anwendung// ihren Ausdruck//." (MS 130, 184–5, 22.7.46.)
10 Zum Begriff der entwickelnden Variation siehe außer dem in Fn. 22 genannten Aufsatz Schulte (2009a); Schulte (2009b); Schulte (2010a); Schulte (2010b).
11 PhO, 378.
12 Ebd.

Handlungsweisen lernt, werde dazu angehalten, jedem Alltagsgegenstand mit Zweifeln zu begegnen. Dann wäre die Welt wirklich eine andere, eine, in der es beispielsweise wie folgt zuginge: Das Kind nähert sich einem Tisch, kneift kritisch die Augen zusammen, geht um den Tisch herum und sagt: „Vermutlich könnte man behaupten, dass hier ein Tisch steht" oder „Mir kommt es so vor, als stünde hier ein Tisch" oder dergleichen.

Wittgenstein will keineswegs sagen, dass dergleichen in irgendeinem Sinne *unmöglich* ist. Dennoch ist die vorgestellte Möglichkeit absurd und lächerlich. Woran liegt das? Zunächst muss man deutlich erkennen, dass der Zweifel etwas Hinzukommendes ist. Wenn ein Sprachspiel, das wir kennen, wirklich funktioniert, sind darin nicht nur manche Formen des Zweifels vorgesehen, sondern auch Kriterien dafür, ob der Zweifel berechtigt ist. Damit sind aber zugleich Kriterien für den Ausschluss des Zweifels gegeben – Kriterien, die erfüllt sein können, ohne in Anspruch genommen werden zu müssen.

Der Zweifel hingegen ist ohne legitimierenden Grund kein Zweifel; jedenfalls keiner, den wir als solchen gelten lassen. Natürlich *kann* man in gewissem Sinn an praktisch allem zweifeln, auch daran, ob der Boden, auf dem man gerade steht, in der nächsten Sekunde halten wird.[13] Aber ohne erfindlichen Grund zum Zweifel wäre zweifelndes Verhalten kein wirklicher Zweifel, sondern Albernheit oder nervtötende Wichtigtuerei. In diesem Sinne schreibt Wittgenstein:

> Der Zweifel kann kein *notwendiger* Bestandteil des Spiels sein, ohne den das Spiel offenbar unvollständig und unrichtig ist. Denn es gibt in deinem Spiel Kriterien für die Berechtigung des Zweifels *nicht anders*, wie es Kriterien für sein Gegenteil gibt. Und das Spiel, welches den Zweifel einschließt, ist also nur ein noch komplizierteres als eines, welches ihn nicht einschließt.[14]

---

13 Vgl. PhU §84–87. Dort schreibt Wittgenstein: „... Aber das sagt nicht, daß wir zweifeln, weil wir uns einen Zweifel *denken* können. Ich kann mir sehr wohl denken, daß jemand jedesmal vor dem Öffnen seiner Haustüre zweifelt, ob sich hinter ihr nicht ein Abgrund aufgetan hat; und daß er sich darüber vergewissert, eh' er durch die Tür tritt (und es kann sich einmal erweisen, daß er recht hatte) – aber deswegen zweifle ich im gleichen Falle doch nicht" (§84). Der methodische Zweifel à la Descartes wird in §87 in Frage gestellt: „Es kann leicht so scheinen, als *zeigte* jeder Zweifel nur eine vorhandene Lücke im Fundament; so daß ein sicheres Verständnis nur dann möglich ist, wenn wir zuerst an allem zweifeln, woran gezweifelt werden *kann*, und dann alle diese Zweifel beheben."

14 PhO, 380.

Mit anderen Worten: Der Zweifel ist im Sprachspiel etwas, was hinzukommt, nachdem das Spiel – in Situationen ohne jeglichen Zweifel – in seinen Grundzügen gelernt wurde. Dieses „nachdem" ist ein problematischer Ausdruck, denn natürlich lernt man Sprachspiele in einer Welt, die alle möglichen Zweifel kennt. Aber diese Zweifel finden in Situationen des Lernens noch keinen Ansatzpunkt – sie leisten keine Arbeit. Wir würden das Kleinkind, das Tische und Stühle mit Äußerungen des Zweifels bedenkt, nicht als frühreifen Skeptiker bezeichnen, sondern als Produkt einer verfehlten Erziehung.

Sogar in den keineswegs zur Veröffentlichung bestimmten Notizen des hier betrachteten Manuskripts ist Wittgenstein vorsichtig und beansprucht keine gleichsam „logische" Geltung seiner These. Er fragt: „Was ist nun daran – ›man kann nicht mit dem Zweifel anfangen‹?" Und die Beinaheantwort lautet: „So ein ›kann‹ ist immer verdächtig".[15] Es wäre richtiger zu sagen: „Das Spiel *fängt* nicht mit dem Zweifel an",[16] oder darauf hinzuweisen, dass *wir* es nicht „Zweifel" nennen würden, wenn sich die Menschen einschließlich der Kleinkinder ständig so verhielten, wie wir es tun, wenn wir einen „berechtigten" Zweifel haben.

4. Auch im Rahmen seiner Erörterung des Begriffs „Zweifel" will Wittgenstein den Menschen als Lebewesen betrachten – ein Wesen, dessen „biologische Funktionen"[17] in Betracht gezogen werden müssen, wenn wir beurteilen wollen, welche begrifflichen Fähigkeiten ihm zugeschrieben werden dürfen.[18] Vor diesem quasi „biologisch" gesehenen Hintergrund kann das Reden von mehr oder weniger *primitiven* Stadien des Lebens, von *instinktiven* Reaktionen und dergleichen Sinn bekommen. Ein viele Komplikationen dieses Gedankens berücksichtigendes

---

15 PhO, 378.
16 PhO, 380; vgl. auch die ähnliche Gedankenbewegung in ÜG §232: „›Jedes einzelne dieser Fakten könnten wir bezweifeln, aber *alle* können wir nicht bezweifeln.‹/Wäre es nicht richtiger zu sagen: ›*alle* bezweifeln wir nicht.‹/Daß wir sie nicht alle bezweifeln, ist eben die Art und Weise, wie wir urteilen, also handeln." Vgl. BPhPs II §393 = Z §351.
17 PhO, 380.
18 Vgl. die folgenden Stellen: „Der Instinkt ist das Erste, das Raisonnement das Zweite. Gründe gibt es erst in einem Sprachspiel" (BPhPs II §689). Und: „Ich will den Menschen hier als Tier betrachten; als ein primitives Wesen, dem man zwar Instinkt, aber nicht Raisonnement zutraut. Als ein Wesen in einem primitiven Zustande. Denn welche Logik für ein primitives Verständigungsmittel genügt, deren brauchen wir uns auch nicht zu schämen. Die Sprache ist nicht aus einem Raisonnement hervorgegangen" (ÜG §475).

Beispiel ist der berühmte §244 der *Philosophischen Untersuchungen*, in dem Wittgenstein schreibt, die sprachliche Bezugnahme auf Schmerzen trete an die Stelle des „ursprünglichen, natürlichen Ausdrucks der Empfindung": Indem man dem Kind Wörter für Empfindungen beibringt, lehrt man es „ein neues Schmerzbenehmen".

Diese Betrachtungsweise motiviert Wittgenstein dazu, sein Verfahren der „entwickelnden Variation" so anzuwenden, dass wir – von unserer normalen Situation ausgehend – bei vorsprachlichen oder nichtsprachlichen Situationen landen. Ein besonders frappierendes Beispiel ist die folgende Schilderung mit ihren drei Varianten der Grundsituation des Kindes, das offenbar Schmerzen äußert. Zunächst schreibt Wittgenstein:

> Denken wir uns den Zweifel und die Überzeugung nicht durch eine Sprache, sondern bloß durch Handlungen, Gebärden, Mienen ausgedrückt. So könnte es etwa bei sehr primitiven Menschen oder bei Tieren sein. Denken wir also eine Mutter, deren Kind schreit und sich dabei die Wange hält. *Eine* Art der Reaktion ist also die, daß die Mutter das Kind zu trösten trachtet und es, auf irgendeine Art und Weise, pflegt. Hier ist nichts, was dem Zweifel daran entspricht, ob das Kind wirklich Schmerzen habe.

Ein zweiter – ebenfalls leicht auszumalender – Fall wäre der folgende:

> ... die Reaktion auf die Klage des Kindes ist für gewöhnlich die eben beschriebene, unter gewissen Umständen aber verhält sich die Mutter skeptisch. Sie schüttelt dann etwa mißtrauisch den Kopf, unterbricht das Trösten und Pflegen des Kindes, ja: äußert Unwillen und Teilnahmslosigkeit.

Die dritte Variante sieht so aus:

> Nun aber denken wir uns die Mutter, die von vornherein skeptisch ist: Wenn das Kind schreit, zuckt sie die Achseln und schüttelt den Kopf; manchmal sieht sie es prüfend an, untersucht es; ausnahmsweise macht sie auch vage Versuche des Tröstens oder Pflegens. – Sähen wir ein solches Verhalten, so würden wir es durchaus nicht das der Skepsis nennen, es würde uns nur seltsam und närrisch anmuten. „Das Spiel kann nicht mit dem Zweifel anfangen" heißt: Wir würden es nicht ›Zweifel‹ nennen, wenn das Spiel damit anfinge.[19]

Das entscheidende Resultat dieser Betrachtung ist, dass wir ein Verhalten, das wir in anderen Zusammenhängen als charakteristisch für den Zweifel ansehen, in diesem Kontext von Mutter und Kind *nicht* als „Zweifel" oder „Skepsis" bezeichnen würden. Wittgenstein vergleicht die Absurdität der geschilderten dritten Variante mit der Unverständlichkeit einer Situation, in der das Gewinnen und Verlieren der erste Zug im Spiel sein soll. Hier

---

19 PhO, 382.

wären wir, wie Wittgenstein schreibt, wohl nicht bereit zu „sagen: ›Diese Leute gewinnen und verlieren zu *Anfang* des Spiels‹".[20] Und damit ist implizit gesagt, dass ein solcher Vorgang für uns gar kein *Spiel* wäre. Diese Veränderung des gewohnten Ablaufs würde unser Spielvokabular so durcheinander bringen, dass wir nicht mehr wüssten, wie wir es anwenden könnten.

5. Wittgensteins Überlegungen sind hier von einem Kontrast geprägt, der für sein Denken in mehrerer Hinsicht wichtig ist. Auf der einen Seite dieser kontrastierenden Begriffe steht das Einfache, Primitive, Grobgefügte; auf der anderen Seite das Komplizierte, Verfeinerte, Ausgetüftelte. Diese Formulierung ist freilich – ebenso wie Wittgensteins eigene Darstellung – nicht unproblematisch. Sie ist nicht zuletzt deshalb problematisch, weil solche Wörter in hohem Maß sowohl vage als auch relativ sind. Das sollte jedoch das Verständnis im Einzelfall nicht behindern, vor allem dann nicht, wenn man mehrere dieser Begriffe so zusammenbringt, dass sie einander erläutern.

Die Grundform des Spiels ist, wie Wittgenstein sagt, eine wesentlich primitive, unkomplizierte Form. Man kann hier an simple Formen denken wie das extrem ausgemergelte Sprachspiel (2) der PhU. Dieses Spiel enthält keine Sätze, sondern nur „Rufe", und es wird vom Bauenden und seinem Gesellen in nachgerade mechanischer Weise gespielt. Aber wie schon das Beispiel von Mutter und Kind andeutet, will Wittgenstein hier auf eine besonders frühe Stufe eines Entwicklungsprozesses zurückgehen. Er spricht vom „Ursprung" und der „primitiven Form des Sprachspiels" und sagt, dieser „Ursprung" sei eine „Reaktion; erst auf dieser können die komplizierteren Formen wachsen".[21]

Wie schon gesagt: Hier wie auch sonst muss der Leser darauf achten, dass Wittgenstein, wenn er von „Wachstum", „Entwicklung" und dergleichen spricht, keine historischen Hypothesen aufstellt oder verfechten will. Die Entwicklungen, von denen an dieser und ähnlichen Stellen die Rede ist, sind Modelle, auseinander „abgeleitete"[22] Stufen möglicher Fortgänge.

---

20 Ebd.
21 PhO, 394.
22 Vgl. Goethes Gebrauch des Worts „ableiten" in seinen morphologischen Schriften. Siehe Schulte (1982).

6. Der „Ursprung" des Sprachspiels liegt im vorsprachlichen Tun und Verhalten. Die „Reaktion", von der Wittgenstein in diesem Zusammenhang spricht, ist das instinktive Reagieren des als Tier gesehenen Menschen. Im Kontext dieses Reagierens haben Zögern und Zweifel keinen Platz; man reagiert unmittelbar, spontan. Allerdings ist dieser vorsprachliche Kontext ein Rahmen, aus dem Handlungen hervorgehen können. „Die Grundform des Spiels", schreibt Wittgenstein, „muß eine sein, in der gehandelt wird". „Die Sprache ist", wie er sagen möchte, „eine Verfeinerung". Und hier führt er ein Faustzitat an, das fast 15 Jahre später auch in einem der Manuskripte notiert wird, aus denen dann das Buch *Über Gewißheit* zusammengestellt wurde: „Im Anfang war die Tat".[23]

Zweifelndes Verhalten ist Zögern und Unsicherheit. Auf ihnen kann kein Handeln beruhen; aus ihnen kann es nicht hervorgehen. Wittgenstein schreibt: „Die primitive Form des Sprachspiels ist die Sicherheit, nicht die Unsicherheit. Denn die Unsicherheit könnte nicht zur Tat führen".[24] Damit hängt auch die folgende, ein wenig paradoxe Formulierung zusammen: „Warum ›muß der Zweifel einmal irgendwo enden‹? – Weil das Spiel nie anfinge, wenn es mit dem Zweifel anfinge?"[25]

Natürlich können wir – spätgeborene und raffinierte Erben der kulturellen Entwicklung – so manches Spiel mit dem Zweifel beginnen. Nicht nur als Forscher, sondern auch als Mitmensch ist der Mensch oft gut beraten, seinen Augen nicht zu trauen und zunächst einmal gar nichts zu glauben. Doch diese Möglichkeit beruht darauf, dass man sich in vielen anderen Hinsichten ohne zu zögern auf den Augenschein verlässt.

Dieser Zweifel (im Sinne des methodisch oder empirisch berechtigten Misstrauens) kann also nicht gemeint sein. Vielmehr geht es wohl darum, dass Zweifellosigkeit eine Rahmenbedingung für die Existenz des Spiels ist: Von Zweifel kann nur da gesprochen werden, wo Sicherheit im Spiel ist. Man mag zwar sagen wollen, dass Zweifeln, Glauben und Wissen Begriffe sind, die miteinander stehen und fallen. Aber was man weiß und was man glaubt sind keine Rahmenbedingungen des Zweifels. Sicherheit im Sinne von Abwesenheit des Zweifels ist eine solche Rahmenbedingung. Diese Form der Bedingtheit ist im Spiel und im Begriff „Zweifel" angelegt. Das heißt: Von Zweifeln kann nur dort sinnvoll geredet werden, wo es im Spiel sicheres, mithin nicht zögerndes Handeln gibt. Es

---
23 PhO, 394, vgl. ÜG §402.
24 PhO, 396.
25 PhO, 394.

muss Aspekte des Spiels bzw. im Spiel Fälle geben, wo der Zweifel nicht ansetzen kann; wo zweifelndes Verhalten unverständlich und albern wirken würde.

Dieses Verhältnis der Bedingtheit drückt Wittgenstein aus, indem er sagt, Zweifel und Unsicherheit seien Charakteristika zweiter Ordnung – im Gegensatz zu den erststufigen Merkmalen des unmittelbaren Reagierens, des instinktiven, „beherzten" Handelns. Wittgenstein erläutert das am Beispiel einer Nähmaschine. Zu deren charakteristischen Eigenschaften gehören zwar auch die Abnutzbarkeit ihrer Teile und die Möglichkeit von Defekten. Aber niemand würde diese Eigenschaften nennen, wenn es darum ginge, das Funktionieren einer solchen Maschine zu erklären. Dazu würde man Merkmale erster Ordnung anführen, also die Wirkungsweise einer richtig arbeitenden Nähmaschine erklären.

7. Dass die Dinge so liegen – dass es einen solchen Kontrast zwischen dem Einfachen und dem Komplizierten, zwischen sicherem und zweifelndem Verhalten gibt – kann erklären, warum man vielleicht versucht ist, dem Zweifel Tür und Tor zu öffnen. Denn gerade weil der Zweifel ein Produkt der Verfeinerung, der späteren Entwicklung ist, möchte man sagen, dass eine Darstellung, die ihn nicht berücksichtigt, an der Wirklichkeit vorbeigeht. Erst durch den Zweifel werde die Darstellung „naturgetreu"[26] – wie der Vertreter dieser Position in Wittgensteins Formulierung sagt.

Auf diese Überlegung reagiert Wittgenstein in einer Weise, die gewiss nicht ohne weiteres einleuchtend ist. Er fragt zurück, ob es offenbar ungerecht oder unsinnig wäre, für lange und kurze Fahrtstrecken mit der Eisenbahn den gleichen Preis bezahlen zu müssen.[27] An anderer Stelle weist er darauf hin, dass jemand, der für lange und kurze Arbeitszeit den gleichen Lohn bezahlt oder verlangt, deshalb „nichts übersehen muß".[28]

Was ist damit gemeint? Ich glaube, die Antwort lautet wie folgt: Wenn wir mögliche Situationen wie das Eisenbahn- oder das Lohnbeispiel betrachten, haben wir den Eindruck, dass die Menschen, die so handeln, ein mehr oder weniger offenkundiges Merkmal ihres Sprachspiels verkehrt einordnen oder in seiner Tragweite falsch einschätzen. Der Grund liegt darin, dass ihre Institutionen (Eisenbahn, Lohnverhältnisse)

---

26 Vgl. PhO, 380.
27 Vgl. PhO, 380.
28 PhO, 386; vgl. auch das bekannte Beispiel der Holzverkäufer in BGM, 94. Die Idee stammt vielleicht aus dem Evangelium, siehe Matthäus 20, 1–16.

sich zum Teil mit den unseren decken, in mancher Hinsicht aber völlig von den unseren abweichen. Das gibt uns das Gefühl, hier *müsse* etwas verkehrt sein. Es scheint, als sähen die Leute etwas nicht, was für uns offensichtlich ist. Aber so ist es nicht. Denn fremde soziale Verhältnisse können so sein, dass dort andere ökonomische Regeln herrschen. Einen Preis oder einen Lohn bezahlen – das sind Dinge, die nicht so funktionieren *müssen* wie bei uns. Selbstverständlichkeiten können ganz unterschiedlicher Art sein. Hauptsache, es gibt Selbstverständlichkeiten, denn dann können die Menschen handeln.

Diese Einsicht sollen wir vermutlich auf den Fall des Zweifels übertragen. Es scheint uns, die wir in vielen unserer Spiele Platz für Zweifel haben, als fehlte einem Spiel, in dem der Zweifel nicht vorkommt, etwas oder als übersähen die Menschen, die so spielen, etwas, was uns aus unserer Perspektive sofort auffällt, nämlich die immer gegebene Möglichkeit, dass man sich täuscht oder getäuscht wird. Das ist natürlich ein Fehler, denn ein *anderes* Spiel, das sich zum Teil mit dem unseren deckt, ist nicht wegen seiner Andersartigkeit ein unvollständiges, ungerechtes, unsinniges Spiel. Es ist ein *anderes* Spiel – Punktum!

Wer diesen Fehler begeht, verkennt nicht nur die Bedeutung der primitiven Sicherheit des zweifelfreien Anfangs, auf die wir bereits eingegangen sind. Er übersieht außerdem, dass der Zweifel, wie Wittgenstein sagt, ein „Gesicht" haben muss. Mag sein, dass diese Metapher nicht von selbst einleuchtet, aber Wittgenstein weist darauf hin, dass die Art der jeweiligen Fragestellung oder Untersuchung den Zweifel prägt. So wie nur bestimmte Möglichkeiten des Mienenspiels mit einer gegebenen Physiognomie verträglich sind, so kann der Zweifel nur dort zum Einsatz kommen, wo sein Gesicht zur jeweiligen Fragestellung und deren Kriterien passt.

8. Auf diesen Gedanken geht Wittgenstein in dem Manuskript von 1937 nicht weiter ein. Aber in späteren Schriften verdeutlicht er ihn, indem er die These vertritt, der Zweifel sei nichts Willkürliches oder, anders formuliert, der Zweifel müsse einen Grund haben. Dieser Gedanke wird häufig angedeutet, aber nur selten klar ausgesprochen. In *Über Gewißheit* heißt es an einer Stelle: „Man zweifelt aus bestimmten Gründen"[29], und in den *Bemerkungen über die Philosophie der Psychologie* impliziert die Frage „Wie kommt es, daß der Zweifel nicht der Willkür untersteht?"[30], dass er

---

29 ÜG §458.
30 BPhPs II §343.

tatsächlich nicht dem Willen unterworfen ist. An einer anderen Stelle von *Über Gewißheit* schreibt Wittgenstein: „Kann ich zweifeln, woran ich zweifeln *will?*"[31] Die mitgemeinte Antwort lautet natürlich „Nein". Anders gesagt: Man kann nicht nach Belieben alles in Zweifel ziehen.

Daraus ergibt sich, wie Wittgenstein festhält, dass auch ein abartig veranlagtes Kind nicht an allem zweifeln kann. Wieso ist das ausgeschlossen? Die Antwort lautet, ganz im Sinne des bisher Gesagten: „Man kann erst zweifeln, wenn man Gewisses gelernt hat; wie man sich erst verrechnen kann, wenn man rechnen gelernt hat."[32]

Demnach wäre das wie Zweifel anmutende Verhalten des Kindes deshalb kein Zweifel, weil dem Verhalten die für den Zweifel erforderliche Umgebung relevanter Kenntnisse und praktischer Fähigkeiten fehlen würde.

Eine weitere Variation dieses Gedankens lautet, dass man, um zweifeln zu können, bestimmte Begriffe erfasst haben muss. So heißt es an einer auch in *Zettel* abgedruckten Stelle: „Zum Bezweifeln, ob der Andere jetzt Schmerz fühlt, muß ich den *Begriff* des Schmerzes haben; nicht Schmerzen."[33]

Es wäre leicht, eine Reihe weiterer Zitate anzuführen, die in die gleiche Richtung gehen. Und wie wir gesehen haben, passt dieser Gedanke gut zu vielen sonstigen Bemerkungen Wittgensteins über die Bedingtheit des Zweifels.

9. Es gibt aber auch Bemerkungen, die nachgerade aufs Gegenteil hinauszulaufen scheinen. So schreibt Wittgenstein: „Glauben, daß der Andere Schmerzen hat, zweifeln, ob er sie hat, sind so viele natürliche Arten des Verhaltens zu den andern Menschen ..."[34] Glauben und Zweifeln werden hier auf eine Ebene gestellt und als natürliche Verhaltensweisen bezeichnet. Das Wort „natürlich" wird offenbar im Sinne von „instinktiv", „ursprünglich" verwendet. Ähnlich heißt es an einer späteren Stelle: „... glauben, bezweifeln etc., daß der Andre Schmerzen

---

31 ÜG §221.
32 BPhPs II §343.
33 BPhPs I §154, Z §548.
34 BPhPs I §151. Die ganze Bemerkung lautet: „Glauben, daß der Andere Schmerzen hat, zweifeln, ob er sie hat, sind so viele natürliche Arten des Verhaltens zu den andern Menschen; und unsere Sprache ist nur ein Hilfsmittel und ein weiterer Ausbau dieses Verhaltens. Ich meine: unser Sprachspiel ist ein Ausbau des primitiveren Benehmens. (Denn unser *Sprachspiel* ist Benehmen.)"

hat, sind natürliche Arten unsres Verhaltens gegen den Andern".³⁵ Hier möchte man sich sogleich fragen, ob diese Bemerkung mit der vorhin zitierten Äußerung vereinbar ist, der Zweifel an den Schmerzen des anderen setze den Begriff der Schmerzen voraus. Ein ähnliches Problem wirft die folgende Stelle auf, an der Wittgenstein schreibt: „Der Zweifel am inneren Vorgang ist ein *Ausdruck*. Der *Zweifel* aber ist ein instinktives Verhalten. Ein Verhalten gegen den anderen".³⁶

Alle drei Zitate sagen, das Zweifeln sei ein Verhalten gegen den anderen Menschen. An zwei Stellen wird dieses Verhalten „natürlich" und an einer Stelle wird es „instinktiv" genannt. Aber wenn dieses Verhalten in dem genannten Sinn „natürlich" oder „instinktiv" ist – wie kann es dann so voraussetzungsvoll sein und verlangen, dass der Zweifelnde bestimmte Begriffe und Fähigkeiten erlernt hat?

10. Diese Frage hat auch Wittgenstein beschäftigt. In dem bereits angeführten Manuskript von 1937 sagt er, man könne sich doch eine primitive Vorform des Kopfzerbrechens denken, beispielsweise eine Form des Suchens. Warum also soll das Spiel nicht doch mit dem Zweifel anfangen können?³⁷ Als Antwort verweist er darauf, dass der Zweifel ein Gesicht haben müsse und dass Zweifel oder Unsicherheit im Spiel stets Merkmale zweiter Ordnung seien. Diese Antwort wird an der folgenden, etwa zehn Jahre später geschriebenen Stelle anschaulich erläutert:

> Ich kann mir wohl vorstellen, daß ein bestimmtes primitives Benehmen sich später zum Zweifel auswächst. Es gibt z. B ein *primitives* Untersuchen. (Ein Affe, der z. B. eine Zigarette zerpflückt. Einen intelligenten Hund sehen wir dergleichen nicht tun.) Das bloße Hin- und Herwenden und Beschauen eines Gegenstandes ist eine primitive Wurzel des Zweifels. Aber Zweifel ist erst da, wenn die typischen Antezedentien und Konsequenzen des Zweifels da sind.³⁸

Einerseits bestätigt Wittgenstein hier, dass es primitive Vorformen zweifelnden Benehmens geben kann. Es kann durchaus vorsprachliche Verhaltensweisen geben, die ganz zu Recht als Argwohn, Zögern oder Unsicherheit beschrieben werden dürfen. Da es solche Vor- oder Urformen gibt (oder geben kann), ist es möglich, unseren Zweifel als „Ausdruck" zu begreifen, wie Wittgenstein das an einer schon zitierten

---

35 LS §874.
36 BPhPS II §644.
37 Vgl. PhO, 394.
38 BPhPS II §345.

Stelle tut.[39] Das heißt: So ähnlich wie man unsere normalen Formen des Schmerzausdrucks als Weiterentwicklung eines ursprünglichen, primitiven Schmerzverhaltens sehen kann, so kann man auch unser zweifelndes Verhalten im Sprachspiel als Weiterentwicklung eines primitiven Suchens, Untersuchens oder Misstrauens auffassen.

Es gibt aber einen wesentlichen Unterschied zwischen diesen beiden Arten von Fällen: Während das ursprüngliche Schmerzbenehmen Züge an den Tag legt, die auf unser enorm viel komplizierteres Sprachspiel vorausweisen, hat das primitive Untersuchen des Affen noch keine den Zweifel antizipierenden Merkmale. Das ursprüngliche Schmerzbenehmen ist, streng genommen, keine Vorform, sondern eben eine Form von Schmerzbenehmen. Das primitive Untersuchen dagegen erscheint erst im Lichte des sprachspielimmanenten Zweifels als eine Vorform zweifelnden Verhaltens. Ohne die von Wittgenstein genannten „typischen Antezedentien und Konsequenzen des Zweifels" liegt gar kein Zweifel vor.

Man kann sich zwar vorstellen, dass das primitive Untersuchen eines Affen oder unserer Urahnen zu allen möglichen weiteren Handlungen führt. Es enthält sozusagen das Ausgangspotential für mannigfaltige Komplikationen und Verfeinerungen, die sich dann beispielsweise als Formen des Forschens oder Zerlegens deuten lassen. Aber keine dieser Verfeinerungen wäre wesentlich ein Zweifeln oder nähme vom Zweifel seinen Ausgang. Allenfalls lassen diese Verfeinerungen, sobald sie kompliziert genug sind, Raum für Zweifel. Solche Zweifel kämen aber erst auf, nachdem die ersten Formen des Forschens und Zerlegens etabliert sind.

Dass wir in bestimmten Äußerungen des Zweifels – beispielsweise in misstrauischen Reaktionen gegenüber Gefühlsäußerungen fremder Personen – etwas Instinktives sehen können, liegt daran, dass wir den Sprachspielkontext, in dem diese Äußerungen als Zweifel erscheinen, bereits mitberücksichtigen. Unabhängig von diesem Kontext haben solche Äußerungen nichts Charakteristisches, woraus man wirklichen Zweifel durch entwickelnde Variation hervorgehen lassen könnte. Erst der relativ komplizierte Kontext verleiht dem Zweifel so etwas wie ein „Gesicht". Deshalb ist der Zweifel ein Merkmal zweiter Ordnung. Um als Zweifel zu gelten, braucht unser Verhalten eine Umgebung, die eingeübte Praktiken und angewandte Methoden enthält. Ohne eine solche Umgebung ist das, was in ihr als Zweifel gilt, keine Form des Zweifels, ja nicht einmal eine Vorform.

---

39 Vgl. BPhPs II §644.

11. Ein Grund, weshalb viele Sätze unzweifelhaft für uns feststehen, obwohl sie nie überprüft oder nachgewiesen wurden, besteht darin, dass sie in vielfältiger Weise mit anderen Sätzen zusammenhängen, an denen wir unter normalen Umständen nicht zweifeln würden. Hierin liegt, wie man durchaus sagen darf, ein *holistisches* Element. Aber mit welcher Berechtigung darf man *normale* Umstände unterstellen? Und gibt es, wenn man die Normalität suspendiert, nicht Gründe für radikale Zweifel, die gerade wegen des holistischen Ausgangspunkts extreme Folgen hätten? Denn wenn man den richtigen Faden erwischt, kann man den ganzen Strumpf aufribbeln.

So fragt sich Wittgenstein, der zur Zeit der Niederschrift dieses Texts in England lebte, was es mit der eigentümlichen Gewissheit des Satzes „Ich lebe jetzt in England" auf sich hat. Natürlich ist dieser Satz kein Irrtum! Man wüßte gar nicht, wie man hier auf die Idee eines Irrtums kommen könnte. Aber kann ich nicht dennoch „ganz in meinem Urteilen fehlgehen"? Schließlich weiß ich nur wenig von England, und vielleicht mache ich mir aufgrund dieses Wenigen ein völlig falsches Bild davon, so dass ich mit dem Satz „Ich lebe jetzt in England" etwas meine, was gar nichts mit der Wirklichkeit zu tun hat. Hier öffnet sich anscheinend eine theoretische Kluft, in die der Skeptiker einen Keil treiben könnte. Aber wie ließe sich die Situation konkret ausmalen? Wittgenstein erwägt die folgende Möglichkeit:

> Wäre es nicht möglich, daß Menschen zu mir ins Zimmer kämen, die Alle das Gegenteil [von „Ich lebe jetzt in England"] aussagten, ja, mir ›Beweise‹ dafür gäben, so daß ich plötzlich wie ein Wahnsinniger unter lauter Normalen, oder ein Normaler unter Verrückten, allein dastünde? Könnten mir da nicht Zweifel an dem kommen, was mir jetzt das Unzweifelhafteste ist?[40]

Die Möglichkeit eines solchen Zweifels ist nicht auszuschließen. Aber zu bedenken ist, dass die Vorstellung von dieser Möglichkeit nicht ohne die Annahme des Wahnsinns und die Konsequenz der völligen Isolation auskommt. Extreme Zweifel an meinem Urteil, die ich nicht hegen könnte, „ohne alle andern Urteile mitzureißen",[41] sind zwar möglich, doch die Möglichkeit ist ihrerseits kaum denkbar, ohne den Gedanken an Geisteskrankheit ins Spiel zu bringen.

12. Der von der Möglichkeit des Irrsinns affizierte Zweifel ist ein pathologischer Zweifel. Eine andere Form des pathologischen Zweifels, die

---

40 ÜG §420.
41 ÜG §419.

Wittgenstein in Betracht zieht, ist der „hoffnungslose" Zweifel, von dem er hin und wieder spricht. Gemeint ist nicht der Zweifel des Hoffnungslosen, sondern ein Zweifel ohne Aussicht auf Antwort oder Klärung. Wittgensteins Beispiele sind nicht dem Bereich empirischer Untersuchungen der nichtmenschlichen Natur entnommen, sondern dem Bereich des menschlichen Verkehrs. Vermutlich würde er einen solchen Zweifel, wenn er sich auf eine naturwissenschaftliche Untersuchung bezöge, schlicht für unsinnig erklären. In diesem Fall wäre vielleicht die Frage falsch gestellt, oder es könnte sein, dass sich jemand nicht an die üblichen Untersuchungsmethoden hält.

Im interpersonellen Bereich dagegen, so Wittgenstein, ist ein solcher Zweifel nicht nur denkbar, sondern kommt (wie er andeutet) tatsächlich vor. An einer Stelle schreibt er, nachdem er auf die Sicherheit hingewiesen hat, mit der wir normalerweise über die Empfindungen des anderen reden:

> Und nun – möchte ich sagen – gibt es hier allerdings den Fall des hoffnungslosen Zweifels. Wenn ich sage: „Ich habe keine Ahnung, was er wirklich denkt —". Er ist mir ein verschlossenes Buch. ~~Welcher Fremde empfindet nicht so, wenn er nach England kommt?~~ Wenn das einzige Mittel, den Andern zu verstehen, wäre, die gleiche Erziehung wie er durchzumachen, – was unmöglich ist. Und hier ist keine Verstellung.[42]

Dass es sich nicht um Verstellung handelt, ist wichtig, denn der Verdacht, dass sich die anderen Menschen verstellen, wäre ein guter Grund zum Zweifeln. Ein solcher Zweifel wäre mit der Aussicht oder zumindest mit der Möglichkeit verbunden, herauszubekommen, wie es in Wirklichkeit um den anderen bestellt ist. Jedenfalls wüsste man, was geschehen müsste, um die Wahrheit zu erkennen. Genau diese Möglichkeit ist im Fall des hoffnungslosen Zweifels ausgeschlossen: Der andere ist mir „ein völliges Rätsel". Diese Situation beschreibt Wittgenstein an einer bekannten Stelle wie folgt:

> Wir sagen auch von einem Menschen, er sei uns durchsichtig. Aber es ist für diese Betrachtung wichtig, daß ein Mensch für einen andern ein völliges Rätsel sein kann. Das erfährt man, wenn man in ein fremdes Land mit gänzlich fremden Traditionen kommt; und zwar auch dann, wenn man die Sprache des Landes beherrscht. Man *versteht* die Menschen nicht. (Und nicht

---

42 BPhPS II §568, gestrichener Text in MS 137, 43b.

darum, weil man nicht weiß, was sie zu sich selber sprechen.) Wir können uns nicht in sie finden.[43]

Was ist so wichtig an diesem Fall des bodenlosen Nichtverstehens, der völligen Rätselhaftigkeit? Das Besondere ist, dass die normalen Kriterien des Verstehens erfüllt sind: Ich sehe den anderen vor mir; ich kann erkennen, was er treibt; und ich verstehe die Sprache, die er spricht. Dennoch kann ich mir auf seine Handlungen und seine Äußerungen keinen Reim machen. Ich bin ständig im Zweifel über das, was er meint, fühlt und denkt.

Dabei handelt es sich nicht um einen Fall von permanenter Unsicherheit, wie er beispielsweise dann vorkommen kann, wenn ich Grund zu der Annahme habe, dass sich die anderen verstellen und mir etwas vormachen. In einem solchen Fall gehört die Unsicherheit mit zum Sprachspiel.[44] Nein, wer hoffnungslos zweifelt, weiß nicht, wo er ansetzen könnte, um den Zweifel zu beheben. Wittgenstein fragt: Wie würde jemand handeln, „der den Andern gegenüber in einem ernsten, hoffnungslosen Zweifel wäre"? Und seine Antwort lautet: „Wie ein Geistesgestörter".[45] Die Situation wäre also in ähnlicher Weise pathologisch wie im Fall des Verrückten.

13. Die Wichtigkeit dieser Betrachtungen liegt darin, dass sie eine problematische Seite der relevanten Begriffe erkennen lassen. Ist der Begriff „Zweifel", den wir zur Beschreibung des Verhaltens eines Verrückten verwenden, *unser* Begriff des Zweifels? Fällt hoffnungsloser Zweifel unter den normalen Begriff, oder handelt es sich um einen ungewöhnlichen – vielleicht in irgendeinem Sinn metaphorischen – Gebrauch dieses Worts? Umgekehrt könnte man die Frage aufwerfen, ob unser normaler Begriff „Zweifel" komplett beschrieben ist, solange die pathologischen Formen des Zweifels nicht berücksichtigt sind.

Es macht sicher keinen großen Unterschied, ob man diese Fragen so oder so beantwortet, sofern es gelingt, die Beispiele in verständlicher Weise zu beschreiben. Aber gerade das wird schwierig oder gar unmöglich, wenn man den Zweifel zu weit treibt. Wittgenstein veran-

---

43 PPF §325 = PhU II, 568; PPF (=*Philosophy of Psychology – Ein Fragment*) ist der Titel der neuen Ausgabe des früheren Teils II der PhU. Siehe die von P. M. S. Hacker und Joachim Schulte herausgegebene 4. Auflage der PhU, Oxford 2009. In dieser Neuausgabe sind die Bemerkungen durchnummeriert.
44 Vgl. LS §877.
45 LS §248.

schaulicht das an Beispielen der Verstellung, wie sie im Kriminalroman oder anderen Geschichten vorkommen: Was zunächst harmlos wirkt, erregt Verdacht, sobald man den Kontext erweitert, so dass ganz andere und durchaus nicht harmlose Motive in den Blick kommen.[46]

Diese Kontexterweiterung kann man natürlich iterieren, doch wenn die Sache bodenlos wird – das heißt: wenn man keinen „Urgrund" der Wahrheit erkennen kann – ist das Reden von „Verstellung" (und den entsprechenden „Zweifeln") nicht mehr verständlich.[47] Wenn jemand Böses im Schilde führt und, um seine schlimmen Absichten zu kaschieren, sein Leben lang nur Gutes vollbringt, droht das Reden von „Verstellung" seinen Sinn zu verlieren. (Nehmen wir an, von einem bekannten Wohltäter, über den nichts Nachteiliges bekannt ist, werde folgendes behauptet: „Seine philanthropischen Taten dienten bloß der Tarnung, denn eigentlich wollte er den X um sein Vermögen prellen".[48] Wenn es keinen erkennbaren Grund für diese Behauptung gibt, werden wir sie darauf zurückführen, dass der Sprecher seinen Realitätssinn verloren hat.)

In ähnlicher Weise droht der pathologische Zweifel den Begriff des Zweifels übermäßig zu strapazieren. Wir verstehen zwar, wie es dazu kommen kann (z. B. durch Verrücktheit oder kulturelle Fremdheit), aber ob man hier noch von „Zweifel" reden möchte, ist eine Frage, deren Antwort sicher nicht auf der Hand liegt.

Was dagegen auf der Hand liegt, ist die Parallele, an die wir hier zu denken aufgefordert sind: Der philosophische (sei es skeptische oder methodische) Zweifel trägt offenkundig pathologische Züge. Wo ist die Sicherheit, die der Zweifel voraussetzt? Wo ist der Bezug zum menschlichen Handeln? Wo ist die Methode zur Beantwortung? Wo kommt der Zweifel zu Ende? Wittgenstein legt den Gedanken nahe, dass die Brauchbarkeit eines am philosophischen Modell ausgerichteten Zweifelsbegriffs ähnlich eingeschränkt sein dürfte wie ein Begriff, der sich am irren oder am hoffnungslosen Zweifel orientiert.

---

46 Vgl. LS §254.
47 Vgl. LS §269.
48 Vgl. LS §270.

Literatur

ABKÜRZUNGEN	WERKE WITTGENSTEINS
BGM	Bemerkungen über die Grundlagen der Mathematik (Werkausgabe 6)
BPhPs (I , II)	Bemerkungen über die Philosophie der Psychologie (Werkausgabe 7)
FF	Frühfassung (der PhU)
LS	Letzte Schriften über die Philosophie der Psychologie (Werkausgabe 7)
MS, MSS	Manuskript, Manuskripte (nach der von-Wright-Nummerierung)
PhU	Philosophische Untersuchungen (Werkausgabe 1)
PPF	Philosophie der Psychologie – Ein Fragment (= PhU II, Werkausgabe 1)
PhGr	Philosophische Grammatik (Werkausgabe 4)
PhO	Philosophical Occasions
TS, TSS	Typoskript, Typoskripte (nach der von-Wright-Nummerierung)
UF	Urfassung (der PhU)
ÜG	Über Gewissheit (Werkausgabe 8)
Z	Zettel (Werkausgabe 8)

Bibel: Evangelium, siehe Matthäus 20, 1–16
Carroll (1895): Lewis Carroll, *What the Tortoise Said to Achilles*, in: Mind 4, 278–280.
Rhees (1976): Rush Rhees, „Ursache und Wirkung: Intuitives Erfassen", in: J. Klagge/A. Nordmann (ed.), *Ludwig Wittgenstein: Philosophical Occasions 1912–1951*, Indianapolis.
Rhees (2006): Rush Rhees, *Wittgenstein and the Possibility of Discourse*, Oxford
Schulte (1982): Joachim Schulte, „Chor und Gesetz: Zur ›morphologischen Methode‹ bei Goethe und Wittgenstein", in: J. Schulte, *Chor und Gesetz. Wittgenstein im Kontext*, Frankfurt/Main.
Schulte (2009a): Joachim Schulte, „Philosophy of Psychology – A Criticism of a Young Science?", in: Akten der Leipziger Tagung: „Wittgenstein: Philosophie und Wissenschaft".
Schulte (2009b): Joachim Schulte, „Ideen mit den Augen sehen. Goethe und Wittgenstein über Morphologie", in: J. Maatsch (ed.), Band der Weimarer Tagung „Morphologie und Moderne".
Schulte (2010a): Joachim Schulte, „Concepts and Concept-Formation", in: N. Venturinha (ed.), *Wittgenstein After His Nachlass*, Houndmills, 128–142.
Schulte (2010b): Joachim Schulte, „Does the Devil in Hell Have a Form of Life?", in: A. Marques/N. Venturinha (eds.), *Wittgenstein on Forms of Life and the Nature of Experience*, Bern, 125–141.
Wittgenstein (2001): Ludwig Wittgenstein, *Philosophische Untersuchungen*, J. Schulte/H. Nyman/E. v. Savigny/G. H. v. Wright (eds.), Frankfurt/Main.

Wittgenstein (2009): Ludwig Wittgenstein, *Philosophical Investigations/Philosophische Untersuchungen*, P. M. S. Hacker/J. Schulte (eds.), 4. Auflage der PhU, Oxford.

Skepticism, Contextualism and Entitlement

Sebastian Schmoranzer

I

Who is to deny that we know a lot about the external world? It seems to be a truism that we know there to be chairs, to have hands etc. Yet, once we are seriously immersed in a philosophical discussion with the skeptic, our self-image is put into doubt by means of a simple and prima facie compelling argument. In order to have knowledge we should be able to rule out that we are falling prey to a perfect illusion. This, however, seems impossible since every piece of evidence we might refer to could be part of the very illusion we are trying to dismiss. Consequently, we do not have the kind of knowledge that we commonly take for granted.

One way to spell out the skeptical reasoning in more detail while, at the same time, applying it to a case that we consider to be a paradigmatic example of external world knowledge is as follows:

(I) In order to know that I have a hand, I have to be internally justified in believing that I have one.

(II) But I am only internally justified in believing that I have a hand, if I am also internally justified in believing that I am not a handless and perfectly deceived brain in a vat.

(III) However, I am not internally justified in believing that I am not a brain in a vat.

(IV) Therefore, I do not know that I have a hand.[1]

---

1 How might the skeptic motivate the premises of his argument? A full answer to this question will lead us too far from the topic of this paper. The following short remarks, however, might give you an idea. As to the first premise: It is not enough that our true beliefs are the result of a reliable belief forming process for them to count as knowledge. Otherwise, someone who was in fact a reliable clairvoyant but had overwhelming evidence to the contrary would have knowledge which is implausible. (Cf. BonJour 1985, 40.) As to the second premise: Internal justification is closed under internally justified entailment. Furthermore, in order to be justified in believing that I have a hand I also have to

Presumably, most of us are puzzled. How can it be that, on the one hand, we do know a lot — this much still seems true — while on the other hand the skeptical argument is so convincing? One feels the need to find out where exactly the skeptical argument goes wrong — if fault can be found at all. Some philosophers even see the challenge not only in identifying an unjustified or false premise but in explaining the initial grip of the skeptical argument as well.[2]

Contextualism about knowledge seems to promise well in addressing the latter demand. In general, contextualists hold the view that a person can know that something is the case relative to one context whereas she does not know it relative to another context although the evidence for her true belief is the same.[3] Based on this idea contextualists try to solve the above puzzle by arguing as follows: In a way, the skeptical reasoning is compatible with our everyday knowledge. In ordinary contexts we know a lot and relative to such contexts the skeptical argument is defective. There is therefore no need to revise our self-image. Yet, in a philosophical context in which we are seriously discussing matters with the skeptic her argument is faultless. It is, thus, no surprise that it is so convincing once we muse about it.

For this explanation to succeed the contextualist has to show which of the premises in the skeptical argument is problematic with regard to everyday contexts. The strategies to fulfill this task can be as multifarious as there are premises. A contextualist with externalist leanings might criticize the first premise and argue as follows: Normally, knowledge does not presuppose internal justification. A reliably formed true belief constitutes knowledge no matter whether, from an inner perspective, it is epistemically reasonable to hold the belief in question. But doing philosophy creates a highly reflective context in which "knowledge" is to be understood as "highly reflective knowledge" that stands in need of

---

be justified in believing that handless brains in a vat do not have hands. Therefore, I am only justified in believing that I have a hand if I am also justified in believing that I am not a brain in a vat. (Cf. Schmoranzer 2010, ch. II.2.) As to the third premise: From an internal perspective everything would be just the same whether I was a brain in a vat or a normal person.

2   Cf. Williams (1996a), 10; Williams (2001), 458 and Willaschek (2003), 185.
3   Relative to what kind of context, due to which contextual feature and with respect to what condition of knowledge? This is where contextualists part company.

internal justification.[4] A contextualist defending a relevant alternatives approach to internal justification might say that in order to be justified one has to be able to rule out all relevant alternatives that far fetched skeptical alternatives usually do not belong to.[5] Only if we are seriously considering the skeptical error possibilities do they become relevant after all. Finally, instead of criticizing one of the first two premises of the skeptical argument the contextualist about knowledge could question the third. It is this kind of contextualism that I want to focus on here.

For a contextualist of this kind it might be tempting to reason as follows: Internal justification is a gradual concept. One can be more or less justified because there can be more or less internally accessible evidence for a belief. If Peter tells me that Suzy and Billy are throwing rocks at a bottle, this is good evidence for my respective belief. If Hanna confirms Peter's story, my belief is even better justified. How strong my justification has to be in order for me to have knowledge depends on context-sensitive standards. Typically, those standards are quite moderate and we are internally justified in denying skeptical hypotheses. But in philosophy classes, in contexts of pure intellectual inquiry or moments of meditation standards tend to rise and we are no longer within our rights to dismiss skeptical scenarios.

This reasoning, though, is problematic. By mentioning scenarios of perfect illusion the sceptic is not claiming that we are to some extent justified in believing skeptical hypotheses to be false but that our justification is not good enough for knowledge. He rightly insists that in light of such scenarios there is absolutely *no* internally accessible evidence that they are wrong.[6] *Every* piece of evidence I might refer to in order to rule them out could be part of the very delusion I want to reject.

---

4   This should not be misunderstood. I am not saying that philosophers like DeRose (1995), (1999) or Lewis (1996) who combine externalism with contextualism give this kind of answer. In fact, they do not. They flat out deny the first premise of the skeptical argument. But they continue and try to explain why there are contexts in which *another* kind of skeptical reasoning – this time concerned with external justification – sometimes succeeds.
5   Cf. Rheinwald (2004). In my view Austin (1962) can be read this way as well.
6   More carefully phrased: *Unless* we are entitled to think these scenarios do not hold, there is absolutely no evidence. For the notion of epistemic entitlement and the relation between evidence and entitlement see the rest of this section and section II.

Another way for the contextualist to put the third premise of the skeptical argument into doubt could be to marry contextualism to a theory of epistemic entitlement. The problem with the traditional debates in epistemology, one might say, seems to be that we are tying internal justification too closely to the possession of internally accessible evidence.[7] Instead, one should adopt a more liberal view and define internal justification as follows:

> S is internally justified in believing that p (in context C) if and only if in light of the information available to S (in C) and with regard to the aim of increasing the amount of true beliefs while keeping the amount of false beliefs as small as possible S's believing that p (in C) is responsible.

The general idea is not new: internal justification consists in epistemic responsibility. Yet, contrary to the traditional view, there are – in principle – two ways the demand for epistemic responsibility can be respected: one can possess evidence or one can be entitled to hold a belief for non-evidential reasons. Two examples might help elucidate this idea. If Peter tells me the story about Suzy and Billy, I have good evidence for believing that Suzy and Billy are throwing rocks at a bottle. In this case I am internally justified because I am *evidentially justified*. Yet, the possession of evidence – even if sufficient – is not necessary for epistemic responsibility. How can this be? Different theories of epistemic entitlement offer different answers to this question and an elaborated discussion of one such theory will be our subject in the following sections. Without entering into the details of any specific theory yet, the following example might give you an idea of how non-evidential justification *could* be thought of. Suppose Jack knows next to nothing about leopards whereas Pamela is an expert on this matter. Now Pamela proposes him the following deal: If he makes himself believe that every even number greater than two is the sum of two primes, she will tell him whatever he wants to know about leopards. Jack knows that she will keep her word and that she is a reliable source on this topic. But he, like anyone else, has no idea whether the mathematical thesis in question is true or false. Still, given that he will significantly increase his stock of true beliefs while – maybe – holding a false belief it is, from a purely epistemic point of view, a good idea for him to accept Goldbach's conjecture. Jack is *epistemically entitled* and thereby internally justified in believing

---

7 Wright (2004) defends a non-contextualist theory of epistemic entitlement along the lines indicated below. For a critique on Wright see Schmoranzer (2010), ch. III.4 and Schmoranzer (forthcoming).

that Goldbach's conjecture is true even if he has absolutely no evidence.[8]

This way of distinguishing two kinds of internal justification – evidential justification and epistemic entitlement[9] – seems to open a way to counter the skeptic. There might be no evidence for the claim that we are not brains in a vat. However, at least in non-skeptical contexts, we are nonetheless entitled to think that our senses are reliable and that we are not the victim of an undetectable skeptical delusion. To be sure, the success of this approach to skepticism hinges on how convincingly the following questions can be answered: What are sufficient conditions for epistemic entitlement? Why are we usually entitled to deny skeptical hypotheses?

As I see it, Michael Williams tries to meet the skeptical challenge along the lines just indicated.[10] I therefore want to examine his position in more detail. To begin with, I will establish the claim that Williams criticizes the third premise of the skeptical argument by defending a contextualist-cum-entitlement conception of internal justification (section II). Subsequently, I will reconstruct his conception of epistemic entitlement as methodological entitlement (section III). It will turn out that Williams' alleged answer to skepticism is unconvincing for two reasons: First, the theory of methodological entitlement faces counter-examples (section IV). Second, even if one was willing to adopt a hang-tough-strategy with respect to these examples, the reply to the skeptic then amounts to the thesis that we are justified in believing that we are not brains in a vat only because we are in fact already convinced that we are not (section V).

---

8   Nota bene: I am not claiming that it is plausible to suppose that Jack is in fact internally justified. Neither is this something that has, to my knowledge, been defended by proponents of theories of epistemic entitlement. The sole function of the example is to illustrate in how far the definition of internal justification given above opens the space for non-evidential kinds of internal justification.
9   Unless otherwise indicated entitlement simpliciter is epistemic entitlement.
10 Williams (1993a), (1993b), (1996a), (1996b), (1999) and (2001). For a similar interpretation of Williams (1993a) and (1993b) cf. Brueckner (1994).

II

What premise of the skeptical argument is Michael Williams aiming at in his anti-skeptical writings? Examining Williams' conception of knowledge it becomes clear that he agrees with the skeptic on the first premise. Knowledge always presupposes internal justification in the rather liberal sense described in the previous section.

In accordance with the Platonic tradition Williams takes knowledge to be justified true belief. In contrast to this tradition he sees justification as consisting of two components: personal justification and adequate grounding. In order to be personally justified in believing something to be the case it has to be epistemically responsible to do so. Personal justification requires reasonable epistemic diligence. If, for example, I have good internally accessible evidence that no one is clairvoyant, then I am not personally justified in believing something on the basis of my clairvoyance even if my supernatural capacities are – unbeknown to me – in fact reliable.

Adequate grounding on the other hand consists in truth-conduciveness. One's belief is adequately grounded if and only if the belief is the result of a reliable belief-forming process. If I was in fact clairvoyant, my beliefs would be adequately grounded despite the fact that they are not personally justified.[11]

The possession of internally accessible evidence may be sufficient for personal justification. And in cases in which the evidence available is a reliable indicator of truth it is sufficient for adequate grounding as well. But, according to Williams, it is not necessary for either. My clairvoyance adequately grounds my respective beliefs even though I have no citable and commonly accepted evidence for them. And I can also be personally justified in believing something despite a lack of internally accessible evidence. In order to explain how this is possible Williams distinguishes two concepts of personal justification while opting for the second one himself. The first conception is based on the principle he calls "Prior Grounding Requirement" according to which a belief is jus-

---

11 Instead of adequate grounding Williams also speaks of evidential justification. Yet, this kind of justification is not to be confused with the possession of internally accessible evidence. Williams' use of the term "evidential justification" is therefore misleading. In order to avoid confusion I reserve the term "evidence" for internally accessible evidence. This is the kind of evidence one can refer to in a discussion about why a belief is probably true.

tified only if it can be backed up by quotable evidence. Adherents to the second conception are defending a default-and-challenge approach to personal justification according to which a belief is prima facie personally justified as long as there is no reason to think that it is false. Williams writes:

> The difference between the two conceptions of justification is like that between legal systems that treat the accused as guilty unless proved innocent [Prior Grounding Requirement] and those that do the opposite, granting presumptive innocence and throwing the burden of proof onto the accuser. Adopting the second model, epistemic entitlement is the default status of a person's beliefs and assertions. One is entitled to a belief or assertion (personally justified) in the absence of reasons to think that one is *not* so entitled [default and challenge approach].[12]

This short introduction to Williams' theory of knowledge reveals two points that he seems to agree on. First, knowledge presupposes internal justification understood as epistemic responsibility. In Williams' terminology, knowledge presupposes personal justification which demands for epistemic diligence. Secondly, this kind of internal justification does not presuppose the availability of positive evidence – a point we will come back to in a moment. (From now on justification simpliciter is internal justification as defined in section I. Evidence simpliciter is internally accessible evidence.)

Before, we have to find out about Williams' attitude towards the second skeptical premise according to which our external-world beliefs are justified only if we are justified in denying skeptical hypotheses. As far as I can tell Williams sees no fault with that premise either. He explicitly defends the view that in ordinary contexts we are justified in believing that skeptical hypotheses are false.[13] There is therefore no need for him to reject the second premise. Furthermore, Williams proclaims: "I have no wish to make a denial of closure the basis of my response to skepticism."[14] What does that mean and what does this have to do with the second premise? Williams is talking about the following principle: If S knows that p and if S knows that p entails q, then S also knows that q. Williams does not want his reply to the skeptic to imply that this principle does not hold. Since knowledge, according to Williams, presup-

---

12 Williams (1999), 51. Cf. Williams (2001), 25. My presentation of Williams' concept of knowledge is especially based on Williams (1999), 50–54 and (2001), 22–25.
13 Williams (2001), 187.
14 Williams (1996a), 318.

poses justification, he presumably also does not want his reply to skepticism to imply that the following closure principle for justification does not hold: If S is justified in believing that p and if S is justified in believing that p entails q, then S is also justified in believing that q. But this is exactly what happens if one denies the second premise of the skeptical argument.

Let p be the thesis that I have a hand and let q be the proposition that I am not a handless brain in a vat. It is obvious, and Williams certainly agrees, that I am justified in believing that p entails q. And, at least with respect to normal contexts, Williams also agrees that I am justified in believing that p. If he therefore denied that I was justified in believing that p only if I was also justified in believing that q, he would be rejecting the general validity of the closure principle for justification.[15]

Thus, I conclude that neither the first nor the second premise of the skeptical argument is criticized by Williams. Yet, he definitely objects to the third premise as far as everyday, legal and (non-philosophical) scientific contexts are concerned:

> My inability to rule out skeptical possibilities on the basis of purely experiential evidence affects my entitlement to believe that I am not a brain in a vat – and here I mean *epistemic* entitlement – only if that entitlement is hostage to a prior – and context-invariant – commitment to provide any and every belief about the world with an experiential grounding. [...] But the availability of contextualism as a coherent alternative shows that this doctrine is not self-evidently true.[16]

We have to be careful about what *exactly* Williams is saying here. He is not agreeing with the skeptic on the thesis that we have *no* evidence at all. Ultimately, Williams is defending the following position: In ordinary contexts we do have evidence that we are not brains in a vat because in those contexts we are entitled to believe that our senses are reliable.

---

15 My argument has the following form with "J" standing for "I am justified in believing that ...", "p" standing for "I have a hand" and "q" standing for "I am not a brain in a vat":
 (1) $J(p \supset q)$
 (2) Jp
 (3) $\neg(Jp \supset Jq)$
 (4) $\neg(Jp \,\&\, J(p \supset q) \supset Jq)$

To avoid this problem, Williams could argue that (3) only holds in those cases in which (1) or (2) do not hold. But that would be a rather implausible view. Why should my ignorance decrease my epistemic duties?

16 Williams (2001), 188.

In other words: There is evidence that skeptical hypotheses are false. But we have this evidence only due to the fact that we are non-evidentially justified in dismissing skeptical error possibilities.

This might sound confusing. But let me explain. Williams differentiates between purely experiential evidence and observational evidence. True sentences like "It appears to me as if I have a hand" or "It seems to me that I am not a handless brain in a vat" express purely experiential evidence. Once we are asked to justify our everyday beliefs (e.g., that I have a hand) exclusively on the basis of this kind of evidence the skeptic wins. Such justification cannot be had because everything would appear to me just the same if I were cleverly deceived.

On the other hand, there are what Williams calls observational reports. When I am looking at my hand and spontaneously utter the sentence "I have a hand", that sentence expresses an observational report. Justified observational reports in turn constitute observational evidence. And the justified observational report that I have a hand is evidence for the claim that I am not a handless brain in a vat. However, according to Williams, observational reports are justified on a given occasion only if one is justified in believing that the senses are reliable on that very occasion. In his words: "We need reliability-knowledge to have any observational knowledge of particular facts."[17]

This poses the threat of circularity. How can we be justified in trusting our senses without our observational beliefs being justified in the first place? Williams' solution consists in endorsing a default-and-challenge principle of justification with respect to the assumption that our senses are reliable:

> To be in the game of observational reporting we must know things about our observational capacities. But that knowledge does not provide evidential back-up. More importantly, in entering an observation report, we may often properly presuppose that conditions are sufficiently normal for our reporting dispositions to be reliable. Epistemic responsibility does not require that we first ascertain that such conditions are normal. Such an inquiry is required only if reasons emerge for thinking that conditions may not be normal.[18]

We are prima facie justified in believing that our senses are reliable because we are entitled to do so as long as there is no evidence to the con-

---

17 Williams (2001), 176. For Williams' theory of observational knowledge see Williams (2001), ch. 15.
18 Williams (2001), 177.

trary. Therefore, our observational reports are justified. And this qualifies them as observational evidence for other claims. With respect to skeptical hypotheses this means: I am entitled, i.e. non-evidentially justified, to believe that my senses are reliable and that I am not a brain in a vat. Because of this the observational report, that I have a hand, constitutes observational evidence. This evidence in turn can be used to evidentially justify the claim that I am not a handless brain in a vat.[19]

As we can see, Williams' rejection of the third skeptical premise depends on the claim that in normal contexts we are epistemically entitled to deny skeptical hypotheses. Thus, Williams is pursuing exactly the contextualist-cum-entitlement approach to skepticism I described in the first section. But what makes for entitlement?

III

Why, according to Williams, are we normally entitled to believe that we are not brains in a vat? The quotes given suggest that he is defending the following simple entitlement principle:

> (Simple Entitlement) S is entitled to believe that p if there is no evidence against p.

Unfortunately, this cannot be right. In ordinary contexts there is no evidence against the hypothesis that my senses are in general reliable. But there is no evidence against the hypothesis that I am a brain in a vat either. Certainly, it cannot be that both theses are justified at the same time.[20] Or can it? What if epistemic permissibility is sufficient for epistemic entitlement? Might there not be situations in which it is epistemically allowed to accept a thesis and in which it is also epistemically allowed to accept an obviously incompatible thesis exactly because our evidence is neutral with respect to both?[21] I do not think so. Imagine a situation in which I have good evidence only for the thesis that *either*

---

19 At least if one accepts that evidential justification is closed under justified entailment.
20 Besides: If this was true, one could not explain why we are not entitled to deny skeptical hypotheses in skeptical contexts since in those contexts there is still no evidence against the reliability of the senses.
21 This is not to be confused with the claim that we are allowed/it is permitted to accept a thesis and a contradicting thesis at the same time. From p being justified and q being justified it does not follow that p-and-q is justified.

Peter *or* Jim has eaten my birthday cake but in which I have absolutely no idea which one of them is the culprit. If it was epistemically permissible to believe that (it is *true* that) Peter has eaten the cake it would be appropriate to blame Peter – which it is not. Peter is completely right to protest: "You do not have the slightest reason to accuse me because you do not have the slightest evidence for thinking that I am the perpetrator." The absence of counter-evidence might be necessary but it is not sufficient for epistemic entitlement. The popular slogan "Innocent until proven guilty" is catchy but misleading.

Fortunately, a closer look reveals that Williams has more to say about epistemic entitlement. In this regard he brings into play the notion of methodological necessities. According to Williams, justification is to be relativized to contexts of inquiry. Those contexts are characterized by a method of inquiry that helps to determine with respect to a specific subject whether a thesis is to be classified as true or false. When we are doing history, we are within a context in which, for instance, we are to decide whether Napoleon knew at Waterloo that Blücher's army was on its way. And we have to answer such questions on the basis of historical sources. That is the historical method of inquiry. There are permissible doubts within this context. One may ask whether a diary entry can be trusted or whether a letter was forged. However, if we want to do history at all, the assumption that not all historical sources are misleading has to be exempted from doubt. Otherwise our investigations would not get off the ground and *historical* questions could not be answered. For methodological reasons it is therefore inappropriate in a context of historical research to ask whether we can rule out that all historical sources have been manipulated. Discussing such matters changes the direction of inquiry turning a historical investigation into an epistemological one. Williams writes:

> I shall call propositions that have to be exempted from doubt, if certain types of question are to be pursued, *methodological necessities*. [...] Methodological necessities are a source of default entitlement because they determine the *direction of inquiry*. [...] What we are looking into is a function of what we are leaving alone. We can no more inquire into everything at once than we can travel simultaneously in all directions. [...] The point of such constraints is to make focused questioning possible.[22]

---

22 Williams (2001), 160. Cf. Williams (1996a), 23–25, 117, 122–125. Williams sees himself inspired by Wittgenstein's remarks in *Über Gewißheit*. Cf. Wittgenstein (1989), §§ 163, 341–343.

> These commitments, which must be accepted, if what we understand by historical inquiry is to be conducted at all, have the status, relative to the form of inquiry, of *methodological necessities*.[23]

In light of those remarks we can define methodological necessities as follows: A proposition p is a methodological necessity with respect to a context of inquiry C if and only if asking for a justification for p amounts to putting into doubt the method characterizing the inquiry conducted in C which in turn changes the kind of inquiry. Correspondingly, since such propositions are said to be a source of epistemic entitlement we can define a special kind of epistemic entitlement we might lable "methodological entitlement":

> (Methodological Entitlement) S is methodologically entitled to accept that p in a context of inquiry C if and only if asking for a justification for p amounts to putting into doubt the method characterizing the inquiry conducted in C and thereby changing the kind of inquiry.

Let us grant for a moment that methodological entitlement implies epistemic entitlement – and consequently epistemic justification as well. In how far does this notion help Williams to explain that in ordinary contexts we are justified in believing that we are not brains in a vat whereas in certain philosophical contexts we are no longer justified?

Suppose I was asking my friend whether there was any milk left in the fridge. In this context of inquiry one appropriate method for settling my question is to check the fridge by looking inside. Asking whether our senses are in general reliable, results in putting into doubt this method and thereby leads to an altogether different debate. With respect to this context, propositions expressed by sentences such as "I am not a brain in a vat" are methodological necessities which we are entitled to accept. (The same goes for scientific or legal contexts.)

Yet, in a context of pure intellectual inquiry the skeptic – according to Williams – somehow gets us to agree on the following methodological constraint: Classify as true only those beliefs the negations of which are incompatible with our purely experiential evidence. With respect to this constraint we are no longer justified in believing that we are not brains in a vat since that belief neither has the status of a methodological necessity nor is its negation incompatible with our purely experiential evidence.[24] But the skeptic's victory is elusive. Leave the study and

---

23 Williams (1996a), 123. Cf. Williams (1996b), 372.
24 Williams (1996a), 129 f.

your knowledge returns. Contextualism teaches us that the skeptic is wrong to think that just because there is one context of inquiry in which we have no knowledge, there is no context in which we do.

Thus, Williams seems to offer an elegant solution to the skeptical challenge. However, a closer look will show that he is wrong. Methodological entitlement does not imply epistemic entitlement.[25]

IV

Let me start by questioning the considerations on which the general idea of methodological entitlement is grounded. As far as I can see, Williams offers two reasons why we are contextually entitled to accept methodological necessities.

First, we have to exempt them from doubt to make focused questioning possible. This *by itself* cannot make for epistemic entitlement. If we want to do history, it is certainly epistemologically wise not to ask questions that have nothing to do with our subject. You cannot make any progress if you want to travel into all directions at once. Who is to deny that? But this only entitles us *not to discuss* certain prop-

---

25 One critical comment on how well the story told by Williams explains the initial plausibility of the skeptical argument: We have to explain our initial impression that the skeptical conclusion conflicts with our everyday certainties. It is not only that we find no fault with the skeptical reasoning at first sight. It is also that we are puzzled and think that it puts our self-image into doubt. If Williams were right, the skeptic would impose quite unusual methodological constraints. But if this was the case, we would not be too worried about the results. One can argue for a lot of radical conclusions if one is willing to make the right presumptions. But if those presumptions are obviously silly, that does not bother us at all. If someone argued that there was no doctor in New York City because there was no one who could cure every disease within two minutes, we could, for reasons of cooperative communication, agree on his peculiar definition. And we could, for a moment, accept his conclusion. But we would not be worried because we would not think his conclusion to stand in any conflict with our everyday beliefs. Yet, the situation seems to be different when it comes to Cartesian Skepticism. Thus, the methodological constraints the skeptic applies cannot be too absurd. Cf. Craig (1993), 219–222.

Williams therefore seems to be facing the following difficulty: If according to his theory skeptical doubts are too unnatural, he cannot explain our confusion. But if those doubts are somehow convincing, the question comes up whether they are not grounded in our ordinary way of thinking about knowledge and justification.

ositions. It does not allow us to *accept them as true*. If I want to learn something about Napoleon, I should *not* care about whether Golbach's conjecture is right. However, this does not justify me in accepting it as true.

Second, Williams claims that we are, with respect to a given inquiry, entitled to accept the methodological necessities because otherwise we could not apply the method characterizing our cognitive project. The project could not even get started. This remark should be taken with a grain of salt. One can do history *under the provisional assumption* that not all sources are misleading. Accordingly, one can accept the results of our investigation conditionally by tacitly adding the proviso: "If not all sources are misleading then....". In that case we would not be committed to *accept* the methodological necessities. Nonetheless, Williams could argue that one cannot – on pain of being epistemically irrational – *seriously* do history and *unconditionally* believe in its results if one does not also believe in the general reliability of the historical sources. Yet, even if we agree on this, this alone does not make my acceptance of the methodological necessities epistemically respectable. Only if it is epistemologically responsible to seriously conduct a cognitive project, is it epistemically appropriate to accept its characteristic methodological necessities. This becomes obvious when we consider the following counterexample to our definition of methodological entitlement.[26]

Peter is an astrologist discussing matters with his colleagues at a conference entitled "The love-life of Aquarius". The participants at the conference all presuppose that the celestial constellations influence our lives. Their method for settling certain questions about human beings consists in consulting the stars. With respect to this context of inquiry it is a methodological necessity that the stars influence our lives. Asking for a justification of this presupposition amounts to doubting the adequacy of the method applied and changes the subject. All this notwithstanding, the people at the conference are not justified in believing that the stars influence our lives because they have no reason to think that their cognitive project is epistemically respectable.[27] Furthermore, there is good empirical evidence that astrology is humbug.

---

26 More precisely, it is a counterexample to the claim that methodological entitlement implies epistemic entitlement. In what follows this is what I mean by saying that something is a counterexample to methodological entitlement.
27 If you are a radical contextualist about epistemic justification, you might reply that with respect to *their* context they are justified even if with respect to the

In reaction to this example the following modified version of methodological entitlement comes to mind:

> (Methodological Entitlement – Modified Version 1) S is methodologically entitled to accept that p in a context of inquiry C if and only if i) asking for a justification for p amounts to putting into doubt the method characterizing the inquiry conducted in C and thereby changing the kind of inquiry and *ii) there is no evidence against p.*

This fits well with what Williams writes himself:

> [M]ethodological necessities are a source of *default* entitlement [...].[28] (My emphasis)

> [O]bservational evidence operates cross-contextually. Of course, such evidence is not mechanically determinative of what we ought to think, for it is always potentially subject to considerations of relevance and reliability. But it is always there and is not simply to be dismissed.[29]

According to our new definition, the astrologers are not entitled to believe that the stars influence our life even if this proposition is a methodological necessity because there is evidence that it is false.

Nevertheless, two questions are still to be answered. Is being an uncontradicted methodological necessity sufficient for epistemic entitlement? And in how far does the fact that a proposition has to be accepted in order to seriously pursue a certain form of inquiry contribute to its being justified? Discussing the latter question will lead us to answering the first.

As the definition now stands there are two features a proposition has to have in order for it to earn the title of methodological entitlement. First, there must not be evidence against it. Second, it has to be a methodological necessity. The upshot of our discussion concerning the simple entitlement principle was that the absence of contradicting evidence is a necessary but not a sufficient condition for epistemic entitlement. Therefore, the question still stands why being a methodological necessity makes it in any way epistemologically *more* permissible to accept the proposition in question. A possible reply might go as follows: If there is no evidence against a methodological necessity, there is no evidence

---

context from which *we* are assessing their behavior they are not justified. But this is not convincing. We are trying to elucidate *our* concept of epistemic justification. And – as the example shows – applying our concept to the astrologists' beliefs is inadmissible. See also section V.

28 Williams (2001), 160.
29 Williams (2001), 227.

against the truth-conduciveness of the method applied. This in turn makes it epistemologically permissible to conduct the inquiry. And since that inquiry cannot seriously be executed if one did not accept the methodological necessity, that acceptance in turn is epistemologically permissible as well.

But now the problem reappears which confronted the simple entitlement principle. There being no evidence against the truth-conduciveness of a certain method might be necessary but it is not sufficient for the application of the method to be epistemically permissible. Consequently, it does not make it epistemically permissible to accept the respective methodological necessities either.

This will become clear when we consider the following counterexample to our modified version of methodological entitlement: Anne and Miriam know that either Peter or Jim has eaten the cake. But they have no idea which of the two it was. Anne and Miriam do not like Peter very much and believe that he is to blame. Discussing what happened after the cake had been eaten, they apply a method of inquiry (partly) consisting in obeying the following maxim: Unless there is evidence to the contrary, classify as false any proposition that is incompatible with the thesis that *Peter has eaten the cake*.

The italicized sentence expresses a methodological necessity with respect to Miriam's and Anne's cognitive project of finding out (not about who has eaten the cake but) about what happened *after* Peter has eaten the cake by applying their peculiar method of inquiry. Wondering whether it was really Peter who has eaten the cake amounts to wondering whether obeying the maxim leads to true beliefs. Furthermore, there is no evidence against the thesis that Peter is the culprit. (And there is no evidence that the method applied is not truth-conducive.) Still, neither is it epistemically permissible for Anne and Miriam to proceed as they do nor is it epistemically permissible for them to accept the claim that Peter has eaten the cake.

One might be reluctant to call Miriam's and Anne's procedure "a method of inquiry". But that attitude is unfounded for several reasons: First, a method of inquiry is determined by a set of rules used to classify propositions as true or false. And the maxim mentioned in our example is one such rule. Second, Anne's and Miriam's method is general because it applies to all empirical propositions. Every empirical proposition fulfilling the conditions mentioned above is to be classified as false. Of course, the rule remains silent with respect to a lot of beliefs. But that does not disqualify it as being part of a set of rules that, taken together, constitute the basis of their method of inquiry. Third, compare the maxim Anne and Miriam are obeying to the following maxim that we are respecting in normal contexts: "Unless there is evidence to the contrary classify as false those propositions that are incompatible with the thesis that our senses are reliable". If following this maxim amounts to the application of a method, so is Anne's and Miriam's procedure.[30]

---

30 With respect to this counterexample one might argue as follows: According to Williams there are more contextual features determining the epistemological status of my beliefs than the methodological aspects discussed so far. With respect to personal justification Williams mentions the following: economic constraints, dialectical features and semantic constraints. Someone, my opponent might argue, is methodologically entitled to accept a proposition only if this does not conflict with one of these other constraints. Yet, this is exactly what happens in Miriam's and Anne's case.

In order to counter this objection we have to take a look at the three features mentioned. First, there are the so-called economic constraints. How well my evidence has to be in order for my belief to be evidentially justified or in order for a proposition to be evidentially put into doubt depends on how much is at stake, how much time is available to settle a question etc. (Cf. Williams 1996a, 117 f. and 2001, 161 f.) It is obvious that this rule has no bearing on our example. We are not dealing with the question whether Miriam's and Anne's methodological assumption is *evidentially* justified. And ex hypothesis there is absolutely no evidence against it.

Second, there are what Williams labels "dialectical features". Whether a belief is justified in a certain context depends on what the participants of the debate let each other get away with. If, in a given context, I claim that p is the case and no one objects, then this claim is prima facie justified – at least as long as there is no evidence to the contrary. (Cf. Williams 1996a, 117 f. and 2001, 161 f.) This rule is of no importance to our example either. We are free to assume that all participants in Anne's and Miriam's investigation are letting them get away with their assumption. Furthermore, this is a permissive rule. It does not tell us when an assumption is not justified or ceases to be so. It does not impose any constraints on what Anne and Miriam are allowed to accept as true. Finally, this rule is anything but convincing. If all members of a debate share the assumption that Goldbach's conjecture is true, they are still not justified in believing it to be so.

Third, there are semantic constraints. If a proposition can only be understood if it is false, then I may safely assume that it is. And I am not allowed to accept it as true. (Williams 2001, 159 f., 197 f.) Are we to say that Anne's and Miriam's assumption can be understood only if it is false? No way.

But wait. Do not the semantic constraints offer a way out of the skeptical predicament? Can we not say that skeptical hypotheses can only be understood if they are false? And if so, could we not say that we are *semantically* entitled to believe that skeptical hypotheses are false? These are extremely intricate ques-

Of course, their method is strange and unacceptable. It is not embedded in a long standing practice of truth-seeking. Maybe this is the reason why we are unwilling to classify the respective methodological necessity as justified. We could therefore try to solve the problem posed by the Anne-Miriam-example by amending our definition once again:

> (Methodological Entitlement – Modified Version 2) S is methodologically entitled to accept that p in a context of inquiry C if and only if i) asking for a justification for p amounts to putting into doubt the method characterizing the inquiry conducted in C and thereby changing the kind of inquiry, ii) there is no evidence against p and *iii) the method applied has a long tradition in S's community*.

But why should it become *epistemologically* permissible to enter into a certain form of inquiry just because it is a procedure that has *in fact* been commonly applied for quite some time? With respect to the aim of increasing the number of true beliefs while decreasing the number of false beliefs, it is by no means responsible to apply a method *just because* everyone else does.[31] Even if Miriam and Anne lived in a world

---

tions to answer and I am not addressing them here. Besides, it is doubtful whether Williams is willing to pursue this line of reasoning. Cf. Williams (1996a), xiv, xvi, xvii and (2001), 150 ff., 190 f., 197 ff.

31 Objection: Is not the (known) fact that everyone in my community applies a certain method good evidence for its truth-conduciveness? How could they all be wrong? Is it, therefore, not also epistemically reasonable for someone to apply that method and to accept its specific methodological necessities?

Reply 1: We have to keep in mind that we are trying to discover a non-evidential justification for the proposition that we are not brains in a vat. That is, we are looking for an epistemic warrant for that proposition which does not presuppose the availability of internally accessible evidence. Now let us suppose we were methodologically entitled to believe that we are not brains in a vat because we are applying the traditional method of consulting our senses with respect to which the proposition that we are not brains in a vat is an uncontradicted methodological necessity. That this method is (known to be) commonly applied, implies that we have good evidence for its truth-conduciveness. Our methodological entitlement for the claim that we are not brains in a vat therefore already presupposes evidence for the claim that our senses are to be trusted and that we are not perfectly deceived.

Reply 2: It certainly does not suffice that the method is in fact commonly applied. That by itself does not make it epistemically responsible for me to apply it. It has to be a known fact. But in order to know that the method I apply is in fact applied by other people I would already have to know that I was not a brain in a vat. (Notice: If we give the sentence "It is a common meth-

where it was commonly accepted to act on the maxim that, unless there is evidence to the contrary, Peter is to blame for everything, it would still be epistemically irresponsible for them to believe that he has eaten the cake. One might try to circumvent this peculiarity by stipulating that the method applied has to have a long standing tradition not in S's but in *our* community. Yet, what should be so special about our biases?[32]

In light of the counter-examples given I thus conclude that there is no satisfying way to define the notion of methodological entitlement in such a way that it implies epistemic entitlement.

V

Yet, what if one were willing to bite the bullet? A radical contextualist might claim that in the counterfactual situation described above Miriam and Anne are justified in believing that Peter has eaten the cake even if from the point of view of our actual epistemological practice they are not.

Let us see where this will lead us in our reply to the skeptic. We are not justified in believing that we are not brains in a vat if it is epistemologically equally justified to think that we are. The skeptic claims that the skeptical hypothesis and its negation are rationally seen on a par since the evidence we have is compatible with both theses. Proponents of a theory of epistemic entitlement therefore try to find other reasons why we are allowed to favor the normal world hypothesis over the skeptical hypothesis. In this dialectical situation Williams brings into play the concept of methodological entitlement. In his eyes it is epistemologically permissible to deny the skeptical hypothesis because in ordinary contexts we are applying certain commonly accepted methods with respect to which the proposition that we are not brains in a vat is an uncontradicted methodological necessity.

Now imagine that we ordinarily applied a different method (partly) characterized by the following rule: Unless there is evidence to the contrary, interpret your sensory experience in accordance with the assump-

---

    od" a neutral reading which is compatible with me being a brain in a vat which is "observing" that it is a method "commonly applied", my evidence that this method is "commonly applied" is no evidence for its truth-conduciveness.)

32 Cf. the last three paragraphs of section V.

tion that you are a brain in a vat. With respect to this skeptical method the brain in a vat hypothesis constitutes an uncontradicted methodological necessity. In this scenario we are therefore justified in believing that we are brains in a vat.

There is a third scenario. This time we are commonly obeying the following rule: Unless there is evidence to the contrary, interpret your sensory experience such that the resultant beliefs are compatible with the skeptical hypothesis as well as with its negation. In this scenario neither the proposition that we are brains in a vat nor its denial are justified.

The only reason, therefore, why we are justified in believing that we are not brains in a vat is that we are in fact in the first situation. And the only epistemologically important difference between the first and the other two situations is that we are *de facto* applying a different method. But what is the reason for our behaviour? We are only interpreting our experience the way we actually do because we are already convinced that we are living in a normal world. Therefore, the only reason why we are justified in believing that skeptical hypotheses are false is that we do in fact believe that they are.

This is implausible. With respect to the aim of increasing our true beliefs without increasing our false beliefs, it is by no means epistemically responsible for me to prefer the normal world hypothesis to the skeptical hypothesis just because all of us in fact accept the first.

There is one last exit the Anti-Skeptic might take. He can disagree on my reading of the term "epistemic responsibility". The way I am deploying the expression it means something like "being a good idea with respect to our epistemic aim of finding the truth in the light of the information we have". Instead, my opponent could give it a different reading: Epistemic responsibility consists in epistemic behaviour that conforms to the way most of us are *in fact* playing the game of giving and asking for reasons. What is commonly accepted is legal as it were. Within our game of giving and asking for reasons there are certain moves that are for free. We are getting away with them without further ado. And since no one in fact objects, it is thereby permissible. One such move is to believe/assert/reason according to the assumption that our senses are generally reliable. One *could* play a different game. But this is the game as it *is* played. And that is what counts when it comes to *our* notion of internal justification. "Epistemic responsibility" is to be spelled out as "complying with the epistemic practice of our community".

I am not sure whether this is what we eventually mean by epistemic responsibility. Of course, we treat someone's behavior as epistemically responsible if it conforms to our practice. But the reason we do so is that we are convinced that this practice is epistemically seen a good idea with respect to our aim of discovering the truth. In the end, it is therefore the latter that determines the responsibility of our behavior. And the skeptic has shown that treating as true those propositions that assume the role of methodological necessities is not responsible with respect to our fundamental epistemic concerns.

Furthermore, I doubt whether the skeptic and the Anti-Skeptic still disagree. The skeptic knew all along that we are in fact treating certain assumptions as unproblematic. Yet, he tries to show that with respect to our epistemic goal of finding out about the truth there is no reason to do so. It is in this sense that our external-world beliefs are problematic. If one replies that this leaves us within our rights to call such beliefs "epistemically justified", the skeptic can, with an impish smile on his lips, give in.[33]

References

Austin (1962): John L. Austin, "Other Minds", in: J. O. Urmson/G. J. Warnock (eds.), *Philosophical Papers by the late J. L. Austin*, Oxford, 44–84.
BonJour (1985): Laurence Bonjour, *The Structure of Empirical Knowledge*, Cambridge/MA.
Brueckner (1994): Anthony Brueckner, "Skepticism and Foundationalism", in: *Noûs* 28, 533–547.
DeRose (1995): Keith DeRose, "Solving the Skeptical Problem", in: *Philosophical Review* 104, 1–52.
DeRose (1999): Keith DeRose, "Contextualism – An Explanation and Defense", in: J. Greco/E. Sosa (eds.), *The Blackwell Guide to Epistemology*, Oxford, 187–205.
Lewis (1996): David Lewis, "Elusive Knowledge", in: *Australasian Journal of Philosophy* 74, 549–567.
Rheinwald (2004): Rosemarie Rheiwald, "Skeptische Herausforderung – Eine Diagnose", in: *Zeitschrift für Philosophische Forschung* 58, 347–372.
Schmoranzer (2010): Sebastian Schmoranzer, *Realismus und Skeptizismus*, Paderborn.
Schmoranzer (forthcoming): Sebastian Schmoranzer, "Skeptizismus und epistemische Berechtigung", in: O. Petersen (ed.), GAP 5 Proceedings.

---

33 I thank Nikola Kompa, Flavia Mormann and the participant of the "Oberseminar Theoretische Philosophie WS 2010/11" at the University of Cologne for comments on earlier drafts of this paper.

Willaschek (2003): Marcus Willaschek, *Der mentale Zugang zur Welt – Realismus, Skeptizismus und Intentionalität*, Frankfurt/Main.
Williams (1993a): Michael Williams, "Epistemological Realism and the Basis of Scepticism", 437–461, in: M. Williams (ed.), *Scepticism*, Aldershot.
Williams (1993b): Michael Williams, "Realism and Scepticism", in: J. Haldane/C. Wright (eds.), *Reality, Representation, and Projection*, Oxford, 193–214.
Williams (1996a): Michael Williams, *Unnatural Doubts – Epistemological Realism and the Basis of Scepticism*, Princeton.
Williams (1996b): Michael Williams, "Understanding Human Knowledge Philosophically", in: *Philosophy and Phenomenological Research* 61, 359–378.
Williams (1999): Michael Williams, Skepticism, in: J. Greco/E. Sosa (eds.): *The Blackwell Guide to Epistemology*, Oxford, 35–69.
Williams (2001): Michael Williams, *Problems of Knowledge – A Critical Introduction to Epistemology*, New York.
Wittgenstein (1989): Ludwig Wittgenstein, *Über Gewißheit*, G. E. M. Anscombe/G. H. v. Wright (eds.), Baden-Baden.
Wright (2004): Crispin Wright, "On Epistemic Entitlement – Warrant For Nothing (And Foundations for Free)?", in: *Proceedings of the Aristotelian Society Supplementary* 78, 167–211.

Wittgenstein and Williamson on Knowing and Believing[1]

Marie Mcginn

1. One of the central claims in Timothy Williamson's *Knowledge and Its Limits* is that '[k]nowing is a state of mind'[2]. He writes:

> There is a mental state of believing that it is raining, and there is—on the present account—a mental state of knowing that it is raining, but there is no intermediate mental state of believing truly that it is raining.[3]

The view that Williamson here expresses appears to be the direct opposite of the one expressed by Wittgenstein in the following remarks from *On Certainty*:

> One can say 'He believes it, but it isn't so', but not 'He knows it, but it isn't so'. Does this stem from the difference between the mental states of belief and knowledge? No.—One may for example call 'mental state' what is expressed by tone of voice in speaking, by gestures, etc. It would thus be *possible* to speak of a mental state of conviction, and that may be the same whether it is knowledge or false belief.[4]

> We are asking ourselves: what we do with a statement 'I *know*...'? For it is not a question of mental processes or mental states.[5]

There is, however, a question whether in claiming that knowing is a mental state Williamson is affirming the view that Wittgenstein is denying when he asserts that it is not one. The apparent opposition is real only if what Williamson is claiming about knowing in calling it a mental state is what Wittgenstein means to deny in claiming it is not. And until we know what each of them means in claiming, or denying, that knowing is a mental state, the conclusion that they are disagreeing about the truth of a single thesis is premature. In this paper, I want to look more

---

1   I would like to thank Stephen Everson for helpful comments on an earlier draft of this paper.
2   Williamson (2002), 21.
3   Williamson (2002), 27.
4   Wittgenstein (1977), 42.
5   Wittgenstein (1977), 230.

carefully at what each of the above claims amounts to and thereby try to clarify the extent, if any, to which Williamson and Wittgenstein are in disagreement.

2. One of the things that Williamson means to assert in claiming that knowing is a mental state is that the traditional analysis of knowledge as justified true belief is incorrect. The concept of a justified true belief is a complex concept which conjoins mental concepts (belief and having a justification) with a non-mental concept (truth); someone has a justified true belief insofar as he is in a certain mental state and a certain non-mental condition obtains. Thus, one of the things that saying knowing is a mental state amounts to is that 'knows is not a complex concept of the kind traditionally envisaged'[6]. It may be necessarily true that someone is in the mental state of knowing only if he is in the mental state of believing and the non-mental condition that what he believes is true is met, but the mental state of knowing cannot 'be factored…into a combination of mental states with non-mental conditions'[7].

In place of the traditional analysis, Williamson offers what he calls 'a modest positive account of the concept'. He first introduces the idea of a factive propositional attitude: 'A propositional attitude is factive if and only if, necessarily, one has it only to truths'[8]. Factive propositional attitudes include knowing that A, seeing that A, and remembering that A; these all constitute states in which a subject stands in a cognitive relation to a true proposition. Williamson's proposal is that 'knowing is the most general factive stative attitude, that which one has to a proposition if one has any factive stative attitude to it at all'[9]. He fills this idea out further by introducing the concept of a *factive mental state operator* (FMSO), which he characterizes as follows:

> Syntactically, an FMSO Φ has the combinatorial properties of a verb. Semantically, Φ is an unanalysable expression; that is, Φ is not synonymous with any complex expression whose meaning is composed of the meaning of its parts.

A sentence containing Φ has the form 'S Φs that A', which typically attributes a propositional attitude to a subject; and Φ is factive insofar as 'S Φs that A' entails A. Thus, if Φ is an FMSO, one may infer A from 'S Φs

---

6 Williamson (2002), 30.
7 Williamson (2002), 28.
8 Williamson (2002), 34.
9 Ibid.

that A'. Summarizing, Williamson proposes that the following two principles can be used to characterize the concept of knowing uniquely:

(1) 'Know' is an FMSO
(2) If Φ is an FMSO, then one may infer 'S knows that A' from 'S Φs that A'.

Understood in this way, the primary target of Williamson's claim that knowing is a mental state is a conception of the mental on which no environmental factor enters into the determination of the identity of a mental state. The internalist is committed to analysing any natural language locution which attributes mental states, and which incorporates an environmental circumstance in its truth-condition, into a mixture of genuinely mental states, whose identity is independent of environmental factors, and conditions on the external environment. As Williamson observes, many philosophers who reject internalism in respect of the content of mental states are committed to internalism in respect of locutions which attribute factive propositional attitudes. Williamson's claim that knowing is a mental state amounts to a rejection of both forms of internalism: environmental circumstances enter into both the determination of the content of a subject's propositional attitudes and into the identity of the attitude that a subject has to that content. That is to say, if S knows that A, anyone who is in the same mental state as S also knows that A.

Insofar as this is what Williamson's claim that knowing is a mental state amounts to, it clearly is not what Wittgenstein is to be understood as denying when he claims that it is not a mental state. The internalism that Williamson is opposing is clearly alien to Wittgenstein's philosophy; whatever the view is that Wittgenstein is expressing in the remarks quoted at the beginning it is *not* that knowing is a combination of a mental state and an environmental circumstance. There are, moreover, remarks in which Wittgenstein appears explicitly to acknowledge that the concept of knowing is not analysable in terms of the concept of believing. At OC 42, he remarks of know and believe that 'the concepts are different'. He also observes that "I know" has a primitive meaning similar to and related to "I see" ("wissen", "videre"). And "I knew he was in the room but he wasn't in the room" is like "I saw him in the room, but he wasn't there"[10]. He also seems to acknowledge that 'know' is what Williamson calls 'factive' in observing that '"I believe…"

---

10 Wittgenstein (1977), 90.

has subjective truth; but "I know…" not"[11]. One of Williamson's reasons for claiming that know is an unanalysable concept is that he holds that factive attitudes play an essential role in explanation of action. Wittgenstein also appears to acknowledge this when he remarks that "I show [my] knowledge [that this room is on the second floor, that behind the door a short landing leads to the stairs, and so on] day in, day out by my actions and also in what I say"'[12]. If there is a disagreement between Williamson and Wittgenstein, the issue of internalism versus externalism is obviously not where it lies.

3. Williamson does not attempt to give the concept of a mental state any formal definition. He remarks, however, that 'to call knowing a mental state is to assimilate it, in a certain respect, to paradigmatic mental states such as believing, desiring, and being in pain'[13]. The claim is that attitudes to propositions are to be included as paradigmatic mental states and that knowing that something is so is an unanalysable attitude to a proposition. Williamson also suggests that the concept mental state can be at least roughly defined in terms of the concept *mental concept of a state*. The claim that knowing is a mental state is thus equivalent to the claim that knowing is a mental concept of a state. It might seem, therefore, that all that Williamson's claim that knowing is a mental state amounts to is that *know* is a psychological concept which exhibits the characteristic grammar of a state, rather than, say, a process. And again it is clear that this is not something that we should take Wittgenstein to be denying in saying that there is 'not a question of mental processes or mental states'. At *PI* 572, he explicitly notes that '[e]xpectation is, grammatically, a state; like: being of an opinion, hoping for something, knowing something, being able to do something'. However, it seems that Wittgenstein believes that we need to make a distinction between stative, psychological concepts of this kind and what he calls a concept of a mental state; it remains to be seen whether the distinction he believes we need to make is one that Williamson's account of knowing requires him to deny.

Wittgenstein recognizes that the fact that one can say 'He believes it, but it isn't so', but not 'He knows it but it isn't so' shows that know and believe are different concepts. The question is whether the difference is explained by the fact that two different mental states correspond to the

---

11 Wittgenstein (1977), 179.
12 Wittgenstein (1977), 431.
13 Williamson (2002), 27.

words *believe* and *know*. Wittgenstein then clarifies what the question amounts to by reference to what he is here taking as a paradigm of a mental state: something that 'is expressed by tone of voice in speaking, by gestures, etc.'. To think that the difference in the concepts of knowing and believing is grounded in a difference in mental state, on this understanding of the term, is to suppose that the difference between knowing and believing is, for example, equivalent to the difference between being certain and being uncertain: two different 'mental states' which are expressed in a subject's tone of voice, gestures, and other ways of behaving. Thus, in denying that the difference between *know* and *believe* stems from 'the difference between the mental states of belief and knowledge', Wittgenstein may be seen as rejecting the idea that the criteria by which we judge whether a subject knows, rather than merely believes, something are simply a matter of his tone of voice, his gestures, or of his sincerely affirming "I know…" or "I believe…". To hold that knowing is a mental state, on this understanding of the term, would be to hold that when a speaker sincerely affirms "I know that A", this expresses the mental state of knowing, in the way in which his sincerely affirming "I am convinced that A" expresses his mental state of feeling certain, so that the question of his being mistaken does not arise. On this understanding, denying that knowing and believing are two mental states amounts to the claim that whether a subject knows or merely believes that A is not something that is settled by his sincerely affirming "I know that A". The point is that '[t]here is no subjective sureness that I know something. The certainty is subjective, but not the knowledge'[14].

Wittgenstein's target here is G.E.Moore's attempt, in *Proof of an External World*, to assure his audience that 'I certainly did at the moment *know* that which I expressed by the combination of certain gestures with saying the words "Here is one hand and here is another", that it would be "absurd…to suggest that I did not know it, but only believed it"'[15]. Wittgenstein objects that this is to treat the concept *know* as if it were 'analogous to the concepts 'believe', 'surmise', 'doubt', 'be convinced' in that the statement "I know…" can't be a mistake', when 'anyone who is acquainted with the language-game must realize this—an assurance from a reliable man that he *knows* cannot contribute anything'[16]. It would, he observes, 'be remarkable if we had to believe

---

14 Wittgenstein (1977), 245.
15 Moore (1963), 146.
16 Wittgenstein (1977), 21.

the reliable person who says "I can't be wrong"; or who says "I am not wrong"'[17]. For '[e]ven if the most trustworthy of men assures me that he *knows* things are thus and so, this by itself cannot satisfy me that he does know. Only that he believes he knows. That is why Moore's assurance that he knows...does not interest us'[18]. Even given a reliable man's sincere assurance that he knows..., '[t]hat he does know remains to be shown'[19]. Thus, one of the things that Wittgenstein's claim that knowing is not a mental state amounts to is a reminder to Moore that, in the face of someone who doubts whether one knows that A, a sincere assurance that one does know it counts for nothing.

It is clear that the distinction Wittgenstein is insisting on here is not one that Williamson, in claiming that knowledge is a mental state, means to deny. Whatever Williamson's claim that knowing is a mental state amounts to, it is clearly compatible with his accepting that there are circumstances in which 'p is false, so one does not know p, even though systematically misleading appearances place one in a state which feels just like knowing p "from the inside", so one is not in a position to know that one does not know p. One falsely but justifiably believes oneself to know p'[20]. Williamson is clearly not committed to the claim knowing is like believing or being certain, so 'that the statement "I know..." can't be mistaken'. However, it may seem that Wittgenstein and Williamson do disagree about what follows from this. For while Wittgenstein appears to see it as grounds for denying that knowing is a mental state, Williamson argues that the conclusion that knowing is not a mental state follows *only* on the mistaken assumption that S is a mental state only if one is always in a position to know whether one is in S. Thus, the suggestion is, what Williamson and Wittgenstein are disagreeing about is whether it follows, from the fact that a subject may believe he knows p when he does not know p, that knowing is not a mental state. And what this comes down to, on this understanding of the matter, is a disagreement about whether S is a mental state only if one is always in a position to know whether one is in S.

There are grounds for caution here, however. First of all, Wittgenstein does not make the distinction between the concepts 'believe', 'surmise', 'doubt', 'be convinced', on the one hand, and 'know', on the

---

17 Wittgenstein (1977), 22.
18 Wittgenstein (1977), 137.
19 Wittgenstein (1977), 14.
20 Williamson (2002), 11 f.

other, by explicit appeal to the claim that one cannot, for example, doubt p without being in a position to know that one doubts p. There is no reason to think that he would, for example, deny that there may be circumstances in which someone's behaviour shows that he doubts a given proposition, p, but for particular reasons (for example, firmly believing p is fundamental to his whole idea of who he is) he is not in a position to recognize—that is, to know—he doubts p. He allows, for example, that 'it is possible to think out circumstances in which [the words] "Judging from what I say, *this* is what I believe" would make sense'[21], which suggests that he accepts that what I believe may not be transparent to me and that I might discover what I believe through the kind of evidence which shows me what someone else believes. If this is right, then there is no reason to think that in making a distinction between 'know' and 'doubt', Wittgenstein is implicitly asserting the thesis that S is a mental state only if one is always in a position to know whether one is in S. And if that is right, then we have still not succeeded in identifying a thesis the truth of which is a matter for disagreement between Wittgenstein and Williamson. In order to shed more light on whether there really is a disagreement here, we need to look more closely at the significance that the distinction he is making has for Wittgenstein.

It is important that the distinction Wittgenstein is making concerns the use of the word 'know' as against the use of the words 'believe', 'doubt', 'surmise', and 'be convinced'. He sums up this difference in use in the following two remarks:

> It would be correct to say: "I believe…" has subjective truth; but "I know…" not.[22]
> Or again "I believe…" is an 'expression', but not "I know"[23].

The question is how are we to understand this, if not as the claim that I am always in a position to know that I believe p, but I am not always in a position to know that I know p? How else are we to understand the claim that belief is subjective, but not knowledge? I believe that one of the things that Wittgenstein is getting at here is that, in ordinary discourse, knowing p means having proper grounds for the asserting p, so saying 'I know p' 'often means: I have proper grounds for my state-

---

21 Wittgenstein (1998), 192.
22 Wittgenstein (1977), 179.
23 Wittgenstein (1977), 180.

ment'[24]. Moreover, what count as proper grounds for a statement is not something that I decide: 'What counts as an adequate test of a statement belongs to logic'[25]. There is, therefore, a question whether I am in a position to know p, and this question is settled objectively, in the sense that it is something that can be confirmed, for example, by others carrying out the requisite tests and confirming my statement, or by others confirming that I was in a position to carry them out reliably.

> Thus:
> One says "I know" when one is ready to give compelling grounds. "I know" relates to the possibility of demonstrating the truth.[26]

Compelling grounds are grounds which, in normal circumstances, are enough to convince another that I am in a position to know p, and what count as compelling grounds will vary from case to case. However, it follows from this that 'Whether someone knows something can come to light, assuming that he is convinced of it'[27]. There are not the same conditions on believing p: it is not the case that whether someone believes something 'can come to light, assuming that he is convinced of it'; being convinced of it is, in normal circumstances, sufficient for belief in a way it is not for knowledge. It is in this sense that 'I believe' has subjective truth and 'I know' not; or 'I believe' is an 'expression' and 'I know' not. Again, the sense that there is any substantial disagreement between Wittgenstein and Williamson here evaporates. For in claiming that knowing is a mental state, Williamson is clearly not intending to deny that there are necessary conditions on knowing which concern how things objectively are, and which include not only that the known proposition is true, but also that the subject is in a position to know that it is. And Williamson will also agree that this distinguishes knowing from both believing and being certain. It seems, therefore, that we still lack a clear thesis whose truth is asserted by one and denied by the other.

It is beginning to look as if we might understand the dispute between Wittgenstein and Williamson as merely terminological. It may seem that Wittgenstein is recommending that the term 'mental state' should be restricted to states such as believing and being certain—that is to say, to states which are such that, content aside, no objective cir-

---

24   Wittgenstein (1977), 18.
25   Wittgenstein (1977), 82.
26   Wittgenstein (1977), 243.
27   Wittgenstein (1977), 243.

cumstance is included in the necessary conditions for being in that state—while Williamson believes that it should not be so restricted. The disagreement seems merely terminological insofar as Wittgenstein does not appear to make this more restrictive use of the term 'mental state' a ground for analysing the concept of knowing into a conjunction of a mental state, in the restricted sense, and objective conditions. He restricts the term merely as a means to mark a distinction which Williamson does not deny. There may be something to be said for this way of looking at things. However, there are also grounds for caution in attributing the above conception of a mental state to Wittgenstein. It would mean, for example, attributing to him the claim that remembering is not a mental state. Yet there is reason to think that this is not a view to which he is committed:

> If someone asks me what I have been doing in the last two hours, I answer him straight off and I don't read the answer off from an experience I am having. And yet one says that I *remembered*, and that this is a mental process.[28]

Wittgenstein also includes memory, but not knowing, in a list of 'various psychological phenomena'[29]. He does not, therefore, appear to see it as an objection to describing memory as a mental process, or psychological phenomenon, that there are objective conditions on whether someone's state is one of remembering, or that 'there is also such a thing as "I believe I remember that"'[30]. His view of whether remembering is properly called a mental state or process seems at best equivocal, which suggests that his reason for denying that knowing is a mental state does not depend upon a commitment to a general thesis that restricts the concept of a mental state or process to concepts which do not include an objective condition in their condition of application. The idea that the significance of Wittgenstein's claim that knowing is not a mental state should be understood as an attempt to restrict the concept of a mental state in a way which puts him in merely terminological disagreement with Williamson is, to this extent, unsatisfactory. To get to the bottom of this issue, we need to return, I believe, to the philosophical context in which Wittgenstein makes his observation about the difference between 'know', on the one hand, and 'believe', 'surmise', 'be convinced', on the other.

---

28 Wittgenstein (1980), 105.
29 Wittgenstein (1980), 129.
30 Wittgenstein (1980), 107.

4. Wittgenstein, as we saw earlier, connects the concept of knowing with the possibility of giving compelling grounds for the proposition I claim to know. What counts as a compelling ground for my statement varies. If it is a mathematical proposition it may be a proof, but it may equally be a statement about my expertise, or about my having recently carried out a calculation, or about my having checked a certain number of times that a calculation is correct. If it is a statement about the past it may be a description of the historical evidence, or it may be an assurance that I was present and distinctly remember what happened, or it may be a statement about my expertise, or about my having checked relevant texts quite recently. This distinguishes the use of 'know' from the use of both 'see' and 'remember'. In general, the truth of the statement 'I see that A' depends upon A's being a true description of what is there to be seen; in the same way, the truth of the statement 'I remember that A' depends upon A's being a true description of an occurrence at which I was present and which I witnessed. In general, being convinced that one sees that A, or that one remembers that A, is not sufficient for either seeing or remembering that A. There are circumstances in which one must withdraw the statement 'I see that A', 'I remember that A', and say 'I thought I saw...', 'I thought I remembered...'. However, it is not the case that the ordinary use of the words 'see' or 'remember' is connected with the possibility of giving compelling grounds for one's statement. Rather, 'I see that A', 'I remember that A', is the sort of thing that we might, in suitable circumstances, give as a compelling ground for a proposition which we claim to know, that is, they can be used to say how it is that we are in a position to know what we assert. There is, therefore, no reason to believe that Wittgenstein is committed to the view that 'know', 'see' and 'remember' function in the same way, even though there are clearly links between them.

Thus, in normal circumstances, asked how I know that there is a piece of paper on the desk, I might reply 'I see it', and this will, in normal circumstances, count as a compelling ground for my statement; it states how I'm in a position to know what I assert. However, Wittgenstein sees Moore's assurance that he knows this is a hand as made in response to a philosophical sceptic who, by appeal to the possibility of the sceptical scenarios, has challenged Moore's right to say that he knows any external fact. Thus, the question is no longer, as it is in an ordinary context, how Moore knows that there is a hand here—whether, for example, by seeing it, or by being reliably informed by someone else—but whether this is the sort of thing that can be known on the basis of experience. Moore's response, therefore, is not to say *how* he knows, but simply to insist that he *does* know, that it would be 'absurd...to suggest that I did not know it, but only believed it'. In an ordinary context, 'I see it' may be used to provide compelling grounds for what one asserts, or to remove what Wittgenstein calls a 'practical doubt', but Moore is dealing with a 'further doubt *behind* that one'[31], one which has nothing to do with the ordinary question of how it is that *Moore* knows what he claims, which would ordinarily be removed by Moore's stating how he is in a position to know it. Wittgenstein's suggestion is that it is this philosophical context which leads Moore into using 'know' as if it were like the concepts 'believe', 'doubt', 'be convinced', and into treating knowing as a mental state which is no more subject to doubt than being certain. Wittgenstein's denial that knowing is a mental state may thus be seen as a way of rejecting Moore's idea that he can respond to the philosophical sceptic simply by assuring him that he does certainly know that there is a hand here. For giving this assurance is to treat 'know' like 'believe', or 'be convinced', and to forget that assurance from a reliable man that he knows counts for nothing. Reminding Moore that knowing is not a mental state is just a way of pointing out to him that it is not a satisfactory response to the philosophical sceptic to insist that we *do* know what the sceptic doubts: that I know something—rather than that I believe, or doubt, or surmise, something—cannot be established like that.

In the previous two sections, it proved impossible to give expression to a thesis whose truth is clearly a matter of dispute between Wittgenstein and Williamson. The focus in those two sections was on how each of them describes the way the concept of knowing functions and the principal conclusion is that there is no real disagreement about how it functions, despite Williamson's claiming knowing is a mental state and Wittgenstein's claiming it is not. However, when we look more carefully at what it is that occasions Wittgenstein remark, it suggests that looking at what each of these philosopher's says about how the concept of knowing functions may not be the right place to look for a disagreement, if there is one. Wittgenstein's reasons for denying knowing is a mental state do not, I've argued, reflect a general restriction of the concept of a mental state to states for which no objective circumstance is included in the necessary conditions for being in that state, but arise in the context of a critique of a certain kind of response to scepticism,

---

31 Wittgenstein (1977), 19.

which ends by treating 'know' as akin to 'believe' and 'be convinced', and regarding knowing as a mental state which is no more subject to doubt than being certain. The question whether there is a real disagreement between Wittgenstein and Williamson might be thought to depend, therefore, not on what each has to say about how the concept of knowing functions, but on the role that Williamson's claim that knowing is a mental state plays in his response to the sceptic. The question is whether Williamson tries to use the idea that knowing is a mental state in a response to the sceptic which leads him, like Moore, into simply insisting, against the sceptic, that we do know about the external world, as if an assurance from a philosopher that we know could establish that we do.

5. The sceptic's argument has its source in two claims which Williamson does not attempt to deny:

(1) For any empirical claim, p, which a subject, S, makes on the basis of his current perceptual experience (good case), it is possible to imagine a sceptical scenario (bad case) in which an analogous judgement is made on the basis of experience which is phenomenally indistinguishable from S's.
(2) In the bad case, the subject does not know p, since p is false.

The sceptic tries to use (1) and (2) as premises in an argument whose conclusion is that S does not know p in the good case. Williamson's response to the sceptic has two parts. The first part argues that the move from (1) and (2) to a general sceptical conclusion depends upon the assumption that the evidence available to S in the good case is equivalent to the evidence available in the bad case. Williamson claims that this equivalence is not obvious and stands in need of an independent argument. He then mounts a direct attack on the conception of evidence which is required for any argument in favour of the equivalence to go through. The aim is to show that the argument from (1) and (2) to a general sceptical conclusion is less than compelling, by showing that it depends upon a conception of evidence that is deeply problematic. The second part of his response puts forward an alternative theory of evidence on which (1) and (2) no longer have the power to threaten S's capacity to know p in the good case.

It is easy to see how the sceptic's conclusion follows from (1) and (2), given the assumption that the evidence available in the good case and the bad case is the same. If all the evidence for p is consistent with one's falsely believing p, then for all one knows p is false and therefore, even in the good case, one does not know p. The question is what independent reason is there to accept the equivalence. Williamson claims that any plausible argument for the equivalence must in the end depend upon the assumption that one is always in a position to know what one's evidence is. With this assumption in place, the sceptic can give an independent argument for the equivalence as follows:

> Suppose that one has different evidence in the [good case and the bad case]. Then one can deduce in the bad case that one is not in the good case, because one's evidence is not what it would be if one were in the good case. But even the sceptic's opponent agrees that it is consistent with everything one knows in the bad case that one is in the good case. Therefore, one has the same evidence in the two cases.[32]

Williamson's attack on the sceptical argument takes the form of an attack on the idea that one is always in a position to know what one's evidence is. This idea amounts to the claim that what constitutes one's evidence is transparent. Williamson argues that this assumption leads to a clearly false conclusion.

Williamson's argument aims to show that '[w]hatever the nature of evidence, rational thinkers do not always know what their evidence is'[33]. The argument turns on the fact that human beings have limited powers of discrimination. Williamson asks us to imagine having the experience of watching the sun slowly rise. One's evidence at the beginning of this process has the property of pitch darkness, and at the end it has the property of broad daylight. If we now break the process down into a long sequence of times, $t_0, t_1, t_2, \ldots t_n$ at millisecond intervals, then we can see that, given our limited powers of discrimination, it is consistent with everything I know by sight about my evidence when I'm in the situation at t_i that I am actually in the situation at t_{i-1}. If we assume that evidence is transparent, then it follows that my evidence at t_i has the same properties as my evidence at t_{i-1}. Although indiscriminability is a non-transitive relation, the assumption of transparency allows us to derive from it a transitive relation of exact sameness of evidence: my evidence at t_i has the same properties as my evidence at t_{i-1}. This now leads to the obviously false conclusion that my evidence at t_0, when it is completely dark, is the same as my evidence at t_n, when it is broad daylight. Williamson's conclusion is that transparency is false: 'One does not al-

---

32 Williamson (2002), 169 f.
33 Williamson (2002), 174.

ways know the...properties of one's evidence, one does not always know what one's evidence is'[34].

The purpose of Williamson's argument is to show that there is no viable conception of evidence on which we are infallible about what our evidence is. He claims that the above argument against transparency is unaffected by the move to the claim that all that one knows is what properties one's evidence *appears* to have. Transparency is false even in respect of what one's evidence appears to be. The sceptic's argument for the view that one's total evidence is the same in the good case and the bad case depends, Williamson has argued, on the assumption of transparency. In effect, the sceptic credits us with an infallible capacity for self-knowledge in order to undermine our capacity for knowledge of the external world. Williamson's argument shows that the idea of a realm of appearances about which we are infallible is an illusion. At first sight, this may appear to motivate a still more radical form of scepticism: we never know even how things appear to us. However, Williamson believes that this simply undermines our sense that scepticism expresses a philosophical insight about the limits of human knowledge. The alternative is to reject the assumption that evidence is transparent and accept that the case for the idea that one's total evidence is the same in the good case and the bad case cannot be independently established. The assertion of the equivalence is, therefore, simply equivalent to an assertion of scepticism and it begs the question against a non-sceptical conception, on which one has more evidence in the good case than in the bad case, and thus in a position to know things in the former which cannot be known in the latter.

Williamson has argued that we are not always in a position to know what our evidence is. A plausible theory of evidence must accommodate the fact that our ability to determine what our evidence is is fallible. Williamson's proposal is that what constitutes S's evidence is all the true propositions that S knows. We are not infallible about what we know, but that is no objection to the identification, given that we are also not infallible about what constitutes our evidence. However, the identification of evidence with knowledge may seem to be threatened from another direction. If knowledge is itself evidence based, then identifying evidence with what is known may appear to threaten a regress: evidence-based belief in a proposition p must always be preceded by evidence-based belief in a proposition that is evidence for p. Williamson

---

34 Williamson (2002), 177.

argues that we can avoid the threatened regress by distinguishing two senses of evidence-based:

> Belief in a proposition *p* is *explicitly* evidence-based if it depends upon prior beliefs about what provides the evidence for *p*
> Belief in a proposition *p* is *implicitly* evidence-based if it is causally sensitive to the evidence for *p*

The claim is that an explicitly evidence-based belief in *p* need not be preceded by an explicitly evidence-based belief in a proposition about the evidence for *p*; it is enough that the latter belief is implicitly evidence-based. This would lead to another regress if it were the case that an implicitly evidence-based belief in *p* always had to be preceded by an implicitly evidence-based belief in a proposition about the evidence for *p*. However, Williamson argues, there is no necessity for one's causally sensitive beliefs to be mediated by any further *beliefs* about the evidence for *p*; it is sufficient for a belief in *p* to be implicitly evidence-based that it is appropriately causally sensitive to evidence for *p*.

What are the implications of this for the judgement, 'This is a hand', made on the basis of my current perceptual experience? On the basis of Williamson's definitions, it seems that the judgement may express either an implicitly evidence-based belief, which is causally sensitive to a property of my evidence, or an explicitly evidence-based belief, insofar as it depends upon the prior belief that I am currently seeing a hand. In the latter case, my belief that I am currently seeing a hand is a belief about what provides my evidence for 'This is a hand'. The belief that I am currently seeing a hand need not itself be explicitly evidence-based, although it must be at least implicitly evidence-based. That is to say, my belief that I am currently seeing a hand must be appropriately causally sensitive to the evidence that I am seeing a hand, but it need not be mediated by any further beliefs about what provides my evidence for 'I am seeing a hand'. The possibility of a realistic hallucination shows that I may believe that I am seeing a hand when I am not, that is, that I may misidentify the evidence for 'I am seeing a hand'. However, Williamson argues that '[c]ausal sensitivity need not be perfect to be genuine. There can be a non-accidental rough proportionality between the strength of the belief and the strength of the evidence, even if distortions sometimes occur'[35]. Thus, when things go well, and my belief that I am seeing a

---

35 Williamson (2002), 192.

hand is the result of a genuine but fallible causal sensitivity to the fact that I am seeing a hand, it constitutes an implicitly evidence-based belief and amounts to knowledge that I am seeing a hand.

Given this conception of evidence, a normal perceiving subject's evidence, that is to say, his knowledge, includes all his true beliefs about his immediate environment which are either explicitly or implicitly evidence-based, and all his true beliefs about his own perceptual states, which will normally be implicitly evidence-based. This clearly entails an asymmetry between the good case and the bad case. In the bad case, the subject has only false beliefs about both his own perceptual states and about how things are in the external world. His evidence, that is to say, his knowledge, extends, at best, only as far as his beliefs about how things appear: the mental states he appears to be in and how things appear to be in his environment. By contrast, in the good case, the subject knows both his own mental states, normally as a result of implicitly evidence-based beliefs about them, and the judgements about the external world, which may be either implicitly or explicitly evidence-based. The fact that a subject is not causally sensitive to the difference between the good case and the bad case is not, on Williamson's conception of evidence, enough to show that the cognitive circumstances of the subject are the same in both cases. Provided the subject is a normal perceiver whose beliefs about his own perceptual states and about the properties of objects in his immediate environment show the appropriate causal sensitivity to what is objectively the case, his cognitive circumstances put him in a position in which he can be said to know about both his own mental states and the external world. This knowledge provides the subject with evidence which can then be used to justify further beliefs about what is the case. The fact that the cognitive circumstances of the subject in the bad case are such that he fails to know, either about his own perceptual states or the external world, has no power to threaten the knowledge of the subject in the good case, for the cognitive circumstances of the two subjects are now seen to be completely different. Thus, not only has the sceptic's attempt to use (1) and (2) to derive a general sceptical conclusion been shown to be question-begging, but a coherent conception of evidence has been developed on which (1) and (2) no longer have any tendency to impact sceptically on our understanding of the good case.

6. One clear difference between Williamson's response to scepticism and Moore's is that Williamson, unlike Moore, does not attempt to respond to the sceptic by producing a particular example in which he does

certainly know a fact about the external world. Williamson's strategy has been to argue merely that the possibility of the bad case, in which a subject's cognitive circumstances are such that he is systematically misled about the nature of his evidence, does not have any tendency to undermine the capacity of the subject in the good case to know, when things go well, true propositions about both his own mental states and the external world. That is to say, he has argued that, despite the possibility of bad cases, we can conceive how knowledge of the world and one's own mental states is possible. A familiar objection to this form of disjunctivism is that the move from the claim that we can conceive of circumstances in which it is possible for a subject to know about the world to the claim that I am currently actually so placed that my beliefs about the world amount to knowledge is problematic. We can accept the disjunctivist conception of the good and bad cases, but, the argument goes, this does not help when it comes to meeting a sceptical challenge to a particular claim to know, for example, the claim to know 'This is a hand'.

According to Williamson, if I am in the good case, then I know that I am seeing a hand and this provides a justification for my true belief, 'This is a hand', which gives it a probability of 1 on my evidence, and which therefore also counts as something known. The objection is that the sceptical challenge exploits the possibility of bad cases to raise a question whether my epistemic circumstances are such that I do know that I am seeing a hand, and am thus in a possession of evidence which justifies my assertion 'This is a hand'. Given that I, as the subject of the claim to know, accept the truth of (1), it seems that I am obliged to concede that all I'm in a position to assert in respect of my current epistemic circumstances is the following:

(A) Either my epistemic circumstances are such that I'm in a position to know both that this is a hand and that I am seeing a hand, or they are such that I know only that I seem to see a hand.

On Williamson's account, if I am in the good case, my mental state is one of knowing both that I am seeing a hand and that this is a hand; my evidence includes the known propositions 'I am seeing a hand' and 'This is a hand'. The problem is that I am in a position to use this evidence as a basis for asserting that I am in the good case only if I can recognize it as the evidence it is, but given the truth of (1), it seems that I am not in a position to distinguish genuine evidence from the mere appearance of evidence. If that's the case, then I cannot assert that I am in the good case, and thus cannot move from (A) to:

(B) I am seeing a hand.
(C) This is a hand.

Thus, the move from the assertion of possible knowledge to the assertion of actual knowledge appears blocked.

Thus, if we conceive scepticism as a challenge to a particular claim to know, then it is unclear how Williamson's non-sceptical account of the good case puts us in a position to assert, without begging the question against the sceptic, that we do know what we claim. It's at this point that Wittgenstein believes Moore is led into assuring the sceptic that he does certainly know, and thereby into using 'know' as if it were akin to 'believe' or 'be convinced'. It is clear, however, that Williamson does not believe that the claim that knowing is a mental state provides a subject with the wherewithal to meet a sceptical challenge to an individual claim to know directly. Thus, he acknowledges that '[o]ne sceptical strategy it to exploit the dialectical effects of challenging propositions', and he responds to it as follows:

> If one is never entitled to rely on something under challenge, one will very soon be left with very little.... We should be sceptical of...a sceptic's reliance on the power of challenge. The sceptic relies uncritically on rules of dialectic engagement which evolved to serve more practical purposes, without questioning their appropriateness to the radical questions which scepticism raises. If challenging something thereby makes it dialectically unusable, then the power of challenge might hinder rather than help the pursuit of truth.[36]

On Williamson's conception of knowledge, the subject in the good case is in the mental state of knowing that he sees a hand and the mental state of knowing that this is a hand; the mental states of the subject in the bad case are different from those of the subject in the good case, although they share the mental state of knowing that it appears to them that they are seeing a hand before them. Insofar as the mental states of the subject in the good case include the states of knowing that he is seeing a hand and of knowing that this is a hand, his evidence includes that he is seeing a hand and that this is hand. This evidence can be used by the subject in the derivation of further known truths or to increase the confirmation of hypotheses. Thus, the idea that knowledge is a mental state is central to Williamson's anti-sceptical characterization of the difference between the cognitive circumstances of the subject in the good case and the bad case. However, it is clear from the above response to the idea of

---

36 Williamson (2002), 188.

a sceptical challenge to a particular knowledge claim that there is no suggestion that the claim that knowledge is a mental state puts a knower in a position to respond to this challenge directly, simply by asserting that he knows. At this point, Williamson appears to fall back on a purely pragmatic response which amounts to something like this: we do rely on our ordinary judgements about what our evidence is (about what we see, remember, or know to be the case) and not relying on them is more likely to hinder rather than help the pursuit of truth.

If Wittgenstein's denial that knowing is a mental state amounts to an objection to what he sees as Moore's attempt to respond to the sceptical challenge to his claim to know that there is a hand before him by assuring the sceptic that he does indeed know it, then it is not in conflict with anything that Williamson says in response to the sceptic. Moreover, it seems fair to say that Wittgenstein's own response to scepticism, understood as a challenge to a specific claim to know, could also be described as pragmatic. There is, of course, no suggestion that we can give reasons that justify our proceeding in the way that we do. However, there is a recognition that we do all, in ordinary circumstances, rely on our own and others judgements about what is happening, or did happen, in our immediate environment, about what we see or remember, about the result of a calculation that we have checked; we also rely on history books, on scientific text books, and a host of other sources of information; relying on these things characterizes our practice, all our methods of confirming or disconfirming hypotheses depends upon it. Someone who did not share our reactions, or trust our own and others judgements in the way we do, could not take part in our practice of enquiry.

It is unclear whether Williamson would take exception to any of this, but it does point to at least one potential area of disagreement. Wittgenstein responds to scepticism, understood as a challenge to justify judgements which we make as a matter of course, with a realistic attention to what is involved in learning to judge, to calculate, to infer, and so on, and in coming to recognize that acting surely and without doubt is part of the essence of these things. However, Wittgenstein argues that if the word 'know' expresses our readiness to give grounds, then it is a mistake to think that the judgements we make as a matter of course, and which constitute the framework within which we confirm or disconfirm hypotheses, are properly understood as cases of knowing something. Part of Williamson's purpose in claiming that knowing is a mental state is to argue that knowing is fundamental and 'one's knowledge serves as the foundation for all one's justified beliefs'[37]. Wittgenstein appears to want to draw a distinction between what is properly understood as a case of knowing something and those judgements which we make straight off, which we do not question, and which, he holds, characterize our way of judging. The fact that it belongs to the essence of our practice of judging that these judgements are ones concerning which there is almost universal accord; the fact that learning to judge means being able to make these judgements confidently, without guidance from others; the fact that the question of our grounds for these judgements does not arise; the fact that we do all trust these judgements as made by ourselves and others; all of these things, Wittgenstein believes, make it at least misleading to call them things we know. For then we elide the distinction between these essentially groundless judgements and judgements for which we can give compelling grounds. The distinction Wittgenstein here means to insist upon is perhaps related to Williamson's distinction between explicitly- and implicitly-justified beliefs, but whether the latter is a means to preserve the difference Wittgenstein describes while at the same time justifying the description of the relevant judgements as things we know is a question that will have to be addressed on another occasion.

References

Moore (1963): George E. Moore, "Proof of an External World", in: *Philosophical Papers*, London.
Williamson (2002): Timothy Williamson, *Knowledge and Its Limits*, Oxford.
Wittgenstein (1977): Ludwig Wittgenstein, *On Certainty*, G. E. M.Anscombe/ G. H. v. Wright (eds.), Oxford. (*OC*)
Wittgenstein (1980): Ludwig Wittgenstein, *Remarks on the Philosophy of Psychology*, vol. 2, G.H. v. Wright/H. Nyman (eds.), Oxford. (*RPP* II)
Wittgenstein (1998): Ludwig Wittgenstein, *Philosophical Investigations*, (trans. G.E.M. Anscombe), Oxford. (*PI*)

---

[37] Williamson (2002), 186.

Notes on Contributors

GÜNTER ABEL is Professor of Theoretical Philosophy at the Technical University Berlin, and director of the Center for Knowledge Research (IZW). He published on epistemology, philosophy of mind, philosophy of science, and philosophy of symbols, signs, and language. Among his numerous books and articles are *Zeichen der Wirklichkeit* (2004) and *"Knowledge Research: Extending and Revising Epistemology"* (2011). He is the main editor (with James Conant) of the book series *Berlin Studies in Knowledge Research*.

PETER BAUMANN is Professor of Philosophy at Swarthmore College, Philadelphia. He published numerous articles, reviews and volumes in epistemology and philosophy of mind, practical philosophy, and contemporary analytical philosophy, including *Practical Conflicts* (with Monika Betzler, eds.), and *Erkenntnistheorie* (2002).

ANTHONY BRUECKNER is Professor of Philosophy at the University of California, Santa Barbara. He has written extensively on the problem of skepticism, transcendental arguments in Kant and in contemporary writers, theories of epistemic justification, and the nature of self-knowledge. His teaching and research areas include epistemology, philosophy of language, metaphysics, and philosophy of mind. He recently published *Essays on Skepticism* (2010). See also *Debating Self-Knowledge* (forthcoming, co-authored with Gary Ebbs).

GERHARD ERNST is Professor for the History of Philosophy and Practical Philosophy at the University of Stuttgart (Germany). He works mainly in the fields of metaethics and epistemology. His books and articles are devoted to various topics in epistemology, moral philosophy and the philosophy of science, including *Das Problem des Wissens* (2002), *Die Objektivität der Moral* (2008).

THOMAS GIL is Professor of Philosophy at the Technical University Berlin, teaching theories of action and of rationality, philosophy of science, ethics, and political theory. He published numerous articles and monographs, including *Practical Reasoning* (2002), and *Actions, Normativity, and History* (2010).

HANS-JOHANN GLOCK is Professor of Philosophy at the University of Zürich, (Switzerland). He is also visiting professor at the University of Reading and has recently held a research fellowship at the Hanse Wissenschaftskolleg in Germany. His main areas of interests are philosophy of mind, philosophy of language, animal cognition, history of analytic philosophy, and Wittgenstein. He has published several books, including *Quine and Davidson on Language, Thought and Reality* (2003) and *What is Analytic Philosophy?* (2008).

JOHN GRECO is Leonard and Elizabeth Eslick Chair in Philosophy at the St. Louis University, Missouri, USA. He published numerous articles and encyclopedic entries on epistemology, skepticism, normativity, and ethics. He is the editor of the *Oxford Handbook of Skepticism* (2008) and the *Blackwell Guide to Epistemology* (1999, with Ernest Sosa). He published recently: *Achieving Knowledge* (2010).

STEPHEN HETHERINGTON is Professor of Philosophy at the University of New South Wales in Sydney. He works in the fields of epistemology and metaphysics. He has published on many questions in epistemology, meta-epistemology, philosophical knowledge, various forms of scepticism, and the Gettier problem, including *Good Knowledge, Bad Knowledge* (2001). His most recent book is *How to Know* (2011).

JOHN HYMAN is Professor of Aesthetics at the University of Oxford. His research interests are epistemology and metaphysics, philosophy of mind and action, aesthetics, philosophy of art, and Wittgenstein. He is author of the book *The Objective Eye: Colour, Form, and Reality in the Theory of Art* (2006) and currently editor of *The British Journal of Aesthetics*.

ANDREA KERN is Professor in History of Philosophy at the University of Leipzig (Germany). Her research focuses on topics in epistemology, skepticism, theory of action, and aesthetics. Her publications include the books *Schöne Lust. Eine Theorie der ästhetischen Erfahrung nach Kant* (2000), and *Quellen des Wissens. Zum Begriff vernünftiger Erkenntnisfähigkeiten* (2006).

PETER KLEIN is an American philosopher widely known for his work on skepticism and on theories of justification. He is Professor of Philosophy at Rutgers University (New Jersey), and the author of *Certainty: A Refutation of Scepticism* (1982). His current research focuses on infinitism, as represented in this volume, and the role of false beliefs in the acquisition of knowledge. See, for example, "*Useful False Beliefs*" (2008).

NIKOLA KOMPA is Professor of Theoretical Philosophy at Osnabrück University (Germany). She works and publishes mainly on philosophy of language and epistemology. Her work has a strongly interdisciplinary character, focusing on linguistic semantics and pragmatics, as well as on cognitive linguistics and theories of language change. She published *Wissen und Kontext* (2001), and *Metasemantik* (in Vorbereitung).

HILARY KORNBLITH is Professor of Philosophy at the University of Massachusetts, Amherst (USA), and one of contemporary epistemology's most prominent proponents of naturalized epistemology (*Knowledge and its Place in Nature*, 2002). Further research interests are metaphysics and the philosophy of mind. His most recent work includes the role of intuitions in philosophical theorizing ("*Appeals to Intuition and the Ambitions of Epistemology*") and the mental states of non-human animals.

DAVID LÖWENSTEIN has studied philosophy, political science and comparative literature at Freie Universität Berlin and Stanford University. He teaches philosophy at Freie Universität and works mainly on philosophy of language, epistemology, and metaphysics, His publications include "*Anaphoric Deflationism and Theories of Meaning*" (2010), and "*Davidsonian Semantics and Anaphoric Deflationism*" (under review).

STEVEN LUPER is Professor of Philosophy at Trinity University, Texas (USA). He defended a version of the safety condition for knowledge in "*The Epistemic Predicament*" (1984). He has also written about ethics and death, most recently in *The Philosophy of Death* (2009).

MARIE MCGINN is Professor Emerita, University of York, UK. Her research interests include epistemology, the philosophy of John McDowell, Wittgenstein, and early modern philosophy. She is author of the book *Elucidating the Tractatus: Wittgenstein's Early Philosophy of Logic and Language* (2009). With Oskari Kuusela, she is editor of the *Oxford Handbook to Wittgenstein*.

DUNCAN PRITCHARD is Professor of Philosophy at the University of Edinburgh, UK. His research is mainly in epistemology with particular focus on scepticism, the epistemic externalism/internalism distinction, and modal and ability based theories of knowledge. His books include *Epistemic Luck* (2005), and (with Alan Millar and Adrian Haddock) *The Nature and Value of Knowledge: Three Investigations* (2010).

CLAUDIO ROLLER is the scientific coordinator of the Center for Knowledge Research (IZW), Technical University Berlin. His research concentrates on philosophy of mind, philosophy of language, epistemology, and philosophy of science. Currently he works on a research project on philosophy of perception, focusing on non-propositional forms of knowledge and on color representation. He published *"Colors as epistemic Objects"* (2009) and (with A. Stenzinger et. al.) *"Would Virchow be a systems biologist? A disourse on the philosophy of science"* (2010).

JONATHAN SCHAFFER is Professor of Philosophy at Rutgers University, New Brunswick (USA). He has published extensively on topics in metaphysics, epistemology, and causation. He is well-known for defending contrastivism in epistemology. Some recent publications are: *"Contrastive Knowledge Surveyed"* (with J. Knobe, 2011), and *"The Internal Relatedness of all Things"* (2010).

SEBASTIAN SCHMORANZER has studied philosophy at the University of Münster, the Université de Paris IV (Sorbonne), and the University of St. Andrews. Since 2010 he is research assistant of the Philosophy Department at the University of Cologne, Germany. His research areas include epistemology and metaphysics. His dissertation, *Realismus und Skpetizismus*, was published in 2010. See also *"Brandom on Knowledge and Entitlement"* (2007).

JOACHIM SCHULTE is author of several books and numerous articles on Ludwig Wittgenstein, including *Ludwig Wittgenstein: Leben Werk Wirkung* (2005), and co-editor of the critical editions of Wittgenstein's major works. He teaches philosophy at the University of Zürich (Switzerland), focusing mainly on classical analytical philosophy. With Peter Hacker he revised the translation of Wittgenstein's *Philosophical Investigations*.

ERNEST SOSA is Professor of Philosophy at Rutgers University, USA. He has developed extensive contributions to contemporary epistemology (for example, in virtue epistemology, modal theories of knowledge, and skepticism), and has also published on metaphysics, modern philosophy, and philosophy of mind. His books include *Reflective Knowledge* (2009), and *Knowing Full Well* (2011).

MATTHIAS STEUP is Professor of Philosophy and Department Head at Purdue University in Indiana (USA). He works on a variety of issues in epistemology such as the nature of epistemic justification, the evidentialist response to skepticism and the foundationalism-coherentism controversy. He is the author of *An Introduction to Contemorary Epistemology* (1999), and together with Ernest Sosa, the editor of *Contemporary Debates in Epistemology* (2005).

STEFAN TOLKSDORF teaches philosophy at the Technical University of Berlin. His main interests are epistemology and philosophy of language, in particular Wittgenstein. He is currently working on epistemic abilities and on insights and limits of non-factual semantics. He published "*Wittgenstein und das Projekt einer pragmatisch-genealogischen Philosophie der Sprache*" (2011). With Holm Tetens, he edited the volume *In Sprachspiele verstrickt – oder: Wie man der Fliege den Ausweg zeigt* (2010).

MICHAEL WILLIAMS is Krieger-Eisenhower Professor in the Philosophy Department at the Johns Hopkins University in Baltimore, Maryland. His numerous books and articles are devoted to epistemology, philosophy of language, Wittgenstein, and the history of modern philosophy. He is particularly well-known for his work on philosophical skepticism, defending a contextualist view of knowledge. His books include *Unnatural Doubts* (1991), and *Problems of Knowledge* (2001).

Index

Index of Persons

Abel, Günter   v, 1, 6, 21–25, 58, 67, 245–266, 589f., 615, 691
Alexander, Joshua   69
Alston, William   94, 97, 461–468, 471f., 475f., 484, 490, 500, 507
Alvarez, Maria   559, 563, 567, 578, 586
Amico, Robert P.   2, 67
Annas, Julia   121, 124
Annis, David   330, 347
Aristoteles / Aristotle   105, 122, 143, 181, 218, 487, 489, 491–495, 498f., 503
Armstrong, David   523, 525
Atli, Can   vi
Audi, Robert   113, 124
Austin, John L.   31, 354, 358, 378, 389, 447, 651
Axtell, Guy S.   162, 175, 435
Ayer, Alfred J.   495, 501, 507

Bach, Kent   391
Bacon, Francis   618, 626
Baehr, Jason   181, 214
Barnes, Jonathan   121, 124
Baumann, Peter   34–37, 214, 395–431, 691
Bealer, George   538, 553
Beckermann, Ansgar   29, 67
Bekoff, Marc   571, 586f.
Belnap, Nuel   363, 379, 391
Bennett, Jonathan F.   482, 484, 562
Bergmann, Michael   505, 507
Bermúdez, José Luis   579, 586
Bezuidenhout, Anne   339, 342f.
Blaauw, Martijn   34, 391, 395, 406
Blackson, Thomas   391
Boer, Steven   368

BonJour, Laurence   8, 499, 549f., 649
Booth, Anthony   476
Brandom, Robert   26, 39, 42, 51, 54, 59, 61, 301f., 358, 435, 447, 450ff., 558
Brentano, Franz C.   582
Brogaard, Berit   157
Brown, D.G.   102
Brueckner, Anthony   42, 44, 47f., 383, 527–531

Call, Josep   547
Carroll, Lewis   296, 630
Castaneda, Hector-Neri   379
Cheney, Dorothy   561, 573
Cherniak, Christopher   550
Chisholm, Roderick M.   2, 73, 104, 165, 439ff., 444f., 447f., 456f.
Chomsky, Noam   362
Chrisman, Matthew   482
Clarke, David S.   309, 315
Cleve, James Van   518
Cohen, Stewart   30f., 45, 329, 335, 380, 383, 388, 509f., 514
Collins, John   391
Conant, James   58
Craig, Edward G.   11, 14ff., 27, 31, 104f., 145, 159, 161, 193, 209, 212f., 310, 324, 359f., 661
Crane, Tim   54, 589ff., 597–600, 611
Cussins, Adrian   579

Dancy, Jonathan   59, 119, 494
Davidson, Donald   113, 122, 561f., 568, 576, 581

DeRose, Keith 30, 309, 329, 335f., 383, 388, 395, 428
Descartes, Rene 122, 396, 442, 492, 551, 633
Dolby, David 576, 585
Dretske, Fred 45, 92, 353, 362, 366, 373f., 378, 381, 383f., 389ff., 395, 521, 523, 572, 613f.
Dummett, Michael 579

Eddy, Timothy 545, 547
Engisch, Karl 621
Ernst, Gerhard 11, 15, 27–30, 214, 307–327, 334, 563
Everson, Stephen 671

Faizi, Hadi Nasir vi, 266
Fantl, Jeremy 146, 157, 296, 310, 331, 503
Feldman, Richard 144, 338, 384, 464, 476
Feldmann, Ute vi, 67, 150, 525, 589
Firth, Roderick 500
Fisher, John A. 561
Fodor, Jerry 558, 562, 578f.
Fogelin, Robert 312f.,325
Fricker, Elizabeth 169
Fricker, Miranda 161, 435
Fumerton, Richard 484, 512

Garfinkel, Alan 375
Garrett, Brian 119
Gelfert, Axel 14, 161
Gendler, Tamar 391
Gettier, Edmund 104, 129, 309, 391, 515, 538, 570
Gil, Thomas 57f., 617–626
Ginet, Carl 167, 288, 290, 494
Glock, Hans-Johann 7, 10, 52ff., 557–585
Goethe, Johann W. von 636
Goldman, Alvin 16, 91, 167, 175, 319, 441f., 444, 457, 539–542, 553
Greco, John 1, 5f., 10–15, 19, 21, 25, 65, 141–157, 161f., 164–167,

175, 180, 195, 199f., 202, 217, 237f., 360
Groenendijk, Jeroen 363

Hacker, Peter M.S. 645
Haddock, Adrian 10, 14, 19, 162, 165, 167–171, 214
Haft, Fritjof 624
Hamblin, Charles L. 363
Hanfling, Oswald 27, 309, 314, 320f., 326
Harman, Gilbert 447, 509, 517, 522ff.
Hawthorne, John 44f., 82, 146, 149, 157, 331, 373, 384, 389, 391, 406
Heim, Irene 370
Heller, Mark 148f., 380, 383, 391
Henderson, David 161, 175, 334
Hetherington, Stephen 1–8, 20, 32, 51, 65, 73–97, 214, 296
Higginbotham, James 363, 368f., 376
Hinrichs, Timo vi
Hintikka, Jaakko 91, 364, 368, 376
Hogrebe, Wolfram 256
Holmes, Sherlock 358f., 361, 376, 379
Hookway, Christopher 359
Huemer, Michael 391
Hume, David 492, 595
Hurley, Susan 571
Hyman, John 1f., 5–8, 10, 29, 52f., 65, 101–125, 316f., 326, 570

Jackson, Frank 277, 539f., 589, 592
Jäger, Christoph 316
Jamieson, Dale 571
Jankovic, Tea 241
Johnsen, Bredo 362, 380, 384, 391, 422f.

Kaplan, David 339, 341
Kaplan, Mark 105
Kappel, Klemens 161, 175
Karjalainen, Antti 355, 362, 391, 395, 406
Kelp, Christoph 161, 175

Index of Persons

Kenny, Anthony   107f., 113, 120, 232f., 567, 581
Kern, Andrea   1, 4, 10f., 14, 17, 19ff., 196, 215–241
Klein, Peter D.   38, 42ff., 51, 312, 383, 487–507
Kleiner, Scott   364
Korcz, Keith A.   378
Kornblith, Hilary   7, 10, 49–52, 161, 175, 437, 535–554
Kusch, Martin   161, 175
Kvanvig, Jonathan   143, 156, 162

Lackey, Jennifer   13, 144, 150ff., 157, 168
Lane, Melissa   161
Laudan, Larry   368
Lehrer, Keith   84, 141, 311, 435
Lenk, Hans   264
Levi, Isaac   364
Levin, Janet   277
Lewis, David   91, 248, 341, 344, 354, 368, 376ff., 380, 382f., 388, 390f., 449, 592, 651
Lipton, Peter   375
Locke, John   492
Löwenstein, David   1, 6, 21f., 24ff., 58, 214, 269–303
Luhmann, Niklas   619f.
Luper, Steven   5, 42, 44–47, 509–524

MacCormick, Donald N.   623
MacFarlane, John   340–343, 347
Malcolm, Norman   91, 389, 561, 563, 571, 576, 580
Marcus, Eric   571, 573ff., 577ff.
Margolis, Joseph   105
Marr, David   249
McDowell, John   55, 566, 579f., 601–608
Mcginn, Marie   5, 59, 64ff., 671–690
McGrath, Matthew   146, 157, 316, 331
Mellor, Hugh   54f., 277, 589ff., 593–597, 601, 608, 611

Millar, Alan   10, 14, 19, 162, 165, 167ff., 171, 207
Montmarquet, James A.   162
Moore, George E.   48, 66, 357, 375ff., 381ff., 389, 391, 518, 675f., 680ff., 686. 688f.
Morgan, C. Lloyd   91, 562
Morton, Adam   355, 362, 391, 395, 406
Murphy, Gregory   542

Nashi, Roald   391
Nemirow, Laurence   249, 277, 592
Neta, Ram   161, 175, 378, 391
Nichols, Shaun   50
Nottelmann, Nikolaj   476
Nozick, Robert   383, 521
Nudds, Matthew   571

Partee, Barbara   374, 391
Peacocke, Christopher   91, 579
Peirce, Charles S.   264, 359, 379
Plantinga, Alvin C.   162f., 180
Plato / Platon   104f., 129f., 502, 535, 618, 654
Poston, Ted   435
Povinelli, Daniel   545ff.
Price, Henry H.   472
Prichard, Harold A.   120
Pritchard, Duncan   1, 9ff., 14–21, 30, 142, 157, 159–175, 179, 182, 184, 186, 189–195, 198ff., 202f., 210, 212f., 229
Pryor, James   383, 449f.

Quine, Willard Van Orman   91, 339, 581f.

Raffman, Diane   602
Rawls, John   234f.
Raz, Joseph   113
Rheinwald, Rosemarie   651
Rhees, Rush   629
Richards, Mark   344
Roller, Claudio   v, 24f., 54–57, 589–615
Rooth, Mats   374
Rorty, Richard   31, 450

Rundle, Bede   573, 576f., 580, 584
Russell, Bertrand   566
Russell, Bruce   484
Ryan, Shane   175
Ryan, Sharon   468
Ryle, Gilbert   5, 22, 24ff., 87, 102, 105, 107, 117, 240, 269f., 285–302, 358, 560, 569f., 577, 617, 619

Salerno, Joe   157
Sanford, David   374
Sartwell, Crispin   29, 318
Schaffer, Jonathan   34–37, 272, 353–397, 406, 411–431
Schantz, Richard   437
Schiffer, Stephen   329, 336, 383f.
Schmoranzer, Sebastian   47, 59, 61–64, 329, 649–668
Schulte, Joachim   59ff., 64, 66, 649–668
Searle, John   57, 477ff., 481, 590f., 608–614
Sellars, Wilfrid   40, 59, 76–81, 87, 95, 252, 441–446, 448–451, 453f., 601
Senor, Thomas D.   435
Sextus Empiricus   121, 490f.
Seyfarth, Robert   561, 573
Sherman, Brett   509, 523
Shettleworth, Sara   546f.
Shope, Robert K.   104
Silins, Nicholas   48, 527ff., 530
Sinnott-Armstrong, Walter   355, 391, 395f., 406, 430
Sintonen, Matti   364
Snowdon, Paul   84, 277, 282, 285
Socrates/Sokrates   96f., 102, 104, 535, 537f.
Sorabji, Richard   121
Sosa, Ernest   1, 5f., 8–11, 14f., 19, 21, 59, 65, 77–80, 90f., 129–139, 141, 157, 162, 166f., 180, 195, 200, 202, 211, 217, 224–229, 232, 234ff., 239, 383, 390, 438, 450, 496, 499, 523
Stalnaker, Robert   358, 371

Stanley, Jason   22, 24f., 82, 87, 146, 149, 250, 269–299, 302, 309, 316f., 329, 331, 336f., 358, 368, 374,   376f., 389, 406
Steel, Thomas   363, 379
Steup, Matthias   38–42, 51, 59, 461–484
Steven, Stanley S.   365
Stich, Stephen   50, 542
Stine, Gail C.   383
Stoecker, Ralf   561f., 565, 568, 581
Stokhof, Martin   363
Strawson, Peter F.   112, 116, 473, 560

Thomas von Aquin   122
Tolksdorf, Stefan   1–69, 175, 179–214, 302, 484, 589, 604
Tomasello, Michael   547f., 571
Tugendhat, Ernst   567
Turri, John   162, 330f.

Unger, Peter   383, 410

Van Fraassen, Bas   375
Vendler, Zeno   574ff., 578
Vogel, Jonathan   383, 390f., 512ff., 515, 518, 522
Vogler, Candace   445

Wayne, Davis   336f.
Weatherson, Brian   391, 476ff.
Weinberg, Jonathan   50
Whitcomb, Dennis   145, 154f., 157
Willaschek, Marcus   650
Williams, Bernard   106, 161
Williams, Michael   5, 30, 38ff., 42, 46, 51, 59, 61–64, 66, 334, 435–460, 650, 653–667
Williamson, Timothy   22, 24f., 64–67, 73, 82, 87, 94, 101, 104, 146, 250, 269–282, 284ff., 287–291, 293ff.,   298f., 302, 333, 358, 368, 376f., 384f., 570, 671–690
Wittgenstein, Ludwig   5ff., 22, 27, 29, 33, 51f., 59–62, 64–67, 105, 107, 112, 123, 182, 206, 208, 254,

256–259, 265, 301, 359f., 375f., 427, 446f., 454, 568ff., 604, 629–647, 659, 671–690
White, Alan   102, 105ff., 565, 568, 570, 576, 582, 584
Wright, Crispin   47f., 333, 344, 527ff., 652
Wright, Georg H. von   113, 629
Wolf, Martin   vi

Yablo, Steve   354
Yourgrau, Palle   335

Zagzebski, Linda   11, 19, 141, 162, 166f., 181, 215–223, 438f., 448
Zippelius, Reinhold   621f.

Index of Topics

ability, cognitive   8, 15, 162–170, 172f.
ability condition   162, 164f., 169ff., 179, 182, 184, 191f., 194, 210f.
ability, epistemic   1, 12, 18, 20, 179–214, 252
ability, intellectual   17, 180, 195
ability (a. meta-ability)   4
ability intuition   15, 17, 164, 170f., 173, 179, 189, 192, 200, 212
absolutism   4f., 90–95
accidental / accidentality (a. non-accidental)   19, 182f., 188f., 203, 215–218, 221f., 224, 228–231, 233f., 237ff., 259, 380, 564, 685
accurate / accuracy / accurateness   9, 74, 86–89, 93, 95, 129, 131f., 135, 137, 160, 195, 202, 205, 229, 358, 385, 413, 479, 497, 537, 539ff., 543, 552
achievement (a. cognitive achievement)   8–13, 23, 56, 179f., 201, 227, 267, 380, 571
act, virtuous   220f., 223
actualize   234f., 240
adroit   9, 129, 131, 195, 202, 247, 249, 251f., 255, 257
agency (a. non-human / animal)   3, 41, 52, 77–81, 83, 85, 87, 95f., 167, 216, 465, 468, 478f., 557–587,
agent reliabilism   200
Agrippa Trilemma   455
Aktualisierung   445

Allgemeinheitsproblem   144, 146–149
alternative, relevant   37, 188, 354, 362, 374, 378, 388, 390, 395, 413, 421, 651
analysis, conceptual   73, 179, 538–542, 549, 553
analysis of knowledge   4f., 7, 25, 50, 94, 277, 279, 308, 310f., 313, 315ff., 325f., 377, 397, 405, 487f., 577, 672
analytic philosophy   179, 567, 692
Anerkennung   13, 141–145, 150–153
animal   2, 5, 7–10, 49, 51–54, 90, 129, 138f., 285, 360f., 495, 497, 537, 545, 546ff., 557–587
anti-luck condition / intuition (a. anti-luck theory / anti-luck virtue epistemology)   14–19, 159–177, 179–214
appearance   18, 172, 209, 312, 676, 684
apt, aptness, meta-aptness   9f., 82, 129, 131–139, 195, 202, 224f., 339
argument, cogent   47
Argument der Flüchtigkeit   522
argument from linguistics   270–274, 276–280, 282
assimilationism   52ff., 558, 581, 585
assurance   60, 65, 478, 675f., 680ff.
ascriber   28, 30–33, 35, 39, 358, 580
assertion   82, 336, 344, 361, 655, 684, 687f.

attitude, action-oriented / object-oriented 566
attitude, factive 674
attitude, intentional 566, 568, 581
attitude, propositional 566f., 571, 578–584, 672f.
attribution / ascription 3f., 18, 27, 29–31, 37, 39f., 51ff., 65, 74, 179, 183, 186, 189, 192, 200f., 205ff., 250, 270, 275, 277, 279, 293f., 295f., 318, 331–335, 337f., 341, 346f., 355, 357–362, 366–377, 384, 386, 389f., 395f., 400f., 403f., 417, 423, 426f., 560ff., 568, 571, 576ff., 580, 585
Ausdruck (der Empfindung) 635

background 11, 57
barn-example / Barney-case 9f., 15–18, 21, 160, 167–173, 198f., 201–213, 319–322, 324–325
Begründung 436f., 447, 456f., 459, 601
behaviourism 557
belief, animal 52, 138f., 577f.
belief, basic 38, 43, 493f., 496
belief, contrastive 379, 406f.
belief, justified 43, 195, 215f., 225, 461f., 487, 490f., 497, 500, 502f., 506f., 549ff., 558, 570, 690
belief forming process 164, 184ff., 194, 218, 649, 654
Bewertung, epistemische 142, 144, 438, 459
binary relation 34, 355f., 368, 414, 417, 424
Binsenweisheit 632
blame 41, 321, 462f., 466f., 659, 664, 667
blindness, semantic 323, 337
bootstrapping 512ff., 518
brain-in-a-vat 58, 61ff., 185, 313, 357, 382ff., 386, 649f., 653, 656ff., 660, 666ff.

capability 245ff., 250ff., 255, 263, 265

capacity 9f., 12, 17, 19f., 40, 180f., 190, 196, 199, 202, 204ff., 208f., 213, 215, 224, 227–241, 245f., 284, 358, 495f., 548, 557f., 562, 565f.,   570ff., 576f., 585, 654, 657, 682, 684, 687
capacity, epistemic 230, 234–239, 358
capacity, fallible 19, 215
category mistake 41, 200
certainty 62, 255, 376, 378f., 504, 661, 671, 675, 693
challenge 39f., 61, 66, 76, 78, 80, 94, 262, 487f., 491, 653, 661, 687ff.
character
(a. cognitive character) 1, 51, 180ff., 192, 199, 203, 387f.
clairvoyance 180f., 190, 212f., 654
closure 5, 44–47, 193, 212, 366, 382–390, 529, 655f.
cognitive science 49, 302, 536f., 539–542
coherentism 488f., 493, 499ff., 503f., 506, 695
commitment 54, 61, 91, 282, 302, 336, 339, 358, 471, 475, 656, 660, 679
compatibilism 41, 472–475
competence / competency 2, 4, 8f., 11, 13, 17, 19ff., 26, 32, 40, 45, 54ff., 58, 61, 129–139, 180f., 190, 193, 195, 199f., 204–207, 211, 224–234, 245–252, 255, 257, 259–262, 264f., 300, 309, 336, 338, 344, 385, 387, 562, 575
concept(s), (a. epistemic / practical concepts) 1f., 4, 8ff., 13, 15f., 19f., 23, 25, 29, 38, 41f., 50–57, 59–63, 65, 67, 77–81, 83, 87f., 94, 160, 181, 186f., 198, 200, 206, 208, 212, 216f., 220, 223f., 227ff., 232, 234f., 240, 249, 251, 261f., 264, 280, 286, 310f., 340, 345f., 360f., 427, 461ff., 538–547, 549, 557f., 560–563, 568, 576, 578ff., 651, 654, 663, 667, 672ff., 676, 681f.

concept of knowledge   2, 11, 14f.,
   27, 29, 37, 49–52, 73, 79, 81, 86,
   90, 159ff., 164f., 171–175, 183f.,
   192f., 209, 212, 215ff., 221,
   224f., 229f., 238, 247, 286, 308,
   310, 323, 334, 338, 354, 411, 487,
   538, 541f., 544, 549, 553, 570,
   654f., 673, 675, 679–682, 688
concepts, classical view of   541f.
conceptual / conceptuality / pre-
   conceptual   3ff., 10, 14, 20f.,
   23f., 40, 49, 51f., 54, 56f., 73, 75,
   77, 80, 83–86, 95, 159, 179, 190f.,
   207, 211, 219, 221, 235. 240f.,
   248, 259–264, 280, 307ff., 345,
   355, 398, 426, 538–542, 549, 553,
   557, 560, 562f., 566, 568, 572,
   585
consciousness /   139, 557f.
self-consciousness
constitution thesis   234f.
content, conceptual   581
content, non-conceptual   54, 56f.,
   566, 579, 581
content, propositional   57, 260,
   500, 502, 578f.
content, proto-propositional   579
content, semantic   4, 249, 333, 339,
   347
context   v, 7, 11–13, 16, 23, 27f.,
   30–34, 36, 41, 51, 61–64, 181,
   187ff., 193, 254, 259, 271–275,
   280f., 307f., 315, 319f., 329ff.,
   333f., 336, 338–347, 355, 358,
   361, 371–374, 377, 381, 384,
   387ff., 391, 396, 399f., 404ff.,
   413, 415ff., 419–423, 425, 428f.,
   494, 503, 559, 566, 583f.,
   650–653, 655f., 658–663, 665ff.,
   679ff.
context, everyday   31, 61, 650, 656
context, attributors'   329, 331f.,
   396
context-sensitivity   313, 332–338,
   341f., 346f.. 651
contextualism   27f., 30f., 34f., 37,
   61, 313, 318, 323, 325, 329–339,
   343, 347, 354f., 357, 366, 368,
   376, 378, 382ff., 387ff., 395f.,
   404, 413, 419, 421, 423, 428, 430,
   493f., 649–653, 656, 658, 661f.,
   667, 695
contextualism, conversational   30,
   33, 36, 329
contextualism, epistemic   27, 333,
   346, 388, 395
contextualism, inferential   30, 61
contextualism, nonindexical   30,
   32f., 329, 340ff., 345, 347
continuum of sense   57
contrast   27, 33–37, 60, 133, 353ff.,
   362f., 365–368, 371f., 374ff.,
   381, 385, 387, 389, 395, 397f.,
   401, 408, 412–414, 416f., 419f.,
   422ff., 428, 497
contrast class   34, 36, 401, 420
contrast proposition   34–37, 353,
   396–400, 402–406, 415–418. 425,
   428, 430
contrastivity   357, 361–366,
   374–379, 381ff., 385, 421
contrastive relation   354, 357, 415,
   417, 419
contrastivism   27, 34–37, 351,
   353–357, 361f., 385–391,
   395–401, 403–408, 411, 413–416,
   419–430, 694
control, voluntary   42, 461, 465,
   468ff., 473–478, 482f.
conversation, conversational   30–34, 36, 44, 329, 331f.,
   344ff., 358, 361, 371, 373
counterfactual   183, 187, 481, 667
credit (a. creditable)   13ff., 131,
   136, 138f., 150, 166ff., 179, 199,
   285, 287, 289, 296, 317, 360, 483,
   558, 560, 565, 567, 570, 575
criteria   63, 73, 200f., 254f., 258,
   296, 301, 343, 495, 581, 675

default status   46f., 61, 655
default-and-challenge model   39f.,
   42, 44, 46, 61, 655, 657
defeater (a. misleading defeater)   172f., 212f., 505
Demonstrativa   602f., 607

deontological   38–42, 461, 464ff., 468
deontological justification   461–466
Deontologisch, Deontologie   435, 437, 440ff., 445, 447, 455, 457, 459
Diagnose   442, 444, 458
diagnostic   58
differentialism   557f., 581, 585
direction of fit   163, 186f.
disagreement   33, 65f., 338f., 491, 672, 674, 676–679, 681f., 689
discrimination   24, 57, 209, 260ff., 357, 365ff., 385ff., 398,683
disjunctivism   18, 66, 197, 687
epistemic disjunctivism   19, 196
Disposition   107, 109f., 113f., 147, 157, 449, 451f., 454
disposition   10, 20, 25, 39, 201, 203, 225ff., 235f., 239f., 248, 316, 384, 449, 657
dissolution   59, 88, 92
dogmatism   43, 257, 383f., 387, 391, 567
doubt   7, 25, 39f., 42, 46, 49, 52, 59–63, 65ff., 258, 311ff., 316, 324, 378f., 385–388, 390f., 413, 426, 546, 649, 652, 659–663, 665f., 675ff., 681f., 689
doubt, pathological   59
dualism   51, 55f.
duty   38, 41f., 575

Empfänger   151
Empirismus   442, 459, 601
entitlement   42, 61, 63, 358, 501, 528, 649, 651, 653, 656, 658f., 663
entitlement, epistemic   62f., 651ff., 655f., 658–663, 667
entitlement, methodological   63, 653, 660–664, 666f.
Entwicklung   590f., 603f., 606, 636ff., 642
epistemic abilities   v, 1, 8, 10, 19, 181f., 187, 189, 197f., 200, 202
epistemic practice   184, 667f.

epistemic realism   59
epistemic regress problem   487f., 506
epistemology, analytical   v, 2, 4f., 11, 20, 22, 34, 49, 52, 54, 64, 182
epistemology, normative   501, 536
equivocationism   388ff.
Erfahrung   441, 456, 458f., 517, 521f., 589, 591–608, 614f., 631
Erfüllungsbedingungen   590f., 593, 599ff., 603, 606, 608–613
Erklärung   105, 107f., 113f., 116f., 119, 121, 145, 150–157, 436f., 453f., 512, 515f.
Erlebniswissen   617
error theory   336, 465, 560
Erste-Person-Perspektive   589, 612
ethology, cognitive   49–52, 535, 537, 544, 546f., 553, 560, 562, 571
everyday language   52
everyday life   30, 61, 560
evidence   3, 41, 43, 48, 61, 66, 80, 93, 133, 255, 275, 311, 315, 331ff., 359f., 362, 365f., 373, 378–382, 421–424, 428, 430, 463f., 467ff., 471f., 475, 478f., 482, 498, 550f., 553, 561, 569, 649–660, 662–668, 677, 680, 682–689
Evidentialismus   442
Evidenz   440, 443
Evidenz, irreführende   157
exercise   20, 79, 137, 190, 194f., 197f., 201, 204, 207, 219ff., 225–234, 237, 239f., 247, 250, 253, 255, 270, 288f., 292, 295, 300f., 358, 569, 576
existential generalization   370f., 373
Experiment   62, 121, 592, 631f.
experimental philosophy   50, 283, 540
experience / experientiality   54–57, 150, 247ff., 253, 255, 261f., 277, 378, 469, 471, 468, 479, 495, 527, 530, 580, 593, 597, 656f., 660, 667f., 679, 682, 685

explanation
(a. intentional /causal)   11, 195, 202, 565f., 568, 582
explicit vs. implicit   26, 36f., 206, 260, 337, 355, 358, 362, 371f., 374ff., 386, 390, 405, 422, 677, 685f., 690
expression   27, 30f., 64, 81, 84, 86f., 95ff., 240, 256, 258, 278, 336f., 339, 343, 346, 546, 560, 565,   581, 672, 677f., 681
extensional   184, 187, 200, 562
Externalismus   450f.
externalism   40, 184, 198, 203ff., 651, 674, 694

faculty   181
fact   1, 3, 6f., 28, 48, 53f., 78, 162ff., 167f., 183, 186, 206, 209, 246, 273, 286, 310–316, 321, 323f., 326, 344f., 492, 504, 537, 551, 559f., 565, 571–576, 582, 585, 657, 666, 674, 680, 687
factive   53, 65, 426, 497, 572, 582, 672ff.
Fähigkeiten   102, 104–111, 121, 123f., 141–148, 151–157, 436, 439, 443, 446f., 449–453, 510, 514, 591–605, 608, 610–615, 617, 619, 634, 640f.
fallibilism   380, 382, 504
fallibility (a. fallible competence)   20, 219, 232, 234, 380
Fertigkeiten   105, 107
first person perspective   196
focus   373f., 376, 659, 661
form   7, 24ff., 32, 57, 60ff., 162–165, 167, 180, 183–191, 194f., 203, 208, 223ff., 229, 239f., 249, 251, 256, 262, 337, 343, 356, 361ff., 366, 368, 371, 375, 378, 398, 400, 417, 424, 541, 566–569, 692
form, logical   337f., 343, 368, 389
form, surface   362, 367, 375
forms of knowledge   v, 1, 5, 8f., 13, 22, 49, 54f., 57, 251, 256, 277, 295, 358, 367, 389f., 533, 570, 694
form of life   569
forms of sense   57
foundationalism   8, 488, 490, 492ff., 499f., 502–506, 550
framework   9, 77, 339, 353, 362, 383, 465, 689
free will   41, 473
function   7f., 14–18, 27ff., 35, 51, 60, 67, 79, 130, 186, 189, 191f., 205, 207, 209, 218, 247, 253, 261f., 265, 334, 339, 376, 389ff., 463, 557, 582, 659
Fundamentalismus   440, 443
Funktion   101, 119, 145f., 149, 458, 590, 603, 605, 609, 612, 618ff., 622, 624, 634

Gebrauch   66, 148, 444, 630
Gedankenexperiment   592, 631 f.
genealogical (story)   14 ff., 55, 57, 59, 159–175, 193, 212, 252, 258
Genealogisch   59, 604, 606f., 612ff., 616
genealogy   14, 159, 161, 174, 262 ff.
generality problem   12 f.
Genese   590, 606
Gesetz   621
Gettier-problem   11, 19 f., 170, 193, 215, 692
Gewissheit   643
Glaube   111, 115, 122, 435–458, 523, 637, 640
good case / bad case   307, 682–688
Grabit-example / Grabit-Beispiel   156, 311–313, 324
Grammatisch   598, 631
groundless   255, 690
Grund   110–124, 633
Grund, zwingender   523

hallucination   394, 685
Handeln / Handlung   114–124, 437, 443–447, 457, 639
high (epistemic) standard vs. low (epistemic) standard   32, 36, 341 f., 345, 347, 417ff.

hinge-proposition 67
Hintergrund 589–615
holiday 208
Holismus 610
Hypothese, skeptische (a. skeptische Herausforderung) 455, 517

illocutionary force 358, 360
illusion 45, 649, 651, 684
Imagination 593–597
imperative, normative 496–499
indexicality, indexical, indexicalism 30 ff., 313, 336–342, 355, 388 f.
indubitabilism, restricted 378
Induktion 512 f.
infallible 232, 380, 684
infallibilism, restricted 378, 382
infallibility, epistemic 232
inference, cogent 527
inferential 22, 54, 56, 62 f., 252, 385, 494, 551 f.
infinitism 42 ff., 487–506
Informant, guter 145
Information / information 13, 15, 28, 30, 160, 172 f., 209, 212 f., 248, 284
Informationsquelle, gute 146 f., 153, 157
informants, good / reliable 11, 15, 28 f., 31, 159 ff., 172 ff., 209, 310 f., 313 f.,317 ff., 324
inheritance principle 493 f., 499, 502
inner state 35, 53
inquiry 357–391, 659–664
Instinkt, Instinktiv 636–642
intellectualism 24 ff., 39, 269–304
intellectualism, linguistic 269–302
intellektualistisch, hyperintellektualistisch 441
intensional 581
intentionality 392, 476–484, 566 f., 572, 578
intentional state 52 f., 567 f., 578, 581, 584 f.
Intentionalität 608–613

interests, practical 308–311, 314, 318, 323, 400, 415, 418
Internalismus 436, 439, 441 f., 444 f., 447, 450, 457, 459
internalism 40, 65, 203, 673 f.
interpretation 256–264, 301, 346 f., 378, 574
intuition 8 f., 15–19, 32 ff., 50 f., 152, 162 ff., 170 ff., 179 f., 189–193, 200–205, 212, 254, 309, 320, 324 ff., 332, 338 f., 373, 422, 426, 488f., 495, 497, 510, 538–541, 607
invariantism 331, 355, 376
Invariantismus, subjektsensitiver 149
involuntarism, doxastic 39, 41 f., 465, 467 ff., 475

justification, doxastic 500, 503
justification, propositional 501

Kennen 276, 358
kinds of knowledge 27, 29, 49, 79, 318, 399f., 411, 413f.
know how 87, 246, 257, 274ff., 279, 285, 298–301, 358, 495, 569
know that 4, 7, 28, 31f., 34f., 45, 63, 65f., 74, 79f., 87f., 173, 181f., 196, 198, 213, 246, 257, 273, 290, 298f., 309f., 314f., 317, 319, 321ff., 325, 330, 335–338, 342, 353f., 357, 362, 364–368, 370f., 373–377, 379–383, 385, 387, 395ff., 399–404, 412, 420, 422f., 425f., 428f., 563, 570, 573ff., 577, 649f., 664, 666, 675–678, 680f., 687, 689
knowing-how 1f., 21–26, 54f., 57f., 65, 245–266, 592f., 596f.
knowing-that 22, 24f., 55, 249f., 252, 254ff., 258, 261, 592, 615
knowledge-how 24, 83f., 86ff., 91, 97, 245, 269–302
knowledge-that 2, 83f., 87f., 91, 225, 247, 249, 257f., 269–302, 377

knowledge, animal   5, 8f., 21, 52f., 138f., 202, 496, 547f., 552, 557f.
knowledge, contrastive   37, 353–391, 395–408, 411–430
knowledge, easy   46
knowledge, experiential   54f., 57
knowledge, legal   57
knowledge, methodological   295–302
knowledge, non-human   52, 557–585
knowledge, objective variety of   315, 325f.
knowledge, ordinary   385ff., 390f.
knowledge, perspective variety of   314f., 324ff.
knowledge, phenomenal   25, 49, 54, 55, 279
knowledge, procedural   22, 26, 245–248
knowledge, reflective   9, 129, 136–139, 497, 650, 695
knowledge, situational   27
knowledge as ability   2, 71
knowledge ascription   37f., 373, 376f., 386, 389f., 403, 417, 423
knowledge attribution   37, 201, 331–338, 346f., 360, 384, 395f., 400
knowledge by acquaintance   55, 276, 308
knowledge in a broad sense   23, 247
knowledge in a narrow sense   248, 264
knowledge for the knower   28, 314–318
knowledge relation   28, 36f., 338, 353–357, 361f., 366f., 401, 405, 418
Kohärenztheorie   448
Kommunikation   58, 620, 626
Kompetenz   447, 618f., 622f.
Kontext   148f., 155, 449, 457, 459, 592, 605f., 637, 642, 646
Kontext praktischer Überlegungen   148
Kontextualismus   148f.
Konvention   604f., 607, 614, 631

Konzeptualismus   602f., 605, 607
Krankheit (Geisteskrankheit)   643
Kriterien, Kriterium   607, 633, 639, 645

language   18, 29, 33, 40, 52f., 55ff., 60, 62, 67, 180ff., 189, 204ff., 208ff., 246, 249f., 253, 255–261, 264f., 273–278, 280f., 307ff., 336f., 339f., 343, 346, 355, 368, 371, 375, 407, 440, 557ff., 561, 576, 578f., 585, 673, 675
language-game   18, 33, 40, 44, 62, 67, 180ff., 189, 204ff., 209f.
language of thought   578f.
law   188, 230f., 233, 249, 342, 365
learning   249, 251, 255, 258, 300, 548, 689, 690
lingualism   557ff., 581, 585
linguistic   15, 22, 24–26, 31, 37, 56, 61, 196, 246f., 249–252, 257–266, 269–302, 307, 309, 318, 336f., 342, 346, 363, 390, 398, 426, 465, 560ff., 566, 569f., 577–581, 585
logic, logical   18, 22, 24, 26, 31f., 34f., 37, 42, 54, 59–63, 67, 139, 190, 196, 202, 207f., 216, 223, 240, 245, 251ff., 263, 265, 279, 286, 337f., 343, 363–366, 368, 389, 398,   426, 574, 585, 678
logical structure   31, 42
Lotterie-Proposition, Lotterieartige Proposition   521–525
lottery case, lottery paradox, lottery proposition   182ff., 193, 212, 287, 379f., 382, 495
luck, environmental   18, 194, 198, 201f., 210
luck, epistemic (a. good luck, bad luck)   5, 16f., 19, 21 168ff., 171, 173f., 179–214, 222, 321
luck, intervening   194, 197, 201f.

manifestation   1, 3–6, 9, 11, 13f., 17f., 20f., 194, 200, 202ff., 206ff., 211, 213, 224, 288, 572

meaning   4, 13, 23, 27, 30, 32f., 42, 50, 55ff., 59f., 187, 197, 200, 205, 208, 212ff., 229, 234ff., 252, 307–310, 314,   318, 322, 346, 461, 489, 561, 672f.
meaning, variations of   27, 307ff., 314, 318, 322
memory   9, 76, 80, 180, 225, 294, 397, 399, 476, 495, 530, 571, 679
Mensch   103, 121, 123, 142f., 437f., 450, 511, 590, 593, 595–598, 600, 606ff., 610f., 613, 615, 617–620, 630, 634f., 637–641, 643f., 646
mental state   5, 59, 64ff., 498, 545ff., 558, 562, 565, 671–690
Mentalismus   604, 608, 612
Metapher   614f., 639, 645
metaphor (a. metaphoric)   53, 62, 96, 131, 261, 561, 563
metaphysics, metaphysical   36f., 86, 253, 255, 273–279, 354f., 489
meta-skepticism   66
methodological   v, 49, 62f., 264, 276, 295–302, 379, 541, 557, 559, 562, 570, 653, 659–669
methodological necessities   62f., 659–662, 664, 666, 669
mind   54, 96, 131, 181, 253, 259, 270, 288f., 326, 333, 472, 503, 538, 540, 542, 551, 557, 561, 571, 617, 671
mind, Cartesian conception of the   188, 395, 455, 496, 589, 661
modal analyses of knowledge   183
modal stability   183f., 186f., 189
mode of presentation   25, 280f., 284
modest vs. robust   9f., 14ff., 29, 33, 164–172, 174, 190–195, 197f., 200, 203, 210, 212f., 445, 540f.
modification strategy   320ff.
mögliche Welten   12, 147, 155f.
myth of the given   56
Mythos des Gegebenen   441f., 445, 591, 601f., 604, 607
Natur   11, 141–157, 618

natural kinds   50, 543f.
naturalism   50, 553
Netzwerk   610
nominalization   575
nonsense   59f., 561
Norm, epistemische   447
normal circumstances /
normal conditions /
favorable circumstances   7, 11f., 20f., 39, 74, 132, 180, 188ff., 196, 200, 204, 206ff., 211, 225, 227f., 239, 404, 471
Normativ, Normativität   142, 604f., 607, 619f., 622
normativity, epistemic   2, 9f., 12, 38, 40, 51, 129, 133, 138

objectification   161
obligation, epistemic   39, 51, 461, 464
ontological   236, 279, 426
ordinary language   29, 309, 355, 440
organism   8, 203f., 564

paradox   58f., 193, 357, 366, 382f., 385–388, 390, 522
perception   9, 24, 46, 74, 76, 88f., 93, 137, 180ff., 188, 190, 194f., 198, 207–211, 233, 249, 260–264, 365f., 475f., 495, 511, 566, 572f., 579,
performance   2, 4, 9f., 41, 64f., 128, 131f., 134–138, 201f., 249f.
performance normativity   129, 133, 138
Person   101, 113, 115, 437, 589, 604, 613, 661
person   23, 64f., 81f., 95, 97, 196, 247ff., 253, 259, 265, 275, 281, 293, 314f., 320, 407, 465, 495
Perspektive / Perspektivisch   150, 452, 589, 612f., 639
Pflicht, epistemische   435, 438, 447
phenomenally indistinguishable   682
philosophy, ordinary language

(a. philosophy of language)   29, 309, 355, 440, 559
philosophy of mind   54, 571, 691–695
philosophy of signs and interpretation   32, 263, 538
Position, epistemische   449, 509–511
position, epistemic   30, 91, 383
possible worlds   183–190, 194, 198, 250, 278, 371
possible-worlds semantic   183, 186–188, 278
power   167, 173, 220f., 223f., 263, 354, 379, 478, 528, 546, 583, 688
practical aspects   29
practical reasoning   3, 11, 13, 206, 692
practicalism   2, 4, 7, 89, 91, 93, 95f.,
pragmatic(s)   1, 11, 14, 30–33 42, 58f., 61, 63f., 66, 78, 255, 263f., 342, 346f., 689, 693
pragmatic-logical order   59, 61
pragmatism   558
Praxis   106, 142, 594f., 610f., 613, 620, 624,   626
praxis   235, 258, 260f., 265f., 559
pre-linguistic pattern   24, 261, 265
Primitiv   438, 604, 634–642
Prinzip der Geschlossenheit
Prinzip von Wissen   509, 519, 522
prior grounding model   39f., 447, 654, 656
Problem des einfachen Wissens   510f., 515
problem of the criterion   2, 73–81, 88–94
proof   245, 255, 274, 378f., 384, 387, 490, 655, 675, 680
proposition, basic   489, 491f., 494f.
propositional / pre-propositional   23, 260, 569
propositionalism   55–57
proto-knowledge   160
psychology   50, 542, 546, 560, 562
puzzle   59, 164, 166, 171, 336

qualia, Qualia   54, 277–279
quietism   29

Realismus, epistemologischer   459
Realität   603, 625, 646
reason-giving / reason-taking   209, 253
reasoning, circular   490–494, 498
reasoning, infinite   492f., 502, 506
Recht   57f., 103, 617–626
Rechtfertigung, intern / extern   439
recipient   13, 28
reductive understanding
of capacities / abilities   20, 240, 255
reduction / reductionism   20, 83, 169, 192, 263, 566f., 596
reflection   225, 253, 496, 550ff., 561
Regel   436, 442–448, 453f., 618, 620, 631f., 639
Regeln, Sollte-Tun u. Sollte-Sein
Regeln   446f., 453–457
Regelwissen   618
regress argument   24ff., 290f., 490, 492, 494, 498f., 501
regress, of application   289–292, 295
regress, of contemplation   25, 287–291
regress, of correctness   25, 291–298, 301
Regularität   445
regularity   23, 255, 258, 260
relativism   14, 340, 342
relativization   339, 360, 400f., 404ff., 429
relevantism   388ff.,
reliabilism   8, 38, 144, 148, 200, 229, 435–438, 441, 451ff., 487f., 492, 495ff., 501, 513, 523
reliability   12, 20, 38ff., 51, 164, 213, 216, 551f., 657f., 662f.
Reliabilismus   8, 38, 144, 148, 200, 229, 435–438, 441, 451ff., 487f., 492, 495ff, 501, 512f.
Responsibilismus   435, 437, 441
revisionism   558, 564f., 573

rule, constitutive / regulative 234, 236f.
rule-following 23f., 40, 51, 250, 253–256, 258ff., 265, 301
rule-following, practice-internal 23, 254ff., 258
rules, ought-to-be / ought-to-do 26, 39

safe, safety (a. unsafe) 8, 16f., 183–188, 190, 194, 198–200, 202f., 211, 693
safe (a. unsafe) environment 16, 18, 198f., 203
salience / salient 14, 64, 160, 237f., 332, 390, 544
Satz 113, 523, 598ff., 622f., 630
Schluß, Schließen 113, 119, 447, 450, 452, 512f., 621ff.
Schließen, praktisches 113
Schmerz, Schmerzbenehmen 7, 112, 123, 635, 640ff.
(simple) seeing 67, 74, 167f., 181, 191, 197f., 261, 354, 406, 412, 527, 530, 545, 572, 613f., 685, 687f.
seeming 203, 226f., 230f., 235ff.
Selbstbewusst / Selbstbewusstsein 445
Selbstverständlichkeit 448, 639
self-knowledge 78, 684, 691
semantic(s) 27, 30, 32f., 37, 61, 249f., 260, 265, 270, 272, 275, 278, 333, 336, 341–344, 346, 354f., 357, 370, 373f., 665
semantics, indexical 33, 336, 341, 342
sense-logical 18, 67, 188, 196, 207f.
sensitivity 8, 31f., 182, 313, 333–338, 342, 347, 474, 580, 684, 686
skeptic / sceptic /
scepticism / skepticism / 26, 31, 40, 45f., 48, 58–67, 76
sceptical scenario 161, 168f., 185, 205, 313, 229, 332f., 336, 357, 380–396, 403, 412, 420, 457, 487–494, 504, 551, 649–670, 680–689
Skeptizismus 441, 455–460, 510f., 515, 518, 520
Skeptizismus, cartesianisch / agrippinisch 455, 456
skill 131, 133ff., 137, 198, 245–255, 258f., 260f., 263ff., 558
Sinn / sinnvoll 57, 105f., 121ff., 142, 150, 444f., 513, 521f., 591, 594, 603–607, 612, 614, 617, 621, 643f., 646
Sinnformen 57
social externalism 17, 194, 203ff.
social phenomenon 51
social science 50, 540, 560
sources of knowledge 181, 240
space of acting 56
space of reasons 56, 180, 185, 200f., 204f., 209, 252f.
speech act(s) 359, 371
Spiel 40, 449, 453, 599, 633–639, 641, 643
Sprache 105f., 120f., 597, 604, 631f., 634f., 637, 640, 644, 645
Sprachgemeinschaft 122, 608
Sprachspiel 603, 606, 608, 613, 630–634, 636f., 640, 642, 645
standard, epistemic / of knowledge 30, 32, 36, 63, 91, 96, 194, 198, 338, 341f., 345, 347, 418, 428, 576, 651
status, epistemic 44, 63, 189, 334, 347, 506
structure of justification 38f., 42, 44, 51, 499
structure of reasons 42, 488
Subjektivismus 436
Subjektkontextualismus 149
Substitution 370f., 373, 566, 586
Subsumtion 624
sub-personal 23, 57, 180
success / successful 2, 8f.,11–21, 30, 53, 59f., 66, 97, 129, 138, 159–170, 175, 180, 183, 188f., 195–208, 218–228, 234, 239f., 245–260, 265, 278, 283, 285, 296,

300, 321, 333, 366, 384, 391, 470, 488, 495, 506, 527, 529, 548, 576
success verb   196
Syllogismus   121, 621 ff.
Syntax / syntax   24, 30, 86, 250, 260, 270, 343

Tätigkeit   143, 624
Tatsache   6, 106, 108, 110–124, 443, 449, 517, 519, 589, 592, 597, 624 f.
technique of knowledge   180 ff., 196, 210
ternary / ternarity   34, 36 f., 355, 357, 361, 395, 400, 405 f., 411, 413 f., 417, 419, 424, 426 f.,
testimony / testimonial knowledge   10, 13, 15, 168 f., 172 f., 199, 312 f., 324, 360, 413, 530
tether   96 f.
theory of action   558, 565
theory of knowledge   2, 8, 10, 14, 16 f., 74, 159, 161 f., 164, 166, 169 ff., 179, 184, 189, 191 f., 263, 271, 440, 655
therapeutic (vs. theoretic)   59
thick concept   52, 56, 200
tracking account   354
traits (a. character traits)   1, 181, 192, 199, 212, 219
transcendental   59, 80 f., 691
transmission (of evidential warrant; a. transmission failure / transmission success)   44, 47 f., 527–531
transparency / transparent   31, 65, 677, 683 f.
true, necessarily   20, 62 f., 185, 194, 196 f., 224, 230 f., 529
trust   89, 168 f., 226, 231, 235, 373, 429, 461, 657, 659, 666, 676, 689 f.
truth condition   271, 275 f., 280, 333, 377 ff., 396, 404, 406 ff., 673
truth-conduciveness / truth-conducive   218 ff., 465 f., 496, 498 ff., 654, 664, 666 f.
truth-guaranteeing   20, 220

truth-value   32, 183, 186, 331 f., 339 f., 346 f., 369–373, 377, 398, 426
Tugend, intellektuelle / kognitive   141 ff., 154 f., 438 f., 448
Tugendtheorie   150 f., 154, 156, 435, 438
two- / three-place relation   341, 343, 353 f.
types of action   42, 59, 63, 181 f., 563

Überlegung, praktische   146–149, 153, 157
Überzeugung   103–106, 113 ff., 118 f., 122, 141–145, 147, 150 ff., 154, 156, 435–452, 455–459, 510, 512–516, 518, 520, 523 f., 601, 604 f., 609 f., 612, 617, 635
use (a. ordinary use)   1, 4, 23, 27 ff., 55 f., 60, 66, 79, 84 f., 96, 100, 206, 233, 245, 248, 259, 264, 269, 275 f., 301, 307–310, 314, 316, 318, 323, 325 f., 334, 337 f., 340, 342, 346, 357, 368, 375, 549, 559 f., 572, 580, 677, 679 f.

value of knowledge (a. value problem)   2, 12, 63, 129 f., 133, 165
Veranschaulichen   631 f.
Verantwortung   38, 435–460
Verlässlichkeit   38, 40, 144, 146, 148, 435–460
Vermögen   106 f., 121, 141, 437, 445, 448, 452 f., 611
Verpflichtung   438, 444, 447
virtue, intellectual   8, 217 f., 223, 238
virtue epistemology   1, 5, 8, 10 f., 13–20, 161 f., 164–174, 180 f., 191 f., 194, 199, 200, 212, 217, 219, 221–224, 228 ff., 234, 237, 240
virtue reliabilism   181
virtue responsibilism   181
virtue theory   8, 15 f., 18, 20, 65, 179

vocabulary 57, 191, 384
Vorschuss-und-Anfechtungsmodell der Rechtfertigung 447 ff., 455 ff., 459
Vorschussberechtigung 447, 449, 453, 459
Vorsprachlich 444, 604, 635, 637, 641

Wahrheit 64, 112, 114, 122, 142, 147, 152, 156, 437, 439, 443, 514 ff., 521 ff., 630, 644, 646
Wahrheitsdienlich 437, 440
Wahrheitsbedingungen 590, 596, 600
Wahrheitswert 598 f.
Wahrscheinlichkeit 522 f., 525
warrant (a. doxastic / propositional) 44, 47 f., 297, 502 f., 505, 527–531, 570, 666
Welt 12, 116, 147, 155 f., 437, 441, 443, 450, 456–460, 592, 596, 598 f., 601–606, 609, 611 f., 631–634
Wert, intrinsischer 143
Wertproblem 143, 145, 154
Wissen-dass / Wissen-wie 102, 105, 108 ff., 111, 115, 120, 144, 154, 276, 436, 509 f., 512, 514–524, 610, 617 ff.
Wissen, begriffliches / nicht-begriffliches 591, 598, 602–607, 614
Wissen der Tiere 106, 120 ff., 437 f., 450, 635
Wissen durch Bekanntschaft 596, 600, 603
Wissen, einfaches 46, 510–512, 514 f.

Wissen, Formen des 266, 449, 590–593, 596 f., 614
Wissen, menschliches 438, 450, 590, 630
Wissen, praktisches 101 f., 617 ff., 621, 624, 626
Wissen, phänomenales 54, 589–615
Wissen, propositionales / nicht-propositionales 6, 101 f., 104, 124, 590 f., 596, 598–601, 603, 608, 614, 617 f.
Wissen, rechtliches 57 f., 617–626
Wissen, subjektives 589, 592
Wissen, theoretisches 618 f.
Wissenschaft (a. Natur-, Sozial- und Kognitionswissenschaft) 101, 458, 597, 604, 606, 618, 644
Wissenszuschreibung 157, 452
Wissenszuwachs 589, 596, 599 ff.
world-picture sentence 67
world, material 48, 66

Zeugnis anderer 144 f., 150–153
Zufall, Zufällig 118, 142 f., 147, 152, 154, 438
Zustand (kognitiver, mentaler, intentionaler) 101, 113 f., 123, 444 f., 591, 599, 608–612, 614
Zuverlässigkeit 436, 441, 512–516, 518, 520 f.
Zuschreiberkontextualismus 148 f.
Zweck von Wissen 11, 141, 145, 147 ff., 153, 156 f.
Zweifel (a. philosophischer / pathologischer) 62, 629–647